Transactions of the Royal Historical Society

SIXTH SERIES

VIII

CAMBRIDGE
UNIVERSITY PRESS

Published by the Press Syndicate of the University of Cambridge
The Edinburgh Building, Cambridge CB2 2RU, United Kingdom
40 West 20th Street, New York, NY 10011–4211, USA
10 Stamford Road, Oakleigh, Melbourne 3166, Australia

First published 1998

A catalogue record for the book is available from the British Library

ISBN 0 521 65009 7 hardback

SUBSCRIPTIONS. The serial publications of the Royal Historical Society, *Royal Historical Society Transactions* (ISSN 0080–4401), Camden Fifth Series (ISSN 0960–1163) volumes and volumes of the Guides and Handbooks (ISSN 0080–4398) may be purchased together on annual subscription. The 1998 subscription price (which includes postage but not VAT) is £50 (US$80 in the USA, Canada and Mexico) and includes Camden Fifth Series, volumes 11 and 12 (published in July and December) and Transactions Sixth Series, volume 8 (published in December). Japanese prices are available from Kinokuniya Company Ltd, P.O. Box 55, Chitose, Tokyo 156, Japan. EU subscribers (outside the UK) who are not registered for VAT should add VAT at their country's rate. VAT registered subscribers should provide their VAT registration number.

Subscription orders, which must be accompanied by payment, may be sent to a bookseller, subscription agent or direct to the publisher: Cambridge University Press. The Edinburgh Building, Shaftesbury Road, Cambridge CB2 2RU, UK; or in the USA, Canada and Mexico: Cambridge University Press 40 West 20th Street, New York, NY 10011–4211, USA. Prices include delivery by air.

SINGLE VOLUMES AND BACK VOLUMES. A list of Royal Historical Society volumes available from Cambridge University Press may be obtained from the Humanities Marketing Department at the address above.

Printed and bound in the United Kingdom by Butler & Tanner Ltd, Frome and London

CONTENTS

TRANSACTIONS OF THE
ROYAL HISTORICAL SOCIETY

PRESIDENTIAL ADDRESS

By P.J. Marshall

BRITAIN AND THE WORLD IN THE EIGHTEENTH CENTURY: I, RESHAPING THE EMPIRE

READ 21 NOVEMBER 1997

BY the end of the eighteenth century Britain was a world power on a scale that none of her European rivals could match.[1] Not only did she rule a great empire, but the reach of expeditionary forces from either Britain itself or from British India stretched from the River Plate to the Moluccas in eastern Indonesia. Britain's overseas trade had developed a strongly global orientation: she was the leading distributor of tropical produce throughout the world and in the last years of the century about four-fifths of her exports were going outside Europe.[2] Britain was at the centre of inter-continental movements of people, not only exporting her own population but shipping almost as many Africans across the Atlantic during the eighteenth century as all the other carriers put together.[3] It is not surprising therefore that British historians have searched for the qualities that marked out eighteenth-century Britain's exceptionalism on a world stage. Notable books have stressed, not only the dynamism of the British economy, but developments such as the rise of Britain's 'fiscal-military state'[4] or the forging of a sense of British national identity behind war and empire overseas.[5]

[1] This paper is greatly indebted to work of the scholars who have contributed to the *Oxford History of the British Empire*, vol. II, *The Eighteenth Century* (Oxford, 1998).

[2] Phyllis Deane and W. A. Cole, *British Economic Growth 1688–1959, Trends and Structures*, 2nd edn. (Cambridge, 1969), 86.

[3] David Richardson, 'Slave Exports from West and West-Central Africa; 1700–1810: New Estimates of Volume and Distribution', *Journal of African History*, XXX (1989), 11.

[4] John Brewer, *The Sinews of Power: War, Money and the English State 1688–1783* (1989).

[5] Linda Colley, *Britons: Forging the Nation 1707–1837* (New Haven, 1992).

Yet formidable as the British overseas undoubtedly were in European terms, it would be a mistake to read back too many nineteenth-century scenarios even into the later eighteenth century. Large parts of the world were still wholly beyond the reach of effective British commercial let alone military penetration, and it hardly needs saying that the history of the British empire was a chequered one rather than a story of uninterrupted growth. Against all contemporary expectations, empire in North America ended in humiliating defeat at about the same time that a great territorial empire was coming into existence in the apparently unpromising soil of India. Assessment of Britain's role in the world therefore needs to take account of the constraints and limitations that shaped it as well as of the British strengths that gave it its dynamism. It thus seems to require other dimensions as well as the British one. Eighteenth-century historians have much to learn from historians of later imperialism, whose work seeks to explain the extent of empire or world-wide influence in terms of conditions in the non-European world as well as those in Britain or Europe.

Such an approach seems to be particularly relevant to what will be the central theme of this address, the problem of why the British empire began to change course from the mid-eighteenth century, as territorial empire failed in America but succeeded in Asia. As late as the Seven Years War, empire in North America appeared to be a resounding success, not only in economic terms, as the rapidly growing colonial population consumed more and more British exports as well as contributing a major share to Britain's re-export trade in tropical commodities, but also in military and in ideological terms. Large numbers of American troops enlisted for the war. Even as the slide towards resistance and insurrection was beginning, American commitment to British values, at least as they interpreted them, and to their conception of a British empire, seemed to be unshaken. By contrast, for most of the eighteenth century, the metamorphosis of a British presence in India that was confined to the East India Company and its few trading enclaves into a territorial empire seemed utterly inconceivable. For Europeans to presume to displace the great Mughals over sizeable parts of their empire would have seemed to be a laughable proposition and in any case, an Indian population, as the supposedly cowed victims of immemorial despotism assumed to be totally alien to British *mores*, would be both improbable and unwelcome subjects for an empire conceived as one of freeborn British people.

Whatever British preferences may have been, the future of the empire ultimately depended on what was possible in America and India. Gordon S. Wood in his distinguished book on *The Radicalism of the American Revolution* is only the most recent of many scholars who have emphasised the role of change within the colonies in bringing down the British empire in America. He argues that, while colonial America in mid-century might appear to be increasingly amenable to government from afar, as it became more hierarchically stratified and its elites became more Anglicised, in reality a 'democratic revolution' was gathering pace that was 'changing everything'. It was to sweep away imperial authority as it radically altered the contours of American society.[6] While change in America undermined empire, change in India seems to have made it possible. Old stereotypes about an unchanging pre-modern Asia now have no standing. Professor Bayly, who has contributed so much to our understanding of them, has written about 'the indigenous processes that made empire possible'.[7] Recent historians of eighteenth-century India have tried to show that it was far from being a society in dissolution, as used generally to be supposed. The rulers of the regional states that succeeded to the authority of the Mughal emperors have been depicted as building up administrative and military structures on which the East India Company and its servants could batten to create new colonial regimes. Some of those who had served the new Indian states evidently found no great difficulty in transferring their allegiance to the British. While men like George Washington, Benjamin Franklin or Henry Laurens, who had applied their military, administrative or commercial skills to the service of the British empire as late as the Seven Years War, were within a few years to become that empire's enemies, at almost the same time it was acquiring a new set of allies, also with military, administrative and commercial skills. Men with names like Yusuf Khan, Ganga Govind Singh or Manohar Das have a right to be put alongside Robert Clive or Warren Hastings as the creators of a British Indian empire.

If developments in North America and India were making European empires of rule increasingly difficult to sustain on one side of the globe, while possibilities of empire, previously undreamed of, were opening up on the other side, what of the role of the British themselves? Were they no more than the victims or beneficiaries of processes beyond their control? To go to that extreme would surely be to fly in the face of all the evidence about Britain's political, economic and military muscle, and of her ambitions, even if the outcome of those ambitions was not always what was intended. Britain's rulers in the eighteenth century had expectations of what was involved in empire which changed during the course of the century. Attempts to give effect to changing expectations had important consequences. It is arguable that an empire as it was operating in the early eighteenth century could have retained the loyalty of the colonial elites and thus have survived at least some

[6] (New York, 1991), 124 ff.

[7] *Imperial Meridian: The British Empire and the World 1780–1830* (1989), 13.

degree of social upheaval in America. Until it was too late and armed resistance had actually broken out, few American notables were, however, willing to exert themselves to preserve the kind of empire that the British seemed to be intent on imposing on them in the 1760s and 1770s. On the other hand, against all expectations, it proved possible to create such an empire in India, significant numbers of Indians of wealth and standing being willing to commit themselves to its support.

I

There is a long-standing debate about change and continuity in eighteenth-century attitudes to empire, which until recently has been almost entirely confined to the thirteen colonies. The case for continuity throughout the century has obvious attractions. From a metropolitan perspective, the configuration of the landed and commercial elite, who wielded power from the late seventeenth until well into the nineteenth century changed little and their underlying objectives can be presumed to have remained more or less constant.[8] More concretely, the Navigation Acts, which defined the commercial purposes of empire, survived with no fundamental change right through the century. Nevertheless, historians have argued for major changes of course within these parameters. The origins of a second British empire have been sought even before the loss of America.[9] Scholars like C. M. Andrews and Lawrence Henry Gipson saw a new 'imperialism', based on rule over territory and people replacing in mid-century what they called the 'mercantilism' of trade regulation as the guiding principle at least of the British American empire.[10] This view has recently been restated by Daniel Baugh.[11]

If concepts such as a new imperialism or a second British empire seem to imply both too sharp and too purposeful a break to be appropriate for the changes that were occurring in mid-century, there can be little doubt that attitudes were changing significantly. In crude outline, the contribution from colonies was being given a much higher

[8] This is the theme of P. J. Cain and A. G. Hopkins, *British Imperialism: Innovation and Expansion 1688–1914* (1993), ch. 2.

[9] Vincent T. Harlow, *The Founding of the Second British Empire 1763–1793*, vol. I, *Discovery and Revolution* (1952), 3.

[10] Charles M. Andrews, *The Colonial Background to the American Revolution: Four Essays in American Colonial History* (New Haven, 1924), 125; Lawrence Henry Gipson, *The British Empire before the American Revolution*, vol. XIII, *The Triumphant Empire: The Empire Beyond the Storm* (New York, 1967), 182.

[11] 'Maritime Strength and Atlantic Commerce: The Uses of "a Grand Marine Empire"', in Lawrence Stone, ed., *An Imperial State at War: Britain from 1689 to 1815* (1994), 210.

place in calculations about Britain's prosperity and, crucially, about her security. Enhanced expectations about the importance of colonies led to an increasing concern that metropolitan authority should be effectively exerted over them. At the same time new territorial acquisitions were making the empire much more diverse ethnically and new patterns of governance were of necessity being devised for new territories.

The British empire of the first half of the eighteenth century developed a powerful rhetoric of liberty. This rhetoric was embodied not merely in conventional political writing but also, as Karen O'Brien has demonstrated for Britain[12] and David Shields for the American colonies,[13] in poetry. The British empire was depicted as an empire over the seas as distinct from the territorial empires of conquest established by imperial Rome or by Spain and to which France was alleged now to be aspiring. Whereas Britain's old rivals for maritime empire, the Dutch were accused of seeking to confine and restrict trade to their own advantage, the British dominion of the seas was conceived, as Dr O'Brien puts it, as a 'cosmopolitan fantasy of the empire as the bringer of a universal British peace and free trade in an era of navigation acts and continuous warfare'.[14] Poets were echoed by writers on political economy, who believed that 'The Power attained either by Policy or Arms, is but of short Continuance, in Comparison to what is acquired by Trade. Commerce is founded on Industry and cherished by Freedom.'[15] Under the peaceful sway of the British empire over the seas, commerce would bring the peoples of the world together for their mutual benefit.

Rhetoric and practice were of course different things. This was indeed the age of restrictive navigation acts and of periodic maritime war. Nevertheless, there is an element of truth, however distorted and exaggerated, behind the rhetoric of British commitment to peaceful dominion of the seas in the first half of the eighteenth century. The concept of a British blue-water strategy, as formulated by Daniel Baugh, is a helpful one, so long as it is used with the precision that he uses it. He sees it as a strategy for national defence through the deployment of naval power predominantly in European waters. Colonial trades were to be defended because they contributed a large proportion of the resources needed to sustain that naval power.[16] A blue-water strategy

[12] 'Protestantism and the Poetry of Empire' in Jeremy Black, ed., *Culture and Society in Eighteenth-century Britain* (Manchester, 1997), 146–62.

[13] *Oracles of Empire: Poetry, Politics and Commerce in British America 1690–1750* (Chicago, 1990).

[14] 'Protestantism and Poetry', 147.

[15] John Harris, ed., John Campbell, *Navigantium atque Itinerarium Bibliotecha; or a Compleat Collection of Voyages and Travels*, 2 vols. (1744–8), I, p. vii.

[16] 'Great Britain's "Blue-Water" Policy, 1689–1815', *International History Review*, X (1988), 33–58.

was not, however, aimed at imposing a naval hegemony throughout the world. This would have been beyond Britain's capacity and was not attempted. There was no regular deployment of warships in Asia before the 1760s or on the West African coast at any time in the century. Even in the Caribbean the peace-time British naval presence was a limited one.

British trade throughout much of the world was thus of necessity conducted outside any imperial context. In Asia for most of the eighteenth century the British were participants in an Asian commercial economy linked to Europe but by no means dependent on it. British trade in textiles or tea was made possible not by force but by the existence of highly organised cash cropping and artisan production on which the British could draw through the expertise of Asian merchants. On the West African coast the British were the largest purchasers of slaves, but there too they were dependent on indigenous merchants, whose prices they could not regulate and who could not be made to submit to their conditions. Even dealings with other European colonies usually took place without much coercion on the British side. The British could exploit their privileged position in Portugal to get access to the Brazilian market and to Brazilian gold in return. Otherwise, such success as the British enjoyed in Latin America largely depended on their ability to meet the needs of the creole communities in competition with other European suppliers, notably the French.

Overseas colonies of British subjects who developed new sources of commodities for Britain and widened the market for British manufactures were seen as an integral part of the early eighteenth-century empire of the seas. Such colonies had their place in the rhetoric of dominion based on liberty. They were to enjoy the rights of their fellow citizens at home. They were, as Charles Davenant put it, 'a free people in point of government' and colonial governors must accept that their subjects 'enjoy the rights and liberties of Englishmen, though not in England'.[17] Authoritarian rule and military garrisons were deemed incompatible with commercially flourishing English colonies.

Rhetoric and reality did not again entirely coincide. If overt designs of Stuart centralisation had perforce to be shelved after 1689, officials throughout the first half of the eighteenth century devised a succession of plans for tighter control over colonies. That these plans were not implemented seems to have owed much more to calculations about domestic British politics than to any ideological commitment by ministers to the liberties of colonial populations or even to any belief on their part that neglect was salutary. The practical consequences of

[17] 'Discourse on the Plantation Trade', in Charles Whitworth, ed., *The Political and Commercial Works of Charles D'Avenant*, 5 vols. (1771), II, 34–5.

relative neglect were, however, that colonies enjoyed a high level of autonomy through their Assemblies. The British fiscal-military state was emphatically not exported across the Atlantic. Metropolitan authority had very limited resources in money, military manpower or official positions that were not dependent on the free grant of colonial Assemblies. Practice was elevated into principle as an American theory of an imperial constitution evolved, based on the assumption that the rights of Englishmen applied in their totality to the colonial populations and that colonial legislatures enjoyed a competence that excluded the British parliament.[18] The rhetoric of an empire of freedom was enthusiastically adopted in the colonies as signifying a partnership of equals for the common objectives of commercial prosperity and the preservation of Protestantism and liberty through the containment of supposed Bourbon aggression.

II

For all its obvious distortions of reality, the rhetoric of a peaceful dominion of the seas founded on liberty helped to consolidate an Atlantic empire at least for the first fifty years of the eighteenth century. It could not, however, survive the strains of the great wars of mid-century and the consequences that were to follow from success in war. A new conceptualising of empire and a different set of imperial practices were to take its place.

The war with Spain that began in 1739 could still be invested with traditional libertarian rhetoric, as vindicating British freedom against Spanish oppression abroad and Walpolean oligarchy at home.[19] Projects for plundering the Spanish Main and seizing new colonies invoked the spirit of the great Elizabethan raids or of Cromwell's Western Design. War with Spain merged, however, into war with France in 1744. Twenty years of war or hostile confrontation followed, which were irrevocably to change the nature of the British empire.

Spanish possessions were presented in British propaganda as objects ripe for plunder: in British demonology France was portrayed as a standing threat to 'the Liberties of Europe' and above all to Britain herself, through a French invasion or the incitement of disaffection in Scotland or Ireland. Moreover, after the formal establishment of peace

[18] This is the theme of Jack P. Greene, *Peripheries and Center: Constitutional Development in the Extended Polities of the British Empire and the United States 1607–1788* (Athens, Ga., 1986), Book One.

[19] Kathleen Wilson, *The Sense of the People: Politics, Culture and Imperialism in England, 1715–1785* (Cambridge, 1995), 140–65.

in 1748 France still seemed to be menacing British interests throughout the world. Admiral Vernon, hero of the war against Spain, warned in 1749 that the French would be masters of the British sugar colonies within two years and that they would then be able to force the North American colonies to put themselves under French protection.[20] Ministers believed that French incursions into Nova Scotia and the Ohio valley were a dire threat to British North America. The East India Company warned that the French were trying to close down their trade in southern India.

The Walpole ministry had yielded to some extent to outside pressure in going to war with Spain in 1739.[21] Ministers were also subjected to pressure in the 1750s, but they had no inclination whatsoever to make concessions to the French overseas. The crucial importance to Britain of colonies and long-distance trades had become an article of faith for them. They did not need to be taught this by Pitt or by any other opposition patriot. In 1750 Newcastle called the 'Northern Colonies ... inestimable to us ... [I]f we lose our American Possessions; or the Influence and Weight of them in Time of Peace' he added, 'France will, with great Ease, make War with us whenever they please hereafter.'[22] By 1754 he was convinced that the French were determined to pen the British colonies into a narrow strip along the sea. 'No War can be worse for this Country, than the Suffering such Insults ... That is what We must not, We will not suffer.'[23] The stake in North America was spelt out in 1755 by Thomas Robinson, then Secretary of State, in papers justifying hostilities: one-third of British exports, naval stores, 'vast Fleets of Merchant Ships, and consequently an Increase in Seamen', a 'vast excess' of American commodities to re-export to foreigners, an influx of silver and gold from the colonial trade with Spanish and Portuguese America. Ultimately 'the whole System of public Credit in this Country' was linked to 'American Revenues and Remittances'.[24] Lord Holdernesse, the minister who chiefly concerned himself with efforts to counter the French in Asia, confessed that, although he had difficulty in persuading his colleagues to give their full attention to India, he was 'too sensible of the consequences of our Trade in India to suffer it to be diminished, much less lost'.[25] The fear

[20] Leo F. Stock ed., *Proceedings and Debates in the British Parliaments respecting North America*, 5 vols. (Washington, 1924–41), V, 369.

[21] See discussion in Philip Woodfine, 'The Anglo-Spanish War of 1739', in Jeremy Black, ed., *The Origins of War in Early Modern Europe* (Edinburgh, 1987), 185–207.

[22] Cited in T. R. Clayton, 'The Duke of Newcastle, the Earl of Halifax and the American Origins of the Seven Years War', *Historical Journal*, XXIV (1981), 576.

[23] Letter to Albermarle, 5 Sept. 1754, B[ritish] L[ibrary], Add MS 32850, ff. 218–19.

[24] Letter to Holdernesse with enclosures, 29 Aug, 1755, BL, Egerton MS 3432, ff. 292–8.

[25] Letter to R. Orme, 14 Oct. 1755, BL, Egerton MS 3488, f. 95.

was that the interruption of colonial trades would lead to a national bankruptcy and therefore to the collapse of the government's capacity to raise loans to finance Britain's defence. This spectre was frequently to be invoked in the future. It was used to justify coercing America in the 1770s and the huge deployment of force in the West Indies in the 1790s.

Failure in the early years of the war stimulated a vigorous anti-aristocratic critique of those entrusted with power, but success rallied opinion behind the government.[26] By 1758 an American observer believed that 'the Court has of late shown great regard to the Voice of the People'. He thought that 'the national Resentment was never carried so high since the days of our Edwards and Henrys ... [B]e the issue what it will our nation seems ready to embrace it, for a sort of Enthusiasm seems to possess all ranks, either to conquer or die.'[27] Many died but great conquests were of course made and a good proportion of them were kept at the peace of 1763.

III

The long confrontation with France transformed the empire that emerged from the Seven Years War. The rationale of resorting to arms in the 1750s had been a defensive one: vital overseas assets had to be protected against French aggression. Success inevitably turned the Seven Years War from a defensive war into one of conquest, even if conquest was almost invariably justified in terms of the need to guarantee security against any future French aggression rather than the seizure of territory for its own sake. British gains at the peace, however, far exceeded even the most generous interpretation of what was needed to guarantee the security of existing interests. In North America Britain now had 'a tract of continent of immense extent' reaching nearly to 'the Russian and Chinese dominions', whose wealth and power this new dominion was likely one day to match.[28] Gains had been made in the West Indies and on the West African coast. The East India Company had taken territory around Madras and Calcutta as the reward for its interventions in Indian politics and it was becoming clear that the peace in 1763 had not produced stability in India. The Company's grip on Bengal was tightening and in 1765 responsibility for the whole province and its millions of people was transferred to it.

[26] Wilson, *Sense of the People*, 178–205.

[27] *Letters and Papers of Cadwallader Colden*, vol. V, *Collections of the New York Historical Society for the Year 1921* (1923), 256–7.

[28] *Annual Register for the Year 1763*, 15.

New territorial acquisitions fundamentally changed the ethnic composition of the British empire that was in any case ceasing to be an exclusively English one, as Scots and Irish came to dominate emigration from the British Isles at every level from indentured servant to colonial governor.[29] After 1763 the British ruled French communities in Canada and Grenada, French creole Africans in Senegal and Caribs in St Vincent and Dominica. They had acquired direct responsibility for an unknown number of Native Americans living outside the boundaries of the existing colonies. Above all, Indians were coming under British rule in vast numbers in Bengal and the adjacent provinces.

Ethnic diversity produced religious diversity and diversity of law and of systems of governance. In the old empire, with limited exceptions, such as Minorca, authority had been devolved to representative bodies of Protestants, mainly of British descent, using variants on English common law. After 1763 the British had to cope with colonial populations in which there was a large Catholic majority, accustomed to French law and for whom representative government was deemed inappropriate. This was some kind of preparation for the challenge to imperial statecraft offered by dominion in India, which was the total antithesis of all the principles of the old empire: despotic rule over a huge non-Christian population, of whose religious festivals and temples the British would become patrons and whose systems of law and land tenure they would endeavour to comprehend and to apply.

The response of British governments and of a wider public to a changed empire was slow and uneven. There was no coherent review of imperial policy, a concept that was hardly recognised. New policies were adapted piecemeal, as specific needs seemed to dictate. Public debate was fitful and unfocused, although there was at least a bemused recognition of unprecedented problems on which the conventional wisdom of the classical past offered little guidance.[30] If new concepts of empire were slow to emerge, language and terminology began to change, as those associated with a dominion of the seas based on liberty no longer seemed appropriate.

By 1763 the term 'British empire in America' was well established usage. Distinctions seem, however, generally to have made between 'empire' in America and British 'establishments' or 'settlements' in Africa or Asia.[31] The expression generally applied to the terms relating to India in the 1763 Peace was that they had given the British a

[29] H. V. Bowen, *Elites, Enterprise and the Making of the British Overseas Empire 1688–1775* (Basingstoke, 1996), ch. 7.

[30] Peter N. Miller, *Defining the Common Good: Empire, Religion and Philosophy in Eighteenth-Century Britain* (Cambridge, 1994), 179–94.

[31] Edinburgh address to King, *London Gazette*, 17–21 May 1763.

'superiority' over the French, but there was as yet no talk of an eastern empire. The Bengal *diwani* was clearly much more than a superiority. Whether Bengal after 1765 had become an integral part of the British empire was, however, a difficult question. In theory it remained a province of the Mughal empire, aspects of whose administration had been entrusted to a private British corporation, not to the British state. But in spite of the difficulties of the lawyers and of the failure of administrations to obtain a clear definition of right from parliament, there seemed to be no escaping the fact that, as far as the Mughal emperor was concerned, as one commentator put it, 'the government of the country is dissolved, the sovereignty annihilated'. While it might be expedient for Bengal to be administered by a private body, 'sovereignty and dominion' could only now be vested in the crown.[32] In 1769 a pamphleteer wrote of 'the Company's dominions in the East' as being 'part of the British Empire'.[33] Edmund Burke was one of those who was quick to recognise this. In 1777 he wrote of 'the natives of *Hindostan* and those of *Virginia*' as equally part of that 'comprehensive dominion which the divine Providence has put into our hands'.[34]

Recognition that Britain was now at the centre of a single worldwide territorial empire was not matched by any systematic design to subject it to an effective central authority. Nevertheless, what were seen as practical imperatives, reinforced by the ideological inclinations of British politicians, meant that things would not be left as they had been. Initiatives to strengthen metropolitan authority were launched, if in a haphazard and uncoordinated way. Enough was, however, done to signal what seemed to be a change in the character of the empire and to plunge the North American colonies into crisis.

The principles enunciated in the run-up to war in the 1750s remained sacrosanct for the rest of the century. The established colonial trades were of fundamental importance for the British economy and therefore for Britain's standing as a European power and ultimately for her national security. Commercial regulations to maximise the advantages of empire must therefore be maintained and colonies must be defended. Britain had gone to war to protect the North American and the West Indian colonies and the East India trade. Although the economic benefits of the new acquisitions being made in India for long seemed

[32] Thomas Pownall, *The Right, Interest and Duty of Government as Concerned in the Affairs of the East India Company* [1773], pp. 25–6.

[33] Cited in H. V. Bowen, *Revenue and Reform: The Indian Problem in British Politics 1757–73* (Cambridge, 1991), 25.

[34] Warren M. Elofson and John A. Woods, eds., *The Writings and Speeches of Edmund Burke*, vol. III, *Party, Parliament, and the American War 1774–1780* (Oxford, 1996), 316.

equivocal and the process of subordinating parts of India's economy to Britain's needs was a slow one, the defence of India now also became a major national concern. India was added to North America and the West Indies as a place where a British defeat would produce a national bankruptcy.[35] There could be no relaxing of vigilance on any front after 1763. In the first place, a Bourbon *revanche* was anticipated and then the threat seemed to come from internal disaffection in the American colonies. The loss of the thirteen colonies in no way diminished the importance attached to the West Indies. Saving them became the highest priority of the American War once the French became involved and they were still regarded as essential for sustaining Britain's European war effort in the 1790s.[36]

Effective commercial regulation and defence of Britain's overseas interests required not only obedience but contributions from the North American and West Indian colonial populations and from the East India Company. If these were not freely given, what was at stake was deemed to be so important that metropolitan authority would have to be exerted to enforce them. The means to make metropolitan authority effective where this was lacking had therefore to be ensured. This was the main impulse behind such attempts as were made to reform the working of the empire.

Reforms were not only deemed a matter of state necessity; they were also congenial to the way of thinking of most of the politicians, civil servants or military men who took an interest in colonies. There is much evidence of impatience with autonomies and privileges that obstructed the uniform working of government. There was an increasing stress on the need for obedience to properly constituted authority, that is to an executive bound by law and responsible to a sovereign parliament whose powers extended to regulating the whole empire if necessary. An older language which stressed the corruption of power and the need to guard against it through the strict observance of customary rights and the sanctity of charters was regarded as being theoretically impeccable but of little practical relevance. Rights could not be in danger from a parliament whose members were confident that they could discern the 'common good' and apply it the whole empire.[37] Danger now lay not in the abuse of state power, but in its weakness and the threats to it from local autonomies and popular claims that undermined the balance of the constitution. There could be no rational fear that Britain might slide towards a French style of absolutism; what must be avoided was a quite different

[35] Bowen, *Revenue and Reform*, 22–3.

[36] Michael Duffy, *Soldiers, Sugar and Seapower. The British Expeditions to the West Indies in the War against Revolutionary France* (Oxford, 1987).

[37] Miller, *Defining the Common Good*, 159–69.

fate, that of the Dutch, whose 'sub-divisions of power' had brought 'Holland to its destruction'.[38]

The arguments used in 1760 when legislation from Pennsylvania was being considered by the Board of Trade are typical of many examples of new thinking about colonial government. Pennsylvania was accused by the crown law officers, acting for the Penn family, of trying to 'establish in place of his Majesty's government a democracy, if not an oligarchy'. The fault went back to its origins. William Penn should not have been permitted to 'grant so great powers to the Assembly'. The situation in Pennsylvania ought to be referred to parliament. The Board of Trade agreed that maintaining 'the just Prerogatives of the Crown' was essential for the 'Tranquillity of the Province itself' and for its continuing 'Dependence upon the Mother country'.[39]

Neither Pennsylvania nor other chartered colonies, such as Rhode Island and Connecticut, regarded as particularly flagrant offenders, were ever brought before parliament. Only one attack was made on colonial chartered rights, the attempt to impose modifications on Massachusetts in 1774. Only in the new colony of Quebec was a serious attempt made to create an executive that was not dependent on an elected legislature. Elsewhere, the Townshend Duties of 1767 succeeded in endowing no more than a handful of offices with salaries from parliamentary taxes.

If very little was achieved in reforming imperial structures, British governments still did enough to give what were taken to be unmistakable indications of the kind of empire that they now envisaged. This seemed to be a very different one from the partnership of equals in a dominion over the seas of early eighteenth-century rhetoric.

It was clearly to be an empire over which parliament's authority could not be questioned. Parliament had proclaimed its sovereignty in the Declaratory Act of 1766. It had voted taxes to be paid by the colonies. The Jamaica Assembly was threatened in 1765 that if it withheld supply, the House of Commons vote them in its place.[40] New York's legislature faced suspension by an act of 1767. Attempts by the colonies to explain their objections to measures like the Stamp Act

[38] Speech of Charles Yorke, 3 Feb. 1766, in R. C. Simmons and P. D. G. Thomas, eds., *Proceedings and Debates of the British Parliaments Respecting North America*, 6 vols. (Milwood, NY, 1982–89), II. 137.

[39] See the report of the Board of Trade of 24 June 1760 in Leonard W. Labaree *et al.* eds., *The Papers of Benjamin Franklin*, 27 vols. to date (New Haven, 1959–), IX. 171–2 and the accounts of the hearings in T. Penn's letters to J. Hamilton, 24 May, 6 June 1760, American Philosophical Society, MS 974.8 P 36c.

[40] Jack P. Greene, 'The Jamaica Privilege Controversy, 1764–66: An Episode in the Process of Constitutional Definition in the Early Modern British Empire', *Journal of Imperial and Commonwealth History*, XXII (1994), 30.

were in the view of many Americans rejected by the Commons with 'an air both of severity and contempt'.[41]

The new empire was to have a centralised system of defence. In the capture of Louisbourg in 1745 the New England provincials had acted in partnership with the Royal Navy and had been generously reimbursed by parliament and honoured for their pains. Great numbers of provincials had been raised during the Seven Years War. Pitt again had ensured that reimbursement was paid, but the sense of partnership had worn somewhat thin as the role of the British regulars became increasingly dominant and American officers lost their independent commands. After the war America lost its autonomy altogether in matters of defence. It was granted a British commander-in-chief with a garrison of regulars for which it was intended that Americans should pay part of the cost.

The empire had always been held together by commercial regulations. After 1763 these were revised and their enforcement was strengthened with new regulations and new Admiralty courts and Boards of Customs. While extolling the empire as a commercial partnership, Americans complained about changes that they regarded as damaging to them and made without adequate consultation. 'Our Opinions or Inclinations, if they had been known, would perhaps have weigh'd but little among you', Franklin wrote bitterly. 'We are in your Hands as clay in the Hands of the Potter.'[42]

British ministers conscientiously saw themselves as custodians in a dangerous world of the common good for an empire which required co-ordination of its defence and commerce and an undisputed source of authority to enforce that co-ordination where necessary. Without an effective state apparatus in the colonies they had, however, no alternative but to rely on the support of local elites to give effect to their decisions The need for such allies was the more urgent in a time of social upheaval caused by massive population increase and an economy undergoing rapid if uneven growth. Unfortunately for them, allies willing to support such policies, however reasonable they might seem in Britain, could not be found. Men who were as used to exercising power over their communities as the British political leaders were over theirs were deeply suspicious of what seemed to be an intrusive metropolitan government and parliament.

The Stamp Act riots of 1765 starkly revealed the total incapacity of British authority to enforce any measure that went against the grain of American opinion. 'The present weakness of the American government is amazing', wrote Governor Bernard of Massachusetts. 'In the case of

[41] J. Watts to R. Monckton, 1 June 1765, Houghton Library, Harvard, Sparks MS 38, f. 30.

[42] Letter to P. Collinson, 30 April 1764, *Franklin Papers*, XI, 181.

a popular tumult I can't command ten men that can be depended upon.'[43] The duties could not be collected in any of the colonies from Georgia to New Hampshire. Some Governors suggested the deployment of troops. Ministers were, however, apparently aware that troops could not enforce the payment of a tax by people unwilling to pay it; anyway the garrisons were too dispersed over the continent to act effectively, while troops from Britain could not be sent in winter.[44] The limitation on military force as the means for maintaining an empire was to become clear at every stage in the American crisis up to and beyond the outbreak of war. Britain's fiscal-military state enabled her to inflict heavy damage on the empires of her rivals, but it could not guarantee the survival of her own. Empire in North America had to be on American terms or not at all.

IV

If an empire obedient to metropolitan supervision and with a strong local executive able to maintain powerful armed forces proved to be unattainable in most of North America, it was to come about in India.

In part this was because of the nature of the East India Company, which, in stark contrast to American colonies, could be turned into a 'fledgling version of John Brewer's domestic state'.[45] Although it was a chartered body, with a sometimes truculent General Court of shareholders who could win wider political support in asserting the Company's autonomy, it ultimately had to yield to coercion. Parliamentary fulminations across the Atlantic could do little harm to American colonies, but parliament could consign the East India Company to oblivion, as it nearly did in 1783. The Company therefore in the last resort had to accept regulation of its affairs at home and, in as far as this was practical, in India, where a strong executive was constructed. Authority was vested in a Supreme Council and later in a Governor-General acting on his own as the agent of the British state as well as of the Company. He was backed by a salaried bureaucracy drawn from the Company's civil service and by standing armies of Indian and European soldiers. When the Company required the support of regular troops, it paid for them, an arrangement formalised by an act of parliament of 1781.[46] Another act in 1788 laid down that ministers could

[43] Letter to R. Jackson, 24 Aug. 1765, Houghton Library, Sparks MS 4/4, p. 19.

[44] John L. Bullion, 'British Ministers and American Resistance to the Stamp Act, October–December 1765', *William and Mary Quarterly*, 3rd ser., XLIX (1992), 89–107.

[45] C. A. Bayly, 'The British Military-Fiscal State and Indigenous Resistance: India 1750–1820' in Stone, ed., *An Imperial State at War*, p. 206.

[46] 21 Geo. III, c. 65, s. 17.

determine the size of the regular garrison in India for which the Company was obliged to pay.[47]

The malleability of the Company in becoming an agent of empire contributed much to the new imperial venture, but its success ultimately depended on conditions in India. To historians of the past the Indian role in the establishment of empire was essentially a passive one. Liberated by the British from despotic misrule, Indians were presumed to have wanted nothing more than security for their lives and property and toleration for their religious observances. They were believed to have no capacity for public life and not to aspire to it. Recent historiography, however, tells a story of active participation by military men, professional administrators, holders of large blocks of revenue rights, bankers and merchants, and of their often successful efforts to manipulate the new regime for their own purposes in return for their indispensable service to it.[48]

Neither the degree of coercion and deprivation involved in the establishment of British rule nor the extent of indigenous resistance to it should be underestimated. Some rulers, like Haidar Ali and Tipu Sultan of Mysore, never compromised with the British. Others formed a concerted if transitory alliance against them in the late 1770s. Within the Company's provinces, the Mughal nobility were the most obvious losers and the war of 1763–4 waged by Mir Kasim of Bengal and Shuja-ud-Daula of Awadh has been seen as their last stand.[49] There were serious uprisings in Benaras and eastern Awadh in 1781 and resistance to revenue extraction in parts of Bengal. Yet with due allowance for all this, co-operation or acquiescence at every level from the sepoy who enlisted in the Company's regiments to the Muslim grandee who tried to instruct British Governors in Mughal statecraft or the ruler who hoped to use the Company as an ally against rival Indian states, is still much more marked than resistance.

Changes in eighteenth-century India had created the conditions in which the British could play a political role. Successor states to the

[47] 28 Geo. III, c. 8.

[48] See, for instance, C. A. Bayly, *Rulers, Townsmen and Bazaars: North Indian Society in the Age of British Expansion 1780–1870* (Cambridge, 1983); *The New Cambridge History of India*, II, 1, *Indian Society and the Making of the British Empire* (Cambridge, 1988); *Empire and Information: Intelligence Gathering and Social Communication in India 1780–1870* (Cambridge, 1996); Abdul Majed Khan, *The Transition in Bengal, 1756–1775. A Study of Saiyid Muhammad Reza Khan* (Cambridge, 1969); P.J. Marshall, 'Indian Officials under the East India Company' in *Trade and Conquest; Studies in the Rise of British Dominance in India* (Aldershot, 1993); Lakshmi Subramanian, *Indigenous Capital and Imperial Expansion: Bombay, Surat and the West Coast* (New Delhi, 1995).

[49] Rajat Kanta Ray, 'Colonial Penetration and the Initial Resistance: The Mughal Ruling Class, the English East India Company and the Struggle for Bengal 1756–1800', *Indian Historical Review*, XII (1985–6), 1–105.

Mughal empire had emerged which could first be infiltrated by the British and then taken over and turned to their own purposes. These states were already employing standing armies of professional soldiers, collecting a high level of taxation in cash, subjecting trades in commodities like opium and salt to government regulation, and using bankers to advance money to the state on the security of future taxation or to remit funds. By comparison with what was possible in America, the machinery which could be adapted to construct a formidable colonial state was already in existence in some parts of India. Early British rule was built on Indian soldiers, on Indian taxes (Bengal in 1765 immediately yielded a public revenue one-quarter of that of metropolitan Britain), on Indian financiers and on a strengthened system of Indian commercial regulation.

V

This brief account of developments in America in India has had at least one linking theme: the strength of British imperial ambitions from the mid-eighteenth century and the fragility of the means of realising them without local collaboration. Is it, however, possible to find links between America and India at a deeper level? Is any kind of explanation feasible for the failure of empire in one and its success in the other in terms of trends affecting the eighteenth-century world as a whole?

Some historians seem tentatively to be reaching for an explanation in their emphasis on the effects of world-wide 'commercialisation'. The dynamic growth of an Atlantic economy in the eighteenth century has long been recognised. It is clear that the mass of colonial Americans were being drawn into the workings of this economy by the middle of the century. The political consequences that followed from this are now attracting attention. 'Sudden commercialisation' is one of the main forces that Gordon Wood sees as 'loosening the bonds of society' and disrupting hierarchies.[50] For Timothy Breen 'a rapidly expanding consumer marketplace' was creating new challenges for Americans and forcing them to reassess many things, including the nature of their connection with Britain.[51]

Historians of Asia are in little doubt that commerce was also expanding on a continental scale during at least a part of the eighteenth century and that this had political consequences too. The picture remains very uncertain in many respects, including the chronology of

[50] *Radicalism of the Revolution*, p. 134.

[51] 'Narrative of Commercial Life: Consumption, Ideology, and the Community on the Eve of the American Revolution', *William and Mary Quarterly*, 3rd ser., L (1993), 483.

the phases of expansion. Some features seem, however, to be agreed. Intercontinental trade with Europe conducted by the European companies was likely to have been an important element in commercial expansion, but it was a subordinate one by comparison with inter-Asian maritime trade, such as that between China and Southeast Asia, or trade within the great land masses of India, China or Japan. It has been suggested that the wealth generated by increasing commercialisation of agriculture and the growth of trade was more accessible to smaller, more compact political entities than it was to the great empires. Hence the rise of the Indian successor states, with their effective administrations and their close alliances with bankers and merchants, at the expense of the Mughal empire, which was increasingly starved of resources. British trade in India had grown with the overall expansion of Asian commercial activity in the seventeenth century. This expansion was the impetus for the emergence of the new political order in the first half of the eighteenth century that gave the British their opportunity to become rulers as well as traders.[52]

If there is any substance to the tentative hypothesis that the effects of global commercial expansion in the eighteenth century were undermining empire in the Atlantic, while creating opportunities for an imperial take-over in India, two final reflections suggest themselves. In the first place, the history of the British empire may have to be seen in a global context, as well as in terms of rising British power. Secondly, it might well be asked why, in a world of expanding commerce, Britain, so obviously well endowed to take advantage of such developments through her shipping, her manufacturing and her capacity to extend credit, should have committed herself so tenaciously to the uncertainties of empire, including the desperate attempt to subjugate the thirteen colonies by war. Empire certainly had a strong commercial rationale as the necessary security for the indispensable North American, West Indian and Indian trades. Yet, especially from the mid-eighteenth century, other calculations intruded. Empire was also about international rivalry, fear of others, above all of France, and increasingly about ambition and regard for Britain's status as a great power. That heady mixture was to spread the British across the globe for a long time to come.

[52] On commercialisation in Asia in general, see Bayly, *Imperial Meridian*; Victor Lieberman, 'Local Integration and Eurasian Analogies: Structuring Southeast Asian History, *c.*1350–*c.*1830', *Modern Asian Studies*, XXVII (1993), 475–572. For the Indian situation, see Bayly, *Indian Society and the British Empire*; Frank Perlin, 'Proto-Industrialisation and Pre-Colonial South Asia' *Past and Present*, XCVIII (1983), 30–95; David Washbrook, 'Progress and Problems: South Asian Economic and Social History, *c.*1720–1860', *Modern Asian Studies*, XXII (1988), 57–96.

THE HEREFORD MAP: ITS AUTHOR(S), TWO SCENES AND A BORDER

By Valerie I.J. Flint

READ 24 JANUARY 1998

THE Hereford Map is drawn upon a single pentangular skin of very high quality and, presumably, expense. It measures some 5'2" by 4'4" at its longest and widest points,[1] and has, in addition to the world map from which it takes its name, a number of ornamented borders, inscriptions in Latin and Anglo-Norman, and illuminated scenes. The map thus has a great many claims to the attention of medieval historians, art historians and linguists, but I would single out three. Firstly, as a result of the loss of the Ebstorf Map, the Hereford Map is now the largest and most elaborate medieval *mappa mundi* known to have survived. Secondly, it is still one of the most difficult there is of the genre definitively to date, place and understand; this in the face of over more than one hundred and fifty years of effort on the part of a whole series of accomplished scholars and cartographers,[2] effort of which the recent short and penetrating book by Professor Harvey is a triumphant example.[3] Thirdly, though the map is rightly now regarded by the Hereford Cathedral Chapter as one of its greatest treasures, and is quite beautifully cared for and displayed in Hereford, we are still all a little hazy about how it got there in the first place. Professor Harvey

[1] Complete with its oak framework and triangular hanger, the whole would reach a height of 8 feet; W. L. Bevan and H. W. Phillott, *Medieval Geography: An Essay in Illustration of the Hereford Mappa Mundi* (London and Hereford, 1873), 13. Photographs reproduced by courtesy of the Trustees of the Hereford Mappa Mundi.

[2] The most complete discussion of the map, albeit now a little out of date, is that of Bevan and Phillott, *Medieval Geography*. An excellent introductory description, bibliography and discussion of some of the problems associated with the map is provided in G. R. Crone, *The World Map by Richard of Haldingham in Hereford with Memoir by G. R. Crone* (London, 1954). This memoir accompanies a large-scale collotype reproduction of the whole, on a scale of approximately 9/10 of the original. The reproduction occupies nine slightly overlapping separate sheets, and is accompanied by a tenth drawn sheet, illustrating the possible cartographical sources of the map. It is a magnificent working tool. The discussion in the memoir is summarised and extended in Crone, 'New Light on the Hereford Map', *The Geographical Journal*, 131 (4) (1965), 446–62. Brief guides are provided by A. L. Moir and M. A. Letts, *The World Map in Hereford Cathedral* (Hereford, 1971), and M. Jancey, *Mappa Mundi: The Map of the World in Hereford Cathedral* (Hereford, 1987).

[3] P. D. A. Harvey, *Mappa Mundi. The Hereford World Map* (London and Hereford, 1996).

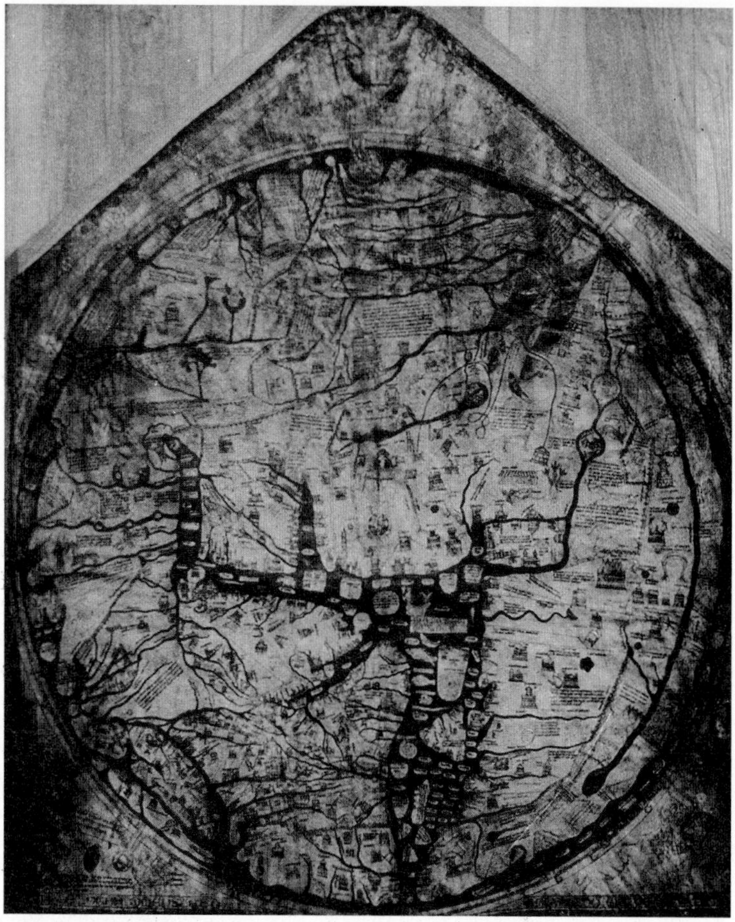

1. The Hereford Mappa Mundi.

suspects it may originally have been made in Lincoln, a suspicion to which I might perhaps now bring a little additional support. But if it was made in Lincoln, how, then, did it come to Hereford, when did it come and, perhaps most importantly of all, why?

I shall attempt to offer answers to these three questions, and I hope, in so doing, to repay the Trustees of the map in some part for their kind hospitality there by showing that the Hereford Map was from the very first integral to the history, and indeed to the very fabric, of that cathedral which is now its home. In preface, I should like briefly to

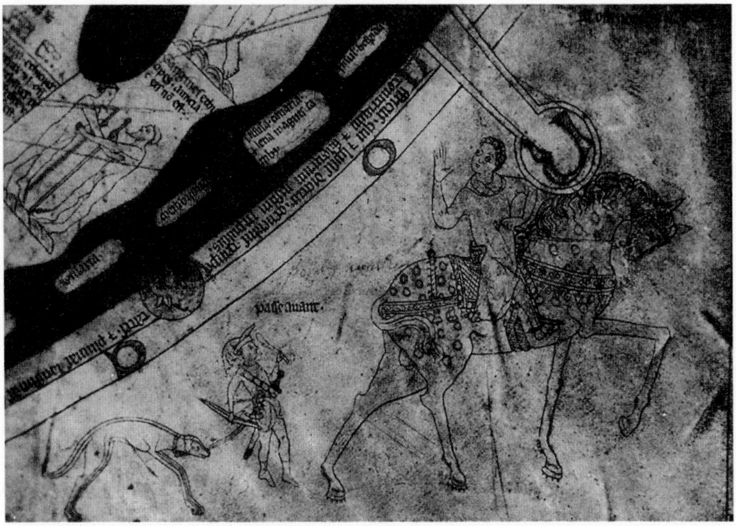

2. *Right-hand corner: hunting scene.*

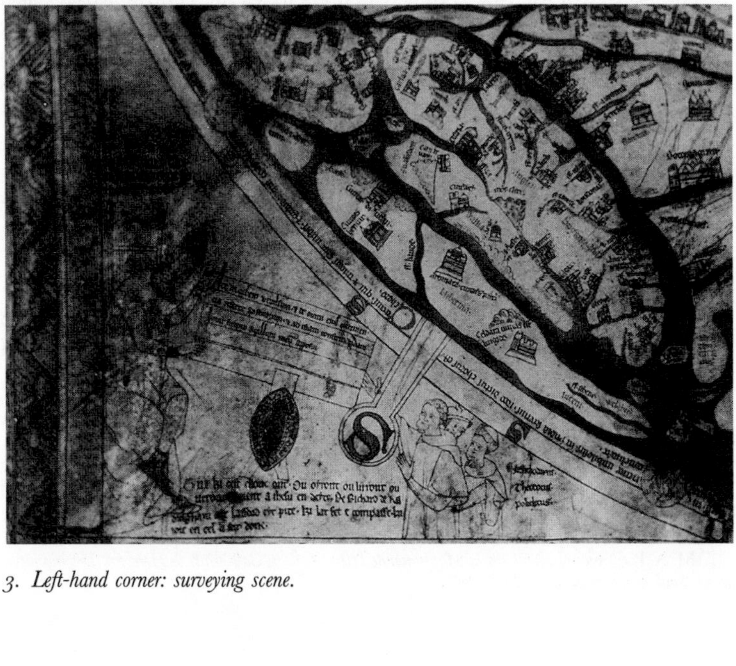

3. *Left-hand corner: surveying scene.*

extricate from the mass of illustration and inscription the two scenes and the border of the title, and to summarise those matters relevant to my argument upon which scholars appear to be agreed.

The two scenes are those on the bottom right- and left-hand corners of the map. At the bottom right-hand corner of the pentangular skin we have a drawing of a man on horseback, followed by a huntsman on foot, with hounds, and, at the corresponding bottom left-hand corner there is a seated figure, representing (or so it would appear from the quotation from Luke 2:1 written above it[4]) the Roman Emperor Augustus. The emperor is here engaged in requiring that the known world be enrolled (in the Vulgate, 'described' or, in the Authorised Version, 'taxed'; a decree which, of course, brought the Holy Family to Bethlehem). Augustus accordingly appoints three commissioners to the task. This scene seems to be related to an outer inscription, tracing the border of the skin; one in which the first known survey of the Roman world is attributed to the Emperor Julius Caesar. We might note immediately that both outer inscription and scene commission only three persons to the task, whereas the map's putative source for Julius Caesar's survey, Ethicus, names four;[5] that the Emperor Augustus of the scene is wearing a tiara, crowned by a cross, seemingly the papal tiara, and that the vesica seal attached to the emperor's instructions also suggests an ecclesiastical connection—an observation I owe to my colleague, Professor Barbara English.

The border of the title is that which encircles the central *mappa mundi* itself, enclosing it from the scenes. Four drawn ligatures stretch out from this frame at its four quadrants. The top two ligatures appear to append the map to the outer surveying inscription. The bottom two are extended into the right- and left-hand scenes. On the ends of the ligatures are written four separate letters, in this order (beginning at the top left and moving clockwise round the map); M.O.R.S. The letters thus spell out 'mors', or death, symbolising, according to d'Avezac, the fact that 'l'empire de la mort environne de toutes parts le monde habité'.[6]

The relevant matters upon which scholars interested in the map are now generally agreed are these. The overall design of the central *mappa mundi* is that of the orthodox medieval TO map, and the Hereford

[4] 'And it came to pass that in those days there went out a decree from Caesar Augustus, that the whole world should be enrolled.'

[5] The three are Nicodoxus, Theodotus and Policlitus; Didymus is omitted. Thus the author of the map may have drawn upon a particular recension of the so-called *Cosmographia* of Ethicus (Bevan and Phillott, *Medieval Geography*, 14–15) or he may have made the change deliberately: see below.

[6] M. A. P. d'Avezac, *Note sur la Mappemonde Historiée de la Cathédrale de Hereford. Determination de sa Date et de ses Sources* (Paris, 1862), 9.

Map is, then, one more example of those tolerably common moralising *mappae mundi* which direct the would-be spiritual journeyer towards the Terrestrial Paradise and the salvation of his soul.[7] This map is, for by far the greater part, the work of a single scribe, but the scribe worked from a draft prepared by the true author, and seems to have been none too good at Latin expansions or, come to that, at sorting out which continent is which, for the names of Europe and of Africa are reversed; a mistake whose dimensions inspire a certain awe.[8] The donkey-work, in other words, was done by a, perhaps inexperienced, amanuensis. Paleographically, the whole may be dated to the late thirteenth or early fourteenth centuries,[9] and the Welsh castles of Conway and Caernarvon are clearly marked upon the *mappa mundi* and are the only Welsh castles represented. This suggests a date close to the conquest of Wales, 1282–3, for the completion of the whole and, perhaps, for its display.[10] On the representations of Europe and of Asia there are imprinted itineraries, some of which are of a thirteenth-century date and relevance, and many of which seem to be meant to illustrate biblical or pilgrimage journeys.[11] The map seems likely at some time to have formed the central panel of a triptych,[12] may at some point have been an altarpiece or *retable*,[13] and was meant to be placed within an ecclesiastical building.[14] There are deep score marks upon certain sections of the map, especially (but not exclusively) over France and Northern Italy. There is some relationship between the Hereford map and the Ebstorf map,[15] but a

[7] A convenient introduction to medieval *mappae mundi*, with some (woefully incomplete) reference to the place of the Hereford Map among them, may be found in V. I. J. Flint, *The Imaginative Landscape of Christopher Columbus* (Princeton, 1992), 5–18.

[8] Harvey, *Mappa Mundi*, 10.

[9] Bevan and Phillott, *Medieval Geography*, pp. 6–8, revised Harvey, *Mappa Mundi*, 7–10.

[10] Though built on the sites of earlier castles and finished years later, both Caernarvon and Conway were fortified in 1283 as the first foundations after the conquest of Wales. J. Morris, *The Welsh Wars of Edward I* (Oxford, 1901), 198.

[11] Crone, *The World Map*, 14–22. For the possible late-thirteenth-century date of certain of the itineraries see especially Crone, 'New light', 452–62. Crone thought it may have been made in aid of persons actually going on a journey: ibid. 462.

[12] See the discussion in *The Observer* 13 and 20 August 1989, 2 and 10 and, especially, by Martin Bailey on 5 November of the same year; also Harvey, *Mappa Mundi*, 12–14.

[13] Richard Gough said that it 'served antiently for an altarpiece in this church' (the church of Hereford Cathedral that is); *British Topography*, i (London, 1780), quoted by Crone, *The World Map*, 1.

[14] The matter is carefully discussed by M. Kupfer, 'Medieval World Maps: Embedded Images, Interpretive Frames', *Word and Image*, 10(3) (1994), 262–88 (especially 271–5). She doubts the altarpiece theory and suggests instead that the map occupied some place 'within the architectural fabric' of an ecclesiastical building which was accessible to the laity.

[15] For a recent discussion of the similarities between the Ebstorf and Hereford maps see P. Gautier Dalché, *La 'Descriptio Mappae Mundi' de Hugues de Saint Victor* (Paris, 1988), 181–92.The dating of the Ebstorf map is fully discussed in H. Kugler, ed. *Ein Weltbild vor Columbus. Die Ebstorfer Weltkarte* (Munich, 1991).

far closer one between the Hereford map and the so-called Henry of Mainz map found in the early thirteenth century Ms. Corpus Christi College, Cambridge, 66 (f.2), where it apparently prefaces an important copy of the *Imago Mundi* of Honorius Augustodunensis and comes from the Cistercian abbey of Sawley in Yorkshire.[16] The name of the map's putative author, one Richard of Haldingham and Lafford, is clearly written upon the bottom left-hand corner of the skin.

I shall begin my attempt to press the matter forward with this author. Between the two outer borders and the surveying scene a verse in Anglo-Norman asks for the prayers of the onlookers for the said Richard:

> May all who have this 'estoire', or shall hear it, or read it, or see it, pray to Jesus, in God, that He may have pity on the soul of Richard of Haldingham and Lafford, who has brought it all about, and grant him the joys of heaven.[17]

This verse suggests that the map was in some way connected with something which could be read; a circumstance which led Denholm-Young to conclude that the Hereford Map was based upon a smaller exemplar, originally accompanying a book.[18] The Latin inscription on the bottom right-hand side of the map, for that matter, suggests this too:

> Descriptio orosii de ornesta mundi *sicut interius ostenditur.*

This might, of course, lead to the conclusion that Richard of Haldingham designed the map for the book, not this map, but this seems an unnecessary complication, even for our tortured profession. We may accept that Richard of Haldingham and Lafford drew up the prescriptions for the Hereford Map and, or so it seems from the emphasis on hearing and seeing as well as reading, for a didactic purpose of some kind. Its purpose may thus be related to that of

[16] Bevan and Phillott, *Medieval Geography*, xxxvi–xxxix. This manuscript is described in V. I. J. Flint, 'The Imago Mundi of Honorius Augustodunensis', *Archives d'Histoire Doctrinale et Littéraire*, 49 (1982), 24 and, more fully, in M. R. James, *A Descriptive Catalogue of the Manuscripts in the Library of Corpus Christi College Cambridge*, i (Cambridge, 1912).

[17] Tuz ki cest estorie ont
Ou oyront ou liront ou veront
Prient a Jhesu en deyte
De Richard de Haldingham e de Lafford eyt pite
Ki lat fet e compasse
Ki ioie en cel li seit done.

[18] N. Denholm-Young, 'The *Mappa Mundi* of Richard of Haldingham at Hereford', *Speculum*, 32 (1957), 308 and 314.

teaching rolls or, more pertinently as I have come to convince myself, to the *Arma Christi* rolls used to guide devout laity and pilgrims through their penitential exercises;[19] hence, perhaps, the pilgrimage itineraries and the score marks. We shall return to this.

The career of Richard of Haldingham and Lafford has long been a cause of anxiety to historians,[20] and rightly so, for clerical Richards de Lafford or de la Ford are by no means a rarity in this period. It may be possible now, however, to extend our knowledge of this career and to enquire a little further into the particular anxieties and ambitions both of Richard of Lafford himself and of his immediate family. It is particularly necessary that we enquire into the latter, for these anxieties and ambitions were, I have come firmly to believe, central to Richard's own directions for the map, and to its eventual completion and home in Hereford.

Haldingham and Lafford are, in more modern terms, Holdingham and Sleaford, neighbouring parishes in the Kesteven and Holland section of the diocese of Lincoln. Lafford/Sleaford was a prebend of Lincoln cathedral and a rural deanery.[21] One Richard 'de Bello' was canon prebendary of Lafford by January 1265. By 1273 this Richard is being described as 'magister'.[22] By this time, then, he had perhaps been to the schools of Oxford, in the diocese of Lincoln.[23] This same Richard was also treasurer of Lincoln Cathedral between the years 1270 and

[19] On the association of the words used with instruction see B. Levy, 'Signes et Communications "Extraterrestres". Les Inscriptions Marginales de la Mappemonde de Hereford (13e Siècle)', in *La Grande Aventure de la Decouverte du Monde au Moyen Age* (Greifswald, 1996), 37–9. On the *Arma Christi* rolls see R. H. Robbins, 'The "Arma Christi" Rolls', *Modern Language Review*, 34 (1939), 415–21. I am grateful to Dr Jeanne Krochialis for the latter reference.

[20] The most recent full discussions of Richard's career are those of Denholm-Young, 'The *Mappa Mundi*', 307–14 and W. N. Yates, 'The Authorship of the Hereford mappa mundi and the Career of Richard de Bello', *Transactions of the Woolhope Naturalists' Field Club* 41(2) (1974), 165–72. The references provided by A. B. Emden, *A Biographical Register of the University of Oxford*, i (Oxford, 1959), 556, are also helpful. Here I shall dissent, however, from the arguments of all three; this as a result of incorporating the more recent editions of *Le Neve* and, in particular, of returning to the sources with the invaluable help of Dr Diana Greenway. Her timely intervention, indeed, led me to rewrite this section of the paper after its delivery to the Society. I am most grateful to her.

[21] The deanery of Sleaford was a large one, later divided into Old and New Sleaford, and the tithes of Holdingham formed part of the endowment of the prebend. An idea of the extent of medieval Lafford, or Sleaford, may be gained from C. R. Humphery-Smith, *The Phillimore Atlas and Index of Parish Registers* (Chichester, 1984). Holdingham had been, it seems, fully absorbed into New Sleaford by the sixteenth century, but a district so named is clearly marked on the 1891 Ordnance Survey map of Lincolnshire.

[22] D. E. Greenway, *John le Neve Fasti Ecclesiae Anglicanae 1066-1300,* iii *Lincoln* (London, 1977), 20 and 73. Hereinafter *Fasti.*

[23] It is possible that Richard held a dispensation from his duties in Lafford after 1265, to enable him to attend the schools, although no such dispensation has survived.

1278 (his name last occurs in this office in the April of 1278). In 1277 Richard de Bello is named clearly both as treasurer of the cathedral and holder of the prebend of Lafford, with Henry of Swindirby as his perpetual vicar at the church at Lafford.[24] A member of the de Bello family is recorded on the dorse of the Lincoln Residentiary Roll for 1278 as receiving a payment 'pro altaria Sancte Lucye', a payment perhaps made by this very treasurer in discharge of his responsibility for the lamps of the cathedral.[25]

The end of Richard's period as treasurer (c. April 1278) appears roughly to correspond with the illness and death of Richard Gravesend (bishop of Lincoln 1258–79). Richard de Bello himself died late in 1278,[26] but there is no notice of a successor to him at Lafford until 1284, when John de Withington was collated to the prebend.[27] We shall return also to the last years of Richard Gravesend, for they are of great importance both to our understanding of treasurer Richard de Bello's ambitions for himself and his family, and to the case I wish eventually to present here.

Richard de Bello appears, in his Anglo-Norman form, as Richard 'de la Bataille' or 'Bat(t)ayl(l)(e)'. His obit is entered, indeed, on the Lincoln Residentiary Roll in this second guise. Such a Richard is also found in the account roll of Richard Swinfield, Bishop of Hereford 1283–1317. There, in 1289, 'Magister Richard de la Batayl' is listed as receiving a gift of meat from Bishop Swinfield's Bosbury estate. Among the incidental expenses recorded on the dorse of this roll, the same Richard's serving man, or 'garcio', is rewarded with a payment of sixpence.[28] Bosbury was one of Bishop Swinfield's favourite manors,

[24] *Rotuli Ricardi Gravesend*, ed. F.N. Davis *et al.* (Lincoln, 1925), 72.

[25] 'Item libet Ade de Belle [*sic*] capelano pro altaria sancte Lucye xiii.s.iiii.d.anno octavo': Lincoln Archives Office, Cv/1. The treasurer was required, among his many other duties 'luminaria ecclesie ministrare'; C. Wordsworth and H. Bradshaw, *Lincoln Cathedral Statutes*, ii (Cambridge, 1897), 160.

[26] I am indebted to Dr Diana Greenway for drawing my attention to his obituary, which is entered in the Lincoln Residentiary Roll of 1278, and dated 4 November. Lincoln Cathedral Archives, Cv/1. This entry remained unnoticed in all previous reconstructions of Richard's career.

[27] Greenway, *Fasti*, iii *Lincoln*, 74. John appointed one Robert of Whitmore to the vicarage on the death of Henry of Swindirby in 1284, and was himself dead by 1286; *The Rolls and Register of Bishop Oliver Sutton 1280–1299* ed. R.M.T. Hill, i (Lincoln, 1948), 58, 90. This Robert may the same 'Master Robert de Laforda' who acquires a licence in 1289 to hold a benefice besides his canonry and Southwell prebend. W.K. Bliss, *Calendar of Entries in the Papal Registers Relating to Great Britain and Ireland: Papal Letters, i 1198–1304* (London, 1893). There is no mention after this of Master Richard de Bello at Lafford.

[28] J. Webb, *A Roll of the Household Expenses of Richard de Swinfield, Bishop of Hereford During part of the Years 1289 and 1291* (London, Camden Society, 1853–4), 20, 151. Denhom-Young ('The *Mappa Mundi*', 309) suggests that the meat was a haunch of venison, but the context implies a large piece of fatted calf.

and he stayed there as often as he could. It seems, then, that a second Richard de Bello, one important enough to have a serving man, was living in the vicinity of Bosbury in 1289, perhaps as a dependent or friend of Bishop Swinfield himself. Sadly, the section from Michaelmas 1289 until Michaelmas 1290 is the only part of Swinfield's account roll which has survived.

In March 1305 (please note), however, Richard Swinfield instituted a Richard de Bello to a Hereford prebend, that of Norton.[29] This Richard then seems to have become steadily (though slowly) prominent in the service of the Bishop of Hereford,[30] but in the meantime a Master Richard de Bello had been acquiring patronage from the Bishop of Salisbury, Simon of Ghent (bishop 1297–1315); this with an even greater speed and *élan*. In March 1298 he obtained the prebend of Beauminster in the cathedral of Salisbury, only to exchange it smartly, in the following June, for the better one of Grantham Australis (a Salisbury prebend in the diocese of Lincoln), with the permission of Bishop Oliver Sutton of Lincoln, successor to Richard Gravesend.[31] Two months later, in August in the same year, Richard de Bello exchanged this too, for the prebend of Coombe Bisset and Harnham, Wilts. (with land in Boscombe). This he held rather longer; until, indeed, September 1305, when he added to the Hereford prebend of Norton his best preferment of all, the Salisbury prebend of Highworth, Wilts., valued in 1291 at £100 *per annum*.[32] The bishops of Hereford and Salisbury seem, then, in the year 1305, to have acted almost in unison to this second Richard's advantage. Richard de Bello held Highworth from 1305 until his death in 1326, against an Italian would-be intruder; this with the assistance of both the Bishop of Salisbury and, a shade more reluctantly, the pope.[33]

Meanwhile, in 1299 Richard de Bello had become Vicar General of Salisbury, an office which perhaps helped him to Highworth. Then, in 1313 he became Rector of Poulshot, Wilts., and of Compton Abbas, Dorset, both of them Salisbury benefices again, which he added to

[29] J. M. Horn, *Fasti 1300–1541*, ii *Hereford* (London, 1962), 38; *Registrum Ricardi de Swinfield Episcopi Herefordensis*, ed. W. W. Capes (London, 1909), 536.

[30] He served, for instance, as proctor for Swinfield, with Adam of Orleton, at a synod in St Paul's in 1313. Capes, *Registrum*, 491.

[31] D. E. Greenway, *Fasti*, iv *Salisbury* (London, 1991), 49; *The Rolls and Register*, ed. Hill, i 229–30.

[32] Greenway, *Fasti*, iv *Salisbury*, 64 and 70.

[33] At the death of the previous holder, William of Savoy, Highworth had been collated to John of Frescobaldi. Bishop Simon of Ghent inhibited the institution of John, and protected Richard's rights with some ferocity against the foreigner, but the matter was not resolved until 1308, when papal intervention adjudged the benefice finally to Richard. J. M. Horn, *Fasti*, iii *Salisbury* (London, 1962), 58.

Highworth and to Norton.[34] He was Archdeacon of Berkshire (a Salisbury archdeaconry) by 1315 and keeper of the temporalities of Salisbury, *sede vacante* in 1315. Between 1294 and 1308 Richard was rector also of Sutton Coldfield in Warwickshire, diocese of Lichfield.[35] Richard de Bello is recorded again as rector of Stoke Talmage in Oxfordshire from 1294–96, during Bishop Oliver Sutton of Lincoln's episcopacy and, interestingly, as receiving major orders at Sutton's hands in 1293, just before this particular preferment.[36] This Richard must have been in minor orders, then, when Bishop Swinfield befriended him, taking major orders only shortly before the minor avalanche of promotions began to descend upon his doubtless happily exposed head.

One branch of the family 'de Bello' came from Sussex, deriving its name, it seems, from Battle itself; but there was another branch to be found in South Yorkshire and Lincolnshire by the early thirteenth century.[37] Both the Richard of Haldingham and Lafford of the map and the Richard de Bello who was ordained by Bishop Sutton are likely to have come, therefore, from the South Yorkshire and Lincolnshire branch of the family,[38] and the second Richard de Bello bids fair to be a close relative and dependant of the first; a relative who subsequently, however, found preferment elsewhere.[39] This second

[34] Richard became prominent in Salisbury affairs from his very first collation there, appearing frequently in Bishop Simon's register as a witness to institutions to canonries. See, for these preferments, *Registrum Simonis de Gandavo Diocesis Saresbiriensis 1297–1315*, ed. C. T. Flower and M. C. B. Dawes (Oxford, 1934), 620, 641, 719–20 and *passim.*

[35] This too may be explained by Richard's Salisbury connections, for the bishop of Lichfield was, at the time, Roger of Longespée (bishop 1257–95), fourth (and natural) son of William Longespée, Earl of Salisbury. M. Gibbs and J. Lang, *The Bishops and Reform 1215–1272* (Oxford, 1934), 190 and 556.

[36] He became subdeacon in 1293 and priest in 1294; Yates, 'The Authorship', 170. Yates points here to the fact that some of the secular cathedrals of England were exceedingly tolerant of deficient orders among their prebendaries, and began to correct these deficiencies only gradually, and after the condemnation of them by the second Council of Lyons, 1274. He suggests, indeed, that Richard of Lafford himself may have resigned his treasurership as a result of these corrections.

[37] Greenway, *Fasti*, iii *Lincoln*, 20. Denholm-Young, 'The *Mappa Mundi*', 311–13.

[38] The Sussex branch may have produced the Richard de Bello who, in 1260, was given a dispensation to hold one benefice with cure of souls as well as the rectories of 'Kingesnade and Demecherethe' (Kingsworth and Dymchurch) in Kent he already held. Bliss, *Calendar*, 370. There was still a de Bello at Kingsworth in the 1290s. *Calendar of Patent Rolls 1292–1301*, 93. This circumstance would, according to Emden (*A Biographical*, 556) have made this Richard too old in 1260 to have been the same as the Richard de Bello of the later preferments. Emden decided, therefore, that the Richard of the southern branch must have been the same as the prebendary of Lafford and the maker of the map, but distinct from the later Richard de Bello who prospered. We should now, however, detach the Sussex branch from the present discussion.

[39] The surname 'de Bello' or 'de la Batayl' appears quite frequently in the registers of the Lincoln diocese (see, for example, *Rotuli Ricardi Gravesend*, ed. Davis, 181; *The Roll and Register*, ed. Hill, v, 32, vii, 12). There was a 'Batayle Hall' in Oxford, of which one 'R.

Richard de Bello prospered during the last decades of the thirteenth century and, even more so, during the first two decades of the fourteenth, and he held benefices in four different dioceses simultaneously. He was a pluralist, in short, and one, furthermore, who seems to have taken major orders comparatively late in his career. Yet, despite these facts (or perhaps because of them?) Richard enjoyed the support of four prominent secular bishops, those of Lincoln, Hereford, Lichfield and Salisbury, and that of the bishop of Salisbury, Simon of Ghent, most of all.

Salisbury, we might mark here, was chosen by King Edward I as the scene of a major parliament in February 1297, during the episcopate of Simon's predecessor, Nicholas Longespee, son of the earl; one before which the king made clear his need and determination to tax his clergy.[40] Simon of Ghent remained a close friend of the king. This need and determination, together with the interest of the bishops of Hereford and Salisbury and the year 1305, bear, as I think, closely upon the prosperity of this later Richard de Bello—and upon the eventual form and placing of the Hereford Map.

The careers of Master Richard de Bello/Richard of Haldingham and Lafford the treasurer (d.1278), and of the second Master Richard de Bello the pluralist began, then, in the diocese of Lincoln, from which their immediate family may have come, and from which they seem to have had good reason to expect preferment. After Richard of Haldingham and Lafford had ceased to be treasurer of Lincoln and had died, however, and before the first manifestation of the friendship of Bishop Richard Swinfield of Hereford towards the second Richard in 1289, there is a silence about them lasting some eleven years. I have said that Richard of Lafford's disappearance from his position as treasurer of Lincoln, and his death, took place during the last years of the episcopate of Bishop Richard of Gravesend, who himself died in December 1279. We may turn now, then, to this troubled time.

Bishop Richard of Gravesend had been ill for some years before his death. In 1275 a coadjutor was sent by Archbishop Kilwardby of Canterbury to assist him,[41] but these interim arrangements were clearly unsatisfactory in some way, for in September 1279 Archbishop John Pecham, newly chosen successor to Kilwardby at Canterbury, addressed

de las Bataylle' (perhaps this one or a near relative) was, in 1300, in charge of the rents; Emden, *A Biographical*, 566.

[40] M. Prestwich, *Edward I* (London, 1988), 415–17.

[41] Emden, *A Biographical*, ii 804. Emden attributes the decision to Pecham, but the date, from the *Annals of Dunstable*, places it within Kilwardby's archiepiscopate. The coadjutor is unnamed; *Annales Monastici*, ed. H. R. Luard, iii (Rolls Series 36, London, 1864), 268.

a blistering letter to Gravesend.[42] Pecham complained in this of Gravesend's activities at Lincoln, accusing him of sequestering benefices, levying fines for concessions, and ordering patrons into speedy presentations in ways which outdid both the canons and common sense; all of this, quite unjustly, under the cover of Pecham's own name, and with (as Pecham spluttered) wholly spurious reference to the council the archbishop had recently held at Reading (July–August 1279), and to its legislation against pluralism, deficient orders and non-residence. We might mark that both Pecham's complaints against Gravesend, and the latter's interpretation of the canons of the Council of Reading, had financial implications; implications of which Gravesend, himself once treasurer of the cathedral of Hereford indeed,[43] would have been very well aware. The whole affair must then, at least in its initial stages, have concerned Lincoln's treasurer, Richard of Haldingham and Lafford, and perhaps his family dependants above all. We cannot know whether the two Richards de Bello fell victim to the over-the-top type of activities of which Pecham now complained, or whether they merely took careful, and nervous, note of them. They could not, however, have remained aloof from them, and the omens were undoubtedly bad for one ambitious of the kind of career the second Richard would come later so successfully to pursue.

There was certainly an upheaval in the chancery of Lincoln in the year 1278. The chancellor, John le Romeyn, moved from the chancellorship to the precentorship in the September of that year, and he was not replaced formally until Bishop Oliver Sutton, Gravesend's successor, appointed Simon de Baumberg to the position in 1281.[44] In the meantime, from at least June 1278, through Gravesend's death in 1279 and until the summer of 1280, Richard Swinfield, later Bishop of Hereford and friend of the second Richard de Bello by 1289 at the latest, administered the Lincoln cathedral chancery.[45] Richard Swinfield and Richard de Bello of Lafford might perhaps have met earlier at Oxford in the late 1260s, for in 1265 Swinfield had entered the service of the redoubtable Thomas Cantilupe, chancellor of the university 1261–3 and 1273–4, and Swinfield's own predecessor as Bishop of Hereford 1275–82.[46] Whether or not he had met him before, Richard of Lafford, newly retired and perhaps ailing Lincoln treasurer, is exceedingly likely to have encountered Swinfield at the Lincoln chancery

[42] *Registrum Epistolarum Fratris Johannis Peckham Archiepiscopi Cantuariensis*, ed. C. Y. Martin, i (London, 1882), 70–1.

[43] Greenway, *Fasti*, iii *Lincoln*, 37.

[44] Simon's name first occurs in the December of that year. Greenway, *Fasti*, iii *Lincoln*, 17–18.

[45] *Acta Sanctorum* Oct. 1, 705b (hereafter *AS*).

[46] Emden, *A Biographical*, i, 348.

in the year 1278,[47] and it is equally likely, as I hope to show, that the second Richard de Bello encountered him there too.

Richard Swinfield had been Thomas Cantilupe's chaplain at Oxford, became Cantilupe's secretary when the latter was elected bishop of Hereford in 1275, and remained Cantilupe's devoted friend for the rest of his life. It must therefore have been with Cantilupe's blessing that Swinfield went up from Hereford to Lincoln in 1278 to administer the cathedral chancery at this crucial time. Indeed, it is by no means beyond the bounds of possibility (and certainly not inconsistent with what we know of Cantilupe's own personality) that Cantilupe sent Swinfield there *specifically* to ensure that Gravesend's interests, and his own, were maintained in Lincoln in the face of the coadjutor sent by Kilwardby, and to stir up trouble if need be with interfering friar-archbishops of Canterbury in general. Cantilupe was familiar with the Lincoln diocese, both as chancellor of Oxford and as recent holder of a benefice there,[48] and Cantilupe and Bishop Richard Gravesend of Lincoln had long been friends.[49] Swinfield had gained a first prebend at the cathedral of Hereford in 1277, and would gain a second in 1279 together with a fistful of other benefices there and in other dioceses.[50] He too swiftly became a pluralist then, Pecham's strictures notwithstanding, and with Cantilupe's support.

Archbishop Kilwardby resigned the See of Canterbury in May 1278 to become Cardinal Bishop of Porto, and there was a contested vacancy there until the nomination of Pecham in January 1279; but Kilwardby had managed to complete a visitation of the Lincoln diocese before resigning and, in 1277, had questioned at least one of Gravesend's presentations to a benefice.[51] Cantilupe and Gravesend may already have been in alliance, then, when Cantilupe sent Swinfield up to Lincoln by June 1278. Thomas Cantilupe, we might note, would never have any truck with archiepiscopal interference in presentations within a diocese, or, come to that, with archiepiscopal attacks upon licensed pluralism.[52] Gravesend, Cantilupe, Swinfield

[47] The residence lists for 1278 show that the treasurer (unnamed) tended frequently to be in residence. Lincoln Archives Office Cv/1. On the Residentiary Rolls see also H. Bradshaw and C. Wordsworth, *Lincoln Cathedral Statutes*, ii (Cambridge, 1897), ccvi–ccix.

[48] Thomas Cantilupe was collated to the Lincoln benefice of Coleby in 1265, and he seems to have held it until he became bishop of Hereford in 1275, when a Master Gilbert of Heywode succeeded him. *Rotuli Ricardi Gravesend*, ed. Davis, 20, 67. The fourteenth-century tomb of the third Baron Cantilupe, still in the cathedral, attests to a continuing family interest.

[49] Richard Gravesend had been a supporter of the baronial cause in 1258–65 with Cantilupe. See Emden, *A Biographical*, ii, 803–4.

[50] Webb, *A Roll*, lxiv. See also Emden, *A Biographical*, iii, 1833–4.

[51] *Annales Monastici*, ed. Luard, iii, 276–9 (*Annals of Dunstable*).

[52] A papal dispensation, though necessary, seems to have been deemed by him sufficient check to abuses, together with local episcopal supervision.

and associated later critics of the canons of Reading[53] were well capable of a concerted and sophisticated, even mocking, campaign against over-officious archbishops (perhaps especially during a vacancy), and, through the use of such words as 'machinationes' and 'subversio' in his blistering letter, Pecham certainly implies that there were plotters about in Lincoln, determined to undermine him.[54] It appears, in sum, that the friends did indeed mean to stir up trouble there for metropolitans with over-zealous interventionist and anti-pluralist intentions, and that they succeeded mightily. All of this added to the urgency of the situation which confronted Richard of Lafford and his relatives in Gravesend's Lincoln in the year 1278; but perhaps to their opportunities too.

This troubled period and these particular contrivances and concerns within the diocese of Lincoln in the years 1277–9 provide, as I think, the clues we need to explain Richard de Bello of Lafford's retirement from the Lincoln treasury, the relationship the second Richard de Bello had established with Bishop Swinfield by the year 1289, and, as I hope at the last to demonstrate, the completion, and ultimate fate, of Richard de Bello of Lafford's map. It is tempting, indeed, to suggest that Swinfield might have encouraged the pluralist-to-be Richard de Bello to move from Lincoln at this very time, especially when his relative, the treasurer, died. Certainly the tensions in the matters of pluralism, presentation, deficient orders and non-residence between Archbishop Pecham and some of his secular bishops on the one hand, and between archbishop and king on the other, assumed alarming dimensions in these years;[55] and it looks as though both of the Richards de Bello may have taken sides on them, the second with an urgent eye to the furtherance of his career.

After his spell at the Lincoln chancery Richard Swinfield went with his friend and master, Thomas Cantilupe, to Normandy in the summer of 1280. The exile was made necessary by Cantilupe's increasingly bitter troubles with (as he saw it) Archbishop Pecham's further objectionable claims to jurisdiction within the Hereford diocese. Both returned in the autumn of 1281. In March 1282 the two departed once

[53] The generally furious opposition to the Council of Reading shows that there were many such critics; cf. F. M. Powicke and C. R. Cheney, *Councils and Synods, ii 1209–1303* (Oxford, 1964), 828.

[54] He begins his letter: 'Frequenter ea quae ad remedium animarum salubriter ordinantur, suadente humani generis inimico, tendunt ad noxam, et per malorum machinationes miserrrime pervertuntur', and goes on to speak of 'subversio' in connection with these schemes.

[55] For an excellent account of King Edward I's hostility towards Pecham's appointment and attitudes see Prestwich, *Edward I*, 249–51.

more on a direct appeal to Rome against Pecham, an appeal for which they had the full support of King Edward I.[56] Whilst returning, however, Cantilupe became ill and died. Swinfield was with him at his death at Ferento, near Orvieto, on 25 August, and he returned to Hereford late in 1282 with Cantilupe's heart and bones.[57] Swinfield, then, was hardly able to foster the second Richard de Bello's interests directly between summer 1280 and autumn 1282. He was certainly in a position, however, to press Cantilupe for some preferment for Richard, and he may already have given Richard hope that he would do this. Then, in 1283 and on his own election to the see of Hereford, Swinfield became able to help this Richard de Bello himself.

It is to this early, anxious, period of the second Richard de Bello's career, and to these hopes this Richard had of Cantilupe and Swinfield, that we should look for an explanation of his move to Hereford. And it is to this same period, and, above all, to the problems of ecclesiastical patronage and rewards which were developing within it, that we should look for our understanding of the ultimate purpose and place of Richard of Lafford's map. Both purpose and place are, I shall now argue, intimately connected with those tensions over pluralism and patronage, diocesan finance and taxation, and the rights of the metropolitan versus the interests of the king we have briefly surveyed; and they are even more intimately linked with the life, and death, and, above all, the supporters of Bishop Thomas Cantilupe, including King Edward I himself.

The origins of the second Richard's later rewarding friendship with Bishop Simon of Ghent may perhaps also be traced to this period, for Simon, appointed Archdeacon of Oxford in 1284, was heavily involved in Hereford affairs before 1289.[58] Bishop Richard Swinfield and Simon of Ghent were in close contact during these years, and Simon was also to show himself deeply in sympathy with the struggles against Pecham's interventions.[59] As judge delegate to the Hereford diocese, Simon actually sat at Gloucester and at Hereford, each of them quite close to

[56] For accounts of Cantilupe's conflict with Pecham see D. Douie, *Archbishop Pecham* (Oxford, 1952), 192–200 and R. C. Finucane, 'The Cantilupe–Pecham Controversy' in *St Thomas Cantilupe Bishop of Hereford*, ed. M. Jancey (Hereford, 1982), 103–23. King Edward sent a letter ahead to the Cardinal Matthew Orsini asking for special attention to be given to the Bishop of Hereford. He also granted him protection and safe-conduct; Finucane, 'The Cantilupe–Pecham Controversy', 108.

[57] Webb, *A Roll*, lxv.

[58] Simon of Ghent was judge delegate in 1286 in Bishop Swinfield's prebendal litigation in Rome and, in 1288, was arbitrator in Swinfield's border disputes with the Bishop of St Asaph. In 1289 Swinfield acted as mediator at Oxford between the masters and the Bishop of Lincoln whilst Simon was still archdeacon there. Capes, *Registrum*, iii, 67 and 190.

[59] Douie, *Archbishop Pecham*, 217.

Bosbury and to Swinfield's favourite manor there, with its gifts of meat to the younger Richard.[60]

The figure of Thomas Cantilupe comes firmly forward upon the stage at this point, and does so, as I think, decisively. To set the scene for this second section of the argument it is now necessary to examine the activities of Cantilupe's devoted friend and admirer, and Richard de Bello's later protector, Richard Swinfield, a little more closely than we have done so far.

The moment he returned to England in 1282 with Cantilupe's heart and bones, and learnt of his own election to the See of Hereford, Richard Swinfield devoted himself to his master's memory. This devotion turned shortly into a campaign for the recognition of Thomas Cantilupe as a Hereford saint, and the gaining of this recognition occupied Swinfield for the rest of his life. Cantilupe's bones were first laid in the Lady Chapel of Hereford Cathedral, but in 1287 Swinfield attended to a better resting-place, and translated them to a stately tomb in the North West transept; a tomb which survives there now. Swinfield may even have rebuilt this transept especially to hold the bones.[61] By 1286 at least four bishops were allowing indulgences for prayers for Cantilupe's soul,[62] and in 1289 Swinfield started the formal process of canonisation by sending a letter of request to Pope Nicholas IV.[63] The suit was prosecuted vigorously but without result until the intervention of King Edward I himself in (please mark) the year 1305. As a result of the royal initiative, Pope Clement V appointed a commission of enquiry. A dossier of Cantilupe's *Vita* and *Miracula* was produced for the commission in 1307,[64] and enquiry and dossier together eventually succeeded. Thomas Cantilupe was canonised in 1320, after, sadly, Swinfield's own death.

[60] One 'Magister Ricardus', perhaps our Richard de Bello, appears in Sutton's *Register* in 1294 as an official of Simon when the latter was at Oxford. *The Rolls and Register*, ed. Hill, vii, 55.

[61] *AS*, 582–4. On this tomb see G. Marchall, 'The Shrine of St Thomas de Cantilupe in Hereford Cathedral', *Transactions of the Woolhope Naturalists' Field Club* (1930), 34–50.

[62] R. C. Finucane, *Miracles and Pilgrims* (London, 1977), 174. The bishops, besides Swinfield, were those of Worcester, London and Rochester. *Registrum Thome de Cantilupo Episcopi Herefordensis (1275–1282)*, ed. R. G. Griffiths and W. W. Capes (London, 1907), lii. The Bishop of Worcester, Godfrey Giffard, had been chancellor to King Henry III and the Bishop of London, Richard Gravesend, was a nephew of Richard Gravesend, former Bishop of Lincoln. See E. B. Fryde *et al.* eds., *Handbook of British Chronology* (Cambridge, 1996), 85.

[63] Capes, *Registrum*, 234–5; Webb, *The Roll*, *Appendix* xxiv.

[64] Capes, *Registrum*, i–ii. The dossier is printed in part in *AS*, 1 Oct., 541–705, but an edition of the fourteenth-century manuscript record (Ms. Vatican City, Vat. Lat. 4015) is still badly needed.

4. Cantilupe's tomb: the sphinx.

The evidence for Swinfield's arrival at the chancery of Lincoln in 1278 comes in fact from this dossier. It so happened, goes the story (recounting the twenty-fifth and final miracle attributed to the living Cantilupe), that Thomas Cantilupe came to celebrate Pentecost in the chapel of the castle of Wallingford (d. Lincoln). He came to Wallingford at the invitation of Edmund, Earl of Cornwall, first cousin of King Edward I, and Edmund had assembled a great noble company there for the festivities. As the would-be saint began to intone the Veni Creator Spiritus at the Mass, a flock of birds, at least thirty (and of strangely mingled species—rooks and doves and starlings), appeared at the windows of the chapel. When the choir took up the refrain, the birds flew away, only to return when Thomas himself began the next verse. This all happened in about the second or third year of Thomas's episcopacy (1277 or 1278, that is), say the witnesses when questioned, and Earl Edmund went up to Lincoln to tell Swinfield all about it whilst the latter was chancellor there.[65]

This 1307 dossier is a major source of evidence about the life of Thomas Cantilupe, and presents with an especial force those aspects of his friend's achievements Swinfield thought most likely to recommend Cantilupe's cause and to attract appropriate pilgrims to his tomb. Numbers of miracles and throngs of pilgrims were both vital to the

[65] *AS*, 1 Oct., 705.

cause of canonisation and a part of its aim, as the dossier makes very plain.[66] It is to this dossier, then, that we should turn for an understanding of Swinfield's ambitions for his friend's memory.

It must be confessed immediately that the dossier has a hard time with Thomas Cantilupe the saint. Most of the miracles have a distinct sense of strain about them. The bird one is, after all, at best a feeble effort (and there is a particularly wonderful resurrection from death by drowning).[67] Though clearly chaste in his life, and generous to the poor, no one could possibly represent Thomas as an unworldly man. Thus, the dossier concentrates instead upon the virtues of Thomas's worldliness. Well born, and well educated (Oxford, Paris, Orléans), chaplain and friend to popes, fostered by his uncle Walter Cantilupe,[68] and present at the two papal councils at Lyons in 1245 and 1274 (with their legislation about pluralism and the papal right to dispense from this legislation), Thomas Cantilupe is the epitome of that nobility, incorruptibility, wealth and power which (or so the dossier clearly implies) is now one of the most precious assets of both Christian church and state. Thomas is shown to be especially honest and forceful in the matter of rights and revenues, their possession, defence and just use.[69] He was thus, as a 'miles Christi', a superior form of 'miles', confiscating knightly arms for bad behaviour, but restoring them *gladly* for good.[70] He particularly appreciated the value of money in just royal and military causes, buying over, for instance, some Welsh rebels for King Edward I at a crucial moment in the Welsh Wars.[71] He was, in short, a ruler's and noble layman's bishop, and was certainly much appreciated as a sympathetic royal councillor and representative.[72] He would be a ruler's and noble layman's saint perhaps, then, too.

The dossier places considerable stress on Cantilupe's helpful contributions to the Welsh wars of Edward I. The message here seems to be one of how well both king and bishop might do against a common

[66] See *AS* 594–5 for the enormous list of gifts to the tomb and attestations of miracles preceding the commission. The 1,000 waxen models of body-parts healed and the three carriages left by the lame who were cured would themselves have required more space than the Lady Chapel could provide, not to speak of the 170 silver ships (in thanksgiving for rescues at sea), the 180 crutches and the 77 models of animals and birds brought back from the dead.

[67] *AS*, 567–8. A child falls into the river and appears to drown. He is pulled out, his mouth is opened with a little knife to let the water out and he is held upside down and shaken. Thomas makes the sign of the cross in his general direction, and the child revives as a result of this last intervention, says the dossier.

[68] Bishop of Worcester, 1236–66, at whose tomb there had also been miracles and pilgrims, it takes pains to tell us; *AS*, 544.

[69] He was strikingly fair, for instance, over his own father's will. *AS*, 543.

[70] *AS*, 544, 546.

[71] *AS*, 565.

[72] *Registrum Thome*, ed. Griffiths and Capes, xxxvi–xli.

enemy, provided they act sympathetically and co-operatively towards one another's needs.[73] Into the context of the struggles with Pecham, the dossier fits, furthermore, some fulsome praise on the part of Cantilupe about the church of Rome.[74] King and pope are drawn together in the dossier as recipients of Cantilupe's good services. The king, his military nobility, right-minded local bishops and the Roman church as whole, will, goes this message, justly triumph for the good of the English realm as a whole, whereas the Archbishop of Canterbury, we might remark, appears only as an obstacle in the way of this.

We have reviewed Richard of Haldingham and Lafford's retirement from the treasury of Lincoln in the turbulence of 1278, and his death in that same year. We have remarked upon his likely connection there with Richard Swinfield, and we have noted the second Richard's developing relationship with Swinfield, bishop of Hereford. We have traced Bishop Swinfield's own friendship for Bishop Thomas Cantilupe, and his deep concern for Cantilupe's canonisation and the embellishment of his resting places, and we have set the whole against the background of a large degree of trouble; trouble over diocesan decision-making and archiepiscopal interference, especially in Lincoln and in Hereford, and particularly over the rights of local diocesans to present to benefices, if need be with a papal dispensation for pluralism. We have remarked upon the praise to be found in the canonisation dossier for the co-operation of English church, pope and king, and the increased interest of King Edward I in the cause of Cantilupe; an interest which resulted, at last, in Cantilupe's canonisation. We may now turn to the two scenes and the one border of the Hereford Map and, finally, to the reasons for its coming to Hereford.

Many of the known manifestations of Thomas's pugnacity are tactfully passed over in the dossier,[75] but one of them, a battle he had with Earl Gilbert of Gloucester, is thought worthy of special emphasis in it. The battle with Earl Gilbert was evidently a great *cause célèbre* at the time,

[73] The buying-over of the Welsh rebels, for instance, was preceded, says the dossier, by a dramatisation of the liturgy of excommunication against the sinning Welsh invaders. Interestingly, reference to some of Thomas's episcopal opponents follows this episode immediately; his battle with Richard Carew, Bishop of St David's, over Hereford's right to consecrate the church at Abbey Dore, won in fact by Cantilupe after reference to the royal courts, and Cantilupe's furious struggles with Pecham over the Council of Reading: *AS*, 565–7. *Registrum Thome*, ed. Griffith and Capes, xxxiv–xxxv.

[74] *AS*, 566–7.

[75] Cantilupe's struggle with Peter of Langona for the prebend of Preston, for instance, and his hearty dislike of 'Burgundians': *Registrum Thome*, ed. Griffiths and Capes, xxiv–xxvii.

for it finds a place too in the *Annals of Worcester*,[76] and is recorded in Swinfield's *Roll*[77] and in the Close and Patent Rolls of Edward I.[78] It happened in the years 1277–8, and the story is this. Earl Gilbert and his family, so Thomas claimed, had long usurped rights to the chase of Colwall and Eastnor, above Ledbury in the Malvern Hills, a chase which belonged to the Bishop of Hereford. Thomas moved against the earl in 1277 with a threat of excommunication for trespass, then required that a jury be empanelled by the sheriff to decide the matter. Champions were employed in case of a duel.[79] Meanwhile, the earl's foresters were withdrawn from the Malvern hills and the bishop was allowed to hunt over the chase and assert his claims. The case was heard before the royal justices Sir Ralph de Hengham and Sir Walter de Helyun, and, before Easter 1278, the jury found for Cantilupe. Swinfield's canonisation dossier makes a very great deal of this event, and it dwells especially upon how the earl, though furious and full of threats, had, in the end, to allow Thomas Cantilupe his right to hunt in the face of his own huntsmen; to pass before them, in fact.[80]

Let us look now again at the hunting scene in the right-hand corner of the Map.[81] This depicts, as we saw at the beginning of this paper, a rider, with, behind him, a huntsman on foot, holding a pair of greyhounds on a leash. The huntsman is wearing and carrying all the appropriate badges of his craft; traditional hat, horn, bow and arrows, sword. He is trimly and expensively turned out. The words 'passe avant' are inscribed above the huntsman's head, and he appears to be addressing these words to the rider. The rider, by a half-backwards, half-upwards glance at the *mappa mundi*, seems, in his turn, to signal his acceptance of the permission to advance, and to be trotting confidently ahead. His mount is a magnificently harnessed horse, and there are, about the harnessing of the horse and the apparel of the rider, two features which, to my knowledge, have not been emphasised before.

[76] *AS*, 563–5; *Annales*, ed. Luard, iv, 476.

[77] See Webb, *A Roll*, i, xxiv, ii, 125 and Appendix I, 201.

[78] *Calendar of the Close Rolls, Edward I 1272–1279* (London, 1900), 490–1. This entry gives a very full account. *Calendar of the Patent Rolls, Edward I 1272–1281* (London, 1901), 284.

[79] The retaining bond for the champion Cantilupe specially engaged to fight, if he must, and the result of the battle are enrolled in his *Register*. *Registrum Thome*, ed. Griffiths and Capes, xxviii–xxix, 201, 227–8.

[80] *AS*, 564: 'Et tunc dictus dominus Thomas, qui fecerat multos venatores et canes venaticos congregari, illa die ac tribus sequentibus fecit palam et publice venari in nemore supradicto. Et licte dictus dominus comes fuisset comminatus in praedicto suo recessu ... nullum tamen tunc, nec etiam postmodum opposuit impedimentum in praedictis domino Thomae vel successoribus eiusdem. Et dixit [i.e. the reporting witness] quod ista fuerunt publice et notorie facta et sunt publica et notoria in partibus illis ...'.

[81] Canon Moir was rightly puzzled by this scene. 'Who is this unnamed rider?'; A. L. Moir, *The World Map in Hereford Cathedral* (Hereford, 1971), 12.

On the rump of the horse there is a raised cross, attached to the crupper strap. Denholm-Young thought the huntsman might represent the foresting background and family badge of his Richard de Bello of South Essex;[82] but there is now a nearer solution. The huntsman must, I think, be held to represent one of Earl Gilbert's splendid huntsmen, giving the signal to pass and so allowing the rider to hunt. And the rider, with hand raised in acceptance of the right to pass before the huntsman, and horse marked by the cross, may be none other than Thomas Cantilupe himself.

Judgement on the Ledbury Chase was made in Cantilupe's favour in April 1278, the year and indeed the month in which the last mention of Richard de Bello as treasurer of Lincoln occurs. The Pentecost miracle of the birds took place shortly after this (Pentecost fell, in 1278, on 5 June) and Swinfield was chancellor of Lincoln when Edmund of Cornwall went up to tell him of it. That a record of this triumph should be incorporated in Richard of Haldingham and Lafford's map is readily reconcilable with that possible association between him and Swinfield to which I have already drawn attention. Interestingly, the estate of Bosbury, which, in 1289, provided the second Richard de Bello with his meat, was in fact supplied by this very disputed chase above Ledbury. And we may find another connection between Cantilupe and this particular scene. In a fascinating exploratory article on the multiple literary and allegorical meanings which may be present in such portrayals, my colleague Dr Brian Levy has pointed to a connection between the rider on the Hereford Map and the iconography of the four riders of the *Apocalypse*, most particularly that of the rider of the white horse (*Apocalypse* 6:2), or Christ.[83] Thomas Cantilupe gave lectures on theology in Paris in the 1260s; and, as the dossier again tells us, his lectures upon the *Apocalypse* were much admired by certain of the Dominican Friars.[84]

Let us now approach the second scene, the border, and, at last, the conclusion I hope that this paper may reach. As we do so, we might recall the sympathy shown to Cantilupe's struggles, and to the eventual canonisation process, by the king. This sympathy was shown, in fact, very early. In November 1283, whilst Cantelupe's bones still rested in the Lady Chapel of the cathedral, King Edward I actually visited them there.[85] Edward was greatly interested in seeking cures at such tombs

[82] 'The *Mappa Mundi*', 312.

[83] Levy, 'Signes', 44–5. He makes no reference to the hunting dispute, but does hazard the guess, through the connection with Richard de Bello, that the rider might be Richard Swinfield. I am most grateful to him for allowing me to read this article in advance of its publication.

[84] *AS*, 548. *Registrum Thome*, ed. Griffiths and Capes, xvii.

[85] H. Gough, *The Itinerary of King Edward I Throughout His Reign* (Paisley, 1900), i, 149–50.

for his sick falcons, and indeed later sought one for a gyrfalcon at Cantilupe's.[86] Thus, Cantelupe's hunting enthusiasms may have made him a sympathetic figure to the king straight away; but there is more still to the point than this. Edward's victories over the Welsh seem to have been noted especially early on the Hereford *mappa mundi*, as we saw, and to have indicated a date close to 1283. Another Welsh landmark on the map may owe its appearance also to the Welsh wars. The appearance of 'Mons Clece', in central Wales, puzzled Crone.[87] He thought it might be Matthew Paris's 'Pinlimon', or even Clee Hill; but Lleyn, the hill jutting out south-westwards from the present county of Caernarvon, seems a far more likely solution. Lleyn was adjudged to Llewelyn's brother after the Treaty of Conway in 1277, and remained a vital section of Llewelyn's lands until his death in 1282.

The second scene, the surveying scene, may be approached with these Welsh wars, with King Edward and, of course, with Cantilupe in mind. My views about it are tentative; but are grounded quite firmly, as I think, both in the dossier compiled for Cantilupe's canonisation and in the case I have put forward so far. Now, this scene may indeed innocently represent the survey of the known world ordered, or thought to be ordered, by the Emperor Augustus, but there are some odd things about it, as we saw; the papal tiara with which the emperor is crowned, and the vesica seal. The survey undertaken by Augustus was in part for taxation, as we know. This scene might, then, have reference as well to taxation; specifically to the Crusading Tenth, decreed in 1274 by the Second Council of Lyons, at which Cantilupe was present, and which was beginning to be collected early in 1278 whilst, we may remember, Richard de Bello the elder was still treasurer of Lincoln. Three supervising collectors were engaged by the pope for this purpose; as three, not four, surveyors were here engaged by Augustus.[88] In March 1283, before his November visit to Cantilupe's tomb, King Edward I seized the tax, albeit briefly, to meet the expenses of the Welsh war. Cantelupe had borrowed from it too for his own Welsh expenses. The pope then openly allowed it to the king for the crusade.[89] Crone drew attention to the fact that the only episcopal sees unrepresented on the map of England were those of Norwich and Chichester—the two, in fact, who argued first and most cogently for a lower valuation than the one both king and pope required.[90] This

[86] L. E. Salzman, *Edward I* (London, 1968), 188. Webb, *A Roll*, xlix–l.

[87] *The World Map*, 8.

[88] W. Lunt, *Financial Relations of the Papacy with England to 1327* (Cambridge Mass., 1939), 311–17.

[89] Lunt, *Financial Relations*, 330–8.

[90] The Bishop of Chichester was still recalcitrant in 1277. Lunt, *Financial Relations*, 257–9, 324–8.

interpretation of this scene is, as I have said, tentative, but the dates, the seal and, especially, the papal tiara are suggestive, and the purpose and the profits of pilgrimage seem both of them, at this point, to have been, once more, popular with the king, and readily reconcilable, by him, with the purposes of just war.[91] It is conceivable that difficulties with the tenth, and with Canterbury's obstructive attitude towards it, as well as problems with presentation, minor orders and metropolitan strictures, affected treasurer Richard de Bello's retirement, and even, perhaps, his death. Richard of Lafford's own name is, we might remember, attached to this particular scene; and it seems to refer, yet again, to both Cantilupe and king.

The clinching evidence as to the ultimate aim of the Hereford Map is, as I think, however, provided by the border. Stretching from the ornamental border of the *mappa mundi* itself, there are, as we have seen, four ligatures with letters at their end, spelling out the word 'mors'. I noted that the top two ligatures, spelling the 'M.O.' of mors, are attached to the frame of the parchment, but that the bottom two are differently disposed, reaching into the right and left hand scenes. These bottom two spell out the 'R' and 'S' of 'mors'; but also the initials of Richard Swinfield.

The conclusion to which this discussion has been directed may now be stated quite baldly. The Hereford Map was designed by Richard of Haldingham and Lafford, alias Richard de Bello the elder, between some unknown point in the 1270s and his death in 1278; and it ended its career as a memorial to Bishop Thomas Cantilupe of Hereford. This leads me to one last suggestion about it. The map was not all made in Hereford; indeed, Swinfield may have seen Richard of Lafford engaged on the *mappa mundi* part of it at Lincoln in 1278. This is another story.[92] But then, Richard of Lafford died, leaving his dependants, and among them the younger Richard to seek their fortunes elsewhere.

This younger Richard may even have been his elder relative's amanuensis. We enter the wilder world of speculation at this point; but

[91] Powicke argues convincingly that Edward I was wholly sincere as a crusader; F. M. Powicke, *King Henry III and The Lord Edward*, ii (Oxford, 1947), 729–30.

[92] Morgan argues for a Lincoln origin for the map; N. Morgan, *Early Gothic Manuscripts ii 1250–1285* (London, 1988), 198. Lincoln certainly figures prominently upon it. In 1280 the bones of St Hugh of Lincoln (canonised 1220) were translated to a new setting, in the presence of Bishop Oliver Sutton and the king. The map may have been begun, then, as a decoration for St Hugh's tomb. I suspect, indeed, that it was, but the further examination of this hypothesis must await another occasion. In further support of a Northern origin we might note that the Yorkshire river system is particularly accurately traced on the map.

this Richard certainly found, as we saw, great fortune in several places, and he found it first of all with Bishop Swinfield. If the younger Richard had indeed been entrusted with the drawing and inscription of the map, then the two scenes additional to the *mappa mundi* of Richard of Lafford we have discussed may easily have been added by him. The famous inscription in the second scene, where Richard of Haldingham and Lafford's authorship of the map is recorded, has always been attributed to Richard of Lafford himself. It asks specifically, however, for prayers for this Richard of Lafford's soul. It is surely conceivable, then, that this was also added by the younger Richard, in piety after the elder's death, and in the course of adapting his relative's work to his own quite different purposes.

In the years 1278–9, I would aver, therefore, Richard de Bello the younger began, in the troubles besetting Lincoln, to adapt the *mappa mundi* of Richard of Lafford to the interests of his own potential new Hereford patrons; Swinfield, temporary Lincoln chancellor, and, behind him, Bishop Thomas Cantilupe. And the whole was completed after Cantilupe's death, in essence by 1283, for the embellishment of Cantilupe's first resting place in Hereford Cathedral. The judgement scene at the top of the map, which deserves (and I hope will receive) separate discussion reinforces this last proposition,[93] and there is another small indication of the relationship between map and Cantilupe's resting places on the existing 1287 Cantilupe tomb in Swinfield's North transept. Within the right and left hand spandrels of the decoration on this tomb are carved two figures—a sphinx (with a bird's wings, a girl's face and a serpent's tail, according to an inscription apparently taken from Pliny)[94] on the right, and of a griffin, or wyvern, on the left. Two such figures are also to be found opposite one another, and at the same height, on the right and left sides of the *mappa mundi*. The correspondence between tomb sphinx and map sphinx is particularly striking. The carver of the new tomb may, then, have deliberately carried with him an image from the map, hung at the old tomb in the Lady Chapel.

The Hereford Map as we know it was perhaps in the Lady Chapel of Hereford Cathedral when King Edward I and his court visited Cantilupe's bones in the year 1283. Richard de Bello the younger received his greatest preferments, we may remember, in the dioceses of Salisbury and Hereford, and, especially, when the king took the canonisation project seriously in 1305. The map thus played a part in, and so may be used in illustration of, a great struggle about pluralism, pastoral care and taxation, about

[93] This judgement scene has echoes, in the Anglo-Norman texts which accompany it, of Anglo-Norman Apocalypses and so, again, of Thomas's interests. Levy, 'Signes', p. 11. The curious image it has of the bare-breasted Virgin is particularly well suited to the Lady Chapel, in which newly delivered mothers were accustomed to be 'churched'.

[94] Bevan and Phillott, *Medieval Geography*, 83.

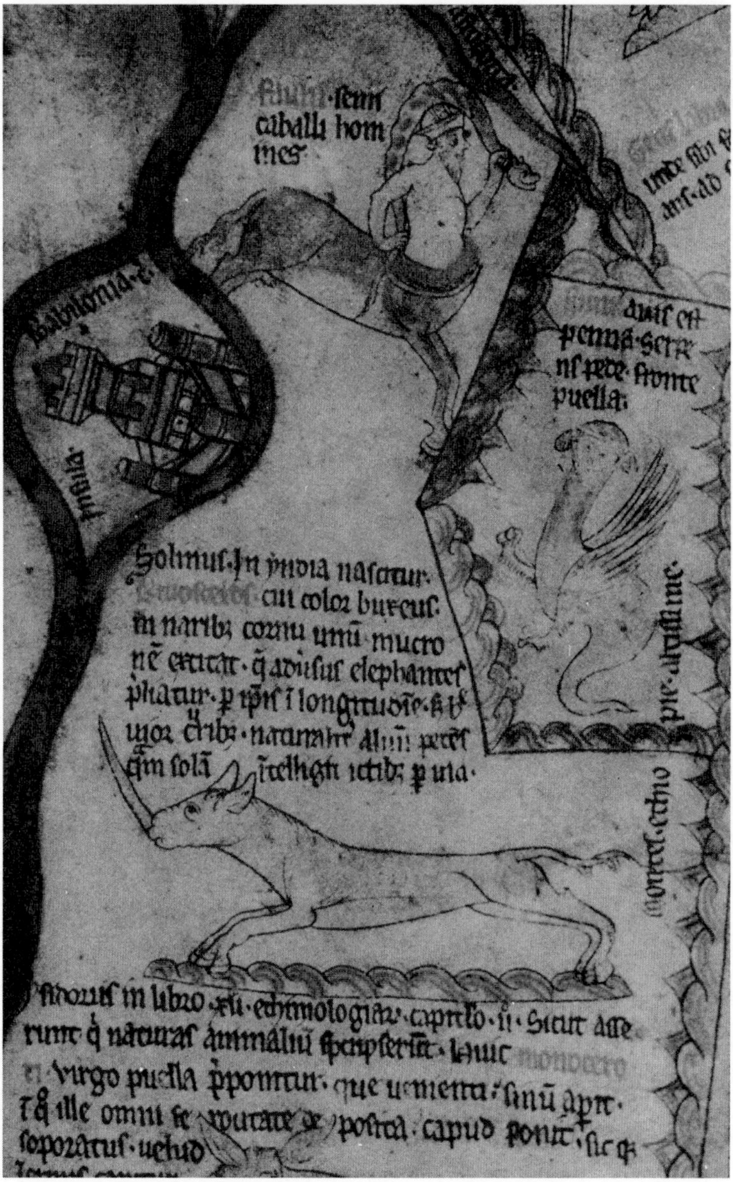

5. The Hereford Map: the sphinx.

diocesan and metropolitan rights and duties, and, perhaps most importantly of all, about the place organised and lucrative pilgrimages and crusades, and their ecclesiastical managers and illustrators, were coming to occupy in all of these concerns. In Hereford and many of the other secular cathedrals of England, it was a struggle for the ear of the king and the respect and the revenues of the laity, rich and poor. But that is yet another, and an even larger, story.

THE MEANING OF IRISH FREEDOM CONSTITUTIONALISM IN THE FREE STATE

By Charles Townshend

READ 7 MARCH 1998

THE performance of Ireland as an autonomous state since 1922 remains a contentious subject. Joseph Lee's withering critique of Irish economic backwardness and cultural parochialism, which he holds to be rooted in a narrow adhesion to the 'possessor principle' against the 'performance ethic', charts a long-term failure to rise to the challenge of statehood.[1] It is not appropriate here to attempt even a summary of his sprawling, bristling account; I want to focus on an aspect highlit by Denis Donoghue when he reviewed it in the *London Review of Books*. 'The first and most important fact about modern Ireland,' Donoghue contended, 'is that, after the Civil War, there was unquestioned transition to democracy.'[2] On this view, modern Irish history is, *pace* Lee, in essence a success story. As Brian Farrell put it, the capacity of the Irish parliamentary tradition to 'encompass, neutralise and institutionalise' the disastrous split of 1922 'makes the Irish experience unique among the new nation-states of the twentieth-century world'.[3] Tom Garvin has recently reinforced this verdict by pointing to the surprising speed with which any tendency to military intervention in Irish politics disappeared. This after a Civil War in which the new Army—lacking any experience of subordination to the civil power—had saved the life of the infant Irish Free State. Indeed, far from witnessing the politicisation of the military, Ireland 'rapidly became one of the most demilitarised societies in Europe'.[4]

Several explanations for the survival of democracy in Ireland have been advanced. While one political scientist has recently dismissed the issue as unproblematical, suggesting that the Irish experience was not deviant, others continue to be impressed by the touch-and-go nature of the outcome, and the seriousness of the threat to democracy posed

[1] J.J. Lee, *Ireland 1912–1985. Politics and Society* (Cambridge, 1989), *passim.*

[2] *London Review of Books*, 5 April 1990, 9.

[3] B. Farrell, 'The Paradox of Irish Politics', in *The Parliamentary Tradition in Ireland* (Dublin, 1972), p. 14. Cf, with the modified 'virtually unique', B. Farrell (ed.) *The Creation of the Dáil* (Dublin, 1994), p. 5.

[4] T. Garvin, *1922. The Birth of Irish Democracy* (Dublin, 1996), ch.4; see also E. O'Halpin, 'The Army and the Dáil', in B. Farrell (ed.), *The Creation of the Dáil*, p. 108.

by a combination of militarist elitism—what Garvin calls the 'public band tradition'—and the authoritarianism of the Catholic social culture.[5] Some of the divergence stems from the slipperiness of the concepts in play here, not least that of democracy itself. One well-known study in the early 1970s, *The Irony of Irish Democracy*, for instance, suggested that the Irish version diverges significantly from the Western norm. Garvin has also indicated that Irish democratic culture was compatible with a surprising array of non-liberal or even illiberal attitudes. The key element of the Irish political system has been variously labelled parliamentary, representative, and responsible government.[6] I should like to consider here whether the common thread running through this terminology is an underlying cultural one, a notion of constitutionalism of the British kind, transmitted through the first Irish constitution in the 1920s. For as Giovanni Sartori observed (in talking of nineteenth-century liberal constitutionalists), 'Every state has a "constitution", but only some states are "constitutional".'[7]

Though the British are famously lukewarm about the value of constitutional inscription, the notion of constitutionality has been salient in modern British public culture.[8] The principal function of the constitution as generally construed was the protection of individual liberty—in the characteristically ambivalent English formulation 'liberty of the subject'—by a set of guarantees against arbitrary government, such as the 1689 Bill of Rights. This defensive function was most typically displayed in the 1672 Habeas Corpus Act, which, as jurists always insisted, did not 'enlarge our liberties' but merely set up efficient judicial machinery to enforce an ancient right.[9] Suspensions of habeas corpus during civil emergencies were not necessarily unconstitutional (as long as they were decreed by the omnipotent parliament), but were regarded as breaches of constitutionality. A second concrete aspect of the constitution which was of fundamental importance was the Protestant nature of the Act of Settlement which established the modern constitutional monarchy. This gave the idea of the constitution a cultural

[5] Bill Kissane, 'The Not-so-amazing Case of Irish Democracy', *Irish Political Studies*, 10 (1995): 43–68; cf. F. Munger, *The Legitimacy of Opposition: the Change of Government in Ireland in 1932* (Beverly Hills, 1975); T. Garvin, 'Unenthusiastic Democrats: the Emergence of Irish Democracy', in R. Hill and R. Marsh (eds.), *Modern Irish Democracy* (Dublin, 1993), 8–23.

[6] Alan J. Ward, *The Irish Constitutional Tradition. Responsible Government and Modern Ireland 1782–1992* (Dublin, 1994).

[7] G. Sartori, 'Constitutionalism: a Preliminary Discussion', *American Political Science Review* 56 (1962), 853.

[8] Giovanni Sartori charmingly described the British avoidance of constitutional normality as 'coquetry'.

[9] Henry Hallam, *Constitutional History of England*, vol. III, p. 11; A. V. Dicey, *The Law of the Constitution* (1905), pp. 231–2.

meaning which has been preserved by Protestants in Ireland more carefully than by their co-religionists in Britain. Less symbolic but more practical functions of constitutionality took shape as patterns of political behaviour expressing the conventions of representative government. Insofar as the British constitution made possible positive as well as negative liberty (to follow Isaiah Berlin's usage) it was through uncodified practices of representation and accountability.

In the late nineteenth century the 'constitution' was widely believed to be delivering an unique compound of representative, effective, and uncorrupt government.[10] But the incapacity of constitutional procedures to accommodate the aspirations of Irish nationalists generated an extended crisis from the 1880s to the First World War. The Irish national movement was antagonistic to British constitutionalism at several levels. Coercive intimidation of communities (boycotting), even more than naked political violence or terrorism, destroyed the liberty of the subject and deformed the notion of representation. As Joseph Chamberlain put it, 'I say that liberty is a mere phantom unless every man is free to pursue his inclinations, to consult his interest within and under the protection of the law.'[11] Unconstitutional opposition nearly got out of control several times in the nineteenth century, and did so finally and decisively in the republican guerrilla campaign of 1918–21. It embodied an Irish political tradition which was not casually but aggressively anti-constitutional, repudiating parliamentary politics and the British culture of compromise—together with everything else lumped together as symptoms of 'Anglicisation'—as alien and deadly to Ireland.[12]

However, the failure of constitutional methods to resolve the Irish question, the absolutism of the Irish nationalist assault on Anglicisation, the strength of anti-parliamentary rhetoric, and the dramatic final collapse of the 'constitutional movement' in 1918 tended to exaggerate the rupture with English political culture and to disguise the extent to which constitutionalism informed the post-revolutionary order in Ireland. The Irish Nationalist Party as it had been shaped by Parnell in the parliamentary context of the 1880s was a formidable machine which did not disappear overnight. Sinn Féin, and in particular the pro-Treaty party, Cumann na nGaedheal, was in many central respects

[10] M. Pugh, *The Making of Modern British Politics 1867–1939* (Oxford, 1982), 3. See more generally G. H. L. LeMay, *The Victorian Constitution. Conventions, Usages and Contingencies* (London, 1979).

[11] J. L. Hammond, *Gladstone and the Irish Nation* (London, 1938), 251.

[12] The destructive impact of alien institutions on the 'hereditary mind' of Ireland was forcefully argued in Darrell Figgis, *The Gaelic State in the Past and Future* (Dublin, 1917), *passim* and pp. 83–4.

its lineal descendant.[13] The constitutional values which had been used over a generation to justify the project of Home Rule for Ireland did not disappear either.

The Free State Constitution preserved much of the imprecision of the English public law tradition (besides smuggling in the whole corpus of English common and statute law along with the judicial system) under an aspect of more exotic abstraction. It incorporated the principle of proportional representation—imposed by Britain through the Government of Ireland Act 1920—while almost unconsciously adapting it to the assumptions of a two-party system. Even dramatic departures such as the referendum and the provision for popular initiative, designed to check the growth of parties, proved ineffective in this.[14] The Irish political parties themselves have manifested a quirky, and in some views unsatisfactory, balance between local obscurantism and national progressivism. The achievement of national 'freedom' remains shot through with ambiguities at every level, theoretical and practical, cultural, economic and political.

The function of the constitution in the shaping of Irish political culture has been rather neglected. Lee's interpretation, however cantankerously *à rebours* it may be in many respects, follows recent convention in its glancing treatment of both the 1922 and the 1937 constitutions. It is deeply and extensively committed to the study of political culture, and of what may better be called public culture. Lee insists that 'political systems, politics and politicians matter'. But this insistence does not entail any systematic discussion of even the cardinal aspects of the 1922 constitution, much less its finer points. The 1937 constitution is brought into harder focus, but principally as an epiphenomenon of public culture. This emphasis, stressing the special role of the Catholic church, is familiar in recent historical and political works.[15]

There is no comprehensive modern analysis of the Free State constitution, and the systematic study by Leo Kohn in 1932 is unlikely to be superseded. This is perhaps not surprising, but it is noteworthy that markedly different assumptions underpin the central position accorded to the constitution in books of the 1930s such as Denis Gwynn's history of the Free State's first five years, or (from the opposite political angle) Dorothy Macardle's *Irish Republic*, and its marginality in, say, the account of the Civil War written fifty years later by Michael

[13] D. Fitzpatrick, *Politics and Irish Life. Provincial Experience of War and Revolution 1913–21* (Dublin, 1977), chs. 3–4.

[14] *The Irish Constitution* explained by Darrell Figgis (Dublin, 1922), 34.

[15] J. H. Whyte, *Church and State in Modern Ireland 1923–1979* (Dublin, 1980), ch. II; D. Keogh, 'The Constitutional Revolution: an Analysis of the Making of the Constitution', in F. Litton (ed.), *The Constitution of Ireland 1937–1987* (Dublin, 1988), 4–84.

Hopkinson.[16] Most recent works share the latter's assumptions. Though Joseph Curran's *Birth of the Irish Free State* devotes a chapter to the constitution, it treats it as a token of Anglo-Irish relations rather than as a constituent element in Irish public life.[17] Amongst modern general histories, only F. S. L. Lyons's *Ireland since the Famine* accords the 1922 constitution substantial treatment, while Ronan Fanning's *Independent Ireland* finds only a paragraph for it, John Murphy's *Ireland in the Twentieth Century* two sentences. Theodore Hoppen's *Ireland since 1800* merely alludes to it in passing, and Roy Foster's *Modern Ireland* relegates it to a footnote.[18]

The same tendency to marginalisation appears even in the work of political scientists. With the exception of Alan Ward's specialised account of *The Irish Constitutional Tradition*, recent scholarship has shifted from the traditional institutional ground of texts like Morley Ayearst's *Republic of Ireland*, Basil Chubb's *Government and Politics of Ireland* or Cornelius O'Leary's *Irish Elections*,[19] to political-cultural inquiries like Mart Bax's *Harpstrings and Confessions* or Paul Sacks's study of *The Donegal Mafia* (which does not mention either constitution except to observe in connection with Catholic influence that the 1937 constitution was 'a self-conscious attempt to combine the liberal-democratic tradition of Great Britain with Catholic social teaching').[20] Most of Tom Garvin's fertile work on Irish politics, like that of Paul Bew, has been unconcerned with constitutions as such.[21]

Should we conclude from this scholarly consensus that the Free State constitution was not really important in itself? Terence Brown's 'social and cultural history' of Ireland after 1922 might lead us to say that it had less impact on the public experience of independence than the string of 'harsh, gloomy and sunless' summers and the dismal surrounding seasons which lasted until June 1925.[22] Writing in 1968, Brian Farrell mused that the persistent disenchantment of 'continuing economic dependence, social inertia and cultural reaction and decay'

[16] L. Kohn, *The Constitution of the Irish Free State* (London, 1932); D. Gwynn, *The Irish Free State 1922–1927* (London, 1928); D. Macardle, *The Irish Republic* (London, 1937); M. Hopkinson, *Green aganst Green. The Irish Civil War* (Dublin, 1988).

[17] J. M. Curran, *The Birth of the Irish Free State* (Alabama University, 1980).

[18] J. A. Murphy, *Ireland in the Twentieth Century* (Dublin, 1975), 52–3; R. F. Foster, *Modern Ireland 1600–1972* (London, 1988), 516.

[19] M. Ayearst, *The Republic of Ireland. Its Government and Politics* (London, 1971); B. Chubb, *The Government and Politics of Ireland* (London, 1970); C. O'Leary, *Irish Elections 1918–1977. Parties, Voters and Proportional Representation* (Dublin, 1979). *Cf* N. Mansergh, *The Irish Free State. Its Government and Politics* (London, 1934).

[20] P. M. Sacks, *The Donegal Mafia. An Irish Political Machine* (New Haven, 1976), 45.

[21] *Cf.* T. Garvin, *The Evolution of Irish Nationalist Politics* (Dublin, 1981); P. Bew, E. Hazelkorn and H. Patterson, *The Dynamics of Irish Politics* (London, 1989).

[22] T. Brown, *Ireland. A Social and Cultural History 1922–79* (London, 1981), 15.

over the next two generations had led Irish people to disparage the first leaders of the new state.[23] Did anyone care much about the constitution except its creators, who had to run it through the gauntlet of British suspicion, and their diehard republican opponents who attacked its failure to enshrine Irish sovereignty and identity? Some of those opponents, who went on to form the Fianna Fail party in 1927, replaced it with their own model ten years later. The relatively short life of the first constitution seems to reinforce its perceived insignificance.

As against this, however, it is beyond dispute that the essential lineaments and mechanics of the Irish political system—electoral, legislative, executive and judicial—were established by the Free State. Many of De Valera's most resonant constitutional changes (the removal of the Governor-Generalship, and the excision of references to the King, for instance) were carried out within the 1922 Constitution, and his replacement constitution of 1937 incorporated—'re-bottled' as John Kelly has put it—large parts of the old one.[24] The very fact that this was the first publicly-ratified Irish fundamental law cannot be without significance. And there remains the challenging fact that after a decade of virtual one-party rule, which had witnessed civil war, repeated use of emergency powers, assassinations, executions and reprisals, accompanied by intemperate demonisation of opponents, in 1932 the party which had created the Free State handed over power peacefully to the man who aimed to undo their work. (They could not guess how much of it De Valera would in the end preserve.) If ever there were an acid test of a 'constitutional culture', this was surely it.[25]

To figure out how this culture emerged requires a kind of analysis which is still in its infancy. Brian Farrell laid out in suggestive, if somewhat sketchy form, the framework of an analysis resting on the modernising role of the catholic church under British rule, and the ingrained acceptance of majoritiarian representative democracy—the principle that the losers accept the results of elections.[26] Frank Munger's pioneering effort to explain the 1932 transfer of power focused on the extensive Irish experience of parliamentary action, and in particular the political experience generated by local government reform in 1898. Garvin has persuasively enlarged this dimension in his recent work.

[23] B. Farrell, 'The New State and Irish Political Culture', *Administration* 16, 3 (1968), 238.

[24] D. Keogh, 'The Irish Constitutional Revolution: an Analysis of the Making of the Constitution', F. Litton (ed) *The Constitution of Ireland 1937–1987* (*Administration* 35, 4, 1987), 66.

[25] As Frank Munger noted, 'From our present acquaintance with political processes in new nations, we know how strange these events are. What seemed to the Irish natural, normal, even inevitable, has occurred in few other places.' *The Legitimacy of Opposition*, 6.

[26] Farrell, 'The New State and Irish Political Culture', 238–46.

But some of the ingredients of political culture are harder to clarify: Munger and Garvin reach very different verdicts on the democratic credentials of the Catholic church.[27] And Garvin's view that Irish society in the 1920s was 'essentially peasant' is markedly at variance with the argument advanced by Brian Farrell in 1968, and recently reiterated by Kissane, that Ireland was already a modern society by 1921.[28]

The most ambitious attempt so far made to read the Free State constitution in cultural context is Jeffrey Prager's *Building Democracy in Ireland*.[29] Despite its pedestrian manner, it achieved a vivid impact by its reduction of Irish culture to two strongly-characterised archetypes, the 'Irish-Enlightenment' and the 'Gaelic-Romantic'. Though Prager never makes quite clear whether these cultural (or subcultural) strains are purely ideal types (at times they are treated as virtually autonomous forces), or how far they are mutually exclusive, there can be little doubt as to their essential plausibility. They are considerably more sophisticated than earlier constructs like, say, the 'British' versus 'peasant' traditions proposed by Sacks. But problems arise in Prager's concrete applications of his ideal types, and in their apparent immobility over time. Working from Keith Michael Baker's view that 'a community exists only to the extent that there is some common discourse by which its members can constitute themselves as different groups within the social order and make claims upon one another that are intelligible', Prager argues that 'the formulation of collective goals or purposes, although historically conditioned, is constantly subject to redefinition and respecification through both debate and social contest'.[30] But how far does redefinition go? In the American example he provides, equality remains a constant value but its concrete applications change over time. Since Prager's 'Irish-Enlightenment' and 'Gaelic-Romantic' ideal types are not abstractions but socially constructed bundles of values, it should follow that they themselves would change. Prager, though, seems to expect them to stay constant. Sometimes it seems that the reason for this is that they are actually back-projections from the conflict that they allegedly created.

Prager's treatment of the Free State constitution displays both the strength and the limitation of his analytical model. He takes the constitution very seriously, and in that alone is a remarkable exception to recent fashion. But his central concern is with the state-building

[27] Munger, *Legitimacy of Opposition*, 23–5; Garvin, *1922*, ch. 2.

[28] Farrell, 'The New State', 241–2 concentrated on the process of land transfer; Kissane, 'Irish Democracy', 53–65, argues that the elimination of landlords and peasants was a concurrent process.

[29] J. Prager, *Building Democracy in Ireland. Political order and cultural integration in a newly independent nation* (Cambridge, 1986).

[30] *Ibid.*, 23.

process, so that although he devotes much space to the constitution he does not provide the kind of systematic exegesis of its provisions which used to be the staple of constitutional history. In fact, his analysis is almost exclusively concerned with the symbolic function of a fairly small number of phrases in the Preamble and the first clause of the draft constitution which was adopted by the Provisional Government but rejected by Britain as inconsistent with the Treaty.

The detailed history of the preparation of the drafts from which Michael Collins selected the version first submitted for British approval remained obscure for many years. The documents were rediscovered in the late 1960s and analysed in two pioneering series of articles by D. W. Akenson and J. F. Fallin, and Brian Farrell.[31] Prager's analysis takes the two rediscovered drafts (labelled A and B by Akenson and Fallin; the first two-thirds of O'Rahilly's draft C remain lost) and puts them into a framework of 'contending ideologies that endorsed radically different values and norms' or 'contending cultural antinomies within Irish society'.[32] This contention, in his view, made it difficult for the Provisional Government to frame a constitution that could carry the large burden which has to be laid on such instruments in modern societies. 'In the industrialised nations of the West, consitutionalism historically has played a key role in mobilising and integrating members of the political community in opposition to autocratic, absolutist rule.'[33] In Ireland, however, the constitution became a partisan document. The first draft, which he sees as being informed by Gaelic-Romantic values, was replaced under British pressure by one which enshrined their opposite.

On the face of it this is an odd view, since all three drafts were prepared by the same—i.e. the pro-Treaty (and in Prager's terminology 'Irish-Enlightenment')—side. Darrell Figgis, placed by Prager on the Irish-Enlightenment side, had produced a vivid argument for Gaelic restoration. It is questionable whether the three members of the drafting committee who produced Draft B can be seen as closet, if not explicit, Republicans, and especially whether it makes sense to argue as he does that the 'democratic' aspects of the Free State constitution were included to secure republican support.[34] Prager describes this as ironic, since the

[31] D. W. Akenson and J. F. Fallin, 'The Irish Civil War and the Drafting of the Free State Constitution', *Eire-Ireland* 5 (1970) nos.1, 2, 4: 10-26, 42–93, 28–70. B. Farrell, 'The Drafting of the Irish Free State Constitution', *Irish Jurist* (1970), 115–40, 343–56, (1971), 345–59.

[32] Prager, *Building Democracy in Ireland*, 30, 31.

[33] *Ibid.*, 68.

[34] *Ibid.*, 88. The Provisional Government certainly seems to have hoped that republicans (in particular Eamon de Valera) would be mollified by the inclusion of a 'separatist', as distinct from 'democratic', strain in the Constitution. Notes by Kevin O'Higgins, June 1922. Irish National Archive [NA], Taoiseach S 6695.

parallel inclusion of British symbols automatically alienated Republicans. The idea that the Republicans were the 'democratic' grouping, with a greater inclination than the Treatyites to 'trust the masses', would certainly have struck those Free State Executive members who portrayed the civil war as a struggle between a democratic government and a militarist dictatorship—above all the Minister for Justice, Kevin O'Higgins—as supremely ironic. The real problem here is that the central political notions at issue are much more ambiguous than Prager's simple antinomies require. Those antinomies themselves, though they are certainly recognisable, were neither so coherent nor so exclusive as he suggests.[35]

The attempt to give constitutional form to Irish public culture was inevitably complex, even to the point of inconsistency. (Jurists immediately noted, for instance, the inconsistency between the constitution's assertion of judicial supremacy [Art. 65] and the provision, inserted at British insistence, of the right of appeal to the Judicial Committee of the Privy Council.)[36] The complexities may be indicated by glancing at one general and one specific element in the constitution. First, at the general level, the power and role of the state was not clearly conceptualised by either side. The two 'cultures' did not divide over the issue of central government versus local autonomy, as Prager has to suggest—and in fact he presents two different, indeed contradictory, 'Irish-Enlightenment' views of the state at different points in his text. Wolfe Tone's Enlightenment movement 'embodied the conviction that individuals need to be protected from coercive authority, and that people possess inalienable rights over and above the state'; later 'Irish-Enlightenment thought encouraged a strong state' (as against local particularism).[37] Either the ideology was undergoing significant change over time, or it was ambivalent on this fundamental issue. Neither sorts well with his thesis.

Second, on the substantive provision of the 'extern' ministers—one of the constitution's most spectacular departures from the British model, providing that half the government would be drawn from outside parliament—in Prager's analysis this innovation figures as a deliberate weakening of the autonomy of the political structure by having the community directly represented in the executive council. (An aspect of the 'common distrust of parliamentary authority' which also inspired

[35] Tom Garvin has recently noted the permeability of these categories, and offered 'by way of supplementing rather than replacing' them, two further labels – 'republican moralism' and 'nationalist pragmatism' – for 'the two subcultures or collective political styles'. *Birth of Irish Democracy*, 145.

[36] Figgis, *Irish Consitution*, ch. VII; Mansergh, *Irish Free State*, 320–7.

[37] Prager, *Building Democracy in Ireland*, 38, 76–7.

the system of popular initiative and referendum.)[38] Kohn, however, more plausibly saw them as being 'designed to invest Parliament with a direct measure of control over the more technical departments of state'.[39] To insist that this provision evinced the 'strong suspicion of political authority' characteristic of the Gaelic-Romantic tradition, and represented 'as much a cultural alternative as a political agenda' seems to be to say far too much.[40] Although it is plain that the long association of the state with British rule did legitimise rejection of some forms of authority, this surely did not apply to 'political authority' as such. The oppositional strategy known in the nineteenth century as 'constitutionalism', resting on the use of parliamentary methods, was of course rejected by exponents of 'physical force', and this Fenian suspicion of everything connected with 'politics' was still very much alive amongst some opponents of the Treaty.[41] The moment at which the defeated minority in the Dail vote to ratify the Treaty left the debating chamber and took to the field looked like a body blow to constitutionalism. But the fact that it was not, in the end, a mortal one argues a much deeper legitimacy of political authority.

In attempting to explain this, it seems necessary to emphasise more clearly than does Prager (or indeed Garvin) the positive effect of constitutionalism in Irish public culture. In fact, Prager chooses rather to de-emphasise it—insofar as he recognises it at all—by subsuming it in the 'Irish-Enlightenment' culture. Set in this frame, constitutionalism practically disappears from sight. The striking absence from his book of any reference to O'Connell or Parnell—much less Redmond or Dillon—can only be a deliberate exclusion for which some theoretical justification might be expected, though none is offered. On his account the Irish Parliamentary Party—on any measure the most substantial Irish political organisation before Sinn Féin—might never have existed. But it played a pivotal role in the political mobilisation of the Irish people and their subsequent political socialisation.[42] Under Parnell it was uncannily successful in containing the tension between 'moral force' and 'physical force' prescriptions for securing Irish independence, and the ambiguities in the notion of independence itself.[43] Parnell's act was a hard one to follow, maybe impossible to repeat, but it was surely

[38] *Ibid.*, 84. Note that Darrell Figgis explained these elements quite differently, as checks on party, not parliamentary, power.

[39] Kohn, *The Constitution of the Irish Free State*, 272–6.

[40] Prager, *Building Democracy in Ireland*, 82.

[41] E.g. Ernie O'Malley, elected on the fourteenth count for the eighth North Dublin seat in August 1923, 'hated to be a T.D.' *The Singing Flame* (Dublin, 1978), 238.

[42] Brian Walker, 'The 1885 and 1886 General Elections: a Milestone in Irish History', *Dancing to History's Tune* (Belfast, 1996), 15–33.

[43] F. S. L. Lyons, 'Charles Stewart Parnell', in Farrell, ed., *Irish Parliamentary Tradition*, 181–94.

never forgotten. The masterly imprecision of his rhetoric on 'the march of a nation' was perfectly adapted to managing the dynamic instability of nationalism, and the party he created made a plausible bridge between popular political consciousness and nationalist ideology.

The obverse of Parnell's contribution to constitutionalism was his personal imperiousness, which became institutionalised as an authoritarian disposition in the party. Philip Bull developed a powerful argument that this strain ultimately ossified and destroyed the party by isolating it from public sentiment.[44] In the circumstances of 1914–18, when a formidable new rival was taking shape, this was a fatal characteristic; but it can also be argued that the authoritarian strain re-emerged in the scions of Sinn Féin—pre-eminently Fianna Fail—and brought them longevity, if not actual immortality. The personalism which a number of political scientists have seen as the special mark of Irish political culture may have been confirmed by Parnell's reputation, but it is not clear that it has been inimical to constitutionalism.[45] The ascendancy of de Valera might equally, indeed more probably, in less lethal circumstances, have been the ascendancy of Michael Collins. Neither quite filled Parnell's boots, but both were capable of an impressive degree of control over the unstable dynamics of the nationalist movement.

When Collins was killed the imaginative flexibility of the Provisional Government was crippled: he can still, as Joseph Lee has demonstrated, be lamented as the lost leader, with whom everything could might been different.[46] But even though Cumann na nGaedheal became narrower and more rigid, it never abandoned his explicit commitment to constitutionalism. The central problem that Collins and his Treatyite colleagues faced was to institutionalise a potent but imprecise notion of freedom in a form acceptable to the British government and satisfying to the Irish people. His own formula, 'the freedom to achieve freedom', was as masterly as any of Parnell's. It immediately alerts us to the complex texture of the political liberation which the constitution had to enshrine. Collins' reference to 'the ultimate freedom to which all nations aspire' sounded more definite than Parnell's open-ended 'no man can set bounds to the march of a nation', but it was equally without concrete specification. In common with the pronouncements of all nationalist leaders it insisted that collective independence was the precondition for individual liberty. This logic made the demand for

[44] P.J. Bull, 'The Reconstruction of the Irish Parliamentary Movement, 1895–1903', Ph.D thesis, Cambridge University 1972.

[45] J. Raven and C. Whelan, *Political Culture in Ireland. The Views of Two Generations* (Institute of Public Administration, Dublin, 1976). D.E. Schmitt, 'Catholicism and Democratic Political Development in Ireland', *Eire-Ireland* 8 (1973).

[46] Lee, *Ireland, 1912–1985*, 63–6.

independence immensely rugged and effective in securing public assent, but its simplicity was not very useful in framing a constitution. Indeed the reverse in this case, because between Parnell and Collins the idea of freedom had been crucially modified.

The special version of national freedom produced by the Irish-Ireland movement around the turn of the century charted new zones of tension between collective and individual liberty. The movement's *leitmotiv*, first sounded by the founder of the Gaelic League, Douglas Hyde, was 'de-Anglicisation'. In Hyde's mind this was a cultural, and above all linguistic, project. But its political implications were more or less inescapable.[47] They were most challengingly expressed in the unminced words of D. P. Moran in 1904: 'the foundation of Ireland is the Gael and the Gael must be the element that absorbs'. This was a radical shift from the long-standing liberal, inclusive view of Irishness. Leaving aside the question of how far a distinctly 'Gaelic' people still existed, or could be recreated, in Ireland—which was to become one of the most contentious questions on the Free State's agenda—this programme was instantly perceived by Protestant loyalists as a direct threat to their civil and religious liberties.[48] And though all nationalists tried to preserve the rhetoric of inclusiveness, the exclusive logic of integral nationalism was confirmed by the movement's greatest ideologue, Patrick Pearse. Pearse's insistence on the mutuality of freedom and Gaelic identity ('Not free merely but Gaelic also ...') was no less of a complication for the fact that he himself, and his string of republican epigones, did not recognise its divisive implications.[49]

Michael Collins, whilst attempting (perhaps a little disingenuously) to sideline the now inconvenient obsession with 'sovereignty'—calling it a 'foreign word'[50]—insisted that 'national freedom' meant 'the right of the whole people to live as a nation'. This imposed a daunting cultural agenda. Shortly before his death he was promising that the 'alien administration' (i.e. civil service) would be scrapped as soon as fresh Gaelic nation-building tools could be forged and tempered; the courts of law too 'will be reorganised to make them national in character'.[51] The key was democracy, which Collins (borrowing from Darrell Figgis) held to have been the basis of the social and economic system of pre-Norman Ireland. It expressed the underlying sense of

[47] O. MacDonagh, 'The Politics of Gaelic', in *States of Mind. A Study of Anglo-Irish Conflict 1780–1980* (London, 1983).

[48] The special Protestant Loyalist sense of 'the constitution' is best analysed in D. W. Miller, *Queen's Rebels. Ulster Loyalism in Historical Perspective* (Dublin, 1977).

[49] D. G. Boyce, *Nationalism in Ireland* (London, 1982), 310.

[50] 'Notes by General Michael Collins, August 1922', *The Path to Freedom* (Dublin, 1922; repr. Cork, 1995), 15.

[51] *Ibid.*, 25.

national unity. In Gaelic civilisation, in contrast to Roman (he suggested) 'the people of the whole nation were united not by material forces but by spiritual ones. Their unity... came from sharing the same traditions.' Despite its political and economic fragmentation, 'in the things of the mind and the spirit the nation was one'.[52] But Collins could hardly, in 1922, fail to notice that some members of the putative Irish nation did not subscribe to this 'common ideal—a united, distinctive Irish nationality'. His hope was that democracy would lead 'by attraction, not compulsion' to a new 'diversity in unity'.[53] It was slender enough.

Collins came to the task of organising the drafting of a constitution under the terms of the Anglo-Irish Treaty from a Fenian-physical-force background which may not have seemed to provide the ideal qualification, but he turned out to be a deep-dyed constitutionalist.[54] Negotiating the constitution was a messy political business. The hope that Britain might accept a document sufficiently separatist in tone to stop the Treaty split deepening into civil war foundered on British suspicions that Collins was sliding back into the Republican camp. British insistence on the symbols of Crown and Empire grew still more rigid as the Provisional Government's internal authority weakened. Indeed Winston Churchill frankly used that weakness to force them into the constitution; whether he knew this would precipitate a violent crisis is not wholly clear. His reaction to the notorious Collins–de Valera electoral pact was to say, 'had the proposed election been a bona fide one, they could have put pressure on us to stretch the Constitution to suit them. As no election of value is contemplated we are in a position to be much more searching in our examination of the Constitution.'[55] Collins regretted British inflexibility and unimaginativeness (not to mention humourlessness)[56] but he clearly believed that the essence of the constitution was distinct from its decorous forms. His own preference seems to have been for a drastically simplified 10-article constitution[57] (in contrast to the 78 articles of his committee's

[52] M. Collins, 'Distinctive Culture. Ancient Irish Civilization', *The Path to Freedom*, 96–8.

[53] M. Collins, 'Advance and Use Our Liberties', *The Path to Freedom*, 37.

[54] Garvin perceptively notes the function of strict legalism as a substitute ideal for those who had been driven to abandon the republic, but he sees Collins' commitment to democracy as more than pragmatic politics. *1922*, 128–9.

[55] Memorandum by W. S. Churchill, 23 May 1922. PRO CAB 21 256.

[56] To Collins' quip that the Viceregal Lodge would make an admirable cancer hospital, Austen Chamberlain primly observed that 'jokes were so dangerous. The question was of the greatest importance to His Majesty's Government who could not consent to the humiliation of the representative of the Crown.' Cabinet Conference with Irish Ministers, 26 February 1922. PRO CAB 21 250.

[57] This draft was not found by Akenson and Fallin. Farrell found a copy in in papers of James Douglas, in Douglas' hand but headed 'M. Collins draft', together with some notes, in which Collins insisted that 'the Constitution should be as simple as possible'.

draft A, and the 81 articles of draft B—or even the 66 articles of the eventual Free State Constitution), which should contain 'no unnecessary sentiment, which might be laughed at'. In a similarly revealing way he thought that mixing English and Irish terminology in the same document would have 'a grotesque effect' (for all that it had been, and continued to be, quite routine in Sinn Féin, Dáil Éireann and Free State documents and correspondence). And he believed that the Treaty was genuinely valuable in specifying that the executive should be responsible to parliament—'in itself a natural and essential feature of a satisfactory constitution'.[58] But Collins thought he was preserving the cultural underpinning of his constitution: 'The essence of a Gaelic polity is there, without the trappings.'

Since the notion of collective freedom, or national independence, which is conventionally regarded as the unique fountainhead (or, in the liberal version, guarantor) of individual liberty, was in the Irish case ambivalent,[59] this ambivalence inevitably percolated into the constitutional provisions relating to individual liberty. In any polity there is a clear conceptual, and a somewhat less clear practical, distinction between the freedom of the individual from coercion or religious persecution, and the freedom of the citizen to participate in the political process. Isaiah Berlin popularised the use of 'negative' and 'positive' freedom to articulate this distinction.[60] Franz Neumann put it rather differently, identifying the view that 'freedom is first and foremost the absence of restraints' as underlying the liberal theory of freedom, 'the key concept of what one understands by constitutionalism'. This he referred to as negative in the Hegelian sense, 'one-sided and therefore inadequate'.[61] In other words, it is only half of real freedom. Neumann held that 'the idea that there are individual rights which political power may restrain and restrict but never annihilate' is made concrete in the catalogues of civil rights in various constitutions—'for practical purposes, juridical freedom largely coincides with these charters'. From the basic supposition that there exists a presumption in favour of the individual's freedom follows all the elements of the liberal

Farrell, 'Drafting of the Irish Free State Constitution: I', 122–5. It seems clear from the fact that Collins wrote the further set of notes in S 6541, which Farrell did not find, that his input at this early stage was more substantial than writers such as Akenson and Fallin have suggested.

[58] Notes by Micéal O. Coileán, March 1922. NA, Taoiseach S 6541.

[59] F. S. L. Lyons also noted of Arthur Griffith that 'his definition of independence was clouded by ambiguities which were to haunt him until his dying day'. 'The Meaning of Independence', *Irish Parliamentary Tradition*, 228.

[60] I. Berlin, 'Two Concepts of Liberty' (Inaugural Lecture, Oxford University 1958); *Four Essays on Liberty* (Oxford, 1964).

[61] F. L. Neumann, 'The Concept of Political Freedom', *Columbia Law Review* 53 (1953), 903.

legal system: the permissibility of every act not expressly forbidden by law; the closed and self-consistent nature of the legal system; the inadmissibility of retroactive legislation; the separation of the judicial from the legislative function. These concepts, Neumann thought, are 'accepted by the civilised world without question'.[62] Listing these conventions leaves open 'the question of what this theoretical system actually guarantees', which in his view depends on the nature of each polity. The difference between German and English doctrines of the rule of law seemed to be related to the self-restraint of the English parliament which in turn was 'the result of a stable party system and a balanced and stable social structure'.[63]

The transmission of British political modes to independent Ireland may have served the same purpose though, as Kohn carefully showed, the international catalogue of civil rights was demonstratively—and hence in an un-British way—incorporated in the Free State constitution.[64] Yet the crucial point in Neumann's analysis was the other, positive half of freedom. He observed that the fact that modern man considers political power a force alien to him was the result of political alienation. He noted that for Aristotle, despite his dislike of democracy, 'some kind of active participation in politics is the precondition for citizenship'. More broadly, Neumann insisted that 'freedom is more than the defence of rights against power; it involves as well the possibility of developing man's potentialities to the fullest'.[65] This view, however, carries a lot more freight in the twentieth century than it did in the nineteenth (when it could have made sense to both Hegel and Mill). Nationalism supposes that potential is developed through collective identity as much as, if not rather than, through individual qualities. National identity is the most precious individual civil right. In the Irish case, where alienation was a visceral as much as a psychological state, this might mean that if there were a possibility of conflict between adhesion to Catholic values and to civic culture, it would be hard to resolve.

This bottom line could be obscured by the heady rhetoric of the armed struggle before 1922. Tom Barry, the commander of the West Cork Brigade flying column of the IRA, and a somewhat less sophisticated political thinker than Neumann, certainly spoke for many when he claimed for the republic 'an aim higher than that of simple political freedom'—'the dignity of man and all mankind'. Such aspir-

[62] *Ibid.*, 907.

[63] *Ibid.*, 911.

[64] As did J. G. Swift MacNeill, whose extensive gloss on the constitution argued that it incorporated the spirit of the British constitution, but 'improved' by inscribing many conventions as law. *Studies in the Constitution of the Irish Free State* (Dublin, 1925), vii–xxiii.

[65] Neumann, 'The Concept of Political Freedom', 901, 927, 915.

ations are the breath of many if not most revolutions. Freedom could mean many things. Addressing the question of how workers would benefit from the national freedom sought by Sinn Féin, *Nationality* offered them 'the chance of winning an independent livelihood in their own land under fair conditions'.[66] (Such attitudes lead Tom Garvin mischievously to label republicanism a 'cargo cult'.) An accretion of vague if not actually conflicting hopes was left to be fulfilled by the new constitution.

In the circumstances it would not have been a matter for great surprise if the constitution had failed, as Prager holds, to achieve full symbolic integration. But it is doubtful whether this is the most illuminating perspective to adopt. Prager's emphasis on the distinction between the phrases 'to renew and re-establish our State and to found it upon principles of freedom and justice' and 'to re-establish our national life and unity' in Drafts A and B hinges on reading the latter as 'unwillingness to endorse a modern form of civility based upon the rights of the individual', deriving from 'a romantic reassertion that the collective will of the Irish community, primordially defined, would and could harmoniously establish patterns of interaction belying any need for hierarchy and authority relations superior to the community'.[67] This extrapolation from conventional *volkisch* nationalism can be directly identified with the views of both Darrell Figgis, the chairman of the constitutional committee, and Hugh Kennedy, the Law Officer of the Provisional Government and later Attorney General of the Free State.[68] Kennedy was probably the leading spirit and predominant legal expert of the minority group which produced Draft B, though oddly enough Prager does not refer to him. But was Kennedy more of a 'Gaelic-Romantic' than Figgis? By contrast Akenson and Fallin saw him and his group on the drafting committee as 'liberals', as against the 'conservatives' of Draft A 'clinging to the British cabinet system'.[69] Admittedly, their attribution of labels is a little slapdash: they say of the 'radicals' who produced (the now mostly lost) Draft C, 'it matters little if they be considered right wing or left wing radicals'. Alan Ward suggests that all the constitution drafters were simultaneously conservative and radical.[70]

The point is that to place Kennedy in a position of antipathy to 'Irish-Enlightenment' values is as misleading as to describe him as a liberal. He was deeply concerned that the new state be given a distinctly

[66] *Nationality*, 30 November 1918.
[67] Prager, *Building Democracy in Ireland*, 79.
[68] Thomas Towey, 'Hugh Kennedy and the Constitutional Development of the Irish Free State, 1922–1923', *Irish Jurist* 12 (1977), 355.
[69] Akenson and Fallin, *The Irish Civil War*, 47.
[70] Ward, *Irish Constitutional Tradition*, 168.

Irish institutional structure, but he was a Treatyite who went on serving (or running) a state which fell far short of his aspirations. Here, as elsewhere in analyses of the Treaty split, an adhesion to pragmatism or realism seems to be the most consistent determinant of the cleavage. Kennedy, like O'Higgins and other founders of the Free State, carried through the 'revolution' an underlying system of values which can best be called constitutionalism. In public he capaciously hinted that the main influences on the Free State constitution had been 'the written constitution of the USA, of Germany and of Switzerland, as well as that body of principles which make up the unwritten constitution of Great Britain'.[71] Kennedy's principal contribution to the evolution of the state forms of the IFS was, in the view of one commentator, a 'curious juxtaposition of constitutional fiction and fact'.[72] Such juxtaposition was characteristic of the British constitution, whose spirit was here transmitted even when its forms were changed.

The transmission of this constitutional spirit was not uniquely the province of the Treatyite administration after 1921. It was, as Brian Farrell trenchantly argued in *The Founding of Dáil Éireann*, the work of Sinn Féin.[73] Since 1926, and until very recently, Sinn Féin has been identified with the most rigorous Fenian repudiation of constitutionalism. Even Fianna Fáil, which split from Sinn Féin in the mid-1920s precisely on the issue of entering Dáil Éireann, achieved cheerful notoriety through the epithet 'slightly constitutional' cannily applied to it by Sean Lemass. The knowing ambiguities of this famous phrase have rather obscured the extent to which the original Sinn Féin (from which Fianna Fail likes to imply lineal descent) was a more than slightly constitutional party.

Sinn Féin's critics found an easy line of attack on the party's grasp of democratic principles in the well-attested rigging of the 1917 *árd-fheis* at which the structure and policy of the movement were laid down.[74] To say that this manipulation was in the tradition of the parliamentary party itself (as in the 'baton convention' bitterly commemorated by the great parliamentarian William O'Brien, whose attempt to reconcile the party with his All-For-Ireland League was silenced by the cudgels of the Ancient Order of Hibernians), projected into the fixing of the 'pact election' of 1922 which so alarmed and scandalised the British, may

[71] Hugh Kennedy, 'Character and Sources of the Constitution of the Irish Free State', *American Bar Association Journal* vol. 14 (1928), 443.

[72] Towey, *op cit.*, 358.

[73] B. Farrell, *The Founding of Dáil Éireann. Parliament and Nation-Building* (Dublin, 1971). The absence of this book from Prager's sources is as puzzling as the absence of Parnell from his text.

[74] M. Laffan, 'The Unification of Sinn Féin in 1917', *Irish Historical Studies* xvii (1971), 353–79.

not look like a very strong defence.[75] But it is fair to say that in the circumstances of armed struggle Sinn Féin's practice of constitutionalism was more remarkable than its departures from it. It is important to recall that Sinn Féin was an abstentionist party not in the later absolutist sense, of refusing altogether to take up any seats it won, but in the special 'Hungarian' sense (as adduced by Arthur Griffith) of collectively removing itself from Westminster and reconstituting itself as an Irish national assembly (Dáil Éireann). Brian Farrell pointed out that the working methods of the first Dáil became in practice 'the constitutional cornerstone of the new Irish state'. He held, too, that the first meeting of the Dáil 'was marked by a moderation surprising in a country on the edge of a war of liberation; its documents bear the stamp of an established set of political values, based clearly on the Westminster model of government'.[76]

Farrell used the minutes of the meeting of the Sinn Féin Executive Committee on 19 December 1918, at which the decision to convene the party's MPs as a separate assembly was taken, to show 'how readily Sinn Féin slipped into parliamentary usage', and 'the willingness with which the conventions of representative government were accepted'. His interpretation of the Constitution of the Dail (*Bunreacht Dala Eireann*), which was adopted at the foundation meeting on 19 January 1919, disputed the views of it taken by Kohn and in a later generation by Basil Chubb. Kohn saw the repeated references to 'the Government of the Irish Republic, which is Dáil Éireann' as embodying 'a curious revival of the old revolutionary conception of parliament as the incorporation of all governmental authority'. Farrell argued that in fact cabinet government was established from the start, but that, *pace* Chubb, the powers of the executive were deliberately made amenable to parliamentary control.[77] It is demonstrable that, whatever the intention, the practice of government usually gravitated to British procedures, as in the apparently instinctive reversion to the word 'Cabinet' in place of the initial 'Ministry'.[78]

Altogether, Farrell made a powerful case for seeing what Cathal Brugha called 'this thing which passed as a Constitution but in reality was not a Constitution' as being more than a parliamentary rule book; a true *Grundgesetz*, as the word *Bunreacht*, basic law, implies. He found in the O Ceallaigh papers an abandoned preamble to the Dáil

[75] A. C. Hepburn, 'The Ancient Order of Hibernians in Irish Politics 1905–14', *Cithara* x (1971). J. V. O'Brien, *William O'Brien and the Course of Irish Politics 1881–1918* (Berkeley, 1976).

[76] Farrell, *The Founding of Dáil Éireann*, 51ff.

[77] *Ibid.*, 67.

[78] *Ibid.*, 68. See also B. Farrell, 'The First Dáil and its Constitutional Documents', in *The Creation of the Dáil*, 61–74.

constitution—rendered supererogatory by the Declaration of Independence—which declared 'We, the people of Ireland, in order to establish justice, insure domestic tranquillity, provide for the common defence, promote the general welfare, and secure the blessings of Liberty to ourselves and our posterity, do ordain and establish this Constitution for the Irish Republic'. Despite the persistence of oddities such as the position of the 'President of the Dáil' as President of the Republic, the system built on it was informed by a core of constitutionalism.

In such a framework, the 1922 constitution must be read as a less contentious document than Prager contends, and also a more successful one. Concentration on a couple of clauses which tried to raise, in face of British intransigence, banners of Irish national sovereignty and identity, necessarily points to failure. Republican and Imperial symbolism were plainly irreconcilable, and the constitutional provisions which enshrined the public function of the Crown and the Governor-General only endured as long as the balance of power that had produced them. They remained contentious until they were more or less peacefully buried by De Valera in the 1930s.[79] But below these symbolic elements which mesmerised republican purists lay the mass of constitutional provisions which reflected a deep-set public constitutional culture. This was tested by the 1922 crisis. The severest test of constitutional culture faced by most states is war; very few have faced a civil war in the kind of circumstances which confronted the Provisional Government in 1922—remembered by Kevin O'Higgins as 'simply eight young men in the City Hall standing amidst the ruins of one administration, with the foundations of another not yet laid, and with wild men screaming through the keyhole'.[80] The new Irish state had to take up a task in which the British state had failed disastrously: the vindication of the rule of law. Everything else depended on this. As Michael Collins insisted, democratic government allows the greatest freedom, but 'like all governments, must be recognised and obeyed. The first duty of the new Government was to maintain public order, security of life, personal liberty, and property.'[81]

It is not hard to mount a substantial indictment of the Free State government's persistent subordination of the constitutional guarantees

[79] E.g. D. McMahon, *Republicans and Imperialists. Anglo-Irish Relations in the 1930s* (London, 1984). B. Sexton, *Ireland and the Crown 1922–1936. The Governor-Generalship of the Irish Free State* (Dublin, 1989).

[80] More specifically, O'Higgins added, 'No police force was functioning through the country, no system of justice was operating, the wheels of administration hung idle, battered out of recognition by the clash of rival jurisdictions.'

[81] M. Collins, *The Path to Freedom*, 20.

of personal liberty to the demands of public security.[82] The essence of this indictment is the charge laid by the labour leader Thomas Johnson: 'you are weakening in fact respect for law by detaining men because they are your political opponents'. The charge is an important corrective to the 'Stater' tendency to lionise Kevin O'Higgins—the man 'cast in bronze'—as the saviour of democracy. (A tendency still noticeable in the defence of Irish special powers laws by both Fine Gael and Fianna Fail administrations.) Stemming from critics within the pale of the constitution, it is more telling than the demonisation of O'Higgins by his republican opponents. Since his death it has been maintained by jurists rather than politicians, and rests on the contention that judges should not be put in the front line of political conflict. Leo Kohn opened this line of argument with his fierce denunciation of the extremist tendency of British emergency powers law in the last years of the Union. 'No emergency, however urgent', he insisted, 'can justify the investment of the representatives of force with the functions of the guardians of justice'; but 'the most invidious feature of the system' as it evolved after the *Marais* case was 'the imposition upon the guardians of objective justice of the essentially political tasks of deciding on the existence of a state of emergency and of interpreting the unspecified powers of the executive organs during internal disturbances'.[83] Kohn admitted that the Free State had not altogether broken away from this British tendency, though he gave the impression that the government had become steadily clearer about the formal means of abrogating the constitution via its successive Public Safety Acts. Some recent writers have been less sanguine about the constitution's 'vulnerability to legislative encroachment' or 'implicit amendment' by these Acts.[84]

The central question is whether 'irreparable damage was done to whatever little respect for law there remained in the public mind'.[85] The issue was squarely put in 1923 by the Labour TD Thomas O'Connell: 'we must first of all establish respect for the law ... You will not make a law-abiding people by fear of the law ... The people must be made to feel that the law is just.' Cathal O'Shannon likewise urged that 'if the Ministry only attempted to show the people that they were going to administer the ordinary law, the people would rally to

[82] C. Magee, 'Uses and Abuses of Law. Political Violence, Law and State in Ireland since 1922' (Ph.D. thesis, Trinity College, Dublin 1987).

[83] Kohn, *The Constitution of the Irish Free State*, 147, 157. The significance of the case Ex parte D.F. Marais (1902) in the evolution of emergency powers is outlined in C. Townshend, 'Martial Law: Legal and Administrative Problems of Civil Emergency in Britain and the Empire, 1800–1940', *Historical Journal* 25 (1982), 182.

[84] C. Campbell, *Emergency Law in Ireland, 1918–25* (Oxford, 1994).

[85] Magee, 'Uses and Abuses of Law', 88.

the administration of that ordinary law'.[86] O'Higgins saw the process of law-keeping as operating the other way round: enforcement was the precondition of public belief in the law. 'Nothing so scandalises and demoralises a community as the spectacle of a man flourishing on ill-gotten gains. Nothing so surely destroys the economic life of a country as the absence of credit and security.' In January 1923, in the midst of civil war, he argued that only a small part of the public violence was 'a struggle to secure a particular form of government'; most was crime of one sort or another, 'fostered by the idea that there is a breakdown of law, that the existing Government is unable to function effectively, and that the sun is shining for the law-breaker'. He told his colleagues on the Executive Council,

> the writ of this Committee is running with a limp in most Counties, and is not running at all in many ... We must face this unorthodox situation in an unorthodox way. We must forget the terms 'Government' and 'Army', 'Civil' and 'Military', and remember that we are, all of us, simply a body of men out to vindicate the idea of ordered society and the reign of law.[87]

This was a far cry from Kohn's procedural rectitude, and it gives plenty of colour to the argument that when the chips were down, the constitution was a scrap of paper.

But it is perhaps better to adopt a less formalistic test of constitutionality in the circumstances of open war. The jurist John Finn has argued that the famous accounts of modern 'constitutional dictatorship' by Clinton Rossiter and Carl Friedrich stressed formal limitations on executive power rather than, as Finn would prefer, the rationality of executive action as the essence of constitutional maintenance. (When Kenneth Wheare said that 'crisis government can seldom be constitutional government' he confused the issue by conflating constitutional with limited government.) Finn suggests that, for issues of civil emergency, constitutionalism 'should be understood not in terms of limited government but rather as a commitment to a public life premised upon the public articulation of reasons in support of particular actions taken for the public welfare'.[88] This criterion can be helpfully applied to the actions of the pro-Treaty governments.

The Free State government was certainly aware of the complex issues involved in the enforcement of public order by constitutional means. The acutest difficulties arose not during the civil war so much

[86] *Ibid.*, 89–90.

[87] Memorandum by Minister for Justice, 20 January 1923. Executive Council Conference on Maintenance of Order, 26 September 1923. NA, Taoiseach S.3306.

[88] J. E. Finn, *Constitutions in Crisis. Political Violence and the Rule of Law* (OUP, New York 1991), 30.

as after its unsatisfactory ending (a unilateral cessation of operations, with no negotiations, or decommissioning of arms; serious if sporadic violence persisted for several years). The 1923 Public Safety Act was designed 'to provide for the better preservation of public order during the period after the cessation of "war or armed rebellion" but before the arrival of normal conditions'.[89] The constitution did not allow for the existence of an intermediate state of affairs between war and peace, the 'middle period' when, as one departmental memorandum graphically depicted it, 'the waves will continue to run high for some time after the storm has blown itself out'.

The Justice Department frankly recognised that habeas corpus was at risk in these circumstances; 'the first instinctive refuge of the Executive in such periods is, precisely, trial of accused persons by judges without a jury'. This was because in even the best-founded polities juries are likely to take the side of the individual against the state. 'If that is so elsewhere, it is bound to be much more so in this country where the relation of the citizen to the state has been so long the relation of slave to master that years must elapse before the ordinary man will realise that when he pinches the State his own flesh will show the bruise sooner or later.' This pessimism was accompanied by an equally frank recognition that

> An Executive saddled with a rigid constitution in dangerous times is affected not only by the real and obvious limitations imposed by the Constitution but also by the perhaps even more disturbing and demoralising uncertainty as to what further unsuspected or uncertain limitations may be hidden in other parts of the Constitution, to be discovered by the Judges on the invitation of an able lawyer.[90]

In the situation where 'the Constitution debars us from one of the most universal and natural remedies against the consequences of general turbulence and poor civic spirit' (i.e. juryless trial), to say nothing of internment without trial, some overriding of constitutional guarantees was inevitable. The government took the view that the acid test of such action was public reaction.

In tracing the evolution of the four emergency powers laws of the Cumann na nGaedheal government, Kohn admitted that not until the third (1927) Act was there any open recognition of 'the incompatibility of legislation restricting or abolishing the fundamental safeguards of individual liberty with the spirit of the Constitution'. This seems to be related to the fact that the *habeas corpus* provision of the Constitution

[89] Aireacht um Gnothai Duithche: memo for Attorney-General by Henry O'Friel, *loc cit.* (May–June 1923).

[90] *Ibid.*

(Article 6), albeit prefaced by an un-English abstract declaration that 'the liberty of the person is inviolable', was substantially drafted in a typically English procedural form 'intelligible only in the light of the evolution of habeas corpus in English legal history'.[91] Judicial interpretation of the first Public Safety (Emergency Powers) Act was consequently confusing and unsatisfactory, though it was far from realising the fears of executive paralysis that had been expressed within the government. It was not until the last (1931) public safety act that a formal constitutional amendment of the sort originally suggested in 1923 was incorporated in the law. In the interim, the government preferred to keep the issue in a less formal area of the public sphere. O'Higgins was happy to argue that the rapid passage of the 1926 Public Safety Act showed that 'The country is preponderatingly in favour of what has been done to restore public order. If this were not so', he added, 'the Government believe that their somewhat drastic step would have resulted in very visible manifestations of disapproval'.[92]

This argument was political rather than constitutional, and it lays bare the grounds on which O'Higgins might be seen as either a tyrant or a democrat. His readiness—even eagerness, as it often appeared—to reduce everything to the maxim *salus populi suprema lex* was not easy to square with strict constitutionality. He exploited an exaggerated antinomy between the 'democratic' majority rule of the government and the 'clique of neurotics' aiming at 'rule by the force of the revolver'. But it is not clear that he perverted the rule of law. Rather, he articulated a public belief in order which undergirded it, and did so rather successfully. The situation in which he was operating was, as he put it without overstatement, 'unorthodox'. Indeed, as Thomas Johnson observed (though with rather different intent), 'the normal conditions in this country are abnormal'. Norms have to be negotiated; constitutions can only go so far in establishing them. As the memorandum earlier instanced warned, 'how can any man pretend to foresee how a future Superior Court may interpret the words of Article 70 "... extraordinary Courts shall not be established ..." What are "extraordinary" Courts? Apparently not "ordinary" ones! But what are "ordinary" Courts?'

How was public negotiation done? We are at last coming to recognise how fundamental to the survival of the constitutional state was the Provisional Government's decision, in the midst of civil war, to create a new unarmed police force, the Civic Guard. The shaping of the decision is still obscure, though it may have been driven by pragmatism

[91] Kohn, *The Constitution of the Irish Free State*, 131.

[92] Press conference (Press Association), London, following Proclamation of National Emergency, 20 November 1926. *Irish Times*, 23 November 1923.

as much as by principle. But there was no question that the idea of constitutionality was put in high profile. The Provisional Government's first recruiting proclamation for the National Guard began with the assertion that the anti-Treaty leadership

> Contrary to all Constitutional practice ... has arrogated to itself powers of legislation ... thereby openly challenging the right of the Irish people to express their will through the medium of the popular franchise. By force of arms its supporters have interfered with the right of free speech ... and have threatened to subvert the authority of the Sovereign Irish People duly expressed in accordance with Constitutional practice.[93]

This was of course propaganda—but that is just the point: it was expected to strike a public chord. The unarmed force finally created, the Civic Guard (eventually the Garda Siochana), rapidly achieved a legitimacy unprecedented in the history of policing in Ireland.[94] Equally importantly, and surprisingly, it was allowed to work unmolested by the anti-treaty forces. There are several likely reasons for this. The Irregulars may have been victims of their own military fixation; they saw an unarmed force as contemptible. Tom Garvin has suggested that the government traded on 'a crucial cultural ace-in-the-hole: the taboo on killing unarmed men and women who could not reasonably be seen as spies and informers'.[95] Garvin adds one or two more cultural credits, such as the Guards' involvement in Gaelic games, and the shift in uniform colours from 'quasi-military RIC green to policeman's blue'. But perhaps the weightiest reason for the IRA's general order (12 December 1922) not to fire on unarmed police was their 'tacit recognition of the unpopularity of their own cause'.[96]

It is interesting that this 'brilliant improvisation' followed a model almost unique in the modern world—that of the English 'bobby'. That is a strange coincidence, highlit by the fact that in the 'British' part of Ireland this model could not be adopted. The Royal Ulster Constabulary has remained an armed semi-military force lineally descended from the RIC. Likewise, it may be suggested, Northern Ireland emergency powers legislation since the 1922 Civil Authorities Act has never shed its contentious aspect, whereas even the most draconian of the Free State's emergency laws, however unpopular, were compatible with ultimate reconciliation. Its legal rhetoric skilfully combined ruthless

[93] Proclamation, May 1922. NA Taoiseach S 1168.

[94] And incidentally indicating what the British government might have achieved if it had disarmed the old RIC, as most RIC men seem to have wished. Garvin, *1922*, 114.

[95] Garvin, *1922*, 105. But he seems unclear whether the 'taboo' was already in existence, or (as he says on p. 108) was actually established during the conflict.

[96] *Ibid.*, 110–11.

logic with sardonic humour. Introducing the 1925 Treasonable Offences Bill, O'Higgins began with the elementary school-civics-course observation that the Bill's purpose was 'to protect the life of the State ... upon the existence of which the lives and liberties of individual citizens depend'. 'I imagine it is unnecessary for me,' he suggested, 'to emphasise the fact that no ordered Government can for a moment permit the organisation of any military or police forces in opposition to the forces lawfully established.' Further, 'it would appear to be an elementary principle of social law and order that the chief functionaries of the State duly appointed by the people, and the courts of the country, should be free from any intimidation.' Finally, 'No country could possibly progress under two conflicting Governments and it seems scarcely fair to ask that the Saorstat should give this dangerous experiment a trial.'

In 1922, after the assassination of Sir Henry Wilson in London, Kevin O'Higgins reflected that 'assassination is a game that two can play, and men may be lost to Ireland of greater potentialities and more constructive abilities' than Wilson. In July 1927 he himself was assassinated, and it fell to Cosgrave to introduce the consequent emergency powers legislation. The rhetoric became more pedestrian; a sense of dispiritedness pervaded the ever-more trivial provisions, as the nut held out against the sledgehammer.[97] But there was still a core of almost painful honesty. 'To preserve the youth of the country, the hysterical, the morbid, the neurotic and the impressionable elements of the country from inoculation with poisonous doctrines and ideas it is in our judgment absolutely essential that the Executive should have the power to suppress all associations of persons who set out to achieve a particular object ... by violent or criminal means.'

> To deal with insults to state authority by criminals who frequently indulge in refusal to recognise the authority of the court, this is made a crime in itself. It is perfectly absurd that persons who enjoy the protection and security of the Constitution and the State should openly flout its authority ... It may quite satisfy certain neurotic people but I think it would be healthy to give these neurotics less opportunity for satisfying their desire for the sensational.[98]

The assassination was 'plotted and carried out as a blow against the security of the State ... it is important to make it clear that the people are not going to be overawed by violence, and that revolutionary

[97] Prager holds that the government's response was disproportional (*Building Democracy*, 166); yet in another context he bears out (p. 189) the government's view that IRA intimidation of juries was a deadly menace to 'the integrity of the public'.

[98] Speech notes, President of the Executive Council. NA D/Justice 4/202/1.

changes in the Constitution are not likely to be achieved by deeds of violence'.

Did the Free State government, as Prager contends, flout both the constitution and public opinion in its determination to vindicate its authority? I would suggest that on the contrary it took on the task of demonstrating the burdensome demands of constitutionalism. It believed that public opinion had to develop if democracy was to function. (Ernest Blythe characteristically insisted that 'the first step towards progress is a clear recognition of the fact that, instead of being a race of super-idealists whose misfortunes are due entirely to the crimes of outside enemies, we are an untrained and undisciplined people with practically everything to learn of the difficult business of organising national life . . .')[99] This message was unlikely to be received with delirious enthusiasm, but as far as I can see it was very largely accepted. In the process of renegotiating the public sphere, the constitution of the Free State was a considerable success. Not, indeed, in delivering cherished symbols of liberation, so much as in tapping a fundamental constitutional consensus far more substantial than a conventional reading of Irish history under the Union might suggest. It is hardly novel to suggest that the Staters' finest hour was their defeat in 1932—immediately occasioned, fittingly enough, by their last emergency law. Nothing in their tenure of power became them like their transfer of it to de Valera. The moment de Valera re-entered constitutional politics he ceased to be a public criminal and became the leader of the opposition. In bringing a more congenial message to the Irish public, he was able to capitalise on Cosgrave's work. He took his place in an orderly and well-understood system of constitutional government whose unmistakably British assumptions survived—as possibly those of Britain itself would survive—the risky experiment of proportional representation virtually intact.

[99] UCDAD, Hayes MSS P53/344, q.; Garvin, *1922*, 60.

THE PROBLEM OF PAUPER MARRIAGE IN SEVENTEENTH-CENTURY ENGLAND

The Alexander Prize Essay

By Steve Hindle

READ 25 APRIL 1997

OVER the last thirty years the work of historical demographers, spearheaded by Sir Tony Wrigley, Roger Schofield and others at the Cambridge Group for the History of Population and Social Structure, has demonstrated the centrality of marriage to explanations of early modern English demographic change: 'a history of English population in this period in which nuptiality did not figure prominently would resemble the proverbial production of *Hamlet* without the prince of Denmark'.[1] Although their 'neo-Malthusian' or 'neo-classical' model of population levels kept in 'dilatory homeostasis' by negative feedback relationships between living standards, age at first marriage and the proportion of the population never marrying has not been immune from criticism, it is now generally accepted that changes in fertility rather than in mortality account for population stagnation in mid-seventeenth-century England, and for its renewed and rapid growth from the 1730s.[2] Moreover, having flirted with, and subsequently discarded, changes in *marital fertility* as a proximate cause of fluctuations in the birth rate, Wrigley and Schofield are now convinced that *nuptiality* was decisive.[3] For Wrigley, 'the crucial importance of the tension between production and reproduction which affected all pre-industrial societies' explains why marriage had a 'significance ... far wider than

[1] E. A. Wrigley and R. S. Schofield, *The Population History of England, 1541–1871: A Reconstruction* (reprinted edn, Cambridge, 1989), 450–3; E. A. Wrigley, R. S. Davies, J. E. Oeppen and R. S. Schofield, *English Population History From Family Reconstitution, 1580–1837* (Cambridge, 1997), 197.

[2] The relationship of Wrigley and Schofield's model to its 'Malthusian' and 'classical' predecessors is helpfully discussed by John Landers, 'From Colyton to Waterloo: Mortality, Politics and Economics in Historical Demography', in *Rethinking Social History: English Society 1570–1920 and Its Interpretation*, ed. Adrian Wilson (Manchester, 1993), 100. For 'dilatory homeostasis', see Wrigley and Schofield, *Population History*, 451.

[3] *Cf.* E. A. Wrigley, 'Family Limitation in Pre-Industrial England', *Economic History Review*, 2nd ser., xix (1966), reprinted in Wrigley, *People, Cities and Wealth: The Transformation of Traditional Society* (Oxford, 1987), 242–69.

the purely demographic'.[4] 'Marriage,' he argues, 'was the hinge on which the [early modern English] demographic system turned.'

The mechanics which governed the operation of Wrigley's nuptial 'hinge', however, remain obscure. In the most important contribution to the debate, David Weir argued that marital behaviour was significantly transformed over time, from a period in which trends in the *incidence* of marriage were dominant to one in which changes in the *ages* of those marrying determined fertility trends.[5] As Wrigley and Schofield conceded in 1989,

> it now seems clear that until the middle of the eighteenth century the substantial swings in nuptiality that occurred were produced almost exclusively by wide variations in the proportion of women never marrying (between about five and twenty-two per cent), whereas after this date there was little change in this aspect of nuptiality but a rapid and substantial fall in age at marriage.[6]

Although, therefore, celibacy has become the focal point of seventeenth-century demographic interest, historians have had little success in exploring its social and cultural dynamics. While the calculation of the proportion of the population never marrying is in itself problematic, the explanation of its variation over time is rendered even more difficult by three separate but related factors.[7] The first two of these are chronologically specific to the 1640s and 1650s: first, changes in the law of marriage, especially under the Commonwealth; and, second, the notorious problem of the defective registration of marriages during the mid-century crisis.[8] These factors naturally complicate the actual measurement of celibacy. The third difficulty, however, is methodological, for the Cambridge Group 'model' places at the centre of analysis rational choices made by the prospective marriage partners themselves. The problem with many such 'rational-choice' models of human behaviour

[4] E. A. Wrigley, 'The Growth of Population in Eighteenth-Century England: A Conundrum Resolved', *Past and Present*, no. 98 (February 1983), reprinted in Wrigley, *People, Cities and Wealth*, 239–40.

[5] D. R. Weir, 'Rather Never Than Late: Celibacy and Age at Marriage in English Cohort Fertility', *Journal of Family History*, ix (1984), 349.

[6] Wrigley and Schofield, *Population History*, xix; Wrigley *et al.*, *English Population History From Family Reconstitution*, 195; For the Cambridge Group's detailed response to Weir, see R. S. Schofield, 'English Marriage Patterns Revisited', *Journal of Family History*, x (1985), 2–20.

[7] Wrigley *et al.*, *English Population History From Family Reconstitution*, 197.

[8] For the Act of 1653 and its consequences see G. B. Nourse, 'Law Reform Under the Commonwealth and Protectorate', *Law Quarterly Review*, lxxv (1959), 512–29; and Christopher Durston, *The Family in the English Revolution* (Oxford, 1989), 71–86. On under-registration of marriages *c.*1640–60, see Wrigley and Schofield, *Population History*, 23–8, especially table 1.4 and figure 1.2.

is evidential: it is very difficult to find examples of marriage partners communicating, let alone planning, in this 'rational' way. Arguably, therefore, the model is not only constructed according to non-empirical criteria, but also decontextualised in social terms. After all, were seventeenth-century couples really so free to choose in this way?

Those historians who have sought to answer this question have generally confined their analyses to three sets of factors: *economic*, *ideological*, and *cultural*. From the *economic* perspective, it has been argued, 'marriage was a movable feast, since both the particular circumstances of individual couples and the general circumstances of the economy changed and fluctuated over time'.[9] Accordingly, the real or perceived living standards of the couple have attracted most attention, and aggregative analysis of the link between age at first marriage and income opportunity has been brought into play. Here, Wrigley and Schofield's postulation of a 'dilatory' relationship (or 'long lag') between real wages and the crude first marriage rate has struck many critics as implausible, leading them not only to modify the standard of living indices used, but (as we have seen) to turn attention away from fluctuations in age at first marriage towards the changing proportions of the population never marrying.[10] Although Weir has estimated that celibacy (measured in terms of the proportion of the population never married at ages forty to forty-four) rose to 21 per cent for the cohort born in 1616 and to 24 per cent for that born in 1641, and Goldstone has argued that this figure reflects the decreasing 'fraction of the total population with incomes sufficient to cross the threshold of eligibility for marriage', neither has been able to convincingly disentangle the strands of the labour market.[11] While, therefore, the late seventeenth-century growth in the proportion of the young in service and apprenticeship undoubtedly had profound implications for the incidence of marriage, economic differences among regions may have exaggerated or reduced the significance of such changes. If marriage depended on economic independence either through inheritance or through the pooling of labour resources of husband and wife, it is clear that much more attention needs to be paid to local and regional factors, especially the nature and development of labour markets, in the operation of marriage patterns.[12]

[9] Wrigley *et al.*, *English Population History From Family Reconstitution*, 125.

[10] For criticisms of the 'long lag', see especially M. W. Flinn, 'The Population History of England, 1541–1871', *Economic History Review*, 2nd ser., xxxv (1982), 443–57; and (David Levine in) D. Gaunt, D. Levine and E. Moodie, 'The Population History of England, 1541–1871: A Review Symposium', *Social History*, viii (1983), 157. For the shift of interest toward celibacy, see Weir, 'Rather Never Than Late'; and J. A. Goldstone, 'The Demographic Revolution in England: A Re-examination', *Population Studies*, xlix (1986), 5–33.

[11] Weir, 'Rather Never Than Late', 342; Goldstone, 'Demographic Revolution', 31.

[12] The best discussion of the changing incidence of service is Ann Kussmaul, *Servants in Husbandry in Early Modern England* (Cambridge, 1981), 97–119. Local studies of the

Of those historians who have been sensitive to the role of *ideology* in the formation of households, most have sought to distinguish the 'individualist-collectivist' ideology of English social relations from the 'familist' orientation of 'peasant' societies. Roger Schofield argues that in England 'an ideology of social relations' which 'located individual economic activity firmly within a structure of reciprocal collective responsibilities' helped the English economy 'to evolve flexible markets in goods and labour and develop productive agriculture', which in turn greatly enhanced 'the quality of its economic space' and enabled those increases in productivity with which to meet the challenge of population growth. The powerful mediation of economic developments and demographic behaviour by social ideology explains why the highly abbreviated nuclear family became so characteristic of early modern English society, despite its lack of suitability for coping with the life-cycle dependency so characteristic of pre-industrial societies. Marriage decisions are, therefore, to be interpreted in the light of individualistic principles which encouraged independence and mobility: 'most children [were] expected to leave home, accumulate their own wealth, choose their own marriage partners, and locate and occupy their own economic niche'.[13] In the ideological model, too, therefore, the English marriage regime is portrayed as flexible, adaptable and permissive, unconstrained by the wider interests of 'family strategy'.

Cultural historians have, it is true, paid more attention to the values and expectations not only of the couple, but also of their kin and their neighbours. In particular, they have convinced us that by the mid-seventeenth century, the wish to marry 'regularly' had become the

relationship between marriage formation and the labour markets include David Levine, *Family Formation in an Age of Nascent Capitalism* (New York, 1977); David Levine and Keith Wrightson, *The Making of an Industrial Society: Whickham, 1560–1765* (Oxford, 1991); and Pam Sharpe, 'Literally Spinsters: A New Interpretation of Local Economy and Demography in Colyton in the Seventeenth and Eighteenth Centuries', *Economic History Review*, 2nd ser., xliv (1991), 46–65. For overviews, see Kevin Schurer, 'Variations in Household Structure in the Late Seventeenth Century: Towards a Regional Analysis', in *Surveying the People: The Interpretation and Use of Document Sources for the Study of Population in the Later Seventeenth Century*, ed. Kevin Schurer and Tom Arkell (Oxford, 1992), 253–78; and Wrigley *et al.*, *English Population History From Family Reconstitution*, 182–94.

[13] Quoting Roger Schofield, 'Family Structure, Demographic Behaviour and Economic Growth', in *Famine, Disease and the Social Order in Early Modern Society*, ed. John Walter and Roger Schofield (Cambridge, 1989), 285, 304. For other influential commentaries on the role of ideology in family formation, see Alan Macfarlane, *The Origins of English Individualism: The Family, Property and Social Transition* (Cambridge, 1978); Ron Lesthaeghe, 'On the Social Control of Human Reproduction', *Population and Development Review*, vi (1980), 542–4; Richard M. Smith, 'Fertility, Economy and Household Formation in England Over Three Centuries', *Population and Development Review*, vii (1981), 618–9; and Richard M. Smith, 'Some Issues Concerning Families and Their Property in Rural England 1250–1800', in *Land, Kinship and Life-Cycle*, ed. Richard M. Smith (Cambridge, 1984), 1–86.

norm: as Martin Ingram has argued, by 1640 the 'wedding service of the Church of England had been absorbed as part of popular culture'.[14] This triumph of ecclesiastical solemnisation is demonstrated by the extent to which the late-sixteenth-century seasonality of marriage reflected the ancient ecclesiastical prohibitions on Lent and Rogationtide weddings even after the prohibited periods had ceased to be part of the law of the church of England.[15] The church, it seems, had succeeded (however temporarily) in ensuring that the only fully satisfactory form of marriage was an ecclesiastically solemnised union, performed in the face of the church after the calling of the banns, or after the procurement of a license exempting the parties concerned from this formality.[16] Under canon law, objections to the banns could be made only on the grounds that the partners fell within prohibited degrees of consanguinity, or affinity, although the frequency with which such issues were raised is itself a matter of debate.[17] While noting that ecclesiastical solemnisation implicitly mitigated the principle that the mutual consent of the couple alone made a 'regular' marriage, historians have proceeded to argue that individuals had an extraordinary measure of freedom to marry: 'the dominant social ideal' in the making of marriage, argues Ingram, 'was not parental dictation, but the multi-lateral consent of all the interests involved'.[18]

From various perspectives, therefore, historians have stressed the relatively unconstrained nature of the early modern English marriage pattern. Provided a couple could accumulate the economic wherewithal to set up an independent household, kin and community would welcome their joint entry into full adult membership of the community, although few historians would deny that economic, ideological or cultural trends

[14] Martin Ingram, 'The Reform of Popular Culture? Sex and Marriage in Early Modern England', in *Popular Culture in Seventeenth-Century England*, ed. Barry Reay (1985), 143.

[15] Wrigley and Schofield, *Population History*, 298–305; Martin Ingram, 'Spousals Litigation in the English Ecclesiastical Courts, *c.*1350–1640', in *Marriage and Society: Studies in the Social History of Marriage*, ed. R. B. Outhwaite (1981), 47–57; and Ralph Houlbrooke, *The English Family 1450–1700* (1984), 85–8.

[16] Legal developments with respect to marriage are usefully summarised in R. B. Outhwaite, *Clandestine Marriage in England, 1500–1850* (1995), 1–17. For the late seventeenth-century flight from ecclesiastical solemnisation, see Roger Lee Brown, 'The Rise and Fall of the Fleet Marriages', in *Marriage and Society*, ed. Outhwaite, 117–36; John Gillis, 'Resort to Clandestine and Common Law Marriage in England and Wales, 1650–1850', in *Disputes and Settlements: Law and Human Relations in the West*, ed. John Bossy (Cambridge, 1983), 261–86; and Outhwaite, *Clandestine Marriage*, 19–74.

[17] On objections to marriage banns on grounds of precontract or 'incest', see Martin Ingram, *Church Courts, Sex and Marriage in England, 1570–1640* (Cambridge, 1987), 245–7; Richard Adair, *Courtship, Illegitimacy and Marriage in Early Modern England* (Manchester, 1996), 162; and David Cressy, *Birth, Marriage and Death: Religion, Ritual and the Life-Cycle in Tudor and Stuart England* (Oxford, 1997), 305–9.

[18] Quoting Ingram 'The Reform of Popular Culture?', 136.

might temporarily discourage marriage. In fact, however, there were other factors in play. It is the contention of this essay that one set of influences tending to the reduction of the rate of household formation has been relatively neglected.[19] *Institutional* factors limited the extent of freedom which couples really had to act in 'rational choice' ways: the 1563 statute of artificers was motivated partly out of a desire for 'the prevention of untimely marriages', and the minimum age of departing apprenticeship (twenty-four for males and twenty-one for women) was intended to defer the entry of the young into the marriage market.[20] Other institutional pressures, I want to suggest, operated relatively crudely (though they were no less effective for all that) in actually *inhibiting* marriages altogether, especially among paupers. The role of the poor law in this context is particularly significant, and it will be explored here in the light of scattered evidence collected during the exploration of the policies and priorities of select vestries.[21] Human reproduction, and especially the public celebration of the marriages which were its only legitimate context, were subject to social regulation. In this case, however, it is possible to develop a model of 'social control' which provides us with empirical evidence of its operation. The context and consequences of such 'social control' will be explored here, first by discussing the evidence for the inhibition of pauper marriage; second, by analysing the role and motivation of parish officers and leading rate-payers in such activity; third, by demonstrating the extent of contemporary concern with the policy; and fourth, by assessing its implications for our understanding of fluctuating nuptiality in particular, and of seventeenth-century social change in general.

I

On 29 May 1642 the minister and churchwardens of Frampton (Lincolnshire) subscribed to a vestry memorandum that

[19] But see, from a general theoretical perspective, Lesthaeghe, 'Social Control of Human Reproduction'; and, more specifically, Smith, 'Fertility, Economy and Household Formation', 602–11.

[20] 5 Elizabeth I, c.4. See S. T. Bindoff, 'The Making of the Statute of Artificers', in *Elizabethan Government and Society*, ed. S. T. Bindoff, J. Hurstfield and C. H. Williams (1961), 56–94. But see now D. M. Woodward, 'The Background to the Statute of Artificers: the Genesis of Labour Policy, 1558–1563', *Economic History Review*, 2nd ser., xxxiii (1980), 32–44; and G. R. Elton, *The Parliament of England, 1559–1581* (Cambridge, 1986), 263–7.

[21] See Steve Hindle, 'Exclusion Crises: Poverty, Migration and Parochial Responsibility in English Rural Communities *c.*1560–1660', *Rural History*, vii (1996), 125–49; and Hindle, 'Power, Poor Relief and Social Relations in Holland Fen, *c.*1600–1800', *Historical Journal* (forthcoming, 1998).

> the banes of matrimony between John Hayes and Ann Archer both of this parish were three severall tymes on three severall sundayes or holy dayes published in the parish church of Frampton without contradiction save only the first time they were published they were forbid by one Robert Pimperton of the parish of Kirton who was then requested and so the other two tymes of publishing. It was openly desyred that he bring witnesses to prove there was some just cause why they might not lawfully be joined but yet he hath not done it, and so we know not why wee may not lawfully proceede to marriage, except he presently prove an impediment or put in a caution to do it.

Robert Pimperton's objection to the banns had the effect of (at the very least) delaying and (probably) of preventing Hayes and Archer from celebrating their marriage in the parish. This was not to be the only occasion on which the Frampton vestrymen recorded an objection to a marriage. Samuel Cony, minister of Frampton, whose duty it had been to record the objection to the Hayes marriage in 1642, noted in the parish register that when 'the intentions of a marriage' between Edward Marten and Jane Goodwin were published in January 1654, John Ayre, Thomas Appleby and William Eldred 'in behalf of them selves and other of the inhabitants' objected on two grounds. First, it seems, Marten's marital history was in question: although he had been in service both in neighbouring Algakirke and in Frampton, it was uncertain 'where he has lived before that time nor what hee is, either a maryed or single man'. They argued that the marriage should be deferred until such time as Marten could certify the truth of these matters. Second, however, was the question of Marten's current economic status:

> for aught they knew and as they verily believed hee was a very poore man and that hee had not then any house to live in, and therefore they did desire that he might ere he married gett some sufficient man to be bound with him to secure the town from any charge by him or his whom they consider they were not bound to keepe hee being till he lately crept into [the parish] a poor stranger to us.[22]

Edward Marten's plans were apparently to be held in suspended animation until he could guarantee never to drain parochial resources.

Ecclesiastical solemnisation of these two couples' unions would have served as a ritual of inclusion, as the whole community witnessed their 'liminal transformation' into the states of matrimony, and therefore of

[22] Lincolnshire Archives Office, Frampton PAR 10/1 [vestry minute book, 1597–1683], unfol. (29 May 1642); 1/1 [parish register], unfol. (Jan. 1654). For the immediate context of these decisions, see Hindle, 'Power, Poor Relief and Social Relations'.

adulthood.[23] 'Inclusion' into the community as a settled member naturally entailed the recognition of communal responsibility for maintenance in the eventuality of poverty. In the case of Hayes and Archer, the reasons for forbidding the banns are unspecified, yet the couple were nonetheless denied, if only temporarily, the recognition that they belonged to the community of the parish. In the case of Marten and Goodwin, it seems, inclusion was to be deferred, and (if tolerated at all) made conditional upon his provision of an indemnity bond, a guarantee that the parish would not be liable for relief of his actual or prospective family.[24] Fragmentary as these references are, the politics of the decisions that generated them can be deduced by considering the circumstances of other such refusals.

The Frampton evidence can indeed be buttressed by other evidence of the quasi-formal inhibition of the marriages of the poor in seventeenth-century England. In Terling (Essex) in 1617, for instance, a labourer presented in the ecclesiastical courts for incontinence protested that he and his paramour were 'contracted in matrimonie ... and that the banes of matrimonie were asked betwene them in Terling church ... and the parish would not suffer them to marry else they had bin marryed ere now'.[25] Another Essex labourer, Robert Johnson, had cohabited for a year with, and had a child by, Elizabeth Whitland in the parish of Upminster, only to run away to London protesting that 'he would have maryed her if the inhabitants would have suffered him'.[26] The minister of the Dorset parish of Nether Compton complained in 1628 that Anne Russed 'hath no house nor home of her own and [is] very like to bring charge on the parish, and therefore will hardly be suffered to marry in our parish'.[27] Richard Guy, a 73-year-old pauper of North Bradley (Wiltshire), defended himself against a charge of clandestine marriage by complaining in 1618 that 'the parishioners' had been 'unwilling' that 'he should marry with his now wife being but young'.[28] In 1570, the parishioners of Adlington (Kent) 'were sore against' Alice Cheeseman's projected match and 'stayed the asking of the banns and marriage and many of the cheefest of the parish counselled her to leave him because the parishioners mislyked of

[23] Cressy, *Birth, Marriage and Death*, 286–92, provides an elegant summary of the transformations involved in matrimony.

[24] The only detailed discussion of indemnity bonds is Philip Styles, 'The Evolution of the Laws of Settlement', *University of Birmingham Historical Journal*, ix (1963), reprinted in Styles, *Studies in Seventeenth-Century West Midlands History* (Kineton, 1978), 180–3. But see now Hindle, 'Exclusion Crises'.

[25] Keith Wrightson and David Levine, *Poverty and Piety in an English Village: Terling, 1525–1700* (2nd edn, Oxford, 1995), 135.

[26] *Ibid.*, 80.

[27] Ingram, *Church Courts*, 131.

[28] Ingram, 'The Reform of Popular Culture?', 145.

[him]'.[29] The sanctions that might be applied in such cases are illustrated by the vestry decision at Finchingfield (Essex) in 1628 that 'if William Byfleet shall marry Susan Crosley contrary to the mind of the townsmen ... his collection shall be detained'; and by one Canterbury deponent's report that 'the parishioners threatened Alice [Cheeseman] to expell her out of the parish' if she defied their 'hinderance' of the marriage.[30]

These examples, of course, take no account of those occasions on which already married couples were prevented from settling together in communities where one or the other, or sometimes both, were born. In 1618, for example, Anthony Adams sought to bring his young wife to dwell with him in Stockton (Worcestershire). Despite the fact that he had been born, bred and apprenticed there, 'his parishioners [were] not willing he should bring her into the parish saying he would breed up a charge amongst them'. The couple were forced to live apart, he in Stockton, she in her home parish of Bewdley. But even this arrangement proved unsatisfactory, since 'doubt of further charge' among the parishioners there led to her expulsion from Bewdley.[31] Such inter-parochial wrangling became particularly vitriolic after the passage of the settlement laws in 1662. As Lawrence Stone has shown, restoration parishes were not above actually forcing pregnant women into marriages with 'strangers', providing that the man had a settlement elsewhere, in order to pass the financial burden of maintaining the child on to someone other than her home parish.[32]

These episodes, almost always described in the most laconic or fragmentary of documents, are remarkable in several ways. First, it must be emphasised that the poverty of bride and groom was not among the justified canonical grounds for objecting to marriage banns. Although both Henrician and late Elizabethan parliaments had flirted with the tighter regulation of marriage, neither criminal nor canon law justified the prevention of pauper marriage.[33] Second, the dubious

[29] Diana O'Hara, '"Ruled By My Friends": Aspects of Marriage in the Diocese of Canterbury', *Continuity and Change*, vi (1991), 28.

[30] *Early Essex Town Meetings: Braintree, 1619–1636; Finchingfield, 1626–34*, ed. F. G. Emmison (Chichester, 1970), 117; O'Hara, '"Ruled By My Friends"', 28.

[31] *Worcestershire County Records: Calendar of the Quarter Sessions Papers, Volume I: 1591–1643*, ed. J. W. Wills-Bund (Worcester, 1900), 266–7.

[32] Lawrence Stone, *Uncertain Unions: Marriage in England. 1660–1753* (Oxford, 1992), 83–92.

[33] G. R. Elton, 'Reform by Statute: Thomas Starkey's Dialogue and Thomas Cromwell's Policy', in Elton, *Studies in Tudor and Stuart Politics and Government* (4 vols., Cambridge, 1974–92), II, 252, notes a policy paper sent to Cromwell suggesting the prevention of the marriages of young men until they were of 'potent age'. David Dean, *Law-Making and Society in Late Elizabethan England: The Parliament of England, 1584–1601* (Cambridge, 1996), 184–5, reports an abortive bill to prevent 'sundry great abuses by licenses for marriages without banes' in the parliamentary session of 1597–8.

legality of the informal prohibition of marriage might apparently be side-stepped by any number of expedient pretexts. Those objecting raised the possibilities that Edward Marten might be a bigamist, or remarrying with several children by any previous union; that the disparity of age between Richard Guy and his intended bride was inappropriate; or even that they genuinely bore Alice Cheeseman 'goodwill and affection'. These justifications, offered where unions looked expedient, disparate in age, or likely to involve young children, were almost certainly only the disingenuous 'public transcripts' of the rationale that underlay them: the desire to ease the parish burden. Third, it seems, those accused of moral lapses might in turn criticise these actions as part of their strategy of self-justification, telling the ecclesiastical authorities just exactly what they wanted to hear: that their honourable intentions had been frustrated by the hard-nosed decisions of others. Fourth, on those rare occasions when explicit references were made to the poor, immigrant, status of prospective spouses, the archival record brings us face to face with the 'social cleavage' between those who paid the poor rate (the 'other inhabitants' in whose behalf vestrymen spoke) and those who were considered likely to be a charge upon it.[34] Fifth, there is the vexed question of the identity of those objecting: just who was responsible for these decisions? The communal language used in these orders is ambiguous: (in Finchingfield) 'the townsmen'; (in Terling) 'the parish'; (in Upminster and in Frampton) 'the inhabitants'; (in Stockton, in North Bradley, and in Adlington) 'the parishioners', were described as the authors of the policy. Such terminology implies that these decisions were made and executed consensually by the whole or the majority of the local community. But the language conceals as much as it reveals, perhaps as it was intended to. 'The parishe', argue Wrightson and Levine, denoted the vestrymen, just as 'the inhabitants' denoted 'the best (or long established) inhabitants'. In both cases 'we may be sure that these labourers meant the notables of the parish concerned, in particular the ministers and parish officers'.[35] This scepticism is borne out both by one Canterbury deponent's reference to the 'counselling' of one would-be bride by 'the cheefest of the parish'; and by the fact that the three men objecting to the Marten–Goodwin marriage in Frampton in 1654 were the most experienced office-holders in the parish, having four years service as overseer and thirteen years service as churchwarden between them. It is most tellingly confirmed, however, by the order of the town meeting at Swallowfield (Wiltshire) in 1596 that all vestrymen 'have an especyall care to speake to the mynyster to stay the maryage

[34] Levine and Wrightson, *Industrial Society*, 352.
[35] Wrightson and Levine, *Poverty and Piety*, 133.

of such as wolde mary before they have a convenient house to lyve in according to their callynge'.[36] The use of the terms 'the parish' and 'the inhabitants' are therefore significant precisely because they made an exclusive social institution (the structure of local office-holding) sound like an inclusive one. Moreover, it is arguable that communal rhetoric of inclusion succeeded only in making the institutions and attitudes it served more exclusive.

Furthermore, of course, these prohibitions entailed personal costs for the couples involved, especially in those circumstances where the poor were inclined to marry (or remarry) as a means of survival, and to avoid being left alone.[37] Worse still, the objecting individuals and groups might employ sanctions which could make life very uncomfortable for any couple wanting to defy them. Presentment for incontinence, fornication or clandestine marriage; desertion or separation; and the threat of destitution were the immediate consequences of the desire of the respective parishes to reduce the burdens on their poor rates. Cumulatively, the effect of such decisions on those of marriageable age who faced sanctions against their full adult membership of the community could be severe. In the Wiltshire village of Keevil, for example, a clutch of clandestine marriage cases involving poor cottagers and under-tenants in 1622 was provoked by an 'exclusion crisis', a series of measures in the local manor court to restrict immigration and control sub-letting.[38] Exclusion could also be devastating for the social order itself: John Walter has argued that it was the inability to marry and settle in their own secure holdings that drove the poor husbandmen and servants of Oxfordshire to foment sedition on Enslow Hill in the long wet summer of 1596.[39]

II

The perceived need for marriage controls in early Stuart England is best explained in terms of widespread fears of population mobility and its implications for the exploitation of generous social welfare regimes.

[36] O'Hara, '"Ruled By My Friends"', 28; Hindle, 'Power, Poor Relief and Social Relations', *passim*; MS Ellesmere 6162, fo. 36; Huntington Library, San Marino, Ca.

[37] Margaret Pelling, 'Old Age, Poverty and Disability in Early Modern Norwich: Work, Remarriage, and Other Expedients', in *Life, Death and the Elderly: Historical Perspectives*, ed. Margaret Pelling and Richard M. Smith (1991), 88.

[38] Ingram, *Church Courts*, 215; *cf.* Hindle, 'Exclusion Crises'.

[39] John Walter, 'A "Rising of the People"? The Oxfordshire Rising of 1596', *Past and Present*, no. 107 (May 1985), 90–143. See the theoretical discussion of the response patterns, including not only obedience and 'deferred gratification' but also deviance and rebellion, of those who lose out in systems where reproduction is subject to social control in Lesthaeghe, 'Social Control of Human Reproduction', 533–34.

This prejudice was eloquently articulated by the Hertfordshire clergyman Alexander Strange in an address to his 'good neighbours and loving parishioners' drafted in 1636. In vilifying covetous landlords for their hospitality to poor migrants, Strange called for greater calculation in the administration of the poor laws. Charity without discrimination was, he argued, 'the readyest meanes to impoverish a towne and make it at length unable to releeve [its] poore because of the multitude of such persons as dayly presse into the parish'. Strange described the predicament of the neighbouring parish of Braughing, where a house left for the rent-free use of the elderly resident poor had been 'crept into' by 'yonge and disordered poore' from outside the parish. 'Some maryed folke with this hope, to have a roome' there.[40] As a threshold of the parochial community, and a very public one at that, it is hardly surprising that marriage should figure so prominently in the thinking of ministers, parish officers and the rate-payers and ancient paupers they represented. When the problems of sedentary families were compounded by the immigration of the under-employed, the parameters of parochial tolerance were stretched to breaking-point.

The evidence for the inhibition of pauper marriage must, therefore, be interpreted in the context of what is known about migration, courtship and marital opportunity among the poor. As Ann Kussmaul and David Souden have shown, sex-specific migration patterns, themselves the consequence of a diversified labour market, helped to produce skewed sex ratios in small, rural parishes where the pool of potential marriage partners was already tiny.[41] In some parishes, this pattern was evident by the early seventeenth century. As Barry Stapleton has demonstrated, the excess of female over male migrants in the Hampshire parish of Odiham provoked a nine-fold increase in the proportion of exogamous marriages from 1.2 per cent (1601–20) to 10.1 per cent (1641–60). Moreover, at least 60 per cent of those coming in to the parish to marry were from within 10 kilometres, usually from adjacent parishes.[42] Exogamous marriages were, therefore, increasingly likely, indeed necessary, in seventeenth-century England. In the predominantly agrarian Leicestershire village of Bottesford only 8 per cent of the 617 marriages

[40] Hertfordshire Record Office D/P 65/3/3, fos. 329–31, cited in Hindle, 'Exclusion Crises', 134.

[41] Kussmaul, *Servants in Husbandry*, 24–7; David Souden, 'Migrants and the Population Structure of Later Seventeenth-Century Provincial Cities and Market Towns', in *The Transformation of English Provincial Towns, 1600–1800*, ed. Peter Clark (London, 1984), 150–61; David Souden, '"East, West–Home's Best"? Regional Patterns of Migration in Early Modern England', in *Migration and Society*, ed. Clark and Souden, 292–332.

[42] Barry Stapleton, 'Marriage, Migration and Mendicancy in a Pre-Industrial Community', in *Conflict and Community in Southern England: Essays in the History of Rural and Urban Labour From Medieval to Modern Times*, ed. Barry Stapleton (Gloucester, 1992), 56, 62.

celebrated in the period 1610–69 were entirely endogamous.[43] In the context of ambiguities in the poor laws, these marriage and migration patterns had profound implications. Only under the settlement legislation of 1662 did it become clear that women took the place of settlement of their husbands at marriage. Until then, the Elizabethan poor laws left considerable doubt among both newly-weds and parish officers about the precise demarcation of responsibility. The migrant poor and their (prospective) spouses were almost inevitably, therefore, seeking to reside in parishes which were already acutely sensitive to the problem of unchecked migration, and the consequent application of parochial sanctions evidently extended even to the frustration of their marriage plans.

The refusal to read, or the objection to, the marriage banns of the poor by the 'parishioners' or 'townsmen' might be read as a process of exclusion in which the representatives of the community ostracised, on behalf not only of those who paid the poor rate but also those who received it, those they considered guilty of imprudent and potentially burdensome marital behaviour. Historians are familiar enough with 'rough music' being applied to marital partners whose behaviour failed in various ways to live up to communal norms.[44] The prohibition of pauper marriages might be read as an institutional surrogate for such *charivari*, arguably a more effective strategy in solidifying the exclusions on which the policy of defending the local 'arena of distinctiveness' was to be built.[45] Parochial endogamy might therefore be a crucial component of the idiom of solidarity in seventeenth-century English communities.[46]

III

Rigorous control of marital opportunity was clearly, therefore, one strategy through which parishes sought to inhibit entitlement to poor relief. But how common was it? By its very nature, the practice has left few traces in ecclesiastical archives, leading those few historians who

[43] Levine, *Family Formation*, 39.

[44] Ingram, 'Reform of Popular Culture?'; Martin Ingram, 'Ridings, Rough Music and Mocking Rhymes', in *Popular Culture*, ed. Reay, 166–97. Edward Thompson, *Customs in Common* (1991), 454, notes the use of rough music against exogamous marriage.

[45] Quoting the definition of culture in A. P. Cohen, 'Belonging: The Experience of Culture', in *Belonging: Identity and Social Organisation in British Rural Cultures*, ed. A. P. Cohen (Manchester, 1982).

[46] Citing Scott K. Phillips, 'Natives and Incomers: the Symbolism of Belonging in Muker Parish, North Yorkshire', in *Symbolising Boundaries: Identity and Diversity in British Cultures*, ed. A. P. Cohen (Manchester, 1986), reprinted in Michael Drake (ed.), *Time, Family and Community: Perspectives on Family and Community History* (Oxford, 1994), 234.

have noticed it at all to minimise both its scale and it significance.[47] Richard Smith, for instance, notes that 'the extent of these actions is very difficult to gauge', and argues that historians 'allied to the social control school' have shown disproportionate interest in the 'scattering of instances' of 'socially discriminating welfare-fund managers'.[48] This perspective ignores the fact that, for the most part, objections to marriage banns would have been made either behind the scenes in the vicarage or *viva voce* in the chancel, leaving no imprint in the historical record. Although others have recognised that objections must have been more widespread than surviving evidence suggests, they have chosen to downplay their implications. Thus Richard Adair recognises that 'such vetoes could obviously be effective, and cases were clearly not uncommon, especially in parishes experiencing economic stresses', yet nonetheless insists that 'all this has to be kept in due proportion'. For Adair, the significance of the practice is to be measured only in aggregate terms: if the inhibition of pauper marriage cannot explain 'the broad secular and regional trends in bastardy' then it can safely be relegated to the footnotes.[49] Martin Ingram implies that discriminatory vetoes became quite common in Jacobean England, yet seems perfectly prepared to condone them, arguing that the 'complaisance of the authorities and the apparent heartlessness of the wealthier sections of parish society' are 'readily understandable'.[50]

Not all contemporaries would have concurred. Moralists were commenting on the practice as early as the 1620s. William Whateley noted in 1623 that the absolute denial of the right to marry on grounds of poverty contravened the Christian principle that marriage was lawful for all persons 'of what calling or condition soever'.[51] By the late seventeenth century, parochial vetoes were sufficiently common to attract the attention of ecclesiastical lawyers and economic and social projectors alike. John Johnson noted that 'some parish officers have presum'd to forbid banns, because the parties have been poor, and like to create charge to the parish, or because the man has not been made

[47] David Cressy's thorough, though not exhaustive, searches of church court materials do not appear to have turned up any additional instances of the practice: Cressy, *Birth, Marriage and Death*, 312.

[48] Richard M. Smith, 'Marriage Processes in the English Past: Some Continuities', in *The World We Have Gained: Histories of Population and Social Structure*, ed. Lloyd Bonfield, Richard M. Smith and K. E. Wrightson (Oxford, 1986), 73 n. 101; Richard M. Smith, 'Charity, Self-Interest and Welfare: Reflections From Demograpic and Family History', in *Charity, Self-Interest and Welfare in the English Past*, ed. Martin Daunton (London, 1996), 24.

[49] Adair, *Courtship, Illegitimacy and Marriage*, 138. *Cf.* Smith, 'Charity, Self-Interest and Welfare', 45 n. 3.

[50] Ingram, 'Spousals Litigation', 55–6; Ingram, *Church Courts*, 131.

[51] William Whateley, *A Bride-Bush: or a Direction for Married Persons* (1623), 175.

an inhabitant according to the laws made for the settlement of the poor'.[52] Carew Reynel noted the 'custom in many country parishes, where they, as much as they can, hinder poor people from marrying'.[53] Sir William Coventry was concerned that 'the laws against cottages, inmates, etc. and the method of obliging poor people to give security to save the parish from charge before they are permitted to inhabit' were 'restraints' hindering the poor from marrying.[54] Dudley North believed that officers 'in defence of their parish from charges not only employ themselves to prevent new settlers, but use great care to prevent the mareage of those that they have, hindering all they can possibly the matching of young ones together'. He even imagined the likely justification for this industry to hinder 'mareage': '"Oh," say the churchwardens, "they will have more children than they can keep, and so increase the charge of the parish".'[55]

It is very significant that most surviving seventeenth-century comment on the control of pauper marriages originates after the Restoration, by which time population pressure in most rural communities had eased, and the settlement laws had begun to clarify the extent of parochial responsibilities. The polemic must therefore be set in the context of the transformation of attitudes in a period of demographic stagnation. As Professor Appleby has pointed out, 'the most significant change of opinion about the poor was the replacement of concern about over-population at the beginning of the [seventeenth] century with fears about a possible loss of people at the end'.[56] By the 1670s, it was felt that marriage should be encouraged in order to foster demographic growth and (in turn) an increase in national prosperity. Thus for Dudley North, 'plenty of people is the cheefest riches of a kingdom'.[57] Sir William Coventry argued that 'encouraging our own people to marry' was a means 'to mend our domestic vent by the increasing of our people'.[58] Others identified the poor as the natural constituency from which national prosperity must emerge. John Johnson argued that 'poverty is no more an impediment of marriage than riches, and the

[52] John Johnson, *The Clergy-man's Vade Mecum* (1709), 186. For Johnson, rector of Cranbrook in Kent, see *DNB* [*s.v.* Johnson, John].

[53] Carew Reynel, *The True English Interest* (1674), 59–67, reprinted in *Seventeenth-Century Economic Documents*, ed. Joan Thirsk and J. P. Cooper (Oxford, 1972), 758–60, at 760.

[54] Sir William Coventry, 'An Essay Concerning the Decay of Rents and Their Remedies' [*c.*1670], reprinted in *Seventeenth-Century Economic Documents*, ed. Thirsk and Cooper, 79–84, at 80.

[55] Dudley North, 'Some Notes Concerning the Laws for the Poor' [British Library Additional Manuscripts, 32512, fos. 124^{v}–130^{v}], fo. 128^{v}.

[56] Joyce Oldham Appleby, *Economic Thought and Ideology in Seventeenth-Century England* (Princeton, 1978), 135.

[57] North, 'Some Notes Concerning the Laws For the Poor', fo. 128^{v}.

[58] Coventry, 'Decay of Rents', 80.

kingdom can no more subsist without poor than without rich'.[59] Carew Reynel suggested not only that 'countenancing marriage' was 'the very origin of the well being and continuance of nations', upon which 'property, families and civil government depends, also trade, riches, populacy; and without this a nation crumbles to nothing', but that 'poor people were the stock and seminary of the kingdom', whose 'marrying apace' ought 'to get a laborious hardy generation, which is best for a nation'.[60] This mercantilist critique crystallised in the debates over the passage of the Marriage Duty Act of 1695. Political arithmeticians and projectors alike advocated the taxing of the unmarried for their neglect of the civic responsibility of childrearing. In practice, however, although parish paupers were exempt from the marriage tax (incidentally leading to the explicit recording of their marriages in some parish registers), the labouring poor fell within its terms, provoking Charles Davenant to observe in 1699 that 'they who look into all the different ranks of men are well satisfied that this duty on marriages and births is a very grievous burden upon the poorer sort'. Although the Marriage Duty Act almost certainly created an incentive for unmarried men to marry, some contemporaries evidently felt that it amounted to a tax on the marital bed.[61]

Hostility to the prevention of pauper marriages was not, however, justified exclusively on mercantilist grounds. Criticism also arose where the demeanour of those objecting to the banns was particularly offensive. Clergymen in particular had to ensure that their procedure in the calling of the banns fell within the terms of canon law. That they did not always succeed is suggested by the presentment in 1636 of William Jackson, rector of North Ockenden (Essex), for departing from the canonical formula when, 'in asking the banes of a poore cupple', he 'signified to the parishe that "they would marry and goe a begging together", and asked "yf anie knewe lawfull cause why they might not so doe", which gave great offence to the parties and to others'.[62] Jackson had obviously failed to carry parochial opinion with him, and his open invitation to the making of an illegal objection lacked subtlety, to say the very least. Only in such exceptional circumstances did the ecclesiastical courts seek to halt the practice, for there is little evidence that

[59] Johnson, *Clergy Man's Vade Mecum*, 186.

[60] Reynel, *True English Interest*, 760.

[61] Colin Brooks, 'Projecting, Political Arithmetic and the Act of 1695', *English Historical Review* lxxxvii (1982), 39; Jeremy Boulton, 'The Marriage Duty Act and Parochial Registration in London, 1695–1706', in *Surveying the People*, ed. Schurer and Arkell, 227; Charles Davenant, *Works*, ed. C. Whitworth (5 vols., 1771), II, 190–1; *London Inhabitants Within the Walls, 1695*, ed. D.V. Glass (London Record Society Publications, ii, 1966), xiv–xv. *Cf.* Wrigley *et al.*, *English Population History From Family Reconstitution*, 139.

[62] W.J. Pressey, 'Essex Affairs Matrimonial (As Seen in the Archdeaconry Records)', *Essex Review*, xlix (1940), 86.

ministers were prosecuted.[63] Nonetheless, the restoration commentators also drew attention to its local social implications. Reynel implied that inhibiting marriage only encouraged the poor to commit the vices of fornication or cohabitation.[64] Coventry advocated the reduction of poor rates ('easing the parish') not by regulating marriage but by building workhouses which would drive down wages by 'banishing laziness in the poor'.[65] Johnson attacked the idea that 'temporal laws relating to the poor were intended to alter the laws of the church', and insisted that 'no person has authority to forbid the minister to proceed in publishing the banns'. 'The curate,' he argued, 'is not to stop his proceeding because any peevish or pragmatical person without just reason or authority pretends to forbid him.' Indeed, he saw 'no reason to doubt but that banns may be published and marriage solemnised betwixt two persons that do at present abide or sojourn within a parish, tho' they be not fixed inhabitants, according to the acts for the settling of the poor'. He was prepared to concede only that 'for cautions sake, the minister in publishing the banns may say, *N* of this parish, sojourner'.[66] Dudley North went further, emphasising the deviousness of officers in circumventing ecclesiastical law. Marriages were inhibited, he argued, 'by judicial meanes however the occasion is given by the law, and when the consequence toucheth the pocket means will be found out right or wrong', a practice which, in tandem with the provisions of the settlement laws, reduced 'the poor inhabitants' to a condition 'little better than slaves', rendering them vulnerable to the danger 'of being sent home with the whipp at their backs'.[67] Despite the attempts of modern historians to whitewash the practice, therefore, the peevishness and pragmatism of parish officers is well attested in the contemporary polemic.

IV

Marriage, then, was not merely a rite of passage subject to economic, ideological or even cultural influences, it was also a social process vulnerable to institutional and political sanctions. The broader factors affecting vestry decisions self-evidently require further investigation. Economic fears of unregulated immigration might be crucial, but there might also be ideological and cultural factors at work in the perception

[63] Ingram, 'Spousals Litigation', 56; Ingram, *Church Courts*, 131.
[64] Reynel, *True English Interest*, 760.
[65] Coventry, 'Decay of Rents', 80.
[66] Johnson, *Clergy Man's Vade Mecum*, 186–7.
[67] North, 'Some Notes Concerning the Laws for the Poor', fos. 128–28^{v}.

of 'who belongs?' Thresholds of tolerance might differ from community to community, but in each there was not only a 'continuum' but also a 'hierarchy' of belonging.[68] The recognition of the right to belong implied decision-making by parish officers, acting on behalf not only of rate-payers, but also of the ancient poor whose interest might suffer through the over-burdening of rates. These decisions must therefore be understood less in terms of impersonal forces than in terms of power and of experience. Peter Solar has recently argued that 'the local financing of poor relief gave English property owners, individually and collectively, a direct pecuniary interest in ensuring that the parish's demographic and economic development was balanced'.[69] This judgement, euphemistically expressed as it is, recognises the significance of social welfare institutions in regulating social and economic life in early modern England, yet at the same time entirely fails to recapture the human experience, the heartbreak and the humiliation, which that regulation implied.

The explanatory categories adopted by modern historians and sociologists, it is increasingly becoming clear, take insufficient account of the notions and practices of the historical actors themselves.[70] Although the concept of 'dilatory homeostasis' is a useful external classificatory system for the comparison of demographic regimes across time and space, it should not be mistaken for a historical structure, least of all when it so signally fails to take account of the dynamics of individual and collective decision-making. The weaknesses of the neo-Malthusian approach are further underlined by the fact that the 'rational choice' model has been progressively attenuated since the moment it was first adumbrated by Wrigley. Greater emphasis on the political context in which decisions over household formation were made would, in effect, mark one more significant modification of the demographic orthodoxy, the trajectory of which can be traced back to Wrigley's seminal essay, 'Family Limitation', published in 1966. In that year, Wrigley argued that changes in fertility were largely to be explained by family limitation *within* marriage. By the time the findings of the Cambridge Group were published in 1981, mid-to-late-seventeenth-century fertility trends were to be explained by fluctuations in the age at first marriage. By 1989, when *The Population History of England* was reprinted, seventeenth- and

[68] Quoting Keith Wrightson, 'The Politics of the Parish in Early Modern England', in *The Experience of Authority in Early Modern England*, ed. Paul Griffiths, Adam Fox and Steve Hindle (Basingstoke, 1996), 19.

[69] Peter M. Solar, 'Poor Relief and English Economic Development Before the Industrial Revolution', *Economic History Review*, 2nd ser., xlviii (1995), 16.

[70] See, for example, the careful criticism of the categories of historical sociology in Naomi Tadmor, 'The Concept of the Household-Family in Eighteenth-Century England', *Past and Present*, no. 151 (May 1996), 111–40.

eighteenth-century marriage patterns had been disaggregated and the key determinant of fertility change for the earlier period was the celibacy rate, which, Weir had estimated, reached unprecedentedly high levels in the 1660s and 1670s.[71] Although Wrigley and his colleagues have recently reiterated the view that 'the decision to marry was peculiarly susceptible to economic pressures', each successive nuance to the argument has had the effect of reducing the extent and significance of the autonomous rational choice of courting couples.[72] This is neither to suggest that fluctuations in celibacy can be explained exclusively in terms of the manipulation of banns by parish officers, nor to discount the significance of economic, cultural and ideological factors in the making of marriage; nor even to rehearse the view that the poor law was exclusively responsible for securing social stability in later Stuart England.[73] It is, however, a salutary warning that the actions, aspirations and decisions of individuals and social groups within local communities are as significant in the explanation of social change as are the impersonal forces of economy, ideology and culture.

The models of historical demographers therefore, especially 'unconscious rationality' and 'Malthusian prudence', are all too often predicated on the explanation of human behaviour by factors drawn from outside the immediate context in which courtship and marriage processes were worked out. In restoring the political context of nuptiality, historians must recognise that marriage choice was not simply a matter for discussion between the marriage partners; that political and institutional factors tended to skew the operation of the marriage market; and that difficult decisions about the recognition of the right to belong were bound to be made in local communities experiencing profound economic stresses. The decisions and actions of *parochiani meliores et antiquiores* are, by definition, difficult to recover, but they are nonetheless crucial to any understanding of seventeenth-century social relations. At their starkest, they belie the extraordinary freedom which is often said to have underpinned the making of marriage in early modern England, and are a potent reminder that the human experiences centring on any act must be wrapped into all historical explanations of social change.

[71] Wrigley, 'Family Limitation'; Wrigley and Schofield, *Population History*, xix, 450–3.

[72] Wrigley *et al.*, *English Population History From Family Reconstitution*, 125.

[73] *Cf.* the scepticism of Paul Slack, *Poverty and Policy in Tudor and Stuart England* (London, 1988), 207–8.

THE AGE OF UNCERTAINTY: BRITAIN IN THE EARLY-NINETEENTH CENTURY

By David Eastwood

READ 16 MAY 1997

ONE does not have to be a card-carrying postmodernist to understand that historical periods do not possess inherent characteristics. 'Eras of Reform', 'Ages of Revolution', 'Triumphs of Reform', and 'Centuries of Reformation' exist only in, and as, texts. They represent, in the simplest of forms, readings of the past. The nomenclatures we employ to demarcate and characterise particular historical moments embody fundamental ideological assumptions, encapsulating an *idée fixe*, and exposing the crux of the creative—or, if you prefer, the scholarly—process. Traditionalists might already be crying foul, insisting that our titles, or period characterisations, reflect rather than impute salience. History, as Geoffrey Elton might have instructed us, reports rather than constructs the past. The writing of history, Elton suggested in 1967, 'amounts to a dialogue between the historian and his materials. He supplies the intelligence and the organising ability, but he can interpret and organise only within the limits set by his materials. And those are the limits created by a true and independent past.'[1] Revealingly, though, our book titles generally describe or construct *processes*, rather than recall events; and processes are abstractions whose full meaning, as Vico told us long ago, is apparent only in retrospect.[2] Of course the Reformation happened, but not in the same way as the Battle of Trafalgar happened. Thus describing the sixteenth century as 'The Age of Reformation' orders the experience of the European West in a very particular way. It was also, and some might say equally, an age of exploration, of empire, of inflation, of hunger, and of the explosion of print culture. Only in certain reconstructions of the past does Reformation eclipse inflation, or print matter more than European col-

[1] Geoffrey Elton, *The Practice of History* (1967), 120, *cf.* 11–20. This position has been restated, albeit with refinements and a more apparently sympathetic reception of the role of theory, in Richard J. Evans, *In Defence of History* (1997).

[2] Giambattista Vico, *The New Science* [3rd edn., 1744] (trans T. G. Bergin and M. H. Fisch, Ithaca and London, 1984); Isaiah Berlin, *Vico and Herder. Two Studies in the History of Ideas* (1976), 3–142; and Bruce A. Haddock, 'Vico and the Methodology of the History of Ideas', in *Vico: Past and Present*, ed. Giorgio Tagliacozzo (Atlantic Highlands, 1981), 227–39.

onisation. It is, of course, fundamental to our understanding of the past that we privilege processes of change, and our textbook titles implicitly recognise this, but often do so in ways which are worryingly unself-conscious, and the abstractions of the title thus become the reifications of the text.

Moving closer to my own field of expertise we seem to encounter an exception to the rule I have just been formulating. The period from 1789 to, say, 1802 is commonly, we might even say uncontroversially, known as the 'Age of Revolution'. What happened in France in and after 1789 was of the profoundest significance, and this is captured by the term 'French Revolution'. Superficially, at least, an event seems to determine and demarcate an historical moment. Yet even here my case holds good. What happened in France did come to be known as the French Revolution, and after Condorcet transformed our understanding of the idea of revolution in 1793, this became as good a shorthand as any, not least because events in France constituted the occasion for the term 'revolution's' modern coinage.[3] But no one, not even Edmund Burke, has understood the French Revolution as an event.[4] It was rather an historical process, and a process which might be described by a variety of soundbites. 'The Age of Revolution' invests it with one meaning, 'the Age of Heresy', 'The Age of Terror', 'A Decade of War', or 'The Age of Reason', would impute quite different meanings to the same complex process. I have undertaken no systematic study, but I strongly suspect that 'The French Revolution' is the commonest single title in modern historical writing. The sheer variety of texts and interpretations which shelter under this titular umbrella amply testifies to the complexity of investing the French Revolution with historical and interpretative meanings. At their most innocent, these kinds of historical shorthands distort as much as they describe. Read without the lens of theory, they subtly subvert historical understanding at deeper levels.

Whatever our reservations, the conventions of publishing, and increasingly the conventions of scholarship itself, demand that we employ the interpretative shorthand embodied in book titles and period descriptors. Problems arise when titular hegemony forecloses interpretative debate. All titles distort; they damage historical understanding when the soundbite crowds out or occludes real consideration

[3] John Dunn, 'Revolution', in Terence Ball, James Farr, and Russell L. Hanson eds., *Political Innovation and Conceptual Change* (Cambridge, 1989), 333–56, esp. 334–5; *idem*, *Modern Revolutions: An Introduction to the Analysis of a Political Phenomenon* (Cambridge, 1972).

[4] Burke's most neutral characterization of the Revolution as 'the late proceedings in France' was uncharacteristically understated, but it captured the idea of process for all that: Edmund Burke, *Reflections on the Revolution in France* [1790] (ed. C. C. O'Brien, Harmondsworth, 1969), 85.

of the nature, meaning, and diversity of historical processes and historical moments. British history in the first half of the nineteenth century is in danger of being parodied in precisely this way. The contours of the classic interpretation of early-nineteenth-century Britain were mapped in the first trio of Elie Halévy's magisterial six-volume *Histoire du Peuple Anglais au XIXe Siècle*, published in French between 1913 and 1923. In their English translations, volume one, *England in 1815*, offered a structural survey of state, society, and culture in 1815; volume two identified *The Liberal Awakening* between 1815 and 1830; and volume three celebrated *The Triumph of Reform* in the decade after 1830.[5] Within a decade of its appearance in English translation, the rich, complex, nuanced progressivism of Halévy's reading had given way to the ponderous Whiggism of Llewellyn Woodward's Oxford History. The sonorities of Woodward's 'Age of Reform' were duller than Halévy's movement towards a 'Triumph of Reform', but the underlying dynamic was largely similar. In a passage which recalled Macaulay, Woodward celebrated the achievement of later-Hanoverian and early-Victorian Britain. 'The public conscience was more instructed, and the content of liberty was being widened to include something more than freedom from political constraint. Taken in the large, the age from 1815 (and in some respects the age before 1815) was a period of reform, and justified a robust belief in progress.'[6] There were, of course, good and noble reasons for celebrating the liberal idea of progress in 1938, but Woodward's pre-war reading became post-war orthodoxy. In 1959 Asa Briggs picked up Woodward's suggestion that reform pre-dated 1815 and pushed nineteenth-century progressivism back into the eighteenth century. In Briggs's limpid textbook the period 1783–1867 became 'The Age of Improvement'. Typically Briggs's historical instincts were refined. 'Improvement' captured the tone of nineteenth-century liberalism rather better than 'Reform', but the teleology was broadly the same.[7] By 1996 Briggs's textbook had sold over 80,000 copies and improvement was established as the leading interpretative theme in the orthodox reading of nineteenth-century Britain.[8]

Since 1959 the theme has been varied but the basic interpretive

[5] Elie Halévy, *England in 1815* (1913, first English edn. 1923); *The Liberal Awakening* (1923, first English edn., 1926); *The Triumph of Reform (1830–1841)* (1923, first English edn., 1927). Interestingly in the cases of volumes two and three a rather different English title was superimposed, indicating the influence of an existing liberal teleology. The French titles of volumes two and three were: *Du lendemain de Waterloo à la veille du Reform Bill* and *De la crise du reform Bill a l'avenement de Sir Robert Peel*. See Myrna Chase, *Elie Halévy. An Intellectual Biography* (New York, 1980).

[6] Llewellyn Woodward, *The Age of Reform 1815–1870* [1938] (2nd edn., Oxford, 1962), 629.

[7] Asa Briggs, *The Age of Improvement, 1783–1867* (1959).

[8] Addison Longman Wesley, *History Catalogue* (1997), p. 12.

melody is still recognisable. In a notable reading, Eric Evans discerned 'The Forging of the Modern State' during the years 1783–1870, and accorded the years 1815–46 their customary place as 'the Crucible of Reform'.[9] Elsewhere 'reform' found its dreary counterpoint in 'reaction', these being the twin organising concepts of John Derry's 1963 account of 1793–1868, but even here the victory of reform seems easily won, even formulaic. Thus whilst Derry happily acknowledged that 'the future for contemporaries was uncertain', that uncertainty was never profound, and as 'dramatic events unfolded ... the sinews of a new life and a larger hope' were emerging.[10] Norman Gash, predictably, modulated this stately progression from Whiggish progressivism to liberal orthodoxy, celebrating the myriad even magical ways in which the old governing elites adapted to the profound social transformation of nineteenth-century Britain. 'The people' acquired rights and entitlements without 'the Aristocracy' losing status. Again the driving forces are reform and transformation, and even if agency and ideology are differently configured, the dominant characteristics of the period were 'astute adaptation', 'good sense', 'resolution', and 'efficiency'.[11] Reading Gash one often senses a story of Tory ends being accomplished by Whiggish means.

So far we have been considering general accounts and the kinds of interpretative shorthand unavoidably employed in even the most nuanced textbooks. Nevertheless the terminologies and concepts we have been exploring hitherto do amount to something approaching an interpretative orthodoxy and, crucially, an orthodoxy which has spawned, and in turn been reinforced by, a substantial monographic literature. It is a literature which has explored the patterns of improvement and the processes of reform. Let us take the 1830s as a case study. Here the leading theme has been reform and, since Halévy's great account, this has been the 'decade of reform'. This despite Britain's teetering on the brink of revolution in 1831 and 1832; the emergence of mass protest in a quite unprecedented form in the Chartist movement; and growing anxiety towards the end of the decade that Britain's industrial advance, at once the harbinger and facilitator of reform, had stalled. Halévy's narrative was a grand narrative of reform. Geoffrey Finlayson's short study of 1969 invested reform with still greater hegemonic significance. His 'decade of reform' was a theatre of reformist energies and reformers' frustrations. Paradoxically, though, where reform failed, either through a lack of ambition or a lack of govern-

[9] Eric J. Evans, *The Forging of the Modern State. Early Industrial Britain 1783–1870* (1983), 177–269.

[10] John Derry, *Reaction and Reform. England in the Early Nineteenth Century* (1963), 4.

[11] Norman Gash, *Aristocracy and People. Britain 1815–1865* (1979), 7,8, 350 and *passim*; *cf.* Norman McCord, *British History, 1815–1906* (Oxford, 1991).

mental means, the reformers' agenda was further entrenched. Thus 'if in the short-term, the limitations of reform were more apparent than its achievements, the events of the decade set a direction and pointed a course which later generations were to follow and even yet pursue'.[12] If the political and ideological foundations of this kind of neo-Whig reformist reading were *sotto voce* in readings such a those of Halévy and Finlayson, they were trumpeted in others. William Lubenow concluded an intelligent account of 'The Politics of Government Growth' between 1833 and 1848 in overtly celebratory terms. 'Taken together,' he assured us, 'the nineteenth-century revolution in government [essentially, of course, a model of governmental reformism] is a comforting paradigm of the way in which peaceful institutional change can occur in traditional political and social structures troubled and torn by massive economic and social dislocation.'[13] Given contemporaries' deep anxieties, such comforts are certainly retrospective and probably contingent, and as so often the owl of Minerva spreads its wings some while after dusk.

Three recent works have offered expansive and often fresh readings of the 1830s as the decade of reform. The most traditionally and statically formulated is Ian Newbould's *Whiggery and Reform.* Here the Whigs' decade in power takes its place as a grand reformist statement in a dreary dialectic between reform and reaction. 'The Whigs were moderate reformers ... It was not Peel who won in 1841, but the reactionary forces which deeply offended him ... Peel's parliamentary defeat in 1846 was only the final signal that what he represented had been similarly defeated in 1841. The process of reaction was inevitable. Reform, with its decade, was ended.'[14] In an important monograph in 1987, Richard Brent both enriched our understanding of the ideological basis of Whiggism and of the scope of its reformist ambitions by carefully identifying the 'liberal Anglican' energies which infused such pivotal Whig leaders as Lord John Russell and Lord Althorp, and which animated the Whig Ministries' Irish, tithe, and church rate policies.[15] By recovering a liberal strand in Anglicanism, Dr Brent has identified an Erastian Anglican reformism to set alongside the fiercely Tory reflexes of conservative Anglicans who were only too ready to

[12] G. B. A. M. Finlayson, *Britain in the Eighteenth Thirties. Decade of Reform* (1969), 107.

[13] William C. Lubenow, *The Politics of Government Growth. Early Victorian Attitudes Towards State Intervention 1833–1848* (Newton Abbot, 1971), 188.

[14] Ian Newbould, *Whiggery and Reform 1830–41. The Politics of Government* (Basingstoke and London, 1990), 321. As a reading this is a more persuasive account of Peelism than Whiggism, and insights into Peelite Conservatism were perceptively developed in Ian Newbould, 'Sir Robert Peel and the Conservative Party, 1831–41: A Study in Failure?', *English Historical Review*, xcviii (1983), 527–57.

[15] Richard Brent, *Liberal Anglican Politics. Whiggery, Religion, and Reform 1830–1841* (Oxford, 1987).

chorus 'the Church in danger' whenever a party of movement threatened constitutional alternation.[16]

In perhaps the most ambitious revision of our understanding of 'The Age of Reform', Peter Mandler has carefully rewound the skein of Whigs, Reformers, Liberals, and Moderates who uneasily comprised the governing coalitions of the 1830s. It would be easy to be diverted into the subtleties of Professor Mandler's argument for seeing the 1830s and 1840s as an aristocratic conjuncture in the emergence of British political liberalism, a moment when Foxite Whig gentlemen briefly supplanted Pittite liberal players, but that is not quite my purpose here.[17] Mandler's model privileges two political styles (aristocratic Whiggism and Pittite managerialism) and two modes of policy-making (the ideologically-tinged improvisations of aristocratic Whigs and the more ruthless bureaucratisation eventually wrought by men such as Edwin Chadwick and James Kay-Shuttleworth). What it marginalises is that other cluster of political and social attitudes conventionally regarded as Tory. The effect is that we see the contests within the 'Age of Reform' but not the contest about the 'Age of Reform'.[18] As with Professor Gash, traditional elites again emerge as the principal agents of modernisation, although Mandler's account focuses on the conscious reformers within the Whig aristocracy rather than the pragmatic Tory trimmers beloved of Gash. 'Viewed from a low political perspective', Mandler suggested, 'the 1830s and 1840s were remarkable for agitations which were *not* easily assimilated by the landed mainstream ... The persistent pressing of these Reform and Condition of England questions perplexed, dismayed, and at points almost paralysed moderate landed politicians. High whig aristocrats, on the other hand, were both temprementally more flexible and politically more amenable to such demands.' Mandler's Whig aristocratic moment, his Age of Reform, is embedded in a grander liberal teleology, and that teleology is at least consonant with some earlier trajectories of a nineteenth-century 'Age of Improvement'. Thus when in 1852 Whiggism, liberalism, and residual Peelism coalesced in the Aberdeen Coalition, liberalism again extended its ideological embrace. 'The new liberalism,' Mandler concluded, 'would eschew oligarchy and democracy, and leave the progress of improvement to

[16] G. I. T. Machin, *Politics and the Churches in Great Britain 1832 to 1868* (Oxford, 1977), 28–111; R.J. Smith, *The Gothic Bequest. Medieval Institutions in British Thought, 1688–1863* (Cambridge, 1980), 171–200; Norman Gash, *Reaction and Reconstruction in English Politics 1832–1852* (Oxford, 1965), 60–118.

[17] Peter Mandler, *Aristocratic Government in the Age of Reform. Whigs and Liberals 1830–1852* (Oxford, 1990), esp. 110–99, 275–82 and *passim*.

[18] See also Jonathan Parry's always suggestive and subtle *The Rise and Fall of Liberal Government in Victorian Britain* (New Haven and London, 1993).

proceed safely along its natural course.'[19] And with that, new wine finds its way into old wineskins.

In a remarkable book, Dr Boyd Hilton has offered a striking reinterpretation of the ideological tone and even the 'public mind' of early-nineteenth-century Britain. At one level Hilton's account is conventional, emphasising the centrality of economic thought to public and private doctrine. In every other way this is a brave, sophisticated, and challenging reading. The rise of classical political economy as an essentially secular discourse of patterns of growth and material allocation gives way to an altogether more powerful, theologically infused, Evangelical political economy. Thus, Hilton argues, patterns of economic development were invested with quite different moral meanings, with economic contraction and recession representing Providential retribution rather than technical adjustments. Thus 'improvement' gives way to 'atonement'. 'The first half of the nineteenth century has been called "The Age of Improvement". But it was also an "Age of Atonement", because improvement, like virtue, was then not thought of as its own reward, merely as a terrestrial fumbling towards public and private salvation.'[20] As an interpretation, Dr Hilton's reading is not without its problems. Early-nineteenth-century evangelicalism was itself a broad church, and Hilton struggles to maintain its analytical purchase, from time to time indulging in a little intellectual excommunication of theologically impeccable evangelicals who fail his strict economic tests.[21] Nor is Hilton's account of the relationship between evangelical thought and policy-making always persuasive. Nevertheless, Dr Hilton has, more profoundly than other historians, heard and attended to the early-nineteenth century's anxieties, its self-doubt, its profound anxiety about material development, and its deep uncertainly as to the moral meanings and ultimate sustainability of improvement.[22] The full implications of Hilton's work have yet to be registered.

Inevitably one caricatures positions by characterising them, and I have tried to do justice to the richness and originality of recent scholarship. My purpose is not polemical but categorical: I want to suggest that recent scholarship on early-nineteenth-century Britain has not so much disturbed as undermined many of the descriptive categories

[19] Mandler, *Aristocratic Government in the Age of Reform*, 119–20.

[20] Boyd Hilton, *The Age of Atonement. The Influence of Evangelicalism on Social and Economic Thought 1785–1865* (Oxford, 1988), 3. See also A.C.M. Waterman, 'The Ideological Alliance of Political Economy and Christian Theology, 1798–1833', *Jnl. Ecclesiastical History*, xxiv (1983), 231–44; A.C.M. Waterman, *Revolution, Economy, and Religion. Christian Political Economy, 1798–1833* (Cambridge, 1991); R.A. Soloway, *Prelates and People. Ecclesiastical Social Thought in England 1783–1852* (1969).

[21] See for example his treatment of Perceval, Copleston, Ashley, Sadler, and Oastler; Hilton, *Age of Atonement*, pp. 29–30, 212–13, 219.

[22] *Ibid.*, p. 65 and *passim*.

which have tended to come easily to hand. Texts have destroyed titles, and new scholarship demands new typologies. At the very least, the tone and texture of our characterisation of early-nineteenth-century Britain requires modification. Let us return for a moment to the forceful prose of Professor Briggs, who briefly opened the door to interpretative pluralism before firmly resolving the case in favour of an almost providentially assured liberalism.

> No single interpretation of these formative years may be regarded as definitive, but in the scope of 'improvement' and the reactions to it we have a clear-cut theme. ... To the men of the 1780s ... the 'discoveries and improvements' of their own generation seemed to 'diffuse a glory over this country unattainable by conquest or dominion' ... By the middle years of the nineteenth century, indeed, the economical, social, and political history of England seemed to be falling into shape ... The great changes which had been accomplished in politics as much as in economics had been produced, as H. T. Buckle ... put it, 'not by and great external event nor by any sudden insurrection of the people, but by the unaided action of moral force'.[23]

This is enormously revealing, offering the narrative of 'improvement' in nineteenth-century Britain as a grand morality tale. Unmistakably it invests the process of political and economical development with an ethical significance, quietly celebrating British evolutionary reformism against revolutionary upheaval or democratic insurrectionism. Moreover, in marginalising the opponents of reform the kind of analysis also morally devalues them, and skews the intellectual history of early-nineteenth-century Britain in favour of reformist or self-consciously modernising ideologies.[24] Moreover these kinds of teleological readings radically understate the extent to which the present state and future condition of Britain was the subject of profound contestation, at least until the 1850s, and underestimate the profound uncertainty which was characteristic both of Britain's political life and social condition.

Early-nineteenth-century Britain was built across the fault lines opened up by the advent of revolutionary politics and convulsive

[23] Briggs, *Age of Improvement*, 2–3.

[24] For a striking and persuasive broadening of the terrain of contemporary debate see A. C. Gambles, 'The Boundaries of Political Economy: Tory Economic Argument 1806–1847' (University of Oxford, D.Phil. thesis, 1996); and *idem*, 'Rethinking the Politics of Protection: Conservatism and the Corn Laws, 1830–52', *EHR* forthcoming, Sept. 1998. Harold Perkin's classic *The Origins of Modern English Society 1780–1880* (1969), 237–52, remains as sane and satisfying as ever. Differently cast are James J. Sack, *From Jacobite to Conservative. Reaction and Orthodoxy in Britain c.*1760–1832 (Cambridge, 1993); and Robert Hole, *Pulpits, Politics and Public Order in England 1760–1832* (Cambridge, 1989).

economic growth. It has, however, recently become fashionable to play down the impact of the French Revolution and industrialisation. The most extreme advocate of this new minimalism is Jonathan Clark, for whom the industrial revolution was massively protracted, sectorally limited, and relatively easily assimilated in cultural and social terms. Britain's transition to an industrial and urban society was, according to Clark, 'slow, partial, belated, complex and irregular'. Thus the idea that the Industrial Revolution was a principal cause of social and political transformation in later-Hanoverian England was dismissed as easily as the Marxist and Fabian historians whose totemic creation, Clark alleges, the Industrial Revolution really was.[25] The conventional view, that the French Revolution had cradled a powerful democratic impulse in Britain, which had dominated the literature between Veitch's *Genesis of Parliamentary Reform* (1913) and Dickinson's *Liberty and Property* (1977), was similarly despatched.[26] A powerful 'conservative consensus' confronted, confounded, and crushed British radicalism in the ideological and political battles of the 1790s. Far from being taken to the brink in the 1790s, Clark suggested that Britain was sustained by 'an ideological consensus of great unity and strength'.[27] Such was the crushing superiority of English loyalism that Clark could hail William Paley's *Reasons for Contentment* (1793), written when the archdeacon was so out of form that he could barely get an outside edge, as a 'classic'.[28]

Given the influence of Clark's work, and the general tendency to diminish the significance of the French Revolution and industrialisation to the reshaping of Britain in the early-nineteenth century, it is worth trying to run to ground the empirical and historiographical foundations of this kind of neo-Tory interpretation. The new economic history took off into self-sustaining publishing in the 1980s. The fruits of this cliometric reinterpretation of Britain's economic growth were presented in Professor Crafts's forceful and lucid *British Economic Growth During the Industrial Revolution*.[29] Although Crafts's reworking of the figures of Britain's economic growth in the period 1700–1831 have themselves subsequently been reworked, their mildly revisionist meanings have been generally accepted.[30] In place of the old picture of rapid, even

[25] J. C. D. Clark, *English Society 1688–1832* (Cambridge, 1985), 64–75, quotation at p. 65. I am uncertain what 'belated' can mean in this context.

[26] G. S. Veitch, *Genesis of Parliamentary Reform* (1913); H. T. Dickinson, *Liberty and Property. Political Ideology in Eighteenth-Century Britain* (1977).

[27] Clark, *English Society*, 199–200.

[28] Clark, *English Society*, 262. For rather different readings see J. R. Dinwiddy, *Radicalism and Reform in Britain 1780–1850* (1992), 195–206, 229–52; and David Eastwood, 'Patriotism and the English State in the 1790s', in *The French Revolution and British Popular Politics*, ed. Mark Philp (Oxford, 1991), 146–68.

[29] N. F. R. Crafts, *British Economic Growth During the Industrial Revolution* (Oxford, 1985).

[30] For critiques see Julian Hoppit, 'Counting the Industrial Revolution', *Ec[onomic]*

convulsive industrialisation, presented by Toynbee, the Hammonds, Ashton, and Rostow, we now had a much more gentle trajectory of growth, building gradually from a remarkably advantageous base in 1700. But even after the computer models of the cliometricians had spoken, British industrial growth in the first three decades of the nineteenth century still averaged 3% *per annum*.[31] Nevertheless Crafts and the cliometricians never argued economically what Clark and the revisionists claimed. Professor Crafts's study still left us with an account of the structural transformation of the British economy between 1750 and 1850, and his comparative methodology underscored the structural distinctiveness of the British economic experience when set against that of early-nineteenth-century Europe. More recently Professor Wrigley has offered a compelling account of the ways in which Britain's shift to new energy sources and new patterns of production in the early-nineteenth century enabled it to escape from the Malthusian trap which had shackled sustained economic growth and demographic expansion since the sixteenth century.[32]

Redefining the industrial revolution was a quite different matter from abolishing it as an analytical concept. Moreover, for early-nineteenth-century Britain what mattered was not so much the pace of sectoral advance when indices of growth were disaggregated, but rather the way which economic and change drove urbanisation. It was the combination of dramatic changes in modes of production and apparently uncontrollable urbanisation which traumatised early-nineteenth-century Britain. The growth of Manchester from 75,000 in 1801 to 303,000 by 1851 or Sheffield from 46,000 to 135,000 in the same period is too well known to need comment. What is often underestimated in the sheer rapidity of year-on-year urban growth. Nottingham, for example, expanded by 25% in the 1820s alone, and this within very constrained boundaries, whilst in the same decade Birmingham grew by 42%, Manchester by 45%, and Bradford by 63%. As a proportion of GDP, expenditure on housing in the 1820s was at an all-time peak of 31.5%.[33] Contemporaries were awestruck. In 1807 Robert Southey

H[istory] R[eview], xliii (1990), 173–93; Maxine Berg and Pat Hudson, 'Rehabilitating the Industrial Revolution', *Ec.H.R.*, xlv (1992), 24–50; Pat Hudson, *The Industrial Revolution* (1992).

[31] David Cannadine, 'The Past and the Present in the Industrial Revolution 1880–1980', *Past and Present*, 103 (1984), 131–72; A. Toynbee, *Lectures on the Industrial Revolution* (1884); J. L. and B. Hammond, *The Town Labourer, 1760–1832* (1917); J. L. and B. Hammond, *The Rise of Modern Industry* (1925); T. S. Ashton, *The Industrial Revolution, 1760–1830* (1948); W. W. Rostow, *The British Economy of the Nineteenth Century* (Oxford, 1948). For figures see Crafts, *British Economic Growth*, p. 32.

[32] E. A. Wrigley, *Continuity, Chance and Change. The Character of the Industrial Revolution in England* (Cambridge, 1988).

[33] Richard Rodger, *Housing in Urban Britain 1780–1914* (new edn., Cambridge, 1995), 19.

summoned up his most coruscating prose to capture what he took to be the new social realities of England's urban manufacturing centres. His retrospective of Birmingham suggests a grim fascination:

> A heavy cloud of smoke hung over the city, above which in many places black columns were sent up with prodigious force from the steam-engines ... the contagion spread far and wide. Every where [*sic*] around us ... the tower of some manufactory was seen at a distance, vomiting up flames and smoke, and blasting every thing around with its metallic vapours. The vicinity was as thickly peopled as that of London. ... Such swarms of children I never beheld in any other pace, nor such wretched ones.[34]

Observing Manchester Southey wove together social description and moral critique. The urban working classes were,

> deprived in childhood of all enjoyment ... of fresh air by day and of natural sleep by night. Their health physical and moral alike is destroyed; they die of diseases induced by unremitting task work, by confinement in the impure atmosphere of crowded rooms ... they live to grow up without decency, without comfort, and without hope, without morals, without religion, and without shame ... The dwellings of the labouring manufacturers are in narrow streets and lanes, blocked up from light and air ... crowded together because every inch of land is of such value, that room for light cannot be afforded to them'.[35]

Politically and aesthetically Southey was repelled by the social transformation wrought by manufacturing and urbanisation. Others would celebrate it, but none denied it. Where Southey condemned, the Swiss observer Hans Casper Escher was enraptured by Manchester in 1814. 'In Manchester there is no sun and no dust. Here there is always a dense cloud of smoke to cover the sun while the light rain ... turns the dust into a fine paste which makes it unnecessary to polish one's shoes. In spite of all the smoke they create one must admire the steam engines here. In beauty and efficiency they bear the same relationship

The expenditure of such as high proportion of national capital on what was often poor-quality housing is explained partly by the sheer pace of urbanisation and partly by the still modest rates of capital formation.

[34] Robert Southey, *Letters from England* [1807] ed. and intro Jack Simmons (Gloucester, 1984), 203. For Southey as a social critic see David Eastwood, 'Robert Southey and the Intellectual Origins of Romantic Conservatism', *English Historical Review*, civ (1989), 308–31; *idem*, '"Ruinous Prosperity". Robert Southey's Critique of the Commercial System', *The Wordsworth Circle*, xxv (1994), 72–76; Alfred Cobban, *Edmund Burke and the Revolt Against the Eighteenth Century* (2nd edn., 1960), 197–232.

[35] Southey, *Letters from England*, 210–11.

to French steam engines as English spinning engines bear to those of Saxony.'[36] The French Comptean, Gustave d'Eichthal, travelling through Britain in 1828, had little doubt as to the power and pervasiveness of the industrial spirit. 'As for the industrial aspect, you can imagine I felt only one thing, admiration, they make machines in this country as we plant cabbages in ours. They are afraid of nothing, so plentiful are funds ... The physical condition of the working class [though] is very uneven.'[37] Sixteen years later, yet another French visitor, Leon Faucher, had no doubt that 'The birth of the manufacturing system, like that of Minerva, was sudden and complete; and in less than a century, its colossal, if not harmonious, proportions were fully developed ... Lancashire was its cradle.'[38] These kinds of observation could be multiplied endlessly, from native observers and from the small army of foreigners who flocked to Britain in the early-nineteenth century to observe the future.

Robert Southey returned to the factory system time and time again as the great fact and symbol of the changing social and culture textures of early-nineteenth-century Britain. Southey himself was no marginal figure: poet laureate from 1813, leading economic contributor to the best-selling quarterly, *The Quarterly Review*, from 1812, a key inspiration for Lord Ashley, Michael Sadler and the factory movement of the 1830s and 1840s, and by any standards a major social commentator.[39] Britain's experience as a populous, manufacturing, urbanising society was a *leitmotif* of Southey's journalism and a central feature of his major work of social commentary, the *Colloquies on the Progress and Prospects of Society* (1829), the work which so stung the equable Whiggism of Macaulay that he responded with his most panglossian of reviews.[40] The new wealth of Britain was, for Southey, bought at the price of a Mephistophelean pact which morally debases as it materially rewards. 'The moral atmosphere wherein [children] live and move and have their

[36] H. C. Escher, 'Escher's Letters from England in 1814', in *Industrial Britain under the Regency 1814–18*, ed. W. O. Henderson (New York, 1968), 34–5.

[37] [Gustave d'Eichthal], *A French Sociologist Looks at Britain. Gustave d'Eichthal and British Society in 1828* eds. Barrie M. Radcliffe and W. H. Chaloner (Manchester University Press, 1977), 7.

[38] Leon Faucher, *Manchester in 1844. Its Present Condition and Future Prospects* ed. and trans. J. P. Culverwell (London and Manchester, 1844), 3–4.

[39] Geoffrey Canrnell, *Robert Southey and His Age—The Development of a Conservative Mind* (Oxford, 1960); Jack Simmons, *Southey* (1945); *Robert Southey. The Critical Heritage*, ed. Lionel Madden (London and Boston, 1972); Kenneth Curry, *Southey* (London and Boston, 1975); Jonathan Mendilow, *The Romantic Tradition in British Political Thought* (1986), 47–82; Eastwood, 'Robert Southey and the Intellectual Origins of Romantic Conservatism'.

[40] Macaulay's unsigned review appeared in the *Edinburgh Review*, l (Jan. 1830), 528–65, and was widely reprinted: see Lord Macaulay, *Critical and Historical Essays* (3 vols, 1878), i, 217–69; Biancamaria Fontana, *Rethinking the Politics of Commercial Society. The* Edinburgh Review *1802–32* (Cambridge, 1985), 76–8.

being, is as noxious to the soul. as the foul and tainted air which they inhale is to their bodily constitution.' Meanwhile the moral feelings of the manufacturing elite are 'petrified' by their 'love of lucre'. 'He who, at the beginning of his career, abuses his fellow-creatures as bodily machines for producing wealth, ends not infrequently in becoming an intellectual one himself, employed in continually increasing what it is impossible for him to enjoy.'[41]

The language of social description pioneered by Southey and early-nineteenth-century social critics, and refined by more scientific investigators such as Peter Gaskell, found its most exquisitely powerful expression in Edwin Chadwick's blue books and Friedrich Engels's red condemnation. There can be few more controlled concatenations of statistical evidence and moral indignation that Edwin Chadwick's 1842 *Report on the Sanitary Condition of the Labouring Population of Great Britain.* The message was stark: the price of manufacturing prosperity in an unregulated urban environment was the physical and moral degeneration of the working classes and an annual cull of Britain's able-bodied men which far exceeded that of the battle of Waterloo.[42] Chadwick's solution was a more systematic version of Southey's: a massive extension of the control of the state over society and social policy. Engels's solution was not to expand but to confront the state. Many of his statistics in *The Condition of the Working Class in England* in 1845 came directly from Chadwick's *Report*; whilst his tone was an intensification of that employed by earlier English social critics. Too often Engels's work is either dismissed as uncontrolled polemic or uncritically embraced as revolutionary truth. In fact it is remarkably similar in style and tendency to Peter Gaskell's *Artizans and Machinery* (1836),[43] and firmly within a tradition of British social criticism. Where Engels was often at his best was, like Southey, in his pointing up the moral effects of manufacturing. Like Southey, Engels believed that 'The middle classes have a truly extraordinary conception of society. They really believe that all human

[41] Robert Southey, *Colloquies on the Progress and Prospects of Society* (2 vols., 1829), i, 166, 169–70.

[42] *Report on the Sanitary Condition of the Labouring Population of Great Britain* [1842] (ed. and intro. M. W. Flinn, Edinburgh, 1965), 78–9. For the *Report* and its influence see R. A. Lewis, *Edwin Chadwick and the Public Health Movement 1832–1854* (1952), esp. 29–105; S. E. Finer, *The Life and Times of Sir Edwin Chadwick* (1952), 209–42; Anthony Brundage, *England's "Prussian Minister". Edwin Chadwick and the Politics of Government Growth, 1832–1854* (University Park Pennsylvania and London, 1988), 79–172.

[43] Itself an expanded version of Gaskell's *The Manufacturing Population of England* (1833). See also J. P. Kay, *The Moral and Physical Condition of the Working Classes Employed in Cotton Manufacture in Manchester* (1832); Andrew Lees, *Cities Perceived. Urban Society in European and American Thought 1820–1940* (Manchester, 1985), 16–39; and Michael Turner, *Reform and Respectability. The Making of a Middle-Class Liberalism in Early Nineteenth-Century Manchester* (Manchester, Chetham Society, 3rd ser., xl, 1995), 164–208.

beings (themselves excluded) ... have a real existance only if they make money or help to make money.' Their private virtues—they 'make good husbands and family men'—is mirrored by a public viciousness. Engels walked into Manchester with one leading manufacturer: 'I spoke to him about the disgraceful unhealthy slums ... I declared that I had never seen so badly built a town in my life. He listened patiently and at the corner of the street where we parted remarked: "And yet there is a great deal of money made here. Good morning, Sir".'[44]

Thus, in response to Jonathan Clark's anything but rhetorical question, 'Did the Industrial Revolution happen?', we can answer confidently that contemporaries thought that it, or something very much like it, had. Moreover, they regarded economic change and associated urbanisation as materially enriching and potentially or actually morally destabilising. Southey's mechanisation of the intellect, first canvassed in 1829, found its analogue in Thomas Carlyle's sense of a mechanisation of morality, brilliantly developed in his *Edinburgh Review* essay 'Signs of the Times' in the same year. 'Were we required to characterise this age of ours by any single epithet, we should be tempted to call it, not an Heroical, Devotional, Philosophical, or Moral Age, but, above all others, the Mechanical Age. It is the Age of Machinery, in every outward and inward sense of that word'. Carlyle never doubted material progress: 'What wonderful accessions have thus been made, and are still making, to the physical power of mankind; how much better fed, clothed, lodged and, in all outward respects, accommodated men now are, or might be, by a given amount of labour.' But Carlyle would never let materialism stand proxy for morality, or allow that prosperity was itself a sufficient justification for economic advancement. Whereas Adam Smith had assured his readers that the poorest English peasant lived better than an African king who enjoyed power of life and death over his subjects, Carlyle identified an ethical challenge arising from prosperity which political economy had either evaded or glossed in the glibbest of Smithean economic relativism. 'What changes, too, this addition of [mechanical] power is introducing into the Social System; how wealth has more and more increased, and at the same time gathered itself more and more into masses, strangely altering the old relations, and increasing the distance between the rich and the poor, will be a question for Political Economists, and a much more complex and important one than any they have yet engaged with.'[45] Carlyle's

[44] Friedrich Engels, *The Condition of the Working Class in England* [1845] (Eng. trans. W. O. Henderson and W. H. Chaloner, Stanford, 1958), 311–12. See also Steven Marcus, *Engels, Manchester and the Working Class* (1974); Terrell Carver, *Friedrich Engels. His Life and Thought* (Basingstoke and London, 1989), 95–132.

[45] Thomas Carlyle, 'Signs of the Times' [1829], reprinted in *Critical and Miscellaneous Essays* (4 vols., 1857), ii, 100–1.

was, perhaps, the most distinctive voice of the second quarter of the nineteenth century. In 1855 George Eliot insisted that 'There is hardly a superior or active mind of this generation which has not been modified by Carlyle's writings; there has hardly been an English book written for the last ten or twelve years that would not have been different if Carlyle had not lived.'[46] Readers may have tired of Carlyle's overtly prophetic mode, even of his resonant prose, by the mid-1850s, but in the previous thirty years he had captured not only the profundity of the crisis facing Britain's political, social, and cultural life, but also the insufficiency of conventional modes of political and economic discourse to frame and analyse that crisis.[47] In the midst of the massive economic recession of the late 1830s, with Chartism orchestrating the dissonant distress of the working class, Carlyle sketched what he took to be Britain's social crisis in Belshazzar fire letters:

> Society, it is understood, does not in any age prevent a man from being what he *can be* ... O reader, to what shifts is poor Society reduced, struggling to give some account of herself, in epochs when Cash Payment has become the sole nexus of man to man! On the whole, we will advise Society not to talk at all about what she exists for; but rather with her whole industry to exist, to try how she can keep existing! That is her best plan. She may depend on it, if ever she, by cruel change, did come to exist only for protection of breeches-pocket property, she would very soon lose the gift for protecting even that, and find her career in our lower world on the point of being terminated.[48]

Carlyle's central point was that England did not understand her condition. It was he who coined the idea of a 'Condition of England question': the idea of a social debate which confronted not aspects of Britain's social condition, but its essence. 'So much is to be ascertained; much of it by no means easy to ascertain! Till among the "Hill Cooly" and "Dog-cart" questions, there arise in Parliament and extensively out

[46] George Eliot, *Passages Selected from the Writings of Thomas Carlyle* (1855) quoted in Gertrude Himmelfarb, *The Idea of Poverty. England in the Early Industrial Age* (London and Boston, 1984), 202.

[47] We currently lack the necessary modern critical study of Carlyle which attends to his inner voice and properly maps his influence, but see Himmelfarb, *Idea of Poverty*, 191–206; J. A. Froude, *Thomas Carlyle: A History of the First Forty Years of his Life* (2 vols., 1882); J. A. Froude, *Thomas Carlyle: A History of His Life in London 1834–1881* (2 vols., 1881); Philip Rosenberg, *The Seventh Hero: Thomas Carlyle and the Theory of Political Activism* (Cambridge Mass., 1974); *Thomas Carlyle: The Critical Heritage* ed. J. P. Seigel (1971).

[48] Thomas Carlyle, *Chartism* [1839] reprinted in Carlyle, *Sartor Resartus. Lecture on Heros. Chartism. Past and Present* (1894), 37–8.

of it a "Condition-of-England question" and quite a new set of inquirers and methods, little of it is likely to be ascertained.'[49]

Carlyle was at his most facile in dismissing other languages of social enquiry. Statistical science, coming into its ascendency from the 1830s, political economy, close social observation, the richly ambiguous languages of English constitutionalism, were by no means as vacuous or redundant as Carlyle was wont to suggest.[50] Indeed it was these more prosaic analytical methods, rather than Carlyle's grand prophesying, which ultimately became the instruments through which Victorian Britain came to know itself. Nevertheless Carlyle's work in the 1820s and 1830s does capture something which is too easily missed: that the conflict in British society was both reflected in, and exacerbated by, a consequential conflict between modes and styles of public discourse. A prior, and fearful, uncertainly persisted as to the appropriate linguistic and conceptual mirrors through which the nature and condition of Britain was to be understood. Nowhere was this clearer than in the debates about and within political economy.

There can be little doubt that political economy was, inherently, a hegemonic social language. Not only was it technically committed to the maximisation of society's aggregate material well-being, but also it embodied a fundamentally moral concept of the market as a means of social exchange. Viewed from the perspective of political economy alternative ideologies, be they statist, mercantalist, High Tory, or orthodox Christian, which privileged non-market entitlements or legitimated strategies limiting profit maximisation, were subversive of society's collective well-being. Nevertheless political economy was itself a contested mode of analysis. Carlyle's famous description of political economy as the 'dismal science' captured not what political economy was, but what it had become. In its classical Smithean formulation, political economy offered the prospect of substantial continuing economic growth.[51] Growth of markets, a consequential intensification of the division of labour, and expanding resource base would, if only lightly regulated, promote sustainable economic growth. The market, whilst not allocating wealth equitably, would do so rationally and in a way which ensured that absolute enrichment was a near-universal experience. As Donald Winch has recently argued, the first great

[49] *Ibid.*, p. 10.

[50] David Eastwood, '"Amplifying the Province of the Legislature": the Flow of Information and the English State in the Early Nineteenth Century', *Historical Research*, 62 (1989), 276–94; *Re-Reading the Constitution. New Narratives in the Political History of England's Long Nineteenth Century*, ed. James Vernon (Cambridge, 1996); David Eastwood, *Making Public Policy in Nineteenth-Century Britain* (Swansea, 1998); Karel Williams, *From Pauperism to Poverty* (London, Boston, and Henley, 1981), esp. 235–308.

[51] Adam Smith, *An Inquiry into the Nature and Causes of the Wealth of Nations* (ed. Edwin Cannan, 1904), esp. bk. 1 chs. 1, 3, 8,; bk. 2 ch. 1; bk. 4 chs. 7, 8, 9.

challenge to Smithean political economy came not just with the Malthusian question but also with a very precise historical moment. Winch has succeeded in repositing Malthus, not as the 'demoraliser' of political economy but as its moderniser. *Pace* Gertrude Himmelfarb, Malthus did not repudiate the Smithean project but sought rather to refine and reconstruct Smithean political economy in the light of wartime dislocations, widespread poverty, and rapid population growth. Malthus's understanding of the pace and limitations of economic growth was determined by pre-industrial conditions and the limitations of agrarian economies, and political economy itself became analytically constrained by the structural and technical limitations which constrained growth in pre-industrial economies.[52]

From Malthus's 1798 *Essay on the Principle of Population* onwards, political economy faced the fearsome problem of a biologically driven demographic imperative which would always tend to absorb new wealth through increased population. One consequence was a renewed debate over agrarian policy which raged until 1846. Malthus's own solutions demanded a profound political, cultural, and ideological shift. The Poor Law should be abandoned, selective public works schemes expanded, and a carefully calibrated Corn Law introduced both to secure food supply and to steady the pattern of economic growth.[53] David Ricardo, whose more technically austere version of political economy eventually carried the day, joined Malthus in demanding the radical remodelling of public welfare and the ending of public relief to the able-bodied, but was passionately opposed Malthus's autarkic preferences, preferring an abolition of all agricultural protection, more intensive mechanisation of industrial production, and vigorous concentration on Britain's relative comparative advantage.[54] In both the Malthusian and Ricardian prescriptions, political economy had lost its innocence, Smithean optimism giving way to something approaching Carlyle's 'dismal science'.[55] Classical political economy had, by the

[52] Donald Winch, *Riches and Poverty. An Intellectual History of Political Economy in Britain, 1750–1834* (Cambridge, 1996); *cf.* Himmelfarb, *Idea of Poverty*, 42–144; William Petersen, *Malthus* (1979), 38–134, 218–40; Patricia James, *Population Malthus. His Life and Times* (London, Boston, and Henley, 1979), 55–159; E. A. Wrigley, 'Malthus and the Prospects for the Labouring Poor', *Historical Jnl.*, 31 (1988), 813–29.

[53] T. R. Malthus, *An Essay on the Principle of Population [1798 edn.]*. ed. and intro., A. Flew (Harmondsworth, 1970); T. R. Malthus, *An Essay in the Principle of Population [1803 edn.]*, ed. and intro. T. H. Hollingsworth (Everyman edn., 1973); T. R. Malthus, *Principles of Political Economy Considered with a View to their Practical Application* (1820); T. R. Malthus, *Observations on the Effects of the Corn Laws* ... (2nd edn., 1814).

[54] David Ricardo, *Principles of Political Economy [1817]*, ed. P. Sraffa (Cambridge, 1951); Maxine Berg, *The Machinery Question and the Making of Political Economy 1815–1848* (Cambridge, 1980).

[55] Stefan Collini, Donald Winch, and John Burrow, *That Noble Science of Politics. A Study in Nineteenth-Century Intellectual History* (Cambridge, 1983), 63–89.

early-nineteenth century, become preoccupied, some might even argue analytically paralysed, by its anxiety that the economy was about to exchange dynamism for an economically inert and socially calamitous 'stationary state'. This was the pall which hung over all economically literate early-nineteenth century finance ministers, notably F.J. Robinson, William Huskisson, and Sir Robert Peel.[56]

In far more than economic terms, early-nineteenth-century Britain can be said to have experienced a 'Malthusian moment'. There was a kind of popular Malthusianism which took root which came to dominate the social imagination.[57] Martin Wiener has suggested 'Malthusian images of unhealthy, self-destructive vitality pervaded early-Victorian social description', and the necessary counterpoint to this came to be seen as a profound, even providential, rediscovery of a socially necessary unhappiness.[58] Early-nineteenth-century Britain thus saw many of the Enlightenment's methodological tools being used to subvert the Enlightenment's social optimism. Crucially, for many who lauded themselves as economically literate, poverty became a object not of pity but of fear, as the vicious idleness of the poor undermined work-discipline and the poor rates threatened to devour the nation's rents and profits. The Royal Commission on the Poor Laws, reporting in 1834, captured something of this social tone with its frequent emphasis on 'pauperised districts' and its darkly conjured spectres of the 'extensive and irremediable mischiefs' to which pauperisation was giving rise.[59] Such social anxieties coloured responses to the apparently remorselessly rising criminal indictments, growing number of lunatics, and far from sanguine impressions of the recidivism rate. Although politicians' solutions—the new poor law, police forces, small armies of inspectors, and a substantial expansion of the domain of the state—were far from Malthusian, the social anxieties which made them politically thinkable owed much to a pervasive popular Malthusianism.[60]

[56] Hilton, *Age of Atonement*, esp. 203–51; Boyd Hilton, *Corn, Cash, Commerce. The Economic Policies of the Tory Governments 1815–1830* (Oxford, 1977); Boyd Hilton, 'Peel: A Reappraisal', *Historical Jnl.*, 22 (1979), 585–614; Alexander Brady, *William Huskisson and Liberal Reform* (Oxford, 1928); Brian Jenkins, *Henry Goulburn 1784-1856. A Political Biography* (Liverpool, 1996); esp. 150–2, 185–214, 288–356; W. D. Jones, *'Prosperity' Robinson. The Life of Viscount Goderich 1782–1859* (1967), 65–134.

[57] See, e.g., *The Trial of Feargus O'Connor and Fifty-Eight Others on a Charge of Sedition, Conspiracy, Tumult and Riot* (Manchester and London, 1843), vii. The case is also compellingly made in Hilton, *Age of Atonement*, p. 65.

[58] Martin Wiener, *Reconstructing the Criminal. Culture, Law, and Policy in England, 1830–1914* (Cambridge, 1990), 29.

[59] *Report from His Majesty's Commissioners for Inquiring into the Administration and Practical Operation of the Poor Laws, Parliamentary Papers*, xxvii (44), 36–55.

[60] David Eastwood, *Government and Community in the English Provinces 1700–1870* (1997), 123–70; David Eastwood, 'Rethinking the Debates on the Poor Law in Early Nineteenth-Century England', *Utilitas*, 6 (1994), 97–116.

Much, then, hung on dispersing these Malthusian fears. The High Tory Right countered Malthus by deploying what they took to be a Christian moral critique and by asserting an altogether more optimistic demographic model. Coleridge, Southey, Samuel Whitbread, and Sir Thomas Bernard of the Society for Better the Condition of the Poor were part of a chorus which insisted that Malthus's softly spoken attack on unrestrained fertility was both a blasphemy and an crude attempt to emancipate the rich from their social obligations. Meanwhile, from the libertarian left William Godwin in 1820 offered a defence of the superabundance of population which anticipated that offered by the Tory Radical Michael Thomas Sadler in 1830.[61] It was, however, the men at Somerset House and the Board of Trade who perhaps did most to confront, and in their terms confound, the Malthusian fear. G. R. Porter's *Progress of the Nation* offered a rigorous but popular presentation of the newly fashionable statistical case for continuing economic development and social improvement.[62] Statistical societies, which sprung up in numerous provincial centres from the 1830s, added a descant to the Board of Trade's statistical optimism.[63] Perhaps the most committed, or at any rate the most ultimately significant, anti-Malthusian was Edwin Chadwick. At first sight the social horrors conjured up in his *Report on the Sanitary Condition of the Labouring Poor* (1842) reflect and reinforce the kind of popular Malthusianism which we have encountered already. Not infrequently this has been implied by commentators who draw a line through Chadwick's barely restrained bureaucratic prose to Dickens's still more prosaic evocation of misery. Nevertheless, Chadwick proceeded from a profoundly anti-Malthusian premise, believing passionately in state rather than market solutions to Britain's social crisis. The avowed aim of his Sanitary Idea was to increase life expectancy and diminish what he called the 'annual slaughter' of thousands as a result of epidemic diseases.[64] In short, the

[61] William Godwin, *Of Population. An Enquiry Concerning the Power of Increase of the Numbers of Mankind* (1820); William Godwin, *Thoughts Occasioned by a Perusal of Dr Parr's Spital Sermon* ... [1801], in *Political and Philosophical Writings of William Godwin* ed. Mark Philp (7 vols., 1993), ii, 163–208; Michael Thomas Sadler, *The Law of Population* ... *In Disproof of the Superfercundity of Human Beings and Developing the Real Principle of their Increase* (2 vols., 1830); Perkin, *Origins of Modern English Society*, 137–52; Eastwood, 'Robert Southey and the Intellectual Origins of Romantic Conservatism'.

[62] G. R. Porter, *The Progress of the Nation* (3 vols., 1836–43); Lucy Brown, *The Board of Trade and the Free-Trade Movement 1830–42* (Oxford, 1958), 27–31, 76–93; Roger Prouty, *The Transformation of the Board of Trade* (1957), 3–10, 99.

[63] Michael J. Cullen, *The Statistical Movement in Early Victorian Britain. The Foundations of Empirical Social Science* (Hassocks, 1975); Thomas S. Ashton, *Economic and Social Investigations in Manchester, 1833–1933* (1934).

[64] *Sanitary Condition of the Labouring Population*, 251–4; R. A. Lewis, *Edwin Chadwick and the Public Health Movement 1832–1854* (1952), 17–18, 62–6; S. E. Finer, *The Life and Times of Edwin Chadwick* (1952), 22–3.

aim of policy was to remove what the Malthusians might have regarded as preventative checks on the population growth. What might be termed the mid-nineteenth-century official mind's assault on Malthusianism reach its apogee in the 1851 and 1861 Census Reports. The Introduction to the 1861 Census launched a sustained attack on the Malthusian principle of population, repudiating all apprehensions of rising population and concluding that 'there is nothing ... in the past or present conjugal condition of the population to inspire any apprehension of a redundancy ... of population in England; but a great deal to encourage a policy of further improvement in this condition ... so that the English race, growing better and greater, may increase in numbers at home, and continue to send out every year thousands of new families to the colonies'.[65] Put like this, the mid-Victorian consensus was ideologically as well as economically won.

The optimism of the 1850s is far removed, both ideologically and politically, from the profound uncertainties and deep anxieties of the 1830s. Carlyle, again, in 1839 captured something of the profound disorientation of the period.

> To whatever other griefs the lower classes labour under, this bitterest and sorest grief now superadds itself: the unendurable conviction that they are unfairly dealt with, that their lot in this world is not founded on right, not even on necessity and might, is neither what it should be, nor what it shall be ... Has not the French Revolution been? Since the year 1789, there is now half-a-century completed; and the French Revolution is still not complete! Whosoever will look at that enormous Phenomenon many find many meanings in it, but this meaning is the ground of all: That it was a revolt of the oppressed lower classes against the oppressing or neglecting upper classes: not a French revolt only; no, a European one ... These Chartisms, Radicalisms, Reform Bill, Tithe Bill, and infinite other discrepancy and acrid argument and jargon that there are yet to be, are *our* French Revolution: God grant that we, by our better methods, may be able to transact it by argument alone.[66]

We have seen something of the ideological contestation which Carlyle both despised and celebrated as 'discrepancy, and acrid argument and jargon'. This was, as Carlyle recognised, crucial to Britain's coming both to understand and govern her new condition. It has been traditional, at

[65] *Census of England and Wales* (1861), 'Report', *Parliamentary Papers*, 1863, liii, 24–7, quotation at 27.

[66] *Chartism*, 26–7, orig. italics. *cf.* 'Signs of Times', 116–18. Carlyle's *Chartism* was conceived whilst working on his *French Revolution*, and this conjunction is crucial to understanding both the language and sense of revolutionary imminence which infuse *Chartism*.

least amongst Tory historians, to focus on the means by which Britain avoided revolution. This is to miss the profundity of Carlyle's insight. The challenge for early-nineteenth-century Britain was not to avoid revolution, but rather to accommodate itself to revolutionary change by non-revolutionary means. In the event, although discourse was central, something more than argument was required.

Twice, within a decade, the massive forces conjured up by Carlyle's apocalyptic prose threatened to intervene decisively to force Britain into a different trajectory of development. The first reached its climax in the Reform crisis of 1830–32. The myth of the 1832 Reform Act is of a measured concession majestically made. It is the essential vindication of English Whiggism. Macaulay himself, recovering from the exertions of the Session and the 'Days of May' by reviewing Etienne Dumont's *Souvenirs sur Mirabeau*, offered a massively assured evaluation of the political meaning of the Reform crisis.

> If we look at the magnitude of the reform, it may well be called a revolution. If we look at the means by which it was effected, merely an Act of Parliament ... In the whole history of England, there is no prouder circumstance than this ... The work of three civil wars has been accomplished by three sessions of Parliament ... To what are we to attribute the unparalleled moderation and humanity which the English people had displayed at this great conjuncture? ... [to] the fruits of a hundred and fifty years of liberty.[67]

Within a decade, Macaulay's faith in English institutions was such that he could reject the Chartists' great 1842 Charter assuring the House that 'England [has] institutions which, although imperfect, yet contained within themselves the means of remedying every imperfection'.[68] This kind of Whiggism has both ideological and political meanings. The revolutionary imaginings of myriad Tories were dispelled, and the revolutionary hopes of Radicals dashed, by the genius of English Whiggism. The Reform of Parliament opened the way to sunlit uplands of liberty. But we would be well not to take either Whiggism or Whig interpretations of history at their own evaluation. If we look more carefully at means, if 1832 was a triumph, it was a triumph which was improvised rather than designed; and, as Roland Quinault has recently reminded us, improvised against the background of very considerable

[67] T. B. Macaulay, 'Mirabeau' [1832], reprinted in *The Miscellaneous Wirings and Speeches of Lord Macaulay* (1889), 275. See also John Clive, *Thomas Babington Macaulay. The Shaping of the Historian* (1973), 142–76.

[68] Macaulay, 'Mirabeau', 630. John Burrow, *A Liberal Descent. Victorian Historians and the English Past* (Cambridge, 1981), 11–93; Collini, Winch, and Burrow, *That Noble Science of Politics*, 91–126; Peter Ghosh, 'Macaulay and the Heritage of the Enlightenment', *EHR*, cxii (1997), 358–95.

domestic violence.[69] The gesture of Reform was emphatic, and perhaps it was gesture which mattered most. Nevertheless, the Whigs' progress through from the opportunities of November 1830 to the victory of June 1832 was anything but certain. They created a £10 borough franchise without any very clear sense of how many people it would enfranchise or even what the social balance of power in new constituencies would be. Inadvertently they created the basis of a sustained, locally organised adversarial political through the registration clauses of the Bill which were intended merely to cut the costs of contested returns. In short, Lord Grey and his colleagues were certain neither of the scale of the revolution they had wrought, nor sure of its enduring impact.[70]

Nor, of themselves, would the Whigs' constitutional concessions have purchased social peace and a new kind of political consensus. The 1832 Reform Act, after all, induced the most massive backlash in British history. Although it was not its sole cause, the Chartist movement would have been unthinkable without the bitter popular disillusionment attended both on the Reform Act of 1832 and the social legislation of the Reformed parliament.[71] 'It must be clear to every sane man,' the Chartist leader Feargus O'Connor wrote in 1842, 'that the Reform Bill was forced from the Tory party by the new-born influence of the master manufacturers; that with their own party in power they have for ten years gone on establishing the details by which their principle of reform was to be made most beneficial to their order. The Poor-law amendment act, the Corporation reform bill, the Rural police bill and, above all, the appointment of Whig magistrates, constituted those details ... a ten year experience by which ... they were merely completing the machinery by which their ascendency was to be insured'.[72] Chartism represented a formidable challenge to the two governing orthodoxies of post-war Britain. Its conceptual imagination placed it far beyond anything which reforming Whiggism could contemplate, still less com-

[69] Roland Quinault, 'The French Revolution of 1830 and Parliamentary Reform', *History*, 79 (1994), 377–93; *cf.* Carlos Flick, *The Birmingham Political Union and the Movements for Reform in Britain 1830–1839* (Folkestone, 1978), 54–92; Michael Brock, *The Great Reform Act* (1973), 161–313; John Cannon, *Parliamentary Reform, 1660–1832* (Cambridge, 1972), 204–41.

[70] Edward Baines, *The Life of Edward Baines* (London and Leeds, 1851), 157–61; Philip Salmon, 'Electoral Reform at Work. Local Politics and National Parties, 1832–1841', (University of Oxford D.Phil. thesis, 1997); Charles Seymour, *Electoral Reform in England and Wales. The Development and Operation of the Parliamentary Franchise 1832–1885* (new edn., Newton Abbot, 1971), 7–164; John Prest, *Politics in the Age of Cobden* (1977).

[71] In a large literature see esp. Dorothy Thompson, *The Chartists. Popular Politics in the Industrial Revolution* (1984); Paul Pickering, *Chartism and the Chartists in Manchester and Salford* (1995).

[72] *Trial of Feargus O'Connor*, vi.

prehend. Like the radicals of the 1790s, the Chartists took the language of parliamentary reform to its democratic apogee, using the terminology and techniques of parliamentary reform to try to transform a patrician parliament into a peoples' convention.[73] Hence the Whig leadership's unanimity in opposition to Chartist demands and their willingness to augment the police powers of the state to resist them. Chartism represented a equally formidable challenge to liberal Toryism. Whether in the hands of Lord Liverpool, F.J. Robinson, and William Huskisson in the 1820s or Robert Peel in the 1840s, liberal Toryism amounted to an attempt to confound both reformist Whiggism and extra-parliamentary radicalism through an ambitious exercise in political managerialism. The not-so-veiled object of liberal Toryism was to prevent or postpone the need for constitutional reform. Its high point was 1823–5 when Liverpool, Peel, Robinson, and Huskisson seemed to offer prosperity, tariff reform, penal reform, and a thorough-going liberalisation of public policy.[74] The Chartist critique of police, the new poor law, the current fiscal mix, and the Union with Ireland raised a agenda which lay far beyond the ameliorating reach of liberal Tory reformism.

Moreover, a key precondition of liberal Toryism—economic dynamism—was cruelly absent after 1837. The depression of 1837–43 was, on most measurements, the deepest and most unrelieved of the nineteenth century.[75] Mass unemployment, exceeding 50% in many northern and Scottish manufacturing centres, revived in acute form anxieties at the insurrectionary potential of an urbanised society, dependent on something close to full employment for social tranquillity. Moreover some began to believe that the age of manufactures, the precondition of Britain's ability to sustain mass urban populations, might have run its course. As much of Britain's industry stood idle in February 1839, Lord Brougham offered the Lords a celebratory retrospect of the period since 1774 when Britain had become 'one large, wealthy, industrious,

[73] Gareth Stedman Jones, *Languages of Class. Studies in English Working Class History 1832–1982* (Cambridge, 1983), 90–178; James Epstein, *Radical Expression. Political Language, Ritual, and Symbol in England 1790–1850* (Oxford, 1994); Miles Taylor, *The Decline of British Radicalism 1847–1860* (Oxford, 1995), esp. 19–123; Margot Finn, *After Chartism. Class and Nation in English Radical Politics, 1848–1974* (Cambridge, 1993).

[74] Hilton, *Corn, Cash, Commerce*, 171–302; Boyd Hilton, 'The Ripening of Robert Peel' in *Public and Private Doctrine: Essays in British History Presented to Maurice Cowling* ed. M. Bentley (Cambridge, 1993), 63–84; Barry Gordon, *Economic Doctrine and Tory Liberalism 1824–1830* (1979); W.R. Brock, *Lord Liverpool and Liberal Toryism 1820 to 1827* (2nd edn., 1967); Norman Gash, *Lord Liverpool* (1984), 171–91, 217–30.

[75] R. C. O. Matthews, *A Study in Trade-Cycle History. Economic Fluctuations in Great Britain, 1833–1842* (Cambridge, 1954), 164, *cf.* 142–7, 219–20; A.D. Gayer, W.W. Rostow, and A.J. Schwartz, *The Growth and Fluctuation of the British Economy, 1790-1850* (2 vols., Oxford, 1953), i, 276–303; G. Kitson Clark, 'Hunger and Politics in 1842', *Jnl. Modern History*, xxv (1953), 355–74.

expert and skilful workshop'. Whilst offering a prayer that the associated prosperity might not cease, he did strikingly conclude that 'These *were* the miracles of manufacturing industry. This *was* the age of manufactures.'[76]

The anxiety that the recession from 1837 might represent not a cyclical downturn but a structural crisis for Britain's manufacturing revolution was crucial to Peel's strategy on resuming office in 1841. Peel brings together the strands of the contestation which had dominated early-nineteenth-century Britain: the fear of revolution, the ambiguity of responses to economic modernisation, the urgent necessity to renegotiate the boundary between state and society, and the necessity of making policy within a unionist rather than a British framework. Seeing Peel as critical to the resolution of the crisis of early-Victorian Britain is hardly novel, but identifying the critical date as 1842 rather than 1846 is. Faced with an economy mired in recession, a collapse of demand, searing poverty, and a resurgence of Chartist activity which was taking Britain to the verge of revolution, Peel responded with the most audacious budget of the nineteenth century. He introduced a peacetime income tax for the first time, ensured that it tapped new manufacturing wealth effectively by revising the schedules, and demonstrated to the Chartists that their passionate opposition to unconstitutional (i.e. indirect) taxation had been heard and understood. More daringly he used the income tax not to balance the budget, in accordance with fiscal orthodoxy, but to fund a massive remission of indirect taxation. This was a grand exercise in fiscal reflation. Moreover, in using an income tax to fund tariff reform it was strikingly progressive in its fiscal stance.[77] As a strategy for reflating the economy, Peel's ambitious exercise in fiscal reflation was strikingly successful, and laid the foundations for the mid-Victorian boom.

Nevertheless its purpose and meaning went far beyond that. It represented a crucial ideological shift. This was the moment when the debate on the nature of British society moved towards closure. In the abstract, as a debate about the moral meaning and social consequences of urban capitalism, the 'condition of England debate' was a debate without an end. It took contemporaries to the core of capitalism's moral

[76] Hansard, 3rd ser., xlv, 543, my ital.; see also William Hardy, 'Conceptions of Manufacturing Advance in British Politics *c.*1800–1847, with special reference to Parliament, Governments and their Advisers' (Univ. of Oxford, D.Phil. thesis, 1994), 279–95.

[77] Hansard, 3rd ser., lxi (1842), 422–66; Sir Stafford Northcote, *Twenty Years of Financial Policy* (1862), 1–58; Sydney Buxton, *Finance and Politics. An Historical Study 1783-1885* (2 vols., 1888), i, 43–63; David Eastwood, '"Recasting Our Lot": Peel, the Nation, and the Politics of Interest', in *A Union of Multiple Identities. The British Isles, c.1750–c.1850* (Manchester, 1997), 29–44, esp. 32–5. For a different and important reading see Hilton, 'Peel: A Reappraisal'.

meaning and material tendencies. Although this debate, as a debate, would continue, through different languages and new ideological formations, in the decades after 1850, the Peelite decade did politically confirm Britain's future as an urban, manufacturing nation. It did so in typically restrained terms, and it did so for pragmatic rather than principled reasons.

> Something effectual must be done to revive the languishing commerce and manufacturing industry of this country. Look at the congregation of manufacturing masses, the amount of our debt, the rapid increase of poor rates within the last four years, which will soon, by means of rates in aid, extend from the ruined manufacturing districts to the rural ones, and then judge whether we can safely retrograde in manufacturers. If you had to constitute new societies, you might on moral and social grounds prefer cornfields to cotton factories, an agricultural to a manufacturing population. But our lot is cast, and we cannot recede.[78]

The uncertainties of early-nineteenth-century Britain were, ultimately, the consequences a profound struggle to understand the public and private meanings of the transformation which British society was experiencing, coupled with a sense that somehow Britain's future as an urban, manufacturing society was negotiable. This reluctant embracing of an urban, capitalist, destiny was the moment when the anxieties which had dominated early-nineteenth-century Britain began to give way to a moment of confidence. The Chartists, like many of Peel's High Tory opponents, harboured a nostalgia for a pre-industrial, rural past, and flirted with the idea that public policy might be re-engineered as an instrument to recover that past. Peelism, which of course gave new meaning to Whig constitutional reformism, foreclosed all such restrospectives. If there was an Age of Improvement in the nineteenth century, it began here.[79]

[78] Peel to Croker, 3 Aug. 1841, pr. in *Sir Robert Peel from his Private Papers* ed. C. S. Parker (3 vols., 1899), ii, 529.

[79] See also Hilton, *Age of Atonemnet*, pp. 255–97.

THE WIDOW'S MITE AND OTHER STRATEGIES: FUNDING THE CATHOLIC REFORMATION

THE PROTHERO LECTURE

By Olwen Hufton

READ 2 JULY 1997

IT is perhaps more usual for the giver of the Prothero lecture to choose a subject which has been a part of his intellectual baggage for a long time. In contrast, what I am about to offer falls more honestly into the category of work in progress. I am presently at a very preliminary stage in a project that may both take me a long time and lead me up many alleyways. I am concerned to understand how the Catholic Reform of the sixteenth and seventeenth centuries was funded.[1] In the term 'Catholic Reform' are included charitable and educative initiatives, the funding of missions, the conversion of the heathen, the expansion of religious orders, the provision of books and images (*biblia pauperum*) to improve and elevate the minds of the simple into mysteries they could not otherwise conceptualise, and the erection and furnishing of new churches. I would argue that taken as a package this funding process, about which I will be presently more specific, represents one of the largest private money-raising processes ever undertaken. It has, perhaps, a particular interest today when attempts are being made to reinvigorate the spirit of private philanthropy and to dismantle or cause to wither away public commitment to assistance or subsidy.

In contrast to our own times, sixteenth-century notions of social responsibility were primed in large part by religious belief in the obligations of the Christian. But if faith was beyond doubt, putting money where the mouth or even the heart is should not be presumed

[1] This project is my central concern during the period of a Leverhulme Personal Research Professorship and I am deeply indebted to the Leverhulme Trust. Although much has been written about charitable and educational initiatives there is no systematic study which looks across their funding as a whole. Works such as L. Châtellier, *The Europe of the Devout: the Catholic Reform and the Formations of New Society*, trans. J. Birrell (Cambridge, 1989) and *idem.*, *The Religion of the Poor* (Cambridge, 1996); J. Delumeau, *Catholicism between Luther and Voltaire* (Cambridge, 1977) and *idem.*, *Sin and Fear: the Emergence of a Western Guilt Culture 13–18th Centuries*, trans E. Nicholson (New York, 1990) are critical to an understanding of the general background. B. Pullan, *Rich and Poor in Renaissance Venice: The Social Institutions of a Catholic State to 1620* (Oxford, 1971) remains inspirational. My thanks are due also to Christopher Black, Gabriella Zarri and the Pentofilo group in Florence for the many ideas on themes integral to the project that they have helped to generate.

to have flowed automatically and the process of channelling money towards a recognised worthy cause could be fraught with problems. Questions such as where did the money come from or what were the motives of donors, though critical to the narrative, are not the only ones.[2] Equally important are those relating to the influences, subtle or otherwise, which determined the focus of the donation and allow some appreciation of why one gave to this rather than that. After all, at least *prima facie*, there is no hierarchy of worthiness of good causes. It is as blessed in the purely abstract sense to lift the minds of poor orphan girls with a didactic print as to put bread in their hands. (In fact, hierarchies of worthiness did establish themselves—it was always harder to raise funds for penitent prostitutes, syphilis hospitals and foundlings than dowry funds for young girls or for schools.) Something of the shifts of priorities that established themselves can perhaps be attributed to an evolution in the debates as to what private charity should be about and the respective relationship of donor to recipient. However, this theoretical approach is not my concern here. Rather I intend to pursue in this essay the development of techniques of persuasion and the use of these techniques by a religious order, the Jesuits, roughly between 1550 and 1650.[3] I do not intend to suggest that the members of the Society of Jesus invented or were unique practitioners of these techniques and would insist that they were in many instances the legatees of modes of procedure. But the early Jesuits were men of incredible energy and initiative and were dedicated with a burning passion not only to the rechristianisation, as they saw it, of Europe but to the conversion of a wider world encompassing South America, Canada and parts of Asia. From a modest group of young zealots honed in the theological disputes and scholastic training of the University of Paris, inured to personal discomforts and physical deprivations of all kinds and committed to a total rejection of worldly goods for themselves, they were to become deeply embattled in the tangled politics of mid-

[2] On these motives excellent recent works include S. Cavallo, *Charity and Power in Early Modern Italy* (Cambridge, 1995); S. K. Cohn, *Death and Property in Siena 1205–1800. Strategies for the After Life* (Baltimore, 1988); G. Politi, M. Rosa, F. della Peruta, eds., *Timore e carità. I poveri nell Italia moderna* (Cremona, 1982); M. Vovelle, *Piété baroque et déchristianisation en Provence au XVIIIe siècle* (Paris, 1973); P. Chaunu, *La Mort à Paris 16e 17e 18e siècles* (Paris, 1978), p. 365 *passim.*

[3] There is a huge bibliography on the work of the early Jesuits which can be broached through the recent study of J. W. O'Malley, S.J., *The First Jesuits* (Cambridge, MA, 1993); J. Lacouture, *Jesuits: a Multibiography* (English trans. London, 1996) is evocative rather than deep. The older nationally specific studies of P. Tacchi Venturi, *Storia della Compagnia di Gesù in Italia*, 3 vols. (Rome 1961), A. Astráin, *Historia de la Compañia de Jesus en la Asistencia de Espana*, 2 vols. (Madrid, 1902–5), F. Rodriguez, *Historia da Companhia de Jesus na Asisténcia de Portugal*, 2 vols. (Oporto, 1931) include many documents and were important to this essay.

sixteenth-century Rome and to develop into an international enterprise of considerable professionalism, a development which could not have occurred without the raising of substantial economic resources.[4]

Wealth was not a central concern of Ignatius's young men in the early days when with their hand to mouth existence, rough robes and sparse food they begged in the streets of Venice hoping to cadge a passage to the Holy Land. Once, however, they had involved themselves in a social programme transcending simple pilgrimage or service to the sick in hospitals and had discovered that the piazza as a space for a sermon was not acceptable to even the middle strata of society, let alone the elites they hoped to reach, they soon identified the limits of personal denial. For example, instructed not to ask for anything in the Spanish parishes where some of the first missions were made and to carry their bread with them so that they asked nothing of their hosts, they quickly discovered that labourers could not take time off from the fields to hear them because of loss of wages.[5] Ships' passages had to be financed: buildings were needed as shelters and hospices for pilgrims or ex-prostitutes dedicated to penitence.[6] Most of all, the acquisition of buildings and running costs for the educational programme integral to the Jesuit plan to raise a new and formidably orthodox generation of Catholics was not cheap. Fr. John O'Malley's recent work properly emphasises how the commitment to founding colleges caused a fundamental division of the Jesuit ministry into two parts. Citing Polanco, Ignatius's right-hand man, O'Malley shows how the educational obligation had a separate and deeply significant identity within the Jesuit mission:

> Generally speaking, there are (in the Society) two ways of helping our neighbours: one in the colleges through the education of youth in letters, learning and the Christian life and the second in every place to help every kind of person through sermons, confessions and other means that accord with our customary way of proceeding.[7]

[4] G. Schurhammer, S.J., *Francis Xavier. His Life, His Times*, vol. 1, *Europe 1506–1541* (Rome, 1973), permits a graphic perception of this development and in particular of the intense physical deprivation practised by the early fathers.

[5] M. L. Copète, *Les Jésuites et la prison royale à Seville: Missions d'évangelisation et mouvement confraternel en Andalousie à la fin du XVIe siècle* (doctoral thesis, European University Institute, Florence, 1994), 76–133.

[6] Jesuit initiatives aimed at persuading high-born women like Vittoria Colonna to donate and endow such shelters are treated in P. Tacchi Venturi, *Storia della Compagnia di Gesu*, 2, 2, 168, 178–91 and S. Cohen, 'Asylums for Women in Counter-Reformation Italy' in S. Marshall ed., *Women in Reformation and Counter Reformation Europe. Private and Public Worlds* (Bloomington, 1989).

[7] Cited by O'Malley, *The First Jesuits*, 200. A full bibliography on the principles behind Jesuit education is given at page 418 footnote 1.

Yet this commitment to education was to entail a radical reordering of attitudes to property and fund-raising strategies within the order. By 1560 the Jesuits were opening schools, demanding buildings, books and food for the pupils and teachers at the rate of four to five a year. As early as 1540 a discussion was afoot on how the existence of the colleges demanded an overturning of the Society's attitudes to property. The group resolved its dilemma by allowing such colleges, unlike the other houses that sheltered the brethren and which were to be sustained by alms, to be endowed.[8] This endowment would, it was hoped (though this did not prove to be the invariable case) result in a fixed annual income sufficient to cover the needs of both teacher and students. The earliest foundations of the 1540s were situated near universities so that mature students who would be future Jesuits could live in the colleges while they studied; such colleges were more dormitories than schools. In these early days (1540–4) seven colleges emerged near the universities of Paris, Louvain, Cologne, Padua, Alcala, Valencia and Coimbra, of which only the last obtained any early financial stability through the patronage and gifts of John III of Portugal, and the Jesuits generally faced great difficulties in finding benefactors since they were largely unknown and unskilled in presenting their case. Skill was something which was acquired more gradually. If the means to pay for the colleges and open them up massively to young boys were to be found, then techniques of persuasion had to be developed and directed at potential donors. Some of these techniques look surprisingly modern.

As the modern state seeks to reduce its commitment to welfare and higher education and the claims of the Third World to assistance are advanced, it has become impossible to live in western society and be free from pressure to contribute to a multiplicity of good causes: begging letters, telephone calls, posters, covenants, titles (friends of this and that), the careful construction of a sociability of giving by ceremonies and events and initiatives designed to bond a donor to a particular cause by regular information about the success of the enterprise and how the money is being spent. To stress success is of the essence—no donor wants to give to a failing enterprise.[9] The potential donor must be pursued and simultaneously sensitised to what he or she can contribute to the extension or even further transformation of the enterprise. Professional fund-raising agencies know how to give a range of large and small donors a sense of participation by fragmenting a

[8] This development did not occur without substantial debate. L. Lukács, 'De origine collegiorum externorum deque contraversiis circa eorum pauperitatem obortis', *Archivum Historicum Societatis Iesu* 29 (1960), 189–245: 30 (1961), 1–89.

[9] At Harvard I was told by the Dean of Harvard College in 1990 that one must never, when one hopes for donations, talk of either difficulties or failures but always of how success could be widened with more funds.

large scheme into carefully personalised segments: a vaccination project can be offered in numbers of children assisted by a specific sum: a college library renewal project can be presented in terms of the cost of restoring a single book. Painless giving which does not affect the pocket, such as holding a credit card whose service charge is paid to the charity, is another way to touch a donor pool. A donor list of those who have given and can be persuaded to give again is important.

Above all, a specialised knowledge of donor psychology is in our times the *sine qua non* of the successful art of money-raising. This knowledge allows the targeting of particular types of individual. One appreciation is of the commemorative instinct, the search for immortality among the wealthy and successful, which lies behind the use by the development offices of modern educational and medical institutions of the 'naming opportunity', whereby a gift, say one in excess of a hundred thousand pounds, puts the donor's name on a building. Sixteenth-century donors were drawn to a cause on which they could write their name or which commemorated them. Alessandro Farnese's name leaps out of front of the Gesù in Rome: Scipione Borghese managed to get his name five times on the front of St Crisogono in Trastevere. The naming opportunity of course leads to the presence of a building which is essential to launching an enterprise: it is less easy for either the twentieth-century or sixteenth-century fundraiser to raise money for running costs in which the donor's name is lost. Many Jesuit colleges were abandoned because money to support teachers and pupils did not follow the gift of a house.[10]

Another window of opportunity in present times is the widow in command of her late husband's assets with a desire to commemorate him. Widows will appear later in this essay. They are fundamental figures in the history of fundraising from its very inception.[11]

Before considering Jesuit strategies let us consider the funds potentially open to solliciation for philanthropic or educative ends in the early sixteenth century. In his *De subventione pauperum* (Bruges 1526) Juan Luis Vivès gave a rather incomplete resumé of potential funds which could be channelled to help the poor: first, gifts from prelates out of the wealth of their benefices: second, poor boxes in churches: third, the labour of the poor: fourth, testaments and donations: fifth, the temporary loans of the rich through monte di pietá (pioneered by the friars): sixth, divine mercy—the biblical text of manna from heaven:

[10] O'Malley, *The First Jesuits*, 200, and H. Rahner SJ, *Saint Ignatius Loyola. Letters to Women* (London, 1956), 224–6 give several instances.

[11] J. Goody, *The Development of the Family and Marriage in Europe* (Cambridge, 1983) and J. Bremmer, 'Pauper or Patroness: the Widow in the Early Christian Church' in J. Bremmer, ed., *Between Poverty and the Pyre* (London, 1995), 31–57.

seventh, better book-keeping by existing hospitals and institutions.[12] There is a great deal missing from this list, such as the granting of privileges by rulers like the profits of justice[13] or the capacity to impose a random tax on Jews or other wealthy but weak social groups.[14] Investments of accumulated funds are not mentioned. Sixteenth-century fund-raisers needed to believe in the category 'manna from heaven', the miracle that would permit God's work to go forward, which was of psychological worth helping the fund-raiser to persist in difficult times. Obviously, to anyone who ever engaged himself with the issue, neither the church poor box nor the industry of the poor could be relied on to make much, but they are of consequence in the first instance in bringing the capacity to give down the social scale, and in the second in assuring the rich that the honest poor are themselves striving for their own sustenance.

The most substantial sources were testaments and donations and, if we set aside prelates as a very specific category, we must recognise that this brought fund-raisers slap bang up against the institution of the family and the capacity of different family members to give. In this giving process men and women were not equal: *prima facie*, men had much more to give. But the position of women at certain times of their lives gave them a capacity for giving and a relationship to exploitable wealth which was 'interesting' to those concerned to raise money, and which will be pursued here as an entrée into fund-raising strategies.

A married woman from the patriciates and aristocracies was attached to wealth in certain ways. The dowry (escalating in Italy from the 16th century and elsewhere from the 17th) was, according to the family, a sum of money equal to up to 20 per cent of its total assets, and was given to the husband or his family for management. It was a statement of the standing of the bride's family: spousal networks were restricted and indeed in Italy often branches of the same family simply circulated a pool of wealth.[15] However, the capital must be invested to provide

[12] M.J.L. Bataillon, 'Jean Luis Vivès, réformateur de la bienfaisance', *Bibliothèque d'Humanisme et Renaissance*, XIV (1952), 141–58 and, more briefly, L. Marz, *Poverty and Welfare in Habsburg Spain* (Cambridge, 1983), 8–9.

[13] Given for example by Philip II to the Carmelites to aid their expansion in the Low Countries. C. Torres Sanchez, *Conventualismo femmenino y expansion contrarreformista en el siglo XVII. El Carmel Descalzo español en Francia y Flandes (1600–1650)*. (Doctoral thesis, EUI, Florence, 1997), 191–4.

[14] Many such ploys were adopted in Italy. A fifth of the testamentary wealth of courtesans went to subvent the establishments for the retrieval of fallen women or girls at risk in Rome. In Florence licenses for prostitutes also funded, in part, houses of retrieval.

[15] For a brief exposé of such dotal practises, see G. Delille, 'Strategie di alleanza e demografia del matrimonio' in M. di Giorgio and C. Klapisch Zuber, eds., *Storia del matrimonio* (Rome/Bari, 1996) 283–303, and 'Consanguinité proche en Italie du XVI au

interest (usufruct) to be used by the husband for the wife's maintenance, giving her also a share for her own disposition (it might be something like 2 per cent of the capital) normally to be used for clothes and entertaining. In her husband's lifetime she could not touch the capital sum but might use her usufruct to contribute to things like the furnishing of a church, the painting of an altarpiece or as a contribution to a designated initiative, perhaps to help the poor. A wife could also own, if not manage, sources of extra dotal property, such as gifts or bequests made to her by relatives, usually on their death, by testament. Some of these bequests might come from female relatives (such as childless aunts) or secular clerical relatives. A wife had some control over these assets and certainly enjoyed the income on them. Somewhat differently, a wife might also use her powers of mediation to sway her husband to part with money or property. The rituals of court life often involved complex procedures of soliciting favours, in which the solicitor began with persuading ladies in waiting to present a case to the princess or duchess who might in turn approach the head of the house himself. Such favours could be gifts or offices for a member of the family of the initial solicitor, but also a house which could be used for a charitable purpose, a money raising privilege or simply straight cash.[16]

No less a person than Thomas Aquinas in the *Summa Theologica*, when giving consideration as to whether 'alms can be given by a person who is subject to another's power', declared that 'if besides the dowry, a wife possesses other goods to sustain the burden of marriage, earned by herself or obtained in some other licit fashion, she may donate them, even without the permission of her husband: moderately however, in order not to impoverish the husband through excess'. She may not make any other offerings without the permission, expressed or presumed, of her husband, beyond those cases of necessity. Moreover, although the wife is equal to her husband as far as the act of matrimony is concerned, regarding the household economy, 'the man is the head of the woman', as the Apostle states. So, not only has she no access to her husband's goods and her own dowry, in this view she has restricted access to her own extra dotal property.[17] The situation is changed when her husband dies, unless she is still young, in which case her family

XIX siècle' in P. Bonte, ed., *Epouser au plus proche. Inceste, prohibitions et stratégies matrimoniales autour de la Méditerranée* (Paris, 1994).

[16] R. Ago, *Carriere e clientele nella Roma barocca* (Rome/Bari 1990) pursues the operations of the Spada family at the Vatican court. W. Reinhardt, 'Der Papstliche Hof um 1600' in *Europaïsche Hofkultur zur Barockforschung* (Hamburg, 1981).

[17] T. D'Aquino, *La somma teologica* (Firenze 1966), vol. 14, 257–61, text commented on by R. Sarti (University of Florence) in an unpublished paper, 'Alms requested, alms denied', Pentofilo group, Florence, 1996. Dr Sarti has a projected work on the capacity of women to give in a *pater familias* system.

can claim her and her dowry back and renegotiate her in marriage. Her state is then a replica of her former condition. If, however, she is older and getting to the end of her child-bearing years, one of two things could happen: first, she could claim her dowry and leave her husband's house or, if there were children, she might stay as their appointed guardian and her money remain invested as it was. If in her husband's will she was left guardian of the children and administrator of the property, she gained access to the family funds as a whole.

Statute law varied in laying down what should happen to a wife or widow's money on her death. In Florence statute law gave a mothers's inheritance to sons, and, in default of sons prioritised the male line from the family of origin over her daughters. In other parts of Italy daughters could expect a share of their mother's property.[18] But a woman could override statute law by a will leaving her money to the people of her choice either within or without her family—frequently to daughters or nieces if she had no children. There was also scope through the appropriate testamentary donation for even a married woman whose husband and children were alive at the hour of her death to make a substantial contribution to the spiritual or philanthropic institution of her choice.[19]

The childless older widow was a person of some concern to her family and became progressively more so in the late 16th and 17th centuries as the amount of wealth to which she had access on her husband's death mounted. She was clearly someone of known wealth, worth targeting by those anxious to fund good works. Moreover, with time on her hands, she herself could be drawn into initiatives on which she was prepared to spend money, as in the case of Ginevra Gozzadini dall'Armi whose story is recounted below.[20]

It is possible from his correspondence and from the biography written by Ribadaneira (1583) to construct an idea of how Ignatius approached raising money for 'the two ministries' and how his notions of where to find assistance evolved.[21] Initially, he thought no further than immediate

[18] I. Chabod, *La dette des familles. Femmes, lignages et patrimoine à Florence aux XIVe et XVe siècles* (doctoral thesis, EUI, 1995), summarily reproduced in I. Chabod, 'Risorsi e diritti patrimoniale' in A. Groppi, ed., *Il lavoro delle donne* (Rome/Bari 1996), 60–70; S. Chojnacki, 'Dowries and Kinsmen in Early Renaissance Venice' in S. M. Stuard, ed. *Women in Medieval Society* (Philadelphia, 1976), 173–98.

[19] L. Ferranti, M. Palazzi and G. Pomata, *Ragnatele di rapporti. Patronage e reti di relazioni nella storia delle donne* (Turin, 1988) particularly part 1., 'Patronesse e patroni nei rapporti di carita'.

[20] G. Zarri, 'Ginevra, Gozzadini dall'Armi, gentildonna bolognese (1520–27–1567), in O. Niccoli, ed., *Rinascimento al femminile* (Roma/Bari, 1991), 117–42.

[21] Much of what follows is documented in H. Rahner S.J., *Saint Ignatius Loyola, Letters*; and Pedro de Ribadeneyra, *Vida de Ignacio di Loyola* (Madrid, 1967), and Tacchi Venturi, *Storia della Compagnia di Gesù*, 3 vols., 2.2.

needs, in first instance his own education and later than of his companions in Paris, which involved fees and enough in the way of food and shelter to give them time to study; or, when on the road, the begging of food to sustain them on the journey. But these simple requirements had to be quickly expanded as colleges, churches and missionary activity demanded ever increasing resources. In his correspondence relating to the early days what is striking is the preparedness of women to help him financially. Soon after his 'conversion' in 1522, as a pilgrim at Montserrat, he begged money from Inès Pascual a noble woman also visiting the shrine. After some discussion in which the woman questioned Loyola on why he was begging, she became a fervent supporter financing his studies in Barcelona where he learned Latin. Inès Pascual writes in 1533 of a cartel of six women, including herself and her mother, who financed his further studies in Paris:

> My mother, to the best of her ability, gave him everything necessary for the journey and the above mentioned ladies did likewise. During the time of his studies in Paris, there was with him father Ramon Pascual OP ... Him I call to witness that during the 4 or 5 years of his stay in Paris my mother sent him annually bills for 100 ducats for books and for his board and lodging. As, however, he was very charitable, he used it all for the poor. To my mother and me he often wrote with great affection and gratitude and said that God had given her to him, like that other widow who supported Elias, so that he might spend his life in poverty without the help of kinsfolk or revenues ...[22]

This biblical reference to the widow helping the prophet was often used in letters to women, as was that of the financing of Christ's disciples by women in the New Testament. Loyola's begging letters were constructed according to a formula. Two letters were sent sequentially. The first contained news, thanks for any help received and personal enquiries about the spiritual well being of the woman in question. The second followed after a well calculated interval and contained requests for money for specific targets. He sent several such letters out at the same time to different people and the personalised begging letter must be considered the first plank of his fundraising strategy. During his Paris studies he went to both Flanders and London to beg from rich Spanish merchants. In order to cover his needs in 1533 when he had passed his licentiate in philosophy he had the right, after a further examination and an inaugural lecture, to be called 'master' provided he could provide a gold piece. He not only wrote to Inès Pascual but to Dona Eleonor Zapila and Isabel Roser.

[22] Rahner, *Saint Ignatius Loyola, Letters*, 179.

Indeed, Hugh Rahner speaks of 'an elaborately planned campaign for money'.[23]

But from the very beginning, if he asked for money he was quick to thank those who contributed it. In a letter to Simon Rodriguez in Portugal in 1542 he developed what Rahner refers to as 'a theology of gratitude', one which his biographer, Ribadaneira, described in the following way:

> Among all the virtues that our father possessed was one by which he was especially distinguished: the virtue of gratitude. In that he was simply wonderful. It was of the utmost importance to him that he should as far as possible equal in generosity and even surpass his pious admirers and the benefactors of the Society. He kept them informed of its progress, he sent them invitations, he visited them, he helped them in whatever way he could; he even undertook for them special commissions which were quite against his inclination, merely in order to please them.[24]

What Ribadaneira sought to explain was the development in Loyola as the years passed, of a very deep conviction that he was making available to wealthy people an unprecedented opportunity. As the Society grew and its successes outnumbered its setbacks, he sought by carefully articulated strategies to bind his supporter-donors to the Society so that they 'shared in' its triumphs. Integral to this process was information, the letter writing that consumed a great deal of the days of both Ignatius and Polanco. It was in due course, at least in part, the belief that the account of the work done would make people want to participate in it and would prompt giving that led to the evolution of the Jesuit *Relations*.[25] These were letters written from the front—what we are doing to rescue the heathen (they are important sources for the early history of Cananda and Latin America and Goa)—which were at first copied—a very time consuming business—and later published to reach a wider audience. They were also initially in Latin but passed very quickly into the vernacular because this widened the audience. In these *Relations* reference was made to need and how to

[23] *Ibid.*, 182.

[24] *Ibid.*, 170, and Ribadaneira, *Dicta et Facta*, no. 75: also *Epistolae et Instructiones S. Ignatii*, 12 vols. (Madrid, 1903–11), 1.192.

[25] From the very beginning the Jesuits were magnificent letter-writers and letters intended to inform the scattered fathers on developments were copied many times. O'Malley argues this practice to be critical in the formation of Jesuit identity (*The First Jesuits*, 63–4). Polanco wrote a circular letter which was much copied two or three times a year. The original *Relations* were reports from missions. The Canadian ones were largely compiled by the Jesuit superior in Quebec and sent to the provincial of the Order in Paris from 1611. In 1632 they were published so as to publicise the missions. *The Jesuit Relations*, ed. and trans. R. Goldthwaite, 73 vols. (Cleveland, 1896–1901).

advance the cause; and the needs expressed were both great and small, from prints of the Holy Family so that the heathen could know what a Holy Family was, to new serge tunics for the embattled brethren in the Canadian snow. The *Relations* engage the imagination in the information that they offer of the exotic, the other. They are about endeavour: the donor, his imagination fired, can feel he is backing a winning, if struggling, enterprise. Although the *Relations* were not developed until after Ignatius's death, they do represent a distillation of the view of the founder that he was offering the donor an opportunity to participate in a divine mission and to be the executor of God's will, if at one remove. The multi-purpose *Relations* are an important and original development of the science of fundraising.[26]

Equally critical, however, to the overall plan was the recognition of the donor in such a way as to commemorate his or her generosity. It is possible to discern a number of techniques which far outstrip the simple thank you letter, such as certificates or letters patent in notarial form to confer the status of special donor: titles, including that of 'Mother of the Church' bestowed on certain women and coveted by many more, and special ceremonies commemorating the founder of a college which were performed as an annual ritual endowed with abundant symbolism. Loyola gave much consideration to how college donors could be appropriately hallowed. In the final text of the Constitutions (1555) for the colleges it is expressly stated:

> It is a genuine obligation for us to respond, as far as in us lies, to the pious reverence and benificence of those whom the Divine goodness uses as instruments for the foundation and endowment of colleges of our society.[27]

He then gives regulations to govern the annual ceremony of presenting a blessed candle to the founder or foundress which must respect the following conditions; first, the candle must bear the arms of the founder's family; second, after his/her death, it must be given to the next of kin (note the respect for memory but with the added value of linking a dead donor with a living powerful figure) third, if the founder lives far away, the candle must be sent to him and fourth, this candle must always burn at the requiem of the dead benefactor. All this made the founder integral to the annual rituals of the college and the blessed candle can be interpreted as an important expression of the 'theology of gratitude'.

Involved in the ceremonies surrounding the colleges and other pious

[26] Their secular modern equivalent might be *Oxford Today* or the highly professional *Universe* produced by University College, London.

[27] Rahner, *Saint Ignatius Loyola, Letters*, 172.

foundations which the Jesuits fostered, but whose financing was not in their management, was a form of elite sociability. Aristocratic women were encouraged to sit on boards and direct and raise money for the keep of penitent prostitutes and girls at risk and so on. The prowess of the college children was put on show in regular performances (doubtless with proud kinsfolk in the audience) so that the benefits of a Jesuit education could be made manifest.[28]

As some of the initial Jesuit foundations disintegrated through insufficient funds and small numbers of recruits in the early years, Ignatius learned the hard way that certain strategies were needful to avoid the loss of face implicit in failure. In particular he became convinced that if courts were uncomfortable places for men who had eschewed worldly pomp and who were committed to minimal comforts for themselves, notwithstanding, Jesuits had from time to time to be courtiers and adopt courtly manners and stratagems. He placed great hope in dukes and princes because he recognised that the more support he had from above, the more acceptable and attractive Jesuit institutions of all kinds would be to the aristocracy. Not only would aristocrats be led into emulation but they would send their sons to a school patronised by the ruler. His stamp upon a Jesuit college was therefore highly desirable and in default of the ruler, that of the ruler's wife or a high court lady. Since the purses of kings, dukes and princes were under constant pressure of solicitation for largesse of one kind or another from many sources, the mediatory techniques of a royal or aristocratic wife could be critical.

Who provided the money behind the building of the numerous colleges of Spain, Portugal and Italy has yet to be systematically analysed. However, for all these countries there are well-documented instances of important establishments made possible by the involvement and generosity of royal personages such as Juana of Spain at Valladolid, or Dona Leonor Mascareñhas, given the title of 'Mother of the Society of Jesus', of whom a contemporary biographer said:

> She did all in her power to assist Ignatius in the founding of the Society of Jesus. She was heartily devoted to him and gave him alms all her life; she helped the Jesuits in their first beginnings, when difficulties were to be expected, and gave them the house in which this College of Madrid was first opened.[29]

[28] Tacchi Venturi, *La Storia della Compagnia di Gesù*, 2, 2, 431–2, describes how the sons of Cosimo de Medici and Eleanor of Toledo were vastly impressed by one such performance in 1553 and he notes that 'I dialoghi degli fancuilli fiorentini' could pull in crowds of 3,000–4,000 at a time, so that the Church of San Giovannino was too small and the Duomo had to be used.

[29] Rahner, *Saint Ignatius Loyola, Letters*, 417. The original is printed more fully in J.

Even more than this, however, as a celibate lady-in-waiting to King Manuel of Portugal's consort, Maria, and of the same age as the Portuguese Infanta, Isabel, she accompanied the latter to Madrid when she married Charles V in 1526. As governess to their children, Dona Leonor Mascareñas had a particular influence over their daughter Maria. Leonor met Ignatius for the first time in 1527 and undertook for him to do all in her power for the Society by soliciting funds and using her contacts at the Spanish and Portuguese courts to promote Jesuit interests. Her charge Maria, after she married the Archduke Maximilian, was very helpful in promoting the Jesuits in Vienna.[30]

The foundress of the first Jesuit College at Toledo was a noblewoman, Dona Estefania Manrique y Castilla (died 1606). Ribadaneira wrote her life probably as exemplum. Though this remained in manuscript it was copied several times. Jodi Bilinkoff has recently analysed this work[31] and finds that what is apparent is that at the pivot of women's giving was a relationship between herself and her confessor. The nature of this relationship was of deeply spiritual and emotional kind in which the woman in question was drawn into a share of Jesuit action through her giving of money, time and energy. She was given in exchange a great deal of attention from the confessor and this, as we shall see, did not pass without notice.

Ignatius' correspondence with Donna Maria Frassoni del Gesso who was very important in the establishment of the College in Ferrara allows us further insights into the strategies of fund-raising. Ferrara was a priority because Renée de France, wife of the Duke of Ferrara (a Gonzaga), was a Protestant and the allegiances of the court needed reaffirmation. The Duke himself was slow to offer much for the founding of a college but the wife of the late *fattor* (Prime Minister), Maria Frassoni del Gesso, was quick to respond. When Ignatius wrote to her directly in 1552, 120 boys were allegedly waiting admission and a building was needed. Maria Frassoni del Gesso, 'begins to save'. She dismissed redundant servants and cut her expenditure on dress and feasting. In short she reduced expenses she had met out of her usufruct or extradotal income. Ignatius's letter in response to her initiatives includes another reference to a further technique to encourage the donor:

> through the same charity and benificence of your ladyship, it seems to me to be our duty that we give you a share in all the graces and merits of the said Society throughout the world, a thing we are wont

March, *El aya del rey D Felipe II y del Principe Don Carlos, Dona Leonor Mascareñas, su vida y obras virtuosas. Relación de una religiosa su contemporanea* (Madrid, 1942).

[30] J. M. March, *Niñez y juventad de Felipe II*, (Madrid, 1941), 1, 226–9.

[31] Forthcoming, *Renaissance Quarterly*.

> to do for our principal benefactors so that in all that our brethren do and suffer, wherever they may be, your ladyship shares in the merit of it ... *If you wish for letters patent to this effect, I will send them.* (my italics)[32]

The letter was in Ignatius's hand and he only offers her a certificate *if she should so wish it.* Certificates did not come free since they were drawn up by a notary and who usually paid for this document is not clear but the Society tried to avoid doing so.[33]

In the instance of Maria Frassoni del Gesso a problem emerged: her annual savings were not sufficient to allow the construction of the edifice to move apace. However, the gap was bridged by her standing as guarantor for a loan taken out by the Jesuits on the banking house Baltassare Olgiati and Co. at 4 per cent. An annual sum was pledged which acted like a modern covenant. By the end of her life Maria Frassoni del Gesso had spent 70,000 gold scudi on the erection of the college and church of the Society of Jesus in Ferrara, a sum which contrasts sharply with the 1,000 scudi given by Duke Ercole himself.

However, Ignatius Loyola expected his female donor to understand that the Duke's imprimatur on the college was essential to its recognition. In spite of the differential in the donations, the founder's candle must go the Duke, but she could have the title of 'foundress by merit'.[34]

The use of titles as rewards to women donors who helped the Jesuits is striking. For example, in 1537 Ignatius Loyola sent Francis Xavier and Nicolas Bobadilla to Bologna to found the first Jesuit base outside Rome. There was to be a church and some housing for the brethren. Their reputation had gone before them as preachers and confessors. In order to fix them in Bologna a group of Bolognese women who included two intrepid widows, Margharita dal Gigli and Violante Gozzadini, organised themselves to promote the establishment of a permanent Jesuit presence. They organised a group of twelve women for furnishing and buying pictures for the church.[35] All these women would have liked the title of Mother of the Church for their endeavours, but the Jesuits explained to them that the title was reserved for that woman who had done the most to forward their endeavours. In the event both Margherita and Violante did secure the title and Margherita

[32] Rahner, *Saint Ignatius Loyola, Letters*, 191. Rome, 7 Jan., 1553.

[33] Rahner, *ibid.*, gives an instance of Francis Borgia soliciting such a document for his sister-in-law and passing on the cost to the then Duke of Gandía.

[34] Tacchi Venturi, *Storia della Compagnia di Gesù*, 2,2, 267–9; Rahner, *Saint Ignatius Loyola, Letters*, 200.

[35] C. P. Murphy, 'Lavinia Fontana and *Le dame della città*: Understanding Female Artistic Patronage in Late Sixteenth Century Bologna', *Renaissance Studies*, 10, (1996) 201–6.

was one of the acknowledged founders of the college, to which she left all her worldly possessions.[36]

How do we explain the relationship between the Jesuits and these wealthy women? Italian gender historians of the early modern period have recently given a great deal of attention to the confessional relationship as it evolved in the sixteenth century as being the first structured attempt to help a women (that is certain women) towards the realisation of her own subjectivity (*autoconscienza*).[37] The confessional relationship as practised by the Jesuits was a careful attempt to guide women along a spiritual path: to encourage them to write down their thoughts and to develop these with their confessor. Gabriella Zarri has focussed on Ginevra Gozzadini dall'Armi, a very unhappy childless wife of an adulterous husband.[38] Bartolini had a close spiritual relationship with a group of Bolognese women. Indeed, he wrote a confessional manuel whose frontispiece had a woman of an overtly aristocratic status toiling behind Christ on the road to Calvary. He thus offered the unhappy wives an analogy between their suffering and His and encouraged them to see this world as a vale of tears and to dedicate themselves to God's work. Many of the aristocratic marriages with which the Jesuits came into contact brought a great deal of pain to the women in question. Margaret of Parma's trials at the hands of Ottavio Farnese secured a lot of attention from Ignatius himself because Ottavio was the grandson of Pope Paul III and Margaret's father was Charles V, so that the cementing of this alliance had great diplomatic weight.[39] He gave similar attention to that of Juana of Aragon with the equally distasteful Don Ascanio Colonna, but here failed.[40]

The close relationship between particular Jesuit confessors and women did not go uncontested by families deeply disturbed at the prospect of the transfer of wealth which they expected to revert to the kin group. Some critical relatives insisted on the abuse of the confessional relationship and, quite often, an element of sexual innuendo was

[36] *Chronicles*, vi, 183.

[37] G. Zarri, 'Il carteggio tra Don Leone Bartolini e un gruppo di gentildonne bolognese negli anni del concilio di Trento 1543–1563', *Archivio italiano per la storia della pietà* 7 (1976), and R. Guarnieri, 'Nec domina nec ancilla sed socia: Tre casi di direzione spirituale tra Cinque e Seicento' in E. Schulte van Kessel, ed., *Women and Men in Spititual Culture* (The Hague, 1986), 111–32.

[38] G. Zarri, 'Il carteggio tra Don Leone Bartolini' and 'Ginevra Gozzadini dall'Armi, gentildonna bolognese (1520/7–1567)', in O. Niccoli, ed., *Rinascimento al Femminile* (Rome/Bari 1991), 117–43.

[39] 'It is a miserable marriage. They live together like cat and dog ...' (Cardinal Lenoncourt to the Constable Montmorency), cited F. Rachfahl, *Margareta von Parma, Statthalterin der Niederlande* (Munich-Leipzig, 1898).

[40] Rahner, *Saint Ignatius Loyola, Letters*, 133–48, gives a graphic account of this violent and terrible marriage.

allowed to intrude into their complaints. A few examples will have to suffice. If we revert to Maria Frassoni del Gesso at Ferrara we see she clearly valorised not only her relationship with Ignatius both at a personal and epistolary level, but she was also attached to, one might say dependent upon, a French Jesuit named Pelletier whom she expected to see to discuss her spiritual journeying every day. It is worth remembering that Maria del Gesso was childless, that she had brought her husband considerable resources and that her family of origin was very concerned as to the future disposition of her wealth. In 1553 we hear that Maria was 'besieged by kinsfolk who saw their aunt's great fortune already in the hands of the Jesuits'. Criticism of Pelletier's daily visits included every possible innuendo. Scandal loomed and Loyola intervened to insist that the daily visits stop and that Pelletier should only see Maria twice and week and then in company.

For her part, Maria was terrified that Pelletier might be sent to France and insisted that she receive Loyola's guarantee in writing that this would not be the case. The donor believed she had a right to her confessor. A text emerges in Polanco's letter, written at Loyola's instruction, from 2 Corinthians 8:21 that the Jesuits must consider 'what may be good not only before God but also before men,' words which were frequently to recur. We need to remember that many of Loyola's early companions were young and very zealous. Shining eyes and enthusiastic dedication gave them great appeal. Loyola sometimes regretted and challenged their impetuosity and failure to think beyond the immediate goal (hence the recurrent need for 2 Corinthians 8:21). Even so, while he sought strenuously to limit the duration and number of occasions on which a particular woman might go to confession with a particular Jesuit father and tried to insist that the confessor should always operate with another fellow priest to hand and should minimise home visiting, he opposed Venetian pressure to insist that the age of confessors to women should exceed thirty six.[41] In practical terms, given the age profile of the Jesuits whose energies were stretched to the utmost in manning their churches and colleges, this would have much reduced their influence over women but it would also have acknowledged a potential for exploitation within the confessional relationship which Loyola was loathe to concede.

At Bologna the Gozzadini clan, (one with numerous branches) studied closely by Gabriella Zarri, considered itself particularly abused by the influence of the Jesuits over their women. Violante Gozzadini who

[41] On the del Gesso case, see Rahner, *ibid.*, 192; O'Malley, *The First Jesuits*, 148, offers many instances of measures enjoined on the early Jesuits to avoid scandal, including (1553) that penitents should kneel at the side of the confessor's chair and that the priest should cover his eyes with his hand so as not to see them.

worked with Margherita del Gigli wanted to leave her money to the Jesuit college as her associate had done. The news got out. The powerful Gozzadini clan closed ranks and Ignatius Loyola hearing of the furore this had occasioned intervened to instruct the Jesuits in Bologna not to encourage the legacy and to avoid implication in any notarial act concerning the disposal of Violante's worldly goods.

Her kinswoman, the unhappy wife Ginevra Gozzadini dall'Armi, intended to leave her money to a woman associate to form a lay community with a charitable direction. Again news got out to her family of origin and to her husband. Tension mounted against the Society in Bologna. Again Ignatius Loyola wrote to his men to discourage the legacy but this time it was too late: she was already dead. Stories ricocheted around the town but a legal document was a legal document and Ginevra's wishes had to be respected.[42]

Ignatius was very concerned to balance the needs of the Society for money to fulfil its ambitious schemes to Christianise the world with good relations with the powerful. After his death resentment against the Society grew among the male members of the patriciates of northern Italy. In 1606, Venice, under interdict, expelled the Jesuits, the Teatini and the Capucins, as papal supporters but also because their financial manoeuvres had made their names synonymous with trickery. False stories, part humorous, part bitter, abounded and suspicion that the Jesuits were involved in plots to strip families of their assets were exaggerated.

> In Nov. 1619 a certain Venetian gentlewoman died and gave instructions in her will that her body be preserved in a coffer until the Jesuit fathers returned to live in this city and that a tomb should then be built for her in their church and her body laid to rest in it; and she left the fathers a large income. For these reasons her will was declared invalid and the woman was buried, and notaries were forbidden under heavy penalties to draw up any will in which the Jesuits were named as beneficiaries. Any such will would be null and void, for (the Lords of Venice) want no one to be able to leave any income to the Jesuits. And the Jesuits themselves were banned from the whole of the Venetian Dominion on pain of death, and so were former Jesuits who had left the order, unless they produced evidence of the time at which they had left the order and their reasons for leaving. This was because there had come a Jesuit of Vicenza of the family of Valmarana, who pretended to have left the order, and he claimed an inheritance, attempting to displace some of his nephews

[42] See Zarri, 'Ginevra Gozzadini dall'Armi . . .' and Tacchi Venturi, *Storia della Compagnia di Gesù* 2, 2, 249, draws attention to a cartoon circulating in Bologna showing a wolf in Jesuit guise and women as sheep.

who were the children of his deceased brother. He sent all the money he could lay his hands on to the Jesuit fathers at Parma. This man was banished. And Cardinal Vendramin when he died, left by his will 600 ducats income to the Jesuits, from the time they returned to Venice. For this reason (the Lords of Venice) do not want any more legacies to be made to the Jesuits, and they do not wish them to do business in this city in the dress of a priest.[43]

It is not difficult to interpret this text. If their support of the papacy was the *prima facie* reason for the expulsion of the Jesuits, the vulnerability of family fortunes to their missionary zeal was also a potent factor in fostering resentment. The widow who left her all, the recruit to the Society who dissimulated about his entry into the order in order to rob the rightful heirs of an inheritance to the profit of the college at Parma, were both representative of figures who raised panic in families anxious to preserve family wealth and standing.

This anxiety was not to remain confined to Italy. Amongst the Jesuits' many initiatives was the development of the Ursulines as a teaching order. This order originated in 1535 in Northern Italy with a holy woman, Angela de Merici, who aimed to provide simple services to care for the sick and perhaps to give some schooling of a vocational nature to village girls.[44] The early Ursulines were women of little education and wealth. Immensely energetic and infinitely flexible because they were not cloistered and no dowries were demanded on entry, large numbers were inspired to join. In the late sixteenth century the Jesuits assumed the spiritual direction of the order. Like many of their actions, this one had an agenda behind it whose full complexities cannot be more than touched on here.[45] The Ursulines were transformed into a teaching order and their schools came to be considered as the equivalent for girls of the Jesuit colleges for boys. The Jesuits were instrumental in pushing the Ursulines into France and proceeded to orchestrate an expansion resulting in the establishment of some three hundred houses over a couple of decades. Who funded the expansion? For each house a wealthy widow or aristocratic lady was found to provide a house large enough to serve as buildings for a boarding school. After the Edict of Nantes and with the approval of the monarchy, the schools were used for the daughters of nobles whose wives had

[43] B. Pullan and D. Chambers, *Venice, a Documentary History* (Oxford, 1992). This story of the Jesuit of Vicenza became the basis of many others exaggerated in the telling. I am indebted to Kate Davies of the European University Institute, currently working on the Venetian Interdict, for this information.

[44] The context of this development is found in O. Hufton, *The Prospect Before Her: A History of Women in Western Europe* (London, 1995), 374.

[45] A. Conrad, *Zwischen Kloster und Welt. Ursulinnen und Jesuitinnen in der katholischen Reformbeweung des 16/17 jarhunderts* (Mainz, 1991).

converted to Protestantism to instruct them in the Catholic faith. The girls were largely paid for by their families.[46]

From the point of view of the Catholic Church, the process was a huge success. Not only were many of the girls made strong Catholics but there was also a gradual process of infiltration of the order by the daughters of the aristocracy which gave it increased financial strength and a series of bequests (some of which may have been Jesuit inspired) to bolster the solidity of the foundations. The simple village girls of Angela de Merici were a thing of the past. The mushrooming of the order was so conspicuous that claustration was enforced. Whether this was with or without Jesuit intervention remains to be studied but the principle of enclosure certainly accorded with their view on what was a fitting role for women in religion.

It was to be the Ursulines who were to be a part of the Jesuit plan for the christianisation of the savages of North America and they play a part in the story behind the financing of the expedition of Mère Marie de l'Incarnation's work among the Indians. This story will be used as a final example in this paper to demonstrate money-raising strategies. Very recently the story was one of three recounted in Natalie Zemon Davis's *Women on the Margins*.[47] As told by Natalie Davis this story is one where women claim agency to do what they want to do. What follows does not dispute that point of view, but reads the story from the point of view of one interested in the financing of the enterprise.

The story of the bringing together of the highly spiritual Mère Marie de l'Incarnation and her companion Madame de la Peltrie is one of Jesuit planning, targeting and maximising fund-raising potential in order to cover a hazardous enterprise aimed at christianising a new generation of Indian mothers. It is at one level about the success of the *Relations* in firing the imagination of two intrepid women so as to inspire them to embark on an adventure no woman had undertaken before. It is also a story about the influence of confessors over the two main protagonists. But it must also be admitted that it is a story of bleeding a family of half of its wealth and a story of deception as far as that family is concerned.

Something is known of how Mère Marie de l'Incarnation was chosen: much less about how Madame de la Peltrie was found. Briefly, at the point of her discovery by the Jesuits, she was a young widow, one whose child had died and who had returned to her family with her

[46] M. Chantal-Gueudre, *Histoire de l'Ordre des Ursulines en France* (Paris 1957–63). The funding behind the expansion of the Ursulines, and the reasons behind the transformation into an enclosed order, will be one of the concerns of this project.

[47] N. Z. Davis, *Women on the Margins: Three Seventeenth Century Lives* (Cambridge, MA, 1995), 80–4.

dowry after her husband's death. She obviously did not want to marry again: the experience may have been unpleasant and the opportunity to join Mère Marie may have seemed very exciting. But for the Jesuits she was a window of opportunity because her dowry was the potential means to pay the passage for the groups of chosen women, to build a convent, a school, a church and to keep the sisters.

A plot was evolved involving much deception. Madame de la Peltrie's father, a Cochon de Sauvigny, had no sons and no wish to see his daughter in religion. He was concerned with progeny and a distinguished matrimonial alliance. He was persuaded to accept an offer for his daughter's hand from Jean de Bernières of Caen. This marriage, Jesuit organised, was a fake and not consummated but the dowry exchanged hands. However, there were further gains to be had. Madame de la Peltrie was one of two heiresses to her father's estate, an inheritance she would have foregone had she become a nun before his death. Her father died in ignorance of the stratagem of the false marriage and, following his death, Madame de la Peltrie picked up her inheritance, her husband handed over her dowry and the pair went their separate ways, leaving her outraged relatives to protest at the loss of a half of a major family fortune.[48]

Mère Marie de l'Incarnation, who must have been aware of how the expedition was financed and the criticism which had been aroused described the ruse as 'playful'.[49] Perhaps not surprisingly, important families did not see such a stratagem in quite the same light. When Michelet in the nineteenth century depicted the Jesuits as destroyers of family harmony, by which he meant the authority of the husband/father over wife and daughter, he emphasised the power of the seventeenth-century confessional in bringing this about.[50]

In conclusion, there existed an often fraught relationship between the funding of good works and family interests. The sixteenth- and seventeenth-century donor could be located in a web of incompatible relationships. The immediate family had interests in promoting above all other considerations the financial standing of the family in the here and now and believed it had a stake in the distribution of money within that family. The external persuasions of confessors and preachers were directed towards an alternative course of serving as God's agent and sharing divine bounty in the life to come. My purpose has been to show that the business of raising money was a skilled and increasingly very professional business which in part depended on a close under-

[48] G. M. Oury, *Madame de la Peltrie et ses fondations canadiennes* (Quebec, 1974), 44–55.

[49] G. Oury, ed., *Correspondence de Mère Marie de l'Incarnation* (Solesmes, 1971), 909.

[50] J. Michelet, *Du Prêtre, de la Femme, de la Famille* (Paris, 1845), ran into three editions within a year and sold 50,000 copies in French before translation.

standing of family finances and on the psychology of the donor. The value of the naming opportunity, the certificate of participation, the founder's candle, titles, the personalised letter, the constructed sociability which bound donor and initiative together, all contributed to the furtherance of a newly extended social programme of reform. Worldly goods were thus cunningly redistributed.

ONE OF US? WILLIAM CAMDEN AND THE MAKING OF HISTORY

THE CAMDEN SOCIETY CENTENARY LECTURE

By Patrick Collinson

READ 7 OCTOBER 1997 AT WESTMINSTER SCHOOL, LONDON*

I

THE Royal Historical Society will not be startled to learn that one of the best-informed essays on William Camden was written by its quondam president, Sir Maurice Powicke:

> A great book might be written about Camden, his life and his works, his wide circle of friends and correspondents and his humanity. It would be a very difficult book to write, for its author would have to be steeped in the social history of the time and to be familiar with the personal life, the friendships and all the correlated activities of scholars all over the western world in Camden's day. To recapture that society with learning and imaginative amplitude might well engage a fine and patient and sympathetic scholar in the work of a lifetime.[1]

This polymath (who has yet to appear) will also need to share the knowledge of classical antiquity which was in the bloodstream of Camden and his contemporaries, and in particular of the historians, Livy, Polybius and Tacitus.

As Powicke reminds us, Camden was a cosmopolitan. So to ask whether he was one of us is to face a paradox. Camden never crossed the Channel, and Continental Europe was for him only a republic of

*This paper was read at a Colloquium on William Camden held at Westminster School on 7 October 1997, celebrating the centenary of the sponsorship of the *Camden Series* by the Royal Historical Society. On the same occasion there were papers from Dr Pauline Croft on 'Camden, Westminster and the Cecils', Professor Blair Worden on 'William Camden and Ben Jonson', and Dr Tom Birrell on 'William Camden and His European Reading Public'. The Royal Historical Society is grateful to Westminster School (where Camden was once headmaster) for its hospitality.

[1] Maurice Powicke, 'William Camden', *English Studies 1948. Being Volume One of the New Series of Essays and Studies Collected for the English Association* (1948), 67–84; this quotation at p. 81.

letters. And yet he wrote in a universal language, primarily for the edification of the learned European rather than English reader.[2] His historiographical model was Jacques-Auguste de Thou, 'historiarum nostri seculi Princeps', author of *Historia sui Temporis*.[3] So the hundreds of letters to Camden published by Thomas Smith, most of them from foreign correspondents, and Camden's own letters to de Thou, would be only the start of the labours of Powicke's exemplary scholar.[4] We, to speak of 'us', the modern historians of Elizabethan England, are jet-lagged globe-trotters. We equally write in a universal language, but that language is now English, which tends to draw us back into an insular version of our own history.

Yet it was with Camden's works that this insular detachment began. The translations of *Britannia* and of his *Annales* of Elizabeth, not translations which he undertook personally,[5] served to create an educated rather than learned English readership which appropriated his scholarship and turned it into a piece of English apartness, exceptionality, and self-discovery. *Britannia* became Philemon Holland's *Britain*, his *Annales* Robert Norton's *Historie of the most renowned and victorious princesse Elizabeth*.

What of the secondary element in my title, 'us'? Not a lifetime ago, when working as an apprentice under the watchfully indolent eye of Sir John Neale, I knew what was meant by 'us'. We Tudor historians of the London school were empiricists and archival positivists (or so we later learned). Postmodernism had not been invented, and we spent our time in search of the realities which were new sources, new facts; and on that basis we presumed to write history as it really (rather than Ranke's 'evidently') was, a true account of a past which had truly existed, an actual essence which became our property. We were not at fault in our desire not to get it wrong, but we were naive (if not arrogant) in our assumption that we, and we perhaps alone, had

[2] This was amply demonstrated by Dr Birrell's contribution to the Camden Colloquium. Camden's *Anglica, Hibernica, Normannica, Cambrica* was published at Frankfurt in 1602 and 1603, but never in translation and never in England.

[3] William Camden, *Annalium Apparatus, Annales Ab Anno 1603 ad Annum 1623*, bound with Thomas Smith, *Vita Clarrissimi Gulielmi Camdeni et Illustrium Virorum ad Gulielmum Camdenum Epistolae* (1691), 25.

[4] Smith, *Epistolae*; De Thou correspondence in the Collection Dupuy in the Bibliothèque Nationale, Paris, noted by D. R. Woolf, *The Idea of History in Early Stuart England* (Toronto, 1990), 294, 333. Bodleian Library MS. 15680 (MS. Smith 74) contains Latin letters from Camden, chiefly to foreign scholars, 1587–1620, not included in *Epistolae*.

[5] But Thomas Fuller wrote (*The History of the Worthies of England* (1662), iii. 128) that Holland's translation of *Britannia* was done not only with Camden's knowledge and consent but with his 'help'. Letters to Camden from Jean Hotman establish that he was kept informed about the French translation of the *Annales* and had some control over it. (Smith, *Epistolae*, nos. 161, 163, pp. 201–3.)

actually got it right. Neale used to say that there are no pundits in history, but his colleague Joel Hurstfield told me that he didn't really mean it, or, if he did, he made an exception in his own case. But we were perhaps an extreme case. Lawrence Stone has told us that at Oxford he was taught historical relativism, and has nothing to learn from postmodernism.[6] Be that as it may, to call Camden one of us will be to credit him with writing a history close to its sources, equivalent to the truth as he saw it, and even as it very probably was. But this may prove to be an inappropriate and anachronistic way to judge Camden, or any other historian of his age.

To read Camden's Preface to his *Annales of Elizabeth* is to be persuaded that he was indeed one of the first archival positivists, and that that constituted his achievement. He made much of his dusty exertions among 'great Piles and Heaps of Papers and Writings of all sorts'; 'Charters and Grants of Kings and Great Personages, Letters, Consultations in the Council-Chamber, Embassadours Instructions and Epistles, I carefully turned over and over; the Parliamentary Diaries, Acts and Statutes, I thoroughly perused, and read over every Edict or Proclamation.' I am not sure that Sir John Neale ever did as much. On these foundations, Camden erected a history which he could presume to consecrate 'at the Altar of Truth'. 'Which Truth to take from History, is nothing else but, as it were, to pluck out the Eyes of the beautifullest Creature in the World.'[7]

Another former president, Sir Geoffrey Elton, nods approval. Thus it was that Fritz Levy made Camden's *Annales* the logical as well as chronological terminus of his Whiggishly progressive *Tudor Historical Thought* (1967). Camden's *Annales* was 'the greatest accomplishment of the school of politic historians'.[8] Powicke wrote that Camden (by implication alone) grasped the fact that the study of history, if it is to be more than a literary amusement or a branch of the study of conduct, is a very serious business, while Hugh Trevor-Roper's verdict was that Camden had placed historical studies 'on a new base of scientific documentation'.[9] There is, of course, a long tradition, so far as this matter is concerned, of cocking one's ear for the first cuckoo in spring.

[6] Lawrence Stone, 'History and Postmodernism', *Past & Present*, 135 (1992); reprinted, in an adversarial context, in Keith Jenkins, ed., *The Postmodern History Reader* (1997), 255–9.

[7] Wallace T. MacCaffrey, ed., *William Camden: The History of the Most Renowned and Victorious Princess Elizabeth Late Queen of England: Selected Chapters* (Chicago and London, 1970), 3–8; hereafter, MacCaffrey.

[8] F.J. Levy, *Tudor Historical Thought* (San Marino, California, 1967), 279.

[9] Powicke, 'William Camden', 79; Hugh Trevor-Roper, 'Queen Elizabeth's first historian: William Camden', in his *Renaissance Essays* (1985), 146. More recently, Daniel Woolf has claimed that the *Annales* is the first English narrative history to have been founded almost entirely on primary sources. (*The Idea of History*, 120.)

Implied in these judgments, and here too Elton would approve, is the doctrine that political history is the last to which the historian-cobbler should stick. History is past politics, and the truth about past politics is discoverable. Ergo, the truest history is political history.[10] When Digory Wheare, the first holder of the chair which Camden endowed at Oxford, found to his dismay that he was expected to lecture on ecclesiastical history, a subject of which he claimed to be ignorant, Camden wrote, reassuringly: 'It ever was and is my intention, that ... he should read a civil history', not the history of churches, except insofar as that impinged on politics.[11]

Nowadays, these are no longer secure certainties. It may be possible to write 'true' history if we define history as high politics, involving the motives, decisions and acts of individuals and committees. Within these limits, the historian may even hope to provide plausible causes for events. As Camden himself wrote, quoting Polybius, history was not history without the why and wherefore and to what end.[12] But the 'truth' about historical questions which are both smaller and larger than the contingencies of high politics, small because they concern what Camden himself called 'small things', which is to say social history; larger because they deal with longer periods and larger chunks of history: this is more elusive. The higher, or at least broader truths and explanations, the master narratives of metahistory, often embodied in the banality of book titles, 'ages' of this and that, exist only in the eye of the beholder and are read into history rather than out of it.[13] Historical positivists are necessarily revisionists, masters of the short to medium term and contingent. Or they write thick descriptional microhistories, *histoires évènementielles*, which through sheer detail are held to contain their own explanatory if anecdotal truth.

This is to defer a little to postmodernists such as Hayden White, who insists on the fictive nature of the historical enterprise, a nature determined by a process of selection and exclusion, and by the attribution of form and shape to what is selected. 'This is essentially a literary, that is to say fiction-making, operation. And to call it that in no way detracts from the status of historical narrative as providing a kind of knowledge.'[14] But what Hayden White might have to tell us

[10] G. R. Elton, *Political History, Principles and Practice* (1970).

[11] H. Stuart Jones, 'The Foundation and History of the Camden Chair', *Oxoniensa*, viii., ix (1943–4), 175.

[12] MacCaffrey, 6.

[13] See the remarks of David Eastwood, elsewhere in this volume of *Transactions*.

[14] Hayden White, 'The Historical Text as Literary Artefact', in *Tropics of Discourse: Essays in Cultural Criticism* (Baltimore, 1978), 81–100. For recent responses to the challenge to 'traditional history' of postmodernism, see Keith Windschuttle, *The Killing of History* (Sydney, 1994), and Richard J. Evans, *In Defence of History* (1997). However, as part of what, to coin a phrase, may be called the 'peace process', Evans's book has not succeeded.

about Camden's fictive powers in his *Annales* is limited by the boundaries and shape of a given subject, the reign of Elizabeth, and the fact that Camden adopted an annalistic method, in principle non-intrusive and neutral.

What did Camden's contemporary and admired friend, Sir Philip Sidney,[15] have to say in his *An Apology for Poetry*? Contrasting three roads to edifying instruction, Philosophy, History and Poetry (which is to say, imaginative fiction), Sidney took as read the Aristotelian/Ciceronian premiss that the historian deals with the truth in the sense that he does not make up his stories. It is almost sufficient that the man should not be a liar.[16] According to Sidney, the historian 'bringeth you images of true matters, such as indeed were done, and not such as fantastically or falsely may be suggested to have been done'. But this was faint and ambivalent praise indeed. For the historian is the prisoner of 'that was', 'his bare was', and since he deals with particulars, he cannot account for events. Even if history could teach lessons, they would not be edifying or useful. The poet, by contrast, derives edification from what never happened, and perhaps never could happen.[17] Most of this comes straight out of Aristotle[18], who was correcting Plato, who thought fiction pedagogically risky.

However, Sidney torpedoed his own argument with the admission that history itself is more than half fictional. The historian tells of events of which he can yield no cause 'or, if he do, it must be poetical'. For even historians, for all their talk of things done and of absolute verities, have been glad to steal the poet's clothes. Herodotus and all who came after him borrowed from poetry their passionate descriptions, details of battles which they dreamed up; and they put speeches into the mouths of their characters 'which it is certain they never pronounced'.[19] Here Sidney anticipated Hayden White.

At once we have some kind of bench-mark for Camden. For Camden, almost alone among his peers, eschewed the practice of *prosopopoeia*: 'Speeches and Orations unless they be the very same *verbatim*, or else abbreviated, I have not meddled with all, much less coined them of mine own Head.'[20]

Patrick Joyce (*Past & Present*, 158 (1998), 211) asserts that it 'spectacularly fails to meet the real challenges of postmodernist thought'. It appears that the jury is still out.

[15] On the Camden–Sidney relationship, see W. A. Ringler, ed., *The Poems of Sir Philip Sidney* (Oxford, 1962), xviii, and G. B. Johnson, ed., *Poems by William Camden, Studies in Philology*, lxii (1975), 90–1, 94–5, 102–3. In *Britain* (1610), 329, Camden lauded 'the glorious starre', 'the lovely ioy of all the learned sort', 'a sample of ancient vertues'.

[16] Satis est, non esse mendacem.' (Cicero, *De Oratore*, II. xii. 51.)

[17] Geoffrey Shepherd, ed., Sir Philip Sidney, *An Apology for Poetry, or, The Defence of Poesy* (1965), 107–14.

[18] Plato, *Republic*, II, III; Aristotle, *Poetics*, IX.

[19] Sidney, *Apology*, 110, 97.

[20] MacCaffrey, 6.

We are now ready to consider whether Camden as a historian was one of us, not neglecting the question, what kinds of historian do we aspire to be, in this centennial year of the appropriation of Camden's name by the Royal Historical Society. How would Camden himself have defined 'historian'? Most would agree that of Camden's two major literary accomplishments, *Britannia* and the *Annales* (never forgetting the remarkable socio-linguistics of his *Remains Concerning Britain*,[21] and other works) the greater was *Britannia*, both in the range and originality of its learning, and in its seminal importance for the developing study of antiquity on the basis of material artefacts as well as of textual evidence.

Yet, as all commentators on Camden have pointed out, the author of *Britannia*, in his own self-perception, was not a historian at all.[22] The only point of difference is whether Camden's true destiny and ambition was to be a historian, or whether he remained suspicious of history as a pursuit and doubtful about his own fitness to pursue it.[23] John Pocock has drawn our attention to what he calls 'a great divorce' between Renaissance antiquarians and historians. The critical techniques evolved by antiquarians were only slowly and belatedly combined with the literary undertaking of writing history.[24] When Camden disclaimed the role of historian in *Britannia*, it was because this great compilation of antiquity and chorography (rather than of history) lacked rhetorical art; and Cicero had written that history was a branch of rhetoric. 'Do you not see how far history must be a job for the rhetorician?'[25]

To be sure, Pocock's divorce was never an absolute decree nisi, and Sidney deliberately blurred the distinction when he simultaneously mocked the historian as antiquary, 'loaden with old mouse-eaten records', and as rhetorician, 'authorising himself (for the most part) on other histories'.[26] And whatever Camden might want us to think, there is much that we should regard as history in *Britannia*, and even a greater care in the deployment of sound historical method. Camden is more

[21] The best modern edition is R. D. Dunn, ed., *Remains Concerning Britain* (Toronto, 1984).

[22] Woolf, *The Idea of History*, 22.

[23] On the one hand, we know that Camden intended some kind of History of England before being diverted by *Britannia* (Levy, *Tudor Historical Thought*, 280); on the other, his correspondence with de Thou suggests antipathy. He could even write: 'History is in the beginning envy, in the continuation labour and in the end hatred.' (J. Collinson, *The Life of Thuanus* (1807), 173.) But this was a highly charged correspondence, the stakes high, the hazards evident.

[24] John Pocock, *The Ancient Constitution and the Feudal Law* (Cambridge, 1987), 6.

[25] 'Videstine, quantum munus sit oratoris historia?' (Cicero, *De Oratore*, II. xv. 62.) My translation is surely closer to the mark that that found in Loeb: 'Do you not see how great a responsibility the orator has in historical writing?'

[26] Sidney, *An Apology*, 105.

explicit in the use of what is technically conjecture, conjecture about, for example, the meaning of place-names (which he often got wrong), or the location of Roman towns, or the distribution of British tribes.[27] There may be conjecture in the *Annales*, but it is formally excluded on Camden's own terms.[28] In *Britannia* we encounter the word 'guess'; not, I think, in the *Annales*. This leads to a paradoxical consequence of the great divorce for historiography and its immediate future, two paradoxes in fact. *Britannia* is a compendium of facts, which Camden's contemporaries with access to the same facts were able to judge and censure. And they did. Some people were made unhappy by the *Annales*, particularly if they were related to the great personages they met in Camden's pages.[29] Francis Bacon was allowed to insert a number of passages helpful to the posthumous reputation of his father, Sir Nicholas Bacon.[30] But there were no savage reviews along the lines of Ralph Brooke's *A discoveries of certain errors published in print in much commended Britannia* (1594). For every letter which Camden received about his *Annales* he got twenty others offering friendly or unfriendly advice on matters of factual detail in *Britannia*.[31] As the historian of the reign of Elizabeth, Camden was on his own. But as antiquary, he was part of an extensive guild of scholars, inside and outside the Society of Antiquaries. Selden praised Bacon's *Reign of Henry VII and Camden's Elizabeth* as the only two royal lives written in his own time which came up to the dignity of the subject.[32] But did Selden have any idea how different these two books were, and did he have much interest in how accurate and truthful they were? This was history, and where history

[27] See Camden's Preface (*Britain*): 'Many happily will insult over me for that I have adventured to hunt after the originals of names by conjectures, who if they proceed on to reject all conjectures, I feare me a great part of liberall learning and humane knowledge will be utterly out-cast into banishment.'

[28] 'Things doubtful I have interpreted favourably; Things secret and abstruse I have not pried into.' (MacCaffrey, 5.)

[29] The son of the Scottish statesman, Maitland of Lethington, wrote: 'in loca quaedam incidi, in quibus parentis mei mentio non satis honesta facta est'. (*Epistolae*, no. 243, pp. 305–6.)

[30] Peter Beal (*Index of English Literary Manuscripts*, i. *1450–1625*, Part I (New York, 1980), 149) reports that the relevant revisions (in Cotton MSS. Faustina F, see n. 71 below) are in the hand of Francis Bacon. But James Spedding (*Works of Francis Bacon*, xi., *Letters and Life*, iv. (1868), 211–14) notes that the hand is not Bacon's.

[31] For example, a letter from Camden's close friend John Saville (25 December 1589) consists of an endless catalogue of *corrigenda*: 'Taunton in Somersetshire a suffragan see; and had never but one Earl'; 'Sussex *contermine Cantio* as well as Surrey' (was Camden an elder in the Society of Antiquaries and knew not such things?); 'Christ Church in Canterbury hath twelve Prebends'; 'Blithe is not upon the river that goeth to Worksop; but to Scrouby, the Archbishop's Town.' (Smith, *Epistolae*, no. 30, pp. 36–9.)

[32] Quoted by Thomas Hearne in *Guilielmi Camdeni Annales* (1717), i. Sig. a2; and by Thomas Smith in his *Vita* (English translation in Edmund Gibson, ed., *Camden's Britannia* (1695).)

was concerned that was hardly the point. But when the poet Michael Drayton turned *Britannia* into verse as *Poly-Olbion*, the same Selden filled the margins with critical censure whenever Drayton played fast and loose with the facts and perpetuated myths.[33]

The fact that antiquarians concerned themselves with the 'small things' for which Camden found little room in his *Annales* makes our second paradox. Insofar as 'us' is not Sir Geoffrey Elton, the early modern springs and roots of history as we know it are to be found almost anywhere but in history as 'politic history'. There is potentially more history in *Britannia* than in the *Annales*, and certainly more social and economic history.[34] Arthur B. Ferguson has argued that Renaissance historical consciousness is to be found in a variety of particular and practical contexts, more so than in 'history', written as an end in itself, as a narrative of deeds done. It follows that what Camden and his contemporaries understood to be history is not necessarily the place to look for the best of Renaissance historiography.[35]

II

The remainder of this paper will address the subject of Camden's *Annales*, in the context of the 'politic history' of its time. But first we may consider *Britannia*,[36] and its historical and prehistorical prolegomenon, which provides revealing examples of Camden's conduct when it came to confronting dubious historical evidence. Having reduced the British History of Geoffrey of Monmouth to rubble, Camden concludes, to the astonishment, not to say scandal, of 'us', that it was not his intention to 'impeach' this improbable tale. Let Brutus be taken for the father and founder of the British nation. 'I will not be of a contrarie minde.' In things of so great Antiquitie, it is easier

[33] Michael Drayton, *Poly-Olbion: Or a chorographical description of Great Britain ... digested in a poem* (1613–22).

[34] Take, for example, Camden's account of the crofting lifestyle of the inhabitants of Thanet, 'as if they were *Ampibii, that is both land creatures and sea-creatures* ... as well Husband-men as Mariners ... According to the season of the year, they knit nets, they fish for Cods, Herring, Mackerels etc ... The same again dung and manure their grounds.' (*Britain*, 340.) However, there is enough non-'politic' history in the *Annales* for Trevor-Roper to have accentuated its colourful detail in his account of the book. (*Renaissance Essays*, 138–41.)

[35] Arthur B. Ferguson, *Clio Unbound: Perception of the social and cultural past in Renaissance England* (Durham, North Carolina, 1979), *passim.*

[36] T. D. Kendrick, *British Antiquity* (1950), chapter 8 '*Britannia*', 134–67; Stuart Piggott, 'William Camden and the *Britannia*', *Proceedings of the British Academy*, xxxvii. (1951), 199–217; F.J. Levy, 'The Making of Camden's *Britannia*', *Bulletin d'Humanisme et Renaissance*, 26 (1964), 70–97.

to proceed by guesswork than by knowledge.[37] Camden's poem *De Connubis Tamae et Isis* makes similar, conventional gestures towards Brutus as founder of the nation, and to Troy as London's mother.[38] Camden's elusiveness on this delicate subject is best conveyed in his Latin: 'Sin autem Britanni nostri, velit, nolit veritas, origine Troiani esse velint, me sane repugnantem non habebunt.'[39] Philemon Holland's translation loses the irony of 'velit, nolit veritas'.[40] And so with the legendary origins of Cambridge University. 'I will be no dealer in this case ... Howbeit, I feare me, they have builded Castles in the aire ...'[41] Yet Camden was prepared to believe that his own university had been founded by King Alfred, and to tamper with the text of Asser to bolster his belief. So it appears that his critical faculties were sharpened more by *parti pris* than by the concerns of disinterested scholarship.[42] Anthony Grafton has taught us that that was how the learned minds of the Renaissance often worked.[43] However, the reign of Elizabeth was not a thing 'of great Antiquitie', and so a different matter.

Three late Elizabethan and Jacobean historians are conventionally bracketed together as representative of the so-called 'new' politic or 'civil' history: besides Camden, Sir John Hayward, who wrote, amongst other things, a history of the usurpation and early years of King Henry IV, and Francis Bacon, for his *Reign of Henry VII*.[44] In fact Camden, Hayward and Bacon have little in common, beyond a shared appreciation of Cornelius Tacitus, whom they put to very different uses.[45] But Hayward and Bacon make admirable foils for the question we are

[37] Camden, *Britain*, 8, 10.

[38] *Poems by William Camden*, 90–103.

[39] William Camden, *Britannia* (1586), 160.

[40] 'But if our Britons will needs be descended from the Trojans, they shall not verily have me to gainsay them.' (Camden, *Britain*, 22.) Does Camden mean by 'Britanni' the Welsh? I think that he does, for deferring to the sensibilities of that nation was a literary *topos* of the time.

[41] Camden, *Britain*, 488.

[42] Powicke, 'William Camden', 78.

[43] Anthony Grafton, 'Invention of Traditions and Traditions of Invention in Renaissance Europe: the Strange Case of Annius of Viterbo', in A. Grafton and A. Blair, eds., *The Transmission of Culture in Early Modern Europe* (Philadelphia, 1990); Anthony Grafton, *Forgers and Critics: Creativity and Duplicity in Western Scholarship* (1990).

[44] John J. Manning, ed., *The First and Second Parts of John Hayward's The Life and Raigne of Henrie IIII*, Camden 4th ser. 42 (1991); Brian Vickers, ed., *Francis Bacon: The History of the Reign of King Henry VII*, Cambridge Texts in the History of Political Thought (Cambridge, 1998). This leaves out of account the poet-historian Samuel Daniel, who is conventionally regarded as an 'artistic' rather than 'politic' historian: which is somewhat anachronistic and undervalues Daniel.

[45] It is also less than clear what was 'new' about these political historians which was self-evidently newer than Thomas More's *History of Richard III*, written a century earlier by a man who had also read his Tacitus; unless it was a further measure of emancipation from 'Providentialism', normally pin-pointed as the essence of 'politic' or 'civil' history.

pressing upon Camden: one of us? For clearly they, at least, were not.

Hayward understood the historian's task to consist of the making of patchwork quilts: the reworking of moral, psychological and political reflections on great events and those who shaped them; and why not in the very words of earlier histories written about other epochs and subjects? Hayward is a subject which belongs to Lisa Richardson.[46] We have always known that Hayward borrowed from Tacitus. Francis Bacon called it stealing, in a famous exchange with Queen Elizabeth herself. Hayward could not be had up for treason, as the queen had hoped. (The first part of his *Life and Raigne of King Henrie IIII*, a sad story of deposition and death, had been dedicated to the earl of Essex, which, when it happened, appeared to implicate the author in the Essex revolt.) But, said Bacon, Hayward was certainly guilty of felony. 'For he had taken most of the sentences of Cornelius Tacitus, ... and put them into his text.'[47] What Bacon said has not hitherto been understood quite literally, and the full extent of Hayward's plagiarism, if that is the right word, has not been appreciated. John Manning, who edited the first and second parts of *Henrie IIII* for the Camden Series as recently as 1991, supposed, as anyone perhaps would, that he was dealing with a more or less original literary composition.[48] Hayward was even credited with inventing a new kind of historiography, 'significant and enduring'.[49]

But Lisa Richardson will demonstrate that Hayward was a master of scissors and paste. Of the *First part*, 72 per cent is traceable to its immediate sources, word for word, and without authorial elaboration, and 18 per cent comes straight from Sir Henry Saville's 1591 translation of the *Histories* of Tacitus, including almost all of Hayward's characterisations. Hayward ingested whole chunks of the relevant medieval chronicles (which could at least be regarded as legitimate 'sources'); as well as a variety of other more recent texts, such as the Memoirs of Philippe de Commynes and even Sir Philip Sidney's *Arcadia*, a fictional

[46] Miss Richardson's forthcoming Cambridge Ph.D. thesis on Hayward will include an 80,000 word appendix which details, remorselessly, all of Hayward's borrowings which she has been able to trace, in *The Life and Raigne* and in his other historical works. She will also correct the arguments of, e.g., David Womersley, 'Sir John Hayward's Tacitism' *Renaissance Studies*, 6 (1992), who tends to exaggerate the subversive topicality of Hayward's use of Tacitus. I am grateful to Miss Richardson for permission to make use of her work.

[47] Manning, *The First and Second Parts*, 2.

[48] Citing another authority, Manning thought that a complete list of Hayward's Tacitean borrowings in *The First Part* might run to a dozen pages. This is a considerable underestimate. (*Ibid.*, 36, n. 121.)

[49] *Ibid.*, 34. S. L. Goldberg, too, found in Hayward 'a new approach to history', consisting in the kind of dispassionate political analysis which substituted 'is' for 'ought'. (S. L. Goldberg, 'Sir John Hayward, "Politic Historian"', *Review of English Studies*, n.s. 6 (1955), 233–4.)

romance, which makes a distinctly Hayden White-ish point. He also recycled some of this material in his own later histories, where, for example, a politician from the reign of Edward VI was made to put on the same Tacitean costume previously worn in the time of Richard II and Henry IV. Since it has been hard work, even for Miss Richardson, to cover all of Hayward's traces, it is perhaps unlikely that as much as 28 per cent of the first part of *The Life and Raigne* will prove to have been, in the words of the pavement artist, 'all my own work'.

Tacitus is of critical importance.[50] Lisa Richardsons can provide hundreds of examples of Hayward's Tacitean shoplifting. Tacitus (in Savile's translation) had written of the ambitious general Antonius Primus: 'peradventure prosperity in a man of that disposition, discovered the secret and inward faultes of his minde, as covetousness, and pride, and other vices that were suppressed before'; and of the unsavoury character of one of the Emperor Galba's minions, Vinius, who, 'carrying an ill minde, and serving in great place a weake master, made open sale of his Princes free grace and favours'.[51] Out of these materials, Hayward invented a pastiche of Michael de la Pole, earl of Suffolk: 'Prosperity laid open the secret faults of his minde, which were suppressed and cloaked before; and serving a weake ruler in great place, with an ill minde, he made open sale of his prince's honour.'[52] The example of Galba provided the commonplace that 'a good prince governed by evil ministers is as dangerous as if he were evil himself'. Of Richard II, Hayward wrote: 'For it is oft times as dangerous to a prince to have evil and odious adherents as to be bee evil and odious himself.'[53]

The irony of this is that Tacitus himself has been exposed as a 'scissors and paste' historian. Tacitus's model was Sallust, and he helped himself freely to Sallust's character sketches. But Tacitus had the talent to transform many of the passages which he ingested.[54] Let us be fair to Hayward. Tacitus, in the perception of the Renaissance, had uttered aphorisms which are eternally true. Peter Burke remarks: 'Men believed that the maxims could be "unlocked", or released from their context,

[50] J. H. M. Salmon, 'Seneca and Tacitus in Jacobean England', in Linda Levy Peck, ed., *The Mental World of the Jacobean Court* (Cambridge, 1991), 169–88; Malcolm Smuts, 'Court-Centred Politics and the Uses of Roman Historians, *c.*1590–1630'; Blair Worden, 'Ben Jonson Among the Historians', in Kevin Sharpe and Peter Lake, eds., *Culture and Politics in Early Stuart England* (Basingstoke, 1994), 21–43, 67–89.

[51] Publius Cornelius Tacitus, tr. Henry Savile, *Histories* (1591), 143; *The end of Nero and the beginning of Galba* (1591), 14.

[52] Manning, *The First and Second Parts*, 72.

[53] Tacitus, *The end of Nero*, 1; Manning, *The First and Second Parts*, 70.

[54] R. H. Martin, 'Tacitus and His Predecessors', in T. A. Dorey, ed., *Tacitus* (1969), 131–4.

without loss of value.'[55] Hayward was no more than an extreme case. But far from being one of us, he would be denied even a third class degree in any modern university. However, to judge him by such a standard would involve a monumental misunderstanding of what this early modern rhetorician thought history was about.

Bacon was the only one of our three politic historians to have written extensively and originally on the nature of historical knowledge and the practice of history. Bacon wanted history in the broadest sense (for his definition embraced what we should call natural history, that is, all science) to be derived from the study of particulars, from which could be constructed what Bacon called a 'perfect history' of some worthy subject, such as the history of England and Britain from the union of the roses to the union of the crowns. But Bacon thought it beneath the dignity of the historian (himself) to do the work of collecting the particulars. That task belonged to 'factors and merchants', research assistants.[56] So the historian's function was perhaps not essentially different from what it had always been: literary and rhetorical.

Bacon preached better than he practised. In the only 'perfect' history which he ever completed, his *History of the Reign of King Henry VII*, a book which has been described as 'an intellectual anticlimax',[57] he fell below his own exacting standards, effectively dispensing with the primary labour of research. That is not to say that Bacon managed without sources. But he wrote in conditions of enforced rustication, depending upon what the Keeper of Public Records and Selden (some 'factors'!) were able to supply.[58] For his narrative core, he followed earlier accounts of the reign and Speed's *History of Great Britaine*, faithfully reproducing some of Speed's mistakes.[59] Here is a good example of Sidney's historian, authorising himself for the most part on other histories. Bacon's own contribution was to create an at least partly imaginary Henry VII. On the one hand he too wrote under a Tacitean spell, the moral degeneration of Henry Tudor resembling that of the Emperor Tiberius, although Bacon was no crude Haywardian

[55] P. Burke, 'Tacitism', in *ibid.*, 162.

[56] Francis Bacon, 'The Dignity and Advancement of Learning' (translation of Bacon's *De Augmentis*), J. Spedding *et al.*, eds., *The Works of Francis Bacon*, iv. (1858). On Bacon's rhetoric in his historical writings, see John F. Tinkler, 'The Rhetorical Method of Francis Bacon's *History of the Reign of King Henry VII*', *History and Theory*, 26 (1987), and Brian Vicker's Introduction to his edition of *The History*.

[57] Daniel R. Woolf, 'John Selden, John Brough and Francis Bacon's *History of Henry VII* 1621', *Huntington Library Quarterly*, 47 (1984), 47.

[58] *Ibid.*, 47–53.

[59] Most notoriously, in repeating Speed's perversion of André's account of Henry's entry into London *laetenter* (happily) as *latenter* (covertly), so that he entered 'in a close chariot'. This fitted Bacon's characterisation of Henry. (Vickers, ed., *The History*, ll, n. 42.)

plagiarist.[60] On the other, Bacon's Henry VII resembled James I. Without the example of James and Anne of Denmark, would Bacon have alleged, without any evidence, that Henry neglected his wife?[61] In the funeral oration with which the book ended, Bacon wrote: 'This King (to speak of him in terms equal to his deserving) was one of the best sort of wonders, a wonder for wise men':[62] in short, Solomon redevivus, James Stuart. *Henry VII* was a political treatise, not learning from the past but teaching from it. It was also the autobiography of a statesman, particularly in the hostility the book expresses for courtiers of the kind who had destroyed Bacon's own career.[63] These were further refractions of the Roman historians, with whom it was virtually a convention to deplore the rise of upstarts.[64] This was not what we should call a history at all. And yet Bacon set the reign of Henry VII in a mould which historians have broken only in recent years.[65]

III

Which leaves us with Camden, who set Henry VII's granddaughter in a mould which has endured for at least three hundred years.

For a book acknowledged to partake of a certain greatness, Camden's *Annales* is a strangely neglected text. Hugh Trevor-Roper used the occasion of a Neale Memorial Lecture to talk about it with characteristic brilliance.[66] Neale himself, whom Trevor-Roper flattered as 'our modern

[60] Whatever the truth of the matter, historically (it was debated between G. R. Elton and J. P. Cooper), Bacon's account of the avarice of Henry's later years and of his 'opportune' death, 'in regard of the great hatred of his people' (Vickers, ed., *The History*, 194–5) was Tacitean. Bacon (*cf.* Thomas More in his *Richard III*) was doubtless aware of the ambivalent hesitation of Tacitus as he approached the reign of Trajan. Would this prove to be a new golden age? Probably not. (Martin, 'Tacitus and His Predecessors', 126–7; Alistair Fox, 'Thomas More and Tudor Historiography: *The History of King Richard III*', in his *Politics and Literature in the Reigns of Henry VII and Henry VIII* (Oxford, 1989), 109–27.) Lisa Richardson informs me that Bacon was very sparing in directly borrowing from Tacitus.

[61] Vickers, ed., *The History*, 201; David M. Bergeron, 'Francis Bacon's *Henry VII*: Commentary on King James I', *Albion*, 24 (1992), 17–26.

[62] Vickers, ed., *The History*, 196.

[63] S.J. Gunn, 'The Courtiers of Henry VII', *English Historical Review*, cviii (1993), 23–49.

[64] Martin, 'Tacitus and His Predecessors', 122.

[65] S. B. Chrimes, *Henry VII* (1972). But as an introduction to studies which break the mould, see now S.J. Gunn, *Early Tudor Government, 1485–1558* (1995).

[66] Trevor-Roper, *Renaissance Essays*, 121–48; first published as *Queen Elizabeth's First Historian: William Camden and the Beginnings of English 'Civil History': Neale Lecture in English History 1971* (1971).

Camden', almost never cited his illustrious precursor.[67] Trevor-Roper's lecture was a typical exercise in investigative scholarship, opening the diplomatic bag and listening in to the whispering galleries of European intellectual life in order to discover why and how Camden's book came to be written, and written as it was: a tangled plot concerning the posthumous reputation of Mary Queen of Scots, not least with her son, James VI and I; George Buchanan's account of Scottish affairs which Jacques-Auguste de Thou was all too inclined to incorporate, *faute de mieux*, in the great universal history of his own time; circumstances directly relevant to the publication of the first three books of the *Annales* in 1615; and, according to Trevor-Roper, no less to James's lack of interest in Book 4, which dealt with matters after the death of his mother. There is no need on this occasion to repeat that story.

But, more recently, the respective roles in this literary and diplomatic game of Camden and Camden's friend and sometime Westminster pupil, Sir Robert Cotton, have been reexamined by Kevin Sharpe, to the advantage of Cotton;[68] while Daniel Woolf has suggested that James I's interest in the work was more enduring than Trevor-Roper supposed, since Camden's Elizabeth in her moderate instinct for middle and pacific courses bore a flattering resemblance to James himself.[69]

However, the bibliographical story of the *Annales* has never been told. Trevor-Roper was indifferent to such matters, failing even to explain to his audience that the book was written and originally published in Latin, and that Camden had nothing to do with the various English translations. Here, at some risk of being tedious, is the barest summary of the biography of the book.

Conception was in 1608, when Camden recorded: 'I began to compile my Annals.'[70] Then follows the story of gestation, the book hidden in the womb, as told by Trevor-Roper and Sharpe. The events of birth, wholly neglected in modern scholarship, are documented in ten stout volumes in the British Library, MSS. Cotton Faustina F.[71] These contain

[67] And since neither Camden nor Neale (in his *Queen Elizabeth* (1934)) provides any references to sources, it would be a fascinating but difficult task to establish the extent to which Neale was indebted to Camden, not as a substitute for research, but in his adoption of Camden's patterning of the reign.

[68] Kevin Sharpe, *Sir Robert Cotton 1586–1631: History and Politics in Early Modern England* (Oxford, 1979), 84–110; Kevin Sharpe, 'Introduction: Rewriting Sir Robert Cotton', in C.J. Wright, ed., *Sir Robert Cotton as Collector: Essays on an Early Stuart Collector* (1997), 12–13.

[69] Woolf, *The Idea of History*, 123–4.

[70] 'Annales digerere coepi.' (William Camden, 'Memorabilia' [Diary], in *Addenda* attached to *Annales ab Anno 1603 ad Annum 1623*, *Epistolae*, 85.)

[71] The Faustina MSS. are not mentioned by Trevor-Roper or Sharpe, nor are they specified by David McKitterick, although he refers in general terms to 'the drafts and the preparatory materials' of the *Annales*, surviving in the Cotton MSS. (David McKitterick, 'From Camden to Cambridge: Sir Robert Cotton's Roman Inscriptions, And

not one but the better part of two autograph MS. copies of the *Annales*, some volumes in the first series authenticated, in Sir Robert Cotton's hand, as 'manu Authoris scripta'.[72] Volume IV of the series is (flamboyantly) headlined with 'Robert Cotton Bruceus' (Cotton claimed descent from Robert the Bruce), 'the first copy after mended'. Camden's Preface is absent from these MSS., and was presumably supplied at the time of publication. The first series contains many substantial corrections and interpolations. There are excised, and inserted, passages, which are not to be found in any printed edition. It would take a competent Latinist and palaeographer some time to collate this material with the printed text.

Cotton, whose own hand appears at many points, has recorded the progress of his copy-editing of the MSS., two or three distinct readings of each part, which began in August and continued until late October 1613. From these notes it is clear that the whole work up to 1603 had been completed by the autumn of 1613, whereas it has been thought that Book 4, from 1589 to 1603, was written later. However, Cotton's notes prefacing Faustina F VI and IX tell us that he was again reviewing Book 4 for publication between November 1618 and May 1620.

Faustina F X contains this intriguing Cotton note: 'The copye of the storye of Queen Elizabeth from 1583 to 1587, not transcribed for my self as yett but sent unto France to Tuanum [de Thou].'[73] There is evidence here and there that these copies were set up for the printer. One important document is endorsed in Camden's hand: 'I praye that this maye be verie fayre wrytten with some golden letters'—presumably for a presentation copy. Another hand, doubtless the printer's, has added: 'it is so done'.[74] It appears only just that the first edition of the

Their Subsequent Treatment', in Wright, ed., *Sir Robert Cotton as Collector*, 115.) Nor are they noticed in J. K. Moore, *Primary Materials Relating to Copy and Print in English Books of the Sixteenth to Nineteenth Centuries*, Oxford Bibliographical Society Occasional Publications 24 (Oxford, 1992).

[72] BL, Cotton MSS. Faustina F I (1558–72), II (1573–86, 1588–90), III (1593–1603), VI (1589–96), VII (1597–9, 1600–3) comprise what are here called 'the first series', 'a manu Authoris scripta' and, elsewhere 'a prima manu Camdeni' (in Cotton's hand). MSS. Faustina F. IV (1558–72), 'the first copy after mended', V (1573–82), VIII (1589–97), IX (1598–1603) are perfected and fair copies. For the nature and contents of MS. Faustina F X, see n. 73 below.

[73] This statement occurs on fo. 254, which was evidently originally a cover sheet/title page to the volume. Fos. 105–70 of MS. Faustina F X, including this statement, are copied (by Thomas Hearne?) in British Library, MS. Add. 6217, which concludes with a list of textual variants, 'deest paragraphus'. Fo. 255 of MS. Faustina F X is a holograph letter from Camden: 'Right worshipfull. I send you by this gent. Mr Quin: the first parte of my Annales of Q. Elizabeth with manifold additions. I praye you playe an Aristarcho therein and note severally what you thinke to be omitted or emended etc. I will follow your directions.' Was this letter written to Cotton?

[74] British Library, MS. Cotton Faustina F X, fos. 247^{r}–9^{t}.

Annales was licensed to Camden and Cotton jointly.[75] Cotton had supplied much of the source material, either from his own collections or from his privileged access to the state archives,[76] but evidently that was not all that he contributed. It appears that we should be as cautious in referring to the *Annales* as Camden's *Annales* as to the play *Henry VIII* as simply Shakespeare's *Henry VIII.* Joint authorship is now acknowledged to have been commoner than we once thought, and no disparagement to the quality of the work in question.

The first three books of the *Annales*, which took the story as far as 1588, were published in London in 1615: *Annales Rerum Anglicarum, et Hibernicarum Regnante Elizabetha.*[77] This volume was translated into French by Phillipe de Bellegent, a native of Poitou, and printed in London in 1624: *Annales des choses qui sont passés en Angleterre et Irland soubs le Regne de Elisabeth.* This was the basis of the first English translation, entered with the Stationers five months later, the hasty and incompetent work of Abraham Darcie, who was born in Geneva and apparently knew no Latin: *Annales: The true and royall history of Elizabeth.*[78] This edition makes no mention of Camden, who is referred to simply as 'the author'; and whereas Camden had rather pointedly dedicated his book not to his sovereign but to the reader, posterity and his country, Darcie's jingoistic dedication was to James as 'Emperour of Great Britanne' (etc.) and to Prince Charles. In 1625, soon after Camden's death, the Fourth Book, which he had been reluctant to publish in his lifetime, most of all in English (and his biographer suggests why, 'the censures he met with in the business of *Mary* Queen of Scots'[79]), was for the first time joined to Books One to Three in an edition published in Leiden.[80] Two years later Book 4 was separately published in London as *Tomus alter annalium, sive pars quarta.* In 1629 a translation of the *Tomus alter* by Thomas Browne was published at Oxford and dedicated to Charles I.[81] Again, Camden was nowhere named. In 1626 a translation of all four books by Robert Norton, presumably from the Latin, was entered with the

[75] Trinity College Cambridge, MS. R.5.20, fo. 112^{v}, dated 25 February 1615.

[76] Sharpe, *Sir Robert Cotton*, 92, n. 40. Cotton later claimed the credit for conserving many of the Scottish materials for the *Annales*, writing of abstracts 'which Sir Robert Cotton hath compyled into a story of Q Eliz time by mr Camden and published in print.' (Nigel Ramsay, 'Sir Robert Cotton's Service to the Crown: A Paper Written in Self-Defence', in Wright, ed., *Sir Robert Cotton As Collector*, 68–80.) See also Woolf, *The Idea of History*, 118.

[77] And in Frankfort in 1616. Hereafter '*Annales*'.

[78] No less than three printers were employed in the collation of the ten copies listed in the *Revised S.T.C.* (no. 4497): a bibliographer's nightmare, or, playground. Hereafter 'Darcie'.

[79] Smith, 'Life', in Gibson, ed., *Britannia.*

[80] There was a further Leiden edition in 1639.

[81] Hereafter 'Browne'.

Stationers, but only appeared from the press in 1630. The title was now altered: *The historie of the most renowned and victorious princesse Elizabeth*, no longer 'Annals'.[82]

We now have three English translations of Camden and they make an odd bunch: Darcie, the expatriate and third-rate man of letters; Browne, learned cleric, student of Christ Church, and chaplain to both Archbishop Laud and Charles I; and Norton, son of the great Elizabethan 'parliament man' Thomas Norton, a military engineer and gunner.[83] Browne, as we might expect, was the most competent of the three. Compare the first sentence of Book 4, taking up from the failure of the Armada, in his version and Norton's:

> Norton:
> After that the expedition of the *Spaniards* against *England* had proved so adverse, dishonourable, and fully frustrate, they to repaire their glory, and divert the cogitations of the English from fixing upon an invasion of the Countryes of the King of *Spaine* ... (and so on).[84]
>
> Browne:
> After that so unexpected a successe had blasted the glory of the Spanish Invasion; they to salve their wounded honour, and to forestall in the English the very thought of the like invasion...[85]
>
> 33 words to Norton's 43, better English, and more faithful to Camden's tight, economical Latin.

However, Browne was to disappear without trace and it was Norton's version which became the *textus receptus* in a further edition of 1635 (calling itself the third and amplified and corrected edition).[86] Forty years later, in 1675, a version based on 1630 rather than 1635, claimed to be a third edition, and to incorporate radical (but mostly harmless) 'improvements' to the text. We may compare the personal appreciation of Mary Queen of Scots in Camden's epitaph for the poor lady: Darcie (1625) 'of surpassing beauty';[87] Norton (1630) 'and passing beauty' (a subtle variant that);[88] (1675) 'and admirable beauty'.[89] Professor Wallace

[82] Hereafter 'Norton 1630'; and Norton's 1635 edition, 'Norton 1635'.

[83] *D.N.B.*, arts. Darcie, Browne, Norton; Michael Graves, *Thomas Norton: The Parliament Man* (Oxford, 1994). Robert Norton's occupation may explain the delay between the licensing and publication of his translation of the *Annales*. In 1627, as gunnery expert, he took part in the ill-fated expedition to the Ile de Rhé.

[84] Norton 1630, Bk. 4, 1.

[85] Browne, 1.

[86] This edition incorporates passages from Camden's amended text, only found otherwise in Hearne's 1717 edition (see below).

[87] Darcie, Bk. 3, 206.

[88] Norton, 1630, Bk. 3, 112.

[89] 1675, 385.

MacCaffrey employed a further edition of 1688 for his 'selected chapters' of Camden (1970), the only version of any kind to have been made available in this century.[90]

Finally, in 1717, Thomas Hearne published in three volumes a Latin text of the *Annales* based on Bodleian Library MS. Smith 2.[91] This is a printed text (the 1615 London edition), containing the revisions and corrections which Camden intended for a second edition which never materialised. Several of Camden's *addenda* are of interest. For example, under 1559, Camden tells us about Elizabeth's old-fashioned veneration for the cross, the Virgin Mary and the saints. In Hearne's 1717 text, there is an additional sentence otherwise only to be found in Norton 1635. 'And least shee should breake the Ecclesiasticall fast in Lent, shee solemnely asked licence every yeere of the Archbishop of *Canterbury*, for eating of flesh.'[92] Hearne's scholarship is impeccable, and any critical modern edition will have to be based on this text (or MS. Smith 2), collated with MSS. Faustina F I-X.

Camden's Latin is the only text to speak with an authorial voice. In translation, much is lost, although only occasionally the actual sense. It is notorious that Camden detested Puritans, so the following examples are significant. The year is 1564, and Camden is discussing the division of opinion over the succession, and in particular about the claims of Mary Queen of Scots. Camden wrote that 'Protestantes efferuescentes' were hostile to Mary's title; whereas her title was favoured by 'Pontificorum alii, et plerique omnes aequi benique'. 'Protestantes efferuescentes' means the wilder sort of Protestants. Darcie makes this less polemical: 'Protestants, transported with an ardent zeal'; Norton is closer: 'the hot Protestants'. 'Pontificorum alii' Darcie and Norton render, reasonably enough, as 'papists'. (That Camden brackets these Catholics with 'plerique omnes aequi benique' puts an interesting spin on public opinion, suggesting that animosity to Mary was a sectarian, minority sentiment. Darcie makes this 'those who had reference to that which was just and equall', Norton, 'and the greatest part of all indifferent men'.)[93] In 1603, with Elizabeth on the brink of death, among those posting north to pay their respects to James were both 'Zeloti' and 'Pontifici'. Browne translates 'Zeloti' as 'the more zealous';

[90] See above, n. 7.

[91] Thomas Hearne, ed., *Guilielmi Camdeni Annales Rerum Anglicarum et Hibernicarum Regnante Elizabetha, Tribus Voluminibus Comprehensi*; hereafter 'Hearne'. This edition derives from Bodleian Library, MS. 15609 (MS. Smith 2), which is inscribed by Hearne: 'Aprilis 2[do] 1717 ... I give this Book to the Bodleian Library when I die as Dr Smith desired me. Tho. Hearne March 28 1719.' MS. Smith 2 is a copy of the printed 1615 (London) edition, with Camden's autograph revisions.

[92] Hearne, i. 34; Norton 1635, 7–8.

[93] *Annales*, 91–2; Darcie, Bk. 1, 111; Norton 1630, Bk. 1, 73.

Norton, who knew what Camden meant, 'Puritans'.[94] But 'Puritani' is not a word which Camden ever used.

More was lost in translation than such small details. The major casualty, the unavoidable consequence of the act of translation itself, was the intense, epigrammatic, often ironical style and tone of the original. This was the essence of Camden's Tacitism, little in the way of naked plagiarism, but style and tone determining interpretation. For an example, we need look no further than the most famous statement in his Preface. '*Manifesta* non reticui, *dubia* mollius sum interpretatus, *occultiora* non indagavi.' The italicised nouns become rather clumsy constructions in English, 'things manifest and evident', 'things doubtful', 'things secret and abtruse'.[95] A modern authority on Tacitus remarks on the difficulty facing his English translators, problems about 'the intransigence of an uninflected language'.[96]

So much for the problematics of Camden's *Annales* as literary texts. But historians will want to know how faithfully such an influential history depended upon its sources, and is itself dependable. If Camden is to be reckoned 'one of us', and posthumously elected to the fellowship of this learned society, it will be because he, unlike Hayward and Bacon, authorised himself, not on other historians, but on the original archival record, those 'Great Piles and Heapes of Writings of all sorts'.

It is worth asking why Camden went into the archives; not, I think, because he wanted to be one of us, the Whiggish answer. The explanation lies in the doctrine, rooted in the Roman historiographical tradition, that a historian ought to be an experienced politician, or at least an ex-politician, with first-hand knowledge of the arcane mysteries of state. Tacitus, after all, was the son-in-law of his first subject, Agricola, and a senator who served as consul and governed a province, Asia no less. The Elizabethan M.P. Francis Alford was aware of this ancient convention when he suggested that he, Alford, should be allowed and funded to do what Camden later achieved, 'write the storie of her Majestie's reign'. Making what he could of his own not very distinguished public service, Alford remarked: 'To write a storie there apertaineth more then a schollers knowledge.' Lord Burghley himself, if he were not too busy, was the obvious man to do it. But failing that, Alford would take it on, if suitably rewarded.[97] Similarly, Camden represents himself in his Preface as virtually Burghley's *amanuensis*. Sir Henry Saville's dedication of his *Tacitus* to the queen refers to her own

[94] *Annales, Tomus Alter* (1627), 284; Browne; Norton 1630, Bk. 4, 223.

[95] *Annales*, Preface; MacCaffrey, 5.

[96] Norma P. Miller, 'Style and Content in Tacitus', in Martin, ed., *Tacitus*, 114.

[97] Francis Alford to F[rancis] W[alsingham], Inner Temple Library, Petyt MS. 538. 10, fol. 11^v; Francis Alford, 'A sute for the writinge of the storie of her Ma[jes]ties reigne', *ibid.*, fols. 14^v–15^r.

'admirable compositions' and 'excellent translations of Histories (if I can call them Translations, which have so infinitely exceeded the originals).' He wished that she might be her own Tacitus.[98] Camden later assumed the same courtly pose. He would be content if James I were to publish the fourth part of his *Annales* over his own name.[99] Evidently, according to this rhetorical conceit, the most suitable historian of Elizabeth's reign was her first minister, or even the queen herself, or her successor. A second best was the scholar capable of making sense of the state archive, to which Camden had been admitted as a special privilege by Burghley himself, and to which he later had access through Cotton's winning ways with their keeper.

Balancing Camden's desire to please, or at least avoid offence, was his celebrated devotion to truth. 'For the Love of Truth, as it hath been the onely Incitement to me to undertake this Work: so hath it also been my onely Scope and Aim in it ... As for Danger, I feared none, no not from those who think the Memory of succeeding Ages may be extinguished by present Power'—a statement with Tacitean resonances.[100] Trevor-Roper thought that Camden was as good as his word. 'The pressure of King James is reflected not at all' in 'this magnificently uncourtly work'.[101] But a more sceptical reader might take Camden's protestations as a health warning. Trevor-Roper conceded that Camden allowed prejudice to overcome impartiality when it came to the earl of Leicester, but believed this to have been a unique lapse of judgment.[102] However, it has recently been shown that Camden was also capable of stretching a point in the other direction, in order to protect the reputation of his principal patron, Burghley.[103]

[98] *The Ende of Nero and Begining of Galba*, Epistle.

[99] Camden to 'N. N.', 'Right Honourable', Smith, *Epistolae*, no. 287, p. 351.

[100] MacCaffrey, 4–5. *Cf.* Publius Cornelius Tacitus, tr. R. Grenewey, *The Annales* (1598), 101, referring to the error 'of such as thinke with the power and authorities they have in their own time, they can also extinguish the memory of former times.' (I owe this reference to Lisa Richardson.)

[101] Trevor-Roper, *Renaissance Essays*, 134–5.

[102] *Ibid.*, 142. The reasons for Camden's hatred of Leicester will repay further reflection and investigation, given his friendship with Sir Philip Sidney and others in that connection, including Leicester's secretary Jean Hotman, who was a valuable continental contact. (Smith, *Epistolae*, pp. 120–1, 124–6, 174–5, 201–3; Eleanor Rosenberg, *Leicester Patron of Letters* (New York, 1955), 269–70; *Poems by William Camden*, 30.) Camden's copy of the *Franco-Gallia* by Hotman's father Francis is in the Bodleian Library, with annotations in Camden's hand.

[103] Hiram Morgan has shown how Camden composed the history of a murky episode, the political assassination of the Lord Deputy of Ireland, Sir John Perrot, in order to cover up what Morgan calls Burghley's 'despicable behaviour' in this case. (Hiram Morgan, 'The Fall of Sir John Perrot', in John Guy, ed., *The Reign of Elizabeth I: Court and Culture in the Last Decade* (Cambridge, 1995), 109–25). Comparison of the various editions of the *Annales* suggests that Camden repented of what he had done to Perrot.

Let us not deny Camden a generous measure of impartiality, but rather seek to account for it. If he was to trespass into the quagmire of recent politics, it provided some protection to follow the path of fidelity to the written record. 'Mine owne Judgment I have not delivered according to Prejudice or Affection, whilst writing with an undistempered and even Mind ...'[104] This may also help to account for Camden's most common, and laconic, rhetorical device: some thought this, some that, which is surely how Burghley himself would have written history. We associate archivally based, ostensibly objective history with the liberal, bourgeois environment of the nineteeth and twentieth centuries, the product of academic freedom. Have we given sufficient thought to the possibility that 'modern', 'scientific' history, was enforced by the hostile environment of the world of Tacitus reborn, a Europe of incipient absolutism?

However 'uncourtly' Camden may have been, he gave James I's mother, Mary Queen of Scots, a good press: 'A Lady fixed and constant in her Religion, of singular Piety towards God, invincible Magnanimity of Mind, Wisedom above her Sex, and admirable [surpassing? passing?] Beauty; a Lady to be reckoned in the List of those Princesses which have changed their Felicity for Misery and Calamity.'[105] It is impossible to say whether this was Camden's own honest appraisal of the lady (we know how much he detested those 'effervescent' Protestants who deserved more of the blame for Mary's downfall than Mary herself); or whether his eulogy took some prudent account of 'present power'.[106]

But Hearne reveals that where Mary Queen of Scots was concerned, Camden made adjustments to the first edition which are significant. In the 1615 text and the translations which derive from it, it is said that Elizabeth, from her heart, as it seemed, 'ut videbatur',[107] misliked the insolency of the Scots in deposing their queen. Camden had second thoughts about 'ut videbatur' and struck it out, leaving Elizabeth's displeasure unqualified.[108] In the text of 1615, it was said that when the

There are passages in Hearne (ii. 425–6, 456–8, 558–9) which place him in a much more favourable light. It is not clear what motivated these changes.

[104] MacCaffrey, 6.

[105] *Ibid.*, 288.

[106] But we know, because he tells us, that Camden feared that James I would take exception to his laudatory if barbed obit for his mother's arch-enemy, Sir Francis Walsingham. (*Epistolae*, no. 289, p. 351.) The obit ran: 'A man exceeding wise and industrious, having discharged very honourable Embassies, a most sharpe maintainer of the pure Religion, a most diligent searcher of hidden secrets, who knew excellently well how to winne mens mindes unto him, and to apply them to his own uses.' (Norton 1630, Bk. IV, 20–1.)

[107] *Annales*, 145.

[108] Hearne, i. 171, noting the correction 'in Camden's own hand'. Norton 1635, Bk. I, 99, retains 'as it seemed', in parentheses.

news of Mary's execution reached Elizabeth, she 'either conceived or pretended grief and great displeasure', grief about the fate of her cousin, anger directed against William Davison, the under secretary who was to carry the can for delivering the execution warrant: 'iram … et dolorem … conceperit aut praesetulerit.'[109] This sentence is written in Cotton's hand in Cotton MS. Faustina F X.[110] But in his revision of this passage Camden crossed out 'aut preasetulerit'.[111] These were the most important two words which Camden ever wrote, or unwrote. For their implication was that Elizabeth was fully complicit in Mary's death and that her grief and anger were synthetic and diplomatic. Hearne's 1717 edition also contains a paragraph, which follows this passage and which had otherwise only occurred in 1635. This tells how letters, messengers and spies were sent into Scotland to sound out James VI's intentions and to put the best face on what had happened, explaining amongst other things that Leicester's part in the affair had been prompted by his need to placate the Protestants ('Puritans'?) and to protect himself against his enemies among papists and courtiers; and that Walsingham was an honest man 'that bare a *true Romane* spirit'.[112] This passage was not an afterthought but was prudently suppressed in the first edition. The question remains unanswerable, whether these textual adjustments were dictated by the apprehension of 'present power', or by respect for Camden's own declared principles: 'Things doubtful I have interpreted favourably; Things secret and abtruse I have not pried into. "The hidden Meanings of Princes (saith that great Master of History [Polybius]) and what they secretly design to search out, it is unlawful, it is doubtfull and dangerous: pursue not therefore the Search thereof." '[113]

It is now a little late to address the question of what Camden's sources actually were. Camden supplies no references and does not tell us. Was that too a deliberate stratagem? Sometimes he is his own authority. He lived through the whole of Elizabeth's reign, seven years of age when it began, fifty-two when it ended. 'Mine own Cabinets and Writings I also searched into … ; … have myself seen and observed many things, and received others from credible Persons that have been before me, men who have been present at the transacting of Matters, and such as have been addicted to the Parties on both sides in the

[109] *Annales*, 466.

[110] British Library, MS. Cotton Faustina F.X, fo. 80^v.

[111] Hearne, ii. 546. Norton's edition of 1635, which incorporates many of Camden's changes, retains, for whatever reason, 'either conceived or pretended'. (Norton 1635, 349.)

[112] *Ibid.*, 550; Norton 1635, 352.

[113] MacCaffrey, 5–6.

contrariety of Religion.'[114] On Francis Drake, Camden writes: 'to relate no more then I have heard from himselfe'.[115] So as the contemporary of the history he wrote, Camden has a huge advantage over 'us'. We were not there when John Stubbs had his right hand struck off by the executioner for that seditious libel, *The Gaping Gulf*. But Camden was. 'I remember (being there present) that when Stubbs, after his Right hand was cut off, put off his Hat with his Left, and said with a loud voice, "God Save the Queen"'; and he tells us about the reaction of the crowd, silent and shaken.[116] Camden's hostile feelings about Leicester are never disguised. 'In a word, people talked openly in his Commendation, but privately he was ill spoken of by the greater part.'[117] Nevertheless, we prick up our ears when Camden tells us that he himself, 'being then a young man', often heard it said that a clause in the Treason Act of 1571 dealing with the succession, 'except the same bee the Natural issue of [the queen's] body', was put there by Leicester on purpose, 'that he might one day obtrude upon the English some bastard sonne of his, for the Queens naturall issue'. This was no more than a good political joke, and it is evidence not of Leicester's actions or intentions, still less of the queen's sexual history, but of what the chattering classes were heard by the young Camden to be saying.[118]

Camden's account of Queen Elizabeth's deathbed is very famous: how she declared that since her throne was a throne of kings, she would not be succeeded by some vile person; and, asked what she meant, '*Rex*, inquit, *mihi succedat volo, et quis nisi qui cognatus proximus, Rex Scotorum*'—who but my cousin, the king of Scots?[119] This passage is heavily worked over in Cotton's hand in MS. Faustina F III.[120] Was it pure invention? Elizabeth is thought by this stage to have been speechless and only capable of signifying her mind by a hand signal. Yet Camden was, if not an observer, very close to those who were. Nine days before the end, he had written to Cotton about the queen's symptoms and the likely prognosis, evidently from the Court: 'I know you are (as we all here have been) in a melancholy and pensive cogitation.'[121]

[114] *Ibid.*, 4. For a 'politic' (*politique*?) historian, Camden is very preoccupied with 'the contrariety of Religion'.

[115] Norton 1630, Bk. II, 110.

[116] MacCaffrey, 138–9.

[117] *Ibid.*, 330. *Cf.* Savile's Tacitus, (of Mutianus): 'openly praiseworthy, his secrete actions were ill spoken of'. (*The Ende of Nero and Beginning of Galba*, 6.) I owe this reference to Lisa Richardson.

[118] Camden admitted that it was a joke: 'Incredible it is what ieasts lewd catchers of words made amongst themselves.' (Norton 1630, Bk. 2. 28–9.)

[119] *Annales, Tomus Alter* (16276)), 285.

[120] British Library, MS. Cotton Faustina F III, fos. 215^v–216^r.

[121] Camden to Cotton, 15 March [1603], British Library MS. Cotton Julius C III, fo. 64^r; printed, T. Wright, ed., *Queen Elizabeth and Her Times* (1838), ii. 494.

But very soon the editor whom Camden deserves will have to penetrate the archives. And he will be wise to begin with the Cotton MSS. According to Smith, 'the Records and Instruments out of which he extracted his *Annales* are most of them, if not all, in *Cotton's* Library.'[122] However the search is unlikely to end there and is certain to take some time.

I end with a vignette. In her first Parliament, Elizabeth was under pressure to marry; and she responded with one of those answerless speeches, famous for its concluding flourish. She would be content if in due course a marble tomb should proclaim that a queen, having reigned such a time, lived and died a virgin. These words come through very well in Camden's taut, sententious Latin: HIC SITA ELIZABETHA, QUAE VIRGO REGNAVIT, VIRGO OBIIT, placed in capitals in the printed text and so corrected in MS. in Faustina F I, Cotton's version of the speech (at least it is in his hand) having been inserted in the earlier version of 1559, in Faustina F IV.[123]

The speech in Camden, while manifestly the same speech, differs from all other known copies.[124] The most interesting variant is a small piece of theatre recorded nowhere else. 'And behold (said she, which I marvell ye have forgotten) the Pledge of this my Wedlock and Marriage with my Kingdom. (And therewith [she stretched forth her finger and shewed the ring of gold] wherewith at her Coronation she had in a set form of words solemnly given her self in Marriage to her Kingdom.)' And then, having made a pause, she said that she should not be upbraided for lack of children: 'for every one of you, and as many as are English-men, are Children and Kinsmen to me'.[125]

Neale and the editor of *Proceedings in the Parliaments of Elizabeth I* deny Camden's version documentary status.[126] The implication is that without further evidence we must regard it as suspect. Did Camden make up the little scene with the ring? Only if he forgot his own declared historiographical principles. Surely he must have received and recorded

[122] Smith's Life in Gibson, ed., *Britannia*.

[123] *Annales*, 35; British Library, MS. Cotton Faustina F I, fos. 39–40, MS. Faustina IV, fos. 27^{r}–29^{v}.

[124] T. E. Hartley, ed., *Proceedings in the Parliaments of Elizabeth I*, i. *1558–1581* (Leicester, 1981), 44–5.

[125] MacCaffrey, 29–30. The passage in square brackets is supplied from Norton 1635, which is more faithful to the original Latin. (Helen Hackett, *Virgin Mother, Maiden Queen: Elizabeth I and the Cult of the Virgin Mary* (Basingstoke, 1995), 274, n. 83.)

[126] J. E. Neale, *Elizabeth I and her Parliaments 1559–1581* (1953), 47, n. 3 ('I Know of no text, I have therefore ignored it'); Hartley, ed., *Proceedings*, 44. Susan Doran calls Camden's account 'little more than a myth', and seems to think that the absence of his version in Cecil's papers ('Camden's source') is conclusive evidence of invention. (*Monarchy and Matrimony: The Courtships of Elizabeth I* (1996), 1–2.

the little play with the ring as a piece of oral testimony, transmitted by some of those 'credible persons'?

But no doubt this was more than a simple piece of reporting. Elizabeth's strategy had been to declare herself ready both to marry and not to marry, while not concealing her preference for the latter. Camden's version differs from what appears to be the canonical text in suggesting that the transition from a private to a public life had actually strengthened this celibate resolve. 'But now that the publick Care of governing the Kingdom is laid upon me, to draw upon me also the Cares of Marriage may seem a point of inconsiderate Folly.'[127] And then follows the little ring scene. The effect of this, when added to 'Virgo Regnavit, Virgo Obiit' was to strengthen Elizabeth's apparent commitment to virginity, and at the age of twenty-five; indeed to project back into 1559 the legend of the Virgin Queen which, as recent scholarship assures us, was in reality invented, for political purposes, some twenty years later.[128] Is it relevant that Camden himself, as Smith tells us, 'chose a single life'?[129] While historians are not allowed to lie, they cannot help being themselves. But whether Camden tampered with the historical record to achieve this effect, against his own declared principles, we shall never know.

Was Camden one of us? Let Sir Maurice Powicke have the last as well as the first word. We do not read Camden for his learning. The philology of his *Britannia*, for example, is 'pitiful'.[130] But then comes this: 'The foundations of historical criticism were not yet laid. What Camden did was to help to create the atmosphere in which they could be laid.'[131] But that can hardly have been what Camden, the historian, intended to do.

[127] MacCaffrey, 29.

[128] Hackett, *Virgin Mother*, 229–30; Doran, *Monarchy*, 154–209; Susan Doran, 'Juno Versus Diana: The Treatment of Elizabeth's Marriage in Plays and Entertainments, 1561–81', *Historical Journal*, xxxviii. (1995), 257–74; John N. King, 'Queen Elizabeth I: Representations of the Virgin Queen', *Renaissance Quarterly*, 43 (1990), 30–74.

[129] Smith's Life, Gibson, ed., *Britannia.*

[130] Powicke, 'William Camden', 75. The greatest eighteenth-century authority on the Welsh language, Lewis Morris, author of *Celtic Remains*, wrote of Camden's 'wild fancies' and 'lame guesses' where matters Welsh were concerned. (Geraint H. Jenkins, 'The Cultural Uses of the Welsh Language 1660–1800', in Jenkins, ed., *The Welsh Language Before the Industrial Revolution* (Cardiff, 1997), 386.)

[131] Powicke, 'William Camden', 78.

FOR REASONED FAITH OR EMBATTLED CREED? RELIGION FOR THE PEOPLE IN EARLY MODERN EUROPE

By Euan Cameron

READ 24 OCTOBER 1997 AT THE UNIVERSITY OF ST ANDREWS

THERE has long been some measure of agreement that European people in the middle ages adhered to a form of Christianity which was 'folklorised', 'enchanted', or 'magical'. Interwoven with the traditional creeds and the orthodox liturgy were numerous beliefs and practices which were intended to ensure spiritual and bodily welfare, and guard against misfortune. To the endless frustration of theologians, 'religion' and 'superstition' stubbornly refused to remain clearly separate, despite the intellectual effort expended in forcing them into different compartments.[1] 'Superstitious' rites or beliefs repeatedly intersected with the official Catholic cult. It was believed that if a talisman were placed under an altar-cloth during mass, it would acquire spiritual potency. Orthodox prayers were constantly adapted to serve the needs of popular magic. Clergy, let alone layfolk, found the line between acceptable and superstitious practice difficult to draw. For a graphic illustration of this problem, one need only look at the following recipe for curing a hailstorm caused by sorcery:

> But against hailstones and storms, besides those things said earlier about raising the sign of the cross, this remedy may be used: three little hailstones are thrown into the fire with the invocation of the most Holy Trinity; the Lord's Prayer with the Angelic Salutation is added twice or three times, and the Gospel of St John, 'In the beginning was the word', while the sign of the cross is made against the storm from all quarters, before and behind, and from every part of the earth. And then, when at the end one repeats three times,

[1] Defining the boundaries between superstition and religion forms the main issue in St Thomas Aquinas, *Summa Theologica*, iia iiae, qq. 92–6. Several treatises on superstition were written because a 'case of conscience' had arisen over whether a particular rite or rites were superstitious or not. See e.g. Martín de Arles y Andosilla, *Tractatus de Superstitionibus*, in Nicolaus Jacquier, ed., *Flagellum Haereticorum Fascinariorum* [and other works] (Frankfurt, 1581), pp. 351ff [but first published 1517]; and Henricus de Gorihem (Henry of Gorcum), *De Superstitiosis quibusdam casibus* (Esslingen, c. 1473). The author gratefully acknowledges the support given by the Leverhulme Trust, in awarding a Research Fellowship which made the preparation of this paper possible.

> 'the Word was made flesh', and says three times after that, 'by these Gospels uttered, may that tempest flee', then suddenly, so long as the storm was caused to happen by sorcery, it will cease.

This recipe might be expected to originate in some peasant's primer; in fact it comes from none other than the notorious witch-hunting textbook, the *Malleus Maleficarum*, written by two German Dominican friars in the 1480s. It was copied, in the complete conviction of its Catholic respectability, by the papal theologian and expert on the hearing of confessions, Silvestro Mazzolini of Priero, in a work published in 1521.[2]

In the past, most historians have simply observed this phenomenon, which is copiously documented and often severely criticised in the writings of early modern commentators, especially Protestants.[3] Some who have tried to explain it have stressed the role played by surviving pagan beliefs, incompletely or even half-heartedly winnowed out by Christian missionaries in the early middle ages and after.[4] The notion of pagan survivals in Europe becomes superficially more attractive if one draws the plausible parallels between late medieval Europe and modern rural Latin America, where the Roman Catholic Church maintains its hold on the animist beliefs of indigenous villagers by a subtle, at times eclectic or syncretic, attitude to their mountain-spirit cults.[5] At the time, however, contemporary observers usually attributed 'superstitious' charms to the degradation of orthodox Christian prayers over time. Most 'charms', they said, had originally been pious prayers, which the devil had abused.[6] Such a falling-away from an imagined

[2] Heinrich Institoris and Jakob Sprenger, *Malleus Maleficarum*, ii.2.7; and compare Silvestro Mazzolini Prierias, *De Strigimagarum Demonumque Mirandis Libri iii* (Rome, Antonius Bladis de Asula, 1521), sig. ff ii[v]. For further evidence see E. Duffy, *The Stripping of the Altars: Traditional Religion in England c.1400–c.1580* (New Haven and London, 1992), 266ff.

[3] See the classic discussion in K. Thomas, *Religion and the Decline of Magic* (London, 1971), 27–57; and the appropriation of his interpretation for continental material in Stuart Clark, *Thinking with Demons: The Idea of Witchcraft in Early Modern Europe* (Oxford, 1997), 533. Further reflections on the Reformation and magical world-views are found in R. W. Scribner, 'The Impact of the Reformation on Daily Life' in *Mensch und Objekt im Mittelalter und in der frühen Neuzeit*, Österreichische Akademie der Wissenschaften, Phil-hist. Klasse, 568 (Vienna, 1990), 315–43, and R. W. Scribner, 'The Reformation, Magic and the "Disenchantment of the World"', in *Journal of Interdisciplinary History* 23 (1993), 475–94.

[4] See the argument of V. I. J. Flint, *The Rise of Magic in Early Medieval Europe* (Oxford, 1991); for enduring paganism, note also the appropriation of evidence from Olaus Magnus, *Historia de Gentibus Septentrionalibus* (Rome, 1556), in C. Ginzburg, *Ecstasies: Deciphering the Witches' Sabbath*, trans. R. Rosenthal (London, 1992).

[5] For Mexican evidence see Jacques Lafaye, *Quetzalcoatl and Guadalupe: the Formation of Mexican National Consciousness, 1531–1813*, trans. Benjamin Keen (Chicago, 1976); N. S. Davidson, *The Counter-Reformation* (Oxford, 1987), 70ff.

[6] E.g. Johannes Nider, *Preceptorium divine legis* (Basle, c.1470), precept i, ch. 11, q. 27. [This edition has neither foliation nor quire signatures.] On the argument that the devil mocked and parodied divine ordinances, see Clark, *Demons*, ch. 6, 80–93.

pristine past came more naturally to them, just as the idea of unfinished evolution offers a more plausible explanation to our world-view.

Wherever medieval 'superstitions' came from, it is widely thought that early modern Europe saw the first concentrated attempt to dissuade the people from this sort of belief-system, or at least to drive a wedge firmly and consistently between orthodox Christianity and its 'folklorised' accretions. Furthermore, it is usually argued that this campaign was waged by Protestant and Catholic reformers alike, in similar terms and with similar arguments. For all sorts of reasons, it does seem to make sense to envisage the early modern period as the one in which Europe's people were, for the first time, deliberately and systematically dissuaded from 'superstitious' patterns of thought. After the Reformation, the Protestant and Catholic confessions embarked on a massive educational enterprise, in which each sought to inculcate a uniform pattern of belief and practice among its people, from the top down.[7] The confessions backed up their educational work by strenuous, if often incomplete, efforts to institute pastoral and spiritual discipline. Such discipline produced the legions of visitation protocols found in reformed Catholicism, and the corresponding Protestant effort, which has been documented in the last generation by historians of German reformed 'confessionalism'.[8] In so far as both Protestant and Catholic educators laid claim to the mantle of Renaissance Christian humanism, both were heirs to the tradition in which Erasmus of Rotterdam had pressed for a personal, ethical piety, in place of a religion based on 'superstitious' cults and ceremonies.[9]

In different ways, the idea that 'superstitions' were first attacked in a thoroughgoing way in the early modern period also fits in with two of the most current models of early modern cultural change: the 'acculturation' model proposed by Jean Delumeau and, in his earlier works, by Robert Muchembled; and the model of a progressive

[7] For catechesis, see e.g. G. Strauss, *Luther's House of Learning: Indoctrination of the Young in the German Reformation* (Baltimore, 1978); Ian Green, *The Christian's ABC: Catechisms and Catechizing in England c.1530–1740* (Oxford, 1996); on the Roman Catholic side, the works of Peter Canisius, *Summa doctrinae christianae* (Vienna, 1555), *Catechismus minimus* (Ingolstadt, 1556), and *Catechismus minor* (Cologne, 1558), and also the Tridentine Catechism, published as *Catechismus ad parochos* (Rome, 1566).

[8] On pastoral visitations see Umberto Mazzone and Angelo Turchini, *I Visiti Pastorali: Analisi di una fonte* (Bologna, 1985); on confessional discipline see R. Po-Chia Hsia, *Social Discipline in the Reformation: Central Europe 1550–1750* (London, 1989), esp. 122–73. A recent contribution to this subject is B. Tolley, *Pastors and Parishioners in Württemberg during the Late Reformation 1581–1621* (Stanford, Calif., 1995), 64ff.

[9] For typical Erasmian satire of vulgar superstitions see *The Colloquies of Erasmus*, ed. C. R. Thompson (Chicago, 1965), esp. 'A Pilgrimage for Religion's Sake' and 'The Shipwreck'. It is noteworthy that Erasmus's works were placed on the Index in the Counter-Reformation, but extensively used as school-texts in Protestantism.

separation of élite and popular cultures proposed by Peter Burke and in Muchembled's more recent writings.[10] The only issue for debate appears to be whether the enterprise of dissuading the masses from their traditional beliefs succeeded or not. If it succeeded, it was 'acculturation'; if it failed, then the outcome was a separate 'élite culture'. Most recently, Dr Stuart Clark has lent further weight to the idea that Protestant and Catholic fought on a common religious front against popular magic. His monumental study of Protestant and Catholic demonologies relegates confessional differences to the sidelines. He continually stresses the shared concepts and the similar purpose behind all demonological writers.[11]

There is considerable evidence to support that view, and this paper certainly does not propose to try to challenge all of it at once.[12] It does, however, entail certain risks, which the homogenising approach of the secular historians of culture may cause to be overlooked. Essentially, it proposes that two separate processes were at work in the religious history of early modern Europe. On the one hand there was the establishment of Protestant and Roman Catholic Christianity, and on the other the campaign to dissuade the people from their traditional sub-Christian beliefs. If there was conflict over the aims of the first enterprise, there may still (so the theory implies) have been agreement over the second. Yet I simply do not believe that the theologians of the sixteenth and early seventeenth centuries saw their task of taking true religion to the people in this fragmented, compartmentalised way. Put another way, it is not sufficient to analyse the Protestant and Roman Catholic responses to popular belief by cutting out all the theological differences between them. The writers and preachers who tried to take a reasoned, 'modern' religion to the people of Europe were also, at one and the same time, the champions of controversial, embattled, rival systems of belief. This essay seeks to put the theological controversy back into the history of the assault on 'popular superstition'. It will do so by examining some of the wide range of literature written by laity and clergy about popular religion, from both sides of the religious

[10] For acculturation, see J. Delumeau, *Catholicism between Luther and Voltaire* (London, 1977), and R. Muchembled, *Popular Culture and Elite Culture in France, 1400–1750* (Baton Rouge, 1985); also the discussion in J. K. Powis, 'Repression and Autonomy: Christians and Christianity in the Historical Work of Jean Delumeau', *Journal of Modern History* 64 (1992), 366–74; for the separation of élite and popular cultures see P. Burke, *Popular Culture in Early Modern Europe* (London, 1978) and his sources, also the more recent work of R. Muchembled, especially his *L'Invention de l'homme moderne: Sensibilités, moeurs et comportements collectifs sous l'ancien régime* (Paris, 1988).

[11] Clark, *Demons*, esp. chapters 29–34.

[12] This traditional view, by ascribing the attack on 'superstitions' chiefly to the early modern period, may also be unfair to late medieval pastoral theologians. That point is to be developed in a separate article.

divide. These works include sermons, pastoral guides, pamphlets, even university theses, and survive in the European vernaculars as well as in Latin. They are important, first because they form a tradition, within which authors borrowed from each other and responded to each other's views; and secondly, because they circulated in a milieu in which future pastors and priests were trained. They bear abundant witness to the desire to inculcate a 'reasoned faith' in place of popular superstition; but their arguments show, as I shall suggest, certain important differences between one confession and another.

II

First, one important point must be conceded to the thesis that there was a common front between Protestant and Catholic reformers. Both groups of theologians started from a shared body of beliefs about the nature of the universe, and about natural causation, which they inherited from their medieval scholastic predecessors, and ultimately from Augustine and other early Fathers of the Church. Protestants concurred with the traditional belief that the universe was filled with spiritual creatures who were either good angels or fallen angels, that is, demons; they thus rejected the popular belief that there were morally neutral spirits (sprites, house-spirits and others of their kind) whose help might be invoked.[13] Demons, they agreed, were insatiably determined to injure people in body and soul. They could do this by using their great intelligence, speed, and physical power to achieve surprising, but essentially natural effects very quickly. They could also generate illusions which tricked the human senses, and convinced people that they were even more powerful and wise than they were. However, they could not perform genuine miracles; that is, they could not suspend the order of nature. They could not raise the dead, foreknow the future with certainty, see into the human heart, or change one created thing substantially into another. These things were the prerogative of God

[13] For demons, see e.g. Augustin Lercheimer, *Ein Christlich Bedencken unnd Erinnerung von Zauberey, woher, was, und wie vielfaeltig sie sey* ... in *Theatrum de veneficis: Das ist: Von Teufelsgespenst, Zauberern und Gifftbereitern, Schwartzkünstlern, Hexen und Unholden, vieler fürnemmen Historien und Exempel* ... (Frankfurt-am-Main, Nicolaus Bassaeus, 1586), 262ff; for a Catholic example compare e.g. Pedro Ciruelo, *Reprouacion de las supersticiones y hechizerias*, translated as *Pedro Ciruelo's A Treatise Reproving all Superstitions and Forms of Witchcraft*, ed. E. A. Maio and D. W. Pearson (Madison and London, 1977), 83–8. The morally ambiguous 'house-spirits' are attested e.g. in the 'duen de casa' described by Alphonsus de Spina, *Fortalitium Fidei* ... (Lyons, Guillaume Balsarin, 1487), sig. Li^{v}, or the 'helekeppelin' described by Martin Luther in his *Decem Praecepta Wittenbergensi praedicata populo*, in *M. Luther, Werke: Kritische Gesamtausgabe*, 58 vols (Weimar, 1883–1948) [hereafter *WA*] i. 406.

alone.[14] Philipp Melanchthon reinforced this point about the limited power of demons with a particularly graphic story in one of his lectures, which was reported by at least three other writers. At Bologna, a female musician died, but was restored to apparent life by a demonic illusion, in which she appeared to eat, drink, and play her instrument as before. Only when a sorcerer saw her, who could see through the trickery with which she had apparently been revived, was it revealed that she was just a corpse whom a demon had caused to move.[15]

Protestant and Catholic theologians then applied their shared 'demonology' to explain and condemn the two main branches of popular 'superstition' as commonly described, namely divination by unlawful means, and magical or superstitious blessing and healing. Protestants, like their medieval antecedents, firmly denied that there was any natural power inherent in words, signs, symbols, or any other inanimate thing to cause marvellous transformations in natural objects. They insisted that words and signs had meaning only to another intelligent being which could draw meaning from them.[16] Since divinations and magical healing had no natural causes, their apparently marvellous effects had to derive from the co-operation of demons, whether these were deliberately invoked in ceremonial magic, or were unconsciously invited to offer their assistance when a superstitious rite or technique was performed. This analysis led the Lutheran Johann Georg Godelmann, for example, to launch a fierce attack on the populist magical healing of Theophrastus Paracelsus (1493–1541), which encouraged the use of amulets, sympathetic magic, and the recipes of gypsies and old women to cure ailments.[17] It is striking that the Jesuit Martin Delrio, who attacked Godelmann bitterly on other issues, plagiarised the Lutheran's attack on Paracelsus more or less wholesale in Book VI of his *Magical Disquisitions*.[18]

[14] Lercheimer, *Christlich Bedencken*, 263; *cf.* Lambert Daneau, *Dialogus de Veneficis*, in Nicolaus Jacquier, ed., *Flagellum Haereticorum Fascinariorum* [and other works] (Frankfurt, 1581), 271–4. For this 'science' of demonic activity see Clark, *Demons*, ch. 11, 161ff.

[15] The story is reported by Lercheimer, *Christlich Bedencken*, fo. 281r; and by Johann Georg Godelmann, *Tractatus de Magis, Veneficis et Lamiis, deque his recte cognoscendis et puniendis* (Frankfurt, 1601), 36, based on Caspar Peucer, *Commentarius, de Praecipuis Divinationum generibus, in quo a prophetiis, authoritate divine traditis, et a Physicis conjecturis, discernuntur artes et imposturae diabolicae, atque observationes natae ex superstitione, et cum hac conjunctae: Et monstrantur fontes ac causae Physicarum praedictionum: Diabolicae vero ac superstitiosae confutatae damnantur...* (Frankfurt, 1607), 14.

[16] On this position see Clark, *Demons*, 281ff; and also e.g. Daneau, *Dialogus*, 265–7.

[17] Godelmann, *Tractatus de Magis*, 80–3, 86–7, 92–8. Godelmann singled out Paracelsus's *De occulta Philosophia*, *De Caelesti Medicina*, *De Philosophia Magna*, and *De Philosophia ad Athenienses*. See Theophrastus Bombast von Hohenheim [Paracelsus], *Opera Omnia*, 3 vols (Geneva, 1658).

[18] Martinus Delrio S.J., *Disquisitionum Magicarum Libri Sex, in tres tomos partiti*, 3 vols. (Lyon, 1599–1600), vi, ch. 2, sect i, in vol. iii, 175ff.

Thus far there is broad agreement; that is, over the nature of the spiritual hierarchy, and the possible causes of supernatural events in the world. This measure of agreement is to be expected, since Protestant and Catholic churchmen were alike *theologians*. As theologians, they were reared in the same tradition of natural philosophy, neo-scholastic Aristotelianism. The natural philosophy which supported the orthodox belief in demons derived from the same roots, whether it was via the reconstructed Lutheran Aristotelianism of Philipp Melanchthon, the Calvinist scholasticism of Lambert Daneau, or the neo-Thomism of the Spanish Jesuits.[19] However, this agreement only extends as far as the broad lines of analysis and diagnosis. It does not take us very far into the realm of prescription. It does not tell us just what sort of religion was deemed acceptable for Europe's people, and conversely, how wide the net was cast to drag in those aspects of religious belief which were to be condemned as 'superstitious'. Once we look at the practical application of these general principles, we find that the religions proposed respectively by Protestants and by Catholics for Europe's people, and the things which they each denounced as 'superstitious', were significantly different.

III

The early Protestant reformers did not write a great deal about popular superstitions in the years when the reformed churches were being established. Martin Luther did offer one of the fullest discussions of such practices as conjuring weapons, love-magic, amulets, observance of unlucky days, or of omens.[20] However, the sermon-sequence expounding the Ten Commandments, where this discussion occurs, dates from June 1516 onwards. For all its critique of saint-cults, it is essentially a late medieval piece. It draws on sources such as Geiler von Kaisersberg and Johannes Nider. Its emphases were not repeated in Luther's later pastoral writings such as the *Catechisms*.[21]

[19] Melanchthon's Aristotelianism is discussed in Sachiko Kusukawa, *The Transformation of Natural Philosophy: The Case of Philip Melanchthon* (Cambridge, 1995); Daneau's scholasticism in O. Fatio, *Méthode et Théologie: Lambert Daneau et les débuts de la scholastique réformée* (Geneva, 1976); that of the Spanish Jesuits in Charles B. Schmitt, Quentin Skinner, and Eckhard Kessler (eds.) *The Cambridge History of Renaissance Philosophy* (Cambridge, 1988), pp. 490–527 and refs.

[20] WA i.401–10.

[21] WA i.409 cites the story of a woman who suffered from an illusion of night-flight, from Johann Geiler von Kaisersberg, *Die Emeis* (Strasbourg, Johannes Grieninger, 1517), fo. 37^{v}, which is in turn based on Johannes Nider's *Formicarius*, consulted as J. Nider, *De Visionibus ac revelationibus* ... (Helmstedt, 1692), bk. 2 ch. 4, 200–1. On Luther see S. Brauner, *Fearless Wives and Frightened Shrews: the Construction of the Witch in Early Modern Germany* (Amherst, Mass., 1995), 53–67.

One of the first Protestant pieces to address popular superstitions directly was the *Short Opinion, as to what should be thought about idolatrous blessings and conjurations*, published at Basle in 1543 by Johann Spreter of Rottweil.[22] *Segen* (which needs to be translated simultaneously as 'blessings' and 'enchantments') included all forms of words and rites used to transform something natural into something supernatural, or to give spiritual potency to any sort of cult object. *Segenspruch* was a particular preoccupation both of German and of Spanish theologians.[23] The wrongness of *Segen*, for Spreter, lay not only in their source, or whether God or the devil was invoked, but in the very essence of what was attempted by them. God blessed all created things, and assigned to them their purposes; to try to add some additional quality to an object by one's own blessing was to try to amend God's work, and would bring a curse on the one who tried.[24] Spreter's argument was taken up in almost the same words in the *Christian Opinion and Remonstrance on Sorcery*, published under the name of Augustin Lercheimer in a manual of treatises on magic in 1586.[25] '*Segnen* and *Beschweren* is to believe that one can with words, gestures, and certain shapes increase or diminish the power of creatures ... or give them another power against their nature and identity, against God's will and ordinance, which in the creation gave everything its power and operation, according to which it stays ...' This, it was argued, was in effect robbing God of his prerogative to assign the properties to each created thing.[26] Or, as the Tübingen academic Johann Heerbrand put it in a set of theological theses in 1570, 'Neither does the Word of God uttered in this way by the magicians confer any new properties or qualities on things, besides those which they received from God at creation.'[27]

Created things, for the Protestants, always remained just that: herbs remained herbs, water remained water. It might be inferred from this that the Protestant critique of superstition would then categorise Roman Catholic cult-objects, such as holy water, as 'superstitious' in the same

[22] Johannes Spreter, *Ein Kurtzer Bericht, was von den Abgoetterischen Saegen und Beschweren zuehalten, wie der etlich volbracht, unnd das die ein Zauberey, auch greuewel vor Gott dem Herren seind* (Basle, 1543).

[23] The Spanish word *ensalmo* most closely corresponds to the German *Segen*. For a sociological and theoretical approach to this issue see Irmgard Hampp, *Beschwörung, Segen, Gebet: Untersuchungen zum Zauberspruch aus dem Bereich der Volksheilkunde* (Stuttgart, 1961). Tolley, *Pastors and Parishioners*, identifies the use of *Segen* as the most common form of superstitious practice *c.*1600.

[24] Spreter, *Kurtzer Bericht*, sigs. A ii^{r-v}, A iii^{r-v}.

[25] Lercheimer, *Christlich Bedencken*, 261–298.

[26] Lercheimer, *Christlich Bedencken*, 289.

[27] Jacobus Heerbrandus, *De Magia Disputatio ex cap. 7. Exo., ... praeside reverendo et clarissimo viro Jacobo Heerbrando, sacrae theologiae Doctore eximio, ac eiusdem in Academia Tubingensi Professore publico ... Nicolaus Falco Salueldensis ... respondere conabitur* (Tübingen, 1570), 12.

way as popular charms. In fact, one does not have to rely on inference. Right from the start, Protestant critics, Lutheran and reformed alike, included Roman rituals among superstitious enchantments. Spreter said that there were two sorts of enchanters, the monks and priests who tried to make a God out of consecrated salt, water, herbs, wax, etc., and the common conjurers.[28] Jakob Heerbrand went further: 'Pontiffs and priests, satellites of the Roman Antichrist ... sin much more seriously in this respect than common magicians and enchanters.'[29] Johann Georg Godelmann agreed that 'papal exorcists are to be numbered with the enchanters'.[30] These theologians and preachers attacked the entire paraphernalia of the Catholic cult as a form of sorcery, both in its purpose and in its details. Lutheran and reformed alike, it must be emphasised, denounced as magical the belief that by utterance of the words of consecration of the Eucharist, the substance of bread was instantly transformed into the body of Christ and the wine into his blood. They then went through the consecrations of the 'sacramentalia', holy salt, holy water, blessed herbs, the *agnus Dei* made of consecrated wax, the oil used in unction and baptism, and the churches, churchyards and church bells themselves.[31] All of these were enchantments, because they aspired to lock up the Holy Spirit into created things, as though they were magical instruments.

Criticism of the formulae by which Catholics blessed their holy things, their *sacramentalia*, was not confined to learned treatises or to academic debating-halls. The ultra-Lutheran Jakob Andreae preached a series of sermons at Esslingen, in which he thus denounced the rite by which the chrism was consecrated:

> The chrism ... is made with magical, enchanters' blessings, and when one seeks to learn the reason for these, it is no more than devil's work, that so often as the bishop consecrates the chrism, so he blows three times crosswise over the phial in which the oil is, and speaks the following words: 'I conjure you, creature of oil, by God the Father Almighty, who made heaven, earth, and sea, and all that therein is, that all power of Satan, and of all the host of the devils, all assaults and all fantasies of Satan, and their roots may be by you be torn up and driven out' ... Who will not think, when he hears these words of the Bishop, that he is hearing an enchanter or conjurer of devils? that he is conjuring the poor created thing of oil, no differently than if it were possessed with a thousand devils? ... he

[28] Spreter, *Kurtzer Bericht*, sig. Aiii^v.

[29] Heerbrand, *De Magia Disputatio*, 13.

[30] Godelmann, *Tractatus de Magis*, 55–6.

[31] Heerbrand, *De Magia Disputatio*, 13–15, theses 83–92; Lercheimer, *Christlich Bedencken*, 289–90; Godelmann, *Tractatus de Magis*, 57–8.

> breathes like an enchanter over the vessel in which the oil is kept; like an enchanter he makes two crosses; he conjures the devil, yea many devils, like an enchanter ... he has also just as little authority to use the name of God and the cross for this purpose, and to conjure the devil out of the oil, as any other enchanter or soothsayer, when they conjure the devil, and will tell to their neighbours where they may find their lost money or goods.[32]

When the sermons of the ultra-Lutheran Andreae and the ultra-Zwinglian Heinrich Bullinger are laid side by side, there is a remarkable measure of agreement between the arguments which they used against Roman rites. In the sixth sermon of the fifth series of his *Decades*, Bullinger devoted much care to an examination of the power of holy words, as applied to the consecrations of sacraments. He denied that in any scripture there was authority to suppose that the mere utterance of certain words could transform the natures of things, in the Eucharist or anything else. 'These imaginations,' he continued, 'do rather seem more to maintain superstition than religion; as though the words, pronounced according to the form conceived, had power to call down out of heaven, to bring from one place to another, to restore health ... or to transform or change.'[33] Catholic arguments, to the effect that a 'consecration' and a 'superstition' were different things, he rebutted with some scorn. They were based on a misunderstanding of the words 'blessing' and 'sanctify'. In any case, God made things holy, not man.[34]

There is more to this Reformation assault on the 'holy things' in the Catholic rite than tendentious rhetoric. In principle, Protestants denied that the power of God could be locked up, by the performance of certain words and ceremonies, into certain physical material objects. This entailed frontal confrontation not only with the Catholic theology of the sacraments, but also with things such as amulets, which belonged to a part of medieval popular religion which the reformed Roman Church protected and favoured. As will be discussed later, the Catholic Church still distributed the consecrated wax emblem called the *agnus Dei*. Its theologians also endorsed the wearing of texts from Scripture around the neck or in the clothing as phylacteries to guard against demonic assaults, albeit with a string of provisos and conditions. Jakob Heerbrand mocked the rhyme which claimed that the *agnus* broke the power of sin as Christ's blood did.[35] Bullinger, in his treatise *Against the*

[32] Godelmann, *Tractatus de Magis*, 58–9; the original edition of Andreae's sermon has not been traced.

[33] Bullinger, H., *The Decades of Henry Bullinger*, trans. 'H. I.' and ed. T. Harding, 4 vols, Parker Society (Cambridge, 1849–52), iv. 254–60.

[34] *Ibid.*, 260–7.

[35] Heerbrand, *De Magia Disputatio*, thesis 89, 14; also cited by Godelmann, *Tractatus de Magis*, 57.

Black Art, asserted that when people crossed themselves, or used fixed forms of words to which they ascribed curative power, it was idolatry and the devil's work.[36] Godelmann said that when St John's Gospel was worn to protect against artillery, then such an amulet became a 'sacrament of the devil' which could only work by demonic pact.[37] Antonius Praetorius, in his *Basic Advice about Sorcery* of 1613, lumped popular charms and Catholic *sacramentalia* together without distinction. If the devil could be hindered by crosses, herbs, salt, bread, and words, he would have to be weaker than a person, or even a dog or a pig. Holy words hung around the neck had nothing holy in themselves, at least not used in this way. 'It would not help against the devil if a man ate ten Bibles, and tied twenty around himself'; much less would a scrap of paper with a few words hung round the neck be of any help. This was a means by which the devil deceived people and drew them into superstition through abuse of his word.[38]

There was a fundamental difference between the Protestant concept of 'holiness' and its Catholic counterpart, which has its roots in the basic teachings of the Reformation about God's work. For Protestants, God always exercised his power directly, immediately, with absolute sovereign authority and all-encompassing providence. For Catholicism, whether medieval or reformed, God's power was often, even ordinarily, delegated: to holy Church, to holy people, into holy things. The very idea of 'Catholic' Christianity embodies the notion that divine power is authoritatively present in certain religious forms, which have been chosen and appointed by God's decree. In consequence, Protestantism was always bound to be far more hostile than Catholicism to the notion that divine power might be located reliably and consistently in certain things and places on earth. Faith in a transcendent God, not the use of *sacramentalia*, would defend Protestants against the devil. As Andreas Althamer preached in 1532, '[St Peter] does not say, have Masses read against the devil and his delusions, or sprinkle yourself with holy water, or light a consecrated candle, or hang St John's Gospel about your neck, as the Papists teach; but "resist him strongly in the faith". Faith must do it, not the holy-water spring, but faith and trust in God through Jesus Christ...'[39]

[36] Heinrich Bullinger, *Wider die Schwartzen Künst, Aberglaeubigs segnen, unwarhafftigs Warsagen, und andere dergleichen von Gott verbottne Künst*, in *Theatrum de veneficis: Das ist: Von Teufelsgespenst, Zauberern und Gifftbereitern, Schwartzkünstlern, Hexen und Unholden, vieler fürnemmen Historien und Exempel* ... (Frankfurt-am-Main, Nicolaus Bassaeus, 1586), 300.

[37] Godelmann, *Tractatus de Magis*, 92.

[38] Antonius Praetorius, *Gründlicher Bericht von Zauberey und Zauberern, deren Urpsrung, Unterscheid, Vermögen und Handlungen, Auch wie einer Christlichen Obrigkeit, solchen schändlichen Laster zu Begegnen* ... (Frankfurt, 1629), 63–5.

[39] Andreas Althamer, *Eyn Predig von dem Teuffel / das er alles unglueck in der welt anrichte* (n.p., 1532), sig. B iii^{v}.

This difference between the two confessions is shown most glaringly in the issue which provoked the most violent disputes between them, that of ecclesiastical exorcism. Exorcism, as will be shown later, was used by militant Counter-Reformation Catholicism as a propaganda weapon against the Protestants. A successful deployment of the apostolic power of the Church to drive out evil spirits could be enormously impressive. The confirmation of Catholic truths sometimes elicited from a demon under interrogation could buttress the claims made by the Church.[40] To rebut these claims, Protestant polemical theologians such as Bullinger, Godelmann, and William Perkins all insisted that the power to exorcise had been an exceptional, miraculous gift. It was given by God directly to buttress the faith in the early days of the Church, and was not based on the use of any specific forms of words. Now that the Church had been long established, Catholic pretensions to cast out demons through such impressive-sounding formulae arose, literally, from diabolical arrogance.[41] Perkins claimed that the true power of exorcising died out after some two centuries; then, when 'Popery that mystery of iniquitie beginning to spring up, and to dilate itself in the Churches of Europe, the true gift of working miracles then ceased; and instead thereof came in delusions, and lying wonders, by the effectual working of Satan, as was foretold by the Apostle, 2. Thess. 2.9. Of which sort were and are all those miracles of the Romish Church.'[42] As Bullinger remarked, all sorts of bizarre things were done in the rites of exorcism, standing someone naked in a bath of cold water, tying a liturgical stole round his neck, sprinkling him with holy water, covering him with vestments, and so forth, which had no rational purpose.[43] Augustin Lercheimer went further: such acts actually served the devil's purposes, as they did no harm to the spiritual being, but made the victim of his possession suffer bodily.[44]

Protestant theologians linked Catholicism and superstitious magic conceptually: they argued that both these belief-systems pretended to alter the divine dispensation of the universe through words and ceremonies. However, they also linked Catholicism and magic by cruder but more memorable methods. Demonic magic, claimed Godelmann, had grown so current in the Catholic Church, that priests and clerics were not regarded as sufficiently learned unless they were magicians. A succession of popes, from Sylvester II through to Alexander VI and

[40] For examples of this see Clark, *Demons*, 138ff.

[41] Bullinger, *Wider die Schwartzen Kunst*, in *Theatrum*, 301; Godelmann, *Tractatus de Magis*, 55–6.

[42] William Perkins, 'A Discourse of the Damned Art of Witchcraft', in his *Works* (Cambridge, 1618), 648.

[43] Bullinger, *Wider die Schwartzen Kunst.*

[44] Lercheimer, *Christlich Bedencken*, 265.

Paul III, were alleged to have been practising sorcerers.[45] According to Augustin Lercheimer, a canon of Halberstadt named Johannes Saxonicus used sorcery to enable him to fly, and thus celebrated three masses on the same Christmas Eve, at Halberstadt, Mainz, and Cologne.[46] Godelmann wrote about a famous practitioner of the wound-salve, called 'the Monk of Chemnitz', who could heal injuries at a distance by anointing the sword which caused them.[47] The Danish theologian Niels Hemmingsen recalled how Catholic priests used a psalter and a key to divine who had stolen lost goods.[48] Catholicism and magic were assimilated to each other, in both directions. If clerics had practised magic, enchanters and sorcerers invariably used ecclesiastical rites and ceremonies. As John Bale said, the mass 'serveth all witches in their witchery, all sorcerers, charmers, enchanters, dreamers, soothsayers, necromancers, conjurers, cross-diggers, devil-raisers, miracle-doers, dog-leeches, and bawds; for without a mass they cannot well work their feats'.[49] Of the sign of the cross, James Calfhill argued against the Catholic Martiall, 'possible it is that, in time past, men did some good by signing them with a cross: now it is not, according to your position, "medicinable against all conjuration, enchantment, sorcery and witchcraft"; *but rather daily used in all these*'.[50]

Finally, Protestant writers asserted that Catholicism and superstition arose together, and fell together. Augustin Lercheimer claimed that since the Gospel had been preached, the black arts had declined in use, and were more widely regarded as sinful; he looked forward to these things disappearing entirely.[51] Niels Hemmingsen agreed that superstitions had declined at the time of the Reformation, but, more pessimistic, he believed that as people grew weary of the Gospel, so they resorted to their old superstitious ways.[52]

[45] Godelmann, *Tractatus de Magis*, 21f; *cf.* Lercheimer, *Christlich Bedencken*, 273ff.

[46] Lercheimer, *Christlich Bedencken*, fo. 279v. [Note: leaves 277–82 of the *Theatrum* are foliated rather than paginated]

[47] Godelmann, *Tractatus de Magis*, 86.

[48] Nicolaus Hemmingius [=Niels Hemmingsen], *Admonitio de superstitionibus magicis vitandis, in gratiam sincerae religionis amantium* ... (Copenhagen, 1575), sigs. B viii^{v}–C i^{r}.

[49] John Bale, *The Latter Examination of Mistress Anne Askewe*, in *Select Works of John Bale* (Parker Society, Cambridge, 1849), 236.

[50] James Calfhill, *An Answer to John Martiall's Treatise of the Cross*, ed. Richard Gibbings (Parker Society, Cambridge, 1846), 338; italics are mine.

[51] Lercheimer, *Christlich Bedencken*, 276.

[52] Hemmingsen, *Admonitio*, sigs. F ii^{r}–iii^{r}.

IV

For at least a generation it has been accepted wisdom that the Roman Catholic Church after the Council of Trent embarked on a campaign to suppress the traditional, popular abuses of the official cult, and to bring popular religion more strictly under the control of the now more educated, less folkloric reformed priesthood. Jean Delumeau described how the midsummer bonfires for St John Baptist's day, to which all sorts of superstitious beliefs had accrued, were domesticated. The clergy presided over the fires, prevented people from taking brands from the fire to use as talismans, ensured that the fire was thoroughly burned to ashes, and then saw to the ashes being raked into the earth.[53] This story has become a sort of emblem of the Counter-Reformation at village level. Yet the story of the Catholic response to popular belief may be a great deal more complex than the stereotype of intellectual domination of popular belief suggests. The Delumeau pattern requires, first of all, that the Catholic élites should have been absolutely clear, much clearer than their medieval forbears, as to where to draw the line between acceptable devotions and unacceptable vain observances and superstitions. Here the literature on superstitions offers a helpful guide. It is surely safe to assume that at grass-roots level Catholicism was unlikely to have been *more* rigorous and intellectual than the literature: though it may well have been less so.

Since I began earlier with a Protestant work dedicated to incantations and charms, it is appropriate to compare it with its nearest Catholic equivalent, the *First Little Work on Incantations or Ensalmos*, published by the Portuguese theologian and Inquisitor Emanuele do Valle de Moura at Evora in 1620.[54] This appallingly mis-named 'little work' (*Opusculum*) of over 560 pages addressed the whole question of charms and spells with unprecedented intellectual precision, and enormous erudition. Valle de Moura himself was a rationalist, whose opinions fit closely into the Delumeau mould. His work explored the issue of enchantments in three parts. In the first part, he defined and summarised the errors of others on the subject. Secondly, he condemned the practice of uttering what he called 'constitutive *ensalmos*', meaning those charms which claimed to operate mechanically, curing or helping by the mere power of the words uttered. On the other hand, 'invocative *ensalmos*', which functioned only as prayers, might be acceptable under certain conditions. In the last part he defended the right of inquisitors to

[53] J. Delumeau, *Catholicism between Luther and Voltaire* (London, 1977), 177–9.

[54] Emanuele do Valle de Moura, *De Incantationibus seu Ensalmis Opusculum Primum* ... (Eborae, Typis Laurentii Crasbeeck, 1620).

involve themselves in these issues after the reforms of Trent.[55]

The interest in Valle de Moura's work lies chiefly in his encyclopaedic treatment of the views of other writers, both theologians and medical writers, on the issue of incantations or healing charms. He cited a whole range of arguments, which claimed to justify and support some, at least, of these controversial charms. Often these arguments worked by analogy with scriptural and ecclesiastical rituals. One argument ran that God might have instilled a special sanctity in many ordinary things, both material objects and words, to help humanity, just as special power was instilled into the water used in baptism, or holy ground after it was consecrated.[56] Likewise, God might have assigned power to certain things through the intercession of saints; he cited the claims made for the *Bulla Sabbathina*, by which it was believed that the Carmelites who observed particular devotions to the Virgin would be released from Purgatory by a personal appearance of the Virgin on their behalf on the first Sunday after their death.[57] Valle de Moura also quoted the opinions of the medical writer Bravus Chamisius, who claimed that the power of words might itself have a natural curative property.[58] Some people had claimed that other natural things might have the power to drive away demons: Luther, Roman Catholics alleged, had driven away devils not only by the power of his doctoral degree but also by breaking wind.[59] Other material things were alleged to have powers against demons revealed by God, by analogy with the incense which the angel Raphael told Tobias to make with the heart and liver of a fish, which drove away a demon from his marriage-chamber.[60] Such opinions were attributed to the controversial theologian Nicolaus Serarius, as well as the medical-theological writer Francisco Valles.[61] Even Pedro Pablo Ferrer, chancellor of Evora and Valle de Moura's former teacher, was cited as taking a moderate attitude to healing spells: they were always suspect, but there might be certain healers who by a special divine grace could use *ensalmos* licitly. Other moralistic authors whose works appeared at least to show some degree

[55] Valle de Moura, *De Incantationibus*, preface, fo. 1^{r} [the work is foliated to fo. 11, thereafter paginated to p. 552].

[56] *Ibid.*, fos. 8^{r-v}.

[57] *Ibid.*, fo. 9^{v}–p. 12.

[58] *Ibid.*, 22ff.

[59] *Ibid.*, 27; in fact the power of flatulence to drive away demons was believed by others, as shown by Mazzolini, *De Strigimagarum ... Mirandis*, sigs. ee ii^{r-v}.

[60] Tobit 6:3–8:3.

[61] Valle de Moura, *De Incantationibus*, 29ff; the references are to Nicolaus Serarius, *Commentarii in sacros Bibliorum libros, Josuae, Judicum, Ruth, Tobiae ...* (Paris, 1611), on Tobit, ch. 8; and to Francisco Valles, *De iis quae scripta sunt physice in libris sacris, sive de sacra philosophia liber singularis* ([Geneva], 1595), ch. 28.

of doubt included confessional writers such as Toletus and Azor.[62] Opinions, it seemed, were various and divided: Llamas and Lessius thought that some divinely communicated healing rites might be accepted, though the former thought they depended on the good morals of the person using them, the latter judged them more according to the circumstances of the action.[63]

Valle de Moura himself did not believe in any of these equivocations; he vehemently opposed any private form of words or ceremony which claimed to secure certain physical or spiritual benefits for the user or anyone else to whom it was applied. He analysed all the stories of special graces granted to saints' cults, certain prayers, or anything like. He finally concluded that any ritual, the mere performance of which was supposed to ensure benefits (for instance the certainty of not dying in mortal sin) was to be rejected.[64] However, the sheer range of controversy in this treatise illustrates two points. First, Valle de Moura thought that Catholic intellectuals, let alone the ordinary people, were often unsteady in their attitude to charms, and tended to equivocate over whether or not special powers might inhere in certain prayers or cult-objects. Secondly, 'superstitious' healing spells were often justified, or excused, by analogy with Catholic rites and practices such as exorcism. Healing powers might be genuinely delegated by God, or spuriously conferred by demonic pact: some people thought that such cures might fall into either category, and appear identical in their effects.

Especially in the Spanish-speaking world, the problem of distinguishing divine and demonic cures was made more acute by the presence of specially gifted healers or *saludadores*. These often claimed to be devotees of St Catherine or St Quiteria, and were commonly regarded as having received by some means a special personal gift to heal illnesses, and especially to close up wounds.[65] They also used particular

[62] Valle de Moura, *De Incantationibus*, 32–4, 42–3; in these passages Valle de Moura refers, amongst others, to Franciscus Toletus, *Instructio Sacerdotum* (Cologne, 1621), bk. 4 ch. 16, and to Johannes Azor, *Institutonum moralium* (3 vols in 2, Lyon, 1602–22), bk. 9 ch. 26 sect 6.

[63] Valle de Moura, *De Incantationibus*, 65; in these passages Valle de Moura refers to Hieronymus Llamas, 'Methodus', [possibly =] *Summa ecclesiastica, sive instructio confessariorum et poenitentium absolutissima* (Mainz 1605); and Leonardus Lessius S.J., 'Lib. 2 de Mag.' The latter reference has not been traced. Lessius wrote many works of theology, and also the *Hygiasticon*, a treatise on preserving health.

[64] Valle de Moura, *De Incantationibus*, 132.

[65] On these healers, see Ciruelo, *A Treatise Reproving all Superstitions*, 255–6; for the cult of St Quiteria see also W. A. Christian, *Local Religion in Sixteenth-Century Spain* (Princeton, 1981), 108–9. Delrio, *Disquisitionum*, i. 37, compares 'saludadores' to the followers of St Catharine or of St Paul, as they were called in Italy, or the 'children of Holy Saturday' in Flanders.

forms of words in their healing. A most interesting discussion of this phenomenon occurs in the highly rationalistic *Six Books of Magical Disquisitions* written by the Jesuit Martin Delrio, a work mostly known for its discussion of witch-hunting (which actually occupies a very small part of the book).[66] Delrio was willing to allow that certain special people might be given the divine gift of healing, as was claimed for children born on Holy Saturday in Flanders. He noted that Vitoria, Veracruz, and Navarrus were willing to approve *saludadores* in certain circumstances, and suggested that bishops examine them. He was nevertheless worried by the claims made by some that they needed to drink plenty of wine before carrying out a cure, or that they could not cure in the presence of another, more powerful healer. Yet he did not condemn all indiscriminately as working by demonic pacts, as one might have expected.[67]

Elsewhere in the work, Delrio listed a whole range of 'vain observances': these were particular things used by ordinary people as omens or rituals to order their lives, which often drew upon the rites of the Church. Most he condemned as superstitious; only exceptionally might devotion to a saint, combined with looking to God for help, excuse them. Here he returned to the issue of *saludadores*. Spanish soldiers would apply a clean cloth to a wound. They would then utter over it a form of words, in the vernacular, which recalled the institution of the Lord's Supper, and then pray to Jesus that 'by these most holy words, and by their power, and by the merit of your most holy passion, this wound (and this evil) may be healed'. This form of words was debated at Ypres before Bishop Simon shortly before Delrio wrote, and judged superstitious. 'This condemnation,' Delrio commented, 'seemed hard to many people, but mistakenly.' The error, he thought, lay in using a healing charm without medicines; because this implied that one routinely expected a miracle from God, without natural means; it lay also in the abuse of the words of the mass.[68]

Catholic commentators experienced several problems in winnowing and purifying 'popular religion' which were not felt by their Protestant counterparts. One, obviously, was the desire to maintain continuity with the early and medieval churches. Much subtlety had sometimes to be expended in sifting claims made for the miraculous powers of holy words or gestures, or the 'certain' benefits accruing to devotees of a cult. These things could not simply be swept away as the remnants of Antichrist. A second problem concerned ecclesiastical remedies against the assaults of evil spirits. In the later middle ages several

[66] Delrio, *Disquisitionum*; see discussion in Clark, *Demons*, e.g. 439ff.
[67] Delrio, *Disquisitionum*, i. 37–42.
[68] *Ibid.*, ii. 98ff, 113ff.

theologians had encouraged people to look for the source of their misfortunes in hostile sorcery or witchcraft, to explain illness, infertility, bad weather, or other problems.[69] Having diagnosed people's problems as the fault of demons working through sorcerers, the Church then offered an arsenal of supernatural techniques, in the shape of *sacramentalia* and exorcisms, to drive away the demons and thereby to solve the problem of ill-health, bad-weather, infertility or whatever. These *sacramentalia* and exorcisms then became, as was discussed earlier, a debating point between Catholics and Protestants. Protestants claimed that they were nothing more than another form of superstitious magic. Catholics not only rejected this claim;[70] they also alleged that the power and success of these rituals and holy things proved that theirs was the true religion. These ecclesiastical rituals and their powers became, in fact, proofs of the status and claims of Roman Catholicism itself.

From very early in the Reformation era, Catholic writers leapt to the defence of ecclesiastical 'holy things' which the Protestants attacked. Francisco de Osuna (d. c. 1540), whose *Scourge of the Devil* was translated into German in Bavaria in 1602, wrote of the effects and workings of malign sorcery in traditional late-medieval fashion. In fact he drew much of the first part of his text from the *Short Work on Witches* by the Tübingen nominalist theologian Martin Plantsch, dating from 1507.[71] In the second part, however, he departed from his source to embark on a vigorous defence of the Catholic Church's claims to exorcise, and to consecrate holy water. While he quoted Plantsch's reservations about the limits to the power of *sacramentalia*, Osuna defended the power of holy water far more fervently. 'Who is there,' he added, 'who does not

[69] For many instances of recommended 'preservatives' against sorcery, see *Malleus Maleficarum*, pt ii, q. 2 *passim*; Geiler von Kaisersberg, *Die Emeis*, fos. 47–51; Mazzolini, *De Strigimagarum ... Mirandis*, bk. ii chs. 9–12 *passim*. According to Robin Briggs, *Witches & Neighbours: The Social and Cultural Context of European Witchcraft* (London, 1996), chs. 2–4 and 9, people did not need much prompting to see the source of their problems in terms of hostile sorcery.

[70] As for instance in Albertus Hungerus, *De Magia Theses Theologicae, in celebri et catholica academia Ingolstadiana An. S. N. M.D.LXXIIII, die 21 Junii per Reverendum et eruditum virum M. Hectorem Wegman Augustanum, SS. Theologiae Baccalaureum formatum, Divae Virginis apud eandem Academiam Parochum, pro impetrando Licentiae gradu, ad publicam disputationem propositae: Praeside Reverendo et Clarissimo viro ALBERTO HUNGERO, SS. Theologiae Doctore et Professore ordinario, Collegii Theologici pro tempore decano* (Ingolstadt, Weissenhorn, 1574), theses 88–95.

[71] Franciscus de Osuna, *Flagellum Diaboli, oder Dess Teufels Gaisl, darin gar lustig und artlich gehandelt wird: Von der Macht uund Gewalt dess boesen Feindts: von den effecten und Wirckungen der Zauberer / Unholdter und Hexenmaister: Warum Gott bewillige / das die Menschen von ihnen werden belaidigt am Leib und Gut: Und was fuer remedi und mittel darwider zugebrauchen. Beschliesslichen von den Teuflischen remediis, superstitionen, Aberglauben, Agoettereyen* [*sic*] / *wie auch falschen Astrologia, Warsagerey / und andern dergleichen verbottenen Kuensten / die an jetzo starck im schwung gehen* (Munich, 1602); fos. 6^r–33^v are based on an often verbatim rendering of Martin Plantsch, *Opusculum de sagis maleficis* (Phorce, 1/1507), sigs. b iv^v–f i^r.

know that this our holy water will remain uncorrupt for a whole year and more, while ordinary water will not remain good for more than about a month? What can be the origin of that other than the blessing?'[72]

Catholic writers learned to include, while denouncing superstitious remedies, a fervent defence of the power of holy water, holy herbs, holy wax, prayers to saints, the sign of the cross, and a range of other ministrations, including the sacraments themselves, as a far more effective defence against harmful sorcery. Just such a defence forms most of Book VI of Delrio's *Magical Disquisitions*, where he specifically replied to the charges collected by the Lutheran Godelmann from several of his own predecessors.[73] Interestingly, Delrio *disagreed* with Nicholas of Cusa's strictures against using holy water, Easter wax, or baptismal water to cure illnesses in people or animals, or sterility in fields: if these were used as a *sacramentale*, in the expectation that God would confirm faith through a marvel, that would be licit.[74] It was customary to prove the miraculous powers of Catholic rites by reference to miracle-stories, usually involving the conversion of non-Catholics. These were sometimes medieval tales from Caesarius of Heisterbach or Thomas of Chantimpré; but in Delrio's case they were often drawn from Jesuit missions, either to the Americas or to Japan, or to Protestant corners of Europe. Baptism freed a Peruvian prince called Tamaracunga from the assaults of demons; the power of the Eucharist had recently driven demons out of Netherlandish Calvinists.[75] The power of the sign of the cross was attested by a range of miracles.[76] Lopez de Gómara reported that among the American Indians the deceits and apparitions of demons amongst the Indians were best dispelled with the presence of the Eucharist, the image of the crucifix, and the sprinkling of holy water, 'and the very evil spirits have themselves confessed this to the Indians'.[77]

This calling-up of the curative and preservative powers of the Church's rites made excellent sermon fodder. Its potential was exploited to the full in a series of sermons entitled *The Panoply of the Armour of God against all the devil-worshipping of superstitions, divinations, and incantations*, preached by Friedrich Forner, suffragan bishop of Bamberg, and published at Ingolstadt in 1626. Alongside a meticulous and standard

[72] Osuna, *Flagellum*, fo. 40^{v}.
[73] Delrio, *Disquisitionum*, iii. 235–320.
[74] *Ibid.*, iii. 191–2.
[75] *Ibid.*, iii. 237ff, 253.
[76] *Ibid.*, iii. 276–8 and refs. including Tommasso Bozio, *De Signis Ecclesiae libri xxiii* (Cologne, 1592) bk. 2 ch. 8, bk. 15 ch. 1; Jakob Gretser, *De Cruce Christi* (Ingolstadt, 1598), bk. 3 chs. 18–19; P. Thyraeus, *De daemoniacis* (Cologne, 1594), pt 3 ch. 44.
[77] *Ibid.*, iii.282–6.

denunciation of do-it-yourself superstitious cures ran a vigorous defence of, and encouragement to use, ecclesiastical remedies. This defence occupied twenty-two of the thirty-five sermons in the cycle.[78] Like Delrio's, this work told colourful tales of successful exorcisms and cures attributed to the holy things of the Church, drawn either from Delrio himself or from Tommasso Bozio's *On the Marks of the Church.*[79]

Of all the spiritual weapons wielded by the Catholic Church in its propaganda war against the Reformation, the power to exorcise demons was the most dramatic and the most contentious. Broadly considered, exorcism might be achieved through any form of prayer or holy gesture or object; but specifically, it was performed through a series of prayers, conjurations of devils, and ritual instructions to the evil spirits to depart, which were accompanied by gestures, above all the repeated signing of the cross, and the use of cult-objects such as holy water or consecrated herbs. There is abundant evidence from recent research to show that in contested areas of Germany especially, exorcisms became celebrated and public trials of spiritual strength between Protestants and Catholics.[80] Both Delrio and Forner reported a list of instances where the devils prevailed over Protestants, only to be defeated by Catholics.[81] This, the reader was told, was how Divine providence wished to demonstrate the greater truth of Catholicism.

In the light of the persuasive role ascribed to exorcism, it is worth considering in more detail what sort of a message this rite sent to the people of Europe about the nature of the spiritual realm. There were various forms and manuals for exorcism published at this period. The multiplicity of these works proves, if nothing else, that the Roman rite established as the official means of exorcising evil spirits was far from being the only one to be used.[82] We are probably entitled, however, to assume that working exorcists would have used something akin to the works of one of the most popular authorities on the subject, the

[78] Friedrich Forner, *Panoplia armaturae Dei, adversus omnem superstitionum, divinationum, excantationum, demonolatriam, et universas magorum, veneficorum, et sagarum, et ipsiusmet Sathanae insidias, praestigias et infestationes* (Ingolstadt, 1626), 134–292.

[79] Tommasso Bozio, Eugubinus, *De Signis Ecclesiae libri xxiii* (Cologne, 1592 and subsequent edns.).

[80] See for instance P. M. Soergel, *Wondrous in his Saints: Counter-Reformation Propaganda in Bavaria* (Berkeley, Calif, 1993), esp. 131ff.

[81] Delrio, *Disquisitionum*, ii. 75ff; Forner, *Panoplia*, 98ff.

[82] E.g. V. Polidoro, *Pratica exorcistarum* (Patavii, 1587); *Thesaurus exorcismorum sique coniurationum terribilium, potentissimorum, efficacissimorum cum practica probatissima: quibus spiritus maligni, daemones maleficiaque omnia de corporibus humanis obsessis, tanquam flagellis, fustibusque fugantur* ... (Cologne, 1626); Maximilian van Eynatten, *Manuale exorcismorum: continens instructiones, et exorcismos ad eiiciendos e corporibus obsessis spiritus malignos* ... (Antwerp, 1626); *Preces et coniurationes contra aereas tempestates* ... (Campidonae, 1667); *Manuale exorcismorum et benedictionum selectorum pro exorcistarum, parochorum, at aliorum quorumvis curatorum* ... (Einsiedeln, 1671).

Observant Franciscan Girolamo Menghi of Viadana, whose works were published several times in Italian and Latin.[83]

Menghi's writings generally fell into two parts, a discursive part which conveyed the theology of sorcery and its remedies, and a liturgical part which contained prescriptions with which anyone might in principle perform a successful exorcism. In his *Compendium of the Exorcist's Art* (published in Italian), Menghi drew his theology of how lawfully to resist sorcery from a pre-Reformation text, Silvestro Mazzolini's *On the Marvels of witch-sorcerers* of 1521.[84] However, he specified the nature of ecclesiastical remedies rather more fully than his predecessors. Herbs, as such, had no natural power to drive away demons; yet if they were combined with ecclesiastical consecration and exorcism, one could make medicines and potions from them.[85] There was unease about amulets which contained unknown names of God; so Menghi helpfully supplied etymologies (often erroneous) for some of the most impressive ones.[86]

The exorcisms in Menghi's *Flagellum Daemonum* must have reinforced, rather than diminished, popular belief in the power of words and rituals to heal all ills. Several of these included the invocation of God in a list of impressive, powerful, and essentially incomprehensible names;[87] the demon was several times exorcised 'through the virtue of all the holy, ineffable, and most powerful names ... and through the power of all those ineffable names'.[88] Earth, air, fire and water were all conjured individually, to prevent them from containing the devil; fire was conjured before it was used to burn an image of the devil, to torment the demon.[89] In the *Most Efficacious remedies for expelling malign spirits*, Menghi supplied a series of formulae for blessing holy oil. For curing ailments in the body caused by demons, he gave this recipe:

[83] Girolamo Menghi, *Compendio dell'arte essorcistica, et possibilita delle mirabili, et stupende operationi delli demoni, et dei malefici. Con li rimedii opportuni alle infirmità maleficiali* (Bologna, 1582); Girolamo Menghi, *Flagellum Daemonum, exorcismos terribiles, potentissimos, et efficaces: Remediaque probatissima, ac doctrina singularem in malignos spiritos expellendos, facturasque et maleficia fuganda de obsessis corporibus complectens; cum suis benedictionibus, et omnibus requisitis ad eorum expulsionem; Accessit postremo Pars secunda, quae Fustis daemonum inscribitur, quibus novi exorcismi, et alia nonnulla, quae prius desiderabantur, superaddita fuerunt* (Bologna, 1589); [its second part entitled] *Fustis Daemonum, adiurationes formidabiles, potentissimas, et efficaces in malignos spiritus fugandos de oppressis corporibus humanis* (Bologna, 1589); [the latter includes a separately paginated section entitled] *Remedia Efficacissima in malignos spiritus expellendos, facturasque et maleficla* [*sic*] *effuganda de obsessis corporibus; cum suis benedictionibus.*

[84] Compare Menghi, *Compendio*, 528ff, 539ff, 545ff, with Mazzolini, *De Strigimagarum ... Mirandis*, sigs. dd iv^r, ee ii^v, ee iv^{rff}, and bk. 2 ch. 11 *passim.*

[85] Menghi, *Compendio*, 570–3.

[86] *Ibid.*, 574–84.

[87] Menghi, *Flagellum*, 112, 125, 147–8, 214, 217, 220, 225, 227.

[88] *Ibid.*, 112, 133, 140ff, 201.

[89] *Ibid.*, 173, 175, 179, 189.

> Take white hellebore, hypericum, rose-sugar, and incense [in specified quantities], and boil them in a pound of white wine until they are reduced to half their volume; then have the boiled wine blessed and exorcised by a priest according to the form as below, and give it to the patient at a suitable time for three days; each day, notwithstanding vomiting, the sick person being duly contrite and confessed, and being in a state of grace, is to be exorcised for the space of three or four hours; because thus he will be healed, if the grace of God is favourable.[90]

Similar prescriptions were made for the preparation of holy salt, incense of blessed herbs, and for the conjuration of parchment on which amulets were to be written. One could tell whether a person was vexed by evil spirits or not by writing a list of the holy names of God on blessed parchment, and placing it on the patient when he or she was unaware of it.[91]

V

It is perfectly clear that Protestants and Roman Catholics both wished to dissuade their people from using do-it-yourself superstitious cures and methods of divination. The arguments by which they proved that these techniques were naturally inefficacious, and that therefore they must depend on the intervention of an obliging but deceptive demon, show close similarities. However, if one looks a little more widely, and asks what they proposed to put in place of popular superstitions, then their programmes appear to diverge rather dramatically.

Protestants taught, essentially, a different doctrine of the power of God. No earthly thing contained, or received delegated to it, one jot of the sovereign power of the Divine providence. All that one could do was to ask God, in humble petition, for one's wants and needs to be relieved, in the knowledge that providence might well have decreed otherwise. In Roman Catholicism, on the other hand, the picture was more complex. It is quite possible to find passages among Catholic authors which also stress the all-powerful nature of providence, and the way in which every religious rite depends for its working on God's will. Nevertheless, Catholics clearly believed that in ordinary circumstances, God had *chosen* to channel his holiness through the approved rites, through particular people, places, things, words, and

[90] *Remedia*, 25–6.
[91] *Ibid.*, 36–66; for further amulets, see *ibid.*, 89–90.

ways of doing things.[92] To be in communion with these holy things on earth was to touch the expressions of the Divine. To use as many as possible of these holy things for one's spiritual and even material benefit was not disobedience, but devotion.

In practice, Protestants tried to reform the people's religion by instilling a radically different vision of God, by turning the whole form of religion into something else. For Catholics, the exercise was more one of purgation, of bringing into line, and under control, rituals and ceremonies which had grown in an uncontrolled fashion over the centuries, and had ultimately become a vulgar magic decorated with Christian names and symbols. This divergence in intent must explain why, in the succeeding centuries, parts of Europe contained no holy places or miraculous manifestations, while other parts still do demonstrate these things today. Protestants and Catholics, even as they used similar arguments and sometimes even plagiarised from each other, did not think that they were about essentially the same business in transforming people's religion. Neither should we.

[92] In late scholasticism, this belief that God confined his omnipotence to working through certain normal procedures was described as God's 'ordained power', *potentia ordinata*. For discussion see E. Cameron, *The European Reformation* (Oxford, 1991), 84, n. 27 and refs.

SLAVERY AND COLONIAL IDENTITY IN EIGHTEENTH-CENTURY MAURITIUS

By Megan Vaughan

READ 26 SEPTEMBER 1997 AT THE INSTITUTE OF HISTORICAL RESEARCH, LONDON

ON 25 May 1785, a M. Lousteau arrived at the police station in Port Louis, Isle de France (now Mauritius) to complain that his slave Jouan had been abducted.[1] He described Jouan as an 'Indien', 'Lascar' and 'Malabar', and said that he had learned that he had been smuggled on to the royal ship *Le Brillant*, bound for Pondicherry in southern India, by one Bernard (whom Lousteau describes as a 'creol libre' but who later is described as 'Malabar, soi-disant libre' and 'Topa Libre'). The story of the escape had been told to him by a 'Bengalie' slave called Modeste, who belonged to the 'Lascar' fisherman, Bacou. A number of people had apparently assisted Jouan's escape in other ways—most importantly his trunk of belongings had been moved secretly from hut to hut before being embarked with him. Lousteau was a member of that ever-growing professional group of eighteenth-century France and its colonies: the lawyers. He was clerk to the island's supreme court, the Conseil Superieur.[2] He supported a large family, he said, and the loss of Jouan represented a serious loss to their welfare. Jouan, it turned out, was no ordinary slave. He was a skilled carpenter who earned his master a significant sum every month; he was highly valued, and Lousteau had refused an offer of 5,000 livres for him. What is more, he could be easily recognised, for he was always exceptionally well turned-out and well-groomed. To facilitate in the search for his slave, Lousteau provided the following description of him:

> He declares that his fugitive slave is of the *Lascar* caste, a *Malabar*, *dark black* in colour, short in height, with a handsome, slightly thin face, *a gentle appearance, with long hair* ... that he is very well dressed, *abundantly endowed with clothes*, such as jackets and shorts ... wearing *small gold earrings*, a pin with a gold heart on his shirt, and on the arm a mark on the skin which he thinks reads DM. He can be easily

[1] National Archives of Mauritius (hereafter NAM) JB 47, Procedure Criminelle, 1785: Evasion of Jouan, slave of M. Lousteau.

[2] Archives d'Outre-Mer, Aix-en-Provence (hereafter AOM), E293 (Personnel): Loustean, contains further information on Lousteau's career.

> recognised by his *gentle demeanour and cleanliness.* (emphasis in original)

Lousteau, like any attentive slave-owner, knew intimately the qualities, physical and otherwise, of one of his most valued possessions. The story, however, deepens. For this we must thank the obsessive attention to detail, and prurient interest in gossip, which the court officers of Isle de France so often displayed. Not that the gossip was irrelevant to the case, far from it. For Lousteau to have any chance of either recovering his slave, or of receiving compensation for the loss of his slave, it was necessary to find out where, exactly, he had gone, and who, exactly, had incited or facilitated his escape. Plenty of Jouan and Bernard's erstwhile friends appeared more than willing to provide information.[3] Modeste, for example: she was summoned to the police station on 27 May, two days after Lousteau had made his initial complaint. Before Modeste is interviewed, her exact identity must be established, and so we are given the following description of who she is:

> Bengalie negress (*negresse*) concubine of Jouan and so-called slave of Bacou Caremy, free black, Lascar, to whom she pays each day a sum of two livres, despite the fact that she claims to have bought her freedom with the help of a certain sailor.

If this were not complicated enough, Modeste is said to live in the house of her former master, Sieur la Vasseur. Modeste confirms, 'purely and simply', Lousteau's complaint. Indeed, it was Modeste who had alerted Lousteau in the first place. She says that she had been arguing with Jouan for some days and had separated from him, but she wanted to get back from him various clothes and jewellery which were in his trunk in her house, but which was removed, in her absence, the previous Tuesday. She adds that she is certain that Jouan escaped on the *Le Brillant* because he was very close to (*tres lié avec*) Bernard, a free black, Topa, a cook by profession, whom she believes went as a servant to one of the vessel's officers. And his (Bernard's) departure had been confirmed by the butcher, Bellegarde, who was the former master of the negress Louise who he had married to Bernard.

Five months later, in October, Jouan is still missing. Lousteau reiterates his complaint. 'My slave, the carpenter Jouan, escaped on the King's vessel, *Le Brillant*, which left port on 20 May, and this Jouan is living in intimacy (*en liaison intime*) with one Bernard, noir Topas'. Lousteau gets specific. This Bernard, he says , has 'debauched' (*debauché*) or led

[3] Of course in analysing such court cases we cannot exclude the possibility that some or all of the witnesses were pressurised, intimidated or otherwise persuaded to give evidence—particularly in this slave-holding society.

astray Jouan and arranged his escape on the vessel by passing him off as free, and by saying that they were brothers. Jouan, he understands, had been known aboard ship as Joseph, and had been taken on as a servant by one of the officers of the Regiment of the Isle de France, with whom he had disembarked at Pondicherry, the French possession in southern India. Bernard, meanwhile, had returned to the island and could be seen around town wearing a hat, a shirt, and a handkerchief, all of which Lousteau recognised as belonging to Jouan, a fact which, in his view, went to prove the great intimacy (*grand intimité*) which existed between the two men.

Other witnesses corroborate this story. Pierre Moussa, a 'Bambara' slave, belonging to the King, who had been involved in the smuggling away of Jouan's trunk, says that the two men had lived for some time in 'intelligence et d'amitié' and that they called each other 'brothers'. Modeste, too, has elaborated her story. She says that Jouan and Bernard had been involved 'intimately' for some time. Furthermore, she too has seen Bernard, since his return, sporting Jouan's shirt, handkerchief, and even the hat which he had had bordered with gold: sure sign of their great intimacy. Lindor, another slave, had known Jouan on the island, and had also been on the same ship, the *Le Brillant*. He had recognised Jouan on board and asked him what he was doing. He had replied that he was going to find his liberty. Lindor says that Jouan and Bernard lived together intimately and ate together on board ship, and called each other brothers. Lindor had asked Bernard it they were really brothers, to which Bernard had replied that they were indeed, from birth. Jouan had given Lindor a blue shirt, in the pocket of which he had found a golden pin with a heart on it.

On 18 October Bernard is arrested. On 8 November he is interrogated by the court. Described as 'black', 'so called free' (*soi-disant libre*) Malabar, and 48 years old, Bernard (who is literate enough to be able to sign his name), says that he usually lives in the area of Port Louis called the Quartier des Yolofs. Asked if he knows how Jouan had managed to board the *Le Brillant*, Bernard replies that about a month before the ship's departure, Jouan had expressed a wish to embark. Bernard had replied that he could organise it if Jouan obtained permission from his master, M. Lousteau. Jouan had replied that his master would never give him permission, and asked Bernard if he could come aboard as his brother. Bernard had asked him if he had a ticket, to which he had replied, no, but that he could get one by selling some merchandise. Bernard is asked why he had not reported this to the Bureau de Police, to which he answers that he was not acquainted with the ways (*usages*) of this colony. He is then asked if it is true that he is 'tres lié' with the said Jouan, and that they sometimes refer to each other as 'brothers', to which Bernard says that they do sometimes call each other brothers, but that he had only known Jouan well for two months, during which period he had let his house to Jouan. The case stagnates. Lousteau reiterates his complaint on 16 December 1785, having now received information on the whereabouts of Jouan. He is, apparently, in the employ of a lieutenant of the Regiment of Isle de France, one M. Brousse, who had employed him on board the *Le Brillant*, and who now continued to employ him in Pondicherry. No doubt, says Lousteau, the Lieutenant had believed that Jouan was a free man but, 'on this island, no black can call himself free who does not have proof of that condition, and it is impudent of him to believe the word of a black whom he does not know ... and thus to compromise the property of the "habitants"'. For this reason, Lousteau believes that Brousse is obliged to pay him damages. In September 1786 Bernard is still in prison and he writes to the Judge protesting his innocence and asking to be freed for the rest of the duration of the case, promising that he will present himself to the court whenever required. On 17 October he is freed. The case appears to have fizzled out. Lieutenant Brousse writes to Lousteau saying that he is distressed to discover that Jouan had deceived him into thinking he was a free man, and he would willingly return Jouan to his rightful owner, but he lacks the means to do so. Bernard, meanwhile, has also said that Jouan is not happy in Pondicherry, that he is unable to practice his profession there for want of tools, and that he would willingly come back to the island, but lacks the means to do so.

The 'evasion' of Jouan is a minor and incomplete footnote to the history of the Indian Ocean in the eighteenth century. But in some ways it seems a good place to start a discussion of colonial identities. To begin with, it challenges us, I think, to examine what we mean by 'identities' in the first place. A commonplace of social historical writing, and perhaps particularly of recent analyses of the colonial and the post-colonial world, the term 'identity' allows us to hang certain narratives together, and yet its meaning is often implicit, assumed. When I employ the term 'identity' in any attempt to reconstruct the social history of eighteenth-century Mauritius, I may be using it in a number of different ways. It may refer to what appear, in the historical records, to be consciously affirmed identities on the part of historical agents, their self-identifications, and changes to these over time. It may refer to the ascription of identities by one group of people to their contemporaries. Or it may refer to my retrospective reconstruction of identities which contemporaries themselves may never have articulated, my piecing together of the components (language, dress, social behaviour, religious practice) which seem to me to have constituted some kind of meaningful demarcation between one group and another: identities which are perhaps 'lived' in the body, but which do not have a discursive equivalent. And what if we place the term 'identity' next to some other categories frequently used by social historians: 'mentalité', for example, or 'community'?

It would be possible to focus our analysis of the case on issues of sexuality and write Jouan and Bernard's relationship and attempted escape to 'freedom' as a chapter of a gay history of the Indian Ocean. Certainly their former friends and acquaintances appear to have noted a degree of closeness which they considered unusual between men. Not all were convinced by the cover of kinship or brotherhood. Lousteau the Frenchman is more articulate on this point than any of the witnesses of Indian or African origin, claiming that Jouan had been 'debauched' by Bernard. Yet the term 'debauchery' was a loose and wide one in the eighteenth century. Historians of France argue that it was only in the nineteenth century[4] that the concept of the 'homosexual' came into being in France, yet there were many other terms which Lousteau could have used if he had wished to be more explicit about the physical nature of Jouan and Bernard's relationship. He chose instead an ambiguous term. And although the prosecutor, in his interrogation of Bernard on the nature of his relationship with Jouan, seems to be pushing him to 'own up' to something, that something is never defined. It may well be that Jouan and Bernard were not only close friends, but were involved in a sexual relationship. It is also possible that they possessed no term, either in an Indian language, or in the French creole spoken on the island, to describe this relationship to themselves.[5] We might nevertheless decide to ascribe to them the term 'homosexual' (or, given the evidence for their relationships with women, 'bisexual'), since limiting our reconstructions to the terms which contemporaries applied to themselves would certainly make for a limited kind of social history. Or we may decide that the central message of this story is ambiguity, and ambiguous it must remain. These issues of identity and identification have been well rehearsed by historians of sexuality, but in fact, they may be equally relevant to other social categories and designations, as the history of slavery and of creolisation demonstrates.

[4] Chronologies differ. See Michel Foucault, *The History of Sexuality*, vol. 1 (Harmondsworth, 1981); Lynn Hunt discusses homosexuality in the writings of Sade in *The Family Romance of the French Revolution* (London, 1992), 45–6; Robert A. Nye, *Masculinity and Male Codes of Honour in Modern France* (New York and Oxford, 1993); Roddey Reid, *Families in Jeopardy: Regulating the Social Body in France, 1750–1910* (Stanford, 1993).

[5] This raises the question of whether an 'identity' can exist without contemporaries possessing a term for it. For this debate as it relates to sexuality, see John Boswell, 'Revolutions, Universals and Sexual Categories' in *Hidden From History: Reclaiming the Gay and Lesbian Past*, ed. Martin Duberman, Martha Vicinus, and George Chauncey Jr. (New York, 1989), 17–36; Nye, *Masculinity*, Introduction.

For it is not only in relation to questions of sexuality that both contemporaries and historians may experience some confusion. Though the evidence brought to bear in the case of Jouan and Bernard is unusual in some respects, in others it is quite typical of cases in this period. Eighteenth-century Isle de France, and particularly in its capital, Port Louis, was a fluid and complex place: one in which, despite the rigidities of colonial life, the binary divisions between slave and free, black and white, it was not always easy to know just who everyone was.

Contemporary French observers perceived colonial identities to be closely connected with economic functions and activities.[6] The precise role of the colony of Isle de France had been a subject of considerable discussion amongst administrators in the Ministère de la Marine in Paris since the moment it was first occupied by the French in 1721.[7] Its main function had always been as a strategic base in the Indian Ocean and as an entrepot for trade, initially governed by the Compagnie des Indes. The dissolution of Company rule, the introduction of free trade in the 1760s, and the wars with England over India brought wealth to the island, but further emphasised the transitory nature of much of the population. Though a small French elite had established itself under Company rule as landowners and merchants, in general, the 'white' population of the island was an unsettled and unsettling one. Amidst the small numbers of nobles and bourgeois, who kept houses in Port Louis and *habitations* in the country, there were larger numbers of French men and women of much lowlier origins—sailors, craftsmen and labourers from poverty-stricken rural Brittany being the most evident. The social hierarchies imported from the métropole, though important, were inevitably modified, challenged and compromised in this colonial setting. Here, as elsewhere in the colonial world, the term 'creole' was first used to describe the identity of those whose ancestry lay in the métropole, but who had been born in the colonies: in this case, those permanent settlers on Isle de France who both looked to France for their political and cultural bearings, and simultaneously kicked against this distant authority, its corruption, venality and monopolistic economic exploitation.

In the eighteenth century there was no shortage of commentators on the society of Isle de France. The Enlightenment produced a string of more or less famous philosophers, geographers, astronomers, and botanists passing through or stranded for longer periods of time, with

[6] For a more detailed discussion of this see Megan Vaughan, 'The Character of the Market: Social Identities in Colonial Economies; *Oxford Development Studies* vol. 24, no. 1 (1995), 61–77.

[7] Isle de France was first appropriated by the French in 1715. In the seventeenth century it had been briefly colonised by the Dutch. In 1810 it became the British colony of Mauritius.

a passion for comparative social commentary.[8] Their accounts of 'identities' in eighteenth-century Isle de France can be read both as evidence for the nature of identities as complex lived realities, and simultaneously as evidence of the compulsion to order a less than orderly world.

Some like the botanist Pierre Poivre (who was later to become Intendant of the island), heavily influenced by Physiocratic thought, were distressed by the island's dependence on trade and its lack of attention to agriculture. For Poivre, this obsession with the world of goods as opposed to the 'arts' of agriculture was bound to produce an inferior society, and he employs the idiom of slavery to make his point: men who do not practice the arts are 'enslaved', he wrote.[9] Many compared the 'white' society of Isle de France with that of the neighbouring Isle Bourbon. This island, settled from the seventeenth century by a group of colonists from Madagascar and later from France, had evolved into a sleepy agricultural backwater next to its fast-moving trading neighbour. Whilst the colonists of Isle de France were described as largely concerned to get rich quick and move on, those of Isle Bourbon were settled, relatively small-scale agriculturalists whose families and slaves were employed on the land. The constant flow of people, goods and news in and out of Port Louis meant that the elite of that city (and some of the lower orders) could at least attempt to keep up with the 'manners and fashions' of the metropole, and indeed, of other parts of the world. By contrast, major shipping traffic bypassed Isle Bourbon, where the colonists were in any case too poor even to pretend to be replicating the changing fashions of Paris. Some commentators admired the 'simplicity' of the Bourbon creoles, their rustic ways and their established family lives, and though their origins in the French possessions and piratic communities of Madagascar meant that all were of 'sang melé', yet they were apparently eager to profess their loyalty to France. As one missionary wrote in 1732, 'despite the fact that both their hair and their manners resemble those of the blacks, they have a distinct aversion to the latter and call themselves French'.[10] Though eighteenth-century visitors inevitably patronised these distant and dark French men and women, in general they compared their society favourably with that of Isle de France, more commonly described in terms of the social disorder which trade, money and war could bring. Opinions certainly differed on the merits and

[8] Amongst whom were the Abbe de la Caille, Bernardin de St Pierre, Pierre Poivre, M.J. Milbert, Guillaume le Gentil, J. Bory de St Vincent, M. Sonnerat.

[9] M. le Poivre, *The Travels of a Philosopher, Being Observations on the Customs, Manners, Arts, Agriculture and Trade of Several Nations in Asia and Africa* (trans. London, 1769), 4.

[10] Congregation de la Mission (Paris), receuil 1504, f. 171: Voyage des trois missionaires, 1732.

demerits of free trade, but many shared the view of one missionary that 'in according freedom of commerce they had also accorded freedom to all sorts of depradations'.[11] Though the colonists of Isle Bourbon might be recognised as less than 'white', this 'mélange' had at least arrived at some kind of stability. Bourbon creole women were described as 'well built, well-made and beautiful' despite being 'brown'. On Isle de France, by contrast, the moral consequences and context of sexual relations between the 'races' were perceived as far more dangerous:

> It causes great disorder on Isle de France to see men of a certain rank publicly associating themselves with negresses whom they treat as wives and with whom they have children who will one day become a bastardised and dangerous race. This shameful *mélange* has been introduced by the *sejours* of troops and sailors ... In this respect it is not so much the established residents who were the most guilty but a vice once introduced by outsiders, does not leave with them, but stays and grows larger.[12]

Attempts to stabilise 'white' family life had been made on Isle de France almost since its birth as a colony. Girls from religious communities in Brittany had been shipped out in the 1730s with the intention that they would marry the single working men who had signed up for a few years in the colony, and whom the Company hoped would stay and settle on the land. The experiment ended quickly when serious doubts were cast on the health and morality of the girls. Concubinage would remain common throughout the century, giving rise, as the missionaries and others warned, to a small community of *metis* who would find a voice during and after the Revolution. Meanwhile, a commentator such as Bernardin de St Pierre (who was to go on to write the best-seller *Paul et Virginie*, which was set on the island) romanticised and idealised the role of the 'white' creole woman whom he erected as an emblem of colonial simplicity, and whose attachment to her children, closeness to nature, and creation of an ordered household (all these tasks, in fact, performed by her slaves), stood in contrast to the disorder of port life.[13]

Of course, the discourse of immorality and disorder which so permeated observations of life on Isle de France must be treated with caution—the trope of the dissolute colonist was a well-worn one—yet it does appear that the constant comings and goings of troops and

[11] Congregation de la Mission, Receuil 1504, f. 195, Caulier(?), 1765.

[12] Congregation de la Mission, Receuil 1504, ff. 189, Teste, 1764.

[13] For discussions of gender and sexual politics in *Paul et Virginie* see Hunt, *Family Romance*, 29–32; Reid, *Families in Jeopardy*, 101–36.

sailors, of slave ships and merchandise, produced a place which was simultaneously very small and very large, which was parochial in the extreme in some of its politics, but which also stood in the middle of an immensely cosmopolitan world. In this way it was possible both for Jouan to escape on the *Le Brillant*, and for him to be traced to Pondicherry. Though he was wealthy enough to indulge his taste for fashion, for gold-rimmed hats and jewellery, yet he was still a slave. In this world social categories were no sooner invented than they strained at the seams, but the invention of those categories went on nevertheless. For the colonial administration here as elsewhere, it was important to continue to struggle to determine a method of knowing who, exactly, everyone was, in part because 'race' was such an unreliable marker. Jouan had no doubt appeared to be vèry plausible when he presented himself on board ship with his fine clothes and gentle manners. A slave was not always recognisable as a slave which is why, as Lousteau reminded Lieutenant Brousse, skin colour, if not definitive proof of social and legal status, was nevertheless a kind of warning sign: 'no black can call himself free who does not have proof of that condition'. Here, as elsewhere in the colonial world of slavery, though the binary divisions of black and white, slave and free, formed the backdrop, the basic contours of the social landscape, in practice many more sub-divisions, differentiations and compromises to principles were necessary if the place were to function at all. Some of these elaborations, of divisions of labour and of ethnicity, were to become more than mere colonial labels and to endure as lived identities, whilst others were overtaken by the constant process of change which characterised the creole world. The invention of social categories and characterisations was not, of course, solely the domain of the authorities—otherwise their task would have been easier, their world less uncertain. Slaves, for example, were well aware of the divisions which existed within the 'white' society of the island, and when they designated white sailors as 'li negres blancs',[14] they alluded both to the fragility of the category 'white' and to the potential breadth of the category 'slave'.

The complexity of social categories and identities on the island, as this example indicates, and as contemporaries observed, derived in some part from the nature of its economy. Isle de France did not become a major plantation economy until it became Mauritius under the British in the nineteenth century.[15] Slavery, then, was a differentiated sort of affair, with many slaves trained and employed as skilled workers

[14] M.J. Milbert, *Voyage Pittoresque a l'Ile de France, au Cap de Bonne-Esperance et a l'Ile de Tenerife* 2 vols. (Paris, 1812), vol. 1: 274.

[15] Though the production of sugar did begin to expand in the 1790s: M.D. North-Coombes, 'Labour Problems in the Sugar Industry of Ile de France or Mauritius, 1790–1842' (M.A. thesis, University of Cape Town, 1978), Chapter 1.

and artisans whose function was to build the infrastructure of the island, to build the city of Port Louis, to build and repair ships, to service the transient white population.[16] Not all were as successful as Jouan, but many, both men and women, had undertaken apprenticeships through which they had acquired highly marketable skills as masons, carpenters, seamstresses, wig-makers, domestic servants and cooks. Mobility of employment and of residence was common amongst this slave elite, since it often made economic sense for a smaller slave-owner to 'hire out' a skilled slave for a period, or to put a slave in charge of a small business enterprise such as a bar or canteen. This practice is probably what made the court suspicious of Modeste's claim that she had bought her freedom, for if that were so it would be unlikely that she would be paying Bacou the sum of 2 *livres* per day. Slaves, 'free blacks' and poor whites lived in close proximity in the narrow streets of Port Louis, and to a lesser extent on some rural *habitations*. Urban planning throughout the century had attempted to assign certain groups of people to certain urban spaces[17]—there was a Camp des Yolofs and a Camp des Malabars,[18] for example—but the people of Port Louis were not so easily ordered, at least not unless they had acquired their own pieces of property.[19] We have seen that Bernard, a 'Malabar', was living in the Camp des Yolofs. Surviving daily diaries of the Port Louis police station give us a sense of life on the street—the disputes between neighbours who might be technically 'free' or enslaved, and the uncertainty attached to both of these labels; the fights occasioned by newly arrived soldiers and sailors drinking and sleeping in the brothels, or simply renting rooms from 'free black' women; the abandoned babies (about which more later); the frequent arguments about money.[20]

Legal categories of the person were hard to enforce, and ethnic and 'racial' categories often slippery. Yet it was not the case that 'anything goes' in eighteenth-century Isle de France—there were some enduring

[16] On the history of slavery on Isle de France and Mauritius see R. B. Allen, 'Creoles, Indian Immigrants and the Restructuring of Society and Economy in Mauritius' (Ph.D. thesis, University of Illinois, 1983); Muslim Jumeer, 'Les Affranchis et les Indiens Libres a l'Ile de France au XVIII siècle' (Doctoral thesis, Université de Poitiers, 1984); Vijaya Teelock, 'Bitter Sugar: Slavery and Emancipation in Nineteenth Century Mauritius' (D.Phil., University of London, 1993); M. D. E. Nwulia, *The History of Slavery in Mauritius and the Seychelles, 1810–1875* (London and Toronto, 1981); Anthony Barker, *Slavery and Antislavery in Mauritius 1810–33* (Basingstoke and New York, 1996).

[17] A. Toussaint, *Port Louis. Deux Siecles d'Histoire (1735–1935)* (Port Louis, 1936).

[18] 'Yolof' or 'Wolof' referred to slaves of West African origin who had been imported in the early part of the eighteenth century (of which more later), while 'Malabar' referred to those, slave or free, who were of South Indian origin.

[19] On the acquisition of property by manumitted slaves, see especially Allen, 'Creoles'.

[20] NAM. OA 58: Bureau de Police, Journal pour la consignation des rapports de police, 15 avril 1785–31 mars 1787; Z2B/6: Journal de police, 1 juillet 1790–29 juillet 1791.

patterns to social interactions and the disputes occasioned by them. To begin with, ethnic labels, though frequently inaccurate, were not always meaningless, particularly when they functioned to reinforce divisions of labour. The extent to which slaves of Indian origin formed an elite within Isle de France slave society may have been exaggerated,[21] but there is nevertheless substantial evidence that certain occupations were more common amongst them than in the slave body as a whole.[22] So, a female 'Bengalie' slave, such as Modeste, or one designated 'Malabar', was very likely to be employed as a domestic servant. The frequency of sexual relationships between them and their masters may have led in turn to higher rates of manumission,[23] and so women of Indian origin came to form an important core of the small 'free black' population of the eighteenth century.[24] This kind of evidence from Port Louis reminds us that 'globalisation', and the complex social identities created by it, has a long and varied history.

The extent to which ex-slaves of Indian origin retained any cultural identity deriving from their backgrounds is hard to discern in the records. Some of the free 'Malabar' living in that part of Port Louis designated as 'Camp Malabar' married within their community. 'Malabar' was a broad colonial label used to refer to Indians from the Malabar south-west coast of India, but also to South Indians in general. Some 'Malabar' families appear to have retained this identity over generations; others were absorbed into a more general 'free black' population of mixed African, Indian, Malagasy and European origin, and might appear in the colonial records of property transactions and marriage as 'noir libre creol', or simply 'creol libre'.[25]

[21] Marina Carter, 'Indian Slaves in Mauritius, 1729–1834', *Indian Historical Review*, XV (1–2): 239.

[22] Indian slaves were always a small minority within the slave population as a whole. In 1761 they formed 7 per cent of the slave population: Carter, 'Indian Slaves': 233–4; D. Napal, *Les Indiens a l'Ile de France* (Port Louis, 1965).

[23] Though Carter argues that the large free 'Malabar' community (rather than 'white' masters) may have been responsible for the growth in manumitted Indians: Carter, 'Indian Slaves': 240.

[24] This is documented by Richard Allen in 'Creoles'. This property-owning class of women of Indian origin was, on a very small scale, not unlike the more famous and enduring 'signares' of eighteenth-century Senegal, also under French Company rule. The origins of this latter group, however, lay in an earlier period of Portuguese influence. See James F. Searing, *West African Slavery and Atlantic Commerce: the Senegal River Valley, 1700–1860* (Cambridge, 1993).

[25] This issue is discussed by Benjamin Moutou in his history of the Christian population of Mauritius. Moutou refers to this Indian free population of the eighteenth century as the 'Pondicheriens' and takes issue with Hazareesingh's claim that they became completely Christianised and Europeanised. The documentary evidence is, in fact, contradictory, indicating perhaps that within the population of Indian origin different responses existed to the circumstances of life on Isle de France. Benjamin Moutou, *Les Chrétiens de l'Ile Maurice* (Port Louis, 1996), 160–1.

Evidence presented in the case of Jouan and Bernard points to the diversity which may have existed within the population of Indian origin in Isle de France. In order that Jouan might be recognised, Lousteau supplies a number of terms to describe him. He is, firstly, an 'Indien'. Secondly, he is a 'Malabar' from south or south-west India. Thirdly, he is a 'Lascar', a term also used in this case to describe the owner of Modeste, the fisherman, Bacou. In early eighteenth-century Isle de France 'Lascar' was both an occupational and a religious category. The first 'Lascars' to arrive on the island were not slaves, but technically free Muslim sailors imported by Governor Labourdonnais in the 1730s as skilled alternatives to more expensive French labour. Their insistence on practising their religion caused deep offence to the clergy on the island, but Labourdonnais (and subsequent governors) valued them highly and defended their right to a degree of religious freedom.[26] As the century wore on, the meaning of this category undoubtedly shifted. The 'Lascar' Bacou was both free and a fisherman, whilst the Lascar 'Jouan' was a slave and a carpenter. Perhaps they still had in common some degree of Muslim identity—we cannot be sure, but Lousteau insists that they conspired together, speaking what he calls the 'Lascar' language. 'Lascar' was one of those categories, or identities, which carried real meaning, though that meaning was never stable. Behind it lay a longer history of cultural change, of 'creolisation' in the cultural sense. 'Lascar' was in fact a category originating in an earlier period of interaction between the peoples of India and Europeans, in this case the Portuguese. Arab traders and navigators, supported by west Asian trading peoples, had spread the Sufi tradition of the Islamic faith along the southern coast of India from the eighth or ninth centuries AD, while elite groups of Sunni Muslims dominated the maritime towns and trading centres of the region.[27] When, from the late fifteenth century, the Portuguese founded their trading stations and settlements on the coast of South India they found Asian Muslims dominating trade, in conjunction with ruling Hindus. Groups such as the 'Lascars' were the product of this and earlier interactions—they arrived into the new context of French eighteenth-century colonialism with a long and

[26] See the entry in Governor Dumas' diary in 1768: 'There are, on Isle de France, several Asian families of the Muslim religion, from two different nations—the Malabars and the Lascars—the former are workers, the latter fishermen.' The Prefet Apostolique (M. Igou) had complained to Dumas about their public practice of the Muslim religion. Dumas observed that: 'these Asians are connected by bonds of blood, of nationality and of religion to the peoples inhabiting the coasts of Coromandel, of Malabar and of Orissa and asked whether it might not be impolitic to remove from those who come to Isle de France their freedom to practice their religious ceremonies'. Archives Nationales, Paris [AN] C/4/21.

[27] Susan Bayly, *Saints, Goddesses and Kings: Muslims and Christians in South Indian Society, 1700–1900* (Cambridge: Cambridge University Press, 1989), 73–9.

varied history behind them. In addition to the Muslim Lascars, there may well have been Christians amongst the early Indians recruited or enslaved to work on Isle de France.[28] Christianity in South India also pre-dated the Portuguese by many centuries, and these 'Syrian' Christian communities were obvious, though contested, allies for the Portuguese.[29] More straightforwardly the product of earlier Portuguese influence in south India were those who, like Bernard, were described as 'Topas'. The 'Topas' or 'Topasses' were a 'Eurasian' population, mostly Catholic, and mostly of mixed Portuguese and Tamil origin:

> These Eurasion Christians are rarely thought of as a group with a distinctive identity or status in south Indian society: it is usually assumed that they were a 'degenerate' and marginalised appendage of the European powers. In fact, though, the Tamilnad topasses constituted a remarkably large part of the region's military population during the pre-colonial and early colonial periods. They too had a reputation for martial prowess, and like the Syrians, they were widely recruited into the armies of the south Indian regional powers.[30]

These two ethnic labels—'Lascar' and 'Topa'—in addition to the wider categories referring to geographical origin—'Malabar, 'Bengali', 'Talinga' and so on—indicate that the religious, cultural and occupational distinctiveness of different groups of people of Indian origin was at least acknowledged on Isle de France by administrators, by slave-owners like Lousteau and by the people themselves. For slaves like Jouan, the label 'Lascar' may well have added to the value he represented to his master.[31] It also appears to be the case that some groups of Indians—the 'Lascars', the Christians, the 'Topas'—were in fact the product of earlier waves of immigration, of colonisation and of cultural interaction resulting from the ancient trading systems of the Indian Ocean.[32]

An important and enduring feature of the colonial system on Isle de France was that cultural and religious differences amongst slaves of African origin were rarely recognised or commented upon. Differences amongst Africans from different sources on the continent were largely described in terms of physique and supposed suitability for certain types of manual work. Whilst Indians, even those who were enslaved, were recognised as having a culture of some sort, one could say that Africans

[28] Carter, 'Indian Slaves', 242.

[29] Bayly, *Saints, Goddesses and Kings*, chapter 7.

[30] Bayly, *Saints, Goddesses and Kings*, 395.

[31] Carter, 'Indian Slaves', 246.

[32] For this point I am indebted to participants in the Imperial and Commonwealth History Seminar, University of Cambridge, and in particular to Timothy Harper and Chris Bayly.

were thought to possess only bodies of varying degrees of usefulness. There were some exceptions, however. Bernard, though a Malabar, lived in that part of Port Louis which is still designated 'Camp des Yolofs'. In the early part of the eighteenth century the 'Wolof' or 'Yolof' slaves, imported from the coast of West Africa, were highly valued, particularly by the Company itself, and were described in terms of an 'aristocracy' of Africans. They came from the Company's possessions on the coast of Senegal, and although one should be careful not to read too much into this ethnic designation (since 'Wolof', like other terms used to label slaves, was undoubtedly somewhat inaccurate), nevertheless the evidence for the role of this group is interesting and suggestive of some similarities with the situation in eighteenth-century south India. As in south India, so on the West coast of Africa, the French were by no means the first outsiders to make their impact felt. The Portuguese had traded here long before the French and English chartered companies came into existence in the late seventeenth century. A creolised group, which Philip Curtin refers to as the 'Afro-Portuguese', had come into being, acting as a trade diaspora in the region.[33] But there were other factors at work in this region too. The 'Wolof' people of the Senegal river valley in the seventeenth century were partially Islamicised, had developed a centralised monarchy and lived under what one historian has described as 'aristocratic despotism'.[34] They also had a highly developed system of slavery, with an elite of royal slaves at court being used as advisors and administrators, and later as warriors. The Wolof also had a 'caste' system—a subdivision of the people into free persons, hereditary occupational groups (notably blacksmiths and 'griots') and slaves, and rules of endogamy designed to maintain social divisions.

By the late seventeenth century the Wolof polity and system of slavery was being influenced by the new demands of the Atlantic slave economy, and by the increasing influence of the French as opposed to the Portuguese. The trading diaspora was now not so much 'Afro-Portuguese' as 'Afro-French' or 'Franco-Wolof', operating from the island of Gorée.[35] The French in Senegal at this time relied heavily on a range of intermediaries in order to pursue the trade in slaves. An elaborate diplomacy of trade existed between them and local political leaders. Markets were controlled and the sale of slaves was taxed. One important group of intermediaries for the French was that of the 'laptots' (from the Wolof words 'lappato bi'). In the late seventeenth and early eighteenth centuries most of this group were free rather

[33] Philip Curtin, *Economic Change in Pre-Colonial Africa: Senegambia in the Era of the Slave Trade* (Madison: University of Wisconsin Press, 1975), chapter 3.

[34] James Searing, *West African Slavery and Atlantic Commerce: The Senegal River Valley, 1700–1860* (Cambridge, 1993).

[35] Curtin, *Economic Change*, 107.

than enslaved. They were skilled sailors, but also interpreters and intermediaries, who worked alongside French officials and sailors on the river fleets.[36] On Isle de France the role of the Wolof (in this case slaves rather than free persons) exhibited some continuity with that on the West African coast.[37] In 1753 administrators on Isle de France emphasised the importance of the 'noirs de Senegal' for the island, particularly for the 'marine' where they could 'substitute to a large extent for the sailors and carpenters of Europe, and for the Lascars of India'.[38] In some of the documentation on Isle de France the terms 'Wolof' and 'Guinée' are used interchangeably, though in theory the latter came from an area extending from the Senegal River, eastwards to Cape Palmas (now on the Liberia/Ivory Coast border). Slaves described variously as 'Guinée' and 'Yolof' were employed on a privately owned forge on the island in the 1750s and much valued for their skills.[39] This is suggestive, given the existence of a 'caste' of blacksmiths amongst the Wolof people. In a 1761 census of slaves owned and employed by the Company, those of 'Guinée' continued to dominate as blacksmiths, carpenters, and in marine-related activities such as caulking.[40] Though in general the proportion of West Africans in the Isle de France slave population had declined by mid-century, they still formed a majority within the slave elite created by the Company.

The 'Wolof' and 'Guinée' of West Africa, then, though enslaved rather than free, were not unlike the 'Lascars' of south India in terms of the specialist roles accorded to them in the slave system, and in terms of the histories of their original societies. Of course, the coasts of West Africa and of South India were very different places in this period, but nevertheless there were some similarities. Against the ancient trading systems of the Indian Ocean, the trade of coastal West Africa seems relatively shallow, but both regions had experienced interaction with the Portuguese, and the creation of creolised groups (the 'Topas' in India; the 'Afro-Portuguese' in Senegambia), as a result. In the late seventeenth and eighteenth centuries French colonial and commercial ventures, operating through a succession of chartered companies, reproduced this pattern and extended it inland as the influence of the Atlantic slave trade made itself felt. The French needed intermediaries,

[36] Searing, *West African Slavery*, 71–2.

[37] M. David, Governor of Isle de France in the 1750s, had in fact been Company director in Senegal in the 1740s.

[38] AOM: C4/7: Lozier-Bouvet, 31 decembre 1753.

[39] AOM: C4/86: Diary of M. Magon, Governor, July 1756, referring to the forge owned by M. M. Rostaing and Hermans.

[40] In the latter case, this group included more women than men: AOM: G1/505, piece 7:recensement general des noirs, negresses et enfants appartenant a la Compagnie, existant au 20 avril 1761.

just as had the Portuguese, and so the 'Lascars' of South India were recognised by French administrators as indispensable allies in their commercial and political confrontation with the British; on the coast and up the river valleys of Senegambia the 'laptots' performed a similar function as skilled sailors and as intermediaries with powerful and sophisticated African rulers. In both regions Islam was a powerful force—established for centuries in South India, its populist character and incorporationist qualities helped ensure its survival there, while in eighteenth-century Senegambia the ravages of the slave trade, civil war, and a crisis of subsistence paved the way for a powerful and enduring Islamic revival movement beginning at the end of the century. By then, few if any West African slaves were being imported into Isle de France: the newer and nearer markets of the East African coast and of Madagascar now provided the major sources of slaves.

Musleem Jumeer has shown that some 'Lascars' continued to play an important role in the Indian and 'free black' communities throughout the century.[41] On the continuum of creolisation[42] at one end were the those who preserved as much as they could of their cultural and religious origins; at the other were those who had converted to Christianity, and had been absorbed into the 'free black' population. Probably most lay somewhere in the middle. Evidence for the continuity of a Wolof ethnicity is so scant as to be almost non-existent. Given the high mortality rates amongst slaves in Isle de France it seems unlikely that even a slave elite would have managed to pass on their culture and traditions in the face of the dramatic decline in slave imports from their region of origin.[43] It is generally thought that when the court artist

[41] Musleem Jumeer, 'Les Affranchis et les Indiens Libres a l'Ile de France au XVIIIe siècle' (Doctoral thesis, Universite de Poitiers, 1984).

[42] I have taken this way of conceptualising creolisation from the very illuminating work of Richard Burton, *Afro-Creole: Power, Opposition and Play in the Caribbean* (Ithaca and London: Cornell University Press, 1997).

[43] In any case, as we have noted, the term 'Wolof', and that of 'Guinée', as used to describe slaves in Isle de France was a broad one which was likely to have incorporated and blurred other West African identities. Although in the court case on Jouan we are introduced to a witness, Pierre Moussa, who is described as 'Bambara', it is also the case that many ethnically Bambara slaves were counted amongst the 'Wolof' and 'Guinée'. Fear of Wolof insubordination and disloyalty led the French on the island of Gorée to rely for some purposes on slaves who came from further up-river, most notably those known as 'Bambara': Searing, *West African Slavery*, 29, 60. An additional complication is the presence on Isle de France of slaves exported from the French post of Ouidah on the Bight of Benin. These slaves were likely to have been culturally very different from those exported from Senegambia and the Guinée coast. Evidence for the presence of slaves from Ouidah in the first half of the eighteenth century is provided by Philip Baker and Chris Corne in their study of the evolution of a creole language on Isle de France: *Isle de France Creole: Affinities and Origins* (Ann Arbor, Michigan, Karoma, 1982): 180–1. On the French slave trade see also J. M. Filliot, *La Traite des Esclaves vers les Mascareignes au*

M.J. Milbert noted, at the turn of the century, a distinct group of 'Wolof' on Isle de France, he must have been mistaken—imports of West African slaves having long dried up. Yet it remains possible that a small group of West African slaves maintained their privileged role within Government service and their status within the slave economy, as well as some modified and creolised form of their ethnicity. Milbert's description is perhaps a little fanciful, but in some details appears quite plausible:

> Les Africains sont les plus propres au travail de la terre. Les Yolofs sont plus grands, plus forts et mieux faits: ce sont les negres par excellence; ils ont plus d'intelligence que tous ceux qui viennent de Mozambique ou de la cote adjacente. Un grand nombre d'Yolofs sont menuisiers, charpentiers, ou exercent d'autres professions mecaniques. Le gouvernement possede plusieurs centaines d'hommes de cette espece; ils se font remarquer au tatonage bizarre par lequel ils s'imaginent decorer certaines parties du corps: ainsi, par exemple, ils se dessinent sur le ventre un large soleil qui le recouvre tout entier, et ressemble a une espece de cuirasse.[44]

If it were the case that a distinct, if small, group of West Africans survived to the turn of the century on Isle de France, they would have done so, not because they had managed to preserve some elemental or originary identity, but rather because they were, like the 'Lascars', already a creolised group, adapted to the circumstances of colonialism, who had created for themselves a specialised role and occupational niche within the slave economy. The story of the 'Wolofs' of Isle de France, then, is not one which traces the survival of what are sometimes called 'Africanisms', but one of the uneven and unequal processes which went to make a new creole culture on the island.

Many of the factors at work which had gone to create these specialised groups were also present in other areas from which Isle de France began increasingly to source its slaves from the middle of the century—that is the coast of East Africa, and the island of Madagascar. Slaves who had been exported from either the Portuguese-controlled area of the east coast of Africa (running roughly from Delegoa Bay to Cap Delgado), or from those ports controlled by the Arabs (from Cap

XVIIIe siècle, ORSTROM (Paris, 1974) and Robert Louis Stein, *The French Slave Trade in the Eighteenth Century: an Old Regime Business* (Madison: University of Wisconsin Press, 1979).

[44] M.J. Milbert, *Voyage Pittoresque a l'Ile de France, Au Cap de Bonne Esperance et a l'Ile de Teneriffe* (Paris: A. Nepven, 1812), vol. II: 163. Milbert's observations were made in 1801. Gamble's ethnographic study of the Wolof makes no mention of any tradition of body tattooing, though this is noted as a feature of Serer culture—the Serer being an ethnic group partially incorporated by the Wolof: David P. Gamble, *The Wolof of Senegambia* (1957) 103.

Delgado to the Gulf of Aden) were known generically as 'les Mozambiques', and although they came from a wide range of east and central African societies, cultural or ethnic divisions amongst them are rarely remarked upon in the documentation.[45] There was no equivalent of the 'Wolof' slave elite amongst the East African slaves, despite the fact that the coastal societies of East Africa had a history not dissimilar in some respects to that of coastal West Africa, or indeed to that of the south coast of India. East African slaves, whose numbers in Isle de France rose rapidly in the 1770s and 1780s, arrived into a society which, though still fluid, had developed some degree of stability and identity of its own. The creole language, for example, though still evolving, had acquired some basic features by this period[46] though East African slaves certainly contributed to its vocabulary.[47] In the hierarchy of the slave economy 'les Mozambiques' lay at the bottom. Valued, not for their skills, but for the strength of their bodies, French commentators and administrators did not recognise them as having any distinct culture. If we think of the process of creolisation as one of losing and learning, but an unequal one, then we can imagine that, despite their numbers, 'les Mozambiques' lost more than others and had to learn fast the ways of this already established island colony. Meanwhile, slaves of Malagasy origin occupied an ambiguous position in the evolving creole culture of Isle de France. The relative proximity of Madagascar and the history of French interests and influence there made it an obvious choice as a source of slaves for Isle de France. Although early governors placed a high value on the services of West African slaves, they also recognised that much could be gained from exploiting a nearer market—not least a lower rate of mortality in passage. As on the coast of West Africa, so in Madagascar, the French relied heavily on intermediaries to negotiate the terms of the slave trade. Madagascar had a long history of interaction with 'outsiders' (Arabs, Portuguese) some of whom had traded in slaves. In the seventeenth century, however, a new set of

[45] Though once again it was Milbert who noted that 'Parmi les Mozambiques, il y en a qui sont originaires de l'etablissment portugais de ce nom; d'autres de Querimbas, sur la meme cote; d'autres de Quiloa et de Zanzibar, parmi lesquels se trouvent quelques Abyssins. Cette classe, selon M. de Cossigny, forme quinze divisions de peuples qui ne s'entendent point, et qui etaient destines a se combattre.' Milbert, *Voyage Pittoresque*, vol. II: 162. In the records of the ships which transported East African slaves to Isle de France the ethnicities of slaves were noted, though no doubt they were very rough categories. See for example NAM: OC71 Bureau de Controle de la Marine: Pieces relatives aux operations de traite de la flute Roi Les Bons Amis sur la cote orientale de l'Afrique, 1779–85.

[46] Baker dates the first identification of Mauritian creole in an advertisement of 1773: Baker and Corne, *Isle de France Creole*: 248.

[47] See entries of 'Bantu' derivation in Philip Baker and Vinesh Y. Hookoomsing, *Diksyoner Kreol Morisyen* (Paris: Editors L'Harmattan, 1987).

foreigners (the Dutch, English and French) began to make their influence felt, stimulating the trade in slaves and offering firearms in return. In the same period three movements towards state formation took place within Madagascar, the most successful being that of the highland Merina who, between 1780 and 1820, came to conquer most of the island. The French had tried unsuccessfully to colonise Madagascar in the seventeenth century from their base at Fort Dauphin, and in the process developed a healthy respect for Malagasy rulers. 'La grande île' was vitally important to the development of the French Indian Ocean islands, not only as a source of slaves, but also as a source of foodstuffs: the fleet of boats which made the journey to Madagascar from Isle de France came back loaded with men, cattle and rice. They also exhibited a grudging respect for the slaves of Malagasy origin who were transported to Isle de France. Though in general 'les malgaches' or 'madecasses' were treated as one group within the slave economy, French administrators and observers recognised divisions within them, particularly between the 'light-skinned' highlanders and the more 'African'-looking lowlanders. It was particularly noted that those from the highland populations had straight, rather than curly hair, a fact which apparently led some to classify them, occupationally, as one group with slaves of Indian origin.[48] The 'malgaches' certainly captured the somewhat feverish imaginations of the white population. Some wore talismans, reinforcing their reputation for sorcery. Even when not numerically dominant amongst the population of escaped 'maron' slaves in the mountains at the centre of the island, they were always thought of as having a particular propensity to both violence and flight. Indeed, every year some Malagasy slaves escaped the island altogether in stolen boats, or ones they had secretly manufactured themselves. In some cases they were recaptured in Madagascar and sold again, reappearing in Isle de France. The determination of the Malagasy to escape was understood to have been linked to their particular attachment to their ancestors, and a dread of dying away from home.[49]

Very occasionally in the trials of runaway slaves, or 'marons', we find evidence for what might be called cultural resistance amongst slaves of Malagasy, and, to a lesser extent, African origin. Escaped

[48] At least this is what Milbert seems to imply: 'La population de Madagascar s'etant formée par le concours de plusieurs nations, il en resulte que ces insulaires n'ont pas tous, a beaucoup pres, les meme caracteres physiques; leur couleur est tres variée, tous n'ont point les cheveux crepus. Ces insulaires font, avec les Indiens, un tier des esclaves de l'Ile de France. Quoiqu'ils apprennent facilement toute espèce de metiers, on prefère les employer comme domestiques.' Milbert, *Voyage Pittoresque*, vol. II: 164.

[49] For Malagasy veneration of ancestors and burial practices see M. Bloch, *Placing the Dead. Tombs, Ancestral Villas and Kinship Organisation in Madagascar* (London, Seminar Press, 1971). For an overview of the complexity of Malagasy history and culture see John Mack, *Madagascar: Island of the Ancestors* (London: British Museum Publications, 1986).

slaves of Malagasy origin sometimes testified that they had reverted to their pre-slave names. In a case of 1746, for example, a captured slave of Malagasy origin, known as Louison, when asked if this is her real name, replies that her Malagasy name is Fonovola and that this is the name she used with other maroon slaves, but that she was known to her various slave-masters as Louison.[50] In a case of 1750 the Malagasy slave Magdalene Marena, who had been a member of the 'Bande de Grande Barbe' says in reply to questions that she practises the 'religion of her country'.[51]

As this brief discussion has made clear, delineating the nature of 'identities' on Isle de France in the eighteenth century is a far from straightforward task. All identities are the product of cultural work, and all are thus is some sense continually coming into being. This is more true of places such as Isle de France in the eighteenth century, where the rigidities of the ideology of slavery came up against the fluidity of a society in the making. This was clearly a highly unequal process in which some groups (notably the French colonial elite) retained much of their history, culture and language, albeit transformed by the experience of being colonists, whilst others (most notably the slaves of East African origin) were rarely recognised as having any culture to lose. The task is of course made doubly difficult by the nature of the evidence at our disposal. Any account of slave identities must be read against the grain of the representations of certain groups produced by French observers, supplemented by whatever fragments of evidence survive in the legal documentation, often produced as asides to the central narrative. In contrast, the colonial elite, though deeply divided, was deeply self-conscious, endlessly reflecting on its own identity.

That the identity of this elite was centrally influenced by their ownership of slaves is not only a retrospective observation, but was frequently remarked upon by contemporaries. In the course of the eighteenth century, the belief grew that slavery was an 'unnatural' state, and one which had the potential to corrupt or barbarise the slave owner. Within Isle de France 'white' society, riven as it was by social tensions, jealousies, and rivalries, 'reputation' was all important. Cases in which reputation was at stake can tell us something about the limits of identities, the boundary markers which social groups placed between themselves and others in an often vain attempt to present to the outside world the picture of themselves which they cherished within. Such cases often revolved around issues of sexuality, of family life, and of the

[50] NAM: JB4: Procedure Criminelle, 1746.
[51] NAM: JB6: Procedure Criminelle, 1750–1.

treatment of slaves. Though slaves who attempted to bring their masters and mistresses to book for ill-treatment were rarely successful, nevertheless, the alleged ill-treatment of slaves was a powerful weapon with which one slave-owner could insult another. As the eighteenth century progressed, so 'respectable' people held the view that the survival of the institution of slavery depended on it moving more definitively from the private to the public domain. Though the institution of slavery had in theory been regulated since 1723 by a version of the Code Noir, in practice the treatment of slaves on the island was largely a private affair. Slaves were private property and many slave-owners guarded jealously what they regarded as an inviolable right to do what they would with that property. But as the eighteenth century progressed, and as the view that slavery was an 'unnatural' state became more widespread, so also did the argument that the punishment of slaves must be removed from the private domain and regulated by public authority. Reason was to be applied to this very unreasonable institution. Allegations of ill-treatment of slaves were much like allegations of wife beating—they only came to the fore under certain circumstances, either because the ill-treatment has caused public disorder, or because there was already some underlying resentment or jealousy against the slave-owner on the part of another. More frequent were charges by a slave-owner against a third party for beating or injuring a slave belonging to the complainant. One such case from 1777 is revealing, not only of norms around the 'proper' treatment of slaves, but also of the degree to which male slaves were regarded as having some right to respect, even from whites, when it came to their own sexual and familial relations.

In November 1777 one Sieur de Clonard, who was a Lieutenant in the King's navy, complained to the police of the 'excès' committed by a certain 'white' against his slave, Joseph, a Malagasy domestic servant, who had received a blow to the head resulting in a great deal of bleeding.[52] Sieur de Clonard presents his complaint in the following terms, arguing that 'such excessive acts are all the more worthy of the attention of the law and all the more reprehensible since, being committed against a slave, they cause the latter to forget, in the first moments of pain and sensitivity, the singular respect which they must show to whites'. De Clonard's argument was a familiar one—that there were limits beyond which it was not reasonable for a slave to maintain the appropriate respect for whites, and that excessively harsh or provocative treatment therefore threatened the whole institution of slavery. In Joseph's case, the original provocation appears to have been an insult or at least an unwarranted intrusion into his private life.

[52] NAM: JB29: Procedure Criminelle 1777, cases against Joseph and against la Poeze.

Joseph, when interviewed by the examining judge, gives the following account. The previous day he had been in the Rue des Limittes with Perrine, a slave belonging to Sieur Bellerose, when a white man, whom he did not recognise, accosted him and demanded to know if this woman was his 'wife', to which he replied that she was his 'wife'. At this the white man said 'So you sleep with her then', to which he had replied, 'yes'. At this point the white man told him to stand back, but Perrine had stopped him from doing this, saying 'don't' and held him by the shirt. The next thing he knew was that the white man had raised the parasol he had in his hand and had begun hitting him hard on the head, neck and left arm. He had then gone to report the incident to his master. Perrine, when asked to recount the event, adds that in response to the white man's questions Joseph had replied that 'ce que cela lui f . . .' and that it was at this point that the man (whom she names as la Poeze) lifted his parasol against him. La Poeze, described simply as an employee of the King and 26 years old, is brought in for questioning. He has himself simultaneously brought a case against Joseph, accusing him of insulting and menacing him on the street and arguing for the danger represented by blacks who dare to insult whites, causing 'disagreeable scenes on the street every day'. His case against Joseph is merged with that against him. He denies that he ever asked Joseph whether he was married to, or slept with, Perrine. The interrogator persists: 'Was it not the case that Joseph's indecent and improper response was not in fact a reply to his own improper question when he had asked Joseph if the woman was his wife and if he slept with her?' La Poeze continues to deny that he ever asked such a question. As was usual in these cases, no action was taken against him and Joseph was reminded of his duty to pay respect to whites, but the message of the proceedings was already clear—that slaves were persons enough to experience insult.

Such cases were rare. More common were those involving the reputation of 'free blacks' and free persons of colour, or 'metis'.[53] Amongst this small group a self-conscious awareness of the rights, and a demand to be recognised as equal to 'whites', becomes more evident towards the end of the century and is further enhanced by the Revolution.[54] These cases remind us that, in the complex melting-pot

[53] There are many such examples: e.g. in 1784 that of Louis Bergincourt, a 'free black' carpenter, who complains to the police that two brothers (the brothers Sieurs le Goy) have composed a song which defames his family and have pinned the text of this song to the door of his house.

[54] My impression (but this is only an impression) is that cases involving the reputations of 'free blacks' increased in the revolutionary years. This would not be surprising given the importance of the issue of 'free blacks' in revolutionary politics and the debate which led to the abolition of slavery in 1794.

of people and identities which was eighteenth-century Isle de France, 'race' could still act as the ultimate arbiter, the bottom line. Though, as I have argued, 'race' was never a reliable or sufficient marker of social difference, neither was it far beneath the surface and could be appealed to at any moment. 'Race' was far from irrelevant when it could be connected to property and inheritance, for example, as many women knew. Cases of abandoned new-born babies were frequent in Isle de France as they were in France itself at the time. Investigations into the circumstances of abandonment sometimes revealed that the baby had been left by its slave or 'free black' mother at the door of a white man, the supposed father, in the early hours of the morning. Though an illegitimate child would have no formal claim to support from the father, a degree of moral pressure could nevertheless be exerted, sometimes with success. In episodes of high tragic-comedy, surgeons were dispatched to examine the new borns and to determine whether they might be in any degree 'white' ('blanchatre').

There were also moments of high drama on the streets of and bars of Isle de France even before the Revolution, when the mythology of 'freedom' could be seen in head-on collision with the reality of racism; in which identification by others was radically at odds with the identity which individuals had created for themselves and which they held internally; in which the simple question 'who are you?' could reveal the both the power and the fragility of an entire colonial system and the fraught nature of colonial identities. I shall end this paper with a discussion of one such case.

In Port Louis in August 1777, a crowd gathered to watch the hanging of a man named Benoit Giraud, also known as 'Hector the Mulatto'.[55] Giraud was described as a 'free-born black' from another island on the other side of the French colonial empire, Martinique. More proximately he came from Paris where, after a spell in the notorious Châtelet prison, he had been, to his immense outrage, exiled to Isle de France by order of the Ministère de la Marine. Arriving on the island in May 1777, Giraud was immediately placed in chains and imprisoned. On 15 August, in the late afternoon, he and another prisoner, a young boy named Cezar, were digging a trench close to the island's administrative headquarters. Benoit Giraud and Cezar were chained together. At about 5 o'clock senior government officials crossed the square in formation, passing as they did so close to the trench where the two men were digging. Amongst them were the Intendant of the colony, M. Maillart Dumesle, and one M. Foucault, the Intendant-elect, due shortly to replace Dumesle. As they walked passed in a group, so a number of witnesses saw Benoit Giraud hurl an object in the direction

[55] NAM: JB27, Procedure Criminelle, 1777 no. 14.

of M. Foucault, the force of which was deflected by M. Dumesle's cane. Having apparently missed his target, Giraud then leapt at Foucault (dragging the unfortunate Cezar with him), and attacked him both physically and with insults. Words in this eighteenth-century world, as we have seen, were barbed weapons. The precise words of the insult reported by witnesses varied somewhat, but most recalled hearing something along the lines of 'You fucking villain, you are the cause of all my misfortunes and you will pay for it.' Finally Giraud was removed by the other officers and he and Cezar were returned to jail, where his ranting and raving could be heard by all. In his testimony the jailer, M. Blanchteste, reported that on being returned to the jail and admonished for the terrible thing he had done, Giraud had replied: 'I have only one thing to say—I promised myself that I would do what I did—let them hang me.' The next day he stood trial.

Giraud's first examination by the judge followed the prescribed form. His answer to the question 'Who are you?' was critical. Giraud stated that he was 37 years of age, that he had been a domestic servant in Martinique, where he had been born, and in Europe, in the service of M. Foucault. He was, he emphasised, of free birth. Asked if he had ever been convicted of a crime, Giraud answered that he had never been subject to a 'punition infamante',[56] but that he had spent fifteen days in the Châtelet prison in Paris following a quarrel with the person with whom he was boarding. Admitting readily that he had thrown something at M. Foucault, he disputed the evidence that this was a stone. In his fury, he said, he had picked up whatever was to hand, and that had been mud. In fact, he went on, he was not entirely sure what he had done the previous day because as soon as he set eyes on Foucault his blood had boiled so much that he had not known what he was doing or saying. But, yes, he had called him a number of names—that he did recall. Asked if he had intended to kill M. Foucault he replied that he had not, but that given the terrible things that Foucault had done to him, he had wanted to humiliate him.[57] He was certain, he said, that his imprisonment had not been at the orders of the Ministère de la Marine. He demanded justice.

On 18 August Giraud was examined again and confronted with the witnesses. Asked if he had not insulted and menaced M. Foucault after having hurled a rock at him, he replied that he had hurled earth and not a rock, and that he had indeed insulted Foucault, but only in

[56] A 'punition infamante' was one which involved the loss of civil rights. In using this term Giraud demonstrates that not only is he well-versed in French law, but that he is a free man with rights which could be lost.

[57] Unfortunately I have not been able to discover from the surviving documentation what had gone on between Giraud and Foucault in the past, through details on Foucault's career can be found in AOM: E Series (Personnel Colonial Ancien): E 190.

response to Foucault's own insults, for Foucault had referred to him as a slave. Asked whether he did not know that M. Foucault had been named by the King as the successor to M. Maillart Dumesle as Intendant of the colony, Giraud replied that he had not known this, and even if he had been told it he would not have believed it, since Foucault had been dressed in plain grey and not in uniform. Asked whether he was not aware of the laws which ordained that free blacks and liberated slaves show particular respect to whites, Giraud responded that he was familiar with the Code Noir, and he had seen the chapter which said that 'noirs mulatres' enjoyed the same rights and privileges as other free persons.[58] His own case, he went on, was that of a free person who had insulted a 'bourgeois', for M. Foucault could not be regarded as anything but a 'bourgeois', having been dressed as one, and not in uniform.

Giraud was found guilty of assault and hanged on the same day. In this case Isle de France justice worked fast—in most other cases people stayed festering in jail for months, if not years. Writing after the event to the Ministère de la Marine, Maillart Dumesle expressed something of the sense of scandal which this case had occasioned. Imagine, he wrote, that even in his last interrogation, this man admitted that he knew M. Foucault, that he had indeed intended to hit him, but that as far as he was concerned this was just a quarrel between one free individual and another. 'You can well see,' he went on, 'how these small pretexts can serve as excuses.' The case only served to underline how important it was that officers of the state should bear marks of distinction, especially in this island where the streets were 'continually full of slaves, of free blacks and mulattoes, of workers and foreigners, such that under the pretext of not recognising an official, anything might be thought permissible'.

Giraud's defence had rested on his identity. He knew that as a 'free-born mulatto' he was entitled, under the Code Noir, to the same rights and privileges as any other free person. His blood had boiled at the sight of his former employer, not only because he attributed to Foucault the injustice of his imprisonment and exile, but because he had heard Foucault refer to him as a 'slave'. He was not a slave, and so he insisted that his dispute with Foucault was merely a dispute between one free-born person and another. When told that Foucault was much more than a 'bourgeois', Giraud's defence was one of mis-recognition. How was he to know that he was the Intendant-elect (and thus about to become a kind of embodiment of the King) when he wore no uniform, no marks of office? Giraud had read the Code Noir and had believed

[58] Here Giraud appears to be emphasising not only his legal status as a free person, but his 'racial' origins as a 'mulatto'.

in the myth of freedom. He had failed to grasp that freedom, truth and culpability were all relative concepts in this eighteenth-century world—everything depended on who you were, and who you were was a great deal more complex that the interdependent ideologies of freedom and slavery implied. Indeed, under Ancien Regime criminal law the importance of who you were in determining the severity of a crime was formally recognised. There were, for example, seven circumstances of the person which could be held to aggravate an offence, a number of which could have been applied in this case.[59] What Giraud had also failed to grasp, or was refusing to recognise, was that who he was still ultimately rested on the colour of his skin. Whilst correctly identifying M. Foucault might, as Giraud argued, depend on what M. Foucault was wearing, in Giraud's own case his identity was written on his body; it was his non-whiteness which set the limits of his freedom in the colonial world. But for Giraud this identification of him as 'black' was a mis-recognition, and it was this which made his blood boil. Nearly two hundred years later, another citizen of Martinique would experience a similar sense of fury as a result of the gap between his own sense of identity and that attributed to him by whites. This was Frantz Fanon.

[59] There were seven circumstances of the person or of the offence which could aggravate culpability and penal severity. These included 'rank or social condition, if the offended was infamous ...'; 'if the victim was an illustrious personage ...'; 'if the crime was committed in ... a public square ...'; 'if the crime was committed by assault or surprise ... or with blatant scandal'. Richard Mowery Andrews, *Law, Magistracy and Crime in Old Regime Paris, 1735–1789* (Cambridge, 1994), vol. 1, 498.

EMPIRE AND NATIONAL IDENTITIES THE CASE OF SCOTLAND

By John M. MacKenzie

READ 26 SEPTEMBER 1997 AT THE INSTITUTE OF HISTORICAL RESEARCH, LONDON

THE modern historiography of the origins of British national identities seems riven with contradictions and paradoxes. First there is a major chronological problem. Is the forging of Britishness to be located in the sixteenth, seventeenth, eighteenth or nineteenth centuries? Second, there is a difficulty in the compilation of such identities. Are they to be found in negative reactions to the perceived contemporary identities of others or in positive, if mythic, readings of ethnic history? Third, can there be a British identity at all when the cultural identities of what may be called the sub-nationalisms or sub-ethnicities of the United Kingdom seem to be forged at exactly the same time? And fourth, did the formation of the British Empire and the vast expansion of British imperialism in the nineteenth century tend towards the confirmation of the identity of Greater Britain or of the Welsh, Irish, English and Scottish elements that made it up?

The number and complexity of these questions, and the equally complicated answers which they stimulate, is a reflection of the extensive multi-disciplinary interest in identities which has emerged in recent times. In order fully to understand these concerns, it is necessary to comprehend their instrumentality. Most modern scholars seem to comply with Sir John Seeley's injunction that history should be read upwards and not downwards.[1] Generally they have accepted the notion that historians have always done this even when they have denied doing so. The practical objects of history seem once more to be recognised, that its study does indeed modify views of the present and consequently influence the framing of the future, and that it should be inseparably bound up with contemporary culture and politics. It is no longer a surprise to find a scholarly discussion of the Union of the Crowns of England and Scotland of 1603 directly linked to the surprises of the 1992 British General Election in an article in the *Transactions of the Royal Historical Society*.[2]

[1] J. R. Seeley, *The Expansion of England: Two Courses of Lectures* (London, 1883), p. 130.

[2] Jenny Wormald, 'The Creation of Britain: Multiple Kingdoms or Core and Colonies', *Transactions of the Royal Historical Society*, sixth series, II (1992), p. 194.

The interest in national identities also inhabits a current scholarly yearning for globalisation. Modern concerns with internationalism and inter-culturalism have turned the spotlight on the national identities which seem to stand in their way. For Europeans, the complex layering of region, nation and supra-nationalism and the inter-relationship of the multiple ethnicities which they represent have become important in the cultural, economic and political formation of the European Union. So have been concerns with the post-imperial and often synthetic nationalisms of Asia and Africa, now sometimes construed as the means for the continued dominance of specific elites, as the source of major ethnic stress and as barriers to material and cultural development.

These problems of multi-ethnic societies within specifically nineteenth-century state configurations have been just as apparent in Europe. In the British case, the renewed propaganda for a patriotic history stimulated by the Thatcher government, with its promotion of a national educational system and curriculum, produced an almost inevitable reaction among scholars. That was certainly the case with the History Workshop group's fascination with patriotism and national identity.[3] Post-colonialism and other multi-disciplinary scholarly alliances have continued to develop concerns with cultural values, myths, constructions of the past and inventions of traditions. The emergence of a new environmental history has also played a key role. Here, a significant shift has taken place from a supposedly realist and scientific approach to a largely constructivist one. Nature, landscape, and perceptions of environmental change have themselves been increasingly recognised as cultural constructs which play their own part in notions of identity.[4]

Perhaps all this helps to explain why the chronological landscape has been so complex, stimulating the four questions posed at the beginning of the paper. First, which century is the key? English and Welsh, and in a more negative form Irish, identities have inevitably looked to the Tudor period for the origins of Britishness. This was the period when the word 'empire' was first used to mean the enlarging state, a time when Welsh figures were influential at the royal court, when both history and the theatre were bent towards propagandist underpinnings of that state, when settlements were begun across the Irish Sea and tentative steps taken towards more distant colonisation. For Scots, the 1603 Union of the Crowns inevitably marks a significant turning-point, leading to a period of intense theorisation about two

[3] *Patriotism: the Making and Unmaking of British National Identity*, 3 vols., ed. Raphael Samuel (London, 1909); 'History, the Nation and the Schools', Special Feature, *History Workshop*, 29 (spring, 1990), pp. 92–133.

[4] Simon Schama, *Landscape and Memory* (London, 1995); Jane M. Jacobs, *Edge of Empire: Postcolonialism and the City* (London, 1996).

nations with a single monarch, with visible representations of such intellectualisation expressed in the court masque, architecture and public pageants, particularly those associated with the visits of the monarch.[5] But the 1707 Union of Parliaments seemed even more significant; for Sir John Seeley it marked virtually the start of Scottish history because it represented both the beginnings of material progress for the Scots (and therefore of the cultural and intellectual achievements of the Scottish Enlightenment) and the true origins of the creation of nineteenth-century Greater Britain.[6] If modern historians have departed from the first proposition, stressing significant economic and intellectual foundations in the seventeenth century, they have perhaps continued to accept the second. And if imperialism brought this Greater Britain to apparent fruition in the nineteenth century, it also helped to form the myth of British national character. This concept of national character relates to the alleged characteristics of individuals rather than the more all-embracing totality of national identity. We can now recognise, however, that national character as formulated in the nineteenth century was a myth that was essentially English and masculine, represented as phlegmatic, unemotional, unintellectual, individualist, eccentric, sporting (both literally and metaphorically), fair-minded and essentially youthful.[7] It was a national character which was often promoted by those who were not English (John Buchan would be a good example), but which was also frequently contrasted with the characteristics both of the English of the eighteenth century and before, and of the other ethnic groups of the British Isles.

If there seems, then, to be a problem of origins, there is equally a difficulty in construction. Many scholars of identity and representation, including Linda Colley, see national identities as constituted of negative elements in relation to Others. Thus, for Colley, the formation of a distinctively British identity was made up in the later eighteenth century in contradistinction to France: Protestantism contrasted with Catholicism, constitutional monarchy with absolutism, a commercial and progressive economy with an agrarian and backward one, an essentially bourgeois with an aristocratic society.[8] For Edward Said and the later post-colonialists, the Others are non-European and the manichean polarities become white and black, rational and emotional,

[5] Wormald, 'Creation of Britain'; *Scots and Britons: Scottish Political Thought and the Union of 1603*, ed. Roger A. Mason (Cambridge, 1994); Charles W.J. Withers, 'Royalty and Empire: Scotland and the Making of Great Britain, 1603–1661', *Scottish Geographical Magazine*, 113 (1997), pp. 22–32.

[6] Seeley, *Expansion*, p. 131.

[7] The most recent examination of this myth of English national character is Jeffrey Richards, *Films and British National Identity: From Dickens to Dad's Army* (Manchester, 1997).

[8] Linda Colley, *Britons, Forging the Nation 1707–1837* (New Haven and London, 1992).

technologically sophisticated and primitive, with subjection to the western rule of law on the one hand and the supposedly arbitrary whims of indigenous rulers on the other.[9] Here identity is formed out of notions of racial difference and a profound sense of superiority already present in the eighteenth century, but considerably developed in the nineteenth.[10] But as Anthony D. Smith has argued, self-formulated national identities in Europe and elsewhere are invariably about fractions of uniqueness as well as about alleged cultural superiority.[11] They therefore have a much greater depth than these contemporary negative reactions: they are forged out of a reading of history upwards into the realm of myth. They search for and construct a unique complex of national ethnic origins, often expressed through linguistic identities and literary formulations of heroic migration and community cohesion, with chivalric encounters and cultural interpretations of a distinctive geography and landscape. They also often appeal to a distant past in order to establish a critique of more recent times. In any case, the binary Other has surely been emphasised too much. We need to pay more attention to the positive referent society, not only the mythic Merrie past, but also the geographically distant positive Other. It is interesting that in the late nineteenth and early twentieth centuries Japan was used in this way, both by British propagandists anxious about the lack of a true social and political coherence, and therefore of national efficiency, in the United Kingdom, and by the re-emerging nationalities of the Celtic periphery. The Meiji political and intellectual myth-making about her own distant past, and her communication of such historical myths to the populace, was indeed keenly followed.[12]

While such readings of mythic origins begin in the late fifteenth century, it was in the eighteenth and early-nineteenth centuries that they became powerfully instrumental. And the uniqueness that they celebrated was not British, but English, Scottish, Welsh and Irish. They often interwove both aristocratic and folk traditions, as in James Fergusson's Gaelic Ossian fabrications of 1762, Joseph Ritson's work on the medieval outlaw hero, Robin Hood, published in 1795, Sir Walter Scott's avowedly fictional recreations of Scottish and English pasts, or the Welsh inventions of Edward Lluyd, William Pughe and

[9] Edward Said, *Orientalism* (London, 1978); *Culture and Imperialism* (London, 1993).

[10] Christine Bolt, *Victorian Attitudes to Race* (London, 1971); Douglas A. Lorimer, *Colour, Class and the Victorians* (Leicester, 1978); *The Expansion of England: Race, Ethnicity and Cultural History*, ed. Bill Schwarz (London, 1996).

[11] Anthony D. Smith, *National Identity* (Harmondsworth, 1991).

[12] See, for example, Arnold White, *Efficiency and Empire*, edited by G. R. Searle (Brighton, 1983, first published London, 1901); Alfred Stead, *Great Japan, a Study in National Efficiency* (London, 1906); Sir Henry Norman, *The Peoples and Politics of the Far East* (London, 1907).

Edward Williams between the 1690s and 1790s.[13] According to Jeanne Sheehy, Irish cultural traditions were being formed at a slightly later date.[14] All these 'Celtic' myths quite specifically contrasted their cultural character with that of the English, in their devotion, for example, to epic poetry and music, with various forms of the harp interestingly turning up in each. How then do these sub-nationalities relate to the imperial identity of Greater Britain? Do they cohere with it or run counter to it? Seeley, of course, had nothing to say about such British ethnicities except to draw some very curious comparisons. He likened Maori resistance in New Zealand to that of Highland Scottish clans, by which he presumably meant the Jacobite revolts of the eighteenth century. He also considered the presence of French in Canada, Maoris in New Zealand and Dutch and Africans in South Africa as being no different from the peoples of Wales, Scotland and Ireland, who had distinctive Celtic blood and similarly spoke, as he engagingly put it, unintelligible languages.[15] Despite its cultural arrogance, this is a curiously non-racial formulation. Moreover, it seems to recognise the essentially romantic character of ethnic identities. And it reflects the coherence between the construction of such identities and Seeley's view of history. His vision was akin to the literary adventure tradition distinguished by the American scholar, Martin Green: lively, dramatic, broad events upon a large canvas, easily captured in story and communicated to the young.[16] Here, imperial history and romantic nationalism meet on a common cultural ground. They also bring together the essentially bourgeois and intellectual character of the construction of both ethnic identities and the ideologies of imperial idealism.

Gwyn Williams, in his impressive book *When Was Wales?*, demonstrated that there was no incompatibility between the continuing construction of Welsh cultural identity in the nineteenth century and the emergence of Wales as a major auxiliary economy of Empire. On the contrary, most Welsh cultural and intellectual figures found in Empire a wider and justificatory stage for the Welsh character.[17] Cardiff's status as the Welsh capital was enormously enhanced by its emergence as a grand imperial city.[18] Early in the twentieth century, the patriotic journal *Welsh Outlook* actually compared the Welsh with the Japanese

[13] Prys Morgan, 'From a Death to a View: the Hunt for the Welsh Past in the Romantic Period', in *The Invention of Tradition*, ed. Eric Hobsbawm and Terence Ranger (Cambridge, 1983), pp. 43–100.

[14] Jeanne Sheehy, *The Rediscovery of Ireland's Past: the Celtic Revival 1830–1930* (London, 1986).

[15] Seeley, *Expansion*, pp. 47, 50.

[16] Martin Green, *Dreams of Adventure, Deeds of Empire* (London, 1980).

[17] Gwyn A. Williams, *When Was Wales?* (Harmondsworth, 1991), pp. 124–5, 139, 225.

[18] *Ibid.*, pp. 221, 223.

as an old people finding a new role on the world stage.[19] Not only were the Welsh dissenting churches strongly implicated in the missionary endeavour of Empire, Welsh liberalism, as Kenneth Morgan has demonstrated, was distinctly of the imperial variety.[20] We should not be confused by the pro-Boer tendencies of Lloyd George. In that respect he was a maverick and, by the time of the First World War, he could marshal imperial rhetoric with the best of them. Even the Irish negotiated their cultural nationalism in relation to Empire, as in the plays of Dion Boucicault or the prominence of both Protestant and Catholic Irish (admittedly often at different levels of the hierarchy) in the military and police forces of the colonial territories.[21]

But there was one great difference between the Welsh and the Irish and the Scots and that was in the levels of emigration. Welsh emigration declined in the course of the nineteenth century and by the 1890s Wales, uniquely, experienced net immigration. Hence, while Welsh names abound in the West Indies from an earlier period, and while the exploits of Welsh regiments and individual missionaries were celebrated in the Empire, the fame of the relatively small Welsh settlements in Pennsylvania or Patagonia indicates the extent to which there was nothing like the interactive experience of homeland and colonial settlement of the Irish or particularly the Scots.[22]

In the Scottish case, another great paradox is the relationship of Scottish participation in Empire to Jacobitism. In the eighteenth century, Scottish commercial involvement in empire was specifically anti-Jacobite. The Scottish burghs resoundingly turned their backs on Jacobitism, often at some temporary cost to themselves.[23] The involvement of Scots personnel in Empire and the formation of London factions connected with such imperial patronage also distanced themselves from romantic Stuart treason. The sons of Highland aristocrats migrated to the Empire to try to reverse the attainders of the post-1745 'pacification', and Highland regiments were formed as evidence of loyalty to the victorious Hanoverian imperial dispensation.[24] Yet, by the later nineteenth century,

[19] *Ibid.*, p. 222.

[20] Kenneth O. Morgan, *Rebirth of a Nation: Wales 1880–1980* (Oxford, 1981), pp. 30–1, 45.

[21] Richard Allen Cave, 'Staging the Irishman' in J. S. Bratton *et al.*, *Acts of Supremacy: The British Empire and the Stage, 1790–1930* (Manchester, 1991), pp. 62–128; *An Irish Empire? Aspects of Ireland and the British Empire*, ed. Keith Jeffery (Manchester, 1996).

[22] Dai Smith, *Wales! Wales?* (London, 1984), pp. 29–32.

[23] Colley, *Britons*, p. 83; Irene Maver, 'The Guardianship of the Community: Civic Authority Before 1833' in *Glasgow: Vol. 1: Beginnings to 1830*, ed. T. M. Devine and Gordon Jackson (Manchester, 1995), pp. 244, 259.

[24] G.J. Bryant, 'Scots in India in the Eighteen Century', *Scottish Historical Review*, lxiv (1985), pp. 22–41; Bruce Lenman, *The Jacobite Clans of the Great Glen, 1650–1784* (London, 1984), pp. 209, 217–18.

as Murray Pittock has argued in relation to domestic Scotland, it was to be partly the romantic signs and symbols of a re-invented Highland culture which were to become the key elements of the interaction of home and Empire in the reconciliation of Scottish ethnic nationalism with its global stage.[25] I say partly, because this imperial interaction was also bound up with the securely Lowland Burns traditions and the effort to construct Scottish heroes, such as David Livingstone, as combining in their persons both Highland and Lowland characteristics.[26] We need to remember that Scots linguistic distinctions embraced Scots as well as Gaelic. Such a cunningly contrived amalgam of Highland and Lowland elements, neatly represented in the Burns societies and Highland games, Caledonian and St Andrews organisations that sprang up around the Empire, in colonies of settlement, India and dependent territories, helped to satisfy what was already clearly perceived as the basic geographic, ethnic and cultural problem in a Scottish nationalist identity. And by the mid to late nineteenth century, the Scots had a very considerable stage upon which it could be worked out.

The eighteenth-century Scottish grasp of imperial opportunities is startling. The city of Glasgow, soon to arrogate to itself a claim as 'Second City of the Empire', expanded mightily and rebuilt itself on the strengths of its American, West Indian and later Asian trades.[27] The Scots' infiltration of the East India Company's marine and medical establishments was notorious.[28] So was their presence at every level of the Company's activities, as soldiers, governors, diplomats and orientalist scholars. As is now well known, Warren Hastings gathered a group of Scots around him, and Scots governors in southern India were later to institute a wholly new land revenue system based upon the peasantry.[29]

[25] Murray Pittock, *The Invention of Scotland: the Stuart Myth and the Scottish Identity, 1638 to the Present* (London, 1991); see also Colin Kidd, *Subverting Scotland's Past: Scottish Whig Historians and the Creation of an Anglo-British Identity, 1689–c.1830* (Cambridge, 1993) and *The Manufacture of Scottish History*, eds. Ian Donnachie and Christopher Whatley (Edinburgh, 1992).

[26] John M. MacKenzie, 'David Livingstone: the Construction of the Myth', in *Sermons and Battle Hymns: Protestant Popular Culture in Modern Scotland*, ed. Graham Walker and Tom Gallagher (Edinburgh, 1990), pp. 24–42; John M. MacKenzie, 'David Livingstone and the Worldly After-Life: Imperialism and Nationalism in Africa' in *David Livingstone and the Victorian Encounter with Africa*, ed. John M. MacKenzie (London, 1996) pp. 201–17.

[27] T. M. Devine, 'The Golden Age of Tobacco' and Gordon Jackson, 'New Horizons in Trade' in *Glasgow*, ed. Devine and Jackson.

[28] George Kirk McGilvary, 'East India Patronage and the Political Management of Scotland, 1720–74' (Ph.D. thesis, The Open University in Scotland, 1989); Michael Fry, *The Dundas Despotism* (Edinburgh, 1992).

[29] John Riddy, 'Warren Hastings: Scotland's Benefactor' in *The Impeachment of Warren Hastings*, ed. Geoffrey Carnall and Colin Nicholson (Edinburgh, 1989), pp. 30–57; Jane Rendall, 'Scottish Orientalism: from Robertson to James Mill', *The Historical Journal*, 25

In the early nineteenth century, the University of Aberdeen supplied most of the doctors and botanists of the Company service.[30] The Hudson's Bay Company famously recruited many of its factors in the Orkneys. The most influential missionaries in southern Africa after the British control of the Cape was confirmed at Vienna were Scots, as were figures active in the press in both India and Cape Town.[31] The most powerful merchant houses in Montreal, Calcutta and the Far East were also Scottish.[32] To all of these were added the large numbers who left Scotland in both the forcible and semi-voluntary migrations of the late eighteenth and nineteenth centuries.

Thus the influence of Scots was to be found in almost all colonies. As I have argued in the past, although the administration and legal systems of empire seemed to be predominantly English, the Scots set about exporting those aspects of their civil culture that had been preserved by the 1707 Act of Union.[33] They asserted their right to develop Presbyterian missions and education in India freed from the established Anglican hierarchy.[34] They developed colleges and schools in India and elsewhere in the dependent territories. Many universities in the colonies of settlement were founded on the Scottish model. The schismatic tendencies of the Church of Scotland, particularly symbolised by the Disruption of 1843, served to enhance rather than inhibit the energy of Presbyterian missions throughout the Empire. In India, Bombay, Madras and Calcutta acquired two Scots colleges each where previously there had been one. The Scottish Episcopal Church was just as influential as its Church of England sister in establishing churches of the Anglican Communion within the Empire. While the Scottish universities passed through a difficult period in the middle decades of

(1982), pp. 43–69; Martha McLaren, 'Writing and Making History: Thomas Munro, John Malcolm, and Mountstuart Elphinstone: Three Scotsmen in the History and Historiography of British India' (Ph.D. thesis, Simon Fraser University, British Columbia, 1992).

[30] John D. Hargreaves, *Academe and Empire: Some Overseas Connections of Aberdeen University 1860–1970* (Aberdeen, 1994), pp. 26, 28, 34–5, 62–5 and *passim.*

[31] John M. MacKenzie, 'On Scotland and the Empire', *International History Review*, XV (1993), p. 734.

[32] David S. Macmillan, 'Scottish Enterprise and Influences in Canada, 1620–1900' and James G. Parker, 'Scottish Enterprise in India, 1750–1914' in *The Scots Abroad*, ed. R. A. Cage; *The Thistle and the Jade: a Celebration of 150 Years of Jardine Matheson and Co.*, ed. Maggie Keswick (London, 1982).

[33] MacKenzie, 'Scotland and the Empire', pp. 732–7; the notion of the Scottish ethic is based upon George Elder Davie, *The Democratic Intellect: Scotland and her Universities in the Nineteenth Century* (Edinburgh, 1961). See also *A Union for Empire: Political Thought and the British Union of 1707*, ed. James Robertson (Cambridge, 1995).

[34] David S. Forsyth, 'Empire and Union: Imperial and National Identity in Nineteenth-Century Scotland', *Scottish Geographical Magazine*, 113 (1997), pp. 7–8.

the century, Scots retained a reputation as a people uniquely trained for medical, technical and environmental services.[35]

Scottish missionaries such as Robert Moffat and David Livingstone had a keen eye for natural historical and environmental concerns. Livingstone of course viewed himself as a scientist as well as a medical missionary and explorer and was accepted as such by great scientific figures of the day like Sir Roderick Murchison, William Whewell and Adam Sedgwick.[36] Richard Grove has suggested that Scots helped to transmit climatic, botanical and environmental ideas from the Continent to the British Empire at a time when English intellectual activity in this area was largely moribund.[37] Certainly, when Robert Croumbie Brown gave evidence to the parliamentary committee on the possibility of establishing a national school of forestry in 1866, he asserted that 'Scotchmen can be most efficiently, and at the least expense, trained up so as to manage our Colonial forests advantageously'.[38]

It is perhaps not surprising that the presence and talents of Scots were much commented upon by such imperial travellers as Anthony Trollope, Sir Charles Dilke, J. A. Froude and many others: clannish, highly visible and often financially successful, they were invariably contrasted with the Irish as colonists.[39] By the final decades of the century, this had an inevitable effect upon Scots' estimation of themselves, not least at home. With the publication of John Hill Burton's *The Scot Abroad* in two volumes in 1864 (with a second edition in 1881) and W. J. Rattray's monumental four-volume *The Scot in British North America* in 1880, a very considerable tradition of celebrating Scots settlement and achievements was begun. In many ways, this was to climax with the publication of Andrew Dewar Gibb's avowedly nationalist *Scottish Empire* of 1937.[40]

[35] Hargreaves, *Academe and Empire, passim*; see also John D. Hargreaves, *Aberdeenshire to Africa: Northeast Scots and British Overseas Expansion* (Aberdeen, 1981).

[36] For the scientific reputation of David Livingstone see *Dr. Livingstone's Cambridge Lectures Together with a Prefatory Letter by the Rev. Professor Sedgwick*, ed. with an introduction, life of Dr Livingstone, notes and appendix by the Rev. William Monk (London, 1858).

[37] Richard Grove, *Green Imperialism: Colonial Expansion, Tropical Island Edens and the Origins of Environmentalism, 1600–1860* (Cambridge, 1995), pp. 312, 347; Richard Grove, 'Scottish Missionaries, Evangelical Discourses and the Origins of Conservation Thinking in Southern Africa, 1820–1900' in *Ecology, Climate and Empire: Colonialism and Global Environmental History, 1400–1940*, ed. Grove (Cambridge, 1997) pp. 86–123.

[38] John Croumbie Brown, *Management of Crown Forests at the Cape of Good Hope Under the Old Regime and the New* (Edinburgh, 1887), p. iii.

[39] See, for example, Anthony Trollope, *Australia* (London, 1873), p. 420; Sir Charles Wentworth Dilke, *Greater Britain* (London, 1872), pp. 373–4 and 533; J. A. Froude, *Oceana or England and Her Colonies* (London, 1886), p. 116.

[40] For a survey of this literature, see MacKenzie 'Scotland and the Empire'. As well as Gibb's *Scottish Empire* (London, 1937), he also published *Scotland in Eclipse* (London, 1930) and *Scotland Resurgent* (Stirling, 1950).

Such pride in imperial achievement, coupled with a sense of duty towards the colonial enterprise, was to be powerfully reflected in the religious, social, intellectual and economic life of Scotland in the late nineteenth and early twentieth centuries. A great deal of work remains to be done on the role of the churches in the dissemination of notions of identity in relation to empire, but there can be little doubt that the missionary societies and missionaries on furlough had a hand in stressing the imperial field as a means to the expression of a distinctively Scots Presbyterian duty. The hero-worship of David Livingstone and the countless biographies written in his memory indicate this strongly.[41] Further evidence comes from the number of missionary memoirs which pointed to Livingstone as the classic Scots exemplar which their authors wished to follow. We now know of the existence of many societies which particularly involved women in the imperial enterprise. These included the Greenock Ladies' Overseas Missionary Association, which raised money for Christina Forsyth's mission school in Fingoland on the eastern Cape, the Glasgow Ladies' Colonial Association and the Glasgow Ladies' Association for the Advancement of Female Education in India.[42] If these represent the strongly imperial orientation of Glasgow and the Clyde region, it should not be a surprise that Mary Slessor, so often depicted as one of the principal heroines of missionary endeavour in Africa, came from the notably imperial city of Dundee, its economy tightly connected with the jute of Bengal, shipping and whaling.[43]

The 1880s, the decade in which the Partition of Africa was pushed forward with particular vigour, are key years in the coming to fruition of these imperial identities. The Boy's Brigade, founded by William Alexander Smith in Glasgow in 1883 and destined to expand throughout Britain and the Empire, as well as to spawn many imitations among other denominations and religions, had a distinctly imperial tone and inevitably venerated the Scots imperial heroes.[44] The Royal Scottish Geographical Society, founded in the four centres of Edinburgh, Glasgow, Dundee and Aberdeen in 1884–5, initially emphasised the intellectual and economic relationships between Scotland and Africa and later promoted wider imperial connections, including Scotland's

[41] MacKenzie, 'Livingstone, Construction of the Myth', pp. 32–5.

[42] Stana Nenadic, 'The Victorian Middle Classes' in *Glasgow: Vol. II, 1830–1912*, ed. W. Hamish Fraser and Irene Maver (Manchester, 1996), p. 288.

[43] Cheryl McEwan, '"The Mother of all the Peoples": Geographical Knowledge and the Empowering of Mary Slessor' in *Geography and Imperialism 1820–1940*, ed. Morag Bell, Robin Butlin and Michael Heffernan (Manchester, 1996), pp. 125–50; Gordon Stewart, *Jute and Empire* (Manchester, forthcoming 1998).

[44] J. O. Springhall, *Youth, Empire and Society* (London, 1977); *Sure and Stedfast: a History of the Boys' Brigade, 1883–1983* (London, 1983).

own expedition to Antarctica.[45] Many of its early speakers suggested that Scots had a particular genius for exploration and colonisation.

This seemed to be reflected in the presence of so many industrial, shipping and commercial figures who represented the self-help ideals of Samuel Smiles, born in Haddington, East Lothian. Smiles was himself heavily influenced by the imperial experience and shifted in his own lifetime from a tradition of domestic radical auto-didacticism to one of personal achievements through Empire.[46] The Indian Mutiny had a profound effect on Smiles and he set about emphasising British heroism in the face of the Revolt, including that of the Scottish hero, Sir Colin Campbell, Lord Clyde. Soon, David Livingstone became Smiles's principal self-help hero, and after the drama of his death and the return of his body in 1873, an engraving of the famous Annan photograph of the missionary was used as the frontispiece for all subsequent editions. In Glasgow and the West of Scotland, figures such as Livingstone's fellow student and friend James 'Paraffin' Young, Sir William Mackinnon, Lord Overtoun, and Sir Donald Carrie became involved both in Scottish enterprise and missionary endeavour (particularly that of the Free Church in Nyasaland, Malawi).[47] The personnel of companies such as the African Lakes, founded by the Moir brothers of Edinburgh to advance Livingstone's ideals, and the Imperial British East Africa, the belatedly chartered brainchild of Mackinnon, stressed their Scottish character, as did the wealthy magnates of the Far Eastern *hong* of Jardine Mathieson.[48]

It has sometimes been objected that the Scottish relationship with Empire reflects different and disconnected regions of the country. The East India Company connections were primarily with the North East. So was much early missionary endeavour. The Western Highlands contributed more than their fair share of migration through the Clearances. Much of the imperial activities of the later nineteenth century were connected with the central belt and in particular with Glasgow and the Clyde. Scots themselves thought regionally rather than nationally. This may have been true in the eighteenth century, a time when the Scots were more powerfully under attack for their opportunistic seizure of imperial enterprise and were therefore eager to seek acceptability through British patriotism. But there can be little doubt that an overall conception of Scotland had been created by the

[45] John M. MacKenzie, 'The Provincial Geographical Societies in Britain, 1884–1914' in *Geography and Imperialism*, ed. Bell *et al.*, pp. 93–124.

[46] Angus Calder, 'Samuel Smiles: the Unexpurgated Version', *The Raven Anarchist Quarterly*, v (1992), pp. 79–89.

[47] John McCracken, *Politics and Christianity in Malawi, 1875–1940* (Cambridge, 1977).

[48] F. L. M. Moir, *After Livingstone: an African Trade Romance* (London, n.d.); Gibb, *Scottish Empire*, p. 147; *Thistle and the Jade*, ed. Keswick.

later nineteenth century. Although regiments supposedly had local or clan connections, they often recruited most successfully among the urban population of the central belt. The resulting iconographic status of the Scottish soldier thus contributed to a sense of an integrated Scottish culture, even if marked out by supposedly distinctive Highland forms of dress. Popular imperial art, in paintings and in engravings in the illustrated press and popular books of heroes and school texts, celebrated the Scottish soldier, easily recognised in his kilt or trews, throughout the century and particular regiments became inseparably associated with such imperial events as the Relief of Lucknow or the Battle of Omdurman. Such associations were equally potent in the Highlands, as so many monuments testify. These would include the striking memorial to the Lovat Scouts in the Boer War in Beauly or the massive tower commemorating 'Fighting Mac', Sir Hector MacDonald, at Dingwall (despite the rather dubious circumstances of MacDonald's death), both erected in Edwardian times. Improvements in communications and the development of the mass market, with the cultural and imperial strategies of its advertising and the projection of distinctive commodities would also have contributed to this.

It might also be objected that regional distinctions would have been matched by differences in class responses. Mary Slessor and David Livingstone were resolutely working-class imperial heroes who were certainly manipulated by middle-class writers. But there can be little doubt that figures such as these, together with the churches, schools and youth organisations which promoted them, had an influence upon working-class identity. They were celebrated as much as such by the auto-didacts of the trade union movement, the working men's clubs and left-leaning politicians. There is also solid evidence that the working class responded to commercial heroes who inhabited the sentimental fantasy land of rags to riches. The classic case would be Thomas Lipton, whose connections with Ireland and the Empire (notably the Ceylon of his extensive tea plantations) were promoted through his shops, advertisements and packagings.[49] Other Scottish-produced commodities, like Camp Coffee, brought together imperial and military iconography in a potent mix.

This negotiation of Scottish identity in relation to Empire was particularly notable in the Scottish imperial exhibitions which took place in both Glasgow and Edinburgh. These consciously vied with their English equivalents and set out to create imaginative geographies in which Scotland was placed at the centre of the empire of trade, heavy industries, settlement and culture. The Glasgow Exhibition of

[49] Sir Thomas J. Lipton, *Leaves from the Lipton Logs* (London, 1931); Bob Crampsey, *The King's Grocer: The Life of Sir Thomas Lipton* (Glasgow, 1995).

1888, which was conceived as a direct competitor of the Manchester Jubilee exhibition of 1887, not only stressed Glasgow and Scotland's role in shipping, technology, heavy industrial manufactures and iron work, but also invoked a Scottish past with a realistic mock-up of the medieval Archbishop's Palace of Glasgow, demolished more than a hundred years earlier.[50] Scottish archaeological and antiquarian concerns were also emphasised, as was a distinctive cultural identity through matching colossal statues of Burns and Scott.

Inevitably, the exhibition also promoted Scotland as a destination for tourism, as a romantic and sublime landscape worthy of being visited in association with the exhibition, particularly by returning imperial migrants. Clyde steamers and Glasgow's Clydeside resorts did well out of this stress upon Scottish scenic and historical heritage. In a conscious aping of South Kensington, the profits of the exhibition were to fund a School of Art and a Museum and Art Gallery. The painting by Sir John Lavery of Queen Victoria opening the exhibition deserves an imperial deconstruction all its own. This didactic and idealistic spirit also ran through the 1901 Glasgow exhibition and the 1907 equivalent in Edinburgh. It reached a considerable climax in 1911 when the Glasgow exhibition was specifically designed to promote the Scottish cultural renaissance which had already been manifested throughout the Empire in the founding of Caledonian societies, the holding of Highland games, and the erection of statues of Burns.

This Scottish Exhibition of National History, Art and Industry laid considerable emphasis on the Scottish past, on distinguished Scotsmen and on Scotland's contribution to the world, and its profits were to fund a chair of Scottish history and literature at Glasgow University. Lord Kelvin's role in the laying of Atlantic and other imperial cables, David Livingstone's appropriation of East and Central Africa for Scotland and the contribution of Scots to Canada were all prominently featured. The reconstructions of the Auld Toun and the Highland Clachan set out to reconcile Lowland and Gaelic culture, while suggesting their joint role in the creation of the Scottish spirit that had produced modern technology and industry. Historical pageants featured the traditional heroes of the Scottish past. It is perhaps not surprising that the exhibition attracted pilgrimages of Scottish Americans and parties of New Zealanders as well as Scots from other colonies.[51]

As Richard Finlay and David Forsyth have shown, a whole range of

[50] Perilla Kinchin and Juliet Kinchin, *Glasgow's Great Exhibitions* (Bicester, 1988), pp. 17–53; *Illustrated London News*, 12 May 1888. The Glasgow Room of the Mitchell Library, Glasgow, holds albums of cuttings and photographs relating to this exhibition.

[51] *Official Catalogue, Scottish Exhibition*, Glasgow, 1911; *Souvenir Album of the Scottish Exhibition of National History, Art and Industry*, Glasgow 1911; *Scottish Exhibition of National History, Art and Industry, Glasgow 1911, Palace of History, Catalogue of Exhibits*, 2 vols., Glasgow, 1911.

Scottish political organisations and their associated journals, including the National Association for the Vindication of Scottish Rights of 1853, the Scottish Home Rule Association and the Scottish Patriotic Association of the Edwardian period and *The Scottish Patriot* claimed Scottish rights precisely in relation to her imperial prominence.[52] This was also emphasised by leading aristocratic politicians like Aberdeen and Rosebery, as well as a host of bourgeois civic leaders. Even figures of the Left like Keir Hardie, James Ramsay MacDonald and James Maxton stressed Scotland's imperial role as part of the legitimation of their political demands. The imperial relationship remained a lodestar of one significant fraction of Scottish nationalism until at least the Second World War and remained central to the myths and symbols of Scottish Conservatism and Unionism.

Finlay, however, argues that these imperial cultural and political relations waned considerably after the First World War, a view which connects with a long-standing interpretation in British history as a whole.[53] The evidence does not, however, seem to support this. All the characteristics of an imperial culture seem, on the contrary, to continue in a relatively unbroken line until after the Second World War.[54] Despite the economic disasters of the inter-war years, for example, Glasgow continued to stress her imperial status and emphasised the municipal socialism that was closely related to it.[55] The cinema and juvenile literature continued in the modes carved out in the later nineteenth century and Scottish nationalism was at its most imperial at this time.[56] The Scottish Empire Exhibition of 1938 was an even grander affair than its predecessors, specifically designed as a means of lifting western Scotland out of the depression by emphasising the potential of imperial preference as laid out in the Ottawa Agreements of 1932.[57] Once again,

[52] Forsyth, 'Empire and Union', pp. 9–11; Richard J. Finlay, 'The Rise and Fall of Popular Imperialism in Scotland 1850–1950', *Scottish Geographical Magazine*, 113 (1997), pp. 13–21.

[53] Finlay, 'Rise and Fall', pp. 19–20.

[54] John M. MacKenzie, *Propaganda and Empire* (Manchester, 1984), pp. 256–7 and *passim.*

[55] See for example, *Scotland's Welcome, 1938*, ed. G.F. Maine (Glasgow, 1938); C.A. Oakley, *The Second City* (London, 1946).

[56] Jeffrey Richards, *Visions of Yesterday* (London, 1973); *Imperialism and Juvenile Literature*, ed. Jeffrey Richards (Manchester, 1989); MacKenzie, 'Scotland and the Empire', p. 738. See also Richard J. Finlay, '"For or Against?": Scottish Nationalists and the British Empire', *Scottish Historical Review*, LXXI (1992), pp. 184–206 and 'National Identity in Crisis: Politicians, Intellectuals and the "End of Scotland", 1920–1939', *History*, 79 (1994), pp. 242–59.

[57] Kinchin and Kinchin, *Glasgow's Great Exhibitions*, pp. 127–85; Bob Crampsey, *The Empire Exhibition of 1938: the Last Durbar* (Edinburgh, 1988); *Empire Exhibition, Official Guide* (Glasgow, 1938); *A Souvenir of the Empire Exhibition* (Glasgow, 1938), among many other sources.

a distinctive Scottish culture was delineated in the Highland clachan and in the pageants held at Ibrox Stadium.

Given the character of the displays in the various pavilions, no visitor could have been in any doubt as to the imperial economic system which was being projected through the exhibition. Although the Glasgow working class—and indeed other classes—would have exhibited a great range of identities, including Protestant, Catholic, Highland, Lowland, Irish, as well as class and professional affiliations linking them to national and international connections through unions, churches or societies, none would have been in any doubt that this was an imperial city whose workforce was highly dependent upon the export opportunities of empire. This was strongly projected through both the working-and middle-class press of the city, even through its architecture, street furniture, public parks and statuary.[58] The common enterprise of Empire, sanctified by Church, school and a broad spectrum of political opinion, surely helped to overlay these social fractures and sometimes competing interests. Shipbuilding and all its related heavy industries was inseparably connected to imperial companies, and noticeably so.[59] The notion that the Clyde was a highway of Empire was much hyped and the highly visible coming and going of ships from and to imperial destinations served to emphasise this. Many of the manufactures of the city were closely connected to the imperial market, and the companies involved in such trades never failed to emphasise such relationships, almost as a patriotic imperative, however short-sighted it may have been in economic terms. By 1953, the various companies that made up the North British Railway Company (amalgamated in 1903), had sent well over half of its total production to imperial territories.[60] It even exhibited a locomotive intended for the by then independent India at the 'Colonial Week' of 1950.

In an earlier article, I argued that Scotland has long required a European or global connection to set over against the dominance of its English neighbour.[61] Until the eighteenth century, this relationship was satisfied both by the Auld Alliance with France and by the trading relationships of Scotland with the Baltic and the Low Countries.[62] From the eighteenth until the mid-twentieth centuries, it was supremely

[58] John M. MacKenzie, 'Glasgow: an Imperial City?' in Felix Driver (ed.), *Imperial Cities* (Manchester, forthcoming).

[59] Michael S. Moss and John R. Hume, *Workshop of the British Empire: Engineering and Shipbuilding in the West of Scotland* (London, 1977).

[60] *A History of the North British Locomotive Company Limited* (Glasgow, privately published, 1953), p. 10 and *passim*.

[61] MacKenzie, 'Scotland and the Empire', pp. 732–7.

[62] *Scotland and Europe, 1200–1850*, ed. T. C. Smout (Edinburgh, 1986); *Scotland and the Sea*, ed. T. C. Smout (Edinburgh, 1992); Th. A Fischer, *The Scots in Germany: Being a Contribution towards the History of the Scot Abroad* (Edinburgh, 1902).

justified by Empire, where the Scots were able to establish a distinctive identity which reflected back upon the survival of her religious, intellectual, legal and ethical civil culture. Today it remains reflected in the currently dominant nationalist cry of Scotland and Europe. Thus, when the Scottish experience is put together with that of Wales, Ireland—both the Republic and Ulster in their very different ways—and, it must be said, the English regions, we arrive at the greatest paradox of all. The British Empire, supposedly central to the forging of the national identity of Britons in opposition to the French, may well have performed a very different function. Instead of creating an overall national identity, it enabled the sub-nationalisms of the United Kingdom to survive and flourish. Each was able to create a loop beyond the English, a loop whereby ethnic myths could be reciprocally nurtured and developed. Perhaps the Empire was more notable in preserving a plurality of British identities than in welding together a common imperial tradition. That may well be the principal lesson of the end of Empire and the discovery of distinctive regionalisms within Europe.

Imperialism is all too glibly depicted as a culturally repressive force. From opposite ends of the political spectrum and with very different intentions, both Tom Nairn and one of the last of the imperial historians, Sir Reginald Coupland, have argued that this was the case. For Nairn, the end of Empire was a necessary precondition for the break-up of Britain.[63] Coupland was expressing similar anxieties in his last book, *Welsh and Scottish Nationalism*, published posthumously in 1954.[64] He had been involved in discussions regarding the status of the Irish Free State and in the constitutional debates leading to Indian independence, and these experiences led him to suggest that decolonisation would test the bonds of the metropolitan state.[65] As an apologist for Empire, it was inevitable that he would be convinced of the beneficence of Union to the development of the British state. It represented 'a great political and psychological achievement', creating an Imperial patriotism both superseding local nationalism and confirming the Hanoverian line.[66] The Celtic fringe had to be absorbed by the Anglo-Saxon heartland to create a complementary economic system, enhance the population available for the imperial enterprise, and ensure that the danger of foreign invasion was reduced or eliminated. Coupland's consolatory reaffirmation, almost a deathbed plea for Union and national greatness, was virtually the last gasp of imperial scholarship.

[63] Tom Nairn, *The Break-Up of Britain* (London, 1977).

[64] Sir Reginald Coupland, *Welsh and Scottish Nationalism* (London, 1954).

[65] See, for example, Coupland's memorandum on Ireland, July 1933, published in *Imperial Policy and Colonial Practice, 1925–45, British Documents on the End of Empire*, ed. S. R. Ashton and S. E. Stockwell (London, 1996), Part I, pp. 281–6.

[66] Coupland, *Welsh and Scottish Nationalism*, pp. xv, 12, 113.

It is true that the imperial state did attempt the suppression of regional ethnicities, particularly through educational and linguistic policies,[67] but these were notably unsuccessful. Indeed, it may be argued that, as such policies invariably do, they stimulated a powerful defensive reaction and fed into the major cultural and language revivals that took place in Wales and Scotland from the later nineteenth century. In the Scottish case, that revival had important imperial dimensions: not only were societies founded throughout the Empire, but there was a realisation that Scottish linguistic and musical traditions has survived among migrant populations eager to maintain their cultural identities in colonies of settlement, notably in Canada and New Zealand.[68]

Imperialism was repressive in many ways, but throughout the British Empire, it had a tendency to perpetuate and enhance regional and ethnic identities among indigenous peoples, whether through indirect rule policies or divide and rule tactics. Clearly, the social, cultural and political objectives of the ruling Establishment were very different at home, but maybe the unintended results were not so distinct. It surely does a disservice to its metropolitan participants to imagine that imperialism always tended towards the suppression of regional and ethnic identity. The end of Empire is too easily seen as the precondition for the rekindling of the suppressed nationalisms of the so-called regions of the British Isles, heading them towards their referenda. In fact, Empire, in establishing those world-wide connections and global loops, had just as much an effect upon the preservation and strengthening of the distinctive identities of the Scots and the other ethnicities of Greater Britain. Diasporas have their origins in considerable distress, but ultimately they invariably strengthen the ethnic and nationalist causes from which they stem. Empire was as capable of producing an enlarged consciousness as a false consciousness.

[67] Tim Williams, 'The Anglicisation of South Wales' in *Patriotism*, ed. Samuel, vol. II, *Minorities and Outsiders*, pp. 193–203; Gwyneth Tyson Roberts, '"Under the Hatches"; English Parliamentary Commissioners' Views of the People and Language of Mid-Nineteenth-Century Wales' in *The Expansion of England*, ed. Schwarz, pp. 171–97.

[68] Ian McKay, 'Tartanism Triumphant: The Construction of Scottishness in Nova Scotia, 1933–1954', *Acadiensis*, XXI (1992), pp. 5–47; Tom Brooking, '"Tom McCanny and Kitty Clydeside"—the Scots in New Zealand' in *The Scots Abroad*, ed. Cage, pp. 156–90.

CHRISTIANS, CIVILISED AND SPANISH: MULTIPLE IDENTITIES IN SIXTEENTH-CENTURY SPAIN[1]

By M. J. Rodríguez-Salgado

READ 26 SEPTEMBER 1997 AT THE INSTITUTE OF HISTORICAL RESEARCH, LONDON

I. Spain

IN January 1556 Charles V renounced his rights to the Iberian kingdoms and passed them on to his son, Philip, who at once assumed the title of King of Spain. To his surprise and consternation, the English council refused to endorse it and pertly reminded him that the Kingdom of Spain did not exist. While the title had long been used, and almost every language had an equivalent for Spain and Spanish, the truth was that legally there was no such entity. Philip II's will reflected this judicial reality. He was, 'by the grace of God, king of Castile, Leon, Aragon, the Two Sicilies, Jerusalem, Portugal, Navarre, Granada, Toledo, Valencia, Galicia, Mallorca, Seville, Sardinia, Cordoba, Corsica, Murcia, Jaen, Algarve, Gibraltar, the Canary Islands, the Eastern and Western Indies, the islands and terra firma of the Ocean Sea; archduke of Austria; duke of Burgundy, Bravant and Milan; count of Habsburg, Flanders, Tirol, Barcelona; Lord of Biscay, Molina etc.'.[2] This lengthy litany partly explains why he and all his contemporaries habitually resorted to the title King of Spain as convenient short-hand. As we will see, however, there was more to it than simple utility. The terms were used because they were broadly understood and accepted. But it will be apparent at once that the concept of a specific Spanish identity in the sixteenth century is likely to be particularly problematic since Spain did not exist.

Recent political events have made the topic highly controversial as

[1] The title of this chapter is a paraphrase of Francisco de Tanara's statement in *El libro de las costumbres de todas las gentes del mundo y de las Indias* (Antwerp, 1556), 5, where he thanked God for 'making us Christians and not heathen; civilised and not barbarians; Spaniards and not Moors or Turks, dirty idolaters'. Cit. in J. H. Elliott, *Spain and Its World, 1500–1700* (New Haven and London, 1989), 57.

[2] D. M. Loades, *The Reign of Mary Tudor* (London, 1991 edn.), 181, 186. Philip's titles from his will: M. Fernández Alvarez, *Codicilio y última voluntad de Felipe II* (Valencia, 1997), 68.

the constituent parts of modern-day Spain assert their distinct, historically based identities largely by denigrating and rejecting the existence of a 'national' Spanish identity. Spain is only one of several European states where the very notion of a national identity has been challenged. In part, this is due to the enduring spell of nineteenth-century political ideology which accustomed us to think of nationalism in terms of an exclusive form of patriotism; a particularly ardent loyalty to the one, eternal nation. We are ill-prepared to understand earlier forms of patriotic and national identity which were acknowledged to be complex, multi-layered, powerful and necessary aspects of human civilisation. Early-modern people, particularly those living in composite monarchies, were sensitive to the multiple layers of association which they, as most of us now, nurtured. Although the term 'nation' was variously used, it was seldom coextensive with a separate state. It frequently designated a group (of students, clerics, soldiers, merchants etc.) from a particular geographical area that might or might not be in the same state; or groups which belonged to the same linguistic region who might belong to different states. At times it can be found in the context of denominating different races. 'Nation' was not as frequently used nor did it have the resonance of the term *patria*, which by the sixteenth century had acquired the powerful, emotive forces we associate with modern patriotism and nationalism.[3] Neither nation nor *patria* were exclusive concepts. In the *Dictionarium Tetraglotton* of 1562 *patria* was defined as 'everyman's country, fatherland, the town, village, hamlet or any other place where one is born'. Some went even further. Hermann von Weinsberg, for instance, included in his definition of what he variously calls *patria*, fatherland and *Heimat*, twelve different levels, from his birthplace, through to his parish, the state he was born in and that where he lived, as well as the Holy Roman Empire of which they were a part, reaching out to Christendom and heaven itself.[4]

In Iberia the issue of identity was complicated during this period by the rapidly changing political, dynastic, religious and social conditions of the peninsula. The concept of *Hispania* was ancient and had endured despite the legal, political and physical fragmentation of the area after the fall of the Roman Empire. Although it was mainly a geographical term which designated the whole of the peninsula, the vague memory

[3] J. A. Maravall, *Estado moderno y mentalidad social. Siglos XV a XVII* (Madrid, 1972) 2 vols., I, esp. ch. IV.

[4] I am most grateful to Dr Alastair Duke for these two references, the *Dictionarium Tetraglotton* (1st edn., Plantin, Antwerp 1562), and the diaries of von Weinsberg on which he is currently working. The excursus into *patria* is *c.*1582: 'Liber Senectutis. Gedenkboich des altertombs Hermanni von Weinsberch' in *Das buch Weinsberg. Kölner Denkwürdigkeiten aus dem 16.Jahrhundert* (Fünfter Band, ed. J. Stein, Publikationen der Gesellschaft für Rheinische Geschichtskunde. XVI Das Buch Weinsbert) (Bonn, 1926), 217–19.

of an ancient political unit did not disappear entirely. All Iberian states claimed at different stages to be *Hispania*. The largest of them, Castile, was particularly eager to subsume its identity within this superior community and its union with Aragon in the latter part of the fifteenth century, supported by an aggressive propaganda campaign led by the Catholic monarchs, finally persuaded Portugal to drop its use of the term.[5] Spain was widely identified thereafter within and outside the peninsula either with Castile or with the Castilian-Aragonese state. As late as 1585 Philip II found it necessary to explain to the Pope that when he spoke of Spaniards he meant the whole of Spain. In Italy, he commented, they think Spain means only Castile.[6] It was during the 1490s that major steps were taken to endow that greater ideal of Spain with racial and cultural unity as the Hispano-Jews were expelled and the Hispano-Muslims subject to ever-tightening restrictions.

When Charles V took power in 1516 the Castilian-Aragonese state was incorporated into a large Habsburg empire scattered throughout Europe and it seemed as if the evolution of a distinct Spanish identity would cease. Loyalty to the monarchy was a powerful pull which lifted many Iberians beyond the boundaries of kin, parish, city and Spain into association with the emperor and service abroad.[7] Equally intense was the attachment to the universalist, increasingly beleaguered Catholic church, which committed them irrevocably to the maelstrom of international politics and distant European battlefields. The arrival of an alien dynasty and incorporation into a state which was beyond most people's imagination might also help to explain why the identification with a home town, city or lordship became particularly intense among Iberians at the time.[8] It is as if they had to take refuge in the familiar and stable local environment. Yet the currents nurturing a specifically Spanish identification among the Castilian-Aragonese states were ironically strengthened by the regular encounters with Charles V's other lands and the need to present a united front against the Netherlanders,

[5] The use of Hispania in the reign of the Catholic monarchs has been dealt with by R. B. Tate, *Ensayos sobre la historiografía peninsular del siglo XV* (Madrid, 1970), and more recently by P. Fernández Albaladejo in the rich and suggestive essays included in sections 1 & 2 of: *Fragmentos de Monarquía* (Madrid, 1992).

[6] Archivo General de Simancas, Estado 946 f. 148 Philip II to the count of Olivares, 22 August 1585.

[7] M. J. Rodríguez-Salgado, 'Patriotismo y política exterior en la España de Carlos V y Felipe II', in F. Ruíz Martín (ed.) *La proyección Europea de la Monarquía Hispanica* (Madrid, 1996); further details on attitudes to the emperor in: J. M. Jover, *Carlos V y los Españoles* (Madrid, 1963); J. Sánchez Montes, *Franceses, Protestantes, Turcos. Los Españoles ante la política internacional de Carlos V* (Madrid, 1951).

[8] I. A. A. Thompson, 'Castile, Spain and the Monarchy: The Political Community from *patria natural* to *patria nacional*', in G. Parker and R. Kagan (eds), *Spain, Europe and the Atlantic World. Essays in Honour of John H. Elliott* (Cambridge, 1995), 125–59.

Germans and Italians who surrounded the emperor. The Iberian states became more conscious of the similarities between them. Despite the evident reluctance of Charles V there was also a seemingly irresistible pressure to continue the process of internal racial and cultural unification which led to forced conversion and harsher restrictions on the remaining Hispano-Muslims. Moreover, the process of integration within the peninsula continued, with regular intermarriage of monarchs and nobles, until Philip II succeeded as king of Portugal in the 1580s and the peninsula was at last under a single ruler.

The unification appeared to give the ideal of Hispania a concrete physical and dynastic reality, yet dynastic union did not herald the destruction of Iberian diversity. The borders, as well as the bewildering linguistic, legal, financial and other divisions within the peninsula remained, jealously guarded as distinguishing marks of ancient liberties and a separate identity. In some areas, at least in periods of conflict, these loyalties were so intense that they seemed to threaten the survival of the composite state as well as the ideal of a Spanish identity. When the Aragonese rebelled in 1590, they justified it on the grounds that they would die, if necessary, to maintain their privileges. Antonio Pérez, who caused the uprising, claimed that one Aragonese woman urged both her son and beloved grandson to fight: 'notable proof that the love we bear for the liberties of our country (*patria*) is greater than the love we have for those dearest to us'.[9] Fernando Bouza argued that Portuguese opposition to Philip II was founded on a sense of pride and of being a 'nation, so distinct and specific that it could not be included within the dominions of any alien king'.[10] But for a long time Iberian union survived, largely because, except in times of crisis, its inhabitants were able to combine a high degree of political and cultural pluralism with a sense of being Spanish. The different levels proved compatible essentially because the relationship between the various states was not one of subjugation and dependence, or, of empire as defined by the *Oxford English Dictionary*—'supreme and extreme political dominion ... by a sovereign state over its dependencies'.[11]

The state of the so-called kings of Spain in the sixteenth century was made up of lands which belonged to the sovereign—the 'proprietor king' as the Castilians termed him. The dominant states of Castile and Aragon were both composite monarchies pieced together by inheritance and conquest. The nature of the acquisition of a territory frequently determined the form by which it was attached, united or federated to

[9] *Relaciones de Antonio Pérez*, ed. P.J. Arroyal Espigares (Madrid, 1989), 198.

[10] F. Bouza Alvarez, 'Portugal en la Monarquía Hispánica (1580–1640). Felipe II, las Cortes de Tomar y la genesis del Portugal Católico' (2 vols., Madrid, Universidad Complutense, 1987), I, 157.

[11] *The Compact Edition* (Oxford, 1979), 854.

the dominant political unit, but the circumstances of the time, the status and the geostrategic position of the area also affected the terms by which it was incorporated. There was no general model, although as a rule lands seized by conquest lost some traditions and privileges in the process and tended to be under more direct control from the royal court. Crucially, however, conquest did not mean the end of sovereignty or the creation of colonies. It was universally accepted that successful rule depended on cooperation rather than force. States such as Portugal, Naples or Navarre, which were taken by force of arms but claimed by dynastic right, were treated like inherited states; their privileges and traditions left almost intact. Whether inside or outside Iberia, Castile and Aragon expanded by loosely attaching lands to themselves in a patchwork system that was more like an uneven federation, where each unit enjoyed a measure of independence. It is significant that when Philip II claimed Portugal, the bishop of Tuy was the only man of note who argued in favour of its subjugation to Castile, and the imposition of a common law and currency. Most of the royal councillors agreed with the king that it should be federated as an equal of Castile, along the lines of the union with Aragon, with 'the Castilians in their homes and we in ours'. Philip's Portuguese supporters were confident of this, and of the fact that 'His Majesty will be as much our king and lord as he is theirs'.[12] In other words, the very nature of the Iberian polity was antithetical to the modern-day notion of empire. Expansion took place by a process of federation and while it was a union of unequal proportions, the king's titles continued to manifest the monarchy's commitment to the principle of diversity and maintenance of separate, sovereign units.

Over the century Iberia had nevertheless drawn closer ethnically, politically and economically. Philip II could claim by 1579 that what separated the Portuguese and Castilians was the name. Both were Spaniards, he asserted. As for key differences between states such as language and customs, these were slight. More important was the fact that most of the nobles were of mixed Iberian blood.[13] John Elliott was rather more guarded when he noted with some caution that we can detect an association with 'the community of the realm' albeit 'very hazily' in Spain. He defined that community as something 'founded on history, law and achievement, on the sharing of certain common

[12] Bouza Alvarez, 'Portugal' I, 229 on Tuy; quote 331. Other Iberian councillors opposed its acquisition out of fear that the king might be tempted to extend his authority beyond present bounds once he had acquired another, powerful state. For the opposition ibid., I, 99 and 105.

[13] *La Historia de España en sus documentos. El Siglo XVI*, ed. F. Díaz-Plaja (Madrid, 1958), Philip II to his ambassador in Lisbon, 24 August 1579, 673–81, quote 680.

experiences and certain common patterns of life and behaviour'.[14] All these factors were indeed present, but often generated a clearly visible, potent form of Spanish identity. The influence of classical texts significantly affected concepts of patriotism, and expressing love of the *patria* in extreme and passionate form became a natural and laudable activity—in fact, an essential sign of humanity and civility in the sixteenth century. 'When God put in our souls such a powerful, natural love of our country (*patria*), he must have thought it just [also] to die for it', noted Antonio Pérez.[15] While for him at that juncture Aragon was the *patria*, for many others it was clearly Spain. The Jesuit Ribadeneira asked at the time of the war against England in 1588: 'If the honour of Spain is at stake, what Spaniard would fail to seek the fame and glory of his nation?' Spain appeared in many sixteenth-century texts as the 'mother', as we can see from Cervantes' anguished cry at the return of the Spanish Armada: 'oh Spain, our mother! you see your sons return to your breast leaving the seas full of their suffering'.[16] So integral was love of country and nation to the individual that its absence was regarded as a rejection or hatred of oneself.[17] Only Philip II, with his huge and diverse composite monarchy, dared argue that he, unlike all other men, had no *patria*.[18] However, after 1559 he and his successors resided in Iberia and this led once more to the identification of the dynasty and Spain, which allowed the fusion of two powerful forms of loyalty and significantly strengthened and accelerated the identification of Spain as the *patria* for many Iberians.

II. Empire and Spanish identity

'Worship God, be loyal to your king, and love your country' became something of a popular mantra.[19] The association of God with Spain was long in the making and closely bound up with early-modern notions of empire. The term 'empire' was widely used at the time, mainly in the context of the Holy Roman Empire, an institution which, along with the papacy, had long fought to assert universalist claims of

[14] *Spain and Its World*, 105 and 106 respectively.

[15] *Relaciones de Antonio Pérez*, ed. Arroyal Espigares, 198.

[16] *La Historia de España en sus documentos*, ed. Díaz-Plaja, Ribadeniera, 760; Cervantes, 776. Maravall, *Estado Moderno*, collected many excellent examples to illustrate the association of Spain with the *patria* and with the mother, esp. I, 474–83.

[17] Maravall, *Estado Moderno*, cites Antonio Agustín's words from 1587: 'no hay hombre tan ageno de sí mesmo que no ame su tierra y su nación', I, 478.

[18] Bouza Alvarez, 'Portugal', I, 242, 339.

[19] The chronicler Pulgar wrote: 'a Dios con devoción, al rey con lealtad e a la patria con amor', cit. Maravall, *Estado Moderno*, I, 475.

sovereignty over European states. Spain, France and England were the largest monarchies which proclaimed themselves empires in the later medieval period. In doing so, they were asserting their sovereign independence and refusing to acknowledge other earthly powers as superiors. To justify and support their claim to sovereignty, the Iberian monarchs fostered propaganda that both proved and nurtured a sense of independent identity. Spain took shape as chroniclers and poets produced histories based on the Bible, on myths and signals of divine favour, on plain fabrication as well as adorned and unadorned facts taken from classical authors, even without royal patronage to prompt them.[20] The rejection of papal and imperial universalism also opened the way for a closer identification of individual monarchs/dynasties and God, who now became the monarch's direct superior and guardian of the kingdom. It was a short step from this to the identification of a 'nation' or peoples of a state with God. Providentialism lay at the heart of all early modern national myths and identities, legitimising and explaining their distinctive existence.

The transformation of Spain into an empire—in the sixteenth-century sense of the word—thus made a significant contribution towards the development of a distinct Spanish identity, both in terms of the ideas and art it generated, and by forging a new relationship between God, on the one hand, and the sovereign and the people on the other. Equally important in this complex process of association was the acquisition of what came to be known in the eighteenth century as a 'colonial empire'. The absence of the term prior to this, as Elliott pertinently stated, does not mean that the Spaniards 'lacked the capacity to think in imperial terms about the widespread dominions of their king' in the earlier period.[21] There were two areas where such attitudes emerged: North Africa and America. They shared many characteristics—they were acquired by conquest without dynastic right, but with full ideological endorsement in the sense of papal grants and theoretical justification by jurists and theologians; they aroused powerful messianic and providential impulses. In both, the Spaniards were confronted with peoples of very different races and divergent religious and cultural habits. The experiences in these areas prompted unity between the usually warring Iberian peoples, transforming, as one

[20] Tate, *Ensayos*, esp. I. Mitología en la historiografía de la edad media y del Renacimiento.

[21] Elliott, *Spain and Its World*, 7. He also points out that it was not until the seventeenth century that one can find the term 'empire of the Indies' (8). In the rare instances one encounters the use of the word empire, e.g. B. Alamos de Barrientos *c.*1600 in his *Discurso político al rey Felipe III al comienzo de su reinado*, ed. M. Santos (Barcelona, 1990), 26 'es necesario en un imperio tan grande', it tends to refer to the totality of the king's dominions.

contemporary noted, extreme hostility into cooperation.[22] They also fostered an overpowering sense of Spain's ethnic, ideological and cultural superiority.[23]

North Africa was considered a natural and necessary area of expansion by the Iberian states, who shared the common belief that whoever controlled one side of the Straits would control the other. The enthusiastic drive southwards after 1492 was halted, however, by stiff opposition from Sa'di, Hafsi and Ottoman sultans, Berber tribes and corsairs. The Spanish and Portuguese succeeded only in establishing maritime outposts (*presidios*) in the Maghreb, which were entirely dependent on Iberia and Italy for survival.[24] As a recent publication states: 'contrary to other areas of hispanic penetration, North Africa was never colonised, or totally occupied ... it was an enterprise with rather mediocre results which ended in failure'.[25] More could have been achieved if they had continued the mediaeval policy of alliance and cooperation with local muslim leaders. But although some cooperation is evident until the mid-sixteenth century,[26] the intensification of messianic and ideological elements on both sides of the ideological divide made such practices increasingly unacceptable. The largely unsuccessful war in this sector nurtured messianic zeal in Spain while enhancing fears of another muslim invasion. These trends had dramatic internal consequences. It was widely believed that the remaining Hispano-Muslims (*moriscos*)—still a large and unassimilated minority—would rebel when the Muslims landed. As Jews served as intermediaries between the Christian and Muslim worlds, they too were thought to be implicated in this conspiracy. Such widespread fears exacerbated hostility towards non-

[22] Suárez de Figueroa: 'Los ánimos más opuestos en la patria, fuera se reconcilian y conforman para valerse', cit. Maravall, *Estado moderno*, I, 472.

[23] It is essential to stress that conquest was not the distinguishing or most important factor in nurturing a sense of superiority. When Barrientos categorised the empire *c.*1600 he included the American possesions with Castile, Aragon, the Mediterranean islands and Flanders as inherited states—as opposed to the 'legitimally inherited' *conquests* of Portugal, Navarre, Milan, Naples and Sicily: *Discurso político*, ed. Santos, 8–9.

[24] The classic work by Fernand Braudel, *The Mediterranean and the Mediterranean World in the Age of Philip II* (2nd edn., 2 vols., London 1972), has much detail to offer, esp. vol. II. A. C. Hess, *The Forgotten Frontier: a History of the Sixteenth Century Ibero-African Frontier* (Chicago, 1978); a detailed analysis of the role of North Africa in Spanish policy in mid-century, M.J. Rodríguez-Salgado, *The Changing Face of Empire. Charles V, Philip II and Habsburg Authority, 1551–1559* (Cambridge, 1988) esp. 253–88.

[25] M. García Arenal and M.-A. de Bunes, *Los Españoles y el norte de Africa. Siglos XV–XVIII* (Madrid, 1992), from the jacket of this up-to-date synthesis of Spanish expansion. The authors blame 'the inertia of ancient habits of frontier war', as well as lack of interest at court, lack of knowledge of the area and a bundle of prejudices and preconceived notions about Islam for this state of affairs, 61.

[26] Charles V's protectorate over Tunis is an obvious example, see Luis del Marmol Carvajal, *Primera parte de la descricion general de Affrica* (Granada, 1573) ff. 260r–v. On the 1550s, Rodríguez-Salgado, *Changing Face of Empire*, 253–88.

Christian groups in Iberia. Intolerance was translated into legislation that gradually excluded mixed race peoples as well as converted Jews and Muslims from the ranks of nobility and higher secular and ecclesiastical positions. By the later sixteenth century, the rejection of Spain's earlier identity as a multi-cultural, multi-racial state was total. A new identity had been forged founded on extreme Christian purity both in racial and ideological terms. The trend was reinforced by the need to counter the vitriolic attacks from competing Christian powers, who taunted and denigrated the Spaniards with references to their Jewish and Muslim past.[27]

The Mediterranean front affected the evolution of a new Spanish identity in other, concrete ways, making it genuinely collective in practice as well as in theory, because it led to regular cooperation between Castile and Aragon—and later Portugal—a fact which many treatises emphasised.[28] The absence of substantial support from other Christian powers also helped to nurture a sense of grievance and uniqueness which was soon reflected in the linguistic and conceptual terms of discourse. Pedro de Salazar's 1570 treatise reflects the uneasy transition: it is titled *Hispania Victrix*, but subtitled a history of relations between 'christianos y infieles'. Increasingly the conflict was presented as the eternal holy war between Spain and the Muslims. 'Let the Spanish arm strike', wrote the poet-soldier, Francisco de Aldana, in an epistle intended to arouse 'our Spanish Atlas' (Philip II), to new efforts against North Africa.[29] Significantly, he died fighting alongside King Sebastian of Portugal in another instance of Iberian cooperation. By the mid-sixteenth century, however, arguments based on secular concepts of civility were also used in the context of North African expansion. The debates over America had given the classical concept of the duty of civilised nations to conquer barbarians a new lease of life.[30] Diego de Torres is typical in this respect, claiming that since the fall of the Roman empire North Africa had been occupied by 'a swarm of base peoples' who lacked the requisite level of civilisation to have sovereign power over the lands they occupied. Conquest was not only just

[27] A. C. Hess, 'The Moriscos: an Ottoman Fifth Column in Sixteenth Century Spain', *American Historical Review*, 74 (1968), 1–25. A. Domínguez Ortiz and B. Vincent, *Historia de los moriscos* (Madrid, 1978), and H. Kamen, *Inquisition and Society in Spain in the Sixteenth and Seventeenth Centuries* (London, 1985) chs. 6 & 7. For an introduction to the main lines of the Black Legend which incorporated these racial attacks, P. W. Powell, *Tree of Hate* (New York & London, 1971), W. Maltby, *The Black Legend in England* (Durham, NC, 1971).

[28] For example, Salazar, *Hispania Victrix*. cap. 33 f. 44 'quexaruanse le [*sic*] Aragoneses, Valencianos, y Catalanes ...'; Marmol Carvajal, *Primera parte*, f. 140r multiple appeals for action, 1564.

[29] Cit. A. Mas, *Les Turcs dans la littérature Espagnole du Siècle d'Or*, 2 vols. (Paris, 1967), I, 244–5.

[30] See below, p. 244.

under such circumstances, it was Spain's duty, and would benefit the vanquished who would be brought once again within the aegis of a civilised world.[31]

In other words, the conditions existed both in broad ideological terms and in terms of specific beliefs in the racial and cultural superiority of Spain, for Spaniards to have developed modern 'imperial' attitudes towards the Maghreb. A number of factors hindered its evolution. First, their inability to make much headway in the region. Second, expansion here was seen as the recovery of an integral part of the ancient Hispania, rather than as the acquisition of alien territory. As late as the 1570s some still thought it possible to recreate a multi-racial Spanish state. Don John of Austria suggested that Tunis should be integrated into Philip II's lands as Granada had been in the 1490s, with freedom of worship for Muslims, preservation of their customs—dress, language etc.—and political rights which included choosing their own leaders.[32] This was the advice of a desperate man. It was no longer ideologically possible. But the notion of federation of new lands was as strong as it had ever been. A third factor intervened: after centuries of cohabitation and warfare, most Spaniards regarded 'the Moor' (the generic term 'African' was limited to negro slaves) as a vile but worthy enemy, often their equal in chivalric terms—and in the case of the Sa'di, Algerian and Ottomans, in terms of power and military technology.[33] Consequently, the Mediterranean remained the preferred setting for tales and legends demonstrating the Spaniard's particular blend of ideological purity and bravery.[34] The vast volume of literature and visual art generated by the North African front projected the widespread and potent identification with Spain and the monarchy. An incident in the famous treatise *Viaje de Turquía* serves to illustrate this widespread pheonomenon. At one point, the Spanish captive was asked by his master, Sinan Pacha, to swear on a cross that he would not escape and

[31] *Relación del origen y suceso de los xarifes y del estado de los reinos de Marruecos, Fez y Tarundante*, ed. M. García-Arenal (Madrid, 1980), 36. Torres spent much of his adult life serving the king of Portugal in the Maghreb. Marmol Carvajal's dedication to Philip II in his *Primera parte* refers to 'los pueblos barbaros Affricanos tan vezinos como crueles enemigos nuestros'.

[32] Letter from don John of Austria to Philip II cit. García Arenal and de Bunes, *Españoles en el norte de Africa*, 94.

[33] Lope de Vega, *La mayor desgracia de Carlos V y hechicerias de Argel*, ed. M. Menéndez Pelayo (Madrid, 1969), 30, dismissed the Indians as 'gente desnuda ... que se espantaba de un caballo y de los ecos de un arcabuz', whereas in North Africa: 'Esta es guerra diferente; / los contrarios son tan diestros/ como nosotros; no saben / tener a las balas miedo'.

[34] G. Cirot called it 'maurophile littéraire'. The classic study remains A. Mas, *Les Turcs dans la littérature Espagnole du Siècle d'Or*, 2 vols. (Paris, 1967); see also García Arenal and de Bunes, *Españoles y el Norte de Africa*, esp. 99–105.

betray him. On reflection, the Pacha thought this an insufficient guarantee, and demanded his word as a good Spaniard, ostensibly declaring that 'no other nation' was trusted with the defence of the *presidios* in North Africa because of the Spaniard's superior valour and loyalty. They preferred to be torn to pieces rather than break their word as Spaniards. The hero admitted that, although it was a sin, he would have broken oaths sworn on the cross but not his word as a Spaniard. Nothing could move him to shatter the 'good opinion' which the Moor had of Spanish soldiers either.[35]

The popularity of such tales, and the well-documented popularity of North African campaigns—which attracted large numbers of volunteers—does not, however, justify the claim that was once so popular, that Spanish identity was wholly defined in terms of North African policy, encapsulated and reduced to the crusade against Mediterranean Muslims. Elite and popular enthusiasm with an equally heady mixture of religious zeal, defensive needs and self-interest, laced with the belief in a uniquely Spanish mission, can also be found in the case of other conflicts, notably the war against England in the 1580s.[36] As Ribadeneira put it: 'to whom does this task belong but to the king, our lord, and the kingdoms of Spain?'. A victory in England would bring honour and glory to 'our Spanish nation'.[37] Although for many Iberians North Africa had a pull and resonance other sectors lacked, it is truer to say that by the latter part of the sixteenth century the self-identity of those calling themselves Spaniards was defined in terms of service to God and king against the enemies of the church. The crusade could be directed as much against the heretic in Europe as against the infidel in North Africa or the Americas. Fernández Albaladejo recently argued that for many Spaniards identity came to be essentially grounded on religious elements, overwhelming those elements based on 'civis' or civilisation.[38]

Faith and civility were also vital components of the burgeoning Spanish identity in the context of America. Columbus and the early

[35] *Viaje de Turquía*, ed. F. García Salinero (Madrid, 1980), 172.

[36] Rodríguez-Salgado, 'Patriotismo y política exterior'. C. Gomez-Centurion, *La Invencible y la Empresa de Inglaterra* (Madrid, 1988).

[37] *La Historia de España en sus documentos*, ed. Díaz-Plaja, 'Exhortación' 747–75, quotes at 752. There was also much opposition to these northern campaigns, and as can be seen by the important study of J. M. Jover Zamora and M. V. López-Cordón Cortezo, 'La imagen de Europa y el pensamiento político-internacional', in *Historia de España de R. Menéndez Pidal. El siglo del Quijote (1580–1680)* (Madrid, 1986).

[38] P. Fernández Albaladejo, 'Católicos antes que ciudadanos. Gestación de una «política española» en los comienzos de la Edad Moderna', in J. I. Fortea Pérez (ed.), *Imágenes de la diversidad. El mundo urbano en la corona de Castilla (s. xvi–xvii)* (Universidad de Cantabria, 1997), 103–27, which develops ideas on Spanish identity he touched on in his *Fragmentos de Monarquía*.

explorers expected to reach the fabled and sophisticated East, and instead encountered indigenous Caribbean societies so different that they were unable to categorise them or resolve the most fundamental question of identity: what is a human being? Armed with classical notions of natural slaves as a sub-species of humanity, many concluded that the cultural and physical similarities between the Amerindians and black African slaves were close enough to place them in this category. Economic, labour and political interests which would benefit from unfettered exploitation of indigenous populations were additional and powerful incentives in favour of the conclusion that the Indians were sub-human.[39] From the start, however, the indigenous peoples had their defenders. A long debate ensued in Spain which sought to resolve the issue of what a human being is and what factors made up human society and civilisation. Issues of *ratio*—reason or understanding of the Christian God—of the nature of sovereignty, of what justified the possession of lands, people and minerals were raised by the discoveries. Their resolution would be as fundamental to order and authority in the Old World as in the New. Classical ideals and models fed the debates about civilisation, especially because many felt that it was acceptable to dispossess barbarians, but not infidels. But what, exactly was a barbarian? What type and levels of organisation and what social relations did a community need to be accepted as civilised? Everything from sexual mores to monetary exchanges and organised warfare was scrutinised, compared and evaluated. In the process, men became far more sensitive and conscious of their own values and civilisation.

Surrounded by diverse indigenous groups and constantly challenged by enemies such as French and English, it was easy to assume a collective identity in the Americas and the most developed and readily available was that of Spaniard. The bulk of emigrants were from Castile and arrived there at a time when Castilians were actively promoting a Spanish identity. Early place names reflect the vogue—Hispaniola, New Spain etc. The number of non-Castilians was initially too small to allow them to project their own distinct regional/national identities, as the Galicians and Basques were to do in the nineteenth century. Necessity also forced emigrants to cooperate, and the ease and success of their collective activity persuaded some at least that they clearly belonged to the 'same nation'—Spain.[40] Moreover, the majority of early settlers had a strong corporative sense and found it both natural and necessary to

[39] There is a vast literature on the subject, which can be approached through the lucid and balanced accounts of Elliott, *Spain and Its World*, part I; A. Pagden, *Spanish Imperialism and the Political Imagination* (New Haven & London, 1990), I: *Dispossessing the Barbarian*; J. A. Fernández-Santamaria, *The State, War and Peace. Spanish Political Thought in the Renaissance, 1516–1559* (Cambridge, 1977).

[40] Maravall, *Estado Moderno* I, 472–3.

embrace a collective identity. Soldiers, ecclesiastics and traders were used to acting under the title of 'Spanish nation' elsewhere, and the trend was strengthened by administrators whose courtly ethos and education had forged in them a Spanish identity. Commanders and governors regularly addressed soldiers and settlers simply as 'Españoles'. Captain Lierno Aguero ordered an attack on the English invaders of Nombre de Dios in January 1596 with the simple injunction: '¡Ea Españoles a ellos!'[41] Troops, clerics and settlers marched under the banner of Spain's patron saint and responded to patriotic battle cries such as: 'Santiago y a ellos' (For St James! Let's get them!)—which encouraged the troops in New Spain in the 1520s—or the '¡Vitoria! ¡España! ¡España!' reported by an author of Basque origin describing a fight between 'our men', 'the Spaniards', and 'the Indians'.[42]

The habitual use of Spain and the Spaniards is one of the more striking elements of the literature generated by the New World, particularly as the writers make it clear that they knew the lands were part of the king of Castile's dominions. Yet it could all have been very different, as the famous 'defender of the Indians', Bartolome de las Casas, demonstrates. Born in Seville and motivated by 'compassion for my country, which is Castile', he reveals some typical Castilian habits, such as the comment that in America 'more than ten kingdoms were bigger than all of Spain, even if we include Aragon and Portugal ...' Yet he seldom acknowledged the Spaniards as his own people.[43] Along with other early pro-Indian writers, Las Casas attempted to restrict the term 'Spaniards' to those soldiers and settlers who exploited the 'Indians' (another striking example of a reductionist term given the range of ethnic, cultural and ideological variations among indigenous peoples). Those he approved of were designated by their proper names or their occupations, so that he and other Iberian clergy were referred to simply as 'religiosos' or friars, as when he contrasts 'the friars and the Spanish tyrants, thieves and bandits'.[44] Non-hispanic settlers such as Italians were called Christians, except 'the Germans'.[45] Significantly, however, these linguistic acrobatics proved short-lived. For the majority, the positive connotations of Spain and their own attachment to the identity of Spaniards led to the adoption of other terminology, notably the use of the term 'conquistador' to distinguish bad settlers from clerics and

[41] *The Last Voyage of Drake and Hawkins,* ed. K. R. Andrews (Cambridge, 1972), report by Miguel Ruiz Delduayen, 207.

[42] Quotes from B. de las Casas, *Breve resumen del descubrimiento y destruicion de las Indias*, ed. E. Escolar (Madrid, 1981), 55; and Alonso de Ercilla, *La Araucana*, ed. M. A. Morínigo and I. Lerner, 2 vols. (Madrid, 1979), I, 182 repectively.

[43] Las Casas, *Breve resumen*, ed. Escolar, 105; an example of 'our Spaniards', 33.

[44] *Ibid.*, 79; examples of religioso, 65, 69, 70.

[45] *Ibid.*, Italians, 34–6, 39–40; Germans, 84.

other 'good' Spaniards.[46] The soldier, courtier and poet, Alonso de Ercilla, born in Madrid of Basque parents, is an admirable example of the compatibility of multiple identities at the time, and of the way in which most commentators could be both critical of Spanish greed and cruelty and yet revel in the shared glory of being Spanish. For Ercilla, colonists and conquistadores, the good and the evil, were uniformly identified as 'Spaniards' and he did not hesitate to associate himself with them, habitually using 'we' and 'our people' even as he lamented the atrocities they committed.[47] Similarly, the Madrid-born Vasco de Quiroga filled his treatise on the rights of the Indians with details of Spanish avarice and cruelty, but acknowledged the Spaniards as 'our nation'.[48]

Pride and confidence combined with something we have largely lost—the sense of awe and amazement at the huge extent of territory which their monarch ruled—to facilitate the adoption of a powerful Spanish identity in the New World.[49] The American experience further deepened the sense of Spain's distinctiveness by fostering a sense of messianic providentialism. The rapid and successful conquest and occupation of vast tracts of land was widely held to be miraculous. Juan de Garnica in his *Epistola ad Hispanos* put it clearly: 'God chose you, O Spain! and was pleased to raise you, so that you should be universal, catholic and perfect'. For him, Spain was the 'patria mía' he loved; 'my most sweet mother'.[50] Ribadeneira reckoned that 'our Spaniards' had 'wrought marvels' and covered themselves in honour and glory by spreading the faith in the New World.[51] Ercilla, like so many others, believed that God had chosen the Spaniards to discover and settle the New World precisely because they were the most ardent Catholics and bravest soldiers.[52]

It has nevertheless been argued that residence in the Americas gave rise to other identities. Pastor Bodmer claimed that critics of the conquest, such as Las Casas, Núñez Cabeza de Vaca and Ercilla,

[46] A good example is Alonso de Zorita's *Relación de los señores de la Nueva España*, ed. G. Vázquez (Madrid, 1992), although he was deeply influenced by Franciscan critics.

[47] Ercilla, *La Araucana*, examples of criticism: I, 146, 174–5, 225; but Spaniards are 'gente nuestra' (I, 149) and he regularly attached positive adjectives to Spanish, such as 'valor' and 'valiente' (e.g. I, 169, 171), 'constante' (I, 179) etc.

[48] 'Tratado de Derecho' printed in Vasco de Quiroga, *La Utopia en America*, ed. P. Serrano Gassent (Madrid, 1992), 63–248.

[49] The point was made by John Elliott, who argued that the overwhelming sense of universal authority of the king bound the bureaucrats together: *Spain and Its World*, 17.

[50] The Latin manuscript in the Biblioteca Nacional, Madrid, mss. 7382. It was published in a two-part, bilingual version by E. Luque under the title: 'La Misión del Imperio Español en una carta política del siglo XVI', quotes I, 717–8; II, 141; I, 726 respectively.

[51] *Historia de España en sus documentos*, ed. Díaz-Plaja, 752–3.

[52] *La Araucana* e.g. II, 18–19.

evolved 'what we could call a Spanish American consciousness'. Despite its label, this is not 'a harmonious fusion or synthesis of the two cultures. On the contrary, it refers to the realisation of the insoluble conflict between the two'.[53] Pastor Bodmer's argument rests on two premises: first, that these writers were alienated by what she labels the 'official ideology' and unable to sustain allegiance to an 'ideological and political system that has lost all credibility', and second that they remained conscious of 'the impossibility of ever belonging to America'.[54] Both are questionable. For decades there was no clearly defined official ideology. The crown allowed itself to be advised and alternatively swayed by different pressure groups and the legislation varied accordingly. In the end it did not so much declare as assume possession of the new continent, leaving vital issues of sovereignty and humanity vague and unresolved. In so far as there was a sustained official policy it was the crown's belief that it had a duty to protect, indoctrinate and civilise the Amerindians and that this was incompatible with their enslavement. Even the most ardent critics could agree with this—which explains why most of them, including Ercilla and Las Casas, far from rejecting the ideological and political system of the day, received office and reward and held officials posts. As for a Spanish-American consciousness, a convincing case can be made that it was emerging, grounded on a profound sense of belonging to America. John Elliott and Anthony Pagden have suggested that the barrage of criticism against the Spanish settlers caused a defensive reaction which stimulated them to develop their own separate and positive identity. This process was reinforced subsequently by the hostility and derision they encountered from new Spanish settlers and by the insensitive actions of central government.[55] It is unclear how far this criollo culture had progressed in the sixteenth century.[56] In any case, we should not assume that those who grew to love America and see it as their *patria* were excluded from a Spanish identity. Just as the distinct groups in Iberia could combine the different identities, so could they.

Men such as Hernan Cortés saw the New World in terms of

[53] B. Pastor Bodmer, *The Armature of Conquest. Spanish Accounts of the Discovery of America, 1492–1589* (Stanford, California, 1992), esp. 207–75; quotes at 262 and 272 respectively. Her close reading of Ercilla's epic is interesting, but underplays the positive associations he has of Spain and the Spaniards, as well as the negative evaluations he frequently gives of the Indians.

[54] *Ibid.*, 272.

[55] J. H. Elliott's introduction to N. Canny and A. Pagden (eds.), *Colonial Identity in the Atlantic World, 1500–1800* (Princeton, 1987), 9; A. Pagden, 'Identity Formation in Spanish America', *ibid.*, 57.

[56] In his *Discurso*, Barrientos categorised Americans as 'naturales, o conquistadores, o forasteros, o eclesiásticos'. Indigenous groups and Spaniards born in America were 'natives', 14–16.

traditional ideology and expected that it would be treated as other areas of the composite monarchy. Initially, settlers imagined the creation of a series of semi-autonomous units federated with Castile. Las Casas argued that the relationship of Spain to America should be as that between Spain and Milan—a conquered area which nevertheless retained a wide measure of independence—while Melchor Cano illustrated his point about sovereignty by equating America to Naples and Aragon. Only a few radicals living in America espoused political aspirations for their own native prince.[57] The crown shared the ideology and expectations of the majority of settlers but its response to the situation was perforce uncertain. It was quickly appreciated that wielding authority over such distant and mixed regions required different solutions. The difficulties of controlling the settlers were at once apparent, suggesting that greater control would have to be imposed. More importantly, the continuing debate over the status of the indigenous peoples did not allow a coherent policy to be drawn from the start. Zorita might have emphasised the similarities between native Indian and Spanish peasant patterns of behaviour,[58] but for most Spaniards, the Amerindians were at best inferior beings akin to children or lunatics. In other words, humans in need of tutelage and control. Consequently, while many elements of European government were transferred to the Americas,[59] and the status of the major regions, with their viceroys (*alter reges* rather than simple administrators) and High Courts, was constitutionally superior to some other Iberian and Italian states within the 'Castilian federation', it was impossible for the American states to be considered as ordinary members of the composite monarchy. Disillusionment with the slow progress of the natives towards Christianity and Spanish civilisation subsequently hardened attitudes and encouraged the imposition of stricter controls.

A recognisably imperial, colonial mentality had emerged in the seventeenth century which was further encouraged by the growing fragmentation of the Americas and the attempts to refine—and redefine—what being Spanish meant. The initial lack of European women had given rise to mixed-race relationships. In Mexico some of the natives were acknowledged to have noble status which facilitated intermarriage there. Even this could not attenuate the opprobrium in which such unions were held in Spain. 'There, it will be considered a serious fault that I have married an Indian,' wrote one settler from

[57] Pagden, *Spanish Imperialism*, 24 Cano, 32 Las Casas. Also ibid., 'Identity Formation', 51–93. The more radical notions were rare and essentially shared by established settlers and mixed-race peoples.

[58] Zorita, *Relación*, 119ff.

[59] See the classic study by J. H. Parry, *The Spanish Seaborne Empire* (London, 1966).

[60] Elliott, *Spain and Its World*, 50–1.

Mexico, 'but here, no honour is lost in doing so, because this Indian nation is highly esteemed.'[61] A decree of 1533 declared that children born of such unions were Spanish and ordered that they should live in Spanish areas and be given a Spanish education. But identity cannot be established merely through legislation. It has to gain widespread acceptance, and neither the new waves of emigrants nor the American-born descendants of Spaniards would accept mixed-race or mestizos as Spanish.[62] At the heart of this rejection was the issue of race, and race, as mentioned earlier, had come to be a crucial feature of the new Spanish identity. By the end of the sixteenth century the concern with purity of blood pervaded Spanish culture, and the exclusion of Muslim and Jew in the peninsula was mirrored in the exclusion of indigenous and mixed races in the New World. Even Vasco de Quiroga, who dedicated his adult life to the Indians and frequently lamented the lack of tolerance and comprehension of 'our Spanish nation',[63] could not overcome these prejudices. While he made provision for Indians to be educated free of charge in the Christian faith and the Castilian language, he specified that free education for the priesthood in the school he founded must only be made available to 'pure Spanish students'.[64] Eventually legislation echoed popular perceptions and Spanish identity in America was defined by origin, race and colour (white) as well as by a distinct religious and political culture. The mestizos had no option but to develop an alternative, differentiated identity of their own.

III. Conclusion

The creation of a distinct, national identity depends on duality. As Maravall put it, it has an 'existential' existence because it requires both the nation and 'the other'.[65] Africa and the Americas were the most notable examples of 'the other' against which a scarcely developed sixteenth-century Spanish identity measured, compared and distinguished itself. Neither of these areas was initially perceived as a colony, but as additions to an already complex, extended and diverse composite monarchy. Yet the gulf that separated the Spaniards from

[61] Andrés García to his nephew Pedro Guiñón, from México, 10 Feb. 1571, in *Cartas privadas de emigrantes a Indias, 1540–1616*, ed. E. Otte (Jerez. s.d., 1992?) n. 27, 61.

[62] On the mestizos, see A. Pagden, 'Identity Formation in Spanish America' in N. Canny and A. Pagden (eds), *Colonial Identity in the Atlantic World, 1500–1800* (Princeton, 1987), 69–80.

[63] 'Tratado de Derecho' in Quiroga, *La Utopia*, ed. Serrano Gassent, 63–248, quote at 130.

[64] *Ibid.*, 288–309 the will of 24 January 1565; quote, 293.

[65] *Estado Moderno* I, 500.

the states, races and civilisations they encountered in these areas was too great. It accelerated the process of differentiation and gave rise to sentiments of racial, cultural and ideological superiority that gradually turned to recognisably modern, imperialist sentiments. By 1588 a contemporary could claim without blushing: 'Since Spain was Spain, it has never enjoyed the reputation it now has among all the nations of the world, because its empire has never been as great as it is now, embracing as it does from East to West and from North to South; and also because of the heroic and notable deeds which the Spaniards have done in the wars in France, Italy, Germany, Flanders, Africa, Asia, Europe and the New World against Moors, Turks, Christians, pagans, Catholics and heretics.'[66] Inexorably, the habit of superior and unbridled command, stoked by pride and arrogance, also changed Castilian attitudes towards lesser states within Europe, as the much-quoted exchange in a letter of 1570 illustrates. A Spanish official ruefully commented that all those 'subject to the Spanish nation and empire' hated the Spaniards. In the margin another noted: 'these Italians, although they are not Indians, have to be treated as such, so that they will understand that we are in charge of them and not they in charge of us'.[67] By the 1590s Garnica blithely referred to the rest of the Monarchy as Spain's 'possessions', God's gift to ensure that the Spaniards were kept busy fighting for the faith and thus free from the cardinal sins of sloth and sodomy! The Italian states were condescendingly accepted as Spain's siblings—but only as long as they continued to make contributions to the common cause.[68]

There can be no doubt that a distinct and powerful Spanish identity emerged in the sixteenth century, and that it was especially evident in the context of North Africa and America. It was broadly encapsulated in Tanara's trinity of Christianity, civilisation and Spanishness, although some would have considered it tautology, since for them being Spanish was, by definition, being an ardent catholic and member of a superior social and political structure. We should not allow current political concerns to negate its existence, or to dismiss evidence with slighting references to Castilian imperialism—which certainly played an important part in its development. Nor should we assume that the existence of powerful emotive attachments to other identities in the peninsula and outside were incompatible with the identification with Spain. John Hale once argued that war was less likely to encourage nationalism than peace, because by its nature war is a cosmopolitan experience

[66] Ribadeneira in *Historia de España en sus documentos*, ed. Díaz-Plaja, 754.

[67] Cit. H. G. Koenigsberger, *The Government of Sicily under Philip II of Spain* (London & New York, 1951), 48.

[68] 'La misión del imperio' I, 727 on sodomy; II, 127 on Italy.

that exposes men to other influences and 'camaraderies that ... broke the spell of national identity'.[69] This implies that nationalism is the antithesis of cosmopolitan. But, as I have argued here, Spanish identity was a cosmopolitan, collective construct. It was precisely that experience of war abroad and camaraderie that forged the bonds that knit hostile Iberians into 'the Spanish'.[70] So much so that, when the Castilian cortes attempted to replace the patron saint, St James, with St Theresa of Avila, there was an uproar. St James's patronage, it was claimed, 'extends throughout all the lands and domains of the king of Spain and the whole of his monarchy', whereas St Theresa was purely Castilian.[71] The vehement defence and ultimate victory of this crucial symbol of Spain demonstrates the depth and attachment to that collective identity. Significantly, while Spain still did not exist *de jure*, from 1600 the extended possessions of the western Habsburgs were known as the Spanish Monarchy. The very absence of a concrete political reality behind a term redolent with traditions and ancient associations made Spain and Spanish malleable and flexible concepts. As a shared ideal and imagined community it could be endlessly adapted and understood. In the sixteenth century, quite extraordinary circumstances of discovery, conquest and war in diverse lands combined with active promotion from the court to give Spanish identity profound and multiple layers of meaning, provided new shared experiences, and a receptive artistic environment to disseminate them. Together they enabled Spain and Spanish to establish deep roots and ensured success and survival to our own day.

[69] J. R. Hale, *War and Society in Renaissance Europe, 1450–1620* (London, 1985), 44.

[70] An argument could be made that other major 'national' identies are similarly collective constructs.

[71] Cit. Thompson, 'Castile, Spain and the Monarchy', 145. It is clear that some Castilians were now conscious that by fostering a Spanish identity they had lost their own.

RUSSIAN, IMPERIAL AND SOVIET IDENTITIES

By Dominic Lieven

READ 26 SEPTEMBER 1997 AT THE INSTITUTE OF HISTORICAL RESEARCH, LONDON

IN a much-cited statement Ernest Renan once commented that the nation was a daily plebiscite.[1] Whereas the state's essence are institutions and laws, the nation exists first and foremost in the consciousness of the population. How strongly a population identifies itself as a nation differs over time and from one section or class to another. The nature of the external challenges facing a community will also help to determine its sense of identity. Though different groups and individuals may all claim membership of the same nation, they may still disagree radically about the institutions, memories, symbols and values which embody that nation and make it worthy of allegiance.

National identity is indeed a complicated matter, much more confusing and fluid than Renan's metaphor of the plebiscite might suggest. Plebiscites occur rarely, concentrate the mind, demand yes or no answers, and usually concern a single political issue of commanding importance. Group identities—including national ones—are usually ill-defined and overlapping. For most people politically defined group identities are not of pre-eminent importance, nor are individuals usually faced with the need to make definitive choices between competing political group allegiances.

Even when this does happen, many extraneous factors may well determine their choice. In 1860–1, for instance, Robert E. Lee was faced with a choice between loyalty to the American nation and the federal army on the one hand, and the Commonwealth of Virginia and the Southern nation on the other. An educated man long aware of the issues involved in the conflict between north and south, Lee was well equipped to make his choice. Since he had been offered top command in both of the rival armies, the dilemma was both especially agonising and doubly important. According to Lee's latest biographer, however, the final decision to opt for the South was owed in part to his liking for a quiet life without personal confrontations and conflicts, including those that would erupt between him and his wife and family should he continue to serve the Union.[2]

[1] For instance in Anthony Smith, *The Ethnic Origins of Nations* (Oxford, 1986), p. 136.

[2] Emory M. Thomas, *Robert E. Lee* (New York, 1995), pp. 187–90.

National identity can to some extent be seen to revolve around two poles, one political, the other cultural. In the former case it is the state and its institutions, perhaps above all its armed forces, which are of primary importance, together with the memories, myths and symbols attached to them. In the latter case language, popular customs, religion and values come to the fore. The distinction between these poles is usually anything but absolute, religion, for instance, clearly linking the two, but it is real and, especially in the Russian context, useful for the scholar. Significantly, the adjective 'Russian' in the English language is a translation of two Russian words with clearly distinct meanings. The first word, *rossiyskiy*, is traditionally associated with the Russian dynasty and state, the institutions through which it ruled and the territory over which it exercised sovereignty. By contrast, the word *russkiy* is linked to the Russian people, culture and language.

Russian statehood and Russian political identity owe their origins to the Moscow branch of the Rurikid dynasty, to the polity they created, to the aristocratic families who dominated this polity over the centuries, and to the territories over which they ruled. The fact that monarchy, aristocracy and polity endured provided the essential continuity between the medieval land of the Rus and the later Russian Empire.[3] The huge success of this polity as an instrument of power and territorial expansion was the essential basis of its legitimacy and of the alliance between monarchy and aristocracy which was its core. That alliance and legitimacy was also embedded in a range of myths, symbols, rituals and institutions.[4] Aristocratic families found it easy to identify with a dynastic state whose history was their own. In the imperial (i.e. post-Petrine) era, for instance, the state created a range of military, administrative, educational and honorific institutions and corporations which aristocratic families dominated and with which they identified.[5]

The tsarist elite was relatively open to new blood, to some extent from ethnically Russian families of the minor gentry and official class, but also from non-Russian minorities within the polity and from abroad. Before the mid-nineteenth century access was often easier for non-

[3] On Muscovite and early modern Russian identity the English-speaking reader should consult: D.J. Halperin, 'The Russian Land and the Russian Tsar: the Emergence of Muscovite Ideology, 1380–1408', *Forschungen zur Osteuropaischen Geschichte* (1976), 23; P. Bushkovich, 'The Formation of a National Consciousness in Early Modern Russia', *Harvard Ukrainian Studies*, X, 3–4 (1986); M. Cherniavsky, 'Russia', in O. Ranum (ed.), *National Consciousness, History and Political Culture in Early Modern Europe* (Baltimore, 1975); J. Cracraft, 'Empire versus Nation: Russian Political Theory under Peter I', *Harvard Ukrainian Studies*, X, 3–4) (1986).

[4] R. S. Wortman, *Scenarios of Power, Myth and Ceremony in Russian Monarchy*, vol. I (Princeton 1995).

[5] D. C. B. Lieven, *Russia's Rulers under the Old Regime* (Yale University Press, New Haven, 1989), chs. 2, 3, 4, 5.

Russians. Subsequently the growth of a Russian middle class and of Russian nationalism contributed to making the imperial polity and its ruling elites more ethnically and culturally Russian. Whereas at the beginning of the nineteenth century non-Russian elites found it easy to combine allegiance to their own cultures with identification with the Russian imperial polity, this was becoming harder by 1914. Nevertheless, in wide sections of the non-Russian aristocracy loyalty to the Russian dynasty, pride in the Russian army, and consciousness of historical links between family and state remained important, as did solidarity between these elites and the tsarist state in defence of property, privilege and culture in the face of threatened social revolution.[6]

To what extent if any, the bulk of the Russian population identified with the tsarist polity is difficult to say. For most of tsarist history the masses were both illiterate and discouraged from expressing political opinions. As in other early modern European states the power and wealth of the royal-aristocratic polity was largely based on the exploitation of the peasantry.[7] In the Russian case serfdom was particularly arbitrary and brutal, as well as having been imposed relatively late on a previously free peasantry. From the late seventeenth century in Russia, as elsewhere in Europe, a gulf opened up between elites who understood the world in increasingly scientific and rational terms, and masses whose cosmology was still religious and magical.[8] In Russia, however, the elites remained relatively smaller and their partial adoption of Western clothes, languages, cultures and values may have made them seem even more alien from the bulk of the population than was true elsewhere.[9] Even in 1914, let alone before 1861, it is certainly wrong to see the tsarist empire as dominated by the Russian nation. Within the Russian community the gulf between elite and mass in terms of power, culture and consciousness makes use of the term 'nation', with its connotations of civic equality or at least spiritual solidarity, distinctly dubious. The sense of national pride and identity which Russian literature had developed in the intelligentsia was by definition meaningless to a peasantry barely, if at all, literate. Russian peasants were certainly not privileged in comparison to their un-Russian peers, indeed

[6] On the tsarist ruling elites see B. Meehan-Waters, *Autocracy and Aristocracy. The Russian Service Elite of 1730* (Rutgers, 1982); J. LeDonne, 'Ruling Families in the Russian Political Order 1689–1825', *Cahiers du Monde Russe et Sovietique*, XXVIII, 3–4 (1987); D. Lieven, 'The Russian Civil Service under Nicholas II: Some Variations on the Bureaucratic Theme', *Jahrbucher für Geschichte Osteuropas*, 29 (1981), 3. For non-Russian elites' relationship with the imperial polity see A. Kappeler, *Russland als Vielvölkerreich* (Munich, 1993).

[7] But see a very interesting short essay by Steven Hoch, 'The Serg Economy and the Social Order in Russia', in M. Bush (ed.), *Serfdom and Slavery* (London, 1996).

[8] E. Weber, *Peasants into Frenchmen* (Stanford, 1976), especially ch. 29.

[9] The classic statement on this was by A. von Haxthausen, *The Russian Empire. Its People, Institutions and Resources* (London, 1968), vol. II, p. 185.

if anything quite the opposite. During the eighteenth century in the Volga region, for instance, Russian peasants could be the serfs of Tatar nobles and were subject to military conscription. Tatar peasants enjoyed the much less burdensome status of state peasants and were free from service in the army.[10]

Tsarist history therefore offered ample reason why the bulk of the Russian population should fail to identify with the dynastic state. This became very important in the early twentieth century when revolutionary movements began to mobilise the masses behind alternative political conceptions. Nevertheless, it would be a mistake to read 1917 back throughout the whole of Russian history or to deny that for much of tsarism's existence the monarchy had a considerable hold on the imagination and loyalty of the peasantry.[11]

The case of the army as a source of mass identification with the polity is more ambiguous. Russian peasants dreaded conscription into the long-service regular army that existed from Petrine days to 1874. Ripped away forever from their families and villages, shock and ill-treatment resulted in the death of a large percentage of the new conscripts even before they reached their regiments. Conditions of service were harsh, medical services before the nineteenth century, for instance, being non-existent. And yet, as the French emigré General Langeron commented, this army, whose conditions of service ought to have made it the worst in Old Regime Europe, was in fact probably the best. Among the explanations for this cited by contemporaries were the unique (for the times) ethnic homogeneity of the army and the strong national loyalties of the soldiers. Certainly no observer ever questioned the deep sense of identification of soldiers with their regiments, with some of their commanders, with the Orthodox Church and with their monarchs. The astonishing morale and capacity for self-sacrifice shown by Russian soldiers and sailors on so many occasions is inexplicable unless such factors are invoked. Moreover, although the rank and file of the pre-1874 armed forces were to a considerable extent divorced from civilian society, it is inconceivable that the loyal and often heroic service of literally millions of ordinary Russian men had no impact on the masses' political identity in the eighteenth and nineteenth centuries. Heroes such as Suvorov and Rumyantsev, great patriotic dramas such as 1812 and the defence of Sevastopol, must have left their mark at the time and certainly provided great potential for

[10] On Russians and Tatars, see A. Kappeler, *Russlands Erste Nationalitäten. Das Zarenreich und die Völker der Mittleren Volga von 16 bis 19 Jahrhundert* (Cologne, 1982).

[11] M. Cherniavsky, *Tsar and People. Studies in Russian Myths* (New York, 1969); M. Perrie, *Pretenders and Popular Monarchism in Early Modern Russia* (Cambridge, 1995). For a sceptical view, D. Field, *Rebels in the Name of the Tsar* (Boston, 1976).

later exploitation by nationalist politicians and intellectuals.[12]

Behind both dynasty and army stood the Orthodox Church, which undoubtedly played the greatest role in creating a sense of unique national identity and community among the Russians, and in legitimising the dynastic polity with which the church was fused. Orthodox rituals, music, icons and belief became intertwined with every aspect of the masses' existence and of their conceptions. Surrounded by Catholics, Protestants, Muslims and pagans, the Russian sense of unique identity rooted in Orthodoxy is unsurprising. Nevertheless although the church was far better placed than any other force to fuse political (*rossiyskiy*) and cultural (*russkiy*) national identity, it nevertheless suffered some weaknesses in this respect. The closeness of state and church meant that the latter inevitably suffered as tsarism's legitimacy declined after 1861. After Peter I's ecclesiastical reforms the church could never generate an autonomous leadership or political voice, which contributed to its helplessness when tsarism collapsed in 1917. Compared to its Ottoman rival one great strength of the early-modern Russian state was its success in overcoming religious conservatism and in adopting European technologies and values. One price paid, however, was a split in the Orthodox community, many of whose most active and fervent members defected to the various traditionalist Old Believer sects. In time too the Europeanised Russian elites often became increasingly dissatisfied with a church which rejected most aspects of European modernity. The defection of much of educated Russia to rival religions or atheism further weakened the national church and therefore the Russian polity and society as well.[13]

In the nineteenth century there emerged a number of political movements which stressed the gap between state and people, and emphasised to an increasing degree that the latter alone embodied the true Russia worthy of service by patriots. Ironically, the Slavophile movement of the 1840s, which played a key role in launching this tradition, was in many ways deeply conservative and was led by mostly wealthy land-owning nobles drawn from the top ranks of Muscovite society. To some extent Slavophilism reflected a split often found in early modern European society between 'court' and 'country'. Muscovite Slavophile aristocrats were asserting a claim as spokesmen for the authentically Russian land and people against a cosmopolitan, alien and impersonal Petersburg court and bureaucracy, which had little

[12] On the army, its morale, and the role of ethnic homogeneity see W. Fuller, *Strategy and Power in Russia 1600–1914* (New York, 1992), esp. Ch. 3, and C. Duffy, *Russia's Military Way to the West. Origins and Nature of Russian Military Power* (London, 1981). In ch. VI of his splendid *When Russia Learned to Read* (Princeton, 1985) J. Brooks barely mentions the army's impact on popular consciousness.

[13] These themes are covered in G. Hosking, *Russia, People and Empire* (London, 1997).

concern for truly Russian values and interests. But, in tune with ideas current in a Romantic and nationalist age, they identified the peasantry, its culture, and its sense of instinctive collectivism and solidarity, as the essence of true Russianness. The Slavophiles were never hostile to the monarchy, let alone the Orthodox Church, and their heirs in the 1860s and later to some extent forged an alliance with the state rooted in support of a foreign policy which would defend Russian power and prestige, and 'protect' Slav interests.[14]

Nevertheless a certain degree of distrust and tension remained between the state on the one hand, and this core element in conservative Russian nationalism on the other. To some extent this merely reflected the fact that the tsarist state after 1861 was too weak to pursue victoriously an expansionist and glorious foreign policy capable of winning the elites' allegiance in Bismarckian style. Conscious of this fact, the state was deeply scared by nationalist, Pan Slav pressure which might expose it to dangerous conflicts with foreign powers. In addition, the survival of autocracy and the absence therefore of any formal controls over government by public opinion and social elites made it impossible to generate a sense of citizenship and civic nationhood, or a firm confidence that the state embodied society's values and aspirations. Public opinion's hysteria about 'dark forces' and treason in court circles during the Great War owed something to these factors.[15]

The Slavophiles' stress on the peasantry as the bearers of a collectivist and essentially Russian identity was taken up by the early Russian socialists in the 1860s. Much of the Russian socialist tradition was in a sense deeply nationalist. Most of the 1860s and 1870s socialists and many of their twentieth-century heirs idealised the Russian peasantry (*narod/volk*), believed in its uniquely collectivist and egalitarian morality, and stressed that Russia would find its own path to modernity through socialism. Unlike the Slavophiles, however, the socialists totally rejected the monarchy, church and even army, denying them any legitimate role as constituent elements or defenders of Russian identity.[16]

The competition between the tsarist regime and its radical opponents to define a legitimate Russian identity was complicated by the fact that nineteenth-century Russia was no longer an ethnically homogeneous community but instead a multi-ethnic empire. Although, however, the 1897 census showed that roughly 46 per cent of the empire's population

[14] On the Slavophiles the best place to start is A. Walicki, *The Slavophile Controversy* (Oxford, 1975). On the social history of the early Slavophiles see also M. Hughes, 'Independent Gentlemen: the Social Position of the Moscow Slavophiles and Its Impact on their Political Thought', *Slavonic and East European Review* (1993), 71.

[15] See ch. 8 of D. Lieven, *Nicholas II. Emperor of all the Russians* (London, 1993).

[16] F. Venturi, *Roots of Revolution* (Chicago, 1983), remains the best introduction to this theme.

were Great Russians, the significance of this fact was a cause for some debate. Roughly 20 per cent of the population were Ukrainians and Belorussians, whom not only the regime but also most of its liberal opponents saw as offshoots of the Russian tribe, with whom they were said to have a common religion and language of high culture. When one considered two-thirds of the population to be Russian, discounted many Muslims and most nomads as too primitive to matter, and believed that the smaller Christian peoples had little alternative but to prefer Russian dominion to that of the rival German and Ottoman empires, it was relatively easy to believe that, given sufficient determination by the government, most of the Russian Empire could be transformed into something approximating to a nation-state.[17]

Important factors existed to sustain this view. As Russian educated society grew in size and nationalism took a greater hold on European public opinion, pressure mounted to make the polity less cosmopolitan and aristocratic, and more clearly Russian in cultural terms and in its leading personnel. A small but symptomatic example of this comes from the world of music in the Petersburg of the 1860s and 1870s. Traditionally, the court and high society had patronised foreign music and musicians. The assault by the 'Mighty Five' on this tradition therefore combined personal ambition and outraged national feeling in a manner very familiar to historians of nationalism.[18] Of more obvious political significance was the growing belief among sections of an increasingly professional and ethnically Russian bureaucracy that Russian economic power, religion, language and culture should be encouraged to dominate as much as possible of the empire, and particularly the Western Borderlands inhabited by east Slavs.

There were also strong prudential reasons for attempting to consolidate the empire around its Russian ethnic core. Everywhere in Europe, as dramatic changes in education, communications and commerce undermined traditional local loyalties and widened horizons, nationalism appeared to be a means to re-integrate society and provide it with common loyalties and values. Conservatives noted the successes of Bismarck and Disraeli in mobilising mass nationalism to defend existing elites and institutions against the radical and socialist challenge.

[17] The literature on this theme is already immense and interest in nationalities' issues since the break-up of the USSR ensures its exponential growth. Kappeler, *Russland als Vielvolkerreich*, remains the best overall study but three recent works well deserve attention: T.R. Weeks, *Nation and State in Late Imperial Russia* (De Kalb, 1996). O. Andriewsky, *The Politics of National Identity: the Ukrainian Question in Russia 1904–12* (Harvard Ph.D., 1991): W. Rodkiewicz, *Russian Nationality Policy in the Western Provinces of the Empire during the Reign of Nicholas II, 1894–1905* (Harvard, Ph.D., 1996).

[18] A very inadequate summary of R.C. Ridenour *Nationalism, Modernism, and Personal Rivalry in Nineteenth-Century Russia* (Bloomington, 1981).

Statesmen could not ignore the impact of nationalism on states' viability and power. The nation-state appeared to be the wave of the future. Germany and Italy overcame resistance to unification. Britain and Germany, both perceived as nation-states, became Europe's greatest powers by 1900. Meanwhile polyglot empires such as Turkey and Austria seemed doomed to weakness and probable dissolution. The greatest single issue facing the Russian state by 1900 seemed to be whether she would become one of the world's leading, dynamic polities along with Britain and Germany, or whether she would decline and ultimately fall along with the other polyglot empires of her day. The answer to this question seemed to revolve, in part anyway, around the extent to which the regime could create a homogeneous national community and legitimise itself in its eyes.[19]

Nevertheless there were always many Russian statesmen who pointed to the impossibility of russianising most of the non-Slav population, particularly when it already possessed a high culture of its own, and who warned of the dire political consequences of attempting to do so. In 1914 the dilemmas of Russian and imperial identity were very far from being resolved, even in the minds of tsarist statesmen. Moreover, these dilemmas could only worsen as previously illiterate peasants and nomads acquired the new consciousness that education and urbanisation would entail, and as the state attempted to penetrate more deeply into society with programmes of, for example, compulsory education for all.[20]

It is instructive to compare English and Russian national and imperial identities on the eve of 1914. At that time the two empires were the largest in the world and both embodied Europe's immense expansion at the expense of the non-Christian continents. In both cases their peripheral position within Europe had greatly facilitated expansion beyond its borders. A large question mark stood against the survival of both empires by 1914, however. Long-term viability depended above all on the extension and consolidation of Russian and British national identity well beyond the limits of England and Great Russia. For the tsarist regime the greatest challenge was to ensure the russianisation of Ukraine and Belorussia. For the English it was to create a genuine British Federation of the White dominions and to defuse the challenge of Irish nationalism at the empire's core. The greatest obvious difference

[19] See e.g. P. B. Struve's writings before 1914: 'Otryvki o gosudarstvei natsii,' (*Russkaya Mysl'*, May 1908) and a further article on the same theme in December 1914: *Collected Works*, vol. VII, pp. 187–98 No. 360 and vol. XI, pp. 176–80, University Microfilms, 1970.

[20] I tackle these issues in much greater detail (and with a large bibliography) in my forthcoming article in the *Journal of Contemporary History* entitled 'Dilemmas of Empire 1850–1918. Power, Territory, Identity'.

between the two empires was that the Russian imperial polity was a homogeneous land mass and therefore much easier to defend and consolidate than its British maritime rival, which was scattered across the oceans. The often terrifying sea voyage which had accompanied emigration and the radically different natural environment which confronted the colonist also contributed to a sense of distance and separateness from the metropolis which the Russian colonist was unlikely to feel to any similar degree. For him it would be hard to say where Russia ended and empire began as he continued his ancestors' age-old pattern of migration across the Steppe. Only perhaps when he reached the Tauride peninsula, the Caucausus mountains and the ancient cities of Central Asia was he confronted with totally dissimilar societies on a par to those subjected by British imperialism.[21]

Nevertheless, particularly where identities are concerned, by far the greatest difference between the two empires was rooted not in geography but in politics. English seventeenth-century colonialism was founded on the principle of colonial self-government, a principle which was strongly reasserted in the Victorian era. In general a clear constitutional and institutional distinction was made between the United Kingdom on the one hand and the overseas' colonies on the other. The one exception, Ireland, showed the huge difficulties involved in attempting to assimilate a colony into the imperial metropolis, particularly where the metropolitan polity was a liberal, and later democratic, one. By keeping empire and metropolis apart the British avoided the Roman trap of allowing republican institutions of self-government to be perverted by the despotic imperatives of empire. But the self-governing institutions they conceded to their White dominions played a huge role in facilitating the creation, articulation and effective defence of a separate colonial, and subsequently national, identity divorced from Britain.

Russian colonists outside the Great Russian heartland, like their British equivalents, created societies and cultures distinctly different to what they had left behind. The egalitarian and anarchic Cossack communities of the sixteenth and seventeenth centuries were far removed from the world of autocratic and serf-owning tsarist Russia. Had these autonomous Cossack communities survived, one can well

[21] For further comparisons between Russian and, *inter alia*, English empire see my 'The Russian Empire and the Soviet Union as Imperial Polities', *Journal of Contemporary History*, 30, 4 (1995) and my forthcoming *Empire and Russia.* As regards the impact on Russian consciousness of imperial conquests two recent English-language books are Y. Slezkine, *Arctic Mirrors. Russia and the Small Peoples of the North* (Ithaca, 1994) and S. Layton, *Russian Literature and Empire. Conquest of the Caucasus from Pushkin to Tolstoy* (Cambridge, 1994). In this context Layton's book is inevitably more useful, since the Caucasus made a vastly greater impact on the Russian imagination than was the case with the Siberian natives.

imagine a separate Cossack political identity being developed on the basis of 'frontier myths'. Indeed to some extent Taras Shevchenko did precisely this when he attempted to articulate a separate Ukrainian identity by defining it against the despotic Russian tsardom and as the legitimate descendant of Cossack democracy. In Siberia too, the regionalist movement that grew up in the second half of the nineteenth century stressed that a new community had developed in Russian Asia: free from serfdom and nobles, and subjected to a uniquely harsh natural environment, the Siberians had become different to the metropolitan Russians, a process aided by inter-marriage with the natives. In both the Siberian and the Cossack case, however, any prospect of a separate political identity's development was nipped in the bud by the tsarist regime, which crushed any attempts to develop such an identity and rejected any institutions of regional self-government. One result of this is that Siberia and the former Cossack territories remained Russian long after Australia, to take but one example, was no longer British. But the Russian determination to retain and assimilate far flung imperial conquests within a centralised, unitary polity undoubtedly contributed to the weakness of liberty and democracy within the Great Russian core.[22]

When the empire went to war the Russians were obviously not a nation, if by nation one means a body of citizens bound together by democratic rights and liberties, and by a sense of shared interests, values and community. Events in the revolutionary years suggest that for the peasantry, still the overwhelming mass of the population, the legitimate political community encompassed the village and *narod* (people), with little place for the cities or the traditional rural elite.[23]

As regards imperial consciousness, much depends on definitions. If one means a sense of racial and cultural superiority over subject peoples, no Russian of any sense was likely to have such an attitude towards the non-Russian but European peoples of the empire, who were not merely White but also very often richer and more cultured than the

[22] On the Cossacks the English-speaking reader must rely on P. Longworth, *The Cossacks* (London, 1969) for a survey, which should be supplemented by H. Stockl, *Die Entstehung des Kosakentums.* On Siberia the place to start is chapter 1 of A. Wood (ed.), *The History of Siberia. From Russian Conquest to Revolution* (London, 1991). On the regionalists, see S. Watrous, 'The Regionalist Conception of Siberia, 1860–1920', ch. 7 in G. Diment and Y. Slezkine (eds.), *Between Heaven and Hell. The Myth of Siberia in Russian Culture* (New York, 1993) and W. Faust, *Russlands Goldener Boden. Der Sibirische Regionalismus in der zweiten. Hälfte des 19 Jahrhunderts* (Cologne, 1980).

[23] On this huge and difficult subject O. Figes, *Peasant Russia, Civil War: The Volga Countryside in Revolution (1917–1921)* (Oxford, 1989), is excellent. See also the essays by Gorky and Chayanov in R. E. F. Smith (ed.), *The Russian Peasant 1920 and 1984* (London, 1977).

Russians themselves.[24] On the contrary, the empire's rulers were if anything exaggeratedly conscious of Russians' inferiority in culture, education and enterprise and were obsessed by the need for the state to make up for their 'natural' inferiority by policies favouring ethnic Russians.[25]

Traditionally the Russian elites had intermarried with the aristocracies of the Tatar Khanates and the Caucasus, readily assimilating them into the tsarist ruling class so long as, in time, they converted from Islam to Orthodoxy. With cultural Westernisation and the vastly enhanced power that technology brought to European states and armies in the nineteenth century there came also, however, a sense of cultural arrogance and civilising mission, at least among the educated classes. Foreign observers noted, however, that Russian peasants and soldiers in central and east Asia had very little of the racial arrogance or sense of inherent superiority to natives which was so marked a feature, especially, of North European Protestants in the colonies.[26]

If, however, by imperial consciousness one merely means a commitment to Russia's position as a great power and to its retention of its imperial borders then clearly not merely the tsarist regime but also the entire liberal opposition and most of middle and lower-middle class Russia fall within this category. The collapse in the masses' commitment to the war effort in 1917 suggests that imperial consciousness was less widespread in the lower classes than among the elites. In the pre-war decades the tsarist state had lacked the resources, cadres or confidence to attempt to indoctrinate the masses in imperialist and nationalist beliefs, along British or German lines. The sharp antagonism between the regime and much of educated society inevitably deterred such efforts and weakened their impact when they were made.[27]

Despite the radical and traumatic changes which occurred in Russia between 1917 and 1921, the Russian polity emerged from these years still in possession of almost all its previous imperial territories. One important reason for this was that tsarism's resolute policy of obstructing the growth of indigenous Ukrainian elites and institutions played a key

[24] See e.g. the comments of Alexsei Kuropatkin, the Minister of War and a great nationalist, on visiting the Baltic provinces in 1903: p. 7 in *Dnevnik A.N. Kuropatkina*, (Nizhpoligraph, N. Novgorod, 1923).

[25] Weeks, *Nation*, and Rodkiewicz, *Russian*, both stress this point as do experts on Russian policy towards the Jews. See chs. 2 and 3 of H. Rogger, *Jewish Policies and Right-Wing Politics in Imperial Russia* (London, 1986) and J.D. Klier, *Imperial Russia's Jewish Question 1855–81* (Cambridge, 1995).

[26] R. Quested, *'Matey' Imperialists. The Tsarist Russians in Manchuria 1895–1917* (Hong Kong, 1987) is usefully compared with Susan Layton's work on an earlier era and region, though a little caution is required given the differences between Layton's literary sources and those deployed by Quested.

[27] See my comments in ch. 8 of Lieven, *Nicholas II* (London, 1993).

role in wrecking efforts in 1917–19 to create an independent Ukrainian nation state. Without Ukraine's grain, coal and heavy industry a post-revolutionary Russia would have been so severely weakened that its ability quickly to reassert itself as a great power would have been questionable. In demographic terms too, then as now, a Russian-dominated imperial polity from which Ukraine was excluded would have rested on an inherently unstable balance between Great Russians on the one hand and Moslem peoples on the other. The re-absorption of Ukraine by Soviet Russia was therefore crucial. Ultimately, however, the Russians—tsarist and Soviet—were not the most decisive element in making this re-absorption possible. The 'independence' of Ukraine, as indeed of most of Russia's European and Caucasian borderlands, could only be sustained under German protection and required the survival of the Brest-Litovsk treaty. American intervention in the Great War and the consequent defeat of Germany doomed the Brest-Litovsk settlement and with it Ukraine's prospects for independent statehood, albeit one constrained by any Ukrainian government's domestic weakness and its inevitably very unequal relationship with Berlin.[28]

The revolution of 1917 destroyed or crippled all the traditional symbols and bearers of Russian identity. The monarchy was abolished, the Romanovs exterminated or forced to flee abroad. The church was disestablished, reduced to a minimal sacramental role, banned from educating children, and saw many of the clergy murdered.[29] The new regime defined itself against religion and most aspects of the Christian world-view. An army of sorts survived but all continuity with its tsarist predecessor and Russia's military heritage was, for the moment, rejected. Even the old radical glorification of peasant institutions and values as the essence of Russianness was now anathema to new rulers who stressed science and rationality and whose roots lay internally in urban Russia. The old bogeymen against which Russian nationalism had defined itself in the tsarist era—the foreign (eg German) threat and the internal enemy (especially the Jews)—were now rehabilitated by a regime that proclaimed its internationalism. Class not nation was to be the true focus of loyalty and identity. The Bolshevik elite contained many non-Russians, and especially Jews. Great Russian nationalism,

[28] On Ukrainian elites see e.g. ch. 1 of B. Krawchenko, *Social Change and National Consciousness in Twentieth-Century Ukraine* (London, 1985) and A. Kappeler, 'A "Small People" of Twenty-Five Million: the Ukrainians circa 1900', *Journal of Ukrainian Studies*, 18, 1–2 (1993). On Germany, see O. S. Fedyshyn, *Germany's Drive to the East and the Ukrainian Revolution, 1917–1918* (New Brunswick, 1971).

[29] On the treatment of the church see e.g. J. Daly, ' "Storming the Last Citadel". The Boshevik Assault on the Church, 1922', in V. N. Brovkin (ed.), *The Bolsheviks in Russian Society* (New Haven, 1997).

denounced as a pillar of tsarism and of the White counter-revolution, became a cardinal sin.

Nevertheless, the fact that the first socialist revolution and polity had come into being on Russian soil was a powerful potential source of national pride and of legitimacy for the new regime in Russian eyes. In its last decades tsarist Russia had suffered from being one of the most backward and least successful of the great powers. Educated Russians made insidious comparisons between their country and the rest of Europe, much to the detriment of tsarism's legitimacy. Now suddenly, for many left-wing Europeans as well as Russians, Europe's stepchild had become mankind's vanguard. A separate national path to modernity had been the dream of many Russians, as indeed was often the case in the post-1945 Third World. Escaping from the constraints and humiliation of junior membership of an international political economy controlled and defined by others had inherent potential appeal to nationalists. Like Sinn Fein and Mazzini's 'Italia fara da se', Russia would cleave to her own path. Unlike them, she would lead the world in her wake.[30]

In one sense therefore the revolution did carry powerful germs of an imperial consciousness, but one defined less in terms of empire's meaning in the twentieth century than by its place in Late Antiquity and the early medieval world. As Arnold Toynbee among others was quick to note, there were parallels between Soviet ideology and an earlier era of would-be universal monarchies proclaiming a global evangelical message in the tradition of dogmatic, monotheistic Judaism. Such parallels are more fruitful than attempts to compare Soviet thinking with the much more modest conceptions of tsarist foreign policy, rooted in European orthodoxies of Realpolitik and balance of power. *Inter alia*, reference to the would-be universal empires of the first millennium AD provided a warning that, in time rival centres of power would emerge within such empires, initially linked often to disagreements over doctrine as well as to factional struggles, and that these separate polities would quickly absorb much of the political culture of the regions where they were based. Had communists come to power in the wake of a successful German revolution after the First World War, conflicts of interest, doctrine and power would quickly have erupted between them and the Bolshevik regime in Moscow, as indeed happened as regards both Yugoslavia and China in the post 1945 era. The hopes invested in the world socialist revolution as the

[30] NB a comment by a delegate to the tenth Party Congress in 1921: 'The transformation of Russia from a colony of Europe into the center of a world movement has filled with pride and with a special kind of Russian patriotism the hearts of all those who are connected with the revolution'; by F. C. Barghoorn, *Soviet Russian Nationalism* (Oxford, 1956), p. 27.

answer to Russia's problems of security, isolation and backwardness were among the most Utopian aspect of early Bolshevik thinking.[31]

In other senses of the word empire it is harder to pin the term 'imperial' on the Bolsheviks. They themselves understood 'imperialism' in terms defined by Lenin and Bukharin, saw themselves as leaders of the anti-imperialist camp, and stoutly denied that Soviet internal arrangements had the least similarity to those of empire. Since the Soviet Union was not a capitalist country, it is obvious that twentieth-century Marxist definitions of imperialism do not apply to it. Nor does it make much sense to see the early Soviet regime as an embodiment of Russian imperialism since the Bolsheviks had imposed themselves on the Russians in the same way that they later extended their rule to non-Russians as well. Moreover, although the basic principles of nationalities policy under NEP, namely rule through indigenous leaders and the encouragement of native cultures, were not uncommon even in contemporary empires, the great stress the Bolsheviks put on modernising the non-Russian republics and raising them to an economic level equal to the polity's core was unique. On the other hand the Bolsheviks showed themselves determined to impose their rule wherever they could safely do so, regardless of the wishes of non-Russian majorities. The doctrine of the party as the vanguard of the working class, which itself had the right to hegemony within society as a whole, legitimised Moscow's rule in regions where the overwhelming majority of the population was indifferent or hostile to the new regime.[32]

The consolidation of a distinctive Soviet identity was above all the product of the Stalinist era. In principle the doctrine of socialism in one country was an intelligent tactical response to geopolitical realities and in no sense an abandonment of the goal of world revolution. In fact, however, Stalinist society was designed to be monolithic within and isolated from the outside world. Terror was used against those who retained pre-Revolutionary memories and values (the old intelligentsia in general and the Old Bolsheviks in particular), allegiances in the non-Soviet world (Jews, elites in Borderlands annexed in 1940) and even Prisoners of War who had years of grim experience of the non-Soviet paradise of Hitler's empire. Infantile cultural xenophobia reached its peak in the years immediately after 1945. At the price of vast suffering and the permanent destruction of agriculture, collectivisation destroyed the autonomous peasant world and brought the bulk of the population

[31] See in particular vol. VII of A.J. Toynbee, *A Study of History* (Oxford, 1954). On empire in the first millennium, G. Fowden, *Empire to Commonwealth. Consequences of Monotheism in Late Antiquity* (Princeton, 1993), provokes many thoughts.

[32] A Brewer, *Marxist Theories of Imperialism. A Critical Survey* (London, 1980) is a useful introduction to this tradition of political thinking. Richard Pipes, *The Formation of the Soviet Union* (Cambridge, 1954), remains the best book on this subject.

into the realm of Soviet values and culture. Huge mobility out of the working class and peasantry not merely contributed greatly to the regime's legitimacy but also created a new middle class which was the true repository of the Soviet identity. Especially in its early decades this middle class was vastly less cosmopolitan and less capable of comparing Russia with the outside world than was the case with the educated classes in the late imperial era. Its mentalities and values were much closer to those of the bulk of the population than had been true in tsarist times.[33] Lenin was Soviet man's chief icon. Although the regime in formal terms derived its legitimacy from the revolution, for the new middle class dramatic industrial development between the 1930s and 1960s, together with the victory over Germany, were the true sources of self-confidence and self-esteem. Soviet identity incorporated a world view that was resolutely optimistic, materialist and scientific, and which gloried in man's conquest of nature. It incorporated too the many unique landmarks and customs of life in a socialist society, including not just the rhythms and imperatives of life under the Plan but also the corresponding jargon. In certain ways, it is true, the Soviet identity included some aspects of the pre-Revolutionary past. Universal literacy combined with Stalinist education's shift back to conservative principles meant that the masses could absorb the rich traditions of pre-revolutionary literature, thereby acquiring access to a common Russian identity in a way denied to their ancestors before 1917.[34] Soviet patriotism, created under Stalin, generated a sanitised, populist and saccharine acceptance of some elements of Russian history, above all in the military sphere. Soviet work styles and communal values owed something to the old village culture. On the whole, however, the new Soviet identity was rather far removed from the Russia either of the villages or of the elites of tsarist days. By the 1980s the world of Old Regime Russia was in every sense very far away.[35]

It is true that by then the Soviet identity was also facing challenges. The regions annexed by Stalin in 1940 had and retained strong national identities. Their incorporation in the USSR was a fatal mistake for which the Soviet regime paid dearly in 1985–91, when democratisation not merely allowed nationalists to come to power legally in these regions but also to act as a model for the other, inherently less anti-Soviet, republics of the USSR. Even in the latter, however, it was clear by the

[33] On the Stalinist middle class and its values see above all V. Dunham, *In Stalin's Time.*

[34] S. Fitzpatrick, 'Culture and Politics under Stalin. A Reappraisal', *Slavic Review* (June 1976), vol. 35, 2, pp. 211–32.

[35] The literature on Stalinism is already immense and is certain to grow greatly, since this is at present the main focus of Western research into Russian history. Of recent works, Stephen Kotkin, *Magnetic Mountain. Stalinism as a Civilisation* (Berkley, 1995) is not merely among the best but also comes closest to the theme of my article.

1970s and 1980s that ethnic nationalism was gaining ground at the expense of identification with the Soviet Union. Within Russia the younger generation diverged increasingly from the Soviet values of its elders, and a current of Russian nationalist thought developed which denounced the Soviet regime's destruction of church and village, joint bearers of Russia's cultural identity and moral values. The Soviet regime defined itself against the capitalist world which it promised to surpass. It was therefore badly wounded by the failure of its predictions about capitalism's demise and the growing gap between Western and Soviet technology and living standards, which was fully evident to members of the Soviet elite of the 1980s.[36]

Nevertheless the bulk of the Russian population was in no sense prepared for the dramatic collapse of communism and of the Soviet Union in 1991, which reduced the Russian polity overnight to its pre-Petrine borders and made essential a search for ethnic Russian symbols, memories and institutions through which the new state might be legitimised. The confusion and bewilderment which resulted was well reflected in 1995 in the great parade to celebrate the fiftieth anniversary of victory over Nazi Germany. Russia's veterans marched in their old Soviet uniforms, but they did so under the command of serving officers dressed in a new uniform, more tsarist than Soviet and bearing the double-headed eagle of the Romanovs on their caps. By contrast the naval units which participated in the ceremony looked more Soviet than tsarist but marched under the flag of Saint Andrew, the standard of the pre-Revolutionary fleet. Given Russia's immense sacrifices during the Second World War, the parade was a highly emotional event. On such occasions, music best captures, symbolises and heightens the feelings of participants and observers alike. At the parade's climax it would have been most appropriate to play the Soviet anthem but in the political circumstances and with Yeltsin present this was impossible. To play the current national anthem would have been meaningless, since few could even recognise it. Instead it was decided to play that great showpiece of Russian patriotism, Chaikovsky's 1812 symphony. In Chaikovsky's original composition, to which after 1917 the rest of the world adhered but the USSR did not, the climax of the 1812 symphony is the Russia Imperial hymn, God Save the Tsar. Whether

[36] On the non-Russian nationalities, see G. Simon, *Nationalism and Policy toward the Nationalities in the Soviet Union* (Boulder, 1991). On Russia, J. Dunlop, *The Faces of Contemporary Russian Nationalism* (Princeton, 1983), traces the rise of dissident Russian nationalism. R. Szporluk is illuminating on the dilemmas faced by Russian nationalists contemplating the USSR's demise: ch. 1, 'Imperial Legacy and the Soviet Nationalities Problem', in L. Hajda and M. Beissinger (eds.) *The Nationalities Factor in Soviet Politics and Society* (Westview, Boulder, 1990). For a balanced over-all survey of the Soviet Union's position on the eve of Perestroyka see P. Dibb, *The Soviet Union: The Incomplete Superpower* (London 1988).

because it was deemed inappropriate or because they simply possessed a Soviet score the massed bands that day followed the Soviet tradition. At the centre of this supremely national day and event there was therefore, very symbolically, a void within a void. As regards Russia's post-Soviet and post-Imperial political identity, that void still very much remains.[37]

[37] I watched the parade and commented on it for Canadian television.

THE BRITISH EMPIRE AND MUSLIM IDENTITY IN SOUTH ASIA

By Francis Robinson

READ 27 SEPTEMBER 1997 AT THE INSTITUTE OF HISTORICAL RESEARCH, LONDON

BRITISH Empire in India saw major transformations in the identities of its Indian subjects. The growth of the modern state, the introduction of new systems of knowledge, the expansion of capitalist modes of production, and the spread of communications of all forms—railway, telegraph, post, press—made possible the fashioning of all kinds of new identities at local, regional and supra-regional levels. One of the identities which developed most strikingly was the Muslim. Indeed, at independence in 1947 it gained the particular accolade of embracing its own modern state in the shape of Pakistan. This political outcome, however, was just part of an extraordinary series of developments in Muslim identities under British rule which shed light not just on the nature of British rule but also on major changes at work in Muslim society.

That Muslim identity would become a prime theatre of activity did not seem likely in the eighteenth century. Amongst Muslims who were descended from, or who liked to claim that they were descended from, those who had migrated to India to seek service at its many Muslim courts—Turks, Persians, Arabs, Afghans—their Muslim identity was not a matter of overriding concern. At the courts of the Mughals they divided not into Hindu and Muslim factions but into Turkish and Persian ones. They shared their Persian high culture with Hindus, including their poetry which rejected Indian life and landscape as fit subjects for poetic response and found its imaginative horizons in Iran and Central Asia. Family was an important source of identity zealously maintained in family histories, most especially if claiming descent from the Prophet. Place of settlement was also a source of identity exemplified by the custom which grew in the eighteenth century amongst scholars, poets and administrators, as they travelled in search of patronage, of adopting the names of their home *qasbah*, hence 'Bilgrami', 'Mohani' or 'Rudaulvi'. As the eighteenth century progressed, and Shias came to assert themselves notably in the Mughal successor states of Murshidabad and Awadh, Shia and Sunni came to be, from time to time, significant badges of difference amongst Muslims. Amongst these, and other possibilities, the category Muslim was not of overriding importance. Learned men (*ulama*), whose job it was to police the boundaries of community behaviour, would make a point of drawing a distinction between what was Muslim religious practice and that of non-Muslims, but this for the most part was as far as things went.

Amongst Muslims who were descended from converts to Islam, that is, the vast majority of Muslims who expressed themselves through the regional cultures and languages of India—Bengali, Tamil, Malayalam, Gujarati, Sindhi, Punjabi and so on—the distinctions of language, metaphor and behaviour between Muslims and the wider society in which they moved have seemed so slight to some that they have referred to an Islamic syncretistic tradition in Bengal[1] or one Indian religion expressed through different religious idioms in the Tamil country of the south.[2] Scholars differ as to precisely what meaning should be attributed to the forms of religious expression of Muslim convert populations. What is clear, however, is that their's was a piety of local sufi cults in which, more often than not, people of all faiths might participate and which might be expressed as much through regional 'Hindu' idioms as through those classically understood to be Muslim. Such was the nature of Muslim identities in the eighteenth century that many have been able to see them as part of a working 'composite culture'.[3] Such an understanding, nevertheless, should always be qualified by noting that some Muslims had a cultural and imaginative reach that went well beyond the borders of South Asia and that the leading Muslim scholar of the first half of the eighteenth century, Shah Wali Allah of Delhi (d. 1762), was able to declare that 'we are an Arab people whose fathers have fallen in exile in the country of Hindustan, and Arabic genealogy and Arabic language are our pride.'[4]

The period of British rule, which eventually became British empire, brought distinct new strands, indeed firmer edges, to Muslim identities. There was a sharpening of the distinction between Muslim and non-Muslim, which was in part an outcome of the impact of British understandings of India and in part that of religious revivalism. There was also the development of a separate Muslim political identity against

[1] Asim Roy, *The Islamic Syncretistic Tradition in Bengal* (Princeton, 1983).

[2] Susan Bayly, *Saints, Goddesses and Kings; Muslims and Christians in South Indian Society, 1700–1900* (Cambridge, 1989).

[3] Jawaharlal Nehru, *The Discovery of India* (Calcutta, 1946); M. Mujeeb, *The Indian Muslims* (1967); Mushirul Hasan, *Legacy of a Divided Nation: India's Muslims since Independence* (Delhi, 1997). For a recent critique of the composite culture thesis see Cynthia Talbot, 'Inscribing the Other, Inscribing the Self: Hindu-Muslim Identities in Pre-Colonial India', *Comparative Studies in Society and History*, 37, 4 (October 1995), 692–722.

[4] Cited in Annemarie Schimmel, *Islam in the Indian Subcontinent* (Leiden, 198), p. 121.

the claims of an all-inclusive Indian national identity. Parallel with this last process a pan-Islamic dimension to Indo-Muslim consciousness emerged, which for a time between 1919 and 1924 threatened to engulf Muslim politics. The gendering of Muslim identity was a feature as women became a key part of the battlefield across which the discourse of Muslim progress was fought. Finally, there were trends towards individualism, towards asserting individual fulfilment against community obligation, which were arguably part of a process of secularising Muslim identity and the emergence of Muslims who were purely Muslim by culture.

That such remarkable developments took place in the nature of Muslim identities during the period of British empire might suggest that the British presence had a powerful role to play. Certainly it was influential. But it is crucial not to ignore the powerful element of Muslim agency at work. Each new strand that went to shape Muslim identities under British rule will be examined, bearing in mind the questions why did they emerge and what do they mean.

The sharpening of the distinction between Muslim and non-Muslim

It has long been part of Indian nationalist historiographical tradition that the British privileged religious identities in India over other possibilities, which inevitably helped to sharpen distinctions between Muslim and non-Muslim. An important part of this process has come to be seen to be the British construction of knowledge about India, and the ways in which this construction not only influenced British governance but also Indian ideas about themselves. From the very beginning of the serious study of India in the eighteenth century, Warren Hastings and the orientalists around him—Jones, Halhed, Wilkins—thought of India in terms of Hindus and Muslims. The former were seen to have enjoyed a great classical civilisation to 1200 AD, while the latter were interlopers in the subcontinent whose empire from the thirteenth century coincided with decline of classical Indian civilisation. The orientalists sought classical texts to guide them in government and the administration of justice, for instance Halhed's *Code of Gentoo Laws* derived from the Sanskrit *sastras* of the Brahmins, or Burhanuddin Marghinani's *Hidaya*, compiled in Central Asia in the twelfth century, rather than grappling with the complexities of the Indian present. When the British came to place a framework of interpretation over India's past they divided it into Hindu, Muslim and British periods. When from 1871 they began their decennial census of their Indian empire, they tabulated its peoples under religious headings. When they described their empire in imperial and provincial gazetteers, they gave substantial consideration to their Indian peoples as religious groupings down to the level of district and small town.[5] For much of the nineteenth century, moreover, this tendency to interpret Indian society in terms of religion was reinforced by the committed Christian beliefs of a good number of administrators and the presence of many missionary organisations.

In this context the category Muslim became a major part of the discourse of the colonial state, both within itself and with society at large. Much social action, whether it be competition for jobs in government offices or riots in town and countryside, was interpreted in terms of Muslim and Hindu rivalry. While Muslims, themselves, when they came face to face with the state more often than not had to define themselves primarily as Muslims. They did so to the census enumerator or when they signed up to join the army; they did so when they went to school or hospital; they did so when they came to vote. The outcome was that men and women, whose Muslimness might not have been prominent in their consciousness of themselves, came to find it increasingly to be so. In the process they became more aware of what might distinguish them from non-Muslims, as for instance those Bengali Muslims of the late nineteenth century who stopped invoking God as Sri Sri Iswar in favour of Allaho Akbar and who dropped their Hindu surnames (Chand, Pal, Dutt) in favour of Muslim ones (Siddiqui, Yusufzai, Qureshi).[6]

It would, however, be wrong to regard the British as playing the only role in privileging the Muslim category and in sharpening distinctions between Muslim and non-Muslim. Of great importance was the movement of revival and reform which has in various ways striven to vitalise Muslim life on the subcontinent from the early nineteenth century to the present. This was not just an Indian phenomenon but an Islam-wide one, as Muslims strove in various ways to find answers to their loss of power in the world, but it did achieve a particular force and variety of expression in British India. Among the manifestations of the movement were: the jihad movement of the *mujahidin* of Saiyid Ahmed Barelwi (d.1831) in northern India,[7] that of Saiyid Fadl Alawi in Malabar,[8] and that of Haji Shariatullah (d.1838) in Bengal;[9] there were the movements of Deoband and the Ahl-i Hadiths in the later nineteenth

[5] David Ludden, 'Orientalist Empiricism: Transformations of Colonial Knowledge', *Orientalism and the Postcolonial Predicament*, ed. Carol A. Breckenridge and Peter Van Der Veer (Delhi, 1994), 250–78.

[6] Rafiuddin Ahmed, *The Bengal Muslims 1871–1906: a Quest for Identity* (Delhi, 1981), 72–133.

[7] Mohiuddin Ahmad, *Saiyid Ahmad Shahid: His Life and Mission* (Lucknow, 1975).

[8] S. F. Dale, *Islamic Society on the South Asian Frontier: The Mappilas of Malabar, 1498–1922* (Oxford, 1980).

[9] Muin-ud-Din Ahmad Khan, *A History of the Fara'idi Movement in Bengal* (Karachi, 1965).

century;[10] and those of the Tablighi Jama'at and the Jama'at-i Islami in the twentieth.[11] Common to all these movements was an attack on all religious practices, which could be conceived of as having a Hindu element, and a concern to assert their understanding of 'pure' Islamic practice. The records of India's learned and holy families speak of the passing of this spirit through the towns and villages of the land, of the debates that were held and of the compromises that were made to accommodate the new boundaries of acceptable 'Islamic' behaviour.[12]

Side by side with the attack on Hindu practices there was also an assault on all behaviour at saints' shrines which suggested that the believer sought the saint's intercession for him with God. At its conception Islam had been profoundly this-worldly, but with the development of its mystical dimensions it had acquired a substantial other-worldly focus. Now, with the assault on intercession, there was to be a profound shift back towards this-worldly piety. Salvation was to be achieved only by action on earth. Particular force was given to this requirement by the colonial context. In the absence of Muslim power to enforce the holy law, Muslims had to use their individual conscience and will to ensure that the law was observed. To achieve this there was a new emphasis on literacy, on the translation of basic works of scholarship on guidance from Arabic and Persian into Indian languages, and on the making of them widely available through the use of the printing press. There began the era of chapbooks and how-to-be-Muslim guides, which can be found down to the present in the bazaars and bookshops of India and the wider Muslim world.[13] When the time came in the early twentieth century to reach beyond the literate, the Tablighi Jama'at or Preaching Society sprang up with the mission to transmit orally its essential Islamic message and to exemplify in the dress and activities of its missionaries the basic standards of 'Islamic' behaviour.[14]

The new 'willed' or quasi-protestant Islam did much to sharpen the

[10] Barbara Daly Metcalf, *Islamic Revival in British India: Deoband, 1860–1900* (Princeton, 1982).

[11] M. Anwarul Haq, *The Faith Movement of Mawlana Muhammad Ilyas* (1972); Seyyed Vali Reza Nasr, *The Jama'at-Islami of Pakistan* (Berkeley, 1994).

[12] Altaf al-Rahman Qidwai, *Anwar-i Razzaqiya* (Lucknow, n.d.), 17; C. Liebeskind, 'Sufism, Sufi Leadership and 'Modernisation' in South Asia since *c.*1800' (PhD thesis, London University, 1995), 317; J. R. I. Cole, *Roots of North Indian Shi'ism in Iran and Iraq: Religion and the State in Awadh, 1722–1859* (Berkeley, 1988), 237.

[13] Francis Robinson, 'Islam and the Impact of Print in South Asia', *The Transmission of Knowledge in South Asia: Essays on Education, Religion, History and Politics* ed. Nigel Crook (Delhi, 1996), 62–97.

[14] Christian W. Troll, 'Five Letters of Maulana Ilyas (1885–1944), The Founder of the Tablighi Jama'at: Translated, Annotated and Introduced', *Islam in India: Studies and Commentaries*, ed. Christian W. Troll (Delhi, 1985), 138–76.

distinctions between Muslim and non-Muslim. But for one Muslim, Saiyid Abul A'la Maududi, who is arguably the most influential Islamic thinker of the twentieth century, it did not go nearly far enough. Responding, as Syed Vali Nasr has recently shown, to threats in the 1920s and 1930s which Hindu assertiveness seemed to represent to Indian Muslims, he created his vision of a hermetically sealed Islamic world in which all human understanding and all human activity would be subject to revelation. State power, moreover, would be used to put into effect the law derived from revelation.[15]

Of course, the Muslim movement of revival and reform and British rule interacted with each other in shaping definitions of Muslim distinctiveness. Muslim jihad movements and fears of the implacable opposition of so-called Wahabis were sources of constant concern to the British down to World War One. 'Fanatical' was the epithet most commonly applied to Muslims, and it was one which only gained force in the late nineteenth century as information flowed into India of British encounters with Muslims elsewhere in the empire, say in the Sudan or Somaliland.[16] Aspects of Muslim revivalism certainly helped to underpin the British construction of India in religious terms. On the other hand, British rule and the cultural challenges it brought also contributed to sharpening Muslim senses of difference. Not only was there a concern to police the boundaries between Muslim and Hindu behaviour but also those between Muslim and European behaviour. The fatwa literature, the writings of the ulama, and the guidance of sufi pirs were full of responses to society's anxieties as to what European customs and innovations it might be permissible to adopt. Could electric light be used in a mosque? Could European customs of eating at table with knives, forks and spoons be followed? Could European dress be worn? How far could women be permitted the freedom of their European cousins? The presence of the British and the stream of changes they brought stimulated a continuing debate about where the boundaries of proper Muslim conduct might be.[17]

The development of a Muslim political identity

If for the Indian nationalist historian the British privileged religious identities in general and the Muslim identity in particular, they are

[15] Seyyed Vali Reza Nasr, *Mawdudi and the Making of Islamic Revivalism* (Oxford, 1996), 27–46.

[16] Francis Robinson, *Separatism Among Indian Muslims: The Politics of the United Provinces' Muslims 1860–1923* (Cambridge, 1974), 126–7.

[17] Liebeskind, 'Sufism', 294–308; K.A. Nizami, 'Socio-Religious Movements in Indian Islam (1763–1898)', *India and Contemporary Islam*, ed. S. T. Lokhandwalla (Simla, 1971), 109–10.

regarded as being even more responsible for the emergence and continuance of a Muslim political identity. The case might begin by showing how the colonial construction of knowledge helped to establish religious categories of thought in the mind of the Raj and then show how setting these groupings against each other was a policy some had very much in mind. '"Divide et impera" was the old Roman motto', declared Elphinstone, the distinguished early-nineteenth-century governor of Bombay, 'and it should be ours.'[18] And, if such views were thought to be an aberration, they remained very much in the minds of late-nineteenth-century administrators, whether it was the vigorous denial of Sir John Strachey in the 1880s that 'nothing could be more opposed to the policy and universal practice of our Government in India than the old maxim of divide and rule ...'[19] or Sir Antony Macdonnell's open consideration of the possibilities, 'we are far more interested in [encouraging] a Hindu predominance', he wrote to Curzon in the 1890s, 'than in [encouraging] a Mahomedan predominance, which, in the nature of things must be hostile to us'.[20]

Most scholars reject a crude 'divide and rule' analysis in favour of noting British concerns to attract powerful allies to their side. Here the focus comes to rest on a particular dynamic which led to the establishment of a Muslim political identity in the developing democratic framework of the Raj. In the 1860s and 1870s the British were particularly concerned about their failure to attract Muslims to their rule; it was a concern summed up in the title of W. W. Hunter's notorious tract *The Indian Musalmans* (1871), which was written in response to Viceroy Mayo's question, 'are the Indian Musalmans bound by their Religion to rebel against the Queen?' This meant that when a group of north Indian Muslims, led by the gifted and energetic Syed Ahmad Khan, strove to build bridges between Islam and modern science and between Indian Muslims and the colonial state, they were looked upon with approval. When this group went on to found MAO College Aligarh in 1877 and the All-India Muhammadan Educational Conference in 1886 to carry the process forward, it received moral and material support from government. When this group, known as the Aligarh movement, made a point of not supporting the Indian national Congress, the organisation of Indian nationalism, the British were not displeased. Moreover, when representatives of this movement went in deputation to the Viceroy in 1906 to ask for special representation for Muslims and recognition of their 'political importance' in the new legislative councils announced by the Secretary of State, they were

[18] Robinson, *Separatism*, 2.
[19] *Ibid.*, 131.
[20] *Ibid.*, 134.

received with sympathy. Furthermore, when they applied enormous pressure as they Morley-Minto Council reforms were going through Parliament, they were granted separate electorates for Muslims with extra seats, over and above their proportions of the population, in those provinces where they were 'politically important'.[21]

British understandings of Indian society, British fears and British styles of rule all played their part in making possible the formal recognition of a Muslim political identity in the developing constitution of their Indian empire. Thus Muslims all over India were given a political identity which had been the concern mainly of the Muslims from the north. Separate electorates, moreover, were to remain a feature of the two subsequent devolutions of power in 1919 and 1935. While no direct line should be drawn between the establishment of a Muslim political identity in the constitution in 1909 and the emergence of Pakistan in 1947, it was one of many enabling developments.

The responsibility for the emergence of a Muslim political identity, however, cannot entirely be laid at the feet of the British. Significant attention needs to be given to processes within Indian society. There was the Hindu movement of revival and reform which, like that of the Muslims, was powered forward by the need to confront colonial rule and Western knowledge. A great ferment of activity was stimulated, which in northern India led to the promotion of distinctive Hindu symbols such as the Nagri script (of Sanskrit) as against the Muslim Persian script then used in government, the increasing sanskritisation of Hindi so as to differentiate it from Urdu, and the assertion of Hindu preferences in many localities with regard to cows or religious processions as against those of Muslims. Agitation for Hindi led Syed Ahmad Khan in 1869 to talk for the first time of working just for Muslims.[22] Recent attempts to make Nagri the script of government, which would put Muslims out of work, and bruising battles over religious preferences on municipal boards were part of the backdrop to the Muslim deputation to the viceroy and its requests for privileges and protection. Indeed, the often close relationship between Hindu revivalism and the Congress was always going to make for a difficult relationship between Muslims and Indian nationalism.[23]

There was also the Muslim movement of revival and reform. Syed Ahmad Khan had his intellectual roots deep in the traditions of the Muslim revival. His Aligarh movement is the expression of that revival that has come to be known as Islamic modernism, which achieved its

[21] *Ibid.*, 84–174.

[22] *Ibid.*, 98.

[23] Francis Robinson 'The Congress and the Muslims', *Indian National Congress and Indian Society 1885–1985: Ideology, Social Structure, and Political Dominance*, ed. Paul R. Brass and Francis Robinson (Delhi, 1987), 162–83.

culmination in British India in the thought of Muhammad Iqbal who succeeded in building a bridge between Islam and the idea of progress, not least in the organisation of a modern state. It was suffused with memories of past Muslim glory and the need to restore that glory in the present. The classic statement of its mood was Hali's *Musaddas*, an elegy on the rise and fall of Islam composed in the 1870s at Syed Ahmad Khan's request. Readings from the poem would often be used to introduce educational and political meetings, and, with verses such as the following, leave audiences in tears:

> There is meanness in everything we do. Our ways are worse than those of the most base.
> Our forefathers' reputation has been eaten away by us. Our step makes our countrymen ashamed.
> We have thrown away our ancestors' credit, and sunk the nobility of the Arabs.[24]

Aligarh was designed to deal with this situation. Its alumni were to be the new Muslim elites of British India. They were to form the All-India Muslim League in 1906, which fought for separate electorates and special privileges for Muslims in the Morley-Minto Council reforms. They were the key supporters of the League as it strove in subsequent years to preserve the Muslim political identity. Nevertheless, the vicissitudes in the support for this identity must be recorded. In the second decade of the twentieth century the young Muslim elites of northern India were firmly behind it. But in the 1920s support drained away: Muslim landlords joining landlord parties, young professionals joining the nationalist movement, and some leaving politics altogether. In the 1930s it virtually disappeared; only once between 1931 and 1936 did the Muslim League meet in full session, between 1931 and 1935. Jinnah, the League's key figure, had his main residence in London, while in the first general election after the 1935 Government of India Act it won only twenty-two per cent of the seats reserved for Muslims. It was only in the special circumstances of the 1940s that the League was able to give the Muslim political identity the broad appeal that enabled it to win over ninety per cent of the reserved Muslim seats in the elections of 1945–46.[25]

[24] Christopher Shackle and Javed Majeed, *Hali's Musaddas: The Flow and Ebb of Islam* (Delhi, 1997), 147.

[25] A. Jalal, *The Sole Spokesman: Jinnah, the Muslim League and the Demand for Pakistan* (Cambridge, 1985).

British empire and the Pan-Islamic strand

Muslims have always had a special feeling for the idea of their community, their *umma*. At one level this might be acknowledged in the salaam to neighbours during the act of prayer or in the particular rites performed at a saint's shrine. An another level community might be understood in the fact that all Muslims belong to a community created by God's grace; they gave alms each year for the support of the community; they endured the privations of the Ramadan fast as one; and that they looked forward to the ultimate celebration of the community in the company of Muslims from all parts of the world during the annual pilgrimage to Mecca.

A feature of the Muslim world over the past century has been that more and more Muslims have developed a pan-Islamic dimension to their consciousness; more and more have engaged imaginatively and emotionally with the fate of Muslims in faraway lands. In India this development was given a particular intensity, in part because the British empire played such a considerable role in the conquest of Muslim peoples and the decline of Muslim power, and in part because Indian Muslims themselves felt especially insecure.[26]

One development which expanded horizons was the increasing ease of travel that owed much to the shipping routes and railway lines that underpinned the trading and communications network of the empire. From the 1860s, increasing numbers of Muslims went to Britain and to Europe to absorb Western learning or to train as lawyers and doctors. Others went to Cairo or Istanbul to pick up the latest in Muslim ideas. Many seized the opportunities created by empire to expand their trading communities around the Indian Ocean shore from Malaysia and Burma through the Gulf to East Africa. Many, too, as they formed half of the Indian army, found themselves fighting the empire's wars in South Africa or on the Western Front, but also against Muslims in Mesopotamia or on the North-West Frontier. But most important was the way in which improvements in sea travel enabled increasing numbers to perform the pilgrimage to Mecca. In good years tens of thousands performed their holy duty, some coming to settle in the Hijaz as scholars or traders.[27]

A second development of particular note was the construction of the Indo-European telegraph line by a British government which had been made powerfully aware of the strategic benefits of the telegraph in the Mutiny Uprising. From 1865 this made possible the rapid transmission

[26] Jacob M. Landau, *The Politics of Pan-Islam: Ideology and Organization* (Oxford, 1990).

[27] F. E. Peters, *The Hajj: The Muslim Pilgrimage to Mecca and the Holy Places* (Princeton, 1994), 266–362; C. Snouck Hurgronje, *Mekka in the Latter Part of the 19th Century* (London, 1931).

of news to and from the subcontinent and gave a massive stimulus to the growth of the Muslim press. Indeed, there was a symbiotic relationship between the growth of pan-Islamic consciousness and the growth of the press, which bears comparison with the relationship which Benedict Anderson has noted between the rapid march of print capitalism and the emergence of national consciousness in early modern Europe. The more Indian Muslims discovered about the fate of their brethren elsewhere in the Islamic world, the more they wished to know. When Russia and the Ottoman Empire went to war in the late 1870s, the press boomed. When the British invaded Egypt in 1882, it boomed again. When the Ottoman Empire entered its terminal stages from 1911 onwards, the press boomed as never before. Great newspapers flourished—Abul Kalam Azad's *al-Hilal*, Muhammad Ali's *Comrade*, Zafar Ali Khan's *Zamindar*.[28]

The new mental horizons were not expressed just in a thirst for news of the Muslim world. They were also expressed in the themes of some of the most successful novels of the time: Sarshar's (1845–1903) *Fasana-i Azad*, written against the background of the Russo-Turkish war of 1877–78 in which the eponymous hero goes off to the Crimean War to fight alongside the British and Muslims against the Russians,[29] or the many historical romances of Abdul Halim Sharar (1860–1926),[30] which were set in all parts of the Muslim world. The leading Muslim historian of the day, Shibli Numani (1857–1914) devoted his energies to reawakening interest in past Muslim lives and culture, especially the achievements of Arabs and Persians.[31] It was symptomatic that much of the more successful poetry had pan-Islamic themes; Hali's *Musaddas*, for instance, took the world by storm after its publication in 1879 by going quickly through six editions,[32] while a vaunting Islam-wide vision pervades the poetry of Muhammad Iqbal. When he wanted to emphasise the decline of Islam, he wrote a tearful poem about the end of Arab rule in Sicily; when he wanted to reflect on human creativity, he wrote his great poem on the mosque at Cordoba; moreover, he wrote much of his verse in Persian so as to reach an audience beyond the confines of India.[33]

Pan-Islamic concerns were also expressed in dress. The Turkish fez

[28] Robinson, *Separatism*, 186.

[29] Ralph Russell, 'The Development of the Modern Novel in Urdu', *The Novel in India: Its Birth and Development*, ed. T.W. Clark (London, 1970), 110–17. It should be noted, however, that Sarshar was a Hindu but his work was successful because of the Muslim market for work of this kind.

[30] Muhammad Sadiq, *A History of Urdu Literature*, 2nd edn. (Delhi, 1984), 430–35.

[31] *Ibid.*, 358–68.

[32] *Ibid.*, 347–51.

[33] *Ibid.*, 450.

was part of the early uniform of Aligarh, as the movement identified with the Ottoman reformers. Muslim scholars in Lucknow followed clothing fashions in Egypt, Syria and Iran.[34] While at the height of pan-Islamist activism in the second and third decades of the twentieth century, Western-educated Muslims made a point of shedding Western dress in favour of Muslim dress bearing distinctive Islamic symbols. Such was the level of identification with the wider Muslim world that men and women were willing to spend huge resources in time and money to further pan-Islamic causes. One, at least, was driven to contemplating suicide when he heard in 1912 that the Bulgarians had advanced to just 25 miles from Istanbul.[35]

The most powerful expression of the pan-Islamic dimension to Muslim identity came with the period which stretched from the Balkan Wars in 1911 through to the abolition of the Turkish caliphate in 1924. Great organisations were founded to carry forward pan-Islamic purposes: there was the Red Crescent Mission in 1912 of Indian Muslim volunteers to provide medical services to Turkish troops; there was the Anjuman-Khuddam-i Ka'aba founded in 1913 to protect and otherwise serve the holy places of Islam; there was the Indo-Ottoman Colonisation Society of 1914 which aimed to establish a pan-Islamic settlement at Adana; and there was the Central Khilafat Committee, founded in 1919 to protect the temporal and spiritual power of the Turkish caliphs. This last organisation swept aside the Muslim League and for two years dominated the Indian National Congress, playing the key role in enabling Gandhi to persuade it to adopt policies of non-cooperation with government. The Khilafat movement, as it came to be known, had mass appeal, attracting not only the Western-educated, traditionally educated, but also women and large numbers from the small towns and even the countryside. The movement went into decline from 1922, as the British arrested its leaders and the Turks moved towards abolishing the caliphate. Nevertheless, it was the most substantial mass movement in India since the Mutiny Uprising. And, even though it was profoundly bound up with Muslim unease about their position in India as well as being an expression of their opposition to British rule, it was also remarkable witness to their sensitivities to the Muslim world beyond the subcontinent.[36]

The failure of the Khilafat movement led to a reassessment of the pan-Islamic dimension of Muslim identity. Realising that there was no political salvation to be found in the wider Muslim world, Muslims

[34] Abdul Halim Sharar, *Lucknow: The Last Phase of an Oriental Culture*, trans. and ed. E. S. Harcourt and Fakhir Husain (London, 1975), 176.

[35] Mohamed Ali, *My Life: A Fragment*, ed. Afzal Iqbal (Lahore, 1942), 35–6.

[36] Gail Minault, *The Khilafat Movement: Religious Symbolism and Political Mobilization in India* (Columbia, 1982).

made their pan-Islamic identity subordinate to a Muslim national identity, or an Indian National identity, or a socialist or even a communist one. Nevertheless, pan-Islam remained an important sub-strand in thought and action. It was expressed in their concern over the future of Arabia in the 1920s, in their support for the Muslim Congress movement—the forerunner of the Islamic Conference Organisation, in their ambitions to create a pan-Islamic university, and in their enormous interest in the fate of the Arabs under the Palestine mandate. It was also expressed in the pan-Islamic missions of Indian Muslim organisations, whether the unorthodox Ahmadiyya or the orthodox Tablighi Jama'at.[37]

British empire and the gendering of Muslim identity

One of the more striking developments in Muslim identity under British rule is its acquisition of a female dimension. Traditionally, if we can risk a brief flirtation with essentialism, Islamic law divided society into public and private realms. The public realm was the key realm. This was the world of the adult man, the place where Islamic social action took place and where the community visibly existed. It was to be distinguished from the domestic world wherein existed the weak—women, children and slaves. Women in particular were seen as sources of *fitna*, social chaos, a threat to the moral order. The man's world was, therefore, the arena of Muslim identity. Here were the distinctive symbols of Muslim identity—mosque, madrasa and sufi shrine. Men, too, as Barbara Metcalf tells us, 'learned Arabic and conventionally carried distinctive Islamic names; women knew the regional languages and their names often evoked only beautiful qualities or flowers'.[38] But under British rule women become both guardians of the shrine of Islam in domestic space and moved into public space. Talk about women, indeed their talk about themselves, increasingly fills public space, and their behaviour and deportment come to range amongst the most potent signifiers of Islamicity. This was a consequence, in part of the new ideas of womanhood and the status of women which were carried to India by official and non-official Britons, and in part of the way in which women became the prime site at which the intersecting discourses of colonialism and modernity (at the social level) took place. The role

[37] Francis Robinson, 'Prophets without Honour: the Ahmadiyya', *History Today*, 40 (June 1990), 42–7; Mumtaz Ahmad, 'Tablighi Jama'at', *The Oxford Encyclopedia of the Modern Islamic World*, ed. John L. Esposito, 4, 165–9.

[38] Barbara D. Metcalf, 'Reading and Writing about Muslim Women in British India', *Forging Identities: Gender, Communities and the State*, ed. Zoya Hasan (Delhi, 1994), 3.

of women became a key issue for Muslims as they considered how they should progress in the world.[39]

From the early nineteenth century the British brought issues regarding women into the public arena with their campaigns against the burning of widows, female infanticide, child marriage and female seclusion. Once the issues of sati and female infanticide had been addressed by the state, missionaries made much of the running. In the case of Muslims their particular concerns were bringing education to women, attacking seclusion, and improving knowledge about health and provision for it. There were zenana missions, zenana clubs, and even magazines especially for women. The twentieth century saw the state increasingly concerned to create greater opportunities for women. By the 1930s there were 2.5m girls in schools, of which 0.5m were Muslims. Substantial attention was being paid to women's health issues, in particular to maternity. Muslim women, moreover, were gaining specific state recognition in the Child Marriage Restraint Act of 1929, the Shariat Application Act of 1937 and the Dissolution of Muslim Marriages Act of 1939. In the Government of India Act of 1935, furthermore, they were acknowledged as having political rights in seats specifically reserved for them. By the 1940s the public existence of Muslim women was widely acknowledged and the business of enlarging the space they occupied was now in the main the task of Muslims themselves.[40]

More important than the ideas that came to India from without in developing a female dimension to Muslim identity was the response of Muslim society to colonial rule. Reformist ulama, confronted with the power of non-Muslims in public space, transform their womenfolk from being threats to the proper conduct of Islamic society to being central transmitters of Islamic values and symbols of Islamic identity. The classic statement of this new position is Maulana Ashraf Ali Thanvi's *Bihishti Zewar*, written in the first decade of the twentieth century, whose volume sales since are probably second only to the Qur'ān. Thanvi's Muslim woman was to be able to read and write Urdu, perhaps to read Arabic, to fulfil her religious obligations, to keep her house in order, to bring up her children with due care, and to be able to sustain appropriate relations with those outside the household. She was regarded in being equal in responsibility and in human potential to men. But in a world in which the Muslim male might well be sullied by the compromises necessary to successful operation under colonial

[39] Gail Minault, *Secluded Scholars: Women's Education and Social Reform among Indian Muslims in the Late 19th and Early 20th Centuries* (Delhi, Oxford University Press, forthcoming); Azra Asghar Ali, 'The Emergence of Feminism Among Indian Muslim Women 1920–47' (Ph.D. thesis, University of London, 1996).

[40] Ali, 'Emergence of Feminism'.

rule, she and her sisters became key sustainers of Islamic values.[41]

In the 1930s Maulana Maududi, the founder of Islamic revivalism in India, gave a new twist to the central role of Muslim women. Whereas the reformist ulama had generated their new role for Muslim women, as far as can be ascertained without reference to Western models, Maududi, as the classic statement of his position *Purdah and the Status of Women in Islam* reveals, was obsessed by the freedoms permitted to women in the West.[42] He emphasises the natural superiority he saw Islam giving men over women. The task of women was to run the home and their education should be limited to what was necessary to enable them to do so; they should not think of leaving it very much. This home, moreover, in the context of British rule and the films, dress, music and morals that came with it, had a very special part to play: 'the *harim*', he declared, 'is the strongest fortress of the Islamic civilization, which was built for the reason that, if it ever suffered a reverse, it may then take refuge in it'.[43]

While for the reforming ulama and for Maududi women and their world became fortress Islam, for those Muslims who made Western standards a key criterion of progress the 'Western' education of their women and their entry into public space became increasingly a measure of their progress and modernity. This was very much part of the thinking of the Aligarh movement as it developed. If Syed Ahmed Khan, himself, thought that men deserved priority, this was less the concern of his followers, Nazir Ahmed, Hali, Sheikh Abdullah and Begum Shah Jahan of Bhopal. Their efforts led to the foundation of the Aligarh Girls School in 1906 which grew by 1937 to a college offering degree classes. Women in this circle and others carved out for themselves a literary space in short stories, novels and magazines such as *Khatun*, *Ismat* and *Tehzib un-Niswan*. They also began to organise in public. In 1914 the All-India Muslim Ladies Conference was founded. Then for two decades Muslim identities tended to be subsumed within the larger female identities of the leading women's organisations: the All-India Women's Conference, the Women's India Association and the National Council of Women of India. In the late 1930s, however, the common feminist front was destroyed by the communalisation of politics. In the campaign for Pakistan women played an active role on the streets.[44]

Colonial rule both brought Muslim women into public space and led

[41] Barbara D. Metcalf, *Perfecting Women: Maulana Ashraf 'Ali Thanawi's Bihishti Zewar: a Partial Translation with Commentary* (Berkeley, 1990).

[42] Abul A'la Maududi, *Purdah and the Status of Women in Islam* (New Delhi, 1974).

[43] Cited in Faisal Fatehali Devji, 'Gender and the Politics of Space: the Movement for Women's Reform, 1857–1900', in Hasan, ed., *Forging Identities*, 35–36.

[44] Ali, *Emergence of Feminism*, 259–381.

to some Muslims elevating them into the bulwark of their capacity to defend their civilisation. One way or another women came to represent a substantial part of the Muslim identity. For Muslims and for Westerners the different roles which women filled in their social orders became prime markers of the differences between them. Equally for Muslims the different freedoms they gave their women became key markers of the differences amongst themselves. Of course, this is not a situation confined to British India, but one experienced in societies throughout the Muslim world. It is one, however, which has come to bear particularly heavily on Muslim women in the independent states of India and Pakistan. In the former women have had to suffer, as in the Shah Bano case of 1986, because to subordinate Muslim personal law to the common civil code would mean an assault on Muslim identity. Indeed, for Hindu revivalists they have become the very epitome of what is wrong and bad about Muslim society.[45] In the latter women have had their freedoms sacrificed on the altar of the state's 'Islamic identity'.[46]

British empire and a new sense of individualism

A further development of no little interest was the emergence of a new sense of self, of growing individualism. Of course, this development was in very large part restricted to a small elite literate, for the most part, either in English or in Urdu, but it is nonetheless observable. Paradoxically, British rule and the Muslim movement of revival and reform both served to heighten forms of Islamic/Muslim identification, which in principle should have meant heightened willingness to subordinate individual will to that of the community, but they also created the conditions in which some Muslims increasingly came to assert their desire for individual fulfilment as against the broader claims of the Muslim community and its law. We see these developments in the emergence of Muslims who assert their right to interpret Islam for themselves, as opposed to accepting the interpretations of the ulama, through to the emergence of growing numbers of those who were Muslims merely by culture. In the later years of British rule such Muslims often held leftist views as progressive writers, socialists or communists. Amongst them there were also women concerned to raise and discuss in public issues which Muslims had traditionally kept concealed.[47]

[45] Paola Bacchetta, 'Communal Property/Sexual Property: on Representations of Muslim Women in a Hindu Nationalist Discourse', ed. in Hasan, *Forging Identities*, 188–225.

[46] Ayesha Jalal, 'The Convenience of Subservience: Women and the State of Pakistan', ed. Deniz Kandiyoti, *Women, Islam & the State* (Basingstoke, 1991), 77–114.

[47] Francis Robinson, 'Religious Change and the Self in Muslim South Asia since 1800', *South Asia*, XX, 1 (1997), 1–15.

In a broad sense the contributions of British rule to this development are not hard to discern. It was, of course, the prime channel through which the post-Enlightenment ideas of the West reached India—ideas of the rights of man and of personal fulfilment, vindications of earthly existence and earthly pleasures, and growing tendencies to celebrate not model lives but lives of all kinds. Such ideas were instinct in much Western literature and some of the institutions exported to South Asia. They were also represented in the behaviour and the attitudes of a good number, though certainly not all, of the colonial British. These, however, were not the only sources of incipient Indian Muslim individualism. There was the spread of capitalist modes of production with their erosion of old communal loyalties and their empowerment of individuals. There was the emergence of the modern state with its growing capacity to reach down to each individual citizen. There was also the changes in the technology of communication, in particular the adoption of print, which enabled Muslims to command knowledge as never before and also to begin, as never before, the exploration of their inner selves.[48]

It would be simple to see the emergence of individualism as the outcome of the projection of British power into India. But it is also the outcome of major changes in Islamic culture, which we have already characterised as the shift from 'other-worldly-' to 'this-worldly-' Islam. The willed or 'protestant' Islam, which was the central feature of 'this-worldly' religion, required Muslims to take action for Islam on earth if they were to achieved salvation. The link between salvation and work for Islam on earth, with no chance whatsoever of intercession, helped to set in motion processes that might underpin the development of a more individualistic Muslim self. Many of these processes bear comparison with those that led in the direction of individualism from the Reformation of Christian Europe.

Muslims were empowered by the thought that they and only they were responsible for shaping the earthly world. God gave his guidance, but they were the actors. The overwhelming responsibility placed on Muslims to act on earth runs through all manifestations of their movement of revival and reform. It is well expressed in the challenge which Iqbal makes man throw at God:

You created the night—I lit the lamp.
You created the clay—I moulded the cup.
You made the wilderness, mountains and forests
I cultivated the flowerbeds, parks and gardens.[49]

[48] *Ibid.*

[49] Translation of part of Iqbal's poem 'God's Talk with Man' in N. P. Ankiyev, 'The Doctrine of Personality', ed. H. Malik, *Iqbal: Poet-Philosopher of Pakistan* (New York, 1971), 274.

Muslims who will their religion make their own choices. The more they do so the more they affirm their own autonomy, their own individuality. Once Muslims move down this path, there must always be the possibility that they will choose to express their individuality by choosing not to believe. With the affirmation of the self, however achieved, there also comes the affirmation of the ordinary things of the self. A striking feature of twentieth-century Indo-Muslim culture has been the increasing valuing of ordinary human things: biographies of the Prophet talk about Him no longer as the Perfect Man but as the perfect family man; women have moved out of seclusion to demand that they and all things to do with them are given respect; even religious philosophers talk of finding God in all the mundane things of life. Then a willed religion had to be a self-conscious one. Muslims had to ask themselves regularly whether they had done all in their power to submit to God and carry out His will in the world. The ground was thus prepared for the 'inward turn'; the self's inner landscape increasingly lay open for exploration.

'This-worldly' Islam made man the chief actor on earth, made his life the prime centre of meaning, and made it clear that he chose whether to enjoin the good and forbid the evil or not. Although designed to reinforce Islam, it also underpinned a valuing of individual desire which might run counter to community requirement. The tension, potential or actual, between individual and community is acknowledged in much twentieth-century Muslim writing. Indeed, the tension is notably expressed in the stridency of some women's writing. It is a tension, moreover, which is broken as from time to time some Muslims burst through the bounds of community to embrace the world of unbelief and other beliefs that lies beyond. In such ways the long-term and unintended outcomes of Islamic reform might work together with influences channelled by the British from the West to bring various 'secular' strands to Indo-Muslim identities.[50]

The period of British rule saw the emergence of new strands of identity among Indian Muslims. For many their religious identity became their prime identity. For a good number, too, their religious identity became their political identity. Muslim imagination expanded to embrace the lives and fate of Muslims elsewhere in the world; for some this became an all-absorbing concern. Increasingly Muslim identity in public space acquired a feminine dimension. Moreover, individuals were beginning to emerge who wished to be treated as individuals; they rejected the demands made upon them by their 'community' and resisted all stereotyping from without. It should be clear that not all Muslims were

[50] Robinson, 'Religious Change', 13–15.

affected by all of these processes, and some by none of them. In sum the period of British rule saw a particular privileging of the religious dimension of Muslim identities, but at the same time it also saw other strands emerged which Muslims might choose to emphasise.

In each of the new strands of Muslim identity we have identified, we have discovered processes set going both by British rule and by religious and cultural change within Muslim society. These processes have been both independent of each other and have interacted with each other. Thus the sharpening of the distinction between Muslim and non-Muslim was both a consequence of British views of Indian society and of the impact of the Muslim movement of revival and reform; the development of a Muslim political identity was both a consequence of British policies towards Indian society and the fears of the north-Indian Muslim elite; the emergence of a pan-Islamic dimension to Muslim identity was in part the outcome of the new world of Muslim communication enabled by British empire but in part too of the values and fears of Indian Muslims; the gendering of Muslim identity owed its development in part to new ideas of women's rights brought to India from the West but also to the new and special role given to women as Muslims sought to respond to British rule; and the new individualism (of at this stage but a few) certainly derived some impetus from the manifold impact of British empire on Indian society but also was instinct in the path of individual responsibility which 'this-worldly' Islam set out for Muslims.

Finally, it may be instructive to place the Indo-Muslim experience in the wider context of British interactions with Muslims elsewhere in the empire. It is arguable that India's Muslims were unique in the intensity of their self-conscious identity as Muslims. They were notable in their development of a Muslim political identity. They were notable, certainly for a short period, in the intensity and impact of their pan-Islamic identity. On the other hand, they were less notable in the gendering of their identity and in the emergence of claims to individual expression as against community obligation. This said, India appears unusual in the extent to which these latter two processes were also underpinned by developments within Muslim society itself.

AM I MYSELF? IDENTITIES IN ZAIRE, THEN AND NOW

By Wyatt MacGaffey

READ 27 SEPTEMBER 1997 AT THE INSTITUTE OF HISTORICAL RESEARCH, LONDON

At the point where two cultures cross, truth and error dwell together.
Merleau-Ponty

IT is useful, for the sake of my topic today, that since I declared my title the Republic of Zaire (in May 1997) changed its identity, or at least, resumed one of its former names, the Democratic Republic of Congo. The change is also a nuisance, because the new/old name revives the likelihood of confusion not only with ex-Zaire's neighbour across the Zaire River, the Republic of Congo, but also with the people called BaKongo, who owned the name in the first place. I will try to explain all that in a moment.

In the 1950s, Erik Erikson described a fragile sense of identity as a peculiarly American problem.[1] His book *Childhood and Society* was widely adopted as a college text, with the result that large numbers of students who, until then, had generally known who they were, lost their identities and were said to be spending considerable amounts of time looking for them. This carelessness has now reached the proportions of a global epidemic, if we are to judge by the number of conferences called to discuss it. The curious anthropologist, observing this development, notices that most of the areas in which identity is reported to be an issue used to be called social structure: race, class, nationality, religion, gender and ethnicity, for example. Elsewhere in his notebook, however, he has already recorded that, in the opinion of many highly articulate natives, social structure has been unmasked as a modernist deceit, part of the apparatus of control imposed by an unidentified Them on the world in general. In the newly enlightened postmodern, individuals and groups are free to engage in social contracts and to define themselves as they choose.

The alleged newness of all this is suspect. 'Identity' as a topic is constructed in highly traditional terms, the debates concerning it torn between the wearisomely opposed perspectives of the social and the

[1] Erik Erikson, *Childhood and Society*, 2nd edn. (New York, 1963).

subjective. Is identity internal or external, mine or yours? Is it a sense of self or a political claim on others? If it is the property of a group, what happens to the identity of individual members? The assertion that individuals are or should be free continuously to negotiate their own identities clearly corresponds to the curious combination in the United States of resurgent political conservatism with what Jonathan Spencer calls 'sentimental radicalism'. The accompanying restatement of free-market ideology masks the real constraints on individual freedom that used to be recognised as social structure.[2]

No matter how much credit we want to give to the creativity, self-inventiveness and resistant capacities of individuals and groups, a serious account of identity in Zaire must refer to three historical moments or levels, each implicated in its successor. They are: the precolonial evolution of the region's cultural forms over many centuries, explicated most effectively by Jan Vansina;[3] the attempted substitution for these forms, by colonial science, of the image of the 'primitive African', in the minds and lives of both colonists and their subjects; and lastly, the practice and ideology of the postcolony, in this case Mobutu and Mobutuism. These are not historical periods, but moments of the past constantly relived in the present. I approach the question of subjective identity in Congo/Zaire from what I can say about its evolving social structure.

In 1483, Portuguese sailors arrived at the mouth of the Zaire River, making contact with the kingdom of Kongo, whose capital, Mbanza Kongo, lay inland in what is now northern Angola. The people of the kingdom have since been known to history as the BaKongo, speakers of the KiKongo language; the name Zaire, applied to the river, was a Portuguese corruption of the KiKongo word *nzadi*, 'large river.'

The kingdom was organised into a number of tributary provinces, each with an appointed governor, and was headed by a king selected by the representatives of noble families residing at the capital. As in Africa polities generally, the centre of power was better defined than the periphery; the indigenous term *bisi Kongo*, people of Kongo, referred to those who dwelt at Mbanza Kongo, as opposed to *bisi vata*, the inhabitants of villages. There is no evidence that the subjects of the king thought of themselves as a discrete nation with a name of its own; chroniclers in the early modern period called them simply 'the people of Kongo,' or 'the natives,' and modern historians have had to invent names for them. The term 'BaKongo' ('MuKongo' in the singular) is an invention of the colonial period, used only when one is speaking a

[2] Jonathan Spencer, 'Post-Colonialism and the Political Imagination', *Journal of the Royal Anthropological Institute*, 3 (1997).

[3] Jan Vansina, *Paths in the Rainforests* (Madison, 1991).

European language. No national boundary existed; the language, social structure and culture of the so-called BaKongo differed from those of the rest of Central Africa west of the Great Lakes only as variations on common themes.

In 1665, as the Atlantic slave trade intensified, Portuguese forces defeated those of the king of Kongo at the battle of Mbwila, reducing the kingdom and its capital to no more than an important village and commercial centre in a network of trade routes linking the interior and the coast. The provinces of the old kingdom disappeared, but at the coast broker states emerged, whose fortunes varied with the movement of trade and the rivalries of European trading powers. Inland, the Zaire not being navigable between the coast and Kinshasa, the BaKongo organised themselves to serve the Atlantic trade and the Central African economy as porters and traders, linking the coastal factories with the interior.

In 1885 the European powers allowed Léopold II, King of the Belgians, to take personal control of an empire occupying the whole, vast basin of the Zaire, called in English 'the Congo Free State.' 'Congo' came from the name given to the inhabitants of the erstwhile Kingdom of Kongo, now distributed through the three colonies of Angola, the Free State, and, north of Kinshasa, Moyen Congo, appropriated by the French. In 1908, after the Free State had become both an international scandal and a financial failure, its territory was taken over by Belgium as Belgian Congo.

The BaKongo are known to anthropology as a matrilineal people, meaning that every individual belongs to his or her mother's clan, a presumptively perpetual corporation recruited by descent in the female line. Clans are exogamous, and therefore every individual's father belongs to a different clan than his own. As a member of a particular clan, the individual has access to land, political support, and judicial representation; in short, the rights of citizenship. BaKongo believe that everybody occupies, or should occupy, an ascribed status, and should both benefit from the rights attached to it and respect its obligations. This model, however, describes how things are supposed to be rather than how they are or ever were.

In a kind of implicit collusion with their informants, but for reasons of their own, ethnographers of the colonial period inscribed a seriously misleading picture of Kongo society as clan-based and ascriptively rigid. They needed to be able to report the presence of hierarchical indigenous organisations that could be incorporated as the lowest level of the apparatus of control, and they were fascinated by the image of matrilineal society, which nineteenth-century anthropology had invented as the primitive predecessor to and antithesis of civilised society. In a cliché which held until the very end of the colonial period, colonial science described the African as identified with his clan and devoid of any sense of the kind of individualism supposed to explain the superiority of Europe.

In reality, Kongo society was and is much more complex. In the nineteenth century, if a man travelled, he needed to be able to list the names of his mother's, father's, father's father's and mother's father's clans, in all of which he could claim a relationship. Kongo clans are thus merely nodes in a network of interclan relations made up of some combination of marriage, patrifiliation and clientage; matrilineal descent is only one element of the social structure, and not necessarily the most significant.

Even this elaborated model is an ideal rather than an adequate description. The assured status it appears to offer to every individual was constantly vulnerable to the threat of enslavement at the hands, not only of strangers, but of precisely those relatives who supposedly guaranteed it. It was the right of his maternal uncles to sell him if they needed to raise money to pay fines, ritual fees, or for some other purpose; it was the duty of his father's and more remotely his grandfathers' clans to protect him from this fate, but in fact they might collude in the sale. Between the two poles of vulnerability, those of the slave and the fully free, many individuals whose parentage was mixed had less than the full complement of four clans to identify and support them. As a result, the clan was anything but solitary. As I have said, it was formally exogamous, but in practice in every clan there was at least one lineage of slaves who, as such, were unable to participate as first-class citizens in the management of their own affairs. Male and female slaves might be married off as their owners saw fit to free members of the clan, which accordingly was not matrilineal at all but cognatic; many of its members could trace their membership in both the male and the female line.

In short, the supposedly fixed and traditional social structure was in fact an arena of constant competition among individuals and groups. The ambiguities of descent were such that the 'slaves,' if they played their cards right, might be able to claim that they and not their supposed owners were in fact free. Most of village politics was devoted to such disputes, which continued well into the twentieth century despite the official abolition of slavery.[4] In this competition, the individual had constantly to defend his rights against what he saw as the deceitful self-seeking and jealousy of others.

The realities of political and economic competition, which constantly corroded their ideal model, were attributed by the BaKongo to the deceitful self-seeking and jealousy of anti-social individuals, who were

[4] Wyatt MacGaffey, *Custom and Government in the Lower Congo* (Los Angeles, 1970).

and are described in words which we translate as 'witchcraft.' Witches supposedly fly about at night to seize the souls of others whom they consume in mysterious feasts. This activity is called *dia bantu*, 'eating people,' and it is believed to explain why some people become ill while others do not, and how some become wealthy at the expense of their neighbours. We attempt to avoid our own sense of embarrassment in the face of these beliefs by describing them as metaphorical, but in the minds of BaKongo witchcraft is much the same thing as slavery; in both, the victims are deprived of life and liberty in order to enrich their masters by working for them or being given in exchange for commodities. The difference is that in slavery the transactions take place visibly, 'by day', whereas the operations of witchcraft supposedly take place in secret, 'at night'.

The discourse of witchcraft can be read more broadly as a theory of the legitimate and illegitimate uses of power; it includes something like a labour theory of value, explaining why some get rich by exploiting the labour of others. In the nineteenth century, commodities such as ivory and rubber, exported to Europe and the Americas, were said to be merely containers for the vital souls of Africans in transit to the plantations and factories of the other world.[5] This theory is a better account of economic relations between the developed and under-developed world than several well-known Western economic theories, and it remains dominant in the minds of Congolese despite massive changes in political conditions in the twentieth century.

The reality of competitive collusion, treachery and greed in ordinary life, dramatised in the language of witchcraft, induced a high degree of anxiety in personal experience; witchcraft beliefs may look like paranoia, but the enemies were real. Names recorded an individual's trials and escapes in a career of social competition. In the nineteenth century a MuKongo would be given in the course of his life a number of names, several of which—especially in the case of a man, whose political and ritual career was likely to be more eventful than a woman's—would refer to his successful participation in ritual procedures of accusation, divination, ordeal and initiation. None of these was his single, 'real' name; all were situational, each used by different people in appropriate social contexts.

A similar flexibility was provided by kinship terms, although in the colonial period the anthropological theory of kinship rested on the ethnocentric assumption that there is one right and proper term for any given relative of Ego, corresponding to his unique identity. The kinship terms a MuKongo used to specify his relationship to other people have been identified by anthropologists as conforming to the

[5] W. MacGaffey, *Modern Kongo Prophets* (Bloomington, 1983), 134–40.

Crow type, as is usually the case in so-called matrilineal societies. Crow usage treats all members of the clan as one person, with the result that a man's father's clan are all his 'fathers' and he calls 'child' the children of all male members of his own clan. He likewise calls anyone 'sibling' who stands in the same relationship as he does to any other clan, such as that of his father or mother's father. On an anthropologist's kinship diagram of Crow terms, Ego's siblings are identified with his parallel cousins on both sides, but his father's sister's child is called 'father' and his mother's brother's child is 'child.'

I could elaborate all this with helpful diagrams and bore you with analyses and qualifications, but instead I will spare us all the trouble. The apparent complexities are largely the output of anthropological conventions and ethnocentric habits of mind; real Kongo kinship is much simpler. The ethnocentrism lies in the assumption, ingrained in kinship theory, that there is one right and proper term for any given relative of Ego, corresponding to his unique identity. The whole notion of unique identity arises in Europe in conjunction with the development of the nation-state and of capitalism; in its anthropological projection, kinship diagrams and the analysis of 'kinship systems' take it for granted that Ego is unambiguously a son in relation to his mother, a nephew in relation to his uncle, and so on.

In reality, a MuKongo may trace a relationship to any other MuKongo and has a choice of paths through which to trace it; he can accordingly be father, grandfather, child, mother's brother or sibling, for example, to the target relative, and will choose the label that implies the kind of relationship politically or affectively most appropriate to his circumstances. His relatives have reciprocal options. I have startled more than one kinship expert by telling him that in Kongo your 'mother's brother' is not necessarily a member of your maternal clan. The guiding principle is that all those who, for whatever reason, can be considered to occupy the same social status are treated, in the context of the moment, as siblings, as 'one person'. With equal facility one could emphasise their categorical differentiation.

All this seems admirably postmodern. There is no fixed point; all individual identities are negotiable, within the practical limits imposed by the distribution of real power. Not that the MuKongo revels in his freedom. To him or her the idea of an autonomous, self-contained individual, able to enter into social contracts in pursuit of personal advantage, and of a society made up of such people, perfectly describes anarchy, or witchcraft rampant. The Kongo ideal, as I have shown, is preeminently social, emphasising ascribed duties and privileges; it was this model, rather than the reality, that colonial ethnographers were happy to inscribe.

Why bother to spend time on the peculiarities of one traditional society among the dozens identifiable in Zaire, most of them not even matrilineal? The question takes ethnic identities for granted and the answer should concern historians as much as anthropologists. The apparently numerous social systems of Central Africa are not independent iterations but local versions of one another, diverse outgrowths of a single historical process analogous to that which formed European societies.[6] If we look past the models of ascriptive descent in these societies, as advanced by their members and, for different reasons, by their ethnographers, we can see the 'matrilineal' and 'patrilineal' variations as much more similar in historical and sociological reality than we thought. Kongo is not a discrete entity with either an independent history or a distinctive social structure; it is a representative sample of the indigenous social system that prevails in most of Central Africa.

My last point here is that far too much of the study of Africa continues to accept a division between the traditional and the modern, writing off such forms of social organisation as I have been describing as negligible survivals, and the anthropological description of their distinctive features as mere exoticism. I would like to assert, on the contrary, that African institutions and knowledges continuously adapt to current requirements, are as much a part of today's events as others with which we are more familiar, and therefore should be taken just as seriously.[7] The epistemological paradox and problem is still that though African peoples are far away geographically they are nonetheless, as the Congolese scholar V. Y. Mudimbe puts it, 'imagined and rejected as the intimate and other side of the European thinking subject'.[8]

By 1910, the Belgians had managed to impose order on the zone of freewheeling banditry that was Leopold's Congo, although during the next 50 years one crisis after another required successive modifications of that order and stability remained an elusive goal. Local administrators intensified a process begun in the late nineteenth century by European travellers, that of classifying the people. The idea of a tribe as a discrete and manageable unit, preferably headed by a traditional ruler, was already central to European thinking about Africa. Ethnographic questionnaires were issued to missionaries, based on the assumption that there must be units, no matter how small, which worked like miniature nation-states. Inventories of tribes were drawn up, and psychological characteristics assigned to them along with places in the overall economy (for example, 'The Bakongo are a mild and inoffensive race; they have

[6] Vansina, *Paths*; for this argument as applied to Melanesia, see Marilyn Strathern, *The Gender of the Gift* (Berkeley, 1988), 340–3.

[7] Peter Geschiere, *The Modernity of Witchcraft* (Charlottesville, 1997).

[8] V. Y. Mudimbe, *The Idea of Africa* (Bloomington, 1994).

few vices, and their virtues are of a negative order').[9] Districts were designated, chiefs appointed, censuses conducted; it was essential to the *mise en valeur* of the colony to reckon the number of 'healthy adult males,' to record the result of these inquiries and to inscribe them as unique labels on the personalities of individuals. Congolese acquired identity cards labelling them as discrete entities liable to obligatory employment, taxation, and judicial punishment; they also became members of a given tribe, even though in quite a few cases they did not speak the appropriate language and had never lived in their villages of origin. Lastly, they were constantly told that their life situation was the inevitable consequence of their collective primitiveness and personally infantile character.

The term BaKongo, once restricted to those who lived south of the Congo River within reach of Mbanza Kongo, was generalised to include all those who spoke the KiKongo language, itself a somewhat arbitrary grouping of several dialects. Ethnographers divided this new entity into sub-tribes in an effort to fix in time and space the apparent variations of culture, language and social structure, themselves attributed to supposed 'migrations' and 'conquests' which implicitly mirrored the European invasion. The colonial literature of the period is preoccupied with physical marks such as tooth-chipping and 'tattoos' (meaning scarification) which might serve to identify these imagined subtribes.[10] Later on, physical anthropologists attempted to refine these indices by measuring head shape, degrees of prognathism, and thickness of lips, all this in total disregard of the obvious fact that this population had mingled for centuries with Europeans and foreign Africans on the coast and with slave imports from the interior. It was necessary to deny history and fix identity in the realm of the physical.

Members of the Kongo elite became aware of their new collective designation at this time, and understood that it already pitted them against similarly designated 'tribes' in the framework of the colony. In 1910 Kavuna Simon, a Protestant evangelist writing in the mission bulletin, urged his compatriots to respect the KiKongo language, but first he had to explain to his readers who 'the BaKongo' were, and what was the KiKongo they were to respect. To this day, BaKongo have an uncertain sense of their collective identity and tend to think of themselves primarily as from the Mayombe, Manianga, or Ntandu districts. Nevertheless, in the context of national politics, the new ethnic identities became effective realities.

The new order was disrupted by World War I and after that by a

[9] Herbert Ward, *Five Years with the Congo Cannibals* (New York, 1890), 47.

[10] 'The Babwende are a strong, hardy race. Their backs and abdomens are profusely decorated with incisions in the flesh.' *Ibid.*, 49.

new policy containing elements of indirect rule, borrowed from Lord Lugard, which in effect replaced a potentially assimilationist practice with one that insisted on the separation of races. The BaKongo now discovered that they were black, meaning that no matter how Christian they were, how educated they became or how hard they worked, they could not hope to take their place beside white people.[11] Their reactions included the highly disruptive religious movement led by the Kongo prophet Simon Kimbangu and a less-known but at the time equally alarming movement called the Congomen, led by a Protestant business-man, André Yengo, which supported what we would now call the civil rights of Africans; it was denounced as a terrorist organisation.

From the outset, Belgian Congo's incipient apartheid contradicted the evolving social and economic facts, with bizarre results. So many Africans had already been torn loose from their former way of life to supply labour to the armed forces and to commercial and industrial enterprises that the administration was forced to create so-called 'extra-customary' or non-traditional units of local government which were also reserves of the new kinds of labour required by colonial enterprises. Mudimbe, now teaching at Duke and Stanford Universities in the United States, grew up in such an environment, controlled by the Union Minière of Kantanga. As a boy he spoke Songhye to his father, Luba to his mother, Swahili to his companions and French to his teachers.[12]

This configuration was a product of the way Belgian Congo was organised, in the social pluralism it convoked and in the designation of the entities themselves. The languages marked a hierarchy built into the colonial system: Luba and Songhye were the languages of 'primitives,' Swahili was the lingua franca of those whom the colonial regime was to elevate, and French was the language of the civilised. The *centres extra-coutumiers* were the site of an experiment intended to accelerate evolution by inculcating Christianity, European family patterns, and the discipline of clock-time. In reality, the societies called primitive were entirely contemporaneous products of history, and that which called itself civilised was itself an African society shaped by that same history into forms not found in Europe. Congolese in the twentieth century were deprived of control over all but minor matters in their lives, their labour had been redirected to new kinds of production, and they had been handed a fictitious model of their own, supposedly 'traditional', society in which their masters believed.

As part of the apparatus of control, the Belgians were remarkably

[11] Congolese did not adopt the sense of an essential or 'genetic' difference between races that has been common sense in the West since the mid-nineteenth century.

[12] V. Y. Mudimbe, *Les Corps glorieux des Mots et des Etres* (Paris, 1994), 30.

successful in keeping their subjects isolated from the rest of the world; there were no intellectuals meeting with their peers from other African countries in Brussels as there were in London or Paris, no negritude movement, no Jomo Kenyatta, no Seretse Khama, no J. B. Danquah. In World War II Belgium was overrun by the Germans, to whom some Congolese looked for their liberation. Others served in the armed forces in distant countries. Disturbing new ideas circulated, and influential Catholic clergy warned that African aspirations demanded some attention. Ethnic associations led by the Alliance des Bakongo (ABAKO) adopted increasingly political programmes. The ABAKO manifesto of 1950 repeated, without knowing it, Kavuna Simon's call of forty years before, to respect the KiKongo language, and it did so in a similar context of emerging competition between invented ethnicities. The government introduced certificates of civilised status for which suitable Africans could apply; in the 1950s, it began to admit Africans to secondary education for the first time.[13] Concurrently with these developments, the image of the African as childlike savage was constantly publicised; in 1956, when a Belgian socialist suggested that independence might come in 30 years, he was widely ridiculed.

In 1960 Belgian Congo became independent as 'the Democratic Republic of Congo'. At the same time the French colony of Moyen Congo, its capital Brazzaville, also became independent as 'the People's Republic of Congo'. The two became known by the names of their respective capitals as Congo-Léopoldville and Congo-Brazzaville, names which incorporated those of their respective European founders. Because government office at the national or provincial level was the only major source of wealth, control of it was the consuming object of politics. The number of provinces increased from 6 to 21 to provide more jobs for the ambitious, and governments rose and fell to allow those temporarily out of power to invest their gains in business while others took their turn at the trough. The Americans, Russians, French and Belgians pulled strings and distributed more wealth.

Joseph Mobutu, a client of the CIA, took power in 1965 to general acclaim. He was credited with putting down the rebellion that had taken over two-thirds of the country. More importantly, he promised firm government and an end to self-seeking politics. Mobutu was an effective moderniser, though his reforms often failed in their manifest purpose and were indeed motivated by sordid considerations. He created a new sense of national identity transcending the regional and ethnic, in spite of—and indeed partly because of—the fact that he stayed in power by playing off one ethnic group against another at

[13] V. Y. Mudimbe, 'La culture', in *Du Congo au Zaire 1960–1980: essai de bilan*, ed. J. Vanderlinden (Brussels, n.d.), 310–98.

every level. Mobutu renamed the country 'Zaire' in October 1971; 'Congo' was too closely identified with a particular ethnic group, which was moreover a powerful source of potential opposition. Zairian cities were given African names, though they did not thereby become any less European; Zairois were obliged to abandon their baptismal names in favour of ones drawn from the languages and traditions of their ancestors, and to don a new and supposedly more appropriate national costume which owed more to Communist China than to Africa. Mobutu created a single party, the Mouvement National de la Révolution; presiding over cabinet meetings with his feet on a leopardskin, he declared himself to be a 'Bantu chief' rather than a European monarch. The huge statue of Henry Morton Stanley beckoning Europeans into the interior was sawn off at the ankles, leaving two feet on the pedestal; it came to be known as *le monument Bata*, from the name of the shoe company. For a short time, 'Zairois' had a resonance that 'Congolais' never had, something to be proud of.

Given the continuing hold that colonial teaching about their evolutionary backwardness had on the minds of even educated Zairois, the new line was certainly needed, as Mabika Kalanda had said in a book about mental decolonisation from which Mobutu borrowed the idea.[14] To the end, the official voices of Belgian Congo described Congolese as childlike, bound by 'the shackles of the clannish collectivity', pre-political, pre-economic and pre-moral. Colonial science, itself supposedly a token and measure of superior civilisation, presented to every African schoolboy, every convert, every active and thoughtful individual, a fundamentally erroneous view of his society and a relentlessly derogatory view of himself, in support of a system which Belgian liberals denounced as much more severely segregated than one could find in French or British Africa.[15]

For Mobutu, however, his authenticity campaign was, as much as anything, an attack on the Catholic Church, the only body in the country capable of mobilising effective political resistance. The official style of Zaire deployed the grandiose rhetoric of 'the post-colony,' devastatingly documented by Achille Mbembe, and accompanied it with an obscenity of conspicuous consumption on the part of the bandits who had appropriated the state.[16] In the case of Mobutu, and no doubt others, this behaviour was at least in part a resentful reaction

[14] Mabika Kalanda, *La Remise en question: base de la décolonisation mentale* (Brussels, 1967).

[15] The stock images in the colonial mythology included the Slave, the Cannibal, the Chief, the Sorcerer and the Tribe; in the context of *la mission civilisatrice* they included the Soldier, the Evolué, the Boy, the Patient, the Black, the Mother, the Pickaninny, Nudity and the Rhythmic Sense. Coopération par l'Education et la Culture, *Zaire 1885–1985: cent ans de regards belges* (Brussels, 1985), 18–19.

[16] Achille Mbembe, 'Notes on the Postcolony', *Africa* 62 (1992).

to the frustrations and indignities of their experiences under colonial rule; he now wanted it all. It is interesting to note, albeit in passing, that this style is characteristic of francophone Africa, and is regarded by anglophones 'with considerable distaste,' even in Cameroon, from which Mbembe writes.[17]

In 1972 the first cohort of intellectuals with doctorates from various foreign countries, including Mudimbe, returned to Zaire with new perspectives as well as new skills which they found they could not put to use. The repressive aspects of the regime, its failure to provide basic services with any regularity, and increasing favouritism shown to representatives of the President's own home region in the northwest were beginning to be recognised and resented. In private, Christian names continued in use; Mudimbe adopted a pair of generic African words with the same initial consonants, 'V. Y.,' as his baptismal names. Mobutu's policy of 'cultural authenticity' came to be a sour joke. As Mudimbe has written, the irony was that Africans internalised the signs invented for their conquest. 'We speak of our being, our existence, our liberty, in terms produced to objectify us, although to be sure we reverse the signs; our "barbarism" is now "traditional civilisation," our "paganism" has become "ancestral religion".'[18] By 1980, it was hard to find anyone with a good word for the regime, although respect for the monuments and symbols of national identity remained almost reverential, at least among the general population. Talk of an eventual return to the name 'Congo' began to be heard among the elite.

In Zaire, nothing worked as one would expect it to work in a modern state, but that did not mean that it was simply a scene of disorder. Its goals were those of an organised kleptocracy, and for a while it met them with some efficiency. 'Corruption' was a system in which everybody was paid off who needed to be paid off, and in which a large proportion of the public had a share one way or another. Though stronger at the centre than at the periphery, it was moreover a national system through which the major politicians, professors, military personnel and businessmen circulated, and in which, ultimately, everybody was subject to the arbitrary generosity or savagery of 'the Guide.' The language of authenticity, in all its irony, was complemented and subverted by the internationally famous popular music of Kinshasa, much of it expressing in transparent codes the real lives and experiences everybody shared. The government and the musicians together made Lingala a national language, to the point that younger generations of the BaKongo, no less, no longer speak anything else.

[17] Michael Rowlands, 'Inconsistent Temporalities in a Nation-space', in *Worlds Apart: Modernity through the Prism of the Local*, ed. D. Miller (1995), 23–42.

[18] Mudimbe, *The Idea*, 140.

The centralising and homogenising practice of the regime continued in important respects the policies of Belgian Congo, as Congolese fully recognised. Colonial rule supposedly ended both slavery and witchcraft; the Second Republic, officially at least, abolished all indigenous forms of law, kinship, marriage and land tenure in an effort to destroy the colonial legacy of social pluralism.[19] To claim a position as a nation among nations inevitably meant subscribing to a particular sense not only of nationhood but of culture and presence which most Zairois found alienating. Local officials attending a meeting in Kisangani one day in 1980, men of small education for whom even the government's lingua franca, Lingala, was a foreign language, found themselves listening to the music of Vivaldi; that was tolerable because, after all, the meeting was being held at the French cultural centre, but it was something else for the Governor of the Region, who had convened the meeting, to exclaim as he walked in, 'Ah! *The Seasons*! Don't turn it off!' and afterwards to harangue the assembly on their personal failings.

None of the official 'authenticity' had much to do with African tradition or the lived realities of indigenous society in either its nineteenth- or twentieth-century form. Paradoxically, however, as Mobutu steadily destroyed the country's official institutions, people at all levels came to rely almost entirely on forms of social organisation and belief which he had officially abolished. In practice, indigenous institutions such as kinship and divination kept both individuals and local committees going; even in Kinshasa people now depend on what an anthropologist has described as the 'villagisation' of the city.[20] The constant negotiation required to find the means of survival caused the postcolonial subject, as Mbembe puts it, to mobilise 'not just a single identity but several fluid identities which, by their very nature, must be constantly revised in order to achieve maximum instrumentality',[21] but this flexibility is, as I have tried to show, an ancient skill in Central Africa.

Besides the social skills, the ideological tools of the village took over the nation. In the face of a hypocritical kleptocracy, the discourse of witchcraft and slavery provided Congolese with a sophisticated medium to discuss personal and political success and failure at all levels. The association between 'wealth' and 'eating,' which linguistic studies show to be centuries old, dominates the political culture of Zaire and elsewhere in sub-Saharan Africa.[22] It is a premiss of what Jean-François

[19] W. MacGaffey, 'The Policy of National Integration in Zaire', *Journal of Modern African Studies* 20 (1982), 87–105.

[20] René Devisch, '"Pillaging Jesus": Healing Churches and the Villagisation of Kinshasa', *Africa* 66 (1996), 555–86.

[21] Mbembe, 'Postcolony', 5.

[22] M. Rowlands and J.-P. Warnier, 'Sorcery, Power and the Modern State in Cameroon',

Bayart calls 'the politics of the belly' that people admired for their success achieve it by eating the substance of others; 'eating' is polysemous: it means not only to feed oneself, not at all easy in an economy of poverty, wracked by 'structural adjustment,' but also 'to accumulate, exploit, attack, conquer or kill by witchcraft'.[23]

Despite journalistic clichés about Mobutu's 'brutal dictatorship', Zaire could not realistically be described in terms of a simple opposition between oppressors and oppressed. 'Witchcraft', describing the uses as well as the abuses of power, is a medium of political negotiation and accommodation appropriate to the remarkable bargaining processes that went on not only between Mobutu and influential sectors of the society but at every level in Zairian villages and towns. Filip de Boeck, in a vivid account of contemporary Zaire, argues (like Mbembe) that both the current crisis and responses to it are 'to some extent rooted in a moral, social and symbolic matrix that reaches beyond the fractures inflicted by the postcolonial world and the myth of modernity, and that also draws from precolonial sources.' This process is mediated not only by indigenous conceptions of power but also by rituals of chiefship, kinship, tributary payment and divination.[24]

Stories widely circulated in the press as well as by word of mouth accused Mobutu of strengthening his person and his regime by witchcraft and by strange techniques obtained from all over the world. It was believed that he was obliged to hand over the souls of citizens to pay for these secrets and, for example, for the new airport at Kisangani. In popular opinion, the death of prominent politicians was never 'natural', but always the result of some kind of internecine sorcery. In 1992–3, when there appeared to be a chance of constitutional reform and an end to dictatorship, politicians who had profited for decades from the Mobutu system joined prayer groups in which they confessed to having been witches, to having eaten people, participated in blood sacrifices, etc. Their claim was that as *reformed* witches they were particularly competent to form a new government.

Towards the end of 1996, some commentators were surprised that in Kinshasa crowds were demonstrating in favour of Mobutu, or at least in reaction *against* Laurent Kabila, whose military successes in eastern Zaire were beginning to seem serious. The crowds would have been happy to see Mobutu replaced, but not by a foreign army led by

Man 23 (1988) 118–32. Michael Schatzberg, 'Power, Legitimacy and "Democratisation" in Africa', *Africa* 63 (1993), 445–61.

[23] J.-F. Bayart, *The State in Africa: the Politics of the Belly* (1993), 269.

[24] Filip de Boeck, 'Postcolonialism, Power and Identity: Local and Global Perspectives from Zaire', in *Postcolonial Identities in Africa*, eds. R. Werbner and T. Ranger (1996). W. MacGaffey, 'Religion, Class and Social Pluralism in Zaire', *Canadian Journal of African Studies* 24 (1990), 249–64.

a man who might as well have been a foreigner, since he had not been a participant during the 1990s in the long and futile negotiations to develop a new, democratic constitution. Other commentators assumed that with Mobutu gone, Zaire would break into separate countries. It is easy to underestimate the strength of national sentiment in Zaire, formed precisely by the experience of Mobutu.[25] The new Democratic Republic of Congo, announced in May 1997 as Mobutu fled the country, reverts in name only to the condition of its predecessor and namesake.

During the Mobutu years, the ruling class, exiled academics and politicians, and business men and women of every level and kind developed extensive experience of the rest of the world, whether in Brussels, Paris, Québec, London, South Africa or the United States, to name only the principal centres of the Zairian diaspora. The naïveté characteristic of the 1960s as a result of the isolation imposed by Belgian Congo has been replaced by extensive knowledge of the international operations of the World Bank, Swiss banks, the State Department, the French and Belgian governments, South African security forces, CNN, Amnesty International, and the international civil rights movement. The potential labour force now includes considerable numbers of highly trained people. Their experiences at home and abroad, and the contacts they have developed, contributed directly to the struggle for democracy at home. The leader of that struggle, Etienne Tshisekedi, is a national and not simply a regional or ethnic hero. It would be rash to predict the future, but the signs are that Kabila does not sufficiently recognise the positive changes that have reconstructed Congolese identity. A change of name does not permit one to relive history. Nor should one assume that any eventual 'democracy' will conform to a familiar model. 'Democracy' does not mean the same to Congolese as it does to the State Department; they set no great store by 'free and fair democratic elections' and have a low opinion of political parties, which they see (with reason) as self-serving factions. They hope to have a chief of state who will listen to the people, deal equitably with their problems, and distribute good things; they do not much care how he gets the job. Mobutu, after all, was popular at first precisely because he suppressed 'politics' and promised benevolent dictatorship.

The three historical moments or levels that I said were essential to Zairian identity are recognisable in three genres of popular painting current during the 1970s. Under Mobutu, until just before the end, political expression in words was severely censored, but painters, like popular singers, found ways to comment guardedly and ironically on the

[25] Mobutuism may have brought about 'a sociological complex that could last longer than we might believe'. Mudimbe, *The Idea*, 146.

times. Johannes Fabian's title for his study of these genres, *Remembering the Present*, reflects his conclusion from discussions with painters and their customers that the pictures 'served as "reminders" of past experiences and present predicaments'.[26] In the first genre, *pays des ancêtres*, idyllic village scenes with canoes and palm trees report not simply or even primarily the nostalgia of the bourgeois purchasers of such paintings for an idealised past but a problematic vision of their 'Africanity' as represented in colonial ideology and in the Mobutuist doctrine of cultural 'authenticity'. '[They] point to a rural past that is distinct from life in cities but nonetheless present or coexistent, much as the dead are coexistent with the living. The village and the bush ... are invoked as foundations on which present life and consciousness grow, or should grow.' The model for these paintings, however, is to be found in illustrations to books of African travel and adventure published at the turn of the century.[27] The second genre, *colonie belge*, showing the flogging of Africans at a colonial military post, implied that under Mobutu not much had changed; these paintings, as Bogumil Jewsiewicki says, 'cast themselves as drawn from memories of colonial days, but they actually address current political issues'.[28] In the third genre, *la sirène*, the mermaid who represents the temptations of lust and wealth, is usually white because she is not only an icon of corrupt modernity but an indigenous water-spirit. The pleasures she offers are available through the treacherous exchanges of sorcery; connected to all three levels of memory, she serves, in Fabian's words, as 'a "totalising symbol" of urban existence'.[29] In all three genres the painter glances over his shoulder, so to speak, at the West; the pictorial model, taken from the West, 'seems to be accepted as a legitimate language for the painter, as French words are in political speech'.[30] The body of the mermaid has evolved rapidly from that found in traditional sculptures into conformity with the shape favoured by Western pornography.

At a loftier and more articulate level, Mudimbe's memoir of the fifty years of his experiences as a colonised African subject offers a similar ironic and questioning commentary. Its title, *Les Corps glorieux des mots et des êtres*, 'The transfiguration of words and beings,' refers to a tenet of Catholic theology but also to Merleau-Ponty's ideas about the embodiedness of knowledge and therefore the difficulty of knowing

[26] Johannes Fabian, *Remembering the Present: Painting and Popular History in Zaire* (Berkeley, 1996), 195.

[27] For example, Ward, *Five Years*, 106; as Ward himself says, ironically, 'A mighty river, dusky savages and graceful palms, all lit up by a fierce tropical sun' (*Five Years*, 30).

[28] Bogumil Jewsiewicki, 'Painting in Zaire: from the Invention of the West to the Representation of the Social Self', in *Africa Explores*, ed. S. Vogel (New York, 1991), 149.

[29] Fabian, *Remembering*, 197.

[30] Jewsiewicki, 'Painting', 131.

oneself as others know us. Rhetorically he asks, 'Am I myself?' His work is full of references to gaps (*l'écart*), cleavages and distorting distances, and to the alienating effect on African subjects of objectifying discourses; in the end he is unable, perhaps quite rightly, to define an essential identity even for himself.

Some commentators have asserted that the present is exceptionally a time of change, but with respect to the history of Africa, Central Africa in particular, it is hard to identify any period marked by stability.[31] In the 1950s, Erik Erikson described a fragile sense of identity as a peculiarly American problem. He thought that Americans were especially vulnerable to identity problems because the United States 'subjects its inhabitants to more extreme contrasts and abrupt changes during a lifetime or a generation than is normally the case with other great nations'.[32] It is ironic, surely, that we now look back on the time when Erikson was writing as one of exceptional stability and confidence.

[31] T. O. Ranger, 'The Invention of Tradition Revisited: the Case of Colonial Africa', in *Legitimacy and the State in Twentieth-Century Africa*, eds. T. Ranger and O. Vaughan (1993), 62–111.

[32] Erikson, *Childhood*, 285.

IDENTITY, ENLIGHTENMENT AND POLITICAL DISSENT IN LATE COLONIAL SPANISH AMERICA

By Anthony McFarlane

READ 27 SEPTEMBER 1997 AT THE INSTITUTE OF HISTORICAL RESEARCH, LONDON

DURING the long crisis of the Spanish empire between 1810 and 1825, the creole leaders of Spanish American independence asserted a new identity for the citizens of the states which they sought to establish, calling them 'Americanos'. This general title was paralleled and often supplanted by other political neologisms, as movements for independence and new polities took shape in the various territories of Spanish America. In New Spain, the insurgents who fought against royalist government during the decade after 1810 tried to rally fellow 'Mexicans' to a common cause; at independence in 1821, the creole political leadership created a 'Mexican empire', the title of which, with its reference to the Aztec empire which had preceded Spain's conquest, was designed to evoke a 'national' history shared by all members of Mexican society. In South America, the leaders of the new republics also sought to promote patriotic feelings for territories which had been converted from administrative units of Spanish government into independent states. Thus, San Martín and O'Higgins convoked 'Chileans' to the cause of independence in the old Captaincy-General of Chile; shortly afterwards and with notably less success, San Martín called upon 'Peruvians' to throw off Spanish rule. Bolívar was, likewise, to call 'Colombians' to his banner in the erstwhile Viceroyalty of New Granada, before advancing south to liberate Peru in the name of 'Peruvians', and Upper Peru in the name of 'Bolivians', where the Republic which his military feats and political vision made possible was named after him.

Here, it seems, were signs of Latin American nationalism. Indeed, one of principal theses in Benedict Anderson's influential work on nationalism is that its origins are found in the New World during the late eighteenth and early nineteenth centuries, and not in Europe, as Eurocentric analysts have for so long insisted.[1] Anderson acknowledges that the traditional explanations of the rise of nationalism do not work

[1] Benedict Anderson, *Imagined Communities: Reflections on the Origin and Spread of Nationalism* (2nd ed., London and New York, 1991), xiii.

for Latin America: language was not an issue, the independence movements did not stem from the middle classes, nor bring mobilisation of the lower classes. Nonetheless, he insists that Latin American independence were national independence movements because, in colonial provinces which usually contained large, lower-class, non-Spanish-speaking populations, the creoles who led the movements against Spain 'consciously redefined these populations as fellow-nationals'.[2] Why, Anderson asks, were conceptions of the nation found so early among the creole communities of Spanish America, and why did the Spanish empire quickly break down into a number of separate states?

Proceeding from his definition of the nation as an 'imagined political community—and imagined as both inherently limited and sovereign',[3] Anderson argues that, prior to independence, creoles throughout the different regions of Spanish America had formed an image of their communities that was to be conducive to the construction of nation-states. In his view, creoles were able to conceive of national communities because their long experience of Spanish colonial rule had imbued them with a sense of identity based in specific territories. In the first place, the experience of creole colonial functionaries had long fostered a sense of separate identity, different from that of metropolitan Spaniards and linked to the particular territories in which creoles served as officials; secondly, the spread of print-capitalism to the colonies during the late eighteenth century provided the creoles with another, stronger means of envisaging themselves as communities separate from Spain, while also providing a medium for inventing and experiencing a 'public' interest. From here, Anderson argues, it was a short step to claim that these communities should be sovereign, and the occasion arose when the Spanish monarchy collapsed under the pressures of revolution and war in Europe. This is not, of course, intended as an explanation of the origins of independence movements in Spanish America; it aims, rather, to explain why the Spanish American empire divided into states which, because they were based on notions of nationality, proved to be 'emotionally plausible and politically viable'.[4] Nonetheless, because Anderson insists that the construction of creole identity was a crucial element in shaping Spanish American independence, his arguments provide a good starting-point for discussing the issues considered in this paper: namely, the origins and character of creole identity under Spanish rule, its relationship to political change before independence, and its contribution to shaping national states after independence.

[2] *Ibid.*, 50.
[3] *Ibid.*, 6.
[4] *Ibid.*, 47–65.

Consider, first, Anderson's observation that the experience of creole officials—what he calls the 'pilgrimages of creole functionaries'—nurtured a sense of creole identity that was not only different from that of metropolitan Spaniards but also associated with the territory created by the administrative entity within which creole officials moved. This is a very useful observation. For it goes beyond the conventional view that creole desire to hold offices simply generated a negative identity which derived its meaning solely from resentment against metropolitan Spaniards, and focuses instead on the way in which the creole experience of office-holding within a confined territory provided a positive identification with a specific territorial community, and thus later allowed Spanish administrative units to be reconceptualised as American 'fatherlands' capable of commanding an emotional attachment and loyalty. It is, however, also an oversimplified and perhaps misleading account of the ways in which creole cultural identity was both formed and fixed to a particular territory. The confinement of creoles to lateral movement within an official habitat that was territorially cramped (compared to the wider horizons of transient metropolitan officials who moved from colony to colony, and colony back to metropolis) was by no means the sole, nor even the most important, way in which creoles found their identity and identified with particular territories. As David Brading and others have shown, the development of 'creole patriotism' had deeper, more complex origins and characteristics, arising from the fundamental dualism of American identity—European or native—that stemmed from the Spanish conquest of indigenous peoples.[5]

The sense of cultural difference between Spaniards in America and those in Europe was present from the first years of settlement. It arose, first, from the cultural diversity of Spain itself, as Spanish immigrants brought to America their regional and cultural identities as Galicians, Catalans, Aragonese, Navarrese, Andalusians and so on. Indeed, it has even been said that the early sixteenth-century chronicles and missionary works on Indian cultures were 'creole in spirit' because they expressed the difference felt by those of long residence and experience in the New World from newly arrived Europeans. To be 'creole' in this early American world was not necessarily to be born in America, but simply to be physically and culturally acclimatised to it. The conquerers' sense of difference from Europeans was, moreover, underpinned by their view of themselves as the architects of new kingdoms who deserved to be treated as a feudal aristocracy comparable to that of Spain, in return for their services to the crown in bringing new lands under its sovereignty. The disappearance of the conquest elite eroded such claims,

[5] For an early, key essay on creole patriotism, see David A. Brading, *Los orígenes del nacionalismo mexicano* (Mexico, 1978).

but creole elites continued to see themselves as landed nobles who, as the societies and economies in which they lived developed in ways which set them apart from Spain, had rights to political autonomy in their own lands.[6]

The creole elites' sense of affinity with a particular land and *patria* was both expressed and reinforced by creole writers who sought to meet creole needs for a cultural personality that was separate from, but comparable to that of Spain. Throughout Spanish America, especially in Mexico, a tradition of creole writing emerged during the seventeenth and eighteenth centuries to meet this need, through the construction of histories which mythologised the Indian past and the creation of religious cults which claimed that America and its peoples held a special place in the plans of Divine Providence.[7] Creoles also drew on Hispanic political traditions to advance their claims to parity within the Spanish world by drawing on the conception, derived from the theory and practice of government in Habsburg Spain, of the Spanish monarchy as a cluster of kingdoms which were united under a single, Catholic king, but which retained their own identities and forms of government. Thus, Castile, Aragon, the Netherlands and so on were regarded as separate kingdoms, each with a distinctive history and culture, different customs, laws and *fueros*, and a territorial nobility with claims to govern under the overarching sovereignty of the king.[8] This image of the Spanish monarchy as a combination of kingdoms was used by the American elites to stake their own claims to identity and autonomy. They professed to be nobles descended from the Spanish conquerers and settlers whose services to the crown had made possible the creation of American kingdoms—in Peru, New Granada, Quito, Chile and so on—and, by the same token, they claimed rights to hold the offices of Church and State in the lands brought under Spanish rule by their forebears. These ideas enabled American Spaniards to see themselves as part of the Spanish 'nation', but distinct from it. They were politically separate from Spain's kingdoms in Europe, but united by political ties to the same monarch; their social milieux and customs made them culturally different from Spain, but shared ethnicity, language and religion also bound them to the mother country.

[6] Anthony Pagden, 'Identity Formation in Spanish America' in *Colonial Identity in the Atlantic World, 1500–1800*, ed. Nicholas Canny and Anthony Pagden (Princeton, 1987), 51–93. Also Bernard Lavallé, *Las promesas ambiguas: criollismo colonial en los Andes* (Lima, 1993), *passim*.

[7] David A. Brading, *The First America: The Spanish Monarchy, Creole Patriots and the Liberal State, 1492–1867* (Cambridge, 1991), 292–390; Jacques LaFaye, *Quetzalcoatl and Guadalupe: The Formation of Mexican National Consciousness, 1531–1813*, trans. B. Keen (Chicago and London, 1976), esp. 51–98; 177–253.

[8] John L. Phelan, *The Kingdom of Quito in the Seventeenth Century. Bureaucratic Politics in the Spanish Empire* (Madison, Wisconsin, 1967), 120.

The underpinnings of creole patriotism were, then, those of an *ancien régime* society. An aristocratic conception of society and a Hispanocentric conception of ethnic hierarchy gave the creole elites a sense of themselves as a ruling class by reason of their noble, Spanish descent. The *History and Genealogies of the Kingdom of New Granada*, written by Flórez de Ocaríz in 1672, reflects this clearly. To establish his credentials as a member of the nobility in Bogotá, Flórez asserted that he descended directly from a Spaniard who had participated in the conquest of New Granada more than a century earlier. The nobility he defined as men who descended from the conquistadors and nobles who had settled New Granada, and who thus had rights to occupy the prime position in society and to provide the dignatories and officers of state which the crown appointed through the king's patronage.[9] Like their counterparts in Europe's nobility and gentry, members of leading American families found a primary identity in claims to nobility which conferred not only prestige but also the right to privileged access to public office.

Creole belief in, and identification with, regional *patrias* did not, however, promote the concept, vital to nationalism, of one 'people' within the territorial *patria*. In the first place, this was a *creole* patriotism, and it was predicated on the belief, implanted at the time of Spanish conquest, that American societies were ordered in a racial hierarchy in which whites occupied the top position. Under Spanish rule, social identities in the Indies were shaped primarily by the Hispanocentric conception of the American social order as a sequence of three major ethnic groups, with *españoles* (Spaniards and their descendants) in the first rank, and Indians and Africans in positions of legal and cultural inferiority. This simple social order became increasingly complicated over the centuries, as the three primary groups were supplemented by intermediate groupings of people of mixed ethnic origin: the mestizos born of Spanish-Indian mixture; the mulattos of Spanish-black miscegenation; the zambos who came from Indian-black unions. By the eighteenth century, the clarity of the system of ethnic categorisation had also been blurred by the Hispanicisation of these subordinate groups. Especially in the urban environments of the more economically developed regions, they became more like each other in language and culture, and, by the same token, more like the Hispanic elites who dominated colonial societies. This trend towards ethnic convergence was reflected in the censuses taken in the late eighteenth century, which enumerated whites or *españoles*, Indians, slaves (or blacks), but employed the generic term of 'castas' to include all other groups formed from

[9] On Flórez de Ocariz, see Juan A. and Judith E. Villamarin, 'The Concept of Nobility in Colonial Santa Fe de Bogotá' in Karen Spalding (ed), *Essays in the Political, Economic and Social History of Colonial Latin America* (Newark, Delaware, 1982), 125–50.

ethnic fusions.[10] The early schema of ethnic classification thus tended to lose its simplicity and clarity, and identification based on supposed biological criteria gave way to ascription defined by local social criteria. Difference defined by birth and blood nonetheless remained an important marker of social standing, since ethnic origins had important practical implications for individuals, especially at the upper and lower ranges of the social order. Indians had to pay tribute and, together with blacks, were not treated equally under the law. Mestizos and mulattos found their origins were a bar to education in the universities and thus to entry into the professions, and to membership of corporations regarded as the exclusive preserve of *españoles*. Conversely, Spanish descent conferred a superior status, opening opportunities to education, to office-holding, the professions, and the priesthood. In short, being *español* brought legal as well as social privilege, and creole concern to protect this status, which intensified with the blurring of barriers and changes in Spanish law, precluded identification with the wider population.[11]

The evolution of creole patriotism into a sense of nationality was also impeded by the character of American political life. According to Anderson, creole involvement in government at the level of the audiencias, with their wide territorial jurisdictions, fostered among creoles the concept of a distinct American identity and the sense of a territorial *patria*. But it is doubtful that this conception of community extended very far beyond small groups of high-ranking creole officials and the equally small creole intelligentsia with which it overlapped. For most creoles, experience of government and politics was at the less exalted level of town and city administration. Unlike North American colonials, Spanish Americans had no representation in regional assemblies, and, aside from the few who were rich enough to secure offices at the regional level, creole political horizons and experience were largely confined to the jurisdictions of urban centres. This did not prevent them from having a lively political life, with a much higher degree of participation than was once supposed. Far from slumbering in a long

[10] For a general analysis of these phenomena, James Lockhart, 'Social organisation and social change in colonial Spanish America' in *Cambridge History of Latin America*, (Cambridge, 1984), II, 265–319; for studies of this process set in two colonial cities, see John K. Chance, *Race and Class in Colonial Oaxaca* (Stanford, Calif., 1978), 144–85, and Martin Minchom, *The People of Quito, 1690–1810: Change and Unrest in the Underclass* (Boulder, San Francisco and Oxford, 1994), 158–90. On the blurring of ethnic and race divisions in colonial Peru, see David Cahill, 'Colour by Numbers: Racial and Ethnic Categories in the Viceroyalty of Peru, 1524–1824', *Journal of Latin American Studies*, 26 (1994), 325–46.

[11] On creoles' concern to protect their superior status against encroachments from people of colour, see Jaime Jaramillo Uribe, 'Mestizaje y diferenciación social en el Nuevo Reino de Granada en la segunda mitad del siglo XVIII', in his *Ensayos sobre Historia Social Colombiana* (Bogotá, 1968), 163–233.

'colonial siesta', the inhabitants of Spanish American cities, towns and villages had an intense political life in which both patricians and plebeians participated actively, which often involved the assertion of village, town and city autonomy, and which did not involve identification with a broader region.[12]

The intense localism of creole politics was reflected in the fact that, until the eighteenth century, regional challenges to royal government were few and far between; unlike the rebellions of the Catalans, Portugal, Sicily and Naples in the mid-seventeenth century, American protests had no nationalist or separatist undertones.[13] Nor, unlike the Catalans, did Spanish Americans take advantage of the crisis of succession at the start of the eighteenth century to press their own political agendas. Throughout the War of Succession, they remained loyal to the monarchy and allowed a smooth, largely unquestioning transition from the Habsburg to the Bourbon dynasty. Creoles' consciousness of pertaining to a *patria* should not, then, be confused with separatist or nationalist aspirations; it referred only to the quasi-aristocratic rights to the prerogatives of local office which members of creole elites claimed to possess, and was perfectly compatible with universal monarchy. The 'creole patriotism' reflected in the literature and culture of colonial elites reflected a cultural effort to resolve the dilemmas faced by whites who felt both Spanish and American: it was a quest for an identity which would reconcile the 'civilised' world of Europe with the 'barbarism' of the New World. Advances in this quest were, however, without any clear political counterpart at the end of the seventeenth century. Creole intellectuals had created histories which legitimated their cultural identity, even to the point where the Mexican creole Carlos de Sigüenza y Góngora affirmed the existence of a 'creole nation' rooted in pre-Hispanic Mexican civilisation. But this was a fragile construct: after the uprising of Indians and *castas* in Mexico City in 1692, Sigüenza y Góngora fell silent, and interest in rooting creole cultural identity in an historic, ethnic past were not revived for decades.[14] Creoles might have identified with a *patria* of their birth and residence,

[12] For examples of local political life, see Anthony McFarlane, 'Civil Disorders and Popular Protest in Late Colonial New Granada', *Hispanic American Historical Review*, 64:1 (1984), 17–54; also Margarita Garrido, *Reclamos y representaciones: Variaciones sobre la política en el Nuevo Reino de Granada, 1770–1815* (Bogotá, 1993), 116–225; and Oscar Cornblit, *Power and Violence in the Colonial City: Oruro from the Mining Renaissance to the Rebellion of Tupac Amaru, 1740–82* (Cambridge, 1995), 37–80.

[13] For a brief comparison of rebellions in the seventeenth-century Spanish monarchy, see Anthony McFarlane, 'Challenges from the Periphery: Rebellion in Colonial Spanish America' in *Rebelión y Resistencia en el Mundo Hispanico del Siglo XVII*, ed. Werner Thomas and Bart de Groof (Leuven, 1992), 250–9.

[14] Anthony Pagden, *Spanish Imperialism and the Political Imagination* (New Haven and London, 1990), 97.

but this was by no means inconsistent with holding another identity as a member of the Spanish 'nation', the source of their common descent. Affirmations of creole identity were cultural, not political, and did not envisage an existence outside the Spanish monarchy. This was a development which arose only late in the eighteenth century, when colonial societies were affected by significant changes to their social, political, and intellectual environments.

How, then, did creole cultural identity become politicised? According to Anderson, the crucial catalyst was the advance of print-capitalism during the later eighteenth century. With the publication of colonial newspapers, he argues, the creoles' sense of an identity rooted in a particular territory became sharper and, with exposure to Enlightenment ideas, capable of conversion into the 'imagined communities' which became the basis of the nation-states which replaced Spain's empire in the early nineteenth century.[15] It is true, as we shall see, that new ideas and new means to receive and disseminate them played a key role in politicising and territorialising the creole sense of identity forged in previous centuries. But this, again, was a more complex process than Anderson's summary argument allows, and did not lead ineluctably towards the expression of Spanish American nationalisms.

The development of a deepening sense of creole identity was bound up, first, with the impact of changes in Spanish imperial policy in societies whose elites felt a growing sense of self-confidence in an era of demographic and economic expansion, and resented the modernised imperialism of the Bourbons, which aimed at turning Spain's American dominions into dependent satellites run in the interests of the metropolitan power.[16] When the Bourbon dynasty succeeded the Habsburgs at the start of the eighteenth century, it inherited an American empire which depended for its government on the active co-operation of American-born Spaniards. Not only did the creole gentry dominate local government through the municipal corporations, but they had also penetrated the royal bureaucracy at many levels, including the upper echelons of the church and the benches of the audiencias (high courts) which were the foremost expression of royal authority in most regions of the Indies.[17] Thus, although Habsburg kings did not formally recognise the rights of the American-born to political office and

[15] Anderson, *Imagined Communities*, 62–5.

[16] Colin MacLachlan, *Spain's Empire in the New World: The Role of Ideas in Institutional and Social Change* (Berkeley and Los Angeles, 1988), pp. 67–88.

[17] On creole penetration of the royal bureaucracy, Mark Burkholder and D. S. Chandler, *From Impotence to Authority: The Spanish Crown and the American Audiencias, 1697–1808* (Colombia, 1977); on creole elites in local government, see Peter Marzhal, *Town in the Empire: Government, Politics and Society in Seventeenth-Century Popayán* (Austin, Texas, 1978).

autonomy, political practice had allowed creoles to take a substantial share of power, particularly within local government. This in turn fostered the creole belief in a pact under which the creoles were entitled, by reason of their place of birth, to control local affairs under the overarching authority of the Spanish king. While the Habsburg monarchy had implicitly accepted that creoles should play a part in their own administration, Bourbon ministers took a different view. Early in the century, they began to try to reverse the 'Americanisation' of colonial government, and in so doing drew on old stereotypes which portrayed creoles as inferiors who were congenitally incapable of administering their own affairs. The official Spanish identification of the creole 'other' tended to reinforce and politicise the creoles' sense of separate and distinctive identity in two ways. It encouraged creoles to embrace their American identity by forcing them to defend it (being caused by birth, creoleness was a condition which could not be escaped, but only defended); secondly, treatment as the 'other' encouraged creoles to use this identity in their political disputes with Spaniards and with Spanish governments.

A clear reflection of the revival of the creole 'other' in official metropolitan circles as a means of both explaining the ills of government in the Indies and justifying closer metropolitan control is found in the famous memorandum which Jorge Juan and Antonio de Ulloa submitted to the crown following their mission to Peru in the 1740s. In it, they reported that a growing gulf divided European Spaniards and creoles:

> In Peru, it is enough to be a European ... to declare oneself immediately against creoles. To be born in the Indies is sufficient for one to hate Europeans. This mutual antipathy reaches such an extreme that in some ways it exceeds the unbridled fury of two nations, completely at odds, who vituperate and insult each other. But if the differences between nations are finally resolved, this is not the case with the whites in Peru. Despite better lines of communication, the welding of kinship bonds, and other good reasons for being conciliatory, united and friendly, discord increases all the time.[18]

To explain this antagonism, Juan and Ulloa offered an analysis which reflected the disdain for creoles felt in metropolitan official circles. The conflict, they argued, had causes which were attributable to the creole characteristics of 'excessive vanity, presumption and pride'. The problem with the creoles was that their 'vanity dissuades them from

[18] Jorge Juan and Antonio de Ulloa, *Discourse and Political Reflections on the Kingdoms of Peru*, trans. John J. TePaske and Besse A. Cement (Norman, Oklahoma, 1978), 217.

working and becoming traders, the only occupation in the Indies capable of maintaining a consistent standard of living', and thus led them into the 'innate vices associated with a licentious, slothful existence'. Spanish immigrants, on the other hand, used enterprise and hard work to amass fortunes, to escape their humble origins, and to become political leaders in their communities. This caused great jealousy, Juan and Ulloa argued, because creoles failed to understand class distinctions. Creoles believed that the Spaniards had prestige and should be well-treated simply because they were from Europe. They therefore went out of their way to help metropolitan Spaniards who, 'because of some disadvantages of birth or upbringing, would not have the opportunities to make their way out of their humble position', were they still in Spain. This, in turn, encouraged Spaniards in the Indies 'to raise their goals to a very lofty plane'. Jealous of such social mobility, creoles ridiculed these metropolitan *parvenus* for their lowly social origins; Europeans then took revenge on creoles 'by throwing in their faces the defects of the exaggerated nobility they boast so much about'.[19]

These observations were of course coloured by traditional metropolitan prejudice against the American-born, and by the proclivity of educated, well-born and condescending metropolitans to dismiss colonials as benighted provincials.[20] The comments made by Juan and Ulloa are nonetheless interesting in two respects. On the one hand, they reflect the extent to which metropolitan Spaniards had constructed a stereotypical image of American-born whites which consisted largely of negative characteristics and was applied indiscriminately to all creoles. On the other hand, by portraying creoles and metropolitans as people with different attitudes and modes of behaviour, Juan and Ulloa also draw attention to the real part which differences in cultural norms played in generating and perpetuating conflict. For, when Spaniards like Juan and Ulloa talked of creole 'vanity, presumption and pride', they were simply belittling the creoles' awareness of themselves as a social elite whose position rested on certain canons of behaviour and demanded recognition and respect. Equally, what seemed to immigrant Spaniards to be their just reward for enterprise, hard work and thrift was to creoles an unfair intrusion into social and political arenas which they believed to be the rightful preserve of the American-born gentry. And when Spaniards disparaged the creoles' excessive concern with genealogy, they failed to recognise that such concern was not simply frivolous, but reflected claims to the political primacy which American

[19] Quotations from Juan and Ulloa, *Discourse and Political Reflections*, pp. 218–22.

[20] For an assessment of Antonio de Ulloa, the report's principal author, and the continuity of his writing with the Spanish imperial tradition of commentary on America, see Brading, *The First America*, 424–8.

social elites believed to be just rewards of their nobility. This Juan and Ulloa ignored. They simply called for control to ensure that only the right kind of metropolitans were able to take office in Peru, through a system of licensing.[21]

Seen from a creole perspective, such portrayals were infuriating, and led creoles, not just to insult and vituperate the Spaniards in order to satisfy their rancorous souls (as Juan and Ulloa scornfully observed),[22] but to defend their creole identity and to invest it with political meaning. A striking and eloquent example of such a politicised defence of creole identity, coupled with a striking rebuttal of the crass stereotypes used to justify discrimination against creoles, is found in the celebrated petition submitted by the Mexico City council to the king in 1771. Written by Antonio Joaquín de Rivadeneira, a creole lawyer who had been a judge on bench of the Mexican Audiencia, the petition was prompted by a report in which a prominent metropolitan official said of creoles that, 'if raised to authority or office, they are prone to the greatest errors', and so recommended creole exclusion from any but 'positions of the middle rank'. In response, Rivadeneira commented bitterly that this was another shot in 'a war we have suffered since the discovery of America', in which creoles had been characterised, like Indians, as lacking in reason. Noting that creoles had recently observed with dismay the tendency of the crown to grant them fewer favours, Rivadeneira went on to argue that to exclude creoles from office was 'to overturn the law of peoples', and he declared 'the rights of the native inhabitants to be appointed to offices in their own countries, not only in preference to foreigners but to their exclusion'. European Spaniards were not, Rivadeneira conceded, foreigners in the Indies from a legal point of view, since they were, with Americans, part of the same body politic under the single head of the Catholic Monarch. However, unlike Americans, they did 'not derive their identity from the Indies', since their homes, families, and ties were all in Old Spain not New Spain. They were merely transients who were primarily concerned 'to return wealthy to their own home and their native land'. Nor was their tendency to use political offices as a means of personal enrichment their only flaw. In countries with 'their own laws of government' which Europeans had not studied, the metropolitan official was incapable of good government because 'he comes to govern a people he does not know, to administer laws he has not studied, to encounter customs he does not understand, to deal with people he has never met. And ... he comes full of European ideas which do not apply in these parts.' American Spaniards, on the other hand, were

[21] Juan and Ulloa, *Discourse and Political Reflections*, 231–2.
[22] *Ibid.*, 217.

worthy of the highest office, since in 'talents, application, conduct and honour, they cede nothing to any of the other nations of the world'.[23]

This paeon of praise for creoles, with its references to creole parity with other nations, was not an unabashed nationalism, however, since it certainly did not embrace all Mexico's people. Rivadeneira made it abundantly clear that he was not speaking of the Indians or people of mixed race who constituted the overwhelming majority of the population, but only of 'Spaniards born in these regions' who traced unbroken descent from conquerors and early colonists or from more recent Spanish immigrants, and 'whose blood is as pure as that of Spaniards from Old Spain'. The Indians, by contrast, were 'victims of their race ... born to poverty, bred in destitution and controlled through punishment'.[24] Here, then, was a claim for the equality of creoles and metropolitan Spaniards as members of the same nation by virtue of their race, or 'purity of blood'. Indeed, 'purity of blood' was a deeply trditional Spanish concept: it derived from the test of 'limpieza de sangre' which Spaniards had used in the sixteenth century to discriminate against, and exclude from office 'New Christians' of Jewish descent.

Creole exasperation at Bourbon realignments of policy did not stop at verbal assertions of creole identity and political rights of the kind made by Rivadeneira. It was much more forcibly expressed in the rebellions which confronted officials charged with implementing government administrative and fiscal reforms during the reign of Charles III (1759–88). Major rebellions occurred in the city of Quito in 1765, and later, on a larger scale, in New Granada and Peru in 1780–2, when lower-class protests against new fiscal demands fused with creole dissatisfaction with administrative and fiscal reform, and allowed creoles to use the sharp edge of popular protests to propel their own claims for redress of grievances.[25] In differing degrees, these rebellions all reflected the way in which Bourbon policies activated the problem of identity which lay at the heart of Spanish American colonial societies. The incursions of the Bourbon state impinged upon both the political authority and economic interests of local creole oligarchies, and, by thus attacking the standing of creoles in their own communities, led them to assert the American part of their dual identity as *españoles americanos*.

[23] 'Representación que hizo la Ciudad de México al rey D. Carlos II al rey D. Carlos III en 1771 ...' in *Latin American Revolutions, 1808–26: Old and New World Origins*, ed. and trans. John Lynch (Norman, Oklahoma and London, 1994), pp. 58–70; quotations from 59, 61, 62–3, 64, 66.

[24] *Ibid.*, 66.

[25] For a general, comparative analysis of these rebellions, see Anthony McFarlane, 'Rebellions in Late Colonial Spanish America: A Comparative Perspective', *Bulletin of Latin American Research*, 14:3 (1995), 313–38.

This rejection of Spanish identity was mirrored in attacks on metropolitan Spaniards. The rebellions of Quito, New Granada and Peru all revealed antagonism towards metropolitan Spaniards, sometimes leading to violent attacks on their property and persons, and demands for their expulsion. This was especially true of Peru and Upper Peru where, during the great rebellion of 1780–2, Spaniards were singled out for violent, systematic persecution. Túpac Amaru, the first rebel leader, called for the expulsion or execution of European Spaniards, and his followers enthusiastically executed his orders by killing 'Spaniards' without discrimination between Europeans and creoles. To justify such slaughter, they invoked a powerful counter-image of 'Spaniards' as traitors to Christianity and the Spanish King, and demonised them as beastly, devilish creatures who deserved inhuman treatment.[26] The rebellion was, moreover, informed by a current of Andean messianic thinking in which anti-Spanish sentiments blended into visions of restoring an Inca kingdom in Peru, ruled by descendants of the ancient Inca dynasty which the Spaniards had deposed in the sixteenth century. This phenomenon, which has been called 'Inca nationalism', was peculiar to the southern Peruvian highlands, particularly in and around the city of Cuzco.[27] There, Indian *caciques* (nobles) and creole families who also claimed noble descent had underpinned their sense of group identity and claims to autonomy from Lima, the viceregal capital, by rooting themselves in a mythologised Inca past. Harking back to an Inca kingdom not only offered a respectable past; it provided an alternative to Spanish monarchy that was in keeping with a traditional, *ancien régime* belief in the necessity of kingship, while also providing a means of mobilising support among the Indian peasantry. Here, then, was a potent blend of creole and indigenous cultural traditions which, because it openly envisaged a new political order outside Spanish rule, sets the Túpac Amaru rebellion apart from the creole-led rebellions of Quito and New Granada. Its potential was severely limited, however. The idea of an 'Inca kingdom', though never clearly formulated, was possible in principle: Indian nobles were members of the privileged classes in Peru, and creoles and mestizos were often eager to emphasise their descent from, and family links with, the ancient Incan aristocracy, since, in an *ancien régime* society, noble blood conferred both prestige and prerogatives of power. But, if the idea that they might come

[26] Jan Szeminski, 'Why Kill the Spaniard? New Perspectives on Andean Insurrectionary Ideology in the 18th Century' in *Resistance, Rebellion, and Consciousness in the Andean Peasant World, 18th to 20th Centuries*, ed. Steve Stern (Madison, Wisconsin, 1987), 166–92; on rebel violence towards both Spaniards and non-Spaniards, see Scarlett O'Phelan Godoy, *La Gran Rebelión de los Andes: de Túpac Amaru a Túpac Catari* (Lima, 1995), 105–37.

[27] John Rowe, 'El movimiento nacional inca del siglo XVIII', *in Túpac Amaru II. Antología*, ed. Alberto Flores Galindo (Lima, 1976), 13–62.

together in a state separate from that of Spain was possible in principle, in practice, it had little appeal outside the Indian world. For, although Túpac Amaru envisaged a place for creoles and mestizos in his putative kingdom, together with a continuing link to the Catholic King of Spain, whites and mestizos found it difficult to take seriously the idea of rule by an Indian rather than a Spanish king. Moreover, the widespread ethnic violence of the rebellion undermined alliances between Peruvians: creoles were terrified by Indian uprisings, while the Indian rebels—themselves a heterogeneous force, divided by regional and ethnic differences—were unable to find any unity of purpose, and were defeated area by area.

So, although creoles involved in the late eighteenth-century rebellions asserted their identity as 'Americans' and explicitly demanded that 'Americans' should be given preference to metropolitans in the distribution of offices, their interpretation of the rights of native-born whites did not generally indicate desire for independence from Spain. It was, rather, a defence of the traditional notion of a 'pact' between the king and his kingdoms, nurtured by the experience of the Habsburg period; it aimed at perpetuating past practices, not overthrowing them. Nor did such protest enlarge the scope for creating a general political identity that embraced not just creoles but the other peoples of their territories. Enmity towards metropolitan Spaniards was insufficiently strong or widespread to underpin nationalistic sentiment or to provide a focus for rebellion against Spain. The heart of the major rebellions was found in the cities, towns and villages which were the primary locus of social identity and political action in Spanish American societies, and rebels rarely succeeded in transcending the concerns of those communities. Essentially, the rebellions of the Comuneros in New Granada and of Túpac Amaru in Peru were clusters of local insurrections, driven by divisions and disputes in local politics and only briefly bound by any sense of allegiance to a wider common cause. Thus, in all the late eighteenth-century rebellions, creole coalitions with lower-class rebels soon foundered, as fear of Indians and other people of colour outweighed creole dislike of Spaniards and Spanish policies. Creoles involved in the rebellions saw the rights of 'Americans' as the rights of creoles within the Spanish 'nation', and were still far from framing a cultural identity which embraced all the populations of their territories, envisaged as potentially unified nations. Moreover, aside from the concept of the Inca kingdom that was briefly promoted by Túpac Amaru in 1780–1, the idea that the colonies might become independent had yet to be voiced. Creole ideas about cultural identity and political rights were still expressed in the political language of the *ancien régime*, and, if creoles accorded themselves distinct identities within the Spanish monarchy, they did not imagine themselves outside it. This occurred only after the ideas of the Enlightenment offered creoles a new medium for understanding and expressing their identity as Americans, and when the dissolution of the Spanish monarchy at its centre provided them with the chance to turn their complaints against Spain to demands for equality.

The part played by Enlightenment ideas in strengthening creole identity was noted by Alexander von Humboldt during his travels in Mexico and South America in 1799–1804. Humboldt observed that following the American and French revolutions, it had become increasingly frequent for creoles to assert that 'I am not a *Spaniard*, I am an *American*'. This Humboldt attributed to 'the workings of a long resentment, which arose from 'the abuse of laws, the false measures of the colonial government, the example of the United States of America, and the influence of opinions of the age ...'[28] These phrases draw attention to the significance of the new elements which entered into the culture and politics in the Spanish world in the closing decades of the century. As the Bourbon reforms reached their apogee, the ideas of the European Enlightenment began to circulate more widely and freely in Spanish America. At the same time, news of the American and French Revolutions entered America by official and unofficial channels during the late 1780s and the 1790s, at a time when, thanks largely to a small but burgeoning press, creoles had unprecedented opportunities for receiving news and absorbing new ideas from the world outside. But what were the political implications and repercussions of this assertion of an 'Americanness' among creoles? Did it signal the translation of a creole sense of cultural identity into a desire for political independence and lead to the foundation of new nations?

One way in which Humboldt's 'opinions of the age' impacted on Spanish American political culture was by supplying creoles with liberal and republican ideas which directly inspired demands for political independence grounded in appeals to universal human rights. As evidence for this, historians have drawn attention to the penetration into Spanish American of the writings of the *philosophes*, the circulation of key texts from the American and French revolutions—such as the Constitution of Philadelphia, the Federal Constitution, and the French Declaration of the Rights of Man and the Citizen—and the activities of that small but famous group of men—Francisco de Miranda, Antonio Nariño, and the Jesuit Juan Pablo Viscardo y Guzmán—who dedicated themselves to preaching and promoting independence from Spain. Tracing the dissemination of ideas through books and the incubation

[28] Alexander von Humboldt, *Political Essay on the Kingdom of New Spain* (1811 edition, reprinted New York, 1966), I, 205.

of separatist sentiments through the careers of a few idealists is, however, a flawed approach to understanding political change in late colonial Spanish America. Reading about new philosophical principles and political experiments was not the same as believing, or wanting to implement them. Indeed, at the end of the century, only a tiny number of creoles took the American and French revolutions as models applicable to Spanish America. The American War of Independence seems to have passed virtually unnoticed in Spanish America at the time that it was happening, even in New Granada and Peru where major rebellions broke out in 1780–1. The French Revolution attracted more attention among creoles, partly because the official Spanish press was so ready to draw attention to the impious horrors which flowed from the overthrow of an anointed king. But the prospect of following this revolutionary path excited only a tiny number of creoles, whose conspiracies were ill-conceived and unsuccessful, and whose idealism found no wider resonance among either their fellow creoles or the larger populations.[29] Moreover, early creole revolutionists such as Miranda and Nariño were republicans rather than nationalists. Their concern was not simply to change government in Spanish America or to affirm the rights of pre-existing Spanish American nations; it was, rather, to overthrow the system of absolutist monarchy throughout the Spanish world (including Spain itself), and to replace it with governments based on the principles of popular sovereignty and consent of the governed.

The inspiration that some creoles took from the radical political ideas of the Enlightenment was, then, only one way in which 'enlightened' ideas influenced creole thinking and behaviour. More important were the slower, more subtle ways in which the Enlightenment emphasis on reason, the rights of the individual, and the possibilities of human progress altered creoles' perceptions of themselves and undermined their respect for Spanish cultural and intellectual leadership. And, if these new perceptions allowed creoles to take a more critical approach to their relations with the metropolitan power, equally important was the development of new means of communicating and disseminating such ideas.

The influence of enlightened thinking in sharpening creole identity came partly through contemporary scientific debate about the New World which raised in new form the old issue of differences about Europeans and Americans, and, by implication, the fitness of creoles for self-government. Denigration of the New World by European

[29] For an account of one of these creole conspiracies inspired by American and French revolutionary ideas, see Anthony McFarlane, *Colombia before Independence: Economy, Society and Politics under Bourbon Rule* (Cambridge, 1993), 285–93.

scientists such as Cornelius de Pauw, who drew highly unfavourable comparisons between the Old and the New World, brought educated creoles to the defence of the American environment, focused their interest in the geography and resources of the regions they inhabited, and thereby stimulated their sense of identity with the lands of their birth.[30] Modern scientific thinking invigorated creole thinking in other ways, too. Reform of university curricula, designed to introduce the 'useful sciences' into the colonies, exposed creoles in leading cities to new ways of thinking as well as creating new areas for contention with European Spaniards. For, while the academic establishment, dominated by the regular orders with their roots in Spain defended the old ways, creoles who were seeking academic positions tended to align with the currents of reform.[31] But perhaps most important was that the new emphasis on improving communication with Spain and disseminating 'useful knowledge' promoted the development of a periodical press which also provided a medium for criticising Spain and for cultivating the American side of creole identity through new circuits of debate and sociability.[32] Although they seem bland politically, the new periodicals published in the major colonial cities made an important contribution to the elaboration and diffusion of new attitudes and ideas. They took up the practice, started by Bourbon officials early in the eighteenth century, of criticising traditional ways and calling for the elite to take up reform, while at the same time strengthening a sense of regional identity by directing news and comment to specific regional audiences. The *Gazeta de Guatemala*, the *Papel Periódico de Santafé de Bogotá*, the *Telégrafo Mercantil* of Buenos Aires, the *Mercurio Peruano*, and so on, aimed at readers who, in the act of reading news of the region, became members of a public identified with it. Editors and authors also assumed that there was a 'public good' which might rationally be pursued, and addressed an 'enlightened' public in the belief that it should promote the public good. In their articles on such topics as improvements to economic life, these journals employed a 'modern' style of criticism,

[30] On creole responses to the debate, see Antonello Gerbi, *The Dispute of the New World. The History of a Polemic, 1750–1900*, trans. Jeremy Moyle (Pittsburgh, 1955), pp. 289–324. For a Mexican response, from the Jesuit Clavijero, see Pagden, *Spanish Imperialism and the Political Imagination*, 104–16; on Chile, see Simon Collier, *Ideas and Politics of Chilean Independence, 1808–30* (Cambridge, 1967), 21–30.

[31] Thomas F. Glick, 'Science and Independence in Latin America (with Special Reference to New Granada)', *Hispanic American Historical Review*, 71:2 (1991), 307–34; Jeanne Chenu, 'De la Terre aux Etoiles: Quête Scientifique et Identité Culturelle en Nouvelle Granade', in *L'Amérique Espagnole a l'Epoque des Lumières*, Centre National de la Recherche Scientifique (Paris, 1987), 247–60.

[32] For a general discussion of the emergence of modern forms of sociability in Spanish America, see François Xavier Guerra, *Modernidad e Independencias. Ensayos sobre las revoluciones hispánicas* (Madrid, 1992), pp. 85–113.

which stressed the superiority of empirical investigation of nature over the repetition of texts invested with only traditional authority. Contributors also reformulated the claims of creoles to participate in government, by stressing the need for educated men to shape and dictate policy. This argument is reflected in explicit attacks on the principles of 'nobility' and family honour, conferred by birth, which stood at the heart of traditional elite political culture. Instead, creole writers proposed an alternative form of nobility, based on merit and the exercise of talent for the public good.[33] The idea of replacing an 'aristocracy' with a species of 'meritocracy' was in effect a modernisation of creole claims to exercise influence and power in their own land, restated in the language of the Enlightenment.

These claims all lend weight to Anderson's proposal that the arrival of print capitalism in Spanish America played a key part in shaping creole nationalism. In his view, the provincial periodicals which were printed in late colonial Spanish America, with their juxtaposition of commercial news, news of events in the world outside, and items pertaining to local society and government appointments, ensured that, when creoles broke with Spain, they thought of their regions as nations. Because these periodicals were published in and for a specific community and aimed at local readers, they were conducive to the formation of a sense of territorial community; secondly, they provided forums of information and discussion which, although often politically innocent, were in time politicised. Thus the presses of colonial Spanish America completed the role played by creole functionaries in shaping the image of the proto-national community which was to assert its interests against the metropolitan power.[34] But, if creoles' confidence in their separate identity and in the potential for economic and social progress in their homelands grew stronger towards the end of the century, did it build into a sense of 'national' identity capable of generating movements of independence and building new states?

There are several reasons for doubting this. First, it is easy to exaggerate the importance of the press as a force for shaping a proto-national community. It may well be true that these publications generated a more intense creole consciousness, but this effect was concentrated in the very restricted circles of an educated creole minority concentrated in leading cities, and did not spread far beyond their ranks. There were some scientific *savants* and enthusiasts for enlightened ideas in the provinces. In New Granada, for example, creoles educated

[33] This discussion draws on the study of the *Papel Periódico* of Bogotá, in Renan Silva, *Prensa y revolución a finales del siglo XVIII: Contribución a un análisis de la formación de la ideología de independencia nacional* (Bogotá, 1988), pp. 28–5; 104–6.

[34] Anderson, *Imagined Communities*, 61.

in the viceregal capital at Bogotá returned to the provinces but kept up contact with new ideas through correspondence;[35] in Mexico, the provincial parish priest Miguel Hidalgo (later the leader of a rebellion against Spanish rule in 1810) was another striking example of the spread of enlightened ideas beyond a colonial capital.[36] Nonetheless, if enlightened ideas had reshaped attitudes within the educated minority of the creole elites, older structures of thought and feeling continued to prevail within the wider ranks of creole society, particularly in the many small provincial towns where the influence of universities and the new periodical press was slight. Nor had new ideas diminished identification with local communities. In New Granada, for example, concern to promote economic and social progress during the 1790s and early 1800s was conceived largely in terms of local interests. Prominent members of the *cabildo* and *consulado* (the municipal and commercial corporations) of Cartagena de Indias, New Granada's principal port, focused on promoting their own commercial connections with the exterior, and paid little attention the needs of the interior. Towns and cities inland in turn sought to diminish Cartagena's privileges, and pressed the government for policies designed to further their interests.[37]

The influence of new ideas did not, then, necessarily mould creoles into a proto-national community, much less unite them with other social and ethnic groupings in a shared sense of cultural identity. What such ideas did was, rather, to strengthen the self-consciousness and inflate the aspirations of creole patricians in the capital cities of the audiencias; as the leading groups in such cities, these creoles later became 'nationalist' to the extent that they presumed to inherit the power which the high-ranking royal officials who were their social peers exercised over the territories of the audiencias. In provincial towns, creoles clung to localised identities with their towns and their hinterlands, identities which did not necessarily translate into a sense of affinity with the jurisdictions of the larger political entities established under Spanish rule.

Nor did the development of a sense of autonomous cultural identity among creoles lead inexorably to demands for a separate, independent political status. So long as Spain remained politically stable, creoles' defence of their character as Americans, their exaltation of the American environment, and criticism of Spanish government were all comfortably contained within the existing political structure. Even when Spain's economic and political power was visibly deteriorating after the end of

[35] Margarita Garrido, *Reclamos y representaciones*, 36–54.
[36] On Hidalgo's career, see Hugh Hamill, *The Hidalgo Revolt; Prelude to Mexican Independence* (Gainesville, Florida, 1966), pp. 53–88.
[37] McFarlane, *Colombia before Independence*, 314–21.

the Peace of Amens in 1804, and when leading creoles had increasing reason for complaining about Spain's commercial and fiscal policies, the threat that creoles would rebel against the parent power was slight.[38] Evidently, the incipient 'nationalism' among the creole elites of colonial capitals was insufficiently powerful to propel creoles into the political organisation needed to demand equality with, or independence from the metropolis. That was achieved only after Napoleon's seizure of the Spanish throne in 1808 collapsed the Spanish state at its centre and provoked a crisis throughout the empire. But, if external events rather than internal developments provoked political change, why did Spanish America become a series of nation-states, each with a republican, representative form of government?

This was, Anderson rightly argues, a precocious development, antedating the emergence of nation-states in most of Europe. Seeing this as an early expression of nationalism, Anderson seeks to explain it in largely cultural terms: he suggests that the roots of the nation lay in creole cultural identities formed under colonial rule, in the 'imagined community' created by creole functionaries and consolidated by the effects of print-capitalism. François Xavier Guerra also stresses the precocity of Spanish America, in setting up some of the first modern political regimes, adopting national sovereignty as a legitimating principle and creating the representative republic as a form of government; however, he advances a different, more historically sensitive explanation for the early creation of nation-states in Spanish America. According to Guerra, the transition into nation-states had a fundamental political logic. It began as a quest to legitimise defence of the traditional order by proclaiming that, in the absence of the legitimate monarch, sovereignty temporarily reverted to the 'people' with whom the monarch had, in the terms of traditional Hispanic political thought, formed a 'pact'. Once it was accepted that legitimacy could only be based in society, representation of the 'people' became necessary. Debating representation then prompted debate about who the 'people' were, and what constituted the 'nation'. As this debate unfolded, creole demands for autonomy, based in the traditional 'pactist' political thinking of the colonial period and justified by a traditional notion of popular sovereignty, took on new coloration, influenced by the republican principles of the French Revolution. Defining the 'people' meant creating the 'nation', and thus, as Spanish Americans sought to find representative

[38] See, for example, the response of the Mexican nobility to the Consolidation decree of 1804 in Doris Ladd, *The Mexican Nobility at Independence, 1780–1826* (Austin, Texas, 1976), 95–104.

forms of government, so they engendered nation-states.[39]

The transition from defence of the established order into development of nation states was driven, as Guerra shows, by a search for a means of legitimating Spanish resistance to France. Started in Spain itself, this continued in Spanish America with a defence by creole patricians of the Spanish *nación* against France that was rooted in a Spanish patriotism founded in a common language, culture and religion. Thus, for the first two years of the Spanish crisis, political mobilisation in Spanish America initially moved along lines similar to, and largely inspired by, the emergency political reorganisation which took place in Spain itself.[40] There, the war of independence against France was founded first on the corporate groupings of *ancien régime* society. In the absence of the legitimate king, Ferdinand VII, sovereignty was claimed to have reverted to the people (the *pueblo*), but the powers of the sovereign people were taken up by juntas which were largely extensions of traditional municipal corporations and were run by local notables.[41] And, when the Central Junta, focus of Spain's resistance to Napoleon, sought to gather support for their cause in the Americas, they instituted the election of American deputies using the traditional criteria of corporate representation practised in the *ancien régime* Spanish monarchy: the deputies were chosen by, and from the ranks of, urban notables, who received from their cities power to act as spokesmen for the wider communities which were subject to these cities.

Creoles participated enthusiastically in these elections of 1809, showing their firm commitment both to the Spanish nation and to the political concepts of *ancien régime* society. But creole loyalty was soon undermined when government in Spain proved unwilling to accord equality of representation to the overseas dominions. Now the old problem of equality between European and American Spaniards, which had long centred on the issue of access to public office, came to the centre of political debate, and led creoles to assert their rights to self-government through autonomous juntas like those of Spain. Throughout Spanish America, creoles called for the establishment of governments which would represent the 'people' to whom sovereignty had reverted, then moved, from 1810, towards the principle of national representation based in a community of citizens.[42]

[39] For a brief exposition of this position, see François-Xavier Guerra, 'The Spanish American Tradition of Representation and its European Roots', *Journal of Latin American Studies*, 26 (1994), 1–33; for a fuller account, see François-Xavier Guerra, *Modernidad e Independencias* (Madrid, 1992).

[40] For a succinct narrative, see Timothy Anna, *Spain and the Loss of America*, (Lincoln, Nebraska, and London, 1983), 15–63.

[41] Raymond Carr, *Spain, 1808–1939* (Oxford, 1966), 86–92.

[42] Guerra, *Modernidad e Independencias*, 115–225.

The sense of creole identity formed under colonial rule and sharpened by the effects of Bourbon policy played a part in this process of political and ideological change, but it did not easily translate into nationalism or result in the foundation of 'emotionally plausible and politically viable' nation-states. Only in Mexico were demands for autonomous government quickly linked to the revindication of the rights of an existing 'nation', when, in 1810 the priest Miguel Hidalgo raised a great popular revolt under the banner of the Virgin of Guadalupe, and called for the expulsion of European Spaniards, in the name of a 'Mexican nation' which had been oppressed by Spain. Under Morelos, the country cleric who succeeded Hidalgo, rebellion became a prolonged insurgency whose intellectual spokesmen proclaimed the existence of a Mexican nation ready for independence and called for ethnic equality in which all people, regardless of their ethnic origins, would share an identity as Americans. Thus, it is said, 'creole patriotism, which began as the articulation of the social identity of American Spaniards, was here transmuted into the insurgent ideology of Mexican nationalism'.[43] If, however, the ideologues of Mexico's insurgency conjured up a nationalist rhetoric, it was of a peculiar kind, deeply influenced by religious conservatism and the desire to protect the privileges of the Church. The insurgency flourished in only a few regions of Mexico, where it took its energy from local social and political conflicts and the desire of local groups to take advantage of the crisis of the state for their own ends, rather than from any identification with the 'Mexican nation'.[44]

In Spanish South America, identifying the 'people' and the 'nation', and creating 'emotionally plausible and politically viable' nation-states, was also fraught with problems.[45] In some areas, fear of the 'people' long inhibited political change. The Viceroyalty of Peru, for example, remained under royalist control largely because creoles feared a recrudescence of ethnic warfare of the kind that had occurred in Túpac Amaru's rebellion. In other areas, where creole leaders set up autonomous governments based on popular sovereignty, the absence of any widespread sense of commitment to a 'nation' quickly became apparent.

[43] D. A. Brading, *Prophecy and Myth in Mexican History* (Cambridge Centre of Latin American Studies, 1984), 43.

[44] On the regional bases of the Mexican Insurgency, see Brian Hamnett, *Roots of Insurgency: Mexican Regions, 1750–1824* (Cambridge, 1986), 47–67, 178–201; John Tutino, *From Insurrection to Revolution in Mexico: Social Bases of Agrarian Violence, 1750–1940* (Princeton, 1986), 99–122; Peter Guardino, *Peasants, Politics and the Formation of Mexico's National State: Guerrero, 1800–1857* (Stanford, 1996), 44–80.

[45] On the problems of defining the 'people' and the 'nation' see Monica Quijada, 'Que Nación? Dinámicas y dicotomías de la nación en el imaginario hispanoamericano del siglo XIX' in *Imaginar la Nación*, ed. François-Xavier Guerra and Monica Quijada (AHILA, Cuadernos de Historia, Münster and Hamburg, 1994), 19–31.

When creoles sought to define their new condition in proclamations and written constitutions, they were rarely intent on locating an historic 'nation' to legitimate projects for independent states.[46] Indeed, in many regions, creoles had no myths of a glorious Indian past to which to turn.

The absence of any sense of an underlying 'national' unity was also apparent, after 1810, in the civil wars which not only set the defenders of the old order against its challengers, but also pitted newly autonomous cities and towns against each other. For, having cast off Spanish command, their leaders often refused to acknowledge the authority of new governments which attempted to inherit the central command previously exercised by the capitals of viceroyalties, audiencias and captaincies-general from which Spanish officials had once ruled. Such divisions have been attributed to creole political inexperience. Bolívar, for example, thought that the failure of the patriot cause in Venezuela and New Granada was due to a political naiveté which meant that 'Each province governed itself independently; and, following this example, each city demanded like powers, based on the practices of the provinces and on the theory that all men and all peoples are entitled to establish arbitrarily the form of government that pleases them'.[47] Bolívar repeated the point in his famous 'Jamaica Letter', in which he stated that America had not been ready for secession, and had 'risen rapidly, without previous knowledge of, and, what is more regrettable, without previous experience in public affairs ...'[48] But such political fragmentation was not so much the result of political inexperience as an extension of the political experience common in Spanish America under colonial rule. For, as we observed above, political life had focused primarily on towns and cities during the colonial period, and the habit of asserting local autonomy and pursuing local interests died hard. Thus, although leaders like Bolívar insisted on the importance of creating a sense of nation which would override other ties, the creoles who provided local leadership were unable to see their political struggle as embedded in a people who shared a history and culture.[49] If creoles shared a sense of affinity and identity, this did

[46] Venezuela moved quickly to secession, and in 1811 became the first, very short-lived independent republic in Spanish America. Elsewhere constitutions of a republican kind were drawn up without declarations of independence from Spain. Excellent examples of such constitutions are found in Manuel Antonio Pombo and José Joaquín Guerra (eds), *Constituciones de Colombia* (2 vols, Bogotá, 1951).

[47] Simon Bolívar, 'Memorial to the Citizens of New Granada' (1812), in *Selected Writings of Bolívar*, ed. Vicente Lecuna and H. A. Bierck (2 vols., New York, 1951), I, 21.

[48] Simon Bolívar, 'Reply of a South American to a Gentleman of this Island (Jamaica, 1815), in *Selected Writings*, I, 112.

[49] On Bolívar's nationalism, see Simon Collier, 'Nationalism, Nationalism, and Supranationalism in the Writings of Simón Bolívar', *Hispanic American Historical Review*, 63:1 (1983), 37–64.

not easily extend to other ethnic groups, nor beyond the boundaries of their own cities. The first movements towards independence foundered on this disunity; lack of common cause among the 'patriots' allowed Ferdinand VII to reaffirm his authority over most of Spanish America with only a moderate military effort. There were no 'nations-in-arms' to defy Spanish reconquest, only city and regional governments which commanded dwindling allegiance and scarce resources, and by 1816 the River Plate region was the only major territory that remained outside royalist rule.

In the event, restoration of royal control was short-lived. This was not, however, a sign that incipient nations, forged in the crucible of war, rose from the ashes of defeat. For, while renewed resistance to Spain owed something to the sense of freedom kindled in the first phase of independence in 1810–15, the political errors and weaknesses of the restored royalist regime played a large part in provoking the empire's second collapse. In Spain, Ferdinand's absolutism won brief popular acclaim but few lasting adherents, while his policy towards Spanish America was ill-informed, poorly conceived, and badly financed.[50] In 1820, the struggle between absolutists and liberals in Spain pushed the metropolis into another political crisis, which, combined with the efforts of 'patriot' guerrillas and generals in America, reopened the way towards independence. Power was, however, usually seized at the top, by military leaders whose power came more from their successes in arms than from the popularity of their political ideas.

The new states were generally inaugurated amidst fanfares of optimistic and reformist rhetoric, as the heirs of the creole enlightenment sought to create nation-states in which centralised, neo-Bourbonist governments would reform society from above, along lines learned from the Enlightenment. But the political ideals of the Enlightenment enthusiastically espoused by men like Bolívar did not fit easily into the social, political and cultural contexts of Spanish America. 'Bolívar's *patria*' was, as Pagden points out, 'an "Enlightened Illusion" ... generated by a body of texts';[51] as such, it did not command much understanding or commitment outside the small circles of educated and Europeanised elites in the leading South American cities. And, however much they tried to create a sense of collective, national identity, the creole liberals' political projects attracted scant support.[52] Indeed,

[50] Michael Costeloe, *Response to Revolution: Imperial Spain and the Spanish American Revolutions, 1810–1840* (Cambridge, 1986), pp. 52–116.

[51] Pagden, *Spanish Imperialism and the Political Imagination*, 151.

[52] On efforts to replace colonial with republican images and rituals in Mexico, see Annick Lempérière, 'Nación moderna o república barroca? México, 1823–1857' in *Imaginar la Nación*, ed. François-Xavier Guerra and Monica Quijada (AHILA, Cuadernos de Historia, Münster and Hamburg, 1994), 135–77; on New Granada, Hans-Joachim

centralist reformers intent on promoting their project for reform provoked antagonism among provincial elites who wanted government to express their identity and interests, while also failing to find popular support, since the political and legal reforms of the new regimes had little practical meaning to the common people.[53] In 1815, after the first failures to achieve independence, Bolívar had likened the state of America in 1810–15 to that of Rome after its fall, when 'each part of Rome adopted a political system conforming to its interest ... or was led by the individual ambitions of certain chiefs, dynasties or associations'.[54] And, for all Bolívar's efforts to prevent it, the new states which emerged after the second crisis of the Spanish monarchy in 1820, when Ferdinand was forced to return to constitutional government, generally followed the same pathway into fragmentation and civil conflict between warring provinces.

Such fragmentation cannot be attributed to a failure among creole leaders to imagine the political future of their countries as nation-states. The fusion of creole patriotism with the ideals of the Enlightenment had nurtured an American identity, the experience of 'patriotic' war against 'foreign' Spaniards had promoted projects for independent states, and the republican ideals of popular sovereignty and equal citizenship legitimated the constitutional bases of independent states. Moreover, the construction of the new liberal states was not solely the work of urban creole elites. For, recent revisionists insist, the peasantry in Mexico and Peru were willing to adopt the political language of the creole elites and to engage in the politics of the new states for their own purposes, and thereby shared in national political life and contributed to shaping the nation-state.[55] But, if it is true that the new nation-states of Mexico and Peru developed from processes of negotiation across class and ethnic lines, it is equally true that generating a sense of national identity continued to be highly problematic in

Köenig, 'Símbolos nacionales y retorica política en la independencia: El caso de la Nueva Granada', in *Problemas de la Formación del Estado y de la Nación en Hispanoamérica*, ed. Inge Buisson *et al.* (Cologne and Venna, 1984), 389–406; also, at greater length, his *En el camino hacia la nación: Nacionalismo en el proceso de la formación del estado y de la nación de la Nueva Granada, 1750–1856* (Bogotá, 1994), 189–415.

[53] For a study of the alienation of the enlightened political elites from their 'national' constituencies, see the analysis of Rivadavia's government in Argentina during the 1820s in Nicholas Shumway, *The Invention of Argentina* (Berkeley and Los Angeles, 1991), 81–111.

[54] *Selected Writings of Bolívar*, I, 110.

[55] See Guardino, *Peasants, Politics and the Formation of Mexico's National State*, 81–109. On the linkages of popular, local and national politics later in the nineteenth century, see Guy Thomson, 'Popular Aspects of Liberalism in Mexico, 1848–88', *Bulletin of Latin American Research* (1991), 265–92; Antonio Annino, 'Otras naciones: sincretismo político en el México decimonónico' in *Imaginar la Nación*, ed. Guerra and Quijada, 215–55; Florencia Mallon, *Peasant and Nation: The Making of Post-Colonial Mexico and Peru* (Berkeley, 1995), esp. chaps. 2–3.

countries where, under Spanish colonial rule, people had acquired social and cultural identities which tended to separate rather than unite them, and where post-independence political leaders invariably reflected the outlook of social elites which, while they proclaimed a shared national identity, continued to see the social order as an ethnic hierarchy. Their idea of a nation was based in the identity which the white elites had formed under colonial rule, and, by failing to encompass the ethnic diversity of their countries, proved too narrow to underpin the foundations of any shared sense of commitment to new nation states.

The frailty of Spanish America's newly independent states was soon reflected in civil conflicts, as *caudillos* asserted family and regional interests, federalists fought centralists, and conservatives fought liberals. Frustrated by such turbulence, the 'enlightened' creoles who tried to build nation-states based on the sovereignty of the people and equality of individual rights were often persuaded that political problems in the new states derived from the inherent incapacity of some of their fellow citizens. Just as 'enlightened' eighteenth-century Europeans had denigrated creoles as racial and cultural inferiors who were incapable of running their own affairs, so 'enlightened' nineteenth-century creoles maligned people of mixed race and Indians as incapable of becoming responsible, economically productive citizens. And, just as eighteenth-century Europeans based their views of Americans on the authority of contemporary biologists, so nineteenth-century creoles appealed to the equally spurious scientific authority of an emerging Social Darwinism.[56] Ironically, moulding nations from native materials seemed so difficult that some creole statesmen concluded that the nation state could only be secured on the basis of European immigration, or even, in the eyes of some disillusioned politicians, through absorption into the United States. Affirmation of creole identity had facilitated a transition from colonial to independent status and, once formed, the newly independent states had widened the basis of political participation and encouraged commitment to the 'national' order. But nationalism was not yet a hegemonic concept capable of overcoming division; indeed, the efforts of centralising creole elites to impose their vision of the nation was often itself divisive. The new liberal states continued to be fundamentally the creation of creole elites who saw 'reform from above' on the Enlightenment model as the path to the future, and they had yet fully to translate their affirmation of American equality with Europe into a

[56] For examples, see Monica Quijada, 'Que Nación?' 40–51; also Frank Safford, 'Race, Integration and Progress: Elite Attitudes and the Indian in Colombia, 1750–1870', *Hispanic American Historical Review*, 71:1 (1991), 20–33. For a contrary example, showing how Social Darwinism could be used to defend people of mixed race as the basis of the nation, see David Brading, 'Social Darwinism and Romantic Idealism: Andrés Molina Enríquez and José Vasconcelos in the Mexican Revolution' in Brading, *Prophecy and Myth*, pp. 63–71.

broader inclusion of the many identities within their ethnically diverse societies. Thus the problems of building a political order based on a clearly defined territory, a sense of political community and shared, national values continued into the nineteenth century and, in some regions, extended into the twentieth.[57]

[57] David A. Brading, 'Nationalism and State-Building in Latin American History' in *Wars, Parties and Nationalism*, ed. Eduardo Posada-Carbó (London, 1995), 89–107.

CONCEPTIONS OF COMMUNITY IN COLONIAL SOUTHEAST ASIA

By A.J. Stockwell

READ 27 SEPTEMBER 1997 AT THE INSTITUTE OF HISTORICAL RESEARCH, LONDON

IT is a commonplace that European rule contributed both to the consolidation of the nation-states of Southeast Asia and to the aggravation of disputes within them. Since their independence, Burma, Cambodia, Indonesia, Laos, Malaysia, the Philippines, and Vietnam have all faced the upheavals of secessionism or irredentism or communalism. Governments have responded to threats of fragmentation by appeals to national ideologies like Sukarno's *pancasila* (five principles) or Ne Win's 'Burmese way to socialism'. In attempting to realise unity in diversity, they have paraded a common experience of the struggle for independence from colonial rule as well as a shared commitment to post-colonial modernisation. They have also ruthlessly repressed internal opposition or blamed their problems upon the foreign forces of neo-colonialism, world communism, western materialism, and other threats to Asian values. Yet, because its effects were uneven and inconsistent while the reactions to it were varied and frequently equivocal, the part played by colonialism in shaping the affiliations and identities of Southeast Asian peoples was by no means clear-cut.

I Colonial rule and plural societies

It seemed that no sooner had a nation achieved independence from colonial rule than it succumbed to civil war. Shortly after its inauguration in January 1948 the authority of the Union of Burma was resisted by minorities located on the margins of 'Burma proper'. First the Karens in 1948, and later the Chins, Kachins, Shans, and the Muslim Rohingyas of North Arakan—each of whom had enjoyed a special relationship with the British and felt little in common with Buddhist Burma—rose in revolt against the government in Rangoon which, after half a century of conflict, is now mastering minorities by military might.[1] The vast Republic of Indonesia, which consists of some 13,000 islands and is currently the fourth most populous country in the

[1] See Martin Smith, *Burma, Insurgency and the Politics of Ethnicity* (1991) and Clive Christie, *A Modern History of Southeast Asia. Decolonisation, Nationalism and Separatism* (1996), 53–80.

world, has been plagued by regional uprisings since its independence won international recognition on 27 December 1949. Sumatra to the west and Ambon to the east have each opposed central control from Java: in 1949 a Muslim-inspired rebellion was mounted from Aceh (north Sumatra) and from April to November the following year Christian Ambonese vainly strove to establish an independent republic of South Maluku.[2] A resurgence of discontent in Sumatra, West Java and the eastern archipelago led to the replacement of Indonesia's parliamentary experiment by Sukarno's authoritarian 'Guided Democracy' in the late 1950s. The geographic fragmentation of the Philippines (some 7,000 islands) has similarly patterned the identities of its peoples and contributed to ethnic risings. In particular, guerilla fighters representing the Muslim Moros of southern Mindanao and the Sulu archipelago (a community of about three million people in a total population of sixty-five millions) have been fighting since the early 1960s for the achievement of autonomy.[3] In its early years Malaysia was buffeted by the storms of regionalism and communalism. In 1965 Chinese-dominated Singapore withdrew from the Federation where Malays were politically transcendent. On 13 May 1969 fighting between Malays and Chinese in Kuala Lumpur and its neighbourhood brought the country to the brink of collapse.[4] The '13 May incident' in fact did more than the achievement of independence twelve years earlier to arouse a sense of national destiny: principles of state (the *Rukunegara*) were promulgated as was the New Economic Policy which, in various versions, has guided national planning ever since 1970. In addition Malaysia's apparently cosy relationship with Britain was reviewed. Mat Kilau, a freedom fighter of the 1890s, was discovered in the jungle of Pahang and lionised, albeit briefly, before he died allegedly at the age of 123. Among the eulogies was a tribute from Tun Abdul Razak, the deputy prime minister, who commemorated him as 'a warrior against colonialism' and said that he hoped 'the spirit of Mat Kilau will serve not only as an example but also as a challenge to the people in facing future problems in defending the independence and sovereignty of the nation'.[5] The riots of '13 May' undermined public confidence in Tunku Abdul Rahman, that great anglophile and 'bapak Malaysia' (father of Malaysia), with the result that in September 1970 he resigned as prime minister, yielding power to a younger generation of politicians.

One of these, the minister for special functions and minister for

[2] Christie, *A Modern History*, 108–26, 140–59.

[3] David Joel Steinberg, *The Philippines. A Singular and a Plural Place* (Boulder, 1994), 126–7.

[4] John Slimming, *Malaysia: Death of Democracy* (1969) and Gordon Means, *Malaysian Politics. The Second Generation* (Oxford, 1991), 4–16.

[5] *Straits Times* (Kuala Lumpur), 17 Aug. 1970.

information, Muhammad Ghazali Shafie, laid Malaysia's racial problems at the door of the British. Maintaining that Europeans first encountered a 'relatively homogeneous area with an appreciably common language and culture', he argued that the British, 'faced with the prospect of a united Malayan nation', resorted to divide and rule. 'It was,' he argued, 'too dangerous to have the local population united and sharing economic and political power.' Therefore, 'by force and subterfuge the colonial authorities established their direct and indirect rule'.[6] Though seminal in the articulation of a post-colonial identity for Malaysians, Ghazali Shafie's indictment of colonialism was neither original nor exclusively polemical. For scholars, too, have argued that imperial expansion, colonial rule and the process of decolonisation preyed on the distinctions between Southeast Asia's communities.

Europeans exploited identifiable divisions between Southeast Asian peoples in order to win control over them. For example, as they advanced eastwards from Bengal into the kingdom of Burma in the late eighteenth and early nineteenth centuries, the British came to rely on disaffected minorities who were traditionally in conflict with the dynasty. Lacking information about Burma, where they were excluded from the inner sanctum of the enclosed royal court, the British concluded military alliances with, and gained political intelligence from, hill communities and others on the outskirts of the kingdom.[7] Culturally and linguistically affiliated with the Thais, the Shans in Burma were recognised as a special group by the British who retained the Shans' system of hereditary princes even after they had abolished the Konbaung monarchy in Mandalay in 1886.[8] The support or 'loyalty' of the Muslim Rohingyas, who were descendants of Arab and Persian traders in the area of north Arakan, ensured them protection from the British regime in Rangoon. Other minorities, who had not been assimilated within Burmese Buddhism, were frequently converted to Christianity and recruited into the colonial army. Chins, Kachins, and Karens were all employed as soldiers. The Karens took part in the suppression of the Hsaya San anti-colonial rising in the Irrawaddy delta in 1930–2. A decade later they vainly resisted the Japanese invasion, suffering reprisals for covering the retreat of British and Indian troops to India.[9] Another example where colonial military needs contributed to ethnic differentiation comes from the Dutch East Indies. The Netherlands, a second-rate European power with a first-rate empire, employed different groups

[6] Tan Sri Dato' Muhammad Ghazali bin Shafie, *Democracy: The Realities Malaysians must face* (Kuala Lumpur, 1971), 3–4.

[7] C. A. Bayly, *Empire and Information. Intelligence Gathering and Social Communication in India, 1780–1870* (Cambridge, 1996), 97ff, 128, 141.

[8] Robert H. Taylor, *The State in Burma* (1987), 91–8.

[9] Smith, *Burma*, 62–4.

of Indonesians in the Dutch East Indian Army (KNIL), the Ambonese of the Maluku archipelago being especially renowned for their fighting prowess. As the KNIL expanded to subdue revolt and extend Dutch power to the outer islands the number of Indonesian soldiers rose from 5,500 in 1815 to 22,000 by the end of the century (an increase from 52 per cent to 61 per cent of the total force).[10]

For Europeans, whose resources were limited, ethnic compartmentalisation was an obvious technique of administration. A mantra of the Brookes, whose dynasty ruled Sarawak from 1841 to the Japanese occupation a century later, was that 'good fences make good neighbours'. Their regime attempted to keep distinct the boundaries between ethnic groups by constraining the mobility of nomads, by restricting intermarriage or by requiring both partners in mixed marriages to opt for membership of the same community.[11] Ethnic fences were erected throughout colonial Southeast Asia and were reinforced by colonial policy and practice. European conceptions of Southeast Asian identities affected the organisation of censuses (for example, Malaya's census for 1921 identified eight categories of Chinese and nine of Malay), led to the establishment of community-specific administrative departments (such as the Chinese Protectorate in the Straits Settlements), regulated the labour force (which often amounted to the management of immigrant Asians), and was a principle directing local recruitment to the colonial police and armed forces. Similarly the growth and management of colonial cities both reflected and reinforced the ethnic divisions of colonial societies.

In pre-colonial times, when Southeast Asian states were hardly defined in terms of territory and when power was exercised through personal relationships rather than bureaucratic structures, cities were constructed as citadels, hill-temples and royal courts. They projected both secular and cosmic order. As kingdoms rose and fell, so new dynasties selected fresh capitals. Beleaguered regimes could be forced to relocate, thus the Konbaung kings of Burma occupied five capitals in the century after 1752 before coming to rest at Mandalay in 1857. When the Thais were driven from Ayuthia by the Burmese in 1767, the Siamese general, Paya Taksin, travelled south to establish his capital at Thonburi on the River Chao Phraya. After Paya Taksin was overthrown, in 1782 his successor (Chakri or Rama I) founded Bangkok

[10] Martin Bossenbroek, 'The Living Tools of Empire: The Recruitment of European Soldiers for the Dutch Colonial Army, 1814–1909', *Journal of Imperial and Commonwealth History*, 23, 3 (Jan. 1995), 29.

[11] Robert Pringle, *Rajahs and Rebels: The Ibans of Sarawak under Brooke Rule, 1841–1941* (1970), 283ff; A.J. Stockwell, 'The White Man's Burden and Brown Humanity: Colonialism and Ethnicity in British Malaya', *Southeast Asian Journal of Social Science*, 10, 1 (1982), 44–68.

on the opposite bank of the river. Cities may have represented the royal and religious authority of enclosed kingdoms, but they also provided points of contact with other worlds. It was in cities and ports that European travellers and traders first encountered Southeast Asians and it was usually in existing towns or indigenous settlements that Europeans set up their forts and factories.

European economic needs and political anxieties significantly altered the functions and design of Southeast Asian cities.[12] Initially seeking to control trade, not to dominate territory, Europeans isolated their cities from a potentially hostile hinterland by building walls round them and restricting entry into them. Furthermore, rather than run the risk of becoming dependent upon unreliable indigenous elites, they chose to employ Asian immigrants (especially Chinese) as collaborators and compradores. From c. 1850 to 1940, however, the size and the function of Southeast Asian cities were transformed: they changed from enclaves perched on river banks or on the coast to centres for the political and economic domination of the interior. By the late 1930s over sixteen cities had populations above 100,000; of these Batavia, Bangkok (which in many ways resembled a colonial city), Manila, Rangoon, and Singapore had between 500,000 and one million inhabitants. They grew spatially, too. As migrants from up-country and overseas were drawn in, so affluent colonial suburbs were developed while shanty towns sprang up on the fringes.

Urbanisation during the 'high colonial period' expanded at such a pace as to require, yet defy, strict control. Though a tiny minority, westerners dominated urban space; they created a colonial order of ethnic 'quarters' and demonstrated their authority by the erection of buildings that were prestigious as well as functional, such as government house, the secretariat, and the cathedral. On the other hand, towns posed problems of disorder: they attracted the landless and dispossessed from the countryside; secret societies ran protection rackets; competing communities clashed with each other; print culture and foreign contact stimulated self-awareness. Indeed, urbanisation contributed to the emergence of new identities. Being cosmopolitan, colonial cities served as conduits for new ideas and as dynamos of change.[13]

In addition to the military, political and administrative practices of

[12] Leonard Y. Andaya, 'Interactions with the Outside World and Adaptation in Southeast Asian Society, 1500–1880' in Nicholas Tarling ed., *The Cambridge History of Southeast Asia* (2 vols., Cambridge, 1992), I, 345, 361–72; Anthony Reid, 'Economic and Social Change, *c.*1400–1800', *ibid.*, 472–76, 494–5; Robert Elson, 'International Commerce, the State and Society: Economic and Social Change', *Cambridge History of Southeast Asia*, II, 168–71.

[13] See Benedict Anderson, *Imagined Communities. Reflections on the Origins and Spread of Nationalism* (1991 ed.).

Europeans, therefore, the dynamics of the colonial economy contributed to the emergence of communal awareness and to the articulation of ethnic identities. These developments occurred not only in towns but in the countryside too. So as not to upset the stability of indigenous societies, immigrant Asians were frequently used to produce export commodities: for example, Chinese and Indians laboured in Malaya's tin mines and rubber plantations; Chinese and Javanese cleared forests and planted estates in Sumatra; Tonkinese were similarly employed in French Cambodia and Cochinchina; and Indian labourers and moneylenders opened up Burma's Irrawaddy as one of the world's principal rice bowls. The Dutch responded to the massive growth of Java's population (by 1930 nearly 70 per cent of Indonesians lived in Java and Madura) by sponsoring emigration to the outer islands of the archipelago and particularly to plantations in east Sumatra (a policy continued after independence as 'transmigration').[14] By the 1920s Burma's economy was in the hands of the British, Indians and Chinese, in that order, while Malaya's economy was dominated by British, Chinese and Indians. Under British rule, Rangoon effectively became an Indian city and Kuala Lumpur a Chinese one. The ancient connections between China and the *nanyang* (southern sea) were enlarged from the mid-nineteenth century as the trickle of Chinese migrants developed into a flood. Fleeing hardships at home and attracted to opportunities in colonial Southeast Asia, overseas Chinese permeated the region. Valued for their enterprise and labour, the Chinese were nonetheless regarded in most colonies (and also to a certain extent in Siam) as transients and legal barriers were erected to prevent their assimilation. Thus were created what J. S. Furnivall defined as 'plural societies' in which ethnic differences were reinforced by the distinct economic functions performed by separate communities.[15]

Ethnicity not only shaped the acquisition and maintenance of empires, it also influenced the process of their decline and fall. European attempts to defeat or delay nationalist campaigns for independence further fostered counter-nationalist identities of race or religion or regionalism. During Indonesia's *perjuangan* or struggle for independence after the Second World War, Ambonese fought on the side of the Dutch against Sukarno's unitarist Republic. Fearful of reprisals—or at least suspicious of a regime perceived to be dominated by Javanese and Muslims—veterans from that campaign were later resettled with their families in Holland. At the same time, the French tried to turn to their advantage the mistrust felt towards the Vietminh by Vietnamese

[14] M. C. Ricklefs, *A History of Modern Indonesia c.1300 to the Present* (1981), 147.

[15] J. S. Furnivall, *Colonial Policy and Practice: A Comparative Study of Burma and Netherlands India* (Cambridge, 1948).

minorities. In May 1946 Admiral d'Argenlieu (France's High Commissioner in Indochina, 1945–7) launched a scheme to create a separate state for the 'Montagnards' or 'hill folk' of Vietnam's Central Highlands.[16] In another move to undermine Ho Chi Minh's exclusive claims upon Vietnamese nationalism, d'Argenlieu fostered separateness amongst the Cochinchinese by declaring an autonomous Republic of Cochinchina on 1 June 1946. He justified this policy as follows:

> Was not the argument of linguistic unity used by the Führer to force German minorities to join the Reich? In Indochina it has always been, and remains, France's mission to protect ethnic minorities against the Annamite tendency to imperialism.[17]

By contrast, after the Second World War the British substituted 'unite and quit' for 'divide and rule'. They supported Aung San in his attempt to assimilate minorities into a Union of Burma, while in Malaya their policy swung dramatically after the Second World War from their former pro-Malay stance to a new commitment to multi-racialism.[18] Their intention was to bind Malays, Chinese and Indians into a Malayan nation to which they might eventually transfer power and with which they might maintain a cordial post-colonial relationship. This strategy was compromised, however, by the deep-seated communalism to which the British themselves had previously contributed.

II Colonial conceptions of identity

Although Europeans assigned roles to Southeast Asian peoples, the view that colonial needs and colonial practices alone determined their identities should be qualified in three respects. First, however sharply colonialism may have intensified ethnic separatism, it did not create it. Such diversity predated European rule. It was a feature of both pre-colonial urban life and the personal rule of indigenous monarchs. Moreover, the conditions which drew immigrants to Southeast Asia and which correspondingly drove them from their homelands, particularly China, were in place long before the establishment of colonial regimes. Second, the capacity of Europeans to restructure indigenous societies, in the manner suggested by 'strategies of divide and rule', was circumscribed. In most parts of Southeast Asia the duration of colonial rule was relatively brief, its resources limited and its impact skin-deep.

[16] Christie, *A Modern History*, 90–1.

[17] Cited in Martin Shipway, *The Road to War. France and Vietnam, 1944–1947* (Oxford, 1996), 192.

[18] See Hugh Tinker ed., *Constitutional Relations between Britain and Burma: The Struggle for Independence 1944–48*, 2 vols. (1983–4) and A.J. Stockwell ed., *British Documents on the End of Empire: Malaya, 1942–57*, 3 parts (1995).

Consequently, Europeans resorted to ethnic differentiation because of a self-conscious weakness rather than in a triumphalist demonstration of power. Third, ethnic compartmentalisation was not simply the product of colonial needs, be they military, administrative, or economic; it also derived from European perceptions of Asian communities.

European perceptions of Southeast Asians were shaped at first by ignorance and later by accumulated knowledge.[19] Early impressions were strongly influenced by ignorance and prejudice, which juxtaposed the rational and the modern of the West against an Orient of superstition, tyranny, corruption, and the exotic. When Conrad's shipwrecked sailor came ashore in the East Indies he saw 'Brown, bronze, yellow faces, the black eyes, the glitter, the colour of an Eastern crowd.'[20] When James Johnston Abraham landed at Penang, he felt he 'was looking on at a theatrical performance—the cosmopolitan crowd composed of every nation in the East appeared so tricked out for effect, the vivid colouring of the Orient smote the eye so insistently'.[21] Differences between East and West were alluded to, though scarcely explained, in metaphors of progress, stagnation and decline. Racial, moral, institutional, or environmental tropes littered the observations of contemporaries who attributed to Southeast Asian societies western paradigms of monarchy and the state, of feudalism and landownership, of community and clan, of religion and criminality. In addition to concepts imported from Europe, they applied models acquired elsewhere in Asia: for example, in both Java during the Napoleonic wars and in Burma after the conquest of 1885 the British introduced a wholly inappropriate administration based upon their experiences of the village in India. The ascription of identities to Southeast Asian communities was also influenced by Europeans' own sense of community. Life on the frontier and contact with the 'other' sharpened self-awareness and strengthened communal bonds. As numbers of Europeans increased, with some families acquiring an almost dynastic position as a result of generations of contact with certain areas, so colonial societies assumed a hierarchy, homogeneity and ideology that marked them off as distinct communities. Though they recreated 'home' in a way of life, whose totems included exclusive clubs and hill stations, colonial communities differed from those at home, not least in the scarcity of poor whites.[22]

[19] Bayly, *Empire and Information*, 52; cf. Edward W. Said, *Orientalism: Western Conceptions of the Orient* (1978).

[20] Joseph Conrad, *Youth: A Narrative* (1927 edn.), 45.

[21] James Johnston Abraham, *The Surgeon's Log* (1911, 1940 edn.), 52.

[22] For the colonial community of Malaya see John G. Butcher, *The British in Malaya 1880–1941: The Social History of a European Community in Colonial South-East Asia* (Kuala Lumpur, 1979); for the hill station's centrality to the identity of the British in India see Dane Kennedy, *The Magic Mountains: Hill Stations and the British Raj* (Berkeley, 1996).

Their own sense of community established criteria by which Europeans identified and regulated non-Europeans. In these and other ways, they sorted the unfamiliar into familiar categories of princes and peasants, merchants and artisans, nomads and villagers, the religious and the pagan, the reliably martial and the irredeemably turbulent.

Many Europeans, therefore, looked at Southeast Asian societies through a glass darkly, staying their eyes upon reflections of their own values. Some penetrated further and, after months spent without European company, felt, as did H. Fielding Hall of his experiences with the Burmese, that they 'had been—even if it were only for a time—behind the veil, where it is so hard to come'.[23] Indeed, in order to compensate for shortages of material power, colonials were obliged to acquire the power of knowledge. Like Meiji Japan, imperial Europe sought knowledge throughout the world in order to strengthen the foundations of their rule.

They went about this in three ways.[24] The first was through the assiduous recording of personal observations, as did John Anderson, Daniel Beeckman, John Cameron, Hiram Cox, John Crawford, Michael Symes, Henry Yule, and many others.[25] Secondly, they employed Asians as guides, scribes, translators, and language teachers. When Raffles moved from India to the Malay world, for example, he depended upon his language tutor or *munshi* as teacher, translator and scribe. Munshi Abdullah was of Indian and Arab background and lived in the Straits Settlements; versed in Islamic learning and Malay literature, he provided the British with a bridge into Malay society. An admirer of the British who drew upon Islamic, Malay and European philosophical traditions, Munshi Abdullah also looked at Malay society afresh and 'helped initiate the process by which the Malays acquired a political discourse'.[26] Half a century later Munshi Mahomed Said ('the best informed Malay of his time', according to Swettenham) taught Malay to Frank Swettenham and collaborated with him in making a Malay translation of the Pangkor Engagement (1874) whereby the British established the

[23] H. Fielding Hall, *The Soul of a People* (1898, 1902 edn.), 2.

[24] *Cf.* Bayly, *Empire and Information, passim.*

[25] John Anderson, *Political and Commercial Considerations Relative to the Malayan Peninsula and the British Settlements in the Straits of Malacca* (Prince of Wales Island, 1824), Daniel Beeckman, *A Voyage to and from the Island of Borneo in the East Indies* (1718), J. Cameron, *Our Tropical Possessions in Malayan India: Singapore, Penang, Province Wellesley, Malacca* (1865), Hiram Cox, *Journal of a Residence in the Burmhan Empire* (1821), John Crawfurd, *Journal of an Embassy ... to the Court of Ava in the year 1827* (1829), Crawfurd, *Journal of an Embassy from the Governor-General of India to the Courts of Siam and Cochin China* (1828), Michael Symes, *An Account of an Embassy to the Kingdom of Ava* (1800), Sir Henry Yule, *A Narrative of the Mission sent by the Governor-General of India to the Court of Ava in 1855* (1858).

[26] Anthony Milner, *The Invention of Politics in Colonial Malaya. Contesting Nationalism and the Expansion of the Public Sphere* (Cambridge, 1995), 11.

residential system in the state of Perak.[27] Charged in 1888 to return to the Malay state of Pahang after a preliminary visit in order to negotiate a treaty with its ruler, the young Hugh Clifford was painfully conscious of the limitations of his local and linguistic knowledge: 'The Malays with whom I was now associating', he later recalled, 'no longer *wanted* [sic] me to understand them.'[28] He therefore recruited a small staff of Malays: Raja Haji Mahmud of Selangor (the Raja Hamid of Clifford's short stories) acted as go-between in the discussions with the Pahang court; Raja Uteh, a descendant of Mendeling royalty from Sumatra, also acted as Clifford's adviser; and Alang Ahmad, a young Perak Malay, served as scribe. Knowledge could generate empathy, though Europeans who were deemed to have identified too closely with their 'adopted people', might run foul of colonial authorities for 'going native' or provoke nationalist politicians on the ground that they were 'subverting' minorities. For example, in 1946 H. N. C. Stevenson, one of the best-informed officials serving in Burma's Frontier Areas, was forced to resign from government service, because he urged the accommodation of Karen claims to partial autonomy. Stevenson was criticised by Aung San's party (the AFPFL, Anti-Fascist People's Freedom League), which demanded early independence for a united Burma, and was ignored by the London authorities which were seeking a quick escape route out of Burma.[29] A similar fate befell John K. Wilson ('Budu Wilson') who, as an education officer in Sarawak after 1949, spent years setting up community development projects for remote Dyak peoples until, having refused to act as a political influence on behalf of the Malaysian federal government, he was served with banishment papers on 24 May 1968 and ordered never to return.[30] The third pathway to knowledge was far more institutionalised; it ran through the agencies which colonial regimes set up to survey, quantify and control the human and material resources of the country, notably the police, land, medical and educational departments. Officials accumulated, classified and evaluated useful knowledge. In so doing, they identified communities and ascribed characteristics to them. They mapped terrain and located communities; they counted heads according to racial or religious categories; they surveyed land, mineral deposits and agricultural production, and established ownership; they traced genealogies and legitimised indigenous rulers.

Information was disseminated not only in government reports but also by learned societies, such as the Straits (later Malayan/Malaysian)

[27] Sir Frank Swettenham, *Footprints in Malaya* (1942), 16, 33. See also Henry Barlow, *Swettenham* (Kuala Lumpur, 1995), 47–9.

[28] Hugh Clifford, Autobiographical Preface to the 1927 edition of *In Court and Kampong*.

[29] Smith, *Burma*, 74–8, Christie, *A Modern History*, 73.

[30] John K. Wilson, *Budu or Twenty Years in Sarawak* (North Berwick, 1969), 279–80.

Branch of the Royal Asiatic Society and the *Ecole Française d'Extrême Orient* which opened in Hanoi in 1900. The peoples of Southeast Asia were also presented to a wider public in travel literature and museums. The museum in Paris, established in 1839 by Louis Philippe to collect colonial 'curiosities', expanded over a century and a half, and was renamed first the Ethnography Museum and later the Museum of Man.[31] In Britain the Royal Geographical Society, the South Kensington complex, the Pitt-Rivers and Horniman museums collected ethnographical material relating to Southeast Asia.[32] In the region itself, archaeological and anthropological findings were displayed from Hanoi to Kuching. In 1920 the French archaeologist and painter, George Groslier, designed the *Musée des Beaux Arts* in Phnom Penh in Khmer style to house a large library and exhibit works largely from the Angkor period. After the Second World War, Tom Harrisson, renowned explorer and co-founder of Mass-Observation, created in the Sarawak Museum, Kuching, one of the finest collections of Southeast Asian ethnography. Administrators became scholars and scholars were employed as administrators. For example, bogged down in the thirty-years' war against Muslim Acehnese (northern Sumatra), the Dutch colonial government appointed their leading Islamicist and ethnologist, Dr Christiaan Snouck Hurgronje (1857–1936), as principal adviser on indigenous Indonesian matters. He advocated crushing the *ulamas* (religious leaders) and building up the authority of secular chiefs. This strategy succeeded as regards the short-term pacification of Aceh, though it exacerbated divisions within Acehnese society. As for Snouck Hurgronje, he went on to a chair at the University of Leiden.[33]

Crucial to the control of knowledge was the command of language. Missionaries joined scholar-administrators in converting spoken languages into written ones (as did Dutch and German evangelists working with the Bataks in the highlands of Lake Toba in northern Sumatra) and in transcribing written languages into the Roman alaphabet. French Jesuits, notably Alexandre de Rhodes, working in Annam during the seventeenth century, converted Vietnamese to Christianity and their script to Roman characters or *quoc-ngu*. British and Dutch administrators romanised the *jawi* or Arabic script of the Malays. Just as the flora and fauna of the region were collected and exhibited to European audiences, so indigenous languages were encased in dictionaries. In Malaya, Frank Swettenham, Hugh Clifford, and especially Richard Wilkinson and Richard Winstedt, were lexicographers as well as administrators. A

[31] Robert Aldrich, *Greater France. A History of French Overseas Expansion* (Basingstoke, 1996), 247.

[32] *Cf.* Annie E. Coombes, *Re-Inventing Africa: Museums, Material Culture, and Popular Imagination in Late Victorian and Edwardian England* (New Haven, Conn., 1994).

[33] Ricklefs, *A History of Modern Indonesia*, 137–8.

senior member of the Malayan Civil Service, Sir Richard Winstedt (1878–1966) played a major part in shaping educational policy. In providing primary, vernacular schools for Malays (to make them better farmers and fishermen) but neglecting the children of immigrant races and in adapting Malay language to modern needs, he focused on the traditional values and virtues of Malay rural life. Amongst his publications are a *Malay Grammar* (1913), *An English-Malay Dictionary* (three volumes, 1914–17) and *A Dictionary of Colloquial Malay* (1920). On retirement from the MCS in 1935 he became lecturer and later reader at the School of Oriental Studies, London. He was elected FBA in 1945 and served as either director or president of the Royal Asiatic Society from 1940 to 1964. During this period he published prolifically, including six new dictionaries. Malays said of him: 'God gave us our language; Sir Richard Winstedt gave us our grammar.'[34]

III Modernisation and Asian values

The colonial mind tended to ascribe characteristics to particular social groups. Although it did not itself create ethnicity, the political, economic and cultural effects of colonialism intensified the demarcation between communities. The impact of colonialism was, however, neither uniform nor consistent. On the one hand, policies could institutionalise some customs and structures of a community to the neglect of its other features, thereby reinforcing and sometimes recreating certain selected traditions. On the other hand, though administrative practice may have generally conserved the old order in the interests of stability, colonialism was a powerful vehicle for change—indeed, it was universally associated with change, whether for good or for ill. Modernisation under colonial rule disrupted customary relationships, destroyed the moral economy of the village, eroded traditional culture, and presented indigenous inhabitants with the challenge of immigrant competition. Thus, the colonial state differed from the pre-colonial state in the increased size, scope and intensity of its government; as it extended its range, so it provided the mould and means for the emergence of new identities. Moreover, the colonial economy differed from the pre-colonial economy. The labour force was concentrated in mines, plantations and towns while an increasing number of peasants were dispossessed to become either labourers on land owned by others or wage-earners outside rural production.[35] Shared predicaments bred common aspir-

[34] *Cf.* John Bastin, 'Sir Richard Winstedt and his writings' in J. Bastin and R. Roolvink eds., *Malayan and Indonesian Studies. Essays presented to Sir Richard Winstedt on his 85th Birthday* (1964).

[35] R. E. Elson, *The End of the Peasantry in Southeast Asia. A Social and Economic History of Peasant Livelihood, 1800–1990s* (Basingstoke, 1997), 239–41.

ations. Furthermore; colonial cities, with their elaborate infrastructure, differed from pre-colonial cities not only in their size but also in the strength of the political and economic grip they exercised upon the countryside. The railways and roads which extended the reach of the rulers also widened the horizons of the ruled. In addition to spreading colonial knowledge, printing and the media broadcast foreign ideas and stimulated indigenous cultural revivals. Colonialism, therefore, sharpened the self-awareness of Southeast Asian peoples who increasingly identified themselves by reference to the 'other'. Reacting to the loss of political power, growth of the colonial state, economic exploitation, Asian immigration, expansion of towns, development of communications, and the spread of print capitalism, Southeast Asian peoples redefined their identities according to a spectrum of values associated with traditional authority, religious revivalism, racial solidarity, and modernity.

First of all, in society after society the colonial take-over provoked a defence of vested interests and a reassertion of traditional authority by monarchs, princes and chiefs who had been deposed or had their authority severely cut. Within a year of the establishment of the residential system in Perak (1875), Malay chiefs rose in a vain attempt to drive out the British who also fought intermittent campaigns against disaffected Pahang *orang besars* (chiefs) between 1890 and 1895. After the deposition of King Thibaw in 1886, princes of Upper Burma tied down thousands of British and Indian troops in a six-year guerilla campaign. Aspirations to restore the monarchy in Burma revived in the early 1930s in the rural uprising led by Hsaya San. In Vietnam, after he had been partly forced and partly duped into territorial concessions, Emperor Tu Doc bemoaned not only the passing of his power but also his inability to fulfil an imperial role ordained by a cosmic order. 'Never has an era seen such sadness,' he lamented, 'never a year more anguish. Above me, I fear the edicts of heaven. Below, the tribulations of the people trouble my days and nights. Deep in my heart, I tremble and blush, finding neither words nor actions to help my subjects.'[36] After the Vietnamese surrender of Tonkin, Phan Dinh Phung and De Tham continued rearguard opposition to the French occupation of the villages. Phan Dinh Phung died in 1897 'suffering from dysentery and clawing at grass roots for food', and De Tham remained free until 1913 when 'his head was cut off and paraded through the recalcitrant provinces'. They failed to save the king and his kingdom from the French.[37] Heirs to a strong, anti-colonial tradition

[36] Quoted in Stanley Karnow, *Vietnam. A History* (1994 edn.), 91.

[37] Greg Lockhart, *Nation in Arms. The Origins of the People's Army of Vietnam* (Sydney, 1989), 35–6.

born of a thousand-year conflict with China, Vietnamese scholar-gentry maintained their opposition to the French for a quarter-century after their country had been occupied and military resistance quelled.[38]

Secondly, anti-colonialism became entwined with religious revivalism. Burman identity, having been dealt a savage blow by the collapse of the Buddhist monkhood under British rule, was resurrected from the early twentieth century by the Young Men's Buddhist Association, the General Council of Buddhist Associations, and by *pongyis* or itinerant monks in the depressed delta area. Islam not only inspired the armed resistance of the Acehnese and Padri of Sumatra but, in its modernist, revivalist form, it also underpinned Indonesia's first mass political organisation, the *Sarekat Islam* (founded in 1912). In the Philippines, Muslims of Mindanao and the Sulu archipelago have mounted successive *jihads* against the Spanish, Americans and post-colonial regimes in Manila, while folk Catholicism was a major ingredient of local protest against Spanish and American colonialism at the end of the nineteenth and early twentieth centuries. Though José Rizal pioneered secular nationalism his memory became fused with Christ. Moreover, the Katipunan's appeal to both independence and redemption contained strong elements of peasant faith and, even in the radical-left Hukbalahap movement of the 1940s, there were echoes of the local religious tradition.[39] In Vietnam, on the other hand, local converts to Roman Catholicism became closely associated with the colonial administration; indeed, the formation in the 1930s of syncretist sects, such as the Cao Dai Church (which borrowed from Confucian, Taoist, Buddhist and Christian traditions) and the Hoa Hao (which 'was the closest that colonial Vietnam came to possessing a Buddhist mass movement') amounted to local rejection of the collaboration between Vietnamese Catholics and the French regime.[40]

Thirdly, immigration during the colonial period reinforced communal bonds, aggravated race relations and particularly encouraged anti-Chinese feeling. The Chinese community was an obvious target of Islamic modernism in Java and the Malay States; one of the motives behind the formation of the *Sarekat Islam* was the desire on the part of Javanese batik traders to protect themselves against exploitation by Chinese middlemen. In Siam, King Vajiravudh (Rama VI, 1910–25) made a bid for popularity by dubbing the Chinese as 'Jews of the East'. Similarly, when he became prime minister in 1938, General Phibunsongkhram proclaimed 'Thailand for the Thai', a confection of '"Thai-ness" and Buddhism which, in turn, provided the foundation

[38] David G. Marr, *Vietnamese Anticolonialism* (Berkeley, 1971).
[39] Steinberg, *The Philippines*, 85–9.
[40] David G. Marr, *Vietnamese Tradition on Trial, 1920–45* (Berkeley, 1981), 89–90, 305–6.

for uniformity of the national culture and social values, and the prescribed way of life'. Although his biographer has argued that 'Phibun's nationalism was not particularly anti-Chinese', he accepts that Phibun's 'measures affected the Chinese more not because they were Chinese but because they were the biggest foreign community in economic activities in Thailand.'[41] In neighbouring Burma riots resulting in Chinese deaths occurred in January 1931 in Rangoon and other parts of the Irrawaddy delta region, though the conflict was on a lesser scale than the bitter communalism between Burmese and Indians during the 1930s.

Fourthly, the modernisation of the governments and economies of colonial Southeast Asia contributed to the development of another type of identity—that of cross-communal nationhood. As the colonial state expanded, so it recruited more Asian functionaries. For example, almost 250,000 indigenes were on the government payroll in the Dutch East Indies by the late 1920s.[42] Government service for the Dutch East Indies contributed to a sense of a wider community embracing the archipelago as a whole, of being Indonesian rather than Javanese or Sumatran. Profiles of emerging national identities were shaped by the language of command used in the new states: English was the official language in Burma, Malaya and the Philippines; French in Indochina where the tradition of the *lycée* supplanted that of the mandarinate; *bahasa Melayu* (Malay) in the Dutch East Indies; and Thai in Thailand. Since the Dutch used *bahasa Melayu* throughout the archipelago, so it became the medium of literary and political expression and a tool for the creation of a sense of Indonesian solidarity. In independent Siam, Prince Damrong (minister of the interior and first director of education) employed the Thai language in mass primary education, monastic schools and specialised colleges for the sons of bureaucrats in order to keep colonialism at bay and combat the western perception that the Thai were uncivilised. In so doing, Prince Damrong made 'a reality of Thai nationhood'.[43]

Although Chulalongkorn, Siam's modernising monarch (1867–1910), was 'convinced that there exists no incompatibility between such acquisition [of European science] and the maintenance of our individuality as an independent Asiatic nation',[44] western education led to conflicts of identity. Not only did it add to the distance between elites

[41] Kobkua Suwannathat-Pian, *Thailand's Durable Premier. Phibun through Three Decades 1932–1957* (Kuala Lumpur, 1995), 107. On Vajiravudh's idea of the nation, see David K. Wyatt, *Thailand. A Short History* (New Haven, Conn., 1984 ed.), 229–30.

[42] Anderson, *Imagined Communities*, 115.

[43] David K. Wyatt, *The Politics of Reform in Thailand: Education in the Reign of King Chulalongkorn* (New Haven, Conn., 1969), 102.

[44] Wyatt, *Thailand. A Short History*, 211.

and the peasant mass of society, it also plunged individuals into uncertainty and sometimes overwhelming turmoil. Attempts to synthesise western and eastern civilisations could founder on contrasting approaches to individualism, as is illustrated by the ideas of Pham Quynh, who dominated Vietnamese intellectual life from 1917 to 1930. A Francophile who worked for greater understanding between French and Vietnamese philosophical traditions, Pham Quynh baulked at the preeminence given to individualism in the West. In his view, individualism and equality struck at the heart of 'a natural order' in which the individual was subordinated to the group. 'Without a fixed set of rules,' he wrote, 'people's hearts are perturbed, society is dangerous'.[45] The appeals of western and eastern values—perceived to be individualism and materialism, on the one hand, and the wider obligations to community and spirituality, on the other—posed all sorts of dilemmas. Take, for example, the contrasts between life in the village and life in the town which are sometimes drawn in the Malay vernacular literature of the interwar years. Whereas the countryside is alleged to embody tradition, conservatism, simplicity and virtue, towns are associated with modernity, change, sophistication, even vice.[46] Another literary theme, this time running through colonial writings about Asia in the late nineteenth and early twentieth centuries, is what Europeans regarded as the unbridgeable gulf between East and West. Saleh, the eponymous Malay prince of Hugh Clifford's novels, loses touch with his own way of life as a result of his education in England, but, having been ostracised by the English when he woos his host's daughter, Saleh returns to Pahang and ends his life running amok in rebellion against British rule. In the foreword to *Saleh: A Sequel* Clifford spells out the potential dangers of the British 'endeavouring to impose on their Oriental brethren education of a purely Occidental type', which the fictional British political officer states more dramatically at the end of the story: 'May God forgive us for our sorry deeds and for our glorious intentions!'[47]

Another example of the inconsistent effects of colonialism and the equivocal reactions to it relates to the position of women. Southeast Asian women customarily enjoyed higher status than those in many other regions of Asia and were prominent in agriculture and trade. Colonialism depressed many to the level of prostitutes, domestic servants

[45] Quoted in Neil L. Jamieson, *Understanding Vietnam* (Berkeley, 1995 ed.), 84.

[46] William R. Roff, *The Origins of Malay Nationalism* (New Haven, Conn., 1967), 253.

[47] The novel was written in two parts: the first, *Sally: A Study* (1904), covers his education and collapse in England; the second, *Saleh: A Sequel* (1908), sees his return to Malaya and the desperate uprising. The two were combined and republished in the USA as *A Prince of Malaya* (1926) which was reprinted, with an introduction by J. M. Gullick, by Oxford University Press, Singapore, in 1989.

and lowly-paid textile workers, yet enhanced the roles of others as go-betweens in a man's world and offered opportunities of advancement to a few.[48] Female emancipation exercised those brought up in either the Islamic or Confucian traditions. Islamic reformists, such as Sayyid Shaykh Al-Hadi of the Straits Settlements, urged that women be freed from traditional constraints so as 'to receive education and participate in social affairs'.[49] In Java the Kartini fund was set up in 1913 in memory of Raden Kartini (1879–1904), a campaigner for women's education. The fund endowed Dutch-language education for young women from well-placed families. In Indonesia, writes Ricklefs, 'Kartini is remembered as an early representative of female emancipation and the national awakening' of the country.[50] In Vietnam, the staunch conservative, Pham Quynh, was hard-pressed to reconcile French egalitarianism with the Vietnamese *yin-yang* distinction between male and female roles, and he advocated education for women only in so far as it would enable them to be better home-makers and stronger supporters of family life.[51]

Southeast Asian communities were unsettled by western challenges. Groups and individuals differed in their responses to the European ideological assault which was transmitted through colonial administration and law, education and printing, immigration and urban settlement, capitalism and class formation. The anxieties and varied reactions of Malays have been examined by Anthony Milner who has scrutinised key Malay texts. His analysis has revealed an unresolved dispute between three principal ideological orientations: *kerajaan* (or the tradition of the authority of the sultanate), *bangsa* (the bond of race), and *umat* (affiliation with the Islamic congregation). It is, he has concluded, the discourse between these ideologies that has shaped the identity of Malays through the colonial and post-colonial periods.[52]

Colonialism aggravated tensions and contradictions between overlapping identities with the result that individuals were frequently torn in different directions according to their allegiances to the affiliations of race, religion, gender, residence, country of origin, ancestry, occupation, and education. In some cases, however, colonially ascribed characteristics were accepted and adopted by Southeast Asian peoples. A glaring example of the assumption by a subject people of an ascribed identity is the stereotypology of the Malay as 'the lazy native'. By succumbing to the 'spell of the colonial image of the Malays', Syed Hussein Alatas has written, some Malays have behaved like 'some

[48] Elson, 'Economic and Social Change', *Cambridge History of Southeast Asia*, II, 177–9.
[49] Roff, *Origins of Malay Nationalism*, 78–9.
[50] Ricklefs, *A History of Modern Indonesia*, 149.
[51] Jamieson, *Understanding Vietnam*, 85–8.
[52] Milner, *The Invention of Politics in Colonial Malaya*.

American negroes who believe what white racialists say about them'.[53] Seeing similarities with 'Fanon's strictures against the nationalist bourgeoisie', Said has drawn attention to '[o]ne of the sharpest attacks in Alatas's *The Myth of the Lazy Native* [which] is against those Malaysians who continue to reproduce in their own thinking the colonial ideology that created and sustained the "lazy native" idea.'[54]

In reaction to post-colonial cultural imperialism, of which the 'myth of the lazy native' is an aspect, and in an attempt to establish a distinctive identity for Southeast Asia as a whole, contemporary leaders of the 'tiger economies' of the Association of Southeast Asian Nations (ASEAN) are propagating 'Asian values' in opposition to western imperialism, individualism and materialism.[55] Determined to resist the currency speculation of foreigners, liberal criticisms of ASEAN's authoritarian regimes, diplomatic pressure over the association's relations with Burma, and what he sees as the 'green colonialism' of environmentalism, Dr Mahathir, prime minister of Malaysia, claims that westerners are still clinging to political paramountcy, economic domination and intellectual hegemony. At the time of the Pergau Dam affair in 1994, when *The Sunday Times* revealed links between British aid and Malaysian arms orders, he condemned some British journalists for having 'colonial brains' and dismissed press freedom as 'a myth invented by the so-called liberal west to serve their own purpose'.[56] The previous year, in May 1993, representatives of Asian nations meeting in Bangkok had issued a new definition of human rights that put more emphasis on social stability and economic development than on individual freedom. Democracy, freedom of the press and human rights were regarded as 'western concepts' which are not necessarily appropriate to Asian societies, at least not in the forms practised in the West. The term 'Asian values' suggests, furthermore, that the countries of Southeast Asia share a common culture. Yet, long regarded as the crossroads of world civilisations or as a palimpsest of alien influences, the region is marked more by its diversity than its unity. A geographical expression, which was first used to designate a military command during the Second World War, Southeast Asia, unlike Europe or Latin America, lacks a common cultural core. Islam, Confucianism, Buddhism—each of which transcends not only the frontiers of Southeast Asian states but also the boundaries of the region itself—neither individually nor in

[53] Syed Hussein Alatas, *The Myth of the Lazy Native: A Study of the Image of the Malays, Filipinos, and Javenese from the Sixteenth to the Twentieth Century and its Function in the Ideology of Colonial Capitalism* (1977), 155, 166.

[54] Edward W. Said, *Culture and Imperialism* (1993), 301.

[55] See the historiographical review by T. N. Harper, '"Asian Values" and Southeast Asian Histories', *The Historical Journal*, 40, 2 (1997), 507–17.

[56] *The Sunday Times*, 6 Feb. 1994.

combination have provided the foundation for a recognisably regional identity. In short, it would seem that the notion of 'Asian values' suffers from the very simplicity, generality and selectivity that were hallmarks of Europe's 'orientalist' attitude to Southeast Asian communities during the colonial period.

THE ROYAL HISTORICAL SOCIETY

REPORT OF COUNCIL, SESSION 1997–1998

THE Council of the Royal Historical Society has the honour to present the following report to the Anniversary Meeting.

1. Developments within the Society during the year

a) The new Editorial Board for *Studies in History* continued its successful start, commissioning further volumes for the new series. Over sixty proposals have so far been dealt with by the Board since it was re-convened in 1995. Four volumes were launched at the reception after the 1997 Anniversary Meeting. Six further volumes will be launched after the Society's 1998 Anniversary Meeting on 20th November at University College London.

b) The Society continued its support for postgraduate research. On the advice of the Research Support Committee 69 individual grants were made to postgraduates and some others to attend training courses and conferences and to undertake visits essential for their research, as well as to the organisers of 17 conferences, primarily to enable younger scholars to attend them. Supplements were paid to 4 holders of awards under the Overseas Research Scheme. The Society continues to provide a Centenary Fellowship at the Institute of Historical Research for a student in the last year of his or her research. A list of those who received awards is attached at Appendix A to this Report.

c) Publications appeared in the Society's series, *Transactions*, *Camden Series* and *Camden* Reprints. In addition to the annual volume of *Transactions*, which included the papers from a conference on the 'Eltonian Legacy', that is on the historical legacy of Sir Geoffrey Elton, not only a great historian but a great benefactor of the Society, two volumes of the *Camden Series* and one volume in the reprint series appeared this year. A new list of 'Fellows, Corresponding Fellows, Associates and Members' has been issued. For the first time this list includes research interests, an innovation that has proved to be of great value. The Society's membership is urged to check their entries and to supply omissions, corrections or additions.

d) The Society has been involved in a wide range of issues of concern to history and historians in Britain. It responded to an invitation to submit names for the History Benchmarking Group that is to work with the Quality Assurance Agency in establishing benchmarks for degree standards and has closely monitored the work of the Group. The Society is giving its full support to the Historical Association's 'Campaign for History', which is aimed at trying to halt the decline in the amount of history taught in British schools and to ensure that all young people are able to choose history as one of the subjects they study. The Society has responded to inquiries into the accessions policy to be pursued by the Public Record Office, the future of Postgraduate Awards in Library and Information Science and the form to be taken by the next Research Assessment Exercise. A submission was made to the Select Committee on Public Administration on the white paper 'Your Right to Know: the Government's Proposals on a Freedom of Information Act'. The Society has made representations for Scottish and Welsh universities to be included on the new Arts and Humanities Research Board.

e) The Society continues to cultivate links with historians in other countries. The decision to double the number of corresponding fellows to approximately one hundred has now been implemented. The new Corresponding Fellows are drawn from a wide range of countries and historical specialisations. Lectures to commemorate the bicentenary of the death of Philip II were held in London and Glasgow for which the Spanish Embassy was joint sponsor. The Society continues to be closely associated with the work of the British National Committee of the International Committee of Historical Sciences. The British National Committee jointly with the British Academy met the costs of the British historians who travelled to Bratislava for a successful conference with Slovak historians on Great Britain and Central Europe c.1867-c.1914 on 9 – 10 September 1997. The Committee uses its very small resources to give subventions to an inevitably limited number of overseas scholars coming to Britain for conferences. Preference is given to scholars from eastern Europe or from non-European countries.

2. Bibliographies

The CD-ROM version of the Society's Bibliography, *The History of Britain, Ireland and the British Overseas*, under the General Editorship of Professor John Morrill, was published by the Oxford University Press in April 1998 and is to receive its formal launch at the Society's annual reception on 1 July 1998. The initial response to the CD-ROM has been enthusiastic and for the successful conclusion of this distinguished project the Society is deeply indebted to the General Editor, to the staff who worked on the project, to the volume editors and to a very large body of contributors who most generously gave their time and learning to compile entries.

The second stage of the project, to produce a new edition of the bibliography that will both be an expanded version of the original and contain new publications down to 2000, is now in its second year under the editorship of Dr. Julian Hoppit. Funding for this project has most generously been provided by the Andrew W. Mellon Foundation, the Esmee Fairbairn Charitable Trust and the Isaac Newton Trust. The *Annual Bibliography of British and Irish History* continues to be published under the editorship of Dr. Austin Gee, who co-ordinates the work of a group of scholars to whom the Society owes a particular debt of gratitude for taking responsibility for the various sections of the bibliography. Through all their efforts, the bibliographies are becoming more comprehensive every year: the volume for 1997 contains over 17 per cent more entries than its predecessor.

3. Meetings of the Society

The Society held six Council meetings, and paper readings and receptions in London. Papers were read to the Society at St. Andrews and Norwich during the session. The Society has arranged papers to be read at Aberdeen and Reading during the 1998–1999 session.

A well-attended Annual Reception was held for members and guests in the Upper Hall at University College London on 2 July 1997.

A two-day conference, 'Empires and Identities since 1500', was held at the Institute of Historical Research, London in September 1997; 60 people attended.

A further two-day conference, 'Memory, Oral and Written Tradition', was held at the University of Sussex in March 1998; over 60 people attended.

A Colloquium on William Camden to celebrate the centenary of the sponsorship of the *Camden* Series by the Royal Historical Society was held at Westminster School, London, on 7 October 1997, with an audience of about 100.

Two lectures entitled 'Philip II: The Man Behind the Legend' by Professor M.J. Rodriguez-Salgado were given at the University of Glasgow and at the Instituto Cervantes, London, in March 1998.

During the 1998–1999 session, a one-day conference, 'Creating New Communities in the Middle Ages' is to be held at the Institute of Historical Research, London, on 26 September 1998, and a three-day [mid-day to mid-day] conference, "Voyages and Journeys: the movement of peoples and cultures across land and sea", is to be held at the University of Hull on Monday 29 – Wednesday 31 March 1999.

4. Prizes

This year has seen the culmination of recent important developments in the Society's ability to award prizes for historical scholarship.

a) The Alexander Prize, for an essay by a younger scholar, attracted nine entries. The Prize for 1998 was awarded to Mr. Neil W. Hitchin for his essay 'The Politics of English Bible Translation in Georgian Britain' which was read to the Society on 24 April 1998.
b) The revised criteria to allow the David Berry Prize to be an essay on any approved topic of Scottish history attracted four entries. The Prize for 1998 was awarded to Dr. Tim Thornton for his essay 'Scotland and the Isle of Man, c.1400–c.1625', which will be published in the *Scottish Historical Review.*
c) The Whitfield Prize for a first book on British history attracted 28 entries. The generally high quality of the entries was commended by the assessors. The Whitfield Prize 1997 was awarded to Dr. Christopher Tolley for his book, *Domestic Biography: the legacy of evangelicalism in four nineteenth-century families*, (Oxford University Press).

> *Domestic Biography* examines the writings of biography in four Victorian families: the Macaulays, Stephens, Thorntons and Wilberforces. Their fathers had been members of the prominent group of Evangelicals and philanthropists known as the Clapham Sect, and their histories were shaped by a cultivated and demanding brand of Evangelicalism, which left its mark even when the parental faith was lost. The family biographers

celebrate this common legacy, testifying to the success of the Evangelical movement in its campaign on behalf of domestic piety. Their tradition of biography is given fact and form by the wealth of documentation produced within Evangelical homes, to which later generations added their significant contribution.

Domestic Biography draws extensively on unpublished material in the family archives, discusses the uses and conventions of nineteenth-century domestic biography, and explores its close relationship with other kinds of private family writing. The result is an illuminating account of the influence of Evangelicalism upon eminent Victorians and their milieu.

The assessors declared Dr. Jacqueline Hill *proxime accessit* for her book, *From Patriots to Unionists: Dublin civic politics and Irish Protestant patriotism, 1660–1840*, (Oxford University Press).

d) Thanks to a generous donation from The Gladstone Memorial Trust, the first Gladstone History Book Prize for a first book on other than British history was awarded. There were 15 entries.
The Gladstone History Book Prize 1997 was awarded to Dr. Stuart Clark for his book, *Thinking with Demons: the idea of witchcraft in early modern Europe* (Oxford University Press).

Unlike most recent contributions to the history of witchcraft this book concentrates on the beliefs of the intellectuals who published on the subject between the fifteenth and eighteenth centuries. It argues that to be understood these writings have to be set in the much broader context of early modern intellectual life as a whole. This is because witchcraft belief at this level was sustained by a range of other commitments. Arguments about witchcraft clustered around broad questions: whether it was possible for it to happen as a real phenomenon in the natural world, why it was afflicting Europe at a particular time, what kinds of sins it involved and how clergymen should counteract them, and why rulers and magistrates should also act to rid the world of the threat. In effect, therefore, the book traces the history of early modern demonology in terms of the concepts and arguments that informed the wider scientific, historical, religious and political debates of its time.

e) Frampton and Beazley Prizes for A-level performances were awarded following nominations from the examining bodies:
Frampton Prizes
The Associated Examining Board: Sarah Joanne Barton, Weald College, Middlesex
Edexcel Foundation incorporating the London Examination Board: Sarah Rose Allen, Haberdasher's Aske's School, Borehamwood, Hertfordshire
Northern Examinations and Assessment Board: William J. Holledge, St. Ambrose College, Altrincham, Cheshire
Oxford and Cambridge Examinations and Assessment Council: Robert Weekes, St. Albans School, Hertfordshire
University of Cambridge Local Examinations Syndicate: Alan Bates, Reigate Grammar School, Surrey

University of Oxford Delegacy of Local Examinations: Rachel Reed, Wycombe High School, Buckinghamshire
Welsh Joint Education Committee: Caleb Frederick Watts, Sir Thomas Picton School, Haverfordwest, Pembrokeshire.
Beazley Prizes
Northern Ireland Council for the Curriculum Examinations and Assessment: Christopher M.D. Middleton, Methodist College, Belfast
Scottish Examination Board: Richard Brash, Stewart's Melville College, Edinburgh.

5. Publications

Transactions, Sixth Series, Volume 7 was published during the session, and *Transactions,* Sixth Series, Volume 8 went to press, to be published in 1998.

The Journal of John Wodehouse first Earl of Kimberley for 1862–1902, ed. A. Hawkins and J. Powell (Camden, Fifth Series, Volume 9) and *Miscellany XXXIV – Chronology, Conquest and Conflict in Medieval England* (Camden, Fifth Series, Volume 10) were published during the session. *Bastille Boy: the Journals of Collin Brooks, 1930–1940*, ed. N.J. Crowson (Camden, Fifth Series, Volume 11) and *Parliament and Politics in the Age of Churchill and Attlee: the Headlam Diaries, 1935–1951,* ed. Stuart Ball (Camden, Fifth Series, Volume 12) are planned to be published in 1998/1999. Further volumes shortly to be published, in the Camden, Fifth Series, are *The Journal of Thomas Juxon, 1643–1647*, ed. K. Lindley, and *Letters of the Archpresbyterate of George Birkhead*, ed. M. Questier.

Cambridge University Press have issued reprints of several Camden volumes which have been out of print for some time, all of which have new introductions. *Kingsford's Stonor Letters and Paper, 1290–1483*, ed. Christine Carpenter, *Thomas Wright's Political Songs of England From the Reign of John to that of Edward II*, ed. Peter Coss, have already appeared and are available in either hardback or paperback editions from the Press. *Richard Symonds's Diary of the Marches of the Royal Army,* ed. C.E. Long, with a supplementary introduction by Ian Roy was added this year. *Encomium Emmae Reginae*, new edn. S. Keynes and *The Political Correspondence of Mr. Gladstone and Lord Granville, 1868–1876*, ed. A. Ramm, with a new introduction by H.C.G. Matthew, went to press during the session.

The Society's *Annual Bibliography of British and Irish History, Publications of 1996*, was published by Oxford University Press during the session, and the *Annual Bibliography of British and Irish History, Publications of 1997* went to press, to be published in 1998.

The Second Series of the *Studies in History* series was launched with the publication of *Medical Charities, Medical Politics: The Irish Dispensary System and the Poor Law, 1836–1872* by Ronald D. Cassell, *Civil War, Interregnum and Restoration in Gloucestershire, 1640–1672* by Andrew R. Warmington, *The Birth of Military Aviation: Britain, 1903–1914* by Hugh Driver, *George Chastelain and the Shaping of Valois Burgundy: Political and Historical Culture at Court in the Fifteenth Century* by Graeme Small, *Nature and Artifice: The Life and Thought of Thomas Hodgskin, 1787–1869* by David Stack, *Britannia's Glories: The Walpole Ministry and the 1739 War with Spain* by Philip Woodfine, during the session. Four volumes *Religious Patronage in Anglo-Norman England, 1066–1135* by Emma Cownie, *Managing the*

South African War, 1899–1902: Politicians versus Generals: by Keith Terrance Surridge, *Red Flag and Union Jack: Englishness, Patriotism and the British Left, 1881–1924* by Paul Ward and *Conversations in Cold Rooms: Women, Work and Poverty in nineteenth-century Northumberland* by Jane Long are currently in the press and will be included in a launch to be held in November 1998.

6. Papers read

At the ordinary meetings of the Society the following papers were read:

'The widow's mite and other strategies. Funding the Counter Reformation'
Professor Olwyn Hufton (2 July 1997: Prothero Lecture)
'For reasoned faith or embattled creed? Religion for the people in early modern Europe'
Dr. Euan Cameron (24 October 1997 at the University of St. Andrews)
'Thatcherism: An Historical Perspective'
Dr. Ewen Green (23 January 1998)
'General de Gaulle and his enemies: antigaullism in France since 1940'
Dr. Julian Jackson (6 March 1998)
'Narratives of Triumph and Rituals of Submission: Charlemagne's Mastering of Bavaria'
Dr. Stuart Airlie (22 May 1998 at the University of East Anglia)

At the Anniversary meeting on 21 November 1997, the President, Professor P.J. Marshall, delivered an address on 'Britain and the World in the Eighteenth Century: I. Reshaping the Empire'.

At the two-day conference entitled 'Empires and Identities since 1500' held at the Institute of Historical Research, London, on 26 and 27 September 1997, the following plenary papers were read:

'The Multiple Identities of the Early Modern Spaniard' by Professor M.J. Rodriguez-Salgado
'Empire and Identity: The Case of Scotland' by Professor John M. MacKenzie
'Russian, Imperial and Soviet Identities' by Professor Dominic Lieven
'Enlightenment, Identity and Political Dissent in Late Colonial Spanish America' by Professor Anthony McFarlane
' "I speak the Queen of England's Dutch." Pursuing settler identities in South Africa, 1795–1853' by Dr. Stanley Trapido
'Mauritius in the Eighteenth Century: The Creation of a Creole Identity' by Professor Megan Vaughan
'What did the British Empire contribute to Muslim Senses of Identity?' by Professor Francis Robinson
'Frontiers of the Mind: Conceptions of Community in Colonial Southeast Asia' by Professor A.J. Stockwell
'Am I myself? Identities in Zaire then and now' by Professor Wyatt McGaffey

Theme sessions were held on:

Metropolitan Identities

New World Identities
African Identities
Asian Identities
Expatriate Communities

At the two-day conference entitled 'Memory, Oral and Written Tradition' held at the University of Sussex on 26 and 27 March 1998, the following plenary papers were read:

'Land, Language and Memory in Europe, 700–1100' by Professor Patrick Geary
'Gender and authority of oral witnesses in Europe, 1100–1300' by Dr. Liesbeth van Houts
'Remembering the Past in Early Modern England: Oral and Written Tradition' by Dr. Adam Fox
'New approaches to memory and oral history' by Dr. Alistair Thomson and Dr. Penny Summerfield
'Anthropology, personal narratives and history: reflections on writing *African Voices, African Lives*' by Professor Pat Caplan
'Resiting French Resistance' by Professor Roderick Kedward

Theme sessions were held on:

War and Resistance
Gender
Politics
Law and Authority

At the Camden Colloquium to celebrate the centenary of the sponsorship of the Camden Series by the Royal Historical Society held at Westminster School, London, on 7 October 1997, the following papers were read:

'One of Us? William Camden and the Making of History' by Professor Patrick Collinson [main paper]
'Camden, Westminster and the Cecils' by Dr. Pauline Croft
'William Camden and Ben Jonson' by Professor Blair Worden
'Camden and his reading public in the 17th and 18th centuries' by Dr. Tom Birrell.

7. Finance

The Society continues to enjoy a healthy financial state overall, as the endowment has increased from £2,164,055 in June 1997 to £2,546,652 in June 1998. A number of the decisions taken in principle last year were implemented this year. In particular, we have changed our fund manager from Cazenove to Cripps Harries Hall and we have modified our investment strategy, with the immediate result that our investment income has increased from £76,332 in the 1996–97 financial year to £124,456 during the 1997–98 financial year. This, plus the Council's decision to support a more rigorous control of expenditure and the Society's decision to support a rise in subscriptions, will enable the Society to continue to carry out its responsibilities without eating away at the endowment. The result this year has been a surplus of £52,774 and increase in the funds available to support postgraduate research.

Council records with gratitude the benefactions made to the Society by:

Mr. L.C. Alexander
The Reverend David Berry
Professor Andrew Browning
Professor C.D. Chandaman
Professor G. Donaldson
Professor Sir Geoffrey Elton
Mrs. W.M. Frampton
Dr. G.L. Harris
Mr. A.E.J. Hollaender
Professor C.J. Holdsworth
Professor P.J. Marshall
Mr. E.L.C. Mullins
Sir George Prothero
Professor T.F. Reddaway
Miss E.M. Robinson
Professor A.S. Whitfield

8. Membership

Council records with regret the deaths of 19 Fellows, 3 Life Members and 1 Associate. They included Dr. G.R.C. Davis, CBE – a Member of Council, 1961–5 and 1966–1967, and Honorary Treasurer, 1967–1974, Dr. A.L. Rowse, CH, Professor Sir Harry Hinsley, Miss N.M. Fuidge and Professor J.A. Phillips.

100 Fellows, 17 Members and 43 Corresponding Fellows were elected. The membership of the Society on 30 June 1998 numbered 2433, comprising 1727 Fellows, 385 Retired Fellows, 28 Life Members, 13 Honorary Vice-Presidents, 81 Corresponding Fellows, 122 Associates and 77 Members.

The Society exchanged publications with 15 Societies, British and Foreign.

9. Officers and Council

It is regretted that Miss V. Cromwell's name was accidentally omitted from the list as a Vice-President of the Society during the session 1996–1997.

At the Anniversary Meeting on 21 November 1997, Professor A.D.M. Pettegree was elected to succeed Professor M.C.E. Jones as Literary Director; the remaining Officers of the Society were re-elected.

The Vice-Presidents retiring under By-law XVII were Miss V. Cromwell and Professor H.C.G. Matthew. Professor A.J. Fletcher and Professor C.J. Wrigley were elected to replace them.

The members of Council retiring under By-law XX were Professor P.R. Coss, Professor L. Jordanova, Professor F. O'Gorman and Dr. J.R. Studd. Following a ballot of Fellows, Dr. I.W. Archer, Dr. G.W. Bernard, Dr. J.C.G.

Binfield and Professor R.H. Trainor were elected in their place.

MacIntyre and Company were appointed auditors for the year 1997–1998 under By-law XXXIX.

10. Representatives of the Society

The representation of the Society upon various bodies was as follows:

Mr. M. Roper, Professor P.H. Sawyer and Mr. C.P. Wormald on the Joint Committee of the Society and the British Academy established to prepare an edition of Anglo-Saxon charters;

Professor N.P. Brooks on a committee to promote the publication of photographic records of the more significant collections of British Coins;

Professor G.H. Martin on the Council of the British Records Association;

Professor M.R.D. Foot on the Committee to advise the publishers of *The Annual Register*;

Dr. G.W. Bernard on the History at the Universities Defence Group;

Professor C.J. Holdsworth on the Court of the University of Exeter;

Professor D. d'Avray on the Anthony Panizzi Foundation;

Professor M.C. Cross on the Council of the British Association for Local History; and on the British Sub- Commission of the Commission International d'Histoire Ecclesiastique Comparee;

Miss V. Cromwell on the Advisory Board of the Computers in Teaching Initiative Centre for History; and on the Advisory Committee of the TLTP History Courseware Consortium;

Dr. A.M.S. Prochaska on the National Council on Archives; and on the Advisory Council of the reviewing committee on the Export of Works of Art;

Professor R.A. Griffiths on the Court of Governors of the University of Wales Swansea;

Professor A.L. Brown on the University of Stirling Conference;

Professor W. Davies on the Court of the University of Birmingham;

Professor R.D. McKitterick on a committee to regulate British co-operation in the preparation of a new repertory of medieval sources to replace Potthast's *Bibliotheca Historica Medii Aevi*;

Professor J. Breuilly on the steering committee of the proposed British Centre for Historical Research in Germany.

Council received reports from its representatives.

16 September 1998

APPENDIX A

ROYAL HISTORICAL SOCIETY RESEARCH SUPPORT COMMITTEE AWARDS SESSION 1997–1998

TRAINING BURSARIES:

Nahfiza AHMED, University of Leicester
to attend the 1998 Gulf South History and Humanities Conference held in Louisiana on 8–10 October 1998.

Denise Marilyn AMOS, University of Nottingham
to attend the Conference 'Health in the City: a History of Public Health' held 4–7 September 1997 at Liverpool.

Kirsty-Ann BUCKTHORP, University of Birmingham
to visit to Siena College, Londonville, USA, 3–5 June 1998.

Steven COLWELL, University of Sheffield
to attend the Social Science History Association Annual Convention, held at Chicago, on 19–22 November 1998.

Lucia DACOME, University of Cambridge
to attend the Conference, 'Medicine, Science and Enlightenment, 1680–1789', held in Edinburgh on 10–13 August 1998.

Stefania GALLINI, Institute of Latin American Studies, University of London
to attend the Conference, 'Culture and Environmentalism', held at Bath Spa University College on 3–5 July 1998.

Emily GILBERT, University of Sheffield
to attend the European Social Science History Conference, subject 'Ethnic Identity among first generation Balts in Britain since 1945', held in Amsterdam, 5–7 March 1998.

Claire Helen GREENE, University of Warwick
to attend the Conference, 'Reading Witchcraft', held at the University of Wales Swansea on 9–11 September 1998.

Karen Louise HARVEY, Royal Holloway, University of London
to attend the Conference, 'After the Body', held at the University of Manchester on 22–25 June 1998.

Anke HOLDENRIED, University of London
to attend the International Congress on Medieval Studies held at Kalamazoo, USA, May 7–10 1998.

Richard Michael HUSCROFT, King's College London
to attend the conference on Thirteenth Century England held at Durham on 1–4 September 1997.

Janet Clare Louise JACKSON, University of Cambridge
to attend the Conference, 'Scotland, Ireland and the "Awkward Neighbour", 1603–1688, held at the University of Aberdeen, on 4–6 September 1998.

Owen David JACKSON, University of Bristol
to attend a conference at the University of Caen, 12–13 December 1997.

Sean Michael KELLY, University of Sheffield
to attend the European Social Science History Conference held in Amsterdam, 5–7 March 1998.

Andrea Elizabeth KNOX, University of Northumbria at Newcastle
to read a paper, '"Women of the Septs": the legal response to female aggression in Ireland, 1630–1690' read to the European Social Science History Conference, held on 4–8 March 1998 at Amsterdam.
Heather Mary MEIKLEJOHN, the Winchester School of Art/University of Southampton
to attend The Women's History Network Annual Conference held, in Glasgow on 12–13 September 1998.
Ilaria MELICONI, University of Oxford
to attend The XVII International Scientific Instrument Symposium held in Soro, Denmark, on 20–25 July 1998.
Craig George SPENCE, Royal Holloway, University of London
to attend the International Conference 'The Social Context of Death, Dying and Disposal', held at Cardiff on 4–6 April 1997
David John TRIM, King's College London
to attend the 'Reformation, Revolution and Civil War in France and the Netherlands, 1555–1585', Colloquium of the Royal Netherlands Academy of Arts and Sciences held at Amsterdam on 29–31 October 1997.
Bjorn Klaus Udo WEILER, University of St. Andrews
to attend The Third Carleton Conference on the History of the Family held 15–17 May 1997 at Ottawa, Canada.
Louise Jane [Hunter] WILKINSON, King's College London
to attend the conference on Thirteenth Century England held at Durham on 1–4 September 1997, and to attend The International Medieval Congress held at the University of Leeds on 13–16 July 1998.
Michelle WINSLOW, University of Sheffield
to attend the European Social Science History Conference held in Amsterdam, 5–7 March 1998. [23]

RESEARCH SUPPORT:

RESEARCH WITHIN THE UNITED KINGDOM:
Alan Bell BRYSON, University of St. Andrews
to visit the Public Record Office, London and Warwick County Record Office.
Andrew Ross BURTON, SOAS, London
to visit Rhodes House, University of Oxford.
Sonia CORRIGAN, Oxford Brookes University
to visit archives at Birmingham and Bristol Universities.
Matthew John FAGG, Canterbury Christ Church College
to visit the Public Record Office, London.
Gal GERSON, University of Oxford
to visit to the British Library and the Colindale Newspaper Library.
Margaret HANLY, Oxford Brookes University
to visit the Public Record Office, London.
Robert Andrew JOHNSON, Exeter University
to visit archives in the London area and Edinburgh.
Natalie Ann MEARS, University of St. Andrews
to visit archives in the London area.

Irina Valeska METZLER, University of Reading
to visit The Wellcome Institute and The Courtauld Institute, London.
Simon James MORGAN, University of York
to visit records in Leeds and Oxford.
Jonathan David OATES, University of Reading
to visit to various archives at Newcastle-upon-Tyne, Sheffield, Leeds, York, Wakefield and Northallerton.
Rhonda Anne SEMPLE, King's College London
to visit the National Library of Scotland.
Anne Margaret STOTT, University College London
to visit to Bristol Record Office.
Charles William TURNER, University of Manchester
to visit the University of Warwick and the Public Record Office, London.
Rebecca Imogen WYNTER, University of Birmingham
to visit archives in Manchester, London, Bath and Bradford. [15]

RESEARCH OUTSIDE THE UNITED KINGDOM:

Sarah BADCOCK, University of Durham
to visit archives in Russia.
Veronica BAINBRIDGE, University of Birmingham.
to visit archives in Chicago and Boston, USA.
Heloise Joanne BROWN, University of York
to visit the League of Nations Archives, Geneva, Switzerland.
Christopher John COLLETT, University of Leeds
to visit archives in Florence.
Jeffrey EAMAN, University of Lancaster
to visit archives in Italy.
Alison Elizabeth FALBY, Oxford University
to visit to special collection at University of California at Los Angeles Library.
Vaswati GHOSH, School of Oriental and African Studies, University of London
to visit the National Library of Scotland, and the National Archive of India and the Maharashtra State Archives in India.
David Stratford GOULD, University of Reading
to visit Archivio Centrale dello Stato, Rome.
Nicholas John GRAY, University of Birmingham
to visit archives in Washington and Abilene, USA.
Carolyn Louise GROHMANN, University of Stirling
to visit archives in Metz, France.
Armin GRUENBACHER, University of Birmingham
to visit the US National Archives, Washington.
Jason Lee HEPPELL, University of Sheffield
to visit the YIVO Institute for Jewish Research, New York.
Shruti KAPILA, SOAS
to visit archives in India.
George David Gwynder LEWIS, University of Newcastle upon Tyne
to visit various archives in USA.
Athanasios LYKOGIANNIS, London School of Economics

to visit archives in Washington.
Pedro A. da S.R. MACHADO, SOAS
to visit archives and libraries in Lisbon.
Lily Anne MO, University of Glasgow
to visit archives at the Vatican.
Fabrizio J.D. NEVOLA, Courtauld Institute of Art, London
to visit archives in Rome and Florence.
Jeremy Richard OSBORN, Lincoln College, Oxford
to visit the National Library of India and the Royal Asiatic Society of Bengal, in India, and libraries in Bangladesh.
John Adrian PALKA, University of Warwick
to visit archives in Germany.
Kumar RAMAKRISHNA, Royal Holloway, University of London
to visit archives at Malaysia and Singapore.
Tobias Frederik RETTIG, SOAS, University of London
to visit archives in France.
Emma Jane ROGERS, University of Reading
to visit archives in France.
Wigan M.W.T. SALAZAR, SOAS
to visit National Archives at College Park, Maryland, U.S.A.
Hilary SIDDONS, University College London
to visit libraries in north or central Italy.
Lisa Wynne SMITH, University of Essex
to visit archives in France.
Silke STRICKRODT, University of Stirling
to visit archives in Benin, Nigeria.
Mark John TAPLIN, University of St. Andrews
to visit to archives in Switzerland.
Apostolos VETSOPOULOS, University College London
to visit archives in the USA.
Clare Elizabeth WHITE, University of St. Andrews
to visit the John Fitzgerald Kennedy Library, Boston, USA. [30]

TRAINING BURSARY TO ATTEND A SOCIETY ORGANISED BY THE ROYAL HISTORICAL SOCIETY:

Kelvin John STREET, De Montfort University
to attend the Society's Conference 'Oral History, Memory and Written Tradition' held at the University of Sussex.

WORKSHOP FUND: [name of organiser in brackets]:

Conference, '1798–Ireland's Year of Liberty', held at the University of Luton on 24–26 July 1998. [N.R. ASTON]
The Association for History and Computing (UK Branch) Annual Conference, 'Computing Local History', held at the University of Teesside, 8–10 September 1998. [Stephen William BASKERVILLE]

The Annual Conference for The Society for the Study of French History, held at the University of York, 7–8 April 1998. [Stuart CARROLL]

The Conference 'Reading Witchcraft: Texts – Idioms – Vocabularies', held at the University of Wales Swansea on 9–11 September 1998. [Stuart CLARK]

The Fifteenth-Century Conference held at the University of Reading on 17–19 September 1998. [Anne CURRY]

Neale Colloquium in British History 1998 'The consciousness of modernity in Britain, c.1860 to 1940', held at University College, London, on 27–28 February 1998. [D.W. FRENCH]

'Reformation Studies Colloquium' held at Wadham College, Oxford, on 30 March and 1 April 1998. [Felicity M. HEAL]

The Conference 'The British World: Diaspora, Culture and Identity, c.1880–1939' held at the Institute of Commonwealth Studies on 26 and 27 June 1998. [Rob HOLLAND]

The Conference, '1848 – A European Revolution?', held at UCL and the German Historical Institute, London, 20–21 February 1998. [Axel KORNER]

The Conference, '1798 Ireland and Europe', held in Belfast, 6–8 February 1998. [John Patrick LYNCH]

The Conference, '"Thirteenth-century Europe" – Political, Cultural and Religious Interaction', held at MacIntosh Hall, St. Andrews, 2–4 July 1998. [Iona McCLERRY and Bjorn WEILER]

The Conference 'Nobles and Nobility in Medieval Europe' held at King's College London on 15–17 April 1998. [Janet L. NELSON]

The Conference, 'Ireland, Scotland and the "Awkward Neighbour", 1603–1688', held at the University of Aberdeen on 4–6 September 1998. [Jane OHLMEYER]

The Conference, 'Early Medieval Rome and the Christian West', held at the University of St. Andrews, 11–14 June 1998. [Julia SMITH]

The Conference 'Hollywood and Its Spectators: The Reception of American Films, 1895–1995' held at University College London 12–14 February 1998. [Melvyn STOKES]

The Gladstone Centenary International Conference held at University College Chester on 5–8 July 1998. [Roger SWIFT]

The Conference, 'Historical Semantics', held at the University of Nottingham on 21 February 1998. [Thorlac TURVILLE-PETRE] [17]

BURSARIES FOR HOLDERS OF ORS AWARDS:

H. ANTONSSON, University of St. Andrews
K. BOYLAN, St. Cross College, Oxford
Megan CLARKE, University of Sussex
Helen Louise DENHAM, Wadham College, Oxford [4]

CENTENARY FELLOWSHIP:

Elizabeth A. BUETTNER, University of Michigan – 1996/1997
Svetlana NIKITINA, SSEES – 1997/1998

ACCOUNTS

PREPARED IN ACCORDANCE WITH THE STATEMENT OF RECOMMENDED PRACTICE OF CHARITIES

THE ROYAL HISTORICAL SOCIETY

AS AT 30 JUNE 1998

MacIntyre & Co
Chartered Accountants
Registered Auditors
London

LEGAL AND ADMINISTRATIVE INFORMATION

Registered Office:	University College London Gower Street London WC1E 6BT
Charity registration number:	206888
The Honorary Treasurer:	Professor K Burk, MA, DPhil
The Honorary Secretary:	R E Quinault, MA, DPhil
Auditors:	MacIntyre & Co Chartered Accountants 28 Ely Place London EC1N 6RL
Investment managers:	Cripps, Harries Hall 14 Buckingham Street London WC1N 6DF
Bankers:	Barclays Bank plc 27 Soho Square London WC1A 4WA

A full list of trustees is given in the Trustees' Report.

THE ROYAL HISTORICAL SOCIETY
REPORT OF THE COUNCIL OF TRUSTEES
FOR THE YEAR ENDED 30 JUNE 1998

The members of Council present their report and audited accounts for the year ended 30 June 1998.

PRINCIPAL ACTIVITIES AND REVIEW OF THE YEAR

The Society exists for the promotion and support of historical research and its dissemination to historians and the wider community.

The Society expects to continue with these aims in the future.

RESULTS

During the year the Fund's income from members' contributions, donations and bequests totalled £125,966 a decrease of £3,350 from that received in 1997. Expenditure and grants relating directly to charitable activities totalled £211,121, an increase of £12,893 on that expended in 1997.

The Society's surplus before surplus from investment activities was £52,774 (1997: £22,488).

FIXED ASSETS

Information relating to changes in fixed assets is given in notes 2 and 3 to the accounts.

INVESTMENTS

The Society's investment policy has been adjusted to produce a higher level of income. Capital appreciation throughout the year was highly satisfactory.

The management of the Society's investment was changed from Cazenove to Cripps Harries Hall with effect from April 1998.

DONATIONS

The Society made donations to other charities in the year of £150 (1997: £200).

STATEMENT OF TRUSTEES' RESPONSIBILITIES

The Council is required to prepare accounts for each financial year which give a true and fair view of the state of affairs of the Society and of the surplus or deficit of income over expenditure of the Fund for that year. In preparing these accounts, the Trustees are required to:

- select suitable accounting policies and apply them consistently;
- make judgements and estimates that are reasonable and prudent;
- state whether applicable accounting standards have been followed, subject to any material departures disclosed and explained in the accounts;
- prepare the accounts on the going concern basis unless it is inappropriate to presume that the Fund will continue in business.

The Trustees are responsible for keeping proper accounting records which disclose with reasonable accuracy at any time the financial position of the Society. They are also responsible for safeguarding the assets of the Society and hence for taking reasonable steps for the prevention and detection of fraud and other irregularities.

MEMBERS OF THE COUNCIL

Professor D Bates, PhD	– Member of Council
G W Bernard, MA DPhil	– Member of Council
J C G Binfield, OBE, MA, PhD, FSA	– Member of Council
Professor J M Black, MA, PhD	– Member of Council
Professor R C Bridges, PhD	– Member of Council
Professor P J Corfield, MA, PhD	– Member of Council
C R J Currie, MA, PhD	– Member of Council
A E Curry, MA, PhD	– Member of Council
Professor A E Goodman, MA	– Member of Council
Professor J A Guy, MA, PhD	– Member of Council
J P Martindale, MA, DPhil	– Member of Council
Professor R I Moore, MA	– Member of Council
Professor J L Nelson, PhD	– Member of Council
Professor P A Stafford, DPhil	– Member of Council
Professor R H Trainor, MA, DPhil	– Member of Council

MEMBERS OF THE COUNCIL

At the Anniversary Meeting on 21 November 1997, Dr A. D. M. Pettegree was elected to succeed Professor M. C. E. Jones as Literary Director, the remaining Officers of the Society were re-elected.

The Vice-Presidents retiring under By-law XVII were Miss V. Cromwell and Professor H. C. G. Matthew. Professor A. J. Fletcher and Professor C. J. Wrigley were elected to replace them.

The members of Council retiring under By-law XX were Professor P. R. Coss, Professor L. Jordonova, Professor F. O'Gorman and Dr J. R. Studd. Following a ballot of Fellows, Dr I. W. Archer, Dr G. W. Bernard, Dr J. C. G. Binfield and Professor R. H. Trainor were elected in their place.

STANDING COMMITTEES 1997

The Society was operated through the following Committees during 1998:—

Finance Committee:	Dr. G. W. Bernard	
	Professor R. C. Bridges	
	Mr. P. J. C. Firth	– non Council Member
	Professor A. J. Fletcher	
	Professor P. Mathias	– non Council Member
	Professor J. A. Guy	
	Professor R. I. Moore	
	The six Officers	
General Purposes Committee:	Professor D. Bates	
	Dr. J. C. G. Binfield	
	Professor P. J. Hennessy	
	Professor R. I. Moore	
	The six Officers	
Membership Committee:	Professor R. D. McKitterick	
	Professor P. J. Corfield	
	Professor A. E. Goodman	
	Professor P. A. Stafford	
	Professor C. J. Wrigley	
	The six Officers	
Publications Committee:	Professor P. Collinson	
	Dr. C. R. J. Currie	
	Dr. A. Curry	
	Professor M. J. Daunton	
	Dr. J. P. Martindale	
	Professor R. Trainor	
	The six Officers	
Research Support Committee:	Professor J. M. Black	
	Dr. I. W. Archer	
	Professor M. D. Biddiss	
	Dr. J. L. Nelson	
	Dr. A. M. S. Prochaska	
	The six Officers	
Studies in History **Editorial Board:**	Professor M. J. Daunton (Convenor)	

	Dr. S. Gunn	– non Council Member
	Professor C. Jones	– non Council Member
	Professor P. Mandler	– non Council Member
	Dr. S. Walker	– non Council Member
	A Literary Director	
	The Honorary Treasurer	
Election of Officers Subcommittee: (Literary Director)	The President	
	The Honorary Treasurer	
	Non-retiring Literary Director	
	Professor R. D. McKitterick	
	Professor P.J. Corfield	

AUDITORS

MacIntyre and Company were appointed auditors for the year 1997–1998 under By-law XXXIX. A resolution to re-appoint Messrs MacIntyre & Co will be submitted to the Anniversary Meeting.

By Order of the Board

25 September 1998

Honorary Secretary

REPORT OF THE AUDITORS

TO THE MEMBERS OF ROYAL HISTORICAL SOCIETY

We have audited the accounts on page 378 which have been prepared under the historical cost convention, as modified by the revaluation of fixed asset investments, and the accounting policies set out on page 380.

RESPECTIVE RESPONSIBILITIES OF THE COUNCIL OF TRUSTEES
As described on page 374 the Trustees are responsible for the preparation of accounts. It is our responsibility to form an independent opinion, based on our audit, on those accounts and to report our opinion to you.

BASIS OF OPINION
We conducted our audit in accordance with Auditing Standards issued by the Auditing Practices Board. An audit includes examination, on a test basis, of evidence relevant to the amounts and disclosures in the accounts. It also includes an assessment of the significant estimates and judgements made by the Board of Trustees in the preparation of the accounts, and of whether the accounting policies are appropriate to the Society's circumstances, consistently applied and adequately disclosed.

We planned and performed our audit so as to obtain all the information and explanations which we considered necessary in order to provide us with sufficient evidence to give reasonable assurance that the accounts are free from material misstatement, whether caused by fraud or other irregularity or error. In forming our opinion we also evaluated the overall adequacy of the presentation of information in the accounts.

OPINION
In our opinion the accounts give a true and fair view of the state of the Society's affairs as at 30 June 1998 and of its surplus of income over expenditure for the year then ended.

MacIntyre & Co
Chartered Accountants
Registered Auditors

28 Ely Place
London
EC1N 6RL

25 September 1998

THE ROYAL HISTORICAL SOCIETY

Balance Sheet as at 30th June 1998

	Notes	1998 £	1998 £	1997 £	1997 £
Fixed Assets					
Tangible assets	2		7,711		4,438
Investments	3		2,498,077		2,112,412
			2,505,788		2,116,850
Current Assets					
Stocks	1(c)	29,968		26,025	
Debtors	4	64,501		35,558	
Cash at bank and in hand	5	100,448		74,718	
		194,917		136,301	
Less: Creditors					
Amount due within one year	6	(154,053)		(89,096)	
Net Current Assets (Liabilities)			40,864		(47,205)
Net Assets			2,546,652		2,164,055
Represented by:					
Unrestricted – General Fund			2,324,814		2,002,048
Unrestricted – *Studies in History*			—		(9,295)
Restricted – E. M. Robinson Bequest			97,517		79,914
Restricted – A.S. Whitfield Prize Fund			42,825		39,072
Restricted – BHB/Andrew Mellon Fund			81,496		52,316
			2,546,652		2,164,055

Approved by the Council on 25 September 1998

President: P. J. Marshall

Honorary Treasurer: K. Burk

The attached notes form an integral part of these financial statements.

THE ROYAL HISTORICAL SOCIETY

Consolidated Statement of Financial Activities for the Year Ended 30 June 1998

	Notes	Unrestricted Funds General Fund £	Unrestricted Funds Studies in History £	Restricted Funds E M Robinson Bequest £	Restricted Funds A S Whitfield Prize Fund £	BHB/ Andrew Mellon Fund £	1998 Total £	*1997 Total* £
INCOMING RESOURCES								
Members' subscriptions —net		49,998	—	—	—	—	49,998	50,233
—tax recovered on Deeds of Covenant and Gift Aid		3,127	—	—	—	—	3,127	2,566
		53,125	—	—	—	—	53,125	52,799
Donations and legacies	7	12,766	—	—	—	60,075	72,841	76,517
Total Voluntary Income		65,891	—	—	—	60,075	125,966	129,316
Royalties and reproduction fees		43,907	3,246	—	—	—	47,153	47,401
Total Income before investment income		109,798	3,246			60,075	173,119	176,717
Investment income		112,813	657	3,063	1,496	6,427	124,456	76,332
Gross Incoming Resources in the Year		£222,611	£3,903	£3,063	£1,496	£66,502	£297,575	£253,049
RESOURCES USED								
Grants and prizes payable	8	(25,817)	—	(2,200)	(1,000)	—	(29,017)	(31,265)
Direct charitable expenditure	9	(145,627)	—	—	—	(36,477)	(182,104)	(166,963)
Administration expenses	10	(32,835)	—	—	—	(845)	(33,680)	(32,333)
Total Resources used		(202,279)	(—)	(2,200)	(1,000)	(37,322)	(244,801)	(230,561)
Net Incoming Resources before transfers		18,332	3,903	863	496	29,180	52,774	22,488
Transfer between funds	22	(5,392)	5,392	—	—	—	—	—
Net Incoming Resources (operating surplus)		**12,940**	**9,295**	**863**	**496**	**29,180**	**52,774**	**22,488**
Gains and Losses on Investment Assets								
—Realised on Investments		38,173	—	—	—	—	38,173	42,607
—Unrealised		271,653	—	16,740	3,257	—	291,650	226,613
Net Movement in Resources in Year		322,766	9,295	17,603	3,753	29,180	382,597	291,708
Balance Brought Forward at 1 July 1997		2,002,048	(9,295)	79,914	39,072	52,316	2,164,055	1,872,347
Balance Carried Forward at 30 June 1998		£2,324,814	—	£97,517	£42,825	£81,496	£2,546,652	£2,164,055
Unrealised Surpluses included in above balances		£898,749	—	£ 32,645	£17,974	—	£ 949,368	£ 774,251

THE ROYAL HISTORICAL SOCIETY

Notes to the Accounts for the Year Ended 30 June 1998

1. Accounting Policies

(a) *Basis of accounting*
The accounts have been prepared under the historical cost convention as modified by the revaluation of quoted investments to market value.

(b) *Depreciation*
Depreciation is calculated by reference to the cost of fixed assets using a straight line basis at rates considered appropriate having regard to the expected lives of the fixed assets.
The annual rates of depreciation in use are:
Furniture and equipment 10%
Computer equipment 25%

(c) *Stocks*
Stock is valued at the lower of cost and net realisable value.

(d) *Library and archives*
The cost of additions to the library and archives is written off in the year of purchase.

(e) *Subscription Income*
Subscription Income is recognised in the year it became receivable with a provision against any subscription not received.

(f) *Investments*
Investments are stated at market value. Any surplus arising on revaluation is charged to the income and expenditure account.
Dividend income is accounted for on a received basis.

(g) *Publication costs*
Publication costs are transferred in stock and released to the income and expenditure account as stocks are depleted.

(h) *E.M. Robinson bequest*
Income from the E.M. Robinson bequest is used to provide grants to the Dulwich Picture Gallery.

(i) *A.S. Whitfield Prize Fund*
The A.S. Whitfield Prize Fund is used to provide an annual prize for the best first monograph for British history published in the calendar year.

(j) *Donations and other voluntary income*
Donations are recognised on a received basis.

(k) *Grants payable*
Grants payable are recognised in the year in which they are paid.

(l) *Allocation of administration costs*
Administration costs are allocated between direct charitable expenditure and administration costs on the basis of the work done by the Executive Secretary.

2. Tangible Fixed Assets

	Computer Equipment	Furniture and Equipment	Total
	£	£	£
Cost			
At 1st July 1996	15,111	1,173	16,284
Additions	9,793	—	9,793
At 30th June 1997	24,904	1,173	26,077
Depreciation			
At 1st July 1997	11,060	786	11,846
Charge for the year	6,226	294	6,520
At 30th June 1998	17,286	1,080	18,366
Net book value			
At 30th June 1998	7,618	93	7,711
At 30th June 1997	4,051	387	4,438

All tangible fixed assets are used in the furtherance of the Society's objectives.

3. INVESTMENTS

	General Fund £	Robinson Bequest £	Whitfield Prize Fund £	Total £
Cost at 1.7.97	1,140,869	59,335	17,571	1,217,775
Additions	437,676	—	—	437,676
Disposals	(325,801)	—	—	(325,801)
Cost at 30.6.98	1,252,744	59,335	17,571	1,329,650
Surplus in revaluation	898,749	32,645	17,974	949,368
Quoted Securities at market value	2,151,493	91,980	35,545	2,279,018
Cash awaiting investment	193,363	16,409	9,287	219,059
	2,344,856	108,389	44,832	2,498,077
Market value at 1.7.97	1,884,498	75,240	32,288	1,992,026
Additions	437,676	—	—	437,676
Disposals	(442,334)	—	—	(442,334)
Unrealised gain on investments	271,653	16,740	3,257	291,650
Market value at 30.6.98	2,151,593	91,980	35,545	2,279,018

4. DEBTORS

	1998 £	*1997 £*
Trade debtors	58,660	*30,462*
Other debtors	238	—
Prepayments	5,603	*5,096*
	64,501	*35,558*

5. CASH AT BANK AND IN HAND

	1998 £	*1997 £*
Deposit accounts	109,420	*82,423*
Current accounts	(8,972)	*(7,705)*
	100,448	*74,718*

6. CREDITORS: Amounts due within one year

	1998 £	*1997 £*
Trade creditors	137,345	*62,319*
Sundry creditors	6,206	*3,050*
Subscriptions received in advance	2,584	*1,823*
Accruals	7,918	*21,904*
	154,053	*89,096*

7. DONATIONS AND LEGACIES

	1998 £	*1997 £*
A. Browning Royalties	189	*527*
G.R. Elton Bequest	7,134	*4,606*
Donations and sundry income	61,232	*65,136*
Conference fees and funding	4,286	*6,248*
	72,841	*76,517*

8. Grant and Prizes Payable

	Unrestricted Funds £	Restricted Funds £	Total 1998 £	*Total 1997 £*
Alexander Prize	421	—	421	*568*
Grants	150	—	150	*2,650*
Research support grants	15,964	—	15,964	*13,920*
Young Historian Scheme	1,907	—	1,907	*1,852*
Centenary fellowship	6,475	—	6,475	*5,975*
A Level prizes	900	—	900	*800*
A.S. Whitfield Prize	—	1,000	1,000	*1,000*
Miss E.M. Robinson Bequest — Grant to Dulwich Picture Library	—	2,200	2,200	*4,500*
	25,817	3,200	29,017	*31,265*

9. Direct Charitable Expenditure

	Unrestricted Funds £	Restricted Funds £	Total 1998 £	*Total 1997 £*
Publishing costs (Note 15)	74,855	—	74,855	*99,161*
Purchase of books and publications	3,605	—	3,605	*3,053*
Binding	5,743	—	5,743	*4,044*
Prothero lecture	352	—	352	*349*
Donations and sundry expenses	—	—	—	*55*
A.S. Whitfield Prize Fund	—	—	—	*40*
Studies in History				
— Executive Editor's honorarium	3,667	—	3,667	*3,500*
— Executive Editor's expenses	985	—	985	*1,289*
— Sundry expenses	1,827	—	1,827	*688*
Other publications (Note 16)	14,452	900	15,352	*7,678*
British Bibliographies	—	35,577	35,577	*12,793*
Salaries, pensions and social security	11,996	—	11,996	*11,210*
Computer consumables, printing and stationery	9,011	—	9,011	*8,060*
Meetings and travel	11,647	—	11,647	*9,428*
Conference costs	7,487	—	7,487	*5,615*
	145,627	36,477	182,104	*166,963*

10. Administration Expenses

	Unrestricted Funds £	Restricted Funds £	Total 1998 £	*Total 1997 £*
Saleries, pensions and social security	17,993	—	17,993	*15,711*
Postage and telephone	1,898	—	1,898	*1,635*
Bank charges	1,303	—	1,303	*1,356*
Audit and accountancy	5,135	—	5,135	*5,611*
Professional fees	596	—	596	—
Insurance	883	—	883	*943*
Depreciation	2,382	845	3,227	*962*
Circulation costs	2,645	—	2,645	*5,767*
Sundry	348	—	—	*348*
	32,835	845	33,680	*32,333*

11. Insurance Policies

The Society was charged with the following amounts relating to committee and employees liability:

	1998 £	*1997 £*
Employees liability	86	*88*
Public liability	86	*87*
	172	*175*

12. Councillors' Expenses

During the year travel expenses were reimbursed to 31 Councillors attending Council meetings as a cost of £5,983.

13. Auditor's Remuneration

	1998 £	1997 £
Audit fee	5,135	5,091
Consultancy fees	—	520
	5,135	5,611

14. Grants Paid

During the year the Society awarded grants to a value of £15,964 (1997: £13,920) to 90 (1997: 72) individuals.

15. Publications

	Transactions Sixth Series 5, 6, 7	*Camden Fifth Series 5, 6, 7, 8, 9, 10*	*Guides and Handbooks Reprint Costs*	*Camden Classic Reprints*	*Total*
Cambridge University Press: Costs	£	£	£	£	£
Opening stock	2,928	4,739	8,344	10,014	26,025
Printing	14,616	28,415	—	6,347	49,378
Offprints	1,972	—	—	—	1,972
Carriage	519	1,316	583	—	2,418
Closing stock	(1,037)	(5,659)	(7,218)	(16,054)	(29,968)
	18,998	28,811	1,709	307	49,825
Society's costs	4,142	5,166	—	—	9,308
Paper					3,820
Sales commission					11,902
					74,855

16. Publications

	1998 £	1997 £
Other publications costs		
Annual Bibliography	17,662	11,268
Less: royalties received	(2,310)	(3,590)
	15,352	7,678

17. Lease Commitments

The Society has the following annual commitments under non-cancellable operating leases which expire:

	1998 £	1997 £
Within 1–2 years	176	1,006
Within 2–5 years	2,517	2,517
	2,693	3,523

18. Capital Commitments

	1998 £	1997 £
At the year end, the Society was committed to expenditure to the sum of	6,842	—

19. Life Members

The Society has on-going commitments to provide membership services to 29 Life Members on a cost of approximately £28 each year.

20. Uncapitalised Assets

The Society owns a library the cost of which is written off to the income and expenditure account at the time of purchase.

This library is insured for £150,000 and is used for reference purposes by the membership of the Society.

21. Analysis of Net Assets Between Funds

	General Fund £	E.M. Robinson Bequest Fund £	A.S. Whitfield Prize Fund £	BHB/ Andrew Mellon Fund £	Total £
Fixed Assets	93	—	—	7,618	7,711
Investments	2,344,856	108,389	44,832	—	2,498,077
	2,344,949	108,389	44,832	7,618	2,505,788
Current Assets					
Stocks	29,968	—	—	—	29,968
Debtors	64,501	—	—	—	64,501
Cash at bank and in hand	2,756	—	—	97,692	100,448
	97,225	—	—	97,692	194,917
Less: Creditors	(117,360)	(10,872)	(2,007)	(23,814)	(154,053)
Net Current Assets	(20,135)	(10,872)	(2,007)	73,878	40,864
Net Assets	2,323,814	97,517	42,825	81,496	2,546,65

22. Transfer Between Funds

It was agreed on 21 May 1998 by the Council to amalgamate the Studies in History Fund with the General Fund as at 30 June 1998.

THE ROYAL HISTORICAL SOCIETY
THE DAVID BERRY ESSAY TRUST

BALANCE SHEET AS AT 30TH JUNE 1998

	1998 £	1998 £	1997 £	1997 £
FIXED ASSETS				
1,117.63 units in the Charities Official Investment Fund (Market Value £9,524: 1997 £8,163)		1,530		1,530
CURRENT ASSETS				
Bank Deposit Account	8,367		7,706	
LESS: CREDITORS				
Amounts falling due within one year	(250)		—	
NET CURRENT ASSETS		8,117		7,706
NET ASSETS		9,647		9,236
REPRESENTED BY:				
Capital fund		1,000		1,000
Income and expenditure reserve		8,647		8,236
		9,647		9,236

INCOME AND EXPENDITURE ACCOUNT

	1998 £	1998 £	1997 £	1997 £
INCOME				
Dividends		389		387
Bank Interest Receivable		272		259
		661		646
EXPENDITURE				
Prize awarded		(250)		—
Excess of income over expenditure for the year		411		646
Balance brought forward		8,236		7,590
Balance carried forward		8,647		8,236

The fund has no recognised gains or losses apart from the results for the above financial periods.

1. ACCOUNTING POLICIES

Basis of accounting.

The accounts have been prepared under the historical cost convention. The late David Berry, by his Will dated 23rd April 1926, left £1,000 to provide in every three years a gold medal and prize money for the best essay on the Earl of Bothwell or, at the discretion of the Trustees, on Scottish History of the James Stuarts I to VI, in memory of his father the late Rev. David Berry.

The Trust is regulated by a scheme sanctioned by the Chancery Division of the High Court of Justice dated 23rd January 1930, and made in action 1927 A 1233 David Anderson Berry deceased, Hunter and Another v. Robertson and Another and since modified by an order of the Charity Commissioners made on 11 January 1978 removing the necessity to provide a medal.

The Royal Historical Society is now the Trustee. The investment consists of 1117.63 Charities Official Investment Fund Income with units. The Trustee will advertise inviting essays every year of the three year period.)

A resolution was approved by the Charity Commission on the 16 August 1997 changing the purpose of the Charity to provide an annual prize of £250 for the best essay on a subject, to be selected by the candidate, dealing with Scottish History, provided such subject has been previously submitted to and approved by the Council of The Royal Historical Society.

Report of the Auditors to the Trustees of The David Berry Essay Trust

We have audited the accounts on page 385 which have been prepared under the historical cost convention an the accounting policies set out on page 385.

Respective responsibilities of the Council and Auditors

The Trustees are required to prepare accounts for each financial year which give a true and fair view of th state of affairs of the Trust and of the surplus or deficit for that period.

In preparing the accounts, the Trustees are required to:

—select suitable accounting policies and then apply them consistently;

—make judgements and estimates that are reasonable and prudent;

—prepare the accounts on the going concern basis unless it is inappropriate to presume that the Trust wi continue in business.

The Trustees are responsible for keeping proper accounting records which disclose with reasonable accuracy a any time the financial position of the Trust. They are also responsible for safeguarding the assets of the Trust an hence for taking reasonable steps for the prevention and detection of fraud and other irregularities.

As described above the Trustees are responsible for the preparation of accounts. It is our responsibility to form an independent opinion, based on our audit, on those accounts and to report our opinion to you.

Basis of opinion

We conducted our audit in accordance with Auditing Standards issued by the Auditing Practices Board. A audit includes examination, on a test basis, of evidence relevant to the amounts and disclosures in the accounts It also includes an assessment of the significant estimates and judgements made by the Trustees in the preparatio of the accounts, and of whether the accounting policies are appropriate to the Trust's circumstances, consistentl applied and adequately disclosed.

We planned and performed our audit so as to obtain all the information and explanations which we considere necessary in order to provide us with sufficient evidence to give reasonable assurance that the accounts are fre from material misstatement, whether caused by fraud or other irregularity or error. In forming our opinion w also evaluated the overall adequacy of the presentation of information in the accounts.

Opinion

In our opinion the accounts give a true and fair view of the state of the Trust's affairs as at 30th June 1998 an of its surplus for the year then ended.

MacIntyre & Co
Chartered Accountant
Registered Auditor
Londor

25 September 1998